THE FEARS OF HENRY IV

Ian Mortimer has BA and PhD degrees in history from Exeter University and an MA in archive studies from University College London. From 1991 to 2003 he worked for Devon Record Office, Reading University, the Royal Commission on Historical Manuscripts, and Exeter University. He was elected a Fellow of the Royal Historical Society in 1998, and was awarded the Alexander Prize (2004) by the Royal Historical Society for his work on the social history of medicine. He is the author of two other medieval biographies, *The Greatest Traitor: The Life of Sir Roger Mortimer* and *The Perfect King: The Life of Edward III*, published in 2003 and 2006 respectively by Jonathan Cape. He lives with his wife and three children on the edge of Dartmoor.

IAN MORTIMER

The Fears of Henry IV

The Life of England's Self-made King

VINTAGE BOOKS
London

Published by Vintage 2008

1 3 5 7 9 10 8 6 4 2

Copyright © Ian Mortimer 2007

First published in Great Britain in 2007 by
Jonathan Cape
Random House, 20 Vauxhall Bridge Road,
London SW1V 2SA

www.vintage-books.co.uk

Addresses for companies within The Random House Group Limited
can be found at: www.randomhouse.co.uk/offices.htm

The Random House Group Limited Reg. No. 954009

A CIP catalogue record for this book
is available from the British Library

ISBN 9781844135295

The Random House Group Limited supports The Forest Stewardship
Council (FSC), the leading international forest certification
organisation. All our titles that are printed on Greenpeace approved
FSC certified paper carry the FSC logo. Our paper procurement
policy can be found at www.rbooks.co.uk/environment

Printed and bound in Great Britain by
CPI Cox & Wyman, Reading RG1 8EX

This book is dedicated to my mother, Judy, mindful of the fact that Henry IV never knew his mother.

In one respect, at least, I have been more fortunate than a king.

CONTENTS

ILLUSTRATIONS

Henry IV and Queen Joan (*Adrian Fletcher, www.paradoxplace.com*).
Archbishop Thomas Arundel (*The British Library, Harley 1319, fol. 121*).
Battlefield Church, Shrewsbury (*author's collection*).
Lancaster Castle gate (*Lancashire County Museums*).

AUTHOR'S NOTE

Although most members of the English royal family were given their place of birth as a surname by chroniclers wishing to distinguish one Henry or one Edward from others of the same name, it was rare for a member of the royal family to adopt his place of birth as a part of his official identity. The earliest references to Henry being referred to as 'Henry of Bolingbroke' are historical: namely, the sections of the fifteenth-century continuation of the Brut chronicle (written about 1430) and his entry in John Capgrave's book *The Illustrious Henrys* which was written a little later. In all official documents for the period 1377–97 he is 'Henry of Lancaster, earl of Derby' or 'the earl of Derby, son of the duke of Lancaster', or a variation on one of these. His own household account books bear the name 'Henry of Lancaster, earl of Derby'. This is also the name by which his father addressed him in official letters and the way his father's treasurer described him in his accounts. The contemporary chroniclers Henry Knighton, Thomas Walsingham and the Westminster chronicler all consistently refer to him as 'Henry of Lancaster', and in claiming the throne he referred to himself as 'I, Henry of Lancaster . . .'. Although the indexes to the Oxford University Press editions of the contemporary chronicles all say 'Henry, earl of Derby: see Bolingbroke' this style of nomenclature is anachronistic. It is also impersonal, comparable to describing Prince Henry as 'Monmouth' or Duke Henry of Lancaster as 'Grosmont'. As a result of this, the name 'Henry of Lancaster' has been used throughout this book. Where appropriate, the same format has been followed with regard to his father's name, although 'John of Gaunt/Ghent' was an occasional contemporary appellation in his case.[1]

With regard to other names, most English surnames which include 'de' in the original source have been simplified, with the silent loss of the 'de'. Where it remained traditionally incorporated in the surname (e.g. de la Pole, de Vere) these have been retained. 'De' has generally been retained in French names.

The first names of members of the French royal family have been Anglicised. French forenames otherwise have been left in the standard French form.

With regard to Aquitaine, the term 'Gascony' has normally been used in a generic sense to mean all the English Crown's possession in south-west France.

ACKNOWLEDGEMENTS

I am very grateful, as ever, to my agent, Jim Gill, and my editors at Jonathan Cape, namely Will Sulkin and Jörg Hensgen. I am also very grateful to the organisers of the 2006 symposium on Henry IV's reign at the University of Nottingham, particularly Dr Gwilym Dodd, for inviting me to participate. I would like to thank all the scholars who took part; their advice and suggestions have proved exceedingly valuable. In addition, I would like to thank Dr Dodd himself for reading through the typescript and making several valuable observations and suggestions. I would like also to thank Susannah Davis, Zak Reddan and Mary Fawcett for accommodating me on research trips to London. Thank you also to Zak for his National Portrait Gallery research. Staff at the library of the University of Exeter proved very helpful, as did staff at the British Library and the National Archives. I am very grateful in particular to Dr Adrian Ailes for his comments on Henry's seals. Also to Dr John Banham, who, when told I was unable to obtain a colour image of Ralph Neville and Joan Beaufort, drove to Staindrop Church and took the photograph included here. I gratefully acknowledge a grant from the K Blundell Trust, administered by the Society of Authors, towards writing this book. Last but most of all, I am profoundly indebted to my wife, Sophie, who put up with me working all hours of the day (and many of the night) on this book, and then had to listen to me complaining about the fact. She also took the lioness's share of looking after our three young research 'assistants', Alexander, Elizabeth and Oliver. This is a book in which she too can take pride.

Necessitas non habet legem

('Necessity has no law' or 'Necessity is above the law': a maxim quoted in French by the chronicler Jean Creton on the arrest of Richard II, and which Henry himself wrote in Latin on a letter in 1403)

INTRODUCTION

Shakespeare has a lot to answer for. While historians today might argue about the significance of the end of Plantagenet rule in 1485, and whether terms such as the Hundred Years War and the Wars of the Roses serve any useful purpose, Shakespeare has dictated the most important cut-off date in English medieval history: 1397. Quite simply, that is the historical point at which his great cycle of history plays begins. It is therefore the start date for our collective familiarity with the leading characters from British history. The well-educated modern reader is familiar with the idea of Richard II and Henry IV as eloquent, intelligent and sophisticated individuals in a way he or she is not with their predecessors. We all know the name of John of Gaunt – 'Time-honoured Lancaster' as he appears in Shakespeare's *Richard II* – but few people recall his father-in-law, the first duke of Lancaster, a more brilliant man in almost every way. The psychological characteristics of political figures before 1397 are known only to those who have studied them whereas, because of Shakespeare, we believe that the English royal family after 1397 was a crucible of glory and terror, and that its individual representatives changed the course of English history through their personal loves, fears, ambitions, vision and courage.

Shakespeare, however, was not a historian. His themes were exclusively living themes: the human struggle against the 'slings and arrows' of personal misfortune and the causes and consequences of political revolution. He was not concerned with accurate descriptions of past individuals or events. He also had little or no understanding of the social and religious differences between the early fifteenth century and his own time. We only have to remind ourselves of his failure to mention the Peasants' Revolt to appreciate that his play about Richard II is not an attempt to provide a full picture of the king's life. Although there are elements of Shakespeare's fictional Henry IV which are closely related to the historical king, the result is an inevitable distortion of his personality and career. In short, the popular view of Henry IV is mainly an Elizabethan embroidery incorporating a few golden threads of historical detail. Henry IV may be a key figure in no fewer than three of the greatest history plays ever written but, as an individual, he lurks in the shadows of the popular imagination, as if still cautious of the judgement of other ages, hardly ever emerging to proclaim himself as the man he was, or openly to explain himself and his actions.

The image of Henry lurking in the shadows of the late middle ages is a good one with which to begin a study of him, for he is perhaps the most enigmatic of all the post-Conquest rulers of England. The great nineteenth-century historian William Stubbs declared that 'there is scarcely one in the whole line of our kings of whose personality it is so difficult to get a definite idea'.[1] Indeed, one of the reasons Henry was so useful to Shakespeare is his very obscurity. In the playwright's hands he could be Bolingbroke, the ruthless commander and ambitious usurper, and yet he could also be King Henry, 'mighty and to be feared', yet somewhat aloof and unengaging, being too full of majesty. This is not a sign of attention to him as a man but rather to his station, as a duke or king. There is no attempt to portray the Bolingbroke/Henry IV characters as having any key trait in common. In 1596 (the year in which *Henry IV Part One* was written) no one had any in-depth understanding of the man's personality. As the historian K. B. McFarlane pointed out, the Tudors in general – and Shakespeare in particular – ignored Henry, and that proved fatal to his historical reputation.[2]

The Tudors had a good reason to ignore Henry, as demonstrated in the career of the one man who did *not* ignore him. This was Dr John Hayward, a Cambridge-educated doctor of law, who in 1599 published a historical study entitled *The First Part of the Life and Raigne of King Henrie IIII*. It was immediately both popular and vilified.[3] The first edition of a thousand copies sold out, but it came to the attention of the queen, Elizabeth I, who saw in it an attempt to compare her with Richard II and to justify her deposition. This was largely paranoia on the aged queen's part, who is supposed to have declared in her fury 'know ye not I am Richard II?'. Nevertheless, she sought to have the author arraigned for treason, and Hayward was accordingly locked up in the Tower of London for daring to write 'a storie 200 yere olde'. The second edition was banned, seized and burned. With that sort of review, all prospective publishers were persuaded that *The Second Part* (up to 1403) was far too dangerous to print, and the third part was never written. Indeed, the whole experiment in writing about the man who deposed Richard II was seen to be so controversial that no one attempted to follow Hayward's example until absolute monarchy was well and truly a thing of the past.

As a result, it is only in recent times that historians have begun to move closer to the historical Henry IV. In 1878, William Stubbs published the third and final volume of his landmark work, *The Constitutional History of England*. In seventy-four pages he provided his readers with an overview of Henry's reign which was both new and positive. Unlike any previous historian, Stubbs presented Henry as 'a great king', albeit troubled at every stage of his reign.[4] The reason for his greatness was only partly because he founded a dynasty; mainly it was because (according to Stubbs) he initiated 'a great constitutional experiment, a premature testing of the strength of the parliamentary system'.[5] Stubbs was particularly impressed by the fact that 'there [was] much treason outside but none within the House of Commons'. This led to his conclusion that, by the time of his death, Henry IV 'had exemplified the truth that a king acting in constitutional relations with his parliament may withstand and overcome any amount of domestic difficulty'.[6]

It has to be said that this is 'greatness' as defined by Stubbs, not as understood by Henry's contemporaries. In the fifteenth century it was Henry's grandfather, Edward III, who was regarded as the model for greatness: a man who took the war to France and Scotland and won, and who presided over peace at home for half a century. Henry IV was not deemed 'great' by his contemporaries for the simple reason that he failed to live up to this example. But even if we go along with Stubbs and accept that a man can be retrospectively 'great' because his constitutional ambitions come into vogue four centuries after his death, we still have a problem in that Stubbs assumed that constitutional achievements necessitate constitutional ambitions. They do not. Some of the most important parliamentary developments of the middle ages were achieved in spite of royal participation, not because of it. Indeed, as this book will show, Henry's vision of kingship was substantially based on that of Edward III, and he approached parliament with a largely conservative agenda. The question of whether or not Henry was a great king in the fifteenth century, or subsequently, is a distraction. A man's character may be obscured as much by the acclamation of greatness as by neglect.

Stubbs's slightly younger contemporary Dr James Hamilton Wylie took the opposite approach to Stubbs. Rather than describing Henry's reign in the context of the development of the constitution, Wylie looked at the administration of England in the context of the reign. *The History of England under Henry the Fourth*, published in four volumes between 1884 and 1898, is an astounding compendium of facts, showing very wide reading on the part of the author and containing many perspicacious judgements. It was also a pioneering work: no one had previously given so much attention to a period of just thirteen years before 1500. It includes a great deal of information about the king and many notes from his accounts prior to his accession, and remains the most complete chronology of the reign even today. However, it is first and foremost a history of England, not a biography, and so there is little or no attempt to reconcile the king's actions, writings and reported statements, or to present a coherent portrait of the man. And there are so many highly detailed digressions that at times it is difficult to remember where we are in Dr Wylie's narrative. Those searching for Henry's character will struggle to find it amid the tangled and seemingly endless documentary undergrowth.

Sir James H. Ramsay's two studies, *The Genesis of Lancaster* (1913) and *Lancaster and York* (1892), were written in the 'constitutional' wake of Stubbs. In these, as in Stubbs's own work, Henry is just one of the players in the political game, not the subject. As such he is adopted into the narrative, but again with no real effort to understand his personality. Only in discussing the end of the king's life does Ramsay try to sum him up, declaring that Henry was 'painstaking and industrious; merciful, temperate, and domestic; a traveller, but not a soldier or a sportsman'.[7] The last words are somewhat surprising considering that Henry won all three of the battles he commanded, habitually led his armies in person, went on crusade, was a famous jousting champion, and regularly engaged in hunting and falconry. Ramsay's books are still useful for their easily accessible narrative structure, but, in terms of searching for Henry, best to move on.

If the ghost of Henry IV was hovering around in the early twentieth century, he (or it) would have despaired of finding a proper representation of his living self. The next writer to address the king, J. D. Griffith Davies, did not greatly help. After completing a popular biography on Henry V, Davies felt inspired to go back a generation and write about Henry IV. The result is an example of the sort of historical biography which gave the genre something of a bad name in the twentieth century. There is a distinct lack of attention to detail. Factual accuracy is sacrificed for an easy-to-read style. There is no examination of the sources on which crucial points of information and interpretation are based. Very few sources are directly cited, and, as for its supposed achievement of 'painting an impartial but living picture of Henry Bolingbroke', it fails to convince, for it does not go far enough into the man's character, being more concerned with the rustling leaves of his 'life and times' rather than the roots, trunk and branches of his personality.

Despite its shortcomings, Davies' book does contain an important idea which causes us to think again about Henry IV, and perhaps put a smile on the face of the dead king's ghost. If Henry V had ascended the throne in 1399 and Henry IV in 1413, would things have turned out differently? Although Davies fails to argue his own view on this, just raising the question implies that he believed the two men might have been of comparable abilities, and only significantly differed from one another with regard to their circumstances. In this Davies echoes a line in Stubbs's evocation of Henry IV's greatness: 'Henry IV, striving lawfully, had made his own house strong; Henry V, leading the forces with which his father had striven, made England the first power in Europe.'[8] If Henry IV secured the stable monarchy and administrative system which Henry V inherited in 1413, and saw off nearly all the opposition which otherwise his son would have had to face, does he not also deserve a portion of the credit for the successes of his son's reign? In addition, while we have traditionally judged Henry IV by the consequences of his actions in relieving Richard II of the throne in 1399, we have not considered the alternatives. What would have happened if he had *not* usurped the throne? This is not just 'virtual history' or a piece of speculation; it was very much the situation which Henry himself faced in 1399. Richard was thirty-two at the time; he might have lived and governed erratically and tyrannically for another twenty or thirty years. The potential danger to the nation as well as to the Lancastrian ducal family was obvious. Moreover, if Henry IV had not taken the throne, Henry V would have had to take on the mantle of the 'usurper', presumably when he came of age, in 1407, after eight more years of Richard's rule. Then he too would have faced the dynastic and political opposition which his father had had to overcome, including the Ricardian faction in the aftermath of the coup, the Welsh, the Scots and the French. So, in raising this question, Griffith Davies gave weight to Stubbs's view of Henry as a great king, not on the basis of nineteenth-century constitutional romanticism but in terms of a royal duke's duty to God, to his family, to his vows of knighthood and to his fellow Englishmen.

By 1961, when E. F. Jacob published his substantial volume *The Fifteenth Century* in the Oxford History of England series, the orthodox view of Henry was that he had received little credit for what had been a demanding struggle against overwhelming odds. Some of Jacob's statements on the progress of Henry's life were open to criticism; for example, his view that the king was 'neurotic' towards the end. But his verdict was that Henry had reigned 'gloriously', as the chronicler Walsingham states, and that for this he had to thank his Lancastrian 'administrative training ground and his own magnificent endurance'. It was a fair judgement, and one which still stands. The successor volume in the New Oxford History of England series, by G. L. Harriss, gives Henry the credit for acting with 'energy and decisiveness' against Richard II and against later rebellions in Wales and the north, and explains his compromises with parliament as the result of bankruptcy and political manoeuvres to bolster his authority. The authors of Henry's entry in the *Oxford Dictionary of National Biography* similarly state that, superficially, his reign appears to be difficult to count a success, but 'once placed firmly in the context of his own reign, Henry IV can be seen as a considerable figure, a humane and cultivated ruler, politically skilled but by no means invariably unprincipled'. After fifty years' consensus, the scholarly verdict on Henry IV as a king seems to be in: overall a successful ruler, despite some major drawbacks and disappointments, whose priority to the end of his life was securing his dynasty, in which he was quietly triumphant.

But what of him as a man? What of his character? This question echoes away into the darkness, and no answer comes. Astonishingly, Henry IV is the least biographied English king to have been crowned since the Conquest.[9] The only monograph wholly devoted to him by a writer familiar with the relevant primary sources is J. L. Kirby's *Henry IV of England*, published in 1970. This is not a biography. Biography means a study of a life and there is no life in Kirby's book. Of its 247 pages of text (excluding the ten-page introduction), only fifty deal with Henry's existence up to August 1399. In other words, just twenty per cent of the book is given over to the first seventy per cent of his life, including his inheritance, childhood and half his adulthood. The remainder is a discussion of the politics of his reign. Kirby shows no understanding of Henry's development from a child into a man and then a king. Yet to ignore the early part of Henry's life and to concentrate on the last fourteen years is dangerously misleading, if only for the reason that Henry was not born or bred to be a king. Moreover, Kirby shows no feeling for some key events in Henry's life. In describing the tragic deaths of the summer of 1394, he says simply 'Anne of Bohemia, Richard's queen, died on 7 June and Mary Bohun, Henry's wife, a few weeks later'.[10] That is all. Heavens above! The coldness is like an experimental scientist noting the deaths of two rodents in a laboratory cage. What about Henry's devotion to his wife, and his shock at the sudden loss of his supportive partner? Even though the evidence is minimal, we cannot assume his feelings were equally slight. Similarly, in describing Henry's decision to invade England in 1399, Kirby does not consider for a moment how much this must have weighed on Henry's mind. There is no suggestion of worry or optimism. There is no discussion even of the cultural context for fearing the removal of a legitimate monarch. Henry just did it, as if he was following a script from which he could not deviate and which guaranteed him success. Kirby's work remains useful as a political guidebook to the reign, but it is little more than that.

Fortunately for Henry IV, and for us, K. B. McFarlane had a far more rounded vision of the king's personality. His six chapters on Henry in the first part of *Lancastrian Kings and Lollard Knights* are the nearest thing to a biography yet to be published. These chapters were originally devised as a series of six lectures which McFarlane delivered at Oxford in the 1930s and rewrote in the 1940s, and which G. L. Harriss edited for publication in 1972. In McFarlane at last we have an intelligent yet humane writer who engages with the man and his problems, and who tries to understand what forces shaped him. He understood that history is the study of living men and women, not merely names in desiccated documents, and that those men and women were individuals. As he himself stated, 'while it is a part of the historian's business to analyse the great impersonal forces at work in society, he must take account of the human instruments, those who held power, through which those forces had in part to find expression'.[11]

One of the most significant aspects of McFarlane's lectures on Henry IV is his understanding of the greater possibilities of a biographical approach as opposed to 'sterile antiquarianism' (as he himself called it). Consider the question of Henry's rivalry with Richard II. There is no evidence of any hostility between the two men until 1386, when they were both nineteen. However, should we presume therefore that they were amicable up to this time? An evidence-based methodology suggests we should, or that we should at least keep an open mind. But McFarlane approached the subject of Henry's youth on the understanding that simple repetition of the evidence (or lack of it) is not enough, and that to understand the relationship between Henry and Richard one has to go beyond the direct evidence and look for hints that they may have distrusted one another long before 1386.[12] In this way McFarlane started to tackle the difficult questions about Henry's personality: questions which up to then had been dismissed as unfathomable depths.

Erudite, well informed and well written as McFarlane's account most certainly is, it still falls short of what we would like to see in a historical biography. Obviously it is too brief and incomplete. It is also too objective, in the sense that it is inextricably linked to a philosophy of history as a judgemental process – seeing Henry in the context of his peers – as opposed to a sympathetic one (seeing his peers through Henry's eyes). There is therefore little attention to emotional development. Also it is significant that McFarlane's Henry IV lectures lack a conclusion. In *Lancastrian Kings*, it is Henry V's achievements which appear to be the conclusion. This, of course, was not McFarlane's intention, for he wrote the lectures on Henry IV and Henry V for different audiences; but even so, one suspects that McFarlane did look back on Henry IV through the distorting lens of Henry V's reign. He was in awe of the younger Henry, declaring that he was 'the greatest man that ever ruled England'.[13] He does not qualify this statement, even though he must have been well aware that Henry V's road to glory was far easier than his father's narrow path of mere survival. Like a race between two sprinters, one of whom attempts the 110 metres hurdles in Wellington boots while the other covers the 100 metres flat in more suitable footwear: if the flat runner is consistently faster than the hurdler, we ought not to be surprised. As a result, McFarlane's book does not reward the reader who picks it up to find out about Henry IV, for despite all the king's efforts in the face of adversity, he does not receive commensurate praise.

Since McFarlane, books about Henry IV have been very few and far between. Two small-press studies appeared in 1986 and 1994, but neither is ground-breaking.[14] The only major contributions are a political study of the reign, *Heresy and Politics in the Reign of Henry IV: the Burning of John Badby* by Peter McNiven (1987) and a volume of essays, *Henry IV: the Establishment of the Regime, 1399–1406*, edited by Gwilym Dodd and Douglas Biggs (2003). The former is, as its title suggests, primarily concerned with the relationship between the political and religious forces of the time. The latter includes a number of important pieces of research but, being a series of contributions to an academic conference, cannot provide the integrated personal story which we look for in a biography. The scholarly overview of the reign suitable for a wide audience is still lacking. It was thought for a long time that A. L. Brown would provide this, and in 1995 it was noted that it was nearing completion.[15] He fell ill, however, before it was finished. It looks as though we must wait a little while yet for the specialist academic overview of the reign of Henry IV.[16]

Nevertheless, research on the period continues to be produced in quantity. Attention to the tyranny of Richard II and the revolution of 1399 has been especially intense. The revolt of the earls in 1400, the Welsh rebellion, the Percy revolt and Henry's parliamentary and financial predicaments have all been subject to detailed scrutiny. However, despite the weight of academic research, the focus is rarely biographical. Except for isolated areas of interest, such as Henry's health, the attention is not on Henry himself but on the political, financial and constitutional aspects of his reign. Even his relationships with his children are examined for political – rather than personal – reasons. Stubbs's constitutional romanticism may have fallen by the wayside, but his view that the most important historical questions of the period are abstract ones concerning the relationship between the monarchy, parliament and the exercise of political authority continues to provide the framework for early fifteenth-century scholarship to this day.

*

This lack of biographical attention is extraordinary, and it is difficult to explain why no one has concentrated on the character of a man who was the first of only four Englishmen since the Conquest to break into the sacred circle of legitimate royal succession (Edward IV, Richard III and Henry VII being the others).[17] He might be enigmatic but that is no reason to ignore him; quite the opposite. It is even more surprising, however, when we reflect that scholars habitually point to Richard II's personality as being the key to his downfall, and have made great efforts to understand him as a man, while not considering what it was about Henry's character which provided the antithesis to this failure. Of course, most scholars have noted Henry's knightly virtues, his intelligence, wit and politeness; but there has not been a single personality-based study of Henry to compare with the many for Richard II. Henry's character has been seen as incidental to his political career whereas Richard II's has been seen as the key to his.

Such a lack of a biographical perspective is one of the reasons for this book. Another reason is that Henry is the obvious next subject in this series of biographies which collectively tell the political history of later medieval England. Following on from *The Greatest Traitor: the Life of Sir Roger Mortimer, 1st Earl of March, Ruler of England 1327–1330* and its successor, *The Perfect King: the Life of Edward III, Father of the English Nation*, this book continues to trace the thread of political power in England. Through this longer temporal framework, it is possible to show how Henry's life connects with both his Lancastrian ancestry and long-term political developments. For instance, the previous two volumes illustrate in greater detail than is possible here the examples of both the Lancastrian rebel Thomas of Lancaster – executed in the reign of Edward II – and the hugely successful first duke of Lancaster, Edward III's most brilliant commander and best friend (he and Edward III both being Henry's grandfathers). Similarly, the earlier books describe the deposition of Edward II, and the awareness in the royal family of his secret survival after his supposed death. These two events have particular resonance in this book, the first in the process whereby Henry IV oversaw the deposition of Richard II and the second in the rumours that first Thomas of Woodstock and then Richard II were kept alive after their deaths.

A third reason to write about Henry IV is to explore what may be termed 'the limits of medieval biography'. There was for many years a general perception that biography was too populist a medium for serious consideration. 'It is despised by the hard and practised by the soft in one discipline after another', wrote a correspondent in the *Times Higher Educational Supplement* in 1987.[18] Sixty years earlier K. B. McFarlane had declared that 'the historian cannot honestly write biographical history; his province is rather the growth of social organisations, of civilisation, of ideas'. One could talk about a king's reign, or the interactions between a king and his people, but biography itself was seen in a negative light on account of its sympathetic (as opposed to objective) approach, or, as other critics have said, because biographical authors 'opt for narrative rather than analysis'.[19] Thus, for most of the twentieth century, academic historians tended to write history books about individuals, not biographies, and justified this on the grounds of the intellectual superiority of the objective, analytical approach. At the same time, there was a widespread belief in literary circles that a 'proper' biography could not be written for a character living before 1500, as personal letters do not normally survive to attest to what the subject thought or felt. This view was seized on by the anti-biographical academics and used as a justification for why it was essential to avoid the biographical medium when writing about medieval political figures: the whole exercise was impossible, they said, 'for the sources to permit such a study have not survived'.[20] For decades no one exposed the weaknesses of this view. It depends on a double assumption: that there is (1) a definite thing called 'a biography', with an established form which a writer could not modify, requiring certain types of primary sources as a *sine qua non*, and (2) that there is a distinction to be made between those whose personal letters are available in large quantities (who are suitable subjects for biography) and all the other people who have walked the planet (who are not). This is surprising, for these assumptions are and were obviously wrong. It is even more surprising when we reflect that, throughout the twentieth century, diversity and experimentation were being encouraged in other forms of serious literature (poetry and fiction, for example) but not biography.

Slowly, things began to change. Historians writing about individuals began to realise that, in order to analyse the past, first one must understand it, and in trying to understand it, issues of character have to be viewed with a degree of sympathy, not complete detachment. For example, in order to understand Roger Mortimer's actions against Edward II in 1322–6, it is necessary to understand his earlier loyalties, disappointments, military experiences and political awareness from *his own* point of view. An analogy with architecture may be made: however much we may hold to the view that it is the external, objective view of an architectural masterpiece which matters most, we cannot properly appreciate a building's merits unless we also see it *from within*. Similarly, the hoary idol of 'biography' began to crack, with dramatic innovations from writers such as Ann Wroe (whose *Pilate* is about a reputation rather than a man, and whose *Perkin* has as its central theme the idea that a man might not know who he actually is) and Peter Ackroyd (whose *The Last Testament of Oscar Wilde* is written as an autobiography, and whose *London: the Biography* stretches our understandings of 'biography' to include the 'life' of a city).

For the historical biographer, the potential benefits of the sympathetic approach to history are obvious. On the one hand we may retain a firm grip on the source material and on the other we may build a coherent picture of a man's life and character based on his actions, his priorities, his political decisions and alliances, and his defiance of (or compliance with) contemporary mores. This in turn leads us to ask why a biography based on a man's actions should not be every bit as 'biographical' as a life based on his letters? Indeed, we delude ourselves if we think that letters prove a man's feelings, or necessarily convey an accurate impression of his inner life. Men and women may misrepresent themselves and their feelings in their letters for any number of reasons, consciously and subconsciously, perhaps due to momentary depression or elation, or even due to their inability to express themselves. In a long summer of happiness, one may take a moment just to write down a single line of regret or bitterness, and what is left of that summer a hundred years later? But although men and women often deceive in what they write, it is rare that they deceive in what they do. A payment for a musical instrument for the lord's personal use is good evidence of a fondness for music; orders for the design of a library to house the king's books is good evidence of a high value placed on literature. The resetting of a medicinal stone to protect the wearer against poison when he is in fear of his life is no less telling. Given enough evidence of his decision-making, one may present a picture of a medieval leader which is as close, or nearly as close, to his actual character as a contemporary biography of a living monarch or prime minister.

It is now, in the present century, that the opportunities afforded by this new form of historical biography are becoming apparent. In the summer of 2003 a whole string of leading medievalists attended a conference at the University of Exeter on 'The Limits of Medieval Biography'. Almost all echoed the conclusion of the keynote speaker: that biography was not only *one* of the most important approaches to the past, it might actually be *the* most important, for 'only through biography could one argue why this had happened, or that had not happened'.[21]

As soon as one accepts this way of seeing past lives, Henry emerges as a prime subject for study. He *personally* changed the government of the country, and thereby he *personally* persuaded the country both to shrug off its allegiance to Richard and to accept him as its king. This goes way beyond the mere changing of the head on which the crown sits. It marks the advent of a totally different form of kingship, for it proves the final failing of one form of rule (Richard II's experiment in autocratic monarchy) and the beginning of another (a return to participatory government). It also demands answers to some very serious questions. What was it about

Henry that made him a preferable choice to the divinely anointed Richard? What was it about him which allowed him to sanction the introduction of the most repressive heresy laws? What was it that equipped him to weather the years of revolution and protest which followed? What was it that made him think he could rule more wisely than his son at the end of his life? When we start to consider these questions, the view of history as a slow socio-economic development is revealed to be just the rocky landscape of the past, as if seen through powerful x-ray glasses that eradicate the presence of every single individual in that landscape, with the loss of every emotion, every bit of pride and every cry of suffering. Take off the x-ray glasses and one is left in no doubt that the 'revolution' which Henry instigated in 1399 was one of the most important events in English history. Its legacy – the question of whether revolution itself can be justified, and, if so, might it be sanctioned by God – was the single most important political concern with which Shakespeare and his contemporaries had to wrestle two hundred years later. We might even go so far to say it remains to this day the ultimate political question: to whom does one owe the greater loyalty, those superiors whom one serves or those dependants for whom one is responsible? Understanding Henry's circumstances and personality helps us to see how the previously accepted order of society (which assumed that one should always remain loyal to one's superiors) could be questioned and found lacking. It helps us to understand the civil wars of the period as well as the Welsh and French conflicts, finance, parliament and sedition. What would have happened if Henry had lost the battle of Shrewsbury? Would we have had a Mortimer on the throne, the reluctant King Edmund? But Henry did not lose at Shrewsbury. So, historically, his survival matters, just as it mattered at the time.

Here, then, is the life of a man whose character profoundly affected the history of the English nation. It may not have been the most glorious reign, but one should not judge the man by the achievements of his reign alone. Unlike all his Plantagenet predecessors, it was an achievement for him simply to become king. Thus his life was certainly not without its moments of glory. He was the man who forced the door shut on the tyranny of Richard II and unlocked the one by which the Lancastrians – most famously Henry V – burst gloriously on to the scene. That he should have been a 'usurper' too (in Shakespeare's eyes at least) has provided us ever since with something of an enigma. It is time to confront that enigma, and to try to understand the man behind it.

ONE

The Hatch and Brood of Time

> There is a history in all men's lives
> Figuring the nature of times deceas'd;
> The which observ'd, a man may prophesy,
> With a near aim, of the main chance of things
> As yet not come to life, which in their seeds
> And weak beginnings lie intreasured.
> Such things become the hatch and brood of time ...
>
> *(Henry IV Part Two*, Act 3, Scene 1)

Their fires had been burning days, most fiercely in Kent and Essex. Maidstone was in flames. Canterbury was under attack. Thousands of rebels were on the march, and rumours were flying in and around London. In every village and town in the south-east people spoke of the outrages committed by royal tax collectors as they went from place to place demanding fourpence or more for the poll tax from every adult man and woman. They went armed, and they were a law unto themselves. They sought out potential evaders ruthlessly. John Legge was one of the worst. He would line all the inhabitants up in a village and inspect them. If told that a girl was under age, and thus exempt from the charge, he would lift up her skirts and find out in his own rough way whether she was 'under age' or not.[1] Most fathers would rather pay than have such an indignity forced on their daughters. The hostility was bitter, and it ran like a seam of anger from rural Essex and Kent right into the heart of the city.

The year was 1381. Henry of Lancaster – the future Henry IV – was fourteen, and in London. He may have been at his father's great house, the Savoy Palace, he may have been at his own house in Coleman Street, or he may have come to London with the king. We do not know for certain. But what we do know is that he was in the capital during those fateful days in the second week of June. He was there when the full force of more than ten thousand aggrieved men tore into the city. The memory of those days would remain with him for the rest of his life.

The advisers with young Henry – his guardian, Thomas Burton, his military tutor, William Montendre, his clerk Hugh Herle and his young companion Thomas Swynford, and possibly the family surgeon, William Appleton – knew that there was no force strong enough to defend their young lord from the rebels. Five hundred men armed with longbows could defeat ten times as many men-at-arms in battle. So what hope did Henry's guards have against several thousand bowmen, roaming at large? As servants of Henry's father, the duke of Lancaster, they were in particular danger. The duke was one of the most hated figures in the realm. He was personally blamed for many of the injustices which had sparked the revolt. Had he not imprisoned Sir Peter de la Mare, Speaker of the House of Commons, for daring to oppose him? Did he not command the council which directed the rule of the young king? Did he not parade in and out of the city in a haughty and conceited manner, squandering money in the pretence that he was the king of Castile? The crowd wanted the duke and all the chief officers of state destroyed. They wanted the nobility disempowered. They believed that they were now the greatest force in the realm. They had shown their strength on the battlefields of France in the service of the late king, Edward III. In return, Edward had shown them the virtue of being English, in their language, in their parliament, in resisting the power of the pope, and in their collective fighting power. That was the most frightening thing of all: these men were not just a rabble, they were an organised fighting force. Moreover, they had a firm belief that King Richard II would understand them, and that he was only prevented from helping them by his advisers. So they paraded the fact that they would have no other king but the fourteen-year-old Richard. They were armed, idealistic and frenzied with anger. Anyone who got in their way was killed, regardless of rank.

As the countrymen marched towards the city, Henry and his guardians went to the Tower of London, the strongest castle in the region. There too the archbishop of Canterbury, Simon Sudbury – who was also the chancellor – sought refuge, and the treasurer, Sir Robert Hales. The duke of Lancaster himself was in Scotland with an army, and so was in relatively little danger. King Richard II and his advisers came downstream from Windsor to the Tower on 11 June, believing they could talk their way out of trouble. But all attempts to persuade the peasant armies to disband failed. The Kentish rebels massed in their march from Canterbury, and although they paused to discuss terms with the bishop of Rochester on Blackheath on the 12th, they were set on demonstrating their destructive power. Likewise the Essex men. The two forces linked up, and coordinated their advance on the capital, as they had been trained to do in campaigns in France. There they had killed and destroyed mercilessly in order to exert political pressure on the government. They might have looked like a rabble of peasants but they were capable of systematic devastation on a scale which London had never seen before.

On the morning of Thursday 13 June the armed countrymen reached Southwark, the suburb of London which lay directly to the south of the Thames. At that moment Richard II was sailing to a point between Rotherhithe and Greenwich to talk with their leaders. His advisers, including Archbishop Sudbury, prevented him leaving the royal barge. Richard called to the rebels from the safety of the river, asking why they had gathered. The leaders sent a list of men whose heads they wanted. First named was the duke of Lancaster, next the archbishop of Canterbury and the treasurer. They also wanted the heads of the keeper of the privy seal, the chief baron of the exchequer and ten other individuals. Obviously, Richard could not agree with such a request. The men of Kent watched the royal barge rowed slowly back to the Tower, their king unwilling to help.

Then the destruction began. Although the mayor of London had given orders for the gates to the city to be closed and the bridge defended, many of the poorer Londoners had every sympathy with the rebels. The men of Southwark did not want a violent mob to be trapped in the streets outside their houses; so they forced the men on the bridge to give way. The gates were opened. Early in the evening of the 13th, crowds of men broke into the city. They were joined by thousands of poor workers within the walls. Overwhelmed, the mayor gave orders that the wine cellars should be left open to the armed mob, hoping that they would drink themselves into a disorganised and confused rabble. But as they drank, half-demented in the heat of what had been a very hot summer's day, the rebels sought out their hated targets. They broke down the gates of prisons, letting everyone go free and killing the custodians, or chasing them to sanctuary. One royal sergeant-at-arms, Richard Imworth, was found in Westminster Abbey, clinging to a pillar. They dragged him outside and cut his throat. The men of Essex ransacked the priory of St John at Clerkenwell, because its prior was Sir Robert Hales, the treasurer. The men of Kent destroyed the manor of Lambeth, which belonged to Archbishop Sudbury. Wherever the citizens pointed out the house of a hated public figure, torches were set to it, the contents were destroyed and the inhabitants killed.

None of the rebels needed any Londoner to point out the house of the duke of Lancaster. The Savoy Palace stood tall and proud in the Strand, halfway between London's city walls and the Palace of Westminster. In the words of one contemporary, it was 'a house unrivalled in the kingdom for its splendour and nobility'.[2] It was, in addition to a residence, the duke's treasury and his wardrobe. Five cartloads of gold and silver were kept there, together with innumerable tapestries, woven cloths, armour, jewels and items of furniture. Now the rebels gathered towards it, like moths attracted to a great beacon of Lancastrian power. In the chambers and hall they cut the rich paintings and tablecloths with their knives and smashed the furniture with their axes. They ripped the tapestries and crushed the gold and silver vessels and threw them into the Thames. They took one of the precious jewel-encrusted padded jackets belonging to the duke and set it up on a lance for the archers to use as target practice. Then the building itself was set ablaze. Those in the wine cellars drinking the duke's wine were crushed to death as the burning building above them collapsed through the floor, probably helped by the barrels of gunpowder stored within. Two men caught looting were thrown into the blaze. It was a systematic destruction of the emblems and insignia of the duke's status and authority.

Henry watched from the walls of the Tower of London. Had he any understanding of what was going on, he would have seen that it was the result of extreme discontent arising from ruthless law enforcement and overtaxation. He could see his father's palace burning and would have heard the explosions as the barrels of gunpowder ignited. Much of Fleet Street was alight. So too was the priory at Clerkenwell, the prisons, the houses of John Butterwick and Simon Hosteler and many other men associated with the regime. Here the shop of a chandler was ablaze, there the shop of a blacksmith.[3] In the streets, men were murdered wherever they met an enemy. The Londoners began to cull their own. A number of houses around the Temple were set on fire, many more to the south of the river, at Southwark. Roger Legget, a royal tax collector, was found and dragged, kicking and shouting, to Cheapside where his head was cut off. Then his house in Clerkenwell was set alight.

Henry would have heard the screams of terror nearby as the citizens took the opportunity to purge themselves of foreigners. Thirty-five Flemish people who had fled to sanctuary in the church of St Martin in Vintry were pulled out of the building, one by one, and dragged across the church-yard to a single block, where they were decapitated, the heads and bodies lying on the ground as the next terrified victim was dragged out of the church. The financier Sir Richard Lyons was sought out and killed.[4] Lombards were pulled from their houses and murdered by the dozen. More than one hundred and fifty Flemings lost their lives. A whorehouse run by Flemish prostitutes was set on fire. Thirteen Flemings were pulled out of the church of the Austin friars and beheaded in the street outside by the drunken rabble, as the burning sun began to set on the burning city.[5]

That night the young king gathered his advisers in the Tower. They had a few hundred men-at-arms with them.[6] Some of the nobles tried to persuade Richard to fight his way out, in a full-scale charge. Others suggested that he should talk to the rebels and draw them away from the city. Henry was there; perhaps he was able to listen as his young cousin accepted the advice of those who suggested another meeting. The next day Richard would ride out from the Tower with the men-at-arms, his half-brothers, his mother and the mayor of London, and talk to the rebels at Mile End.

On the morning of Friday 14 June Richard and his men departed from the Tower, leaving Henry and a few others there with nothing but the stone walls and a few guards to protect them. Most of the lords went with Richard and the mayor. Henry was left with all the men whose heads were sought by the rabble: Archbishop Sudbury, Hales and various other royal enforcers, such as John Legge. They did not know about the jostling of the king's men by the crowds on the way to Mile End. Only when the king's mother returned, escorted back by some men-at-arms when the jeering crowds became too much for her, did they learn about the hostile mood out to the east of the city. Henry would have waited, perhaps looking out for signs of messengers hurrying back. None appeared. Hours passed. Then a mass of armed rebels came running, hungry for blood. In his discussions at Mile End, the king had told the peasants to go through the realm and bring all traitors to justice, wherever they were. Those inside the Tower had effectively been condemned to death.

What Richard had actually said, of course, was that the rebels should go away, or, specifically, 'go through the realm and bring all traitors to him safely, and he would deal with them as the law required'.[7] The rebels' view was that they did not need to go 'through the realm' but only as far as the Tower. They were the law, and judgement was theirs; there was no need for a trial. Armed with longbows and staves, it was not long before the gates to the Tower had been forced and they were going from room to room, looking for their victims. Some went into the king's chamber and lay down on his bed, laughing. The king's mother, renowned thirty years earlier as the most beautiful woman in the land, in whose presence the greatest knights at King Edward III's court had jousted, now found herself roughly kissed and manhandled by the peasants.[8] The few guards remaining were powerless to defend their masters as hundreds of commoners pulled their beards or made faces at them. The archbishop and Prior Hales could do nothing but go down on their knees and pray in the chapel. Henry himself could only watch and wait.

The archbishop could expect no mercy. He had prevented Richard from disembarking at Greenwich to meet the rebels the previous day. On the list of men to die, his name appeared second, just below that of Henry's father, the duke. He knelt and prayed in the chapel of St John in the White Tower. Those who were with him had already heard one Mass; now they listened to another. They could hear footsteps running through the keep. The archbishop chanted prayer after prayer, the seven psalms and the litany. As he said the words 'all saints, pray for us', the rebels burst in. In scenes which must have been truly terrifying for everyone present, the archbishop was seized and dragged out by his arms and hood along the passages of the castle, across the bailey and out to the yelling masses on Tower Hill, where they set up a makeshift block. It was said that they took eight blows to cut off his head. They took Hales too, dragging him away to a similar bloody execution. The Lancaster family physician, William Appleton, was likewise hacked to death for no other reason than that he had served Henry's father. Four others were singled out and butchered.

Then the mob turned to the Lancastrian heir, Henry. If at that moment John Ferrour, one of the remaining guards, had not boldly come between the mob and Henry, and spoken up for him, and persuaded them to let him go, Henry's fourteen-year-old head would have been stuck on a spear on London Bridge, alongside those of the archbishop of Canterbury, Sir Robert Hales and William Appleton.[9] As it was, Ferrour persuaded the crowd, and Henry lived. Many years later, he would repay the debt and save Ferrour's life in return.

*

There is no doubt that seeing the Peasants' Revolt at first hand and coming within an inch of death had the most profound effect on Henry. It affected his thinking about the current reign and conditioned his own policies in later years. But it also leads us to ask one very important question. At that moment, when Richard left him in the Tower, practically unguarded, did Henry blame the young king? And did he forgive him? One chronicle – written by an eyewitness – states that the king told those he left behind to take a boat from the water gate and flee for their lives. But when the archbishop attempted to do this he was spotted by 'a wicked woman', and had to rush back into the Tower.[10] With so many longbows at the ready on the river banks, there was no escape on the water. So it could be said that Richard deserted those in the Tower. In fact it could be said that he did this twice, for when he returned from Mile End he did not go back to the Tower but went to the great wardrobe (one of the offices of his household), situated near Blackfriars.[11] Even if we give him the benefit of the doubt, Richard was guilty of one major error of judgement. By apparently giving in to the rebels, and encouraging them to go off and seek traitors, he placed those in the Tower in very great danger. We may understand what Richard was trying to achieve, but to look at matters from Henry's point of view, having seen the archbishop of Canterbury dragged out and beheaded, would that have been good enough?

The reason why this question is so important is that it is impossible to begin to understand Henry's life without seeing it in relation to that of his cousin, the king. In 1399 Henry took action to dethrone Richard. In so doing he risked not only his own life but the status of his children and the lives of many of his followers and the political stability of the entire realm. No one takes such a decision lightly. But this was not the first time that Henry and Richard had faced each other in anger. Carefully examining Henry's life before 1399 we find a number of instances when Henry and Richard were either weighing one another up or in outright hostility to one another. If we really want to understand why Henry acted the way he did in 1399, and especially in relation to Richard, we need to look far beyond the evidence of that year and understand how these two men saw each other and co-existed, right from the very start of their lives.

Henry and Richard were born rivals. For a start, they were almost exactly the same age. Richard was born at Bordeaux, in Gascony, on 6 January 1367; Henry was born at Bolingbroke, in Lincolnshire, just three months later.[12] Although they would not have met until they were five or six, they were regarded as a pair, on account of their both being the king's grandchildren and the same age. Moreover, they were the *only* two royal children of this age; the next eldest, Roger Mortimer, was seven years younger. They would therefore have seen each other as having very similar royal identities. Each threatened the uniqueness of the other's royal status.

There was a historical dimension to their rivalry too. They were the heirs of King Edward's two most favoured sons, Henry the son of John of Gaunt, duke of Lancaster, and Richard the son of Edward, the Black Prince, the heir apparent. In addition, they were the heirs of the two most important dynasties in England. More than a hundred years earlier, King Henry III had had two sons. The elder had been crowned Edward I. The younger, Edmund, had been endowed with a massive inheritance in the north of England, centred on Lancaster, which gave rise to his title of earl of Lancaster. In time, Edward I's throne passed to his eldest son, Edward II, and the Lancastrian inheritance passed to Thomas of Lancaster, Edmund's eldest son. The resultant rivalry between these two royal cousins – Edward II and Thomas of Lancaster – developed in intensity, to the point of war. Lancaster's incessant attempts to intervene in royal affairs meant he was anathema to the king, and Edward II's bitter hatred for Lancaster following his part in the murder of his best friend, Piers Gaveston, never diminished. That rivalry came to an end at the battle of Boroughbridge in 1322, when Lancaster was captured and beheaded in public, and all his estates were confiscated. After such an outrage the dead earl's younger brother, Henry of Lancaster, had no choice but to join with the arch-rebel Roger, Lord Mortimer of Wigmore, and the queen, who invaded the kingdom in 1326 to put an end to Edward II's tyranny. Together they removed the king from power and, in January 1327, forced parliament to sanction the king's deposition. Edward II then abdicated. That Richard II was the great-grandson and heir of the disgraced king, and Henry the great-grandson and heir of the Henry of Lancaster who had forced him to abdicate, gave a context of ancestral hostility to their relationship of which neither boy could have been ignorant and which neither of them could have totally ignored.

To modern readers coming anew to the story of these two boys, it is easy to forget how characters in the past were so keenly aware of their history. We look back at their lives searching for the seeds of later events, 'our' history. But of course we find the culmination of much earlier developments too. Each boy would have known the above-mentioned stories of rivalry, war, humiliation, execution and deposition. Every chronicle available would have described the deeds of their ancestors. Their intimacy with history was not like that of scholars, aware of the finer points of detail; it was a sense that these chronicles had meaning for them personally. These were not just fanciful tales about knights in days of yore. Edward II had ruled badly and had lost his kingdom. Edward III had ruled well and defeated all his enemies in battle. If you wanted to know how to be a good king, a good knight or a good earl, and if you wanted to know how to avoid failure, you needed to understand the lessons of the past.[13]

And then there were the prophecies. Most people think of prophetic utterances as the stuff of the Old Testament, Nostradamus, or the oracles of the ancient world. In fourteenth-century England prophetic stories were politically relevant, widely circulated and taken very seriously, even by those who did not believe in them. The reason for this is simple: if you happened to be mentioned in one of these prophecies, how you conducted yourself might be interpreted according to your anticipated fate. For example, if you were prophesied to be a great warrior, then acting like one would undoubtedly strengthen the confidence and resolve of your forces. Conversely, a king prophesied to be politically divisive had to tread very carefully in case those whom he disappointed should start claiming or believing that the prophecy was coming true. Therefore it is particularly relevant that the most popular prophecy of the fourteenth century – the Prophecy of the Six Kings – predicted civil war in the next reign.

The Prophecy of the Six Kings was supposedly Merlin's response to King Arthur's question about the ultimate fate of the kingdom. It likened the six kings to follow King John to six beasts. Henry III was portrayed as a lamb, Edward I as a dragon, Edward II as a goat and Edward III as a boar. These emblems and the provenance of the story might seem a very shaky background for any belief system, but it was widely accepted as a framework for God's plan for the English monarchy. It also has to be said that the most recent part had spectacularly come true. The prophecy had originally been written down at the time of Edward III's birth, and various versions written before 1330 reveal it in its near-original form.[14] Edward III was characterised as a boar: the animal which had represented King Arthur himself. He would be renowned for his 'holiness, fierceness and nobility' while at the same time being 'humble, like the lamb'. This was a strange combination of qualities, and one which probably no one could have reasonably expected the infant Edward of Windsor to fulfil. So it was extraordinary that he did.[15] 'Spain would tremble', the prophecy said, and at Winchelsea in 1350 Edward defeated the Spanish fleet. This boar would 'sharpen his teeth on the gates of Paris': Edward's forays into France indeed brought him to the suburbs of the French capital. Ultimately he 'would regain all the lands which his ancestors had held, and more'. For Edward this meant nothing less than reconquering the entire Angevin empire, including more than a third of France. Yet this too came to pass: the territory of the empire was ceded to him in 1360, at the Treaty of Brétigny. At the same time he was humble and pious. That such a remarkable and popular prophecy could be fulfilled in its self-contradicting entirety was astonishing. It also made people look at the continuation of the prophecy with some foreboding.

The king after Edward III was foretold to be another lamb. The land would be at peace at the start of his reign. Within a year of his accession he would found a great city, of which all the world would speak. But then there would be a civil war, and the lamb would lose the greater part of his kingdom to a 'hideous wolf'. Eventually he would recover these lands and give them to 'an eagle of his dominion', who would govern them well until overcome by pride. At that point the eagle would be murdered by his brother, and the lamb would die, leaving his lands once more at peace. He would be succeeded by the next king, a mole, under whose reign the kingdom would be wrenched apart and plunged into civil war, between three warring factions.[16]

The next king a *lamb*? In the 1360s this seemed ridiculous, as no one doubted that the next king would be Edward's son, Edward, the Black Prince. How could he be described as a lamb? He had won one of the most extraordinary battles in European history at Poitiers, capturing the king of France in the process. He had fought in the front line at the battle of Crécy in 1346 and carried on fighting when on his knees. No one on earth was less lamb-like than the Black Prince. To Englishmen this suggested that the prince would not inherit. There would be some calamity and he would die before his father. His successor – whoever that might be – would be the lamb. That in turn gave rise to rumours. Variations on the prophecy sprang up. In late 1361 the chronicler Froissart was at Berkhamsted, immediately after the prince's marriage. Seated on a bench in the hall he overheard Sir Bartholomew Burghersh say to some of the queen's ladies that 'there was a book called the *Brut*, which many say contains the prophecies of Merlin. According to its contents, neither the prince of Wales nor the duke of Clarence [Edward III's second surviving son] will wear the crown of England, but it will fall to the house of Lancaster.'[17]

It is quite possible that the seeds of Richard and Henry's rivalry lie within this ancestral antagonism between their two houses, and that it was exacerbated by the prophecies of political turmoil between them. In later years, Richard certainly took such prophecies very seriously.[18] Obviously this does not mean that their actual hostility to one another was a result of prophetic writing: personal issues such as their shared royal identity were of an even greater importance. But even before they were born, prophecies were circulating about the house of Lancaster supplanting the line of primogeniture, and there was an ancestral precedent for just such a revolution. All of this adds up to a tension which could have gone one of two ways. Either Henry and Richard would be content to share the royal stage, and support each other, or they would look for separate identities of their own, reflecting their maternal ancestries and personal alliances. In short, the ancestral, moral and prophetic rivalry into which they were born was something which only a genuinely close personal friendship could have transcended, and that was something Henry and Richard never shared.

*

Henry and Richard did have one obvious thing in common: they were both grandsons of Edward III, the man regarded in the late fourteenth century as 'Edward the Gracious', the greatest king England had ever had.[19] In life Edward had modelled himself on the legendary King Arthur, the paragon of chivalry, and after his death the enhanced character of the literary King Arthur was based on him.[20] Although in his later years, in declining health, he had to weather some terrible criticism for his steadfast loyalty to his mistress (Alice Perrers), before the age of fifty he had earned the respect of the whole of Christendom. He had taken on the Scots and French in battle and defeated them both, capturing the kings of Scotland and France in 1346 and 1356 respectively. He had overseen the development of a method of fighting which for many years proved unbeatable, earning the nation a pre-eminent position in Europe. He had resisted papal intervention, recognised English as the language of the nation, overseen the development of parliamentary representation and introduced the modern system of local justice. Most of all, he had developed a new form of demonstrative nationalist kingship, in which the unity of nation and royal government was expressed through the king commanding nation and army alike, through building castles and palaces, living in splendour, directing taxation and fighting conflicts on foreign soil to protect the homeland. Perhaps the most eye-catching manifestation of this civil and military kingship was his position as head of the Knights of the Garter, the chivalric order which he had founded at Windsor Castle in 1349.[21] Henry and Richard were not just the grandsons of a king: they were the grandsons of the most successful king Christendom had ever known.

One of the reasons for the phenomenal success of Edward III as a military leader was his ability to command and inspire a band of knights who themselves were able to inspire men to run extraordinary risks. Foremost of all these knights was the man after whom Henry was named: his other grandfather, Duke Henry of Lancaster. In 1337 this Henry was created earl of Derby in a ceremony in which King Edward dramatically created six earls at once. In the early 1340s he became the king's most respected friend and trusted commander. In 1345, having inherited the Lancastrian title, he set out for Gascony and began the campaign which was to change his life. He was stunningly successful. Battles at Montcuq, Bergerac and Auberoche secured him fame which was both lasting and far-reaching. His friendship with King Edward catapulted him even further into prominence. He became the chief English diplomat as well as the principal English commander in war. His piety and sincerity won him widespread admiration: he wrote a book of religious devotion – *The Book of Holy Medicines* – and once, having taken a solemn vow not to depart from the siege of Rennes until he had placed his standard on the battlements, refused to withdraw even when the king himself ordered him to do so. Instead, he negotiated with the garrison to let him into the castle alone so he could put up his standard on their battlements for a minute or two, in fulfilment of his vow. He was the very epitome of the chivalric knight, and it was quite possibly his garter which became the symbol of Edward's great chivalric order.[22]

Young Henry of Lancaster therefore could be very proud of both his grandfathers. Unlike Richard, whose maternal grandfather had died under the executioner's axe in 1330, Henry's maternal grandfather was no less a hero of the golden age of English chivalry than the king himself. He had been of royal blood too, being a great-grandson of Henry III. This gave young Henry a feeling of complete royalty: his lineage was royal on both sides. Moreover, being named after the great Duke Henry of Lancaster meant he did not need to draw attention to this other, maternal line of distinction; it was evident in his name. For this reason, although Henry and Richard were both grandsons of Edward III, this in itself does not fully explain their respective royal standings. It was not what they had in common which mattered; it was what made each of them unique.

The varying degrees of royalty and dignity were equally to be noted in the boys' respective parents. Richard's father was the famous Black Prince, a great warrior – something to be proud of, one would have thought, except that Richard was so unlike his father that the associations may well have been a burden to him. His mother, Joan, 'the Fair Maid of Kent', was renowned for her colourful marital career. This involved having been married to two men at the same time in the 1340s, neither of whom was Richard's father. Richard II himself in later years seems to have been very concerned by his legitimacy, for he kept a strongbox with all the papers and documents relating to his parents' marriage, as well as his mother's divorce documents.[23] It was not just that his mother had already been bigamously married before marrying the prince, and had four surviving children by one previous husband, Sir Thomas Holland; the dispensation for her to marry the prince had not been properly formulated.[24] It could be said that they had married illegally. Both of Richard's parents' legacies were burdensome, the one highlighting his distinct lack of military prowess, the other casting a shadow over his birth.

Henry's mother, in contrast, was popularly regarded as one of the most lovely adornments of the English court. She was Blanche, one of the two daughters of the great Duke Henry. In describing her and Queen Philippa (wife of Edward III), Froissart said, 'I never saw two such noble dames, so good, liberal and courteous, as this lady [Blanche] and the late queen of England, nor ever shall, were I to live a thousand years'.[25] This was praise indeed for Blanche, as Philippa was considered the perfect example of womanly virtue. Henry cannot have been unaware that he alone was the grandson and son of the two most 'noble . . . liberal and courteous' women to have lived in recent times. Chaucer famously paraded Blanche's many virtues in his *Book of the Duchess*, written in her memory. If ever Henry read this poem, or listened as Chaucer read it to him, he would have heard line after line referring to his mother's beauty, and her white-ness 'that was my lady's name right', and her 'goodly sweet speech'. Chaucer likened her to 'Penelope of Greece', called her 'the fairest and the best', and remarked that, when they argued and he was in the wrong, she would always forgive him. In one his most famous passages he described how

> I saw her dance so comely
> carol and sing so sweetly
> laugh and play so womanly
> and look so debonairly
> so goodly speak and so friendly
> that certain I am that evermore
> Ne'er has seen so blissful a treasure.[26]

And he went on to talk of her golden hair, and her wide eyes, 'good, glad and sad', her honesty in everything, her kindness and her wonderful beauty.

Henry thus had every reason to be as conscious of his mother's and grandmother's virtues as his grandfathers' glorious deeds of arms. With such a background, we might regard him as lucky in the extreme. But no. For he never knew his royal grandmother, nor the glorious grandfather after whom he was named, nor his maternal grandmother, or even his mother. The duke of Lancaster died in 1361, in the second wave of plague to hit England. The duke's wife, Isabella Beaumont, died at the same time. Queen Philippa died in 1369, when Henry was just two. And, most tragic of all, Blanche of Lancaster, Henry's mother, died the year after he was born.[27] He would have been reminded in songs and poems of his mother's and grandmother's grace and liberality, their kindness and beauty, but he never saw their faces, except in unfocused babyhood, nor heard their 'sweet voices'. These deaths, and the infant deaths of two of Henry's brothers, Edward and John (both of whom died before he was born), are a sad reminder that in the fourteenth century to be a member of the richest, most celebrated and most powerful family in England was no safeguard from personal tragedy or physical suffering.

*

Henry was born at Bolingbroke Castle, Lincolnshire, in April 1367, almost certainly on Maundy Thursday (15 April). He was placed in the care of a nurse, Mary Taaf of Dublin.[28] His father was out of the country at the time, fighting alongside the Black Prince on behalf of King Pedro of Castile. He did not return to England to see his newborn son until October.[29]

Even this would have been nothing more than a brief visit; John was constantly travelling on royal business and usually stayed at his London residence, the Savoy Palace. In 1369 he took charge of the army at Calais for six months. In 1370 he sailed to Gascony, and remained there for over a year. By the age of four, Henry had probably spent no more than three or four weeks with his father. It is very unlikely that he would have recognised him on his return to England in 1371.

With his mother dead and his father absent, Henry's infancy was not spent in a close family environment. All Henry's grandparents except the king had died by the time he was three. So had all but three of his uncles, and all but one of his aunts. Of these uncles, one, the Black Prince, was resident in Gascony. The prince's sons, Edward and Richard, had never been to England. The elder son, Edward, never came, as he died in Bordeaux in 1371. Following that, the Black Prince did return but by then he was a severely disabled, dying man. Similarly, the king was practically confined in his old age to his palaces, cared for by no fewer than seven physicians and surgeons, the royal household servants, and his mistress, Alice Perrers. Henry's upbringing must therefore have been a little strange. A modern equivalent might be sketched by imagining a boy growing up as the grandson of people like Winston Churchill, President Kennedy and Marilyn Monroe, the son of Princess Diana and the nephew of Field Marshal Montgomery, and to hear people talk about them everywhere – yet never to have seen them or to have known them except by the conversation of adults, and through poetry, chronicles and art.

Henry's closest relations in his infancy were his sisters Philippa and Elizabeth. Philippa, the elder, was seven when Henry was born. She was the steady, dependable one. Elizabeth, four years older than Henry, was more flighty. All three children were looked after by their great aunt, Blanche, Lady Wake. She had no children of her own but, as one of the six sisters of Duke Henry, she was well positioned to introduce her young charges to other members of the extensive Lancastrian family. Besides Henry, Blanche's great-nephews included John and Thomas Mowbray, John Arundel, Henry Percy (the future Hotspur) and his younger brothers, Thomas and Ralph Percy, all of whom were between one and three years older than Henry. It was probably through Blanche that Henry first met his much older cousins, the children of the earl of Arundel: Richard, Thomas, Alice and Joan. In later years Richard and Thomas Arundel had the greatest influence on young Henry, as did their friend and kinsman, Thomas Beauchamp, earl of Warwick. Joan Arundel grew particularly close to Henry, for one of her two daughters by her husband, the earl of Hereford, later became Henry's wife.

In this way we can build up a picture of Henry's early childhood, travelling around the Lancastrian estates with his older sisters in Lady Wake's household. Their governess was a young Hainaulter woman, Katherine Roët, whose sister Philippa was married to Geoffrey Chaucer. Katherine had entered Lancastrian service before Henry's birth, and married a Lancastrian knight, Hugh Swynford. She had two children: Thomas and Blanche.[30] Thomas Swynford was born within a year of Henry, and remained a faithful friend throughout his life. So even though Henry almost entirely lacked the attention of a father and mother, he was not without close companions in his governess, his sisters and all his Lancastrian cousins and companions.

*

In November 1371 Henry and his sisters were taken to London to stay at the Savoy Palace with their father, who had just returned from Gascony. John had not returned alone. While he had been away, he had married Constanza, heiress of the ousted King Pedro of Castile. Two months later he claimed the title king of Castile and León in right of his new wife, and added the arms of Castile to his own.[31]

John did not bring Constanza into his household immediately. Instead he spent the Christmas season at the Savoy with his children and their governess. When he did welcome Constanza to his London palace, all those who saw her remarked on how attractive the new duchess was. But at about this time John fell for the attractions of the young widow Katherine Swynford, whose husband had died in Gascony that November.[32] Quite what twelve-year-old Philippa thought of this introduction of a stepmother into the family, and her father's method of comforting her own widowed governess, we can only guess. But she and her younger siblings now found themselves and their governess transferred from Lady Wake's household to Constanza's, with an allowance of £200 per year for their expenses.[33] The Mowbray brothers now became Lady Wake's full-time charges.[34]

The other collective development for all these young aristocratic children and their cousins was the arrival of Richard of Bordeaux. Until now, the younger son of the Black Prince had been nothing more than a name to them. But in 1371 he returned from Gascony with his parents, and it is highly likely that at some point in 1372, Henry, his sisters and his peer group of four- to seven-year-olds all came face to face with the five-year-old prince.

What did they make of him? He was strange, insecure and very French. His accent was different; and, unlike most of them, he spoke no English. He was both lacking in confidence and extremely self-conscious.[35] Meeting

Henry and the other English noble children cannot have been easy. Here were all these boys and girls who knew each other already, who played together, and spoke differently from him. There were some boys, like Thomas Mowbray, Ralph Stafford and Robert de Vere, with whom he got on well. But there were others – and Henry was probably one – with whom he felt uneasy. These children were confident in their status and surroundings. Furthermore, they were used to each other's company. Richard was not used to any company but that of his father, mother and servants. Until now his closest companion had been his recently deceased elder brother. It is not clear that he was a boy who welcomed a mass of new playmates.[36]

Henry only met Richard occasionally before 1376. Richard remained in the household of his father, the Black Prince, based at Kennington, south of London. Henry, his sisters and governess lived with Constanza, probably at Hertford Castle, twenty-five miles to the north of the city. Their lives and their expectations were very different. Although no memoirs of the period survive, it is not difficult to imagine the Lancastrian hall echoing with children shouting and playing, and a comparatively large number of women in and around the castle attending to them and the duchess. Every time the duke appeared, a mass of Lancastrian men would arrive, for John liked to be surrounded by a huge entourage, maintaining as many as 150 retainers. In contrast, at Kennington there were no other children and very few visitors. Normally there was just Richard, his mother and her ladies, and the regular staff of their household, with physicians and nurses attending his invalid father. Knowing how Richard developed in later years, it would not be surprising if the princess and her ladies made rather a fuss of the boy.

Between Christmas 1371 and April 1373 Henry spent much more time with his father.[37] This must in part have been due to his governess being his father's mistress. John was a great lover of women, and, though proud and haughty, he was also a deeply loyal man. Most mistresses of the royal family were discarded as soon as they had ceased to give delight but John of Gaunt, like his father the king, was different. In fact John showed surprisingly little shame in recognising Katherine as his concubine. In May 1372 the letters in his register refer to her as 'our very dear demoiselle', the 'very dear' echoing the form in which he described his wives and closest companions.[38] In about 1373 Katherine gave birth to her first child by him, John Beaufort, and he acknowledged the child as his own without any qualms.[39] Three more illegitimate children followed: two boys and a girl. In 1372 John also had a daughter by Constanza, baptised Catalina, and a short-lived son by her in 1374. Given that he had already sired five children by Blanche and another illegitimate daughter by one of his mother's ladies-in-waiting, it is easy to appreciate why these four children by Katherine Swynford and two by Constanza caused one medieval writer to refer to him as a 'great fornicator'.[40]

On 13 April 1373, on the eve of Maundy Thursday, Duke John gave out a number of gifts to members of the royal family and Lancastrian retainers. To Henry he gave a silver hanaper (a stemmed drinking goblet with two handles and a lid).[41] That summer he left England at the head of an army. Henry did not see his father for over a year, as he made his brave but ultimately futile march all the way across France from Calais to Bordeaux. It was a miserable expedition, as the French resistance prevented him from approaching Paris or joining up with his allies in Brittany. The English were forced to march east and then south. John forbade his troops from looting, thus depriving them of food, and weakening them. Hundreds of horses died. Men bashed their armour out of shape – to stop the enemy using it – and then threw it away rather than march with so much weight. It took John until December to arrive in English-held Gascony. He did not return to England until the summer of 1374.

John spent several weeks at Hertford in December 1374 and January 1375. Henry was then seven and a half years old, and his father decided it was time for his formal education to begin. On 10 December 1374 he appointed Thomas Burton to be Henry's governor.[42] By so doing, he placed his son in the care of an esquire who had served the great Duke Henry, thus strengthening Henry's Lancastrian identity. At about the same time his clerk and chaplain, Hugh Herle, was given the responsibility of teaching Henry to read and write. Clearly Henry attended to his lessons. Later examples show he had no aversion to writing comments on his own formal letters on occasion (whereas most aristocrats, even those who could read and write, normally delegated the task of writing to others). His writing exists today in three languages: English, Latin and French.[43] There can have been few worries for the young, confident Henry, looking out from the towers of Hertford Castle, attending to his grammar and spending occasional days with his father, hunting and talking, or practising sword-play, and listening to Thomas Burton telling him again how Duke Henry had won his battles in Gascony.

*

It was in 1376 that the first cracks appeared in this picture of privileged existence. Everyone knew that old King Edward was dying; now it became apparent that the prince was even nearer to death. This raised a very important question: if the prince died before the king, who would succeed?

A nine-year-old boy, Richard? Or would it be John of Gaunt, the 'great fornicator'?

Until recently, historians did not consider that there was any doubt about the succession in 1376. Richard was, after all, the eldest son of the eldest son. But although this became the established pattern of legitimacy thereafter, the situation at the time was not so clear. Law books were divided on the issue, even the oldest and most respected ones. In 1199 the throne had passed to Henry II's fifth and youngest son, John, despite the existence of Arthur, the twelve-year-old son and heir of Geoffrey, the king's fourth son.[44] Subsequently the succession had not been interrupted, and so the question had not arisen. In 1290 Edward I had forced his daughters' husbands to swear an oath that the heirs of his eldest son were to take precedence over any other sons he might have, and that his daughters should only succeed to the throne failing his sons and their heirs. But the male line had not failed and so Edward I's provisions had not been put to the test. Richard had been acknowledged as keeper of the realm in 1373, but in 1376 he had yet to be recognised as the official heir over and above Henry's father.

The problem for the Lancastrians was that John of Gaunt was hugely unpopular. Compared to his brother, the dying Prince Edward, hero of the battles of Crécy and Poitiers, he was a disappointment. He had not been a military commander of any great note; his most notable individual achievement had been the great march across France in 1373, during which many men and horses had starved to death. His role in the peace negotiations at Bruges in 1375 was seen as unsuccessful, resulting only in the withdrawal of an English army led by the earl of March. He was considered arrogant and proud, and his claim to be king of Castile did not help. Why did a great English lord need to pretend to be a foreign king? As the richest man in England, he did not need a greater realm, people said, unless it was a matter of greed. Worse still, he had protected and helped a number of unpopular royal officials. As King Edward III slipped further into melancholy he could not help but be manipulated by his mistress Alice Perrers and men like William Latimer (his chamberlain), John Neville (his steward) and Richard Lyons (Warden of the Royal Mint). John's friendship with Latimer especially, at the very moment when people were beginning to realise that their beloved Prince Edward would not live to inherit and that John might be the next king, led to widespread shifting of opinion against him.

Henry, aged nine, was probably only vaguely aware of the political danger his father was facing. For John it was nothing short of a crisis. The king and Prince Edward were both too ill to attend the parliament of 1376, both turning up only for the opening ceremony. John was appointed the King's Lieutenant to hold the parliament.[45] This exposed him to criticism from the Speaker, Sir Peter de la Mare, the steward of the earl of March. De la Mare accused various royal officials of corruption, in particular Latimer and Lyons: men associated with John. With the support of the commons essential for the provision of taxation, John was left with no option but to acquiesce to demands that the corrupt officials be brought to justice. Latimer and Neville were stripped of their offices of state. Lyons was imprisoned for life and Alice Perrers ordered to leave the king's presence. In addition, a council was appointed to oversee all royal business. And John himself was not to serve on it. Instead it was to be led by the earl of March.

While this was going on, the Black Prince neared death. Although he and John had been close in earlier years, their friendship had waned since the prince's weakness had left him bedridden. The prince's dislike of the royal officials now under attack further highlighted their differences. And then there was the succession question. On his deathbed, the prince called both the king and John to him and asked them to recognise the right of his son, Richard, to succeed in his inheritance.[46] Both men solemnly did so, and furthermore swore that they would protect him. Prince Edward died on 8 June and parliament immediately called for the king to recognise Richard as his heir.

John's oath, together with parliament's acclamation of Richard as the heir, eliminated the Lancastrians from the direct line of succession. John could not inherit now, not while Richard lived. But there remained the question of who would succeed Richard if he remained childless. Would it be John? Or would it be Philippa, the daughter and heiress of his deceased older brother, Lionel? John sought to tackle this issue head on, in parliament. He asked for it to be enacted that no woman should be allowed to succeed to the English throne, as was the custom in France.[47] This was a direct threat to the earl of March, Philippa's husband. They now had a son, Roger Mortimer, born in 1374. What John was saying was this: very well, Richard is now the heir – the king and I have both recognised him as such and sworn to support him – but if Richard dies without an heir of his own, who should inherit then? Philippa? Her son, the three-year-old Roger Mortimer? Or me?

John no doubt expected that, in return for ratifying the charges against the royal officials, his own position as second in line to the throne would be ratified by parliament. But he was to be disappointed. Parliament refused to decide on this issue and passed it over to the council. As the council was headed by the earl of March, it is not surprising that its view was contrary to John's hopes. They declared that there was no point even in deliberating such things as the king was not yet dead and his heir was young and could be expected to have children. 'Since they are alive, we have no need to trouble ourselves over matters of this kind.'[48] With that crushing dismissal John not only failed, he was humiliated.

John of Gaunt was not a man to suffer humiliation for long. And he had one enormous advantage over all his adversaries. He was now the king's favourite surviving son. The king himself was distraught at the actions of what later became known by chroniclers as the 'Good Parliament', especially at the banishment of his much-loved mistress and chamberlain, and he welcomed John's presence and attempts to overturn the judgements against the court circle. When Edward fell gravely ill later in 1376, and had to face making a will, John persuaded him to rule on the succession problem once and for all. The dying king had a settlement drawn up for the rightful inheritance of the throne. Only half of this remarkable document survives today, and that in a charred fifteenth-century copy,[49] but what is left is enough to show that in late 1376 the king settled the inheritance of the throne of England upon his male descendants only. This nullified the rights of the Mortimer family and recognised John of Gaunt as next in line after Richard. It also meant that Henry, after his father, was third in line to the throne.[50]

The implications of this for understanding Henry IV's life are huge. At some time, probably in late 1376, young Henry was told by his father that, if Richard died without issue, then he (Henry) would become king. This profoundly affected Henry's thinking, and it allows us to see Henry's life in a wholly different context, so that almost everything written about his character for the last 550 years is open to question. For example, for Shakespeare the single most important fact about Henry was that he was a usurper. But in Henry's mind, he *was* Richard's legal heir. Whether Henry believed in 1376 that he would actually inherit the throne is another matter, as Richard could yet have had sons, but there can be no doubt that Edward III's settlement greatly influenced Henry's thinking about the throne from the moment he was told about it.

*

Until now Henry would have seen Richard and himself as roughly comparable in status: both were royal grandchildren, heirs to great estates and contemporaries in age. But suddenly Richard had been promoted way above him, to become prince of both Aquitaine and Wales, duke of Cornwall and earl of Chester, and to be acknowledged in parliament as next in line to the throne. Great men bowed to him. Henry himself received his father's title of earl of Derby at about the same time, but that did not begin to compare with Richard's elevation.[51] Moreover, Richard's pre-eminence was forced on Henry in a very personal way. John now decided that Henry should live in his cousin's household. Henry would learn how to serve his future king by being educated alongside him.[52]

Henry was not alone in being sent to the young prince's household. John Arundel was also placed there, and probably so were the Mowbray brothers and Robert de Vere.[53] The court of Richard II was gathering around the future king. They did not all like him, and he did not like all of them. In later years John Arundel was never summoned to parliament, even though he should have been entitled to his father's seat. Richard simply never recognised him, let alone advanced him. Much the same can be said for Henry. Richard had plenty of opportunities to show favour to his cousin, if he wished to do so, but he never did. We should thus imagine this entourage in 1377 as a group of boys and young men who were all finding their feet in the world but who at the same time were wary of one another, knowing that the future king had favourites and enemies, and that they all had favourites and enemies of their own.

In April 1377 this band of youths made their way to Windsor Castle for the feast of St George, to attend the annual ceremonies of the Order of the Garter. The dying king, who had just completed his fiftieth year on the throne, was desperate to attend one last ceremony. His sight, dimmed though it was, was fixed on the future. Twelve of the most prominent young men of the realm were to be knighted in a special service. On 23 April 1377, Henry, Richard and ten of their companions, dressed in cere-monial scarlet robes, processed through the doors of St George's Chapel at the heart of the great chivalric palace that was Windsor Castle. They were to receive the honour of knighthood from the white-bearded king.

If ever there was an event which demonstrated Henry's position at the very heart of the English aristocracy, it was this ceremony. Imagine the oak doors to the chapel closing behind them, and each of the twelve youths casting sideways glances at each other as they stood ready to be knighted. No one, not even the king, was so well connected as Henry. He was related to all but one of them. First to kneel before the king was, naturally, his cousin Richard. Then knelt his uncle, Thomas of Woodstock, the king's youngest son. Henry himself was next to go down on his knees and repeat his vows, followed by his second cousin, Robert de Vere, the fifteen-year-old earl of Oxford. Then came John, Lord Beaumont, Henry's second cousin twice over. Of the remainder, John Mowbray and Henry, Thomas and Ralph Percy were all second cousins, and Ralph Stafford was a third cousin once removed. The only boy knighted that day who was not of

Henry's blood was William Montagu, son of the earl of Salisbury. Even the last and least in status – John Southeray (the king's son by Alice Perrers) – was Henry's illegitimate uncle.

This knighting ceremony was just a prelude to a greater honour for Henry and Richard. Both were nominated to become Knights of the Garter. Why Henry was preferred over his uncle Thomas has been something of a mystery until recently. After all, Thomas was the only one of the king's sons not to be a Garter knight in 1377, so why was a ten-year-old boy preferred over him? The discovery of Edward III's settlement of the throne explains why, for it shows that Henry stood higher in the line of inheritance than Thomas, only preceded by his father, John, who was already a Knight of the Garter. Thus it was that Henry and Richard found themselves kneeling side by side in the chapel that day, each looking to the stall which would one day be theirs. Richard would assume the one in which the king now sat. And Henry would taken that of the famous Gascon knight Jean de Grailly, better known as the Captal de Buch, one of the heroes of the battle of Poitiers.

*

Two months later, when Henry and Richard were at Kennington, a messenger brought news. The old king was dead; Richard was now king of England. If Henry observed the niceties of the situation, he would have gone down on his knees immediately and acknowledged his cousin as his lord. So too would everyone else. Suddenly Richard would have found everyone kneeling and making obeisance before him, forbidden from sitting if he was standing, nor permitted to turn their backs on him. For a ten-year-old boy, whose deceased father had been unable properly to prepare him for such a situation, it must have been both intoxicating and frightening at the same time. For Henry it must have been similarly confusing. He had known Richard since he had been an awkward five-year-old recently arrived from Gascony. Now Richard was his sovereign lord. And having lived under the same roof, Henry cannot have been unaware that this final advancement of his cousin would reveal aspects of Richard's character which were not wholly in line with the public expectations of a king.

King Edward's funeral was a magnificent state occasion. For three days his corpse was in procession. The three royal uncles – John of Gaunt, Edmund of Langley and Thomas of Woodstock – processed into the city behind the hearse and the embalmed corpse, with the earl of March alongside them. The king's body rested on a catafalque in St Paul's, viewed by thousands, until taken to Westminster Abbey for the funeral service on 5 July. Three tons of wax was burned in the candle-lit abbey and by the torch-bearing mourning populace. But underlying all this ceremonial solemnity was a hope for the future: that at last England had a young king again who, in time and with luck, would lead them to be victorious once more in every sphere of activity: commercial, diplomatic and martial.

Henry attended Richard's coronation on 16 July, and almost certainly took part in the new king's procession from the Tower to Westminster on the previous day. So many thousands crammed the streets that John of Gaunt had to ride ahead with a body of men-at-arms to clear the route for the young king and his entourage. On the morning of the coronation day itself the new king was led along a covered and carpeted route into the abbey. As the high steward of England, John had the right to bear Curtana in the procession. This was the ancient blunt-tipped sword of mercy which, according to legend, had belonged to St Edward the Confessor. John delegated this responsibility to Henry. So ten-year-old Henry had an official role in turning this cousin into an anointed monarch. He might not have been brought up to be a king but no one was in a better position to see at first hand how kings were made.

*

It was a strange theatre, the court of Richard II. The principal player was a boy, surrounded by many other boys and their more modest but mature advisers interspersed with great lords, all humbling themselves before the king, and bowing before many of the king's under-age courtiers. The council continued to function, and that body made the majority of the governmental decisions. Henry's father – although he had no official position on the council – exercised a heavy influence over proceedings. Sir Peter de la Mare was arrested and thrown into prison at Nottingham Castle, and those he had sought to undermine were restored to power or acquitted. But everything was done in the name of the king. It was thus a court of ceremony, in which there was a universal acceptance that the king was a symbolic figure and an unspoken acknowledgement that real power lay elsewhere.

The mismatch of Richard's regal privileges and regnal responsibilities would have been obvious to Henry. It became even more noticeable soon after the accession, when the French attacked Calais, Gascony and the ports on the south coast of England. It was widely believed that a good king was a fighting king, like Edward III had been in his heyday: a leader who could draw together the forces of the entire nation and inspire them to take the fight to their enemies. If the king was too young or too old, the leadership of the armies fell to men of lesser status who could not easily instil in their men the sort of confidence needed to make expeditions deep into enemy territory. In this way an under-age king like Richard was not only incapable of living up to his regnal responsibilities, his incapability detracted from the authority of the principal military leaders. One tends not to want to fight for a commander who, if he is unsuccessful, will simply be made a scapegoat for a council's poorly thought-out strategy.

The reason why this predicament must have been apparent to young Henry is that his father was given overall command of the English forces in 1377. Criticism of John over the years had weakened people's eagerness to fight for him, and even made them reluctant to provide the ships in which he was to sail.[54] As a consequence, he was delayed, with the inevitable result of further criticism. The chronicler-monk Thomas Walsingham presumed that John was too fond of his womenfolk to set out to fight. But trying to fight an offensive without the king's leadership was like the lion of England lifting a paw but refusing to show its head. Henry, as the nominal lieutenant of the Lancastrian estates during his father's absences abroad, cannot have been ignorant of John's frustrated attempts to gather sufficient ships for an expedition, nor of the vicious circle of popular criticism underlying that failure.[55]

Another reason for Henry to note the mismatch between his cousin's regal privileges and regnal responsibilities lies in the boys' military education. Over the four years between his coronation and the Peasants' Revolt of 1381, Richard revealed himself to be unwilling to practise the art of war. He never took part in tournaments at any time in his career, which is strange considering jousting was regarded as the benchmark of individual military prowess.[56] Given the age at which he became king, it would appear likely that initially his youth excused him this duty, and later he used his royal authority to refuse to take part in such a violent manifestation of kingly responsibility.

Henry, in stunning contrast, stands out as one of the most remarkable exponents of the joust the English royal family ever produced. The reason for this emphasis lies not only in the honours he won in future years but in the very first reference to his jousting, in January 1382. He was at that time just fourteen years and nine months old, and thus the youngest public exponent of the joust in England for whom we have documentary evidence.[57] No one else – not even the Black Prince – is known to have taken part in public jousts at the age of fourteen.[58] Some men are recorded to have won fame in the joust at fifteen, and this suggests that they had been taking part in public jousts at an earlier age, but, even so, Henry's participation is remarkable, especially considering his proximity to the throne and that he was his father's only legitimate son. In fact, he had probably been learning ever since the age of nine, when William Montendre had been appointed as his military tutor.[59] The contrast between Henry's eagerness to become a military leader and the king's reluctance was obvious to all. Henry was learning the skills expected of a king; Richard was refusing to compete.

We do not know for certain how long Henry remained in this situation, living in the royal household, training to be a war leader while the real king shifted uneasily beneath the weight of expectations he could not meet. Henry was still with the king in December 1377, when he, Richard and Robert de Vere visited St Albans Abbey together.[60] From this we may tentatively postulate that he was still in the royal household. But after 1377 there is little trace of him in the royal records. He was present with his father at Windsor in March 1380 for the wedding of the king's half-sister, Maud Holland, to the count of St Pol, but this may well be because he had entered his father's household by then.[61] One would have expected the name of a royal cousin to crop up occasionally if he was continually with the king, even if such references amounted to nothing more than requests by Henry on behalf of his many kinsfolk or servants. But there is only one such reference in the whole period 1377–81, and this was on a day when his father was also present, as parliament was in session.[62] It is possible that Henry remained with Richard from 1377 right up until the Peasants' Revolt, but judging from the lack of evidence it is more likely that he joined his (by now doting) father in 1378.[63] Either way, at Michaelmas 1381 he was no longer in the royal household. By then, whatever advantages John hoped his son would gain from being with Richard were outweighed by the disadvantages and dangers. The direct cause of his removal is very unlikely to have been a breakdown in relations between John of Gaunt and the king, for John remained a trusted adviser. It seems more likely that there was some animosity between Richard and Henry. They were not friends. There were still tokens of respect for each other's rank: Richard lent John the use of ten royal minstrels for use at Henry's wedding in 1381, for example, and Henry always politely included the king in his annual New Year presents, but that was about all.[64] They were chalk and cheese, radically different in outlook, friends, maternal ancestry, personal identity and martial prowess.

As a result of all this, we may say with some confidence that when the fourteen-year-old king left Henry at the Tower on that fateful day in the second week of June 1381, it *may* have been with the best intentions, to protect the life of his cousin and one of the great heirs of the realm. But if so, it was a mark of respect accorded to Henry's rank, not to him personally. It is far more likely that Henry simply did not appear on Richard's list of priorities. To have his cousin and rival there at that time, when his own position was in crisis, was an unwelcome distraction for Richard. As

Henry watched London burn, and heard the gunpowder kegs in the Savoy explode, he may well have wondered whether a Gascon-born boy who showed no aptitude for military leadership and who took the privileges of monarchy without taking the responsibilities, was the right person to be king of England. If so, when the hordes rushed towards the Tower, murdered the archbishop of Canterbury and threatened to kill Henry himself, he had his answer.

TWO

All Courtesy from Heaven

> And then I stole all courtesy from Heaven
> And dress'd myself in such humility
> That I did pluck allegiance from men's hearts
> Loud shouts and salutations from their mouths,
> Even in the presence of the crown'd king.
> *Henry IV Part One*, Act 3, Scene 2

On or about 5 February 1381 Henry married Mary Bohun at Rochford Hall, in Essex. Mary was one of the two daughters of the late earl of Hereford and his wife Joan, a cousin of Henry's mother.[1] It was an arranged marriage; almost all aristocratic marriages in the fourteenth century were organised to benefit both families' economic and political interests. In this case, Henry's father purchased the right for him to marry his youthful second cousin in July 1380 for five thousand marks (£3,333) which the king owed him for his service overseas.[2]

All this appears wholly regular until one realises that John arranged everything despite opposition from his brother, Thomas of Woodstock. Thomas was the guardian of Mary's inheritance, and benefited from her income during her minority. According to Froissart, Thomas had been hoping that he could place Mary in a nunnery, so that the whole of the Hereford inheritance would pass to her sister, Eleanor, and thus to Thomas himself (as Eleanor's husband).[3] John's action prevented this; in fact he purchased the right of Mary's marriage hurriedly, while Thomas was out of the country. Even if Froissart was exaggerating the drama for the sake of a good story, Mary was not the only available bride, and her marriage to Henry was bound to give rise to conflict with Thomas over the Hereford estates.[4] This requires us to pause for a moment and consider why John was so determined that Mary should become Henry's bride.

Mary was about eleven years old: too young to live as Henry's wife but not as young as some of the girls who might have been betrothed to him instead.[5] Her late father had been the earl of Essex and Northampton as well as Hereford, and so there was a sound financial reason for John's investment. But that does not mean that finance was the sole motive for the marriage, especially since the inheritance was certain to be split between her and her sister, and there were substantial proportions of the estate in the hands of their mother, the dowager countess. These encumbrances, combined with Thomas's interest in the estate, suggests that there was another reason. It is perhaps relevant that John's own first marriage had been a deeply loving one. Similarly John's mother and father – Queen Philippa and Edward III – had also been devoted to each other. Thus, despite his affairs, John was no stranger to marital devotion, which makes it more likely that this was a factor borne in mind when considering his son's future wife. Lastly, Henry and Mary had known each other since infancy. So it is reasonable to suppose that Mary was chosen because she was close to Henry. It was a potential love match.

Looking for evidence to support this, we cannot help but note the regularity with which Henry and Mary produced children. Successful aristocratic marriages tended to produce large numbers of offspring, as the mothers did not have to breastfeed (this duty being passed to a wet nurse, allowing wives to conceive again more rapidly). But to have a large number of children very close in age required the parents to be together, and this meant travelling as a couple for a significant proportion of the time. Noblemen who did not particularly enjoy the company of their wives tended not to do this, but happy marriages often resulted in very large numbers of children. Twelve of Roger Mortimer's children by his wife Joan lived to adulthood. Thomas Beauchamp, earl of Warwick, and his wife had seventeen children. Edward III himself sired eleven within the first twenty years of his marriage with Philippa, and then one more a few years later. John of Gaunt and his beloved Blanche had five children in nine years. So it is a very positive indicator that Henry kept Mary pregnant almost continually after they started living together, which was probably in late 1385, when he was eighteen and she was about sixteen. Mary gave birth to six children in eight years and at one point (the summer of 1392) had five children under the age of six. Also Henry sired no illegitimate children during her lifetime: as far as we can tell he remained faithful. Later evidence of presents between them supports this picture of marital bliss. So we may be confident that Henry's closeness to Mary, or potential closeness, was what made John sure she was the right choice for his son.

Henry was fond of books and Mary's family were the foremost patrons of book production in fourteenth-century England.[6] The extant volumes which they commissioned are outstanding examples of English artistry. Two of the most lavishly illuminated books to come from the family workshop were commissioned for Henry's and Mary's marriage. These were both psalters, one for Henry and one for Mary. Both Mary and her sister continued to commission such items, actively involving themselves in the creation of illuminated manuscripts. Henry too gathered valuable books, as revealed by a list of those stolen after his death.[7] That list included two psalters, valued together at twenty marks (£13 6s 8d), one of which may have been his wedding present from the Bohun family.

We know little about the wedding itself. Even the exact date is uncertain. The place – Rochford Hall – was a house of the earls of Hereford. John gave the bride several presents, including a diamond in a clasp (£2 3s 4d), and a great ruby worth eight marks (£5 6s 8d) for which he had a ring made, the fashioning of which – together with the cost of a diamond ring – amounted to a further £1 6s 8d.[8] John also paid for presents from his daughter Philippa to the bride, including a two-handled hanaper and a silver ewer at a cost of £10 8s. Minstrels came from the king and John's brother, Edmund of Langley, earl of Cambridge. Following the wedding, Mary was looked after by her mother. Not long afterwards, Katherine Swynford also joined her household, to assist in the education of the young countess of Derby.[9] Henry himself departed to take his father's place as nominal head of the Lancaster council at the Savoy. Four months later, with his father far away in the north, he found himself facing the smoke of the Peasants' Revolt in London, as the rebels destroyed his father's palace.

*

It is in the year after the Peasants' Revolt that we first get some good evidence about the fourteen-year-old Henry. Most of the documents concerning his life prior to June 1381 were burned in the flames which engulfed the Savoy, but for the year from Michaelmas (29 September) 1381 his account book survives, written up by his treasurer, Hugh Waterton.[10]

Accounts can be awkward documents to use historically. It is important to remember that they only show what was paid for, not those things which were obtained for free. Nevertheless, they are enormously revealing, especially when combined with other evidence; a good set of accounts is often more useful to a historical biographer than a similar bulk of letters. This is because medieval account books do not simply quantify income and expenditure, they seek to justify them too, and therefore normally describe transactions in some detail. Thus we know that Henry's income of £426 9s in the year 1381–2 came predominantly from three manors which John had allocated him: Passenham, Soham and Daventry, plus an allowance from his father's Norfolk estates. His wardrobe expenditure included sections on cloth, furs and skins, mercers' ware, jewellery and goldsmiths' work, leatherwork, shoes, alms-giving, personal gifts, 'necessaries', stipends paid to retainers, stabling of horses, rent, and weapons and arms. The individual entries tell us a great deal about the young Henry, but they also include detailed payments which allow us to establish where he was on a particular day and sometimes whom he was with, what he chose to spend his money on, and to whom he gave presents and from whom he received them. In this way we may build up a picture of his likes and dislikes, his friends, and his patterns of behaviour. Fortunately, we have eight such sets of accounts for Henry prior to his accession: two from the 1380s and six from the 1390s, in addition to two 'day-books'. Using these in conjunction with other evidence we may begin to discover elements of his daily life and character.

The first thing to note is that Henry spent most of the year 1381–2 with his father. In marked contrast to those years of infancy, when John was usually away, father and son were now practically inseparable. Henry travelled with his father, was financially dependent on him, and was educated in courtesy by him. Even where not directly instructed by his father, he learnt from him through example. The accounts note religious oblations and personal gifts made by Henry at his father's direction. When Eleanor, Thomas of Woodstock's wife, gave birth to a son, Humphrey, in April 1382, it was at John's direction that Henry rewarded the messenger and gave presents to the master and nurse of the young infant.[11] Similarly John chose Henry's clothes, directed his own furriers to provide furs for his gowns, and gave special garments to him, whether these be his own cast-offs or newly made gifts.

From these accounts we learn that Henry took part in the January 1382 tournament at Smithfield, held to celebrate the coronation of Anne of Bohemia, Richard's new queen. Henry appeared dazzling: his tournament armour was decorated with silver spangles in the form of roses. Shortly afterwards he appeared jousting in armour covered with golden spangles.[12] Nor was this a one-off. On May Day 1382 Henry (just turned fifteen) entered the lists at Hertford, lance in hand, and rode to the delight of the crowds. He was taking part in the greatest peacetime test of martial skill, drawing attention to himself as a prospective future military leader, and emulating his grandfather, the great Duke Henry, who had been a magnificent tournament fighter. John of Gaunt, who had never won much fame in the lists himself, must have watched his son and heir with great pride.

These entries give us our first real insight into the character of the young Henry of Lancaster. He was close to his father, dutiful and physically resilient. Within a few years he was winning fame in the jousts and earning widespread respect as he travelled around the country in his father's ostentatious cavalcade. One writer later described him as the 'strongest' of the earls of Derby, setting him even above his famous grandfather.[13] That strength is clearly evidenced in his jousting. But perhaps even more importantly, it is good evidence of a high degree of self-confidence. You cannot charge headlong at an opponent in armour on a warhorse – nearly half a ton of man, beast and metal, with a closing speed of more than forty miles an hour – and not falter unless you are a very confident, determined individual.

John impressed upon Henry the importance of looking like a prince as well as being one. Henry's tailors were directed to make short and long gowns, mantles, tunics, paltocks, tabards, kirtles and hoods. His clerks bought scarlet, blue, white and black cloth, of wool, silk, damask, satin, cotton and linen for the purpose. Red damask appears in his accounts alongside golden gowns and ermine furs. Long black gowns furred with ermine must have been particularly elegant. So too must have been the long blue damask tabard which was made for Henry for the occasion of the king's wedding in January 1382, the cloth being given to him by his stepmother, the duchess of Lancaster. Some historians have described Henry at this time as showing 'a certain extravagance in his living'.[14] But Henry was now second in line to the throne: his clothing was no more than what was appropriate for the king's cousin and the heir of the only duke in the realm. The dazzling clothes – the spangles worn at the jousts, the short gown of golden damask, the satin paltock decorated with golden leopards, and the white and gold silk paltock – were made for special occasions, and normally from cloth given to him by his father or stepmother. Compared to some of the lavish clothes brought by Edward III as a young man, or John of Gaunt, this is relatively modest.[15] Most of the time Henry was more likely to be wearing a long gown of wool than damask or silk. Considering what he might have spent as the eldest son of the richest man in the country after the king, a £20 bill for clothes at the end of the year (including the wages of tailors for his clothes at the royal wedding) plus a furriers' accounts of £16 16s 8d are not extravagant.

Much the same can be said for Henry's payments to goldsmiths. We may notice many rings made for him, but plain gold rings were not very costly. Nor were they all for his own wearing: rings were commonly given out as presents. On 29 December 1381 Henry ordered twenty-nine gold rings; he gave them all away on 1 January. There are references to occasional refinements, such as gilt silver rings for a falcon's hood and buckles and pendants of gilt silver; but we also read of mending and cleaning garters, and making new brooches out of old ones. There are only a few references to precious stones, unlike most aristocratic accounts. There are no expensive drinking cups of gold and silver, no enamelware. The entire account of goldsmiths' work amounts to £26 3s. If we add the few pounds paid for leatherwork and shoes, it is clear that Henry spent less than £70 in total on his appearance in 1381–2, less than a quarter of his income. By comparison, Edward III's gifts to Henry's mother at her wedding had cost nearly £390: fifteen times as much as Henry's entire annual goldsmiths' account.[16]

At first the above seems to point to a contradiction. Henry was drawing attention to himself as a jousting prodigy, and dressing in gilded silver spangles and roses, and yet was relatively modest in his usual dress. But there is no real contradiction; Henry was simply being conventional. When expected to dress the part of the second in line to the throne at a royal wedding, he did so. On ordinary days he preferred an elegant long gown. When lifting a lance and fighting in the lists, he wore appropriately decorated costumes, but this did not mean he had to be lavish all the time.

This conventionality is noticeable in his alms payments. Each day he gave a penny to a pauper: a modest sum for a medieval lord. He gave slightly larger amounts – normally fourpence – having heard a mass on a special occasion. He donated extra sums in particular places or when visiting particular shrines. He gave a donation at Hertford marking the anniversary of the death of his grandfather, Duke Henry. Of course, when saying that Henry was conventional in his alms-giving – and thus presumably in his religious outlook – we must remember that to be 'conventional' in a deeply religious age meant to be profoundly religious oneself. In later years Henry's religious sincerity took him beyond the conventional and caused him to be exceedingly conservative. But at the age of fifteen his religious behaviour was more in keeping with his time.

There is just one unconventional religious donation in these 1381–2 accounts. On 3 April 1382 (Maundy Thursday) John of Gaunt made provision for thirteen poor men to receive alms from Henry. This was traditional: similar amounts had been doled out by members of the royal family since at least the reign of King John. But on that day Henry added two more recipients 'because he was fifteen years old', at a cost of an extra two shillings.[17] Henry was marking his birthday, that seems clear; but the real question is, why did he do it in this way? This is the first recorded instance of any member of the royal family making a Maundy Thursday donation equivalent to their age. In later years it became a Lancastrian custom, being followed by Henry's wife and his eldest son, and indeed it remains a royal custom to this day. In the late fifteenth century it was a politically charged act: Henry VII followed it, as did other Lancastrian supporters. Herein lies its interest: if it was a political statement from the outset, why did Henry start to use it now, in 1382? One possibility is that by drawing attention to the religious date of his birth, Henry was countering Richard's boast that he was born on the Epiphany. If so, it is the earliest evidence of the religious dimension to the rivalry developing between the two young men. It may also have had another, more subtle angle, for on that Maundy Thursday Henry took a linen cloth and personally performed the *pedilavium*, the royal washing of paupers' feet. This can only be taken as a sign that he believed that great men – even kings – should be humble. Richard was more concerned with demonstrating his sovereignty than his humility. Thus this payment is evidence of much more than Henry's personal religious observance. It hints at two important divisions between him and his cousin: rivalry for spiritual favour and the expectation of royal humility. As later events were to show, these divisions were never resolved.

*

Henry's religiousness and his conventionality, his jousting prowess and his duty, all suggest that he was an earnest youth. The word which seems to sum him up best is 'conscientious'. This is fully borne out by the evidence relating to his education. Whereas his grandfather King Edward III had laboured with difficulty to form the words 'Pater Sancte' on a letter to the pope, and Richard's hand was neat but awkwardly slow, Henry was a fluent – if not an elegant – penman.[18] His informal handwriting shows signs of regular use. His ability to write in three languages – French, Latin and English – was unusual, to say the least.[19] If we then reflect on other details from his later life, such as the fact that he owned a book with a gloss or commentary in Greek, what begins to emerge is a picture of a man whose education was thorough and wide-ranging.[20] Nor should we be surprised at this: the widely travelled poet Geoffrey Chaucer was a friend of the family, so too was the poet John Gower. When John of Gaunt set about the education of Henry's eldest half-brother, John Beaufort, he did not just have him taught to be an excellent fighting knight, he also sent him to Cambridge.[21] Henry's father can thus be seen as an educational driving force. Henry took full advantage of his educational opportunities, and continued to build on them, showing a conscientiousness in later life consistent with that suggested by his youthful confidence, dutifulness and religious conventionality.

This brings us to an important point about Henry. He was probably the nearest to an intellectual among all the medieval kings of England. He was bookish, as were many young men and women of his class, including his wife's family and his uncle Thomas. But Henry was not just interested in seeing books lavishly decorated, or patronising writers; he was interested in reading too. Gower, in describing learned men who read 'old books', felt obliged to add that he knew that Henry was well learned in such texts.[22] When exiled later in his life, Henry attended and commented on lectures at the University of Paris.[23] Not long after becoming king he personally ordered a magnificent study to be built at Eltham Palace, with cupboards specially designed to house his books. On a visit to Bardney Abbey in 1406, he spent a considerable period of time in the abbey library, reading.[24] We even have some idea what he read, for we have that list of the books stolen from his library after his death. It includes a copy of Gower's work *Confessio Amantis* which was dedicated to him, two histories (including a copy of the popular *Polychronicon* of Ralph Higden), and several spiritual works. This list – which contains nothing which could be called 'light reading' – corresponds with a passage in John Capgrave's later description of him, in which his prodigious memory and willingness to debate moral issues is demonstrated. In Capgrave's words:

> I have known in my time that men of great literary attainments who used to enjoy conversing with him have said that he was a man of very great ability, and of so tenacious a memory that he used to spend a great part of the day in solving and unravelling hard questions ... Let future ages know that he was a studious investigator of all doubtful points of morals ... and that he was always eager to pursue such matters.[25]

It is in this intellectual application that Henry most differs from his contemporaries and royal ancestors. His grandfathers were no less intelligent but they were not inclined to spend prolonged periods in philosophical debate, or reading in abbey libraries. Duke Henry had written a moral treatise, *The Book of Holy Medicines*, it is true, but by his own admission he was not given over to learning. His grandson *was*, or would have been if he had had more time. Moreover, viewed in the context of his determined jousting, his emerging piety and his lack of artistic patronage (on the scale of his father or cousin), for example, one may discern in Henry an intellectual rigour and an aptitude for ideas more than the visual appeal of things. He was, it seems, a man of reason: inclined to logic and justice more than extravagance, artistry and beautiful objects.

There is one further element of his education which needs to be mentioned, even though it does not feature in the 1381–2 accounts. This is Henry's love of music. In one set of annals he is described as 'a sparkling musician'.[26] It was a passion he shared with his wife, Mary, who seems to have arranged choirs, sung and played the cither or harp.[27] Henry did all these things too: in 1387 or 1388 he bought a cover for his cither in London, and the same account records several payments for strings.[28] In 1395 he paid for a *cithara* to be fetched from Leicester and brought to him at Kenilworth.[29] The presence of royal minstrels at his wedding has already been mentioned; but he would have surrounded himself with musicians on a daily basis, eating his meals to the accompaniment of music and encouraging new forms of musical entertainment. He fostered the musical attributes of his sons: he bought a harp for his eldest son and had him taught to play it. He very probably wrote the two pieces of polyphony ascribed to 'Roy Henry' (King Henry) in the Old Hall manuscript, the earliest major collection of English sacred music.[30] One particularly interesting piece of evidence is Henry's purchase in 1388 of the first known 'recorder'. This was obtained specifically for his own use, at a cost of 3s 4d.[31] Flutes and pipes were ubiquitous, and thus it is the use of the term 'recorder' – or, to be specific, 'a pipe called *recordo*' – which is significant. For in its meaning 'I remember', *recordo* relates to a musical memory device, not necessarily as an instrument in itself but a means of being able to gauge pitch. In Mary's accounts for this same year, we find an instrument with a similar purpose: 'an iron to regulate singing', presumably a tuning fork, at a cost of 10d.[32] As later chapters will show, this love of music is revealed in practically all his later accounts, including those while he was overseas. Such an abundance of evidence for his musicianship leaves us in no doubt that he had an aural creative side to his character, and did not just patronise musicians but personally took part in making music too.

All these elements of his development seem to possess a common feature: a sense of order. Jousting was not just a matter of courage and confidence: it required training and structure. Reading and writing in three languages did not come easily to men whose usual occupations were hunting and falconry. The rules of harmony may be very different from those of war and justice, but there is a logical thread running through them all. In what is to come, therefore, we should not picture the young Henry lurking in the shadows like a worried youth but proudly entering the tournament lists, mindful of his duty, and conscientiously reading with his tutor, and singing in chapel or with his companions, guided above all by a logical and resolute mind. By the end of his teenage years he had developed into an exemplary knight: a steadfast champion of God, full of self-confidence, and certain of his place in the social order. Few who met him in his teenage years would not have admired him, or considered him worthy of his grandfather's name.

*

Richard's mid-teenage years were very different from Henry's. In some respects the young king had to educate himself, for there was no one in

England who could actually teach him about kingship from experience. His favourite tutor, Sir Simon Burley, was a man of relatively humble origins who had earned his position through serving Richard's father. Thus when he tried to instruct Richard it was from the point of view of the loyal subject: the man who gladly allows himself to be commanded. Burley may well have been aware of contemporary ideas of kingship; he owned a copy of Giles of Rome's *De Regimine Principum*, for example.[33] But even so, such a work – which stresses the importance of the king exerting his will in government, and demanding total obedience from all his subjects – could only have amplified Burley's natural view of the king's command. Partly as a consequence of this, and partly as a result of his lonely and unnerving upbringing, Richard's very character was being distorted by those around him. The pressure on him was immense: he had been given near-absolute power, educated to believe that the correct application of that power was to force everyone in his kingdom to obey, and told by parliament that his accession was as longed for as the coming of Christ.[34] After such an education, it would have been a miracle if he had developed as a fair-minded, level-headed king.

By 1382 it was already becoming apparent that Richard was very far from the glorious youthful leader that parliament and the rest of the country had hoped for at his coronation. Unlike Henry, who had been able to practise the arts of a chivalric leader privately, Richard was already being tested in public, in council and in parliament. He was already psychologically on edge, wary of expectations he could not live up to, and torn between his education and the advice of the lords in parliament. But he had one great advantage: he was clever, blessed with a very quick and flexible mind. He now began to invent a different sort of kingship, one quite unlike Edward III's, which did not require him to be a jousting champion, or a warrior-king.

It is reasonable to assume that Richard's demands for personal power arose from his intentions to govern well, not just a wilful independent streak. As he toured the south-east counties after the collapse of the Peasants' Revolt, seeing dire punishments inflicted on the rebels, he cannot but have reflected that their demands had been the removal of bad ministers; they had been staunchly royalist. He concluded that the root of the problem was that his rule was too weak.[35] It was his duty to stamp on anyone who threatened his authority, be they bad ministers or overmighty subjects. Ironically, the rebels permitted him to take his first steps towards strengthening his hand. Their universally condemned rebellion meant that he could order severe reprisals without fear of contradiction.[36] It was a first step towards building his personal authority.

Richard knew that the next step – to impose his personal rule over the council and his royal uncles – required a much stronger justification. He needed a body of powerful and influential men who would support him. Such a body of men was already gathering around him. First there were those older men, his tutors. Men like Simon Burley and Michael de la Pole were exhorting him to take power, so they were bound to help him. Then there were the lesser household knights who encouraged him, like Sir Guy Brian, Sir Robert Bardolf and Sir Peter Courtenay. But the most important in the long run were those courtiers and young men of noble birth with whom he had a genuine rapport. Such men and boys included Ralph Stafford, heir of the earl of Stafford, Robert de Vere, earl of Oxford, Sir John Beauchamp of Holt and Thomas Mowbray, who became earl of Nottingham following the death of his brother in February 1383. Quickly they became identified as a set of royal intimates, viewed by non-courtiers with a measure of envy, suspicion and hostility.

Through a natural desire to reward his faithful friends, Richard deepened the divide between those whom he favoured and the rest. After the death of the earl of March in 1381, the major part of the Mortimer inheritance fell into his hands. Rather than keep the whole estate in trust for the heir (his seven-year-old cousin, Roger Mortimer), Richard started breaking it up to distribute among his supporters.[37] When the chancellor, Richard Scrope, refused to countenance these grants of land, Richard sacked him. This was hugely presumptuous for the fifteen-year-old king.[38] Thereafter, many of the Mortimer lands were distributed to Richard's friends, including Burley and the knights of the king's chamber. Similarly, following the death of the earl of Suffolk in September 1382, Richard gave many of the earl's lands to Michael de la Pole, a man not even of noble birth. Nor were these his sole attacks on the magnates' interests in that year. Most shocking of all was his refusal to honour large parts of the will of his grandfather, Edward III. Instead he gave to Burley a number of manors which the late king had intended to be given to religious foundations to pray for his soul. Richard took back estates which had been granted to monasteries by his late grandfather and dismembered certain royal estates, including part of the duchy of Cornwall, again contrary to the late king's charters.[39] It was not behaviour becoming for the grandson of the warrior-king.

The problem for Richard lay in the perception that he was showering rewards on his friends not in return for any great deeds or services to the nation but simply out of favouritism. Simon Burley and his brothers were made Knights of the Garter, and Simon himself received very extensive grants of land. Thomas Mowbray was made a Knight of the Garter and given licence to hunt in all the royal forests. He was also given an heiress to marry (at a cost of a thousand pounds to the royal purse), and allocated his own apartments at two of Richard's favourite royal palaces, Eltham and King's Langley. Robert de Vere likewise was made a Knight of the Garter, given a large number of grants, wardships and offices at Richard's order and installed in private apartments at Eltham and King's Langley. As the criticisms increased, Richard simply put himself physically out of reach of his opponents. Burley, as the acting chamberlain, prevented Richard's critics approaching the king. As teenage rebellions went, this was very serious. Richard was heading quickly for a confrontation with all those who would stand in the way of his assuming complete control of government.

Men cautious of the king now began to discuss historic situations where young leaders who dismissed their councillors met with violent opposition. The case of Rehoboam came to be cited, as it always was when young kings replaced wise old knights appointed for their guidance with a group of young men.[40] More alarmingly, men started to draw a parallel between Richard and Edward II, whose reliance on a small group of intimate companions had eventually led to civil war. By the end of 1382, many people – including a number of lords – were of the opinion that, unless Richard could somehow be brought to heel, all the evils prophesied to occur in this reign would soon take place.

Richard proceeded, undaunted. After all, as he was constantly reminded by Burley, the essence of good kingship was the king's personal control of the realm. It was his duty to face down doubters. His flexibility of mind allowed him to turn his opponents' arguments on their heads. If they said that he would end up like Edward II, why, then he would praise Edward II. His maternal grandfather, the earl of Kent, had been executed for trying to rescue Edward II from wrongful imprisonment, so by championing Edward II he could restore both his grandfather and great-grandfather to a higher level of dignity. We may picture Richard going to the royal book presses in the Tower, and rummaging through them for chronicles which would tell him about the period.[41] And when he found a relevant volume, and read of how Edward II had been forced to work with a royal council, and had resisted all attempts to control his power, and ultimately had fallen due to his refusal to compromise, we can imagine Richard closing the book and holding it tightly, having recognised a royal martyr in the man who had sought to maintain the integrity of the royal will above all his magnates, including Lancaster. Upon opening it again, and reading of how Edward II had preferred his favourites and commoners to the lords who had such different expectations of him, there was no doubt in his mind. At the age of sixteen Richard gave orders that his great-grandfather's anniversary was specially to be celebrated each year. Later he would write to the pope and try to make the man a saint.[42]

*

In 1383 the first opposition to Richard's government began to take form. At first it remained disparate. Those whose prior concern was the management of the royal household petitioned the king 'to choose the most wise, honest and discreet persons of your realm to remain about your honourable person and advise you'; to which Richard responded that he would choose such men as he deemed 'best for his honour and profit'.[43] Those more concerned with the appointments to high offices of state petitioned him 'to elect those endowed with the greatest loyalty and knowledge of the governance of the people ... [and] to exercise office without favour or partiality for any person'. Richard again replied that he would choose such worthy persons as he considered best for the good government of his kingdom. Three days later, after the resignation of the chancellor, he appointed his friend Michael de la Pole, a man who had no right even to attend parliament (not being an MP, a prelate or a lord). Coming on top of his dismissal of the chancellor for daring to disobey him, this was a forceful slap in the face of anyone who expected him not to appoint his personal friends to offices of state.

Such actions concentrated opposition on the king himself. Henry probably met him in the summer of 1383, when his father attended a small council at Nottingham.[44] John was playing a difficult role, balancing his unpopularity with his need to maintain order within the royal family. By the time of the parliament of October 1383 there were a number of lords who were prepared openly to complain that the king was listening to foolish advice. As a chronicler at Westminster Abbey recorded, 'a serious quarrel arose between the king and the lords because it seemed to them that he clung to unsound policies and excluded those offering good guidance from his entourage'.[45] The lords insisted that Richard's royal predecessors had accepted advice from the magnates and prelates. Predictably, the king was of the opposite view; his refusal to follow advice (despite being still only sixteen) confirmed their fears. When Michael de la Pole, the new chancellor, had to apologise in his opening speech for his presence, and announced furthermore that one of the matters to be discussed was the imminent threat of invasion from Scotland and the failure of the previous year's expedition to France, the kingdom could be seen to be trembling. It was far from being the confident and assertive nation which it had been under Edward III.

The opposition lacked leadership. John of Gaunt could not provide a focus of resistance to the king's unsound rule, as he had sworn to the Black Prince on his deathbed that he would protect Richard, and he intended to fulfil that promise. Besides, John was far too unpopular with the commons to act as a spokesman for their cause. The next royal uncle, Edmund, was unambitious and similarly loyal to Richard. Thomas, the youngest son of Edward III, was not yet openly hostile to his nephew's rule. As a result, the nearest approximation to coordinated opposition was the group of lords who continued to press the case of the Mortimer inheritance and who, in December 1383, succeeded in stopping Richard distributing the Mortimer estates among his friends.[46]

To Richard, of course, any man who dared to speak against him was a self-confessed rebel. To Henry, the protectors of the Mortimer inheritance were in the right, safeguarding a great estate for the heir. Just as importantly, these bold lords were his kinsmen. Richard, earl of Arundel, was both his mother's cousin and his wife's uncle. Arundel's close associate in the business, Thomas, earl of Warwick, was a more distant kinsman, but an old comrade-in-arms of Henry's father. Thomas and John were almost the same age, had fought together on Edward III's last campaign in France in 1359–60 and had been on campaign together subsequently, most recently in the summer of 1381. A third earl who joined in this trust overseeing the Mortimer estates on behalf of the young earl of March was Henry Percy, earl of Northumberland, another Lancastrian cousin of Henry's (although a sworn enemy of John of Gaunt). With no love for Richard or his style of kingship, Henry was attentive to the arguments of the opposition lords. While as yet he could not act, he could at least listen.

Henry was still under age, and so was not summoned to the 1383 parliament. He would only have known of the proceedings against Richard from his father. John's own policy with regard to Henry was to keep him in the background, for there could be no possible advantage in bringing him into the political fray too soon. Nevertheless, as a result of John's influence, Henry's name was added to the list of nobles to negotiate a truce with France at the end of the year. Thus Henry received his first (and only) official commission under Richard II. He accompanied his father overseas in December to witness the negotiations with the French at Leulinghen, concluding a truce on 26 January 1384.[47] Herein lies another reason why John was reluctant to take any part in forming an organised opposition to Richard II: he hoped to use his loyalty to gain advantages for his children, especially his eldest son.

Parliament was summoned to meet at Salisbury on 29 April to discuss the terms which Henry had seen formulated at Leulinghen. Writs of summons went out – though not to Henry – on 3 March. But long before parliament actually met, other events had overtaken the original agenda. The Scots had seized the English castle of Lochmaben, removing the last English presence in Annandale. John of Gaunt and his brother Thomas were given the responsibility of carrying out reprisal attacks by the English council, and set off north. Henry, having already proved himself useful in arms, probably went with them.[48] We cannot be certain about this but it seems likely, especially considering that his father believed him old enough to take part in a diplomatic embassy.[49] In the end the expedition proved little more than a punitive raid. By 23 April, John – and presumably Henry too – were back at Durham, and shortly after that they began the long ride south to meet with the parliament already gathered at Salisbury.

Neither father nor son can have had much optimism for the proceedings which lay ahead of them. Each of the last four parliaments had seen a hardening of the stand against the king's personal rule, together with a commensurate increase of the king's defiance of his would-be advisers. But even John could not have expected what would happen at Salisbury. By the time he arrived (shortly after 9 May) there had already been a number of 'astonishing squabbles' between the lords and prelates, so that they 'almost nullified the effect of the parliament'.[50] The commons had had great difficulty deciding whether they wanted peace on the terms agreed in outline by John at Leulinghen. They asked for a committee of lords to help them debate the issue. They felt that the peace gave too much to the French, including the sovereignty of Calais, a near-impregnable town which had taken Edward III eleven months to conquer. But nor were they eager to sanction another term of taxation for a futile war. Suddenly the proverbial elephant in the corner of the debating chamber – the king's inability to lead an army and his reluctance to entrust an army to someone who was capable of military success – raised its trunk and trumpeted loudly in the form of a speech from the earl of Arundel:

You are aware, my lords, that any kingdom in which prudent government is lacking stands in peril of destruction; and the fact is now being illustrated before your eyes, since this country which, as you know, began to lose its strength long ago through bad government, is now almost in a state of decay. Unless remedies are promptly applied for its relief and it is speedily rescued from the stormy whirlpool in which it is engulfed, there is reason to fear that it will very soon suffer enormous setbacks and crippling losses, leading to its total collapse and the removal (God forbid) of all power which may come to its aid.[51]

When Richard heard these words he was uncontrollably furious. 'The king turned white with anger' wrote the chronicler who recorded the earl's speech. Scowling, Richard erupted in fury: 'if you would blame me for this, and say that it is my fault that there is misgovernment in the realm, you lie in your teeth. You can go to the devil!'

A stunned silence followed.

Henry knew Richard well enough from childhood to realise that he was incapable of taking criticism lightly. But shocking though the king's anger was, what happened next was of even greater concern. While celebrating Mass at Salisbury in the chapel of the house commandeered by Robert de Vere, earl of Oxford, a Carmelite friar called John Latimer told Richard that John of Gaunt was plotting against his life. Richard was sent spinning into a fury once more. He ordered that his uncle be put to death immediately. Lords implored him to see reason. Someone ran to tell Thomas of Woodstock who, thrown into a rage, burst into the king's chamber and 'swore a terrible oath that he would attack and kill anyone who intended to accuse his brother John of treason, and no one was excepted, not even the king himself'.[52] Enough of the more moderate lords had their wits about them and were able to divert the king's attention, and make him see that he could not execute the heir to the throne without a trial.

When John heard the charges levelled against him, he too went to Richard, and managed to convince him of his innocence. Richard then ordered the friar to be put to death. This time it fell to John to make Richard see reason, and to try to preserve both the friar's life and the king's reputation. The end of the business is unclear, but one account has John Holland, Simon Burley, Philip Courtenay and others torturing the friar by hanging him by his hands, then suspending heavy stones from his testicles while he was hanging, forcing him to kneel on a fire, draping a sheet over his face and pouring boiling water over it three times, and burning his feet. Whether this torture story was propaganda, salacious rumour or the truth, we cannot be certain – it is hardly likely that the protagonists told the chronicler or anyone else of their misdeeds – but it is likely that the friar was tortured, for he died soon afterwards. Whoever had entreated the friar to say these things against John was never discovered.[53] But the incident had revealed two important things. First, when faced with intense and hostile criticism from the magnates, Richard had no ability to control himself. And second, even though John of Gaunt was his most stalwart defender and his heir, Richard was terrified of his uncle: so much so that he did not think twice before ordering his execution, even though he had no evidence of his guilt, or even of his readiness to commit a crime.

*

Arundel had been right. England in the summer of 1384 was festering with political maladies which were destroying its pride, wealth and security. In June the Scots took advantage of the situation to invade Northumberland, burning the villages and murdering anyone unfortunate enough to get in their way. A great drought parched the country, so that even the deepest wells dried up and many cattle died. When the drought ended, it seemed to rain continuously for four months. Carmelite friars began to declare that John Latimer was a martyr, and publicly preached sedition. Arguments broke out between prelates and temporal lords, with no one to check them. The bishop of Exeter's officers forced a messenger of the archbishop of Canterbury to eat the seal of a letter which he was carrying. In revenge, the archbishop of Canterbury's men forced one of the bishop of Exeter's esquires to eat his own shoes. Such things prompted the monastic chronicler of Westminster to remark that 'all the lamps have gone out in the church of God, and the darkness which shadows her face on every side is great indeed'.[54]

For the purposes of understanding Henry of Lancaster, the importance of the summer and autumn of 1384 is to understand that the rifts were deepening between the Lancastrians and the court of Richard II. Despite John of Gaunt's best efforts to maintain the respect of his nephew, the Lancastrians were powerless to stop Richard himself casting a shadow over his fitness to rule. In coming to judge an ex-mayor of London, a Lancastrian supporter, and being told that he hoped the king would not proceed to judgement until John of Gaunt arrived, Richard shouted that he was competent to sit in judgement on both the accused and John of Gaunt.[55] John himself was out of the country at the time, dutifully attempting to negotiate another treaty on Richard's behalf.[56] Notwithstanding this fact, Richard sentenced John's supporter to death, a punishment only commuted to imprisonment after the queen's intercession.

The original reasons to doubt Richard's fitness to rule – his unwise grants of lordships and lucrative offices, his lack of military leadership in the face of encroaching enemies and his lack of judgement in political and diplomatic affairs – all remained valid. He continued to advance his favourites and friends without regard for lordly or public opinion. For example, he gave the town and castle of Queenborough to Robert de Vere and specified that, if Richard were to die first, then the de Vere family were to keep it as their own inheritance.[57] This was strategically unwise:

Queenborough was of military importance and de Vere had no military experience whatsoever. Moreover, Richard had no qualms about treating one of King Edward III's greatest military constructions as a present for a friend. Similarly when de Vere decided to abandon his royal bride, Philippa, granddaughter of Edward III, Richard did not condemn him, unlike the rest of the nobility. Richard was prepared to belittle his grandfather's memory in order to promote his own vision of kingship. It seems extraordinary that he should not defend the dignity of the royal family but there is no doubt that Edward III's martial legacy bore heavily on him. The late king was not just his predecessor, he was also his rival.

By the end of 1384, after another stormy parliament, relations between the Lancastrians and Richard reached breaking point. John voiced his opinion – which was almost universally shared – that war with France was now unavoidable, and that Richard was well advised to lead an army across the Channel in person. This had been made a condition of the grant of taxation for the war in the recent parliament. But at the council at which John said these things, Richard rebuked him, and blamed him for failing to negotiate a permanent peace treaty. John – who had laboured long and hard in such negotiations – stormed out, together with his brothers.[58] Then Richard, bitter at this flouting of his will, plotted with de Vere and Mowbray to murder John on the night of 14 February 1385. John heard about the plot just in time, and fled with a few companions. Ten days later, when the king was not expecting him, he returned by river. He left his barge in the care of a strong guard, and took more men with him to Sheen Palace, where Richard was staying. He wore a breastplate beneath his robes. At the gate he left a large contingent of armed men, to stop anyone going in or coming out. Then, striding into the hall, and bowing to the king, he launched into a lengthy, well-prepared and heartfelt condemnation of Richard's government and behaviour, condemning him for the bad counsellors whom he kept, and humiliating him with the observation that it was shameful for a king in his own kingdom to stoop to private murder in order to seek revenge. After this, he declared that he would no longer attend the king as he had done previously, for fear of his life.

Hearing of this interview, Richard's mother was distraught, and feared for her son. Once 'the Fair Maid of Kent' – but now so fat she could barely stand up – she went to her son and demanded that he make efforts to restore himself to John's favour.[59] Richard acquiesced. He met his uncle in March 1385 at Westminster, and was reconciled to him, but the damage was already done. Not much later, the archbishop of Canterbury harangued the king on the same theme, accusing him of ordering John to be murdered in the street. How could Richard command the great men of the realm if they feared that he might turn a mere grudge into a reason to murder them? Richard had heard enough criticism of his personal rule, and leapt to his feet. Furious, he launched a tirade of threats at the stunned prelate. Later that same day, Richard met the archbishop again, and drew his sword to kill him, which he would have done had he not been stopped by his uncle, Thomas, assisted by Sir Thomas Trivet and Sir John Devereux. Whatever it was the king yelled at the men who restrained him was not deemed repeatable by the St Albans chronicler, who was clearly deeply shocked to hear such language from an anointed monarch.[60]

*

In 1385, at the age of eighteen, Richard II finally did lead a military expedition. But it did not go to France, as parliament had demanded and as John had advised. Instead the king chose to lead an army to Scotland. Following their reconciliation, John also agreed to serve. In fact, as this was a feudal summons – the last of the middle ages – he had little choice.[61] So John went north, in the summer of 1385, and Henry, now eighteen, went with him.

For Henry the chance to fight in Scotland was probably as good as the chance to fight anywhere. As a tournament champion he was already winning fame and respect, but there was a big difference between being good with a capped lance in the lists and being a successful commander on the battlefield. He rode in the vanguard, in his father's company. Although the English army proceeded to burn and destroy, the Scots remained wary. Years of fighting Edward III had taught them that the best way to preserve their country was to stop the destroying army by starving it. If the Scots themselves undertook the controlled destruction of their crops and livestock before the English got there, and evacuated their people, then the English army could not advance without going hungry, and no leader could wage war with an army of ten thousand empty stomachs. Richard had the choice of advancing through the wilderness to seek out the Scottish leadership and their sixteen hundred French auxiliaries, or to retreat without gain.[62]

John, with the support of the other royal uncles, was all for going after the Scots. He tried to persuade the king, pointing out that the enemy were in flight, and reminding him of the size and strength of their own forces.[63] But Richard did not trust him. De Vere played on the king's paranoia by suggesting that John wished to lure him north in order to murder him in revenge for the two occasions when Richard had threatened his life.[64] So when John suggested advancing, Richard rounded on his uncle and 'blazed with anger', declaring:

'No matter what region you have come to with an army, you have been the ruin of my men because of your bad leadership, your advice, the bad terrain, and because of hunger, thirst and poverty. Always concerned for your purse, you are totally unconcerned for me. And now, it is typical of you to want to force me to cross the Scottish sea, so that I may perish with my men from hunger and destitution, and become a prey to my enemies . . . You will certainly not have your way in this matter. However, you may cross the sea with your men, if you so wish. Never before have you been thronged by so large a number of your men as you are now. But I and my men will return home.'

'But I am also your man', John responded.

'I see no evidence of it!' snapped Richard, whose mood was afterwards one of great distress.[65]

Although the retreat was sounded without any material gain and without even having engaged an enemy, the campaign of 1385 was not without its landmarks. One of these was Richard's creation of two of his uncles as dukes: Edmund as duke of Canterbury and Thomas as duke of Aumale. These titles were short-lived; there may have been hostility to them, not so much arising from the recipients as from the fact that Richard had created them outside parliament. Edward III had been very careful to raise all his higher lords to their dignities within the parliamentary chamber. For this reason, Richard's attempt to make Simon Burley the earl of Huntingdon – having already given him many of the old earl of Huntingdon's lands – failed.[66] He was more successful with his plan to create Michael de la Pole earl of Suffolk, but even here he managed to alienate one of his uncles, Thomas, to whom he had just given a dukedom. He gave de la Pole all the inheritance of the Ufford family, who had previously been the earls of Suffolk. This angered Thomas, who still had no landed inheritance of his own. He began to side more openly with those speaking against Richard's personal form of government.

While the army waited at Bishopthorpe, a quarrel broke out between John Holland – Richard's older half-brother – and Sir Ralph Stafford. Two esquires in the company of Stafford's father, the earl of Stafford, killed two grooms in the service of Sir John Holland. The offenders fled to sanctuary and would have been dragged out and lynched had not Richard intervened. Holland then went to see Richard, to ask for redress, and was assured that the squires would stand trial. But shortly afterwards Sir Ralph chanced upon Sir John. As Ralph Stafford was one of Richard's favourites, probably his closest friend after de Vere, and a great favourite of the queen's too, John Holland should have exercised more caution. But like the king himself, Holland could not stand criticism of any sort, and drew his sword and killed young Stafford. Subsequently, fearing Richard's revenge, John Holland withdrew from the army and sought refuge on his estates in Lancashire.

News of the quarrel between her two sons plunged Joan of Kent into deeper grief. Hearing that one of her sons, the king, had insisted that another of her sons should face the full penalty of the law, she sent messengers to intercede with Richard, and to show pity to her through showing mercy to John. Richard refused. He had promised the dead heir's father – who was understandably distraught at losing his eldest son – that he would not protect the killer even though he was his half-brother. When Joan's messengers returned and told her this, she collapsed.[67] We can sympathise with all parties: the royal family was wrenching itself apart, brother fighting against brother; cousin against cousin. A few days later, on 8 August, Joan died. Although she made due acknowledgement of Richard's place in her affections in her will, describing him there as 'her very dear son', the king cannot have been reassured. She chose not to be buried with his father, the prince, but with Thomas Holland, the father of her other children, including the renegade John.[68]

*

Henry probably remained in the north at the end of the 1385 campaign. His father took on the securing of the northern border against reprisals from the Scots. They had both seen enough of the young king and his entourage for the time being. Although John had been reconciled to Robert de Vere and Thomas Mowbray in June, he did not trust either of them. Nevertheless, he could not remain in the north forever. There was a parliament to be attended. Writs had been sent out as soon as Richard had returned. And this time they included one name which had never before been included on a parliamentary summons: Henry of Lancaster, earl of Derby.

It was a tumultuous parliament. Everything was set for confrontation. The king had led his army, as he had been required to do. Now he wanted free rein to rule as he wished. He had turned his thoughts to how to counter criticisms of his personal rule, and he had a new strategy. Whatever parliament wished to throw at him, he had something to throw back. He was set to make a powerful display of his own vision of chivalric kingship. When the lords, prelates and commons arrived at Westminster Hall, they found themselves confronted by a series of larger-than-life-size statues: one for every king from St Edward the Confessor to Richard himself. Thirteen kings – some good, some bad, some strong and some weak, but all of them kings – were displayed as the inheritors of the throne of a saint, not a conqueror.[69]

The proceedings of the parliament were cold and meaningful. The chancellor made the opening speech, announcing that the parliament had been called to discuss the good governance of the realm and its preservation from threats within and without its borders. But then he announced that the internal 'threats' amounted only to the location of the wool staple and the standard of the currency. What of the appointment of bad ministers, of the raising of unworthy men to peerages, of the alienation of royal property? What of the fact that Richard had promised to give de Vere £45,000 to secure his lands in Ireland? The king was then petitioned repeatedly to revoke his grants to unworthy lords, for the royal purveyors to act within the law, for the royal household to be reviewed, for a committee of lords to be appointed to oversee the operations of the exchequer and to exercise restraint with regard to royal grants. Richard listened as his political opponents read out a blistering attack on his personal government. In thirteen clauses (echoing the thirteen kings, perhaps) it hammered home what exactly the lords wanted from Richard: that he give credence to his council, that he not interfere with the law, that he appoint suitable persons to control access to his chamber and other household offices, that he not appoint anyone to any offices without first seeking advice, that he not grant out lands and offices without advice, nor grant pardons for murder, robbery and rape as lightly as he had done.[70]

After a bitter and long debate, a compromise was reached.[71] A commission of four men to reform the royal household was agreed, with a remit to oversee the operation of the royal finances.[72] The king was prohibited from making further grants which reduced the Crown revenues. Other grants could only be made following an expert valuation, and then only to those who deserved them: the king could no longer simply hand out lucrative offices to his friends. Richard cleverly managed to water down the most excessive demands, but then he rendered the whole compromise utterly meaningless. Having been criticised for raising his friends to high titles outside parliament, he decided that the agreement now gave him the right to demand confirmation of their titles within parliament. On 9 November he announced that he would create his two uncles dukes. Thomas was henceforth to be duke of Gloucester, and Edmund, duke of York (the titles he had given them on the Scottish border were discarded). These were fine but then he declared that Sir Michael de la Pole would receive the earldom of Suffolk and Sir James Butler the earldom of Ormond. Sir Ralph Neville would become earl of Cumberland and Sir Simon Burley earl of Huntingdon. And then he declared that Robert de Vere would become duke of Ireland.[73]

Those present were horrified. They did not know what was more objectionable: Richard handing out a grant of £45,000 of royal revenue to de Vere or making him a duke. Giving Burley, de la Pole and Neville earldoms was hardly any better. They objected. Burley was prevented from receiving his earldom, so too was Neville. De la Pole was grudgingly allowed his, but de Vere's dukedom was out of the question. Richard refused to back down. So the debate raged. Eventually, yet another compromise was suggested. Rather than a dukedom, de Vere could be given a new form of title, a marquisate. Richard agreed. On 1 December, his favourite was created marquis of Dublin.

The earls were bitterly resentful. De Vere now outranked them in the chamber: an unremarkable, inexperienced pleasure-seeking twenty-five year-old! But Richard was not finished yet. To insult his detractors that little bit more, he also gave de Vere the confiscated estates of John Holland, even though the reversion of these meant that they were not his to grant. And then he decided he would not abide by the decisions of the commission to reform his household and finances. Was this not everything which the lords had just sought to prevent happening? Would Richard never learn?

Richard was no fool, however. Instead of working with parliament, he made personal bridges with John of Gaunt. He agreed to pardon John Northampton, the pro-Lancastrian mayor of London. He agreed that John could lead a military expedition to Castile, funded by the subsidy granted in the last parliament. On the last day of the parliament, 5 December – four days after Richard had so controversially raised de Vere to a marquisate – John was dining in his company.[74] Parliament's will had once more been flouted. John was probably looking forward to his Castilian venture, if only because it removed him from threats of being murdered and Richard's shameful political intrigues.

Henry spent Christmas and New Year at Leicester with his father. On 19 February 1386 they were at Lincoln, when Henry was accepted into the confraternity of Lincoln Cathedral. With them too were Henry's half-brother, John Beaufort, now aged about fourteen, and Thomas Swynford, now seventeen.[75] Following the ceremony, the Lancastrian party with all its many followers returned to London, to watch Henry take part in the jousts at Smithfield in early March. All eyes were on him, the champion of the Lancastrians, hoping that he would demonstrate the prestige and power of the family. Henry did not let them down. In front of a huge crowd of Londoners, he swept the field and took the prize as the best jouster of the tournament.

John and Henry remained in London for about three weeks. A royal council on 8 March confirmed support for John's expedition to Castile, and two days later Henry officially received custody of his wife's inheritance.[76] Having made his farewells to the king and queen, exchanging presents with them, John set out on a series of pilgrimages, a preliminary to his expedition to Castile. Henry went as far as Plymouth. In mid-June they were staying at the Carmelites house as the fleet and an eight-thousand-strong army gathered. While waiting for a favourable wind, they gave evidence in the famous heraldic legal case between Robert Grosvenor and Lord Scrope of Bolton as to who should be allowed to bear the arms *azure, a bend or*. On 9 July the wind changed and the fleet was ready to sail. Henry joined his father on board his flagship for one last meal together, and then disembarked.[77]

He was nineteen. The full weight of Lancastrian expectations now lay on his shoulders.

THREE

The Summons of the Appellant's Trumpet

The Duke of Norfolk, sprightfully and bold,
Stays but the summons of the Appellant's trumpet.
Richard II, Act 1, Scene 3

Enmity is a difficult subject for historians. Friendship is much easier. If a king gave a large gift to one of his companions, and showered honours on him, and entertained him regularly, then we may confidently build a picture of the positive rapport between the two men. Not so with enmity. An opponent might still show his face at court, he might continue to receive occasional grants (in order to satisfy the king's debts to him), and he might even receive marks of respect according to his status while all the time plotting against the monarch, or while the monarch was plotting against him. Richard was so mercurial that one reads of him dining or drinking wine with his enemies just after forcing them into open revolt.[1] Thus, historically, relations between lords normally appear as shades of friendship. Enmity is just the darkest, most obscure shade.

Henry was already set on the path which was to lead to enmity between him and the king. Although the crisis had not yet arrived, the parliament of 1385 had shown the level of outrage which Richard could cause through his arrogance and favouritism. Even before that parliament Henry had every reason to be deeply concerned. On top of their childhood rivalry, Richard had attempted to parcel out the inheritance of the Mortimers (Henry's second cousins) and take back the benefactions given under the terms of the will of Edward III (Henry's grandfather). He had sacked the chancellor, raised unworthy men to earldoms, and raised the unworthy de Vere to a higher title than Henry. He had viciously slandered the earl of Arundel (another of Henry's cousins), attempted to kill the archbishop of Canterbury and despite his earlier promises permitted his half-brother John Holland, to go unpunished after murdering the earl of Stafford's son and heir. Worst of all, he had ordered Henry's father to be summarily executed in 1384, plotted to have him murdered in February 1385, and accused him of treason for nothing more than wanting to press ahead with the Scottish campaign. On top of all this the king was ignoring the commission set up by the 1385 parliament to reform the royal household. Richard had frittered away more than a hundred thousand pounds of taxation, having given much of it to his friends. English military obligations overseas were being disregarded, the defence of the realm forgotten. For anyone of the Lancastrian affinity, Richard was both a vicious man and an incompetent ruler.

Henry wisely avoided the court after seeing his father off. Instead he went to Monmouth, a Lancastrian town, where his sixteen-year-old wife, Mary, was preparing to give birth to their first child.[2] Henry would have been able to enjoy the Forest of Dean – a fine hunting ground – while he waited for the child to arrive. Thomas Swynford was with him, as were Hugh Herle (his chaplain), Hugh Waterton (his chamberlain), Simon Bache (his treasurer) and William Loveney (his clerk).[3] Thus he spent the late summer of 1386 with these close companions, hunting, playing dice, feasting, reading, playing music, dictating letters and waiting until 16 September, when Mary gave birth to a boy, the future King Henry V, in the gatehouse chamber of Monmouth Castle.[4]

In normal times, Henry would have attended his wife's churching about a month after the birth, and there would have been celebratory feasting and jousting for three days. But these were not normal times. More than a month earlier, writs had gone out to the lords and commons to attend parliament on 1 October. The forthcoming assembly would be the opposition lords' first opportunity to challenge Richard since the ultimatum of the 1385 parliament. To add to the pressure, intelligence reported that a French army and fleet was gathering at Sluys, ready to invade England. The time for direct action had come.

The early stages of Richard's reign had seen no effective opposition, mainly due to the lack of effective leadership. Now a sort of hereditary responsibility came into play. The last time a wilful and irresponsible king had proved a threat to the kingdom, Edward II in 1312, the earls of Lancaster, Hereford and Warwick had taken action against him. In 1386 the heirs of these three earls were gathering again for the same reason. Henry was one of the key figures, although he was yet to declare his hand. Not only was he the heir of Lancaster, he also represented half of the earldom of Hereford, in right of his wife. The rest of that earldom was represented by his thirty-three-year-old uncle Thomas, duke of Gloucester, the leader of the opposition. The earl of Warwick was with them. Also coming from the same Lancastrian tradition of opposition were Henry's cousins, the Arundels: Richard, earl of Arundel, and his brother, Thomas, bishop of Ely. Their sister Joan was the dowager countess of Hereford, mother of the wives of Henry and Thomas. It was a close-knit, resolute and proud family which was preparing to challenge the king. Henry could not attend his son's baptism and Mary's churching for the simple reason that his presence was required at Westminster. He waited at Monmouth as long as he could, until 24 September.[5] Then he began the 130-mile ride to Westminster.

On 1 October the chancellor opened parliament with the customary speech. At the great council held in Oxford in August, he declared, the king had decided that he would lead an army into France. According to the chancellor, his principal reason for this was, 'because it would entail much less injury and expense to the people in many ways if the king were to fight his enemies overseas than if he were to resist them within the kingdom'.[6] This was a deliberate repetition of Edward III's foreign policy. Indeed, it was practically a quotation from Edward III's letter to the pope of 1339 in which he had explained why he had invaded France.[7] The chancellor added that the king had three other reasons for fighting: to disprove the rumours that he refused to fight in person, to pursue his right to the French throne and to prevail in battle and conquer 'humanely'. The sum of money the king needed was £155,000. Four years' wartime taxation, to be paid in one instalment.

No one in that parliament had any doubt what Richard was trying to do. Quoting Edward III's key policy, and offering to go to France at the head of an army . . . He was offering to sell them – for four 'tenths and fifteenths' of their income (depending on whether they lived in a town or the country) – the sort of kingship they expected of him. But no one believed he had it to sell. Victory in France was well beyond his reach, and thus his bargaining position was ridiculous, insulting even. The newly created earls and dukes and the marquis of Dublin could not defend him. Indeed, Thomas, duke of Gloucester, now stepped forward as leader of the opposition lords. They would not grant this taxation. The king had been poorly advised, badly led, and had failed to fulfil his promises at the last parliament. Had he observed the commission of 1385? No. Why was he in need of so much money now? Because he had failed to accept advice in sorting out the royal finances. And what was this about a 'humane' invasion of France? Edward III had not been humane. He had savaged the country, massacring and burning. That was the nature of war. Richard understood nothing about war.[8]

Richard, enthroned, took the rebuke badly. He demanded total obedience from his subjects, and expected no one to reprove him. But the lords responded with a single voice, calling for the chancellor and treasurer to be sacked. Parliament was determined to take action against Michael de la Pole, and it could not do so while he was still in office.

Richard was furious. 'This is none of your business,' he retorted. 'We will not sack even the humblest of our kitchen staff at your behest'. Having rebuked the lords, he spoke with his friends, including the chancellor, and then announced that he would leave Westminster, thereby dissolving the parliament. He would listen to no petitions. He stormed out of the chamber, followed by Robert de Vere, Michael de la Pole, Simon Burley, John Beauchamp, John Salisbury and a few other friends. They went to the river and took the royal barge to Eltham Palace.

The king clearly expected that the parliament would apologise and ask him to return; either that or disperse. After all, he or his official representative needed to be present for the parliament to be in session. But the lords and commons were seething with fury. They had seen the chancellor step up to the throne and inform the king that he could dissolve the parliament simply by walking out.[9] They had seen John Beauchamp do likewise. And they were not prepared to let the matter drop. They remained in the chamber.

The duke of Gloucester took the lead in organising parliament's response.[10] With strong support from the other opposition earls, and with Henry present, he was able to instil confidence in the assembly, so that the vast majority remained in their seats. They consulted chronicles and statutes, and argued about whether or not the king should be deposed. On 13 October they heard that Richard had created Robert de Vere duke of Ireland, despite all their arguments about creations being in parliament, and despite their protests at the ducal title in the previous session. That infuriated them even more. A few days later, they decided they would send a deputation to the king, demanding his return. Forty knights were selected, and the king was told to expect them. But a short while later a messenger came from the mayor of London, Nicholas Exton, to say that the king was preparing a force of men to ambush the forty knights on their way to Eltham. Given Richard's attempts to murder the duke of Lancaster and the archbishop of Canterbury, parliament judged the risk too great. Instead, the duke of Gloucester and Thomas Arundel, bishop of Ely, were deputed to speak to the king.

Gloucester and Arundel saw Richard at Eltham on or about 21 October.[11] Their opening message was simple. If you stay away from parliament, the commons will refuse to sanction taxation, and depart. Richard was, of course, prepared for such an attack. 'We have long been aware that our people and commons intend to resist and to rise against us,' he replied, 'and in face of that threat it seems to us best to turn to our cousin of France, and seek his support and aid against our enemies, and better to submit ourselves to him than to our own subjects'.[12]

This was nothing but antagonism to Gloucester. Arundel was hardly any less outraged. 'The king of France is your chief enemy and your kingdom's greatest foe, and if he once set foot in your land he would rather work to undo you, and usurp your kingdom, and expel you from your royal throne, than extend his hand to help you,' declared the bishop. The two men went on to remind Richard of how his father and grandfather had fought against the French, and how his people had given their lives, and 'poured out ungrudgingly their goods and possessions to sustain the war'. They were not playing upon Richard's sympathy. Both envoys were far harder men than that. They were preparing the way for the powerful ultimatum which had already been agreed. Parliament had consulted the means by which Edward II had been deposed, and was prepared to follow the same process to get rid of Richard, if necessary. As Arundel put it:

> We have an ancient law, which not long since, lamentably had to be invoked, which provides that if the king, upon some evil counsel, or from wilfulness or from contempt, or moved by his violent will, or in any other improper way, estrange himself from his people, and will not be governed and guided by the laws of the land, and its enactments and laudable ordinances . . . but wrong-headedly, upon his own conclusions, follows the promptings of his untempered will, then it would be lawful, with the common assent and agreement of the people of the realm to put down the king from his royal seat, and raise another of the royal lineage in his place.[13]

Richard was fully aware of the deposition of his great-grandfather, a man he regarded as a saint. But it was a matter to which he had already given some thought. If they did depose him, who would replace him? His official heir, John of Gaunt, was out of the country. Henry could hardly inherit during his father's lifetime. So what then? Gradually Richard perceived a weakness in their plan. He himself had never recognised an heir. Not many people – probably only a handful – knew of Edward III's settlement of the crown on John and then Henry, and that was not a document which Richard was likely to circulate. He could divide and rule. Yes, he agreed to come to parliament within three days. Yes, he would dismiss his officers. But he would have the final word.

It would appear that Richard re-entered the chamber to confront parliament on 24 October. He sacked the chancellor and treasurer, and appointed Thomas Arundel and John Gilbert, bishop of Hereford, in their respective places. It was probably also on this day that he uttered a declaration which would prove the biggest bone of contention for the next one hundred years. If he had been forced to resign, he declared, the new king would not have been John of Gaunt. Nor would it have been his uncle, Edmund of Langley, nor his other uncle, the duke of Gloucester. The new king would have been the twelve-year-old earl of March, Roger Mortimer. The boy was powerless, unable to lead an army. He was incapable of delivering the sort of government parliament wanted, through no fault of his own. What did the representatives think they would achieve by putting him on the throne?

This declaration has been hitherto overlooked for a number of reasons. It only appears explicitly in one chronicle, and there it follows immediately after a section of text dealing with the parliament of 1385. Historians have noticed that it could not purposefully have been made in that parliament as it implies the demotion of John of Gaunt in the line of succession, and there are a number of signs of reconciliation between John and Richard in and after that parliament. But a recent re-examination of the text shows that the section relating to the 1385 parliament is an interpolation, inserted by a later writer. When the original text is restored, the declaration clearly relates to this parliament of 1386.[14]

Most people at the 1386 parliament would not have been very surprised to hear Richard's declaration. Edward III's entail was a secret document, never publicly declared or shown. The populace already assumed that the Mortimers were Richard's heirs, and so there was nothing newsworthy in the king's statement. Besides, they were more interested in bringing Michael de la Pole to justice. The rest of the parliament was spent impeaching him: a momentous event in its own right, especially as it ended with him being found guilty and imprisoned. Thus the chroniclers concentrated on this trial and the ordinances imposed upon the king on 19 November, which put the king back under the guidance of fourteen lords. Richard's statement about the inheritance was taken up by only one other chronicler, a monk of Westminster Abbey. The fact that it barely scratched the surface of writers' consciousness, however, should not delude us into thinking that it was of little or no importance. The effect on Henry was nothing short of life changing. Richard's declaration that Roger Mortimer was his heir, and after him his brother Edmund Mortimer, effectively ruled Henry and his father out of the succession. It was a profound and real threat to his entire dynasty, including his father. What would John say on his return when he learned that Henry had allowed this to happen? But how could Henry dispute Richard's declaration? If the king declared Mortimer was his heir, how on earth could Henry reassert the Lancastrian claim to the throne?[15]

*

Henry left Westminster after the end of the parliament, on 28 November 1386. He was not one of the fourteen lords who remained to oversee the government. Still not yet twenty, the reason was undoubtedly his youth. Instead, he returned to Mary and his young son. Within a few weeks, another baby was on the way.[16] The family passed the summer together at the great Lancastrian fortress-palace of Kenilworth.[17] Apart from his customary attendance at the Garter feast on St George's Day at Windsor (23 April), there is no evidence of Henry coming face to face with the king until the end of 1387.[18] It is possible that they met at the installation of Richard Scrope as bishop of Lichfield on 29 June, as Lichfield is only a day's ride away from Kenilworth.[19] But if they did meet then, Henry kept his anger private.

The commission of fourteen appointed to oversee the king was based at Westminster, so Richard did his best to disempower them by continuously travelling. This did not ease the tension. At Westminster the lords realised that they were being purposefully prevented from carrying out their duties. Their period of office was only one year, and in November 1387 it would come to an end. Similarly Richard – still only nineteen – realised that he could not traipse around his kingdom forever. He started to lay plans so that, in November, he would not have to continue this game, but would repudiate the authority of the council.

In August Richard summoned the judges of the realm to him at Shrewsbury, and put to them a series of questions. Was the new ordinance governing the king lawful, and did it contravene royal authority? What should be done with those who forced this measure upon him? Did parliament have the right to impeach office holders? Could the king dissolve parliament? What should be done with those who had threatened the king with deposition? Was the judgement against Michael de la Pole legal? At Nottingham Castle, on 25 August, the judges were asked to deliver their answers, or rather to ratify the answers which Richard had determined they should deliver. Robert Tresilian, Robert Bealknap and four other justices, plus two lesser legal men, agreed that the ordinance, being against the king's will, was damaging to his kingship, and those who had forced this on him deserved capital punishment. Likewise they declared that parliament had no right to impeach office holders, that the king could dissolve parliament whenever he wanted, and that the king was correct to raise questions about the proceedings of the 1386 parliament. Not all the judges were willing. Robert Bealknap bravely refused several times to fix his seal to the declaration, but the duke of Ireland and Michael de la Pole told him they would kill him if he did not. Poor Bealknap knew exactly what the implications were. Having done what was required of him, he declared, 'Alas, now I need only a hurdle, a horse, and a rope to bear me to the death that I deserve, and yet if I had not done that, I should have met death at your hands.'[20]

With this document, Richard set himself firmly against parliament. He was claiming that the officers of the realm were answerable to him, not parliament. Parliament had no right to act or even assemble without his permission. Anyone trying to diminish the king's authority in any way was guilty of treason. This was patently wrong: Edward III had laid down the law determining what was and what was not treason in the Statute of Treasons in 1352. But even laying this aside, it was an extraordinary attempt to return parliament to its subsidiary role as a purely tax-granting and advisory body, which it had been a hundred years earlier. In Edward III's reign, the members of the commons had come to regard themselves as representatives of the people. No one who knew of Richard's questions can have had any doubt that when parliament next assembled, certain lords would be summarily judged and executed. Parliament was not likely to acquiesce to such an imposition of tyranny, and there would be a bloody revolution. Pre-emptive action was necessary.

Richard was not unaware of the dangers. He took steps to make sure that the questions to the judges remained secret. Even without this information, the duke of Gloucester and the earls of Arundel and Warwick had reason to be fearful of his approach. At the Garter feast in April, Richard had been stirred up against Gloucester, who only escaped with his life by marching out of the hall unexpectedly halfway through a feast.[21] The approaching end of the commissioners' period of authority also created a feeling of unease. For those who knew about the questions to the judges, the tension must have been terrible. Someone's nerve was bound to break.

That someone seems to have been the archbishop of Dublin.[22] He met Gloucester and began by asking to be pardoned for his actions against him. He then revealed the questions to the judges, and the responses given at Nottingham. Gloucester informed his fellow lords. Bishop Arundel went to see the king at Woodstock in mid-October, probably to test the truth of the matter. Richard moved to Windsor, and from there sent a messenger to the mayor of London to find out how strong royalist support was in the capital. Reassured, at the start of November, he began to move towards Westminster. He arrived there on the 10th, and waited for the authority of the fourteen commissioners to run out.[23]

The next day Richard ordered Gloucester and the earl of Arundel to come to him. They refused on the basis that 'their arch-enemies were at the king's elbow'.[24] They were prepared for war, encamped with armed retinues. So too was the earl of Warwick, stationed at Harringay Park (now Hornsey, in north London). Richard instructed the earl of Northumberland to arrest Arundel, and to kill him if he could, but when Northumberland found that his quarry was armed to the teeth, at Reigate Castle, he wavered.[25] In that moment of indecision, Arundel seized the initiative and marched to join with the other lords at Harringay Park. Many lesser lords and knights joined them. So did many commoners, including disgruntled peasants who now realised that the loyalty of the 1381 rebels had been misplaced. Even those lords who did not take up arms against Richard refused to defend him. By 13 November the forces ranged against Richard also included an armed retinue from the Mortimer estates, headed by Sir Thomas Mortimer, guardian of the earl of March whom Richard had declared heir to the throne.

Richard was shocked by the support the lords received. He realised that he had miscalculated. On 14 November he despatched an embassy to the lords, now at Waltham Cross. They stood firm: 'they clearly foresaw the speedy overthrow of the kingdom of England by the traitors who haunted the kings presence', namely Alexander Neville (the archbishop of York), Robert de Vere, Michael de la Pole, Justice Robert Tresilian and Sir Nicholas Brembre of London.[26] The following day they put their complaint in writing. They accused these five men of being enemies of the realm and traitors. On 17 November they rode to Westminster to meet the king. They travelled in full armour, accompanied by three hundred men-at-arms. Richard received them in Westminster Hall, seated on his raised throne, and listened as Richard Scrope – whom Richard had sacked as his chancellor in 1382 – read out the lords' challenge to the five men to trial by combat. Unsurprisingly, such a challenge was ignored. But the king was forced to agree that the charge of treason would be heard in parliament. The date was set for 3 February 1388.

Where was Henry in all this? Given his family ties to all of the leading opposition lords, one might have expected to find him encamped in Harringay Park. However, it seems he was at Westminster when the lords rode there in arms.[27] This begs the question, why did he not join with Gloucester and his fellow opposition lords? Indeed, given that we know Henry joined them shortly afterwards, what was he doing?

It is unlikely that his hesitation had anything to do with the recent birth of his second son, Thomas, or the evacuation on 25 November of Mary and the children from London.[28] We might speculate that he was waiting to see whether Richard would compromise, or would publicly reverse his declaration in the previous parliament that the Mortimers were the heirs to the throne. Alternatively, it is possible that a severe illness is the answer, for his accounts show that he was suffering from a skin disease ('the pox') at about this time.[29] However, the most likely explanation is that he was waiting for authority from John of Gaunt, in Castile, for it is difficult to believe that the dutiful Henry would lead the Lancastrians into a rebellion without consulting his father.

Faced with the prospect of trial in parliament, the king's favourites mostly ran away. De la Pole, Tresilian and Archbishop Neville went into hiding. Brembre stayed with the king. De Vere went to Cheshire. There, assisted by Sir Thomas Molyneux, constable of Chester Castle, he raised an army of between four and five thousand men. Now Henry joined the opposition lords, and so did his second cousin and close friend, Thomas Mowbray, earl of Nottingham. Although the payments noted in his account book are mostly undated, from the relative positions of certain entries, combined with locations known from other sources, we can reconstruct his route.[30] At the end of November or the beginning of December he rode north through Hertford, and attended a war council with the other lords at Huntingdon on 12 December. Sir Thomas Mortimer and Thomas Mowbray were also there. Together they resolved to attack de Vere in the field, if he rode against them. At the same time they discussed whether they should depose Richard. They decided not to, following Warwick's advice that such a move would bring shame on their families.[31] Besides, as Henry knew, if Richard was deposed it would only raise the question as to who would be his successor. With his father out of the country, the duke of Gloucester would probably be seen as the strongest contender. And the duke had a son and heir. If Richard was deposed, the Lancastrians might lose their position in the succession forever.

Henry and the other lords moved to intercept de Vere. They knew he was marching down the main road to London – Watling Street – so they moved westwards to stop him. They were probably at Northampton on 15 December, and at Henry's own manor of Daventry on the 16th. De Vere learned that they blocked his path to London. They in turn learned of his movements from Mary, Henry's wife, who sent several messages to her husband from Kenilworth.[32] De Vere had the choice of turning east or heading directly south. He chose the latter, marching down the Fosse Way to Moreton-in-Marsh. Gloucester and the earls took a parallel southwest path, to Banbury. There Henry split off from the main army. If de Vere was heading south, he would eventually come to the Thames, where he would either have to turn and face the lords with his back to the river or cross a bridge. It was Henry's task to cut him off, and hold the bridges across the Thames.[33]

The exact course Henry pursued is not clear. It is possible that he went south, around the east side of Oxford, and approached the bridges across the Thames from Berkshire. However, this would have taken a considerable amount of time in December, when the daylight hours are few and the roads muddy. Given that he paid for a horse to be returned to him from Banbury, and that his wife sent a letter to him in Oxfordshire at this time, it would appear that he simply rode on ahead of the other lords, to the west of Oxford.[34] Either way, it was an excellent strategy. The main army was forcing de Vere to move southwards while Henry and his men were securing the strategically important bridges, Newbridge and Radcot Bridge, which lay ahead.

On 19 December de Vere was at a manor of the abbot of Evesham near Stow-on-the-Wold, probably Broadwell. The lords had occupied all the places around: Banbury, Brailes, Chipping Norton, Chipping Camden, Blockley and Bourton-on-the-Hill. Now they drove him further south, trusting that Henry would do his duty. The weather was dark and foggy. On went de Vere, not suspecting that Radcot Bridge was held against him. Henry had his force out in the open, between him and the bridge. As for the bridge itself, it was 'broken in three places' so that only a single horseman could cross, and blocked by three barricades. Henry had also posted archers there.[35] The trap into which the lords had led de Vere was about to snap shut.

The most reliable account of the encounter which took place the next day comes from the pen of Henry Knighton, who seems to have heard an eyewitness account, albeit a sketchy one.[36] De Vere marched his men hard towards Radcot Bridge, probably believing he could get there in advance of his pursuers. When he saw the banners of Henry of Lancaster arrayed before him, he realised he had been outmanoeuvred. He decided to fight, and ordered his men to stand their ground. He unfurled the royal banner, a sign of war. He ordered his trumpets, pipes and drums to start playing and 'with a cheerful voice exhorted his men to prepare for instant battle'. But few of the Cheshire men wanted to fight. They had not believed until this moment that it would actually be necessary. Faced with the banners of Henry of Lancaster, which incorporated the royal arms, their courage evaporated.

The first of the lords to join Henry on the scene was Sir Thomas Mortimer, leading the vanguard of the earl of Arundel's army.[37] In response to shouts and threats, de Vere's men raised their hands and let go of their bows. Seeing that all was lost, de Vere dismounted from his war horse, grabbed the reins of his swiftest steed, mounted, and galloped off along the river bank. Sir Thomas Molyneux, constable of Chester Castle, tried to follow him, but Thomas Mortimer was watching and pursued him. After some fighting Molyneux was forced down the bank into the shallows. Mortimer shouted at him to get out of the water, or be pierced with arrows where he lay. 'If I climb out,' responded Molyneux, 'do you promise to spare my life?' 'No, I do not,' replied Mortimer coldly, 'but unless you climb out, you will die straightaway.' Molyneux, seeing he had little choice, announced he would join Mortimer on the bank, and fight like a man, one to one. But Mortimer grabbed his helmet as he climbed out, ripped it off and jabbed a dagger into the side of his skull, killing him instantly.[38] After that, no one else put up any resistance.

Molyneux was almost the only fatality at the battle of Radcot Bridge.[39] De Vere stripped off his armour and swam his horse across the River Thames, near Bablock Hythe, and escaped to his castle of Queenborough in Kent, from which he fled abroad.[40] His armour was later recovered, as were his horse, treasure and other possessions. The Cheshire men in his army were forced to give up everything they possessed – arms, bows, arrows, gold, silver, swords, horses, armour and clothes – and in this state were dismissed and told to walk back to their own lands, naked. The victorious five lords travelled together to Oxford, and from there went to Notley Abbey. Passing his manor of Henton, Henry took all the animals he could find for the army's Christmas feast. According to his accounts, three hundred and twelve sheep, eighty pigs, eighteen oxen and two cows later had to be replaced.[41] The feast was eaten at St Albans. On Christmas Day itself, Henry provided twelve masks in the form of knights' visors for 'disguising games' at the feast.[42] The next day they marched on London, arrayed for war.

Henry, Gloucester and the earls of Arundel, Warwick and Nottingham all met Richard in the Tower on 27 December 1387. What followed was a protracted private discussion. The king agreed to allow the arrest and trial of his favourites. Henry took Richard up on to the walls of the castle at some point and showed him the mass of armed men they had with them, and Gloucester added that these amounted to less than a tenth of those who were willing to take arms against the traitorous favourites.[43] They talked about the future of the monarchy. It appears that at least two of the lords – Gloucester and Arundel – withdrew their homage for the duration of their stay in the Tower. In other words, they deposed Richard and discussed the alternatives.[44]

This was the real showdown. Radcot Bridge had been merely the precursor. The core of the problem was not a favourite's abuse of his position, or even the king's personal government. The fundamental issue was that the king was weak, and, without a clear heir, there were three if not four potential alternatives, two of whom were definitely stronger characters. Weakest of all (on account of his age) was Roger Mortimer, just turned thirteen, whom Richard had named as his heir the previous year. There was the unpopular John of Gaunt. He undoubtedly had the best legal case (considering Edward III's settlement of the throne) but he was absent, in Castile. So Edward III's next eldest son, Edmund, duke of York, had to be considered. He had taken no part against the favourites, was not a strong character, had very little ambition, and he too was unpopular. That left Gloucester, who clearly fancied his chances. In such circumstances, and with Richard's reign hanging in the balance, it is not surprising that the lords publicly insisted that the heir to the throne – whoever he was – was of full age.[45] It was either John of Gaunt (by right of inheritance) or Gloucester (by right of conquest).

If Henry had not joined with his uncle in opposing de Vere things would have been very different. If Gloucester had been alone with Richard, he would have shown scant respect for Edward III's settlement, and even less for the young Mortimer. But Henry would not let his father's interest – and thus his own – be overlooked. It is easy to imagine his line of argument. Why could his father not be recalled from Castile to be crowned? The Lancastrians had, after all, done their part to correct Richard's poor government. Besides, if Gloucester were to take the throne, in defiance of Edward III's settlement, he would have to face the opposition of the Lancastrians, and that would mean a civil war. As the hours passed, Henry managed to persuade his uncle of the necessity of recognising the Lancastrian claim. Eventually the five lords decided that the best course of action for them all was to retain the status quo. Richard would be restored to his throne, but constrained in his kingship. Edward III's settlement would be honoured.

When Gloucester departed, Richard asked Henry to remain with him at the Tower.[46] In all probability it was because Henry had prevented Gloucester and Arundel from deposing him. Richard realised that Henry might be his rival and enemy, but in John of Gaunt's absence he could also be manipulated to become his protector.

*

The relationship between Henry and Richard had been irreparably damaged over the previous two months. They both had every reason to hate one another, and Richard's dislike of Henry was probably only exceeded by that he felt for Gloucester and the earl of Arundel. Yet ironically Henry and Richard needed each other more than ever before. Without Henry, Richard would have lost his crown. Without Richard, Henry and his father might yet lose their position in the succession. Hence it is not surprising to read that Henry and Richard exchanged traditional New Year presents on 1 January 1388. Even though they would never forgive each other for the events of 1386–8, the niceties of diplomatic friendship had to be observed.[47]

Much the same can be said of Henry's relationship with his uncle, Gloucester. In 1377, Henry had been made a Knight of the Garter and Gloucester had not. Subsequently the two men had been rivals for the estates of Mary Bohun. Now they were rivals in the matter of the succession. But despite these problems, Henry and Gloucester also exchanged New Year gifts on 1 January 1388. Of course, we might say, the duke was one of Henry's most prestigious relations. But what then about his other uncle, the duke of York? Henry never exchanged presents with him. Similarly one finds the name of William Bagot regularly in Henry's accounts; one day he would be part of a plot to murder Henry's father.[48] The words with which this chapter began – about enmity being the darkest, most obscure form of friendship – seem particularly relevant with regard to the early months of 1388.

Henry had every reason to be fearful of those around him, not just the king. This was the most damaging aspect of Richard's rule. With a mercurial, unstable and sometimes vicious king, the entire top rank of society was made to feel insecure. It was difficult to know whom to trust. Henry had few close male kin to support him, and he could not even wholly depend on those. His sister Elizabeth had fallen in love with John Holland, Richard's half-brother – the man who had murdered the earl of Stafford's son and heir – and would have eloped with him had not Henry's father allowed them to marry and taken them both to Spain. As for his other sister, Philippa, she was now married to King João I of Portugal. His eldest half-brother, John Beaufort, was similarly of dubious loyalty, being made a knight of the king's chamber by Richard, and later raised to high rank. Apart from the handful of steadfast Lancastrian knights, such as Thomas Erpingham, Robert Waterton and Thomas Swynford, there were few men whom he could wholly trust.

It is in this atmosphere of distrust and suspicion that we should visualise Henry and the other four leading opposition lords entering parliament on 3 February 1388. They entered the White Chamber in a line, all wearing a livery of cloth of gold, with their arms linked.[49] When Thomas Arundel, the chancellor, had made his opening address, and had called for an end to the disputes which had beset the kingdom, Henry and his four colleagues made their declarations of loyalty to the throne. Everyone else watched in silence and nervous anticipation. The five of them then 'appealed' the five favourites of treason. From this they acquired the title by which they are usually known, the 'Lords Appellant', although an alternative name was 'Lords of the Field'.[50] The method of prosecution by appeal was highly unusual.[51] Certainly their accusations had historical references, for as the clerk of parliament read out the appeal he repeatedly accused de Vere and de la Pole of 'accroaching' royal power, a phrase which had been rarely used since the trial of the first earl of March in 1330, and was employed specifically to portray de Vere and his associates as enemies of the Crown.[52] The accused were all summoned to plead. Three times over the next three days they were summoned, but only Brembre turned up. Subsequently, the absent four were given a week-long trial. All were found guilty. De Vere, de la Pole and Tresilian were sentenced to death. Neville as a clergyman was spared death but forced to surrender his temporal estates.

According to the parliament roll, Brembre was denied legal counsel and was only allowed to say 'guilty' or 'not guilty' when the charges were read out. He offered to defend himself in battle, and the king spoke up on his behalf, but a wave of outraged voices silenced him. Twelve lords were eventually deputed to try Brembre. They decided that his crimes were insufficient to merit the death penalty. The Appellants were not satisfied, and apparently used other methods of prosecution, all of which failed. Finally, they hit on the idea of charging him with concealment of the others' treasons, of which they found him guilty. He was drawn to the gallows as a traitor, and hanged, despite the shouts, tears and pleas of the onlookers.

Nervous anticipation had given way to uninhibited anger. Now that mood in turn gave way to vindictiveness. In the course of Brembre's trial, Justice Tresilian was found hiding in Westminster Abbey. He was dragged out by the duke of Gloucester and immediately hanged as a traitor. More trials followed: those of men who had aided and abetted the protagonists, or simply been considered bad advisers for the king. These men were not appealed of treason but impeached. First there were the other justices who had set their seals to Richard's questions of the previous August. They were found guilty, as Bealknap had predicted. The parliament was turning into a judicial mass lynching, a bloodbath. Some of the Appellants themselves were among those who pleaded for the lives of the judges, recognising that they were the unwilling accomplices of Richard's tyranny. They had some success. Their two helpers – those who had actually drafted the questions – were convicted and executed, but Bealknap and his colleagues were spared the rope.

The leading Appellants were not finished yet, however. As the weeks went by, more trials took place. After breaking for Easter, parliament went into a second session, and listened to the cases of four knights: Sir Simon Burley, Sir John Beauchamp of Holt (recently created Baron Beauchamp of Kidderminster by Richard), Sir James Berners and Sir John Salisbury. These men too were accused of 'accroaching' royal power, of misdirecting the king in his youth, of abetting the principal favourites in their plots and attempted murders during the previous parliament, of advising the king to leave that parliament, and – in the case of Sir John Salisbury – of plotting with the French. Eventually all were condemned to death as traitors. Berners, Burley and Beauchamp were beheaded, and Salisbury hanged.[53]

If the Lords Appellant are viewed as a group, there is little doubt that they used tyrannical methods to bring an end to Richard's tyranny. Their definition of treason, like Richard's own, bore no resemblance to the articles of the Statute of Treason drawn up by Edward III. Their processes were based largely on military strength, not the law. Their judgement was in places arbitrary and often prejudiced. Clearly Brembre's crimes did not merit the death penalty. It is not surprising that the parliament came to be known as the Merciless Parliament: it deserved the title. In all, eight of the king's friends were executed. Two others (de Vere and de la Pole) were sentenced to death in their absence. Seven more lost all their goods and were exiled. Nor was the term 'merciless' applied by a Ricardian sympathiser: it comes in fact from the pen of Henry Knighton, whose abbey was patronised by the Lancastrians.

But the Lords Appellant showed signs of breaking up even in their moment of triumph. As noted above, one or more of them called for the judges' death sentences to be commuted, which they were. Although they had entered parliament with a show of unity, they were divided as soon as the first five traitors had been dealt with. Such divisions became even more apparent after Easter, when the case of Simon Burley was heard. Burley was fifty-two, relatively old for the time. He had been in the retinue of the Black Prince, for whom Henry had a high regard. He was also a very well-educated man, and had read treatises of the kind that would have appealed to Henry's logical mind. He was a thinker, and Henry had appreciated his thinking at first hand at the age of ten, when he had been in Richard's household under Burley's tutelage. When the matter of his sentence was raised, on 27 April, the duke of York rose from his seat and declared that Burley had always been loyal to the king and the realm, and he challenged anyone who disagreed to fight him in single combat. Gloucester was outraged at his brother's intervention, and shouted back that Burley was false to his allegiance, and he would prove it with the point of his sword. 'At this,' wrote the Westminster chronicler, 'the duke of York turned white with anger and told his brother to his face that he was a liar'. Gloucester was not the sort of duke who accepted being publicly branded a liar, and was uncontrollably furious. In the chronicler's words, the two dukes 'would have hurled themselves on each other' if the king had not ordered them to stop arguing.[54]

The particularly interesting thing about this event is not just the dissent itself but Henry's reaction. He sided with the duke of York – a man for whom he had no great affection and to whom he never gave presents – and supported the case for Burley to be spared. He did this against the consensus of his fellow Appellants. On this basis, Henry would appear not to have been the author of the list of those to be accused. It follows that he was probably one of the unnamed Appellants who called for mercy to be shown to the justices. As Capgrave later wrote of him, he loved to debate moral issues. He believed passionately in the difference between right and wrong, and was not prepared to succumb to another man's prejudices, even those of his uncle and comrades-in-arms.

When this most shocking and dramatic of parliaments drew to a close, Richard invited all the lords to dine with him at Kennington on the last day of May. It was no more than an act of formal politeness. Richard's half-brother, John Holland, at this point returned from serving with John of Gaunt in Castile and was created earl of Huntingdon. What Henry thought of this rehabilitation of his sister's seducer and Ralph Stafford's murderer is not clear, but it is noticeable that there are no gifts to Holland in his account book. On 2 June the Lords Appellant were granted £20,000 towards their expenses in raising armies to bring the traitors to justice, and soon afterwards all the participants in the parliament departed. Henry's bargemen – equipped in his red and white livery – rowed him back up the Thames to his house in London.[55] He was still there on 15 June but left shortly afterwards.[56] He had won the war, as it were. Yet Richard was still on the throne, and his fellow Appellants had proved themselves as vindictive as the king. They also now knew Henry would not always agree with them, nor follow their guidance. He would follow his own mind. When the time came for Richard to seek revenge, would they all defend one other?

*

Henry left London in June 1388 with plans to fight the Scots.[57] For some, this will summon up a picture of him fighting at the battle of Otterburn – 'the battle won by a dead man' – but in fact Henry was not there. Instead the name we associate with that battle is that of his cousin, Henry 'Hotspur' Percy, the heir of the earl of Northumberland. Hotspur had acquired his nickname on account of his fast and daring escapades against the Scots.

He was the Warden of the East March, and thus he was in command when the Scots invaded Northumberland in late July or early August. At Otterburn the Scottish commander, the earl of Douglas, was mortally injured; but before he died he ordered his body to be concealed beneath a bush and his banner to be borne into the thick of the fighting. As the battle continued into the evening and after dusk, and even by moonlight, so his men took heart and pushed the English back. Hotspur's brother, Ralph Percy, was badly wounded and Hotspur himself was captured after a protracted encounter with Sir John Montgomery.

Given the involvement of two of his Percy cousins in the battle, and considering that the third Percy brother, Thomas, was acting as an intermediary between John of Gaunt and Henry at that time, it would not have been surprising if Henry had intended to be at Otterburn.[58] After all, he was young, and eager for action. However, Jean Froissart, who supplies most of the information we have for the campaign, does not mention Henry at Newcastle before the battle, although he names a number of leaders on both sides. Nor does he mention him at Otterburn itself.[59] At the very least, one would have expected the chronicler Henry Knighton to mention Henry in his account of the battle, if he had been present. He does not. It seems therefore that he was not there, nor in any way connected with Hotspur's campaign.

At the same time as the earl of Douglas invaded Northumberland, a second Scottish force under the earl of Fife invaded Westmorland and Cumberland, and wrought terrible destruction on the town of Appleby and many of the villages in the vicinity. This alternative field of hostilities may have been Henry's destination. The man in command of the West March was Lord Beaumont, an eminent tournament fighter and Henry's second cousin twice over. However, close examination of the evidence shows that Henry was not there either. In all probability, he did not get further than Nottingham.[60] His reason for failing to reach his destination may have been his wife's illness, for about this time the physician Geoffrey Melton was summoned from Oxford to attend her at Kenilworth, to which place Henry now returned.[61]

*

When parliament assembled at Cambridge in September 1388, the members had every reason to be disappointed in the Appellants. The last time they had met they had seen Henry and the four other lords enter in their cloth of gold suits, arm in arm. They had seen them put themselves forward as the agents of good government. Now, seven months later, England had suffered serious attacks in Scotland, and had squandered the taxation for the war. Hotspur was a prisoner, Beaumont a disappointment. The earl of Arundel had been exposed as a profiteer, having taken expenses for four months at sea when he had only served for three.[62] Men wearing the livery collars and insignia of these lords were committing crimes in various places around the country, and the common people felt powerless to resist them. The practice of lords protecting their supporters in this way – usually referred to as 'maintenance' – had supposedly been stamped out fifty years earlier. Now it had come back, and the Appellants were as guilty as the king. To add to the difficulties, employment was in crisis, with beggars tramping from parish to parish, looking for work and resorting to crime if they failed to find it. Far from governing well, the Appellants had apparently resigned their responsibilities and were acting in their own self-interests.

From 9 September to 17 October, the commons led discussion on these issues. No one should be permitted to issue livery badges and collars, they claimed. Henry's was one of the most noticeable livery insignia. The famous Lancastrian livery collar of interlaced esses was in use by this time; the previous year he had distributed collars with 'swages' (circular metal designs) to his supporters, William Bagot, John Stanley and Lord Darcy.[63] His gold-smith's account for 1387–8 is positively dripping with references to lordly collars and badges, including a mulberry design (Mowbray's livery badge). The king offered to stop his retainers using livery badges if it would encourage others to do likewise; but the lords objected. The commons' petition was carried over to the following parliament, pending an investigation.

This piece of lordly obstructionism was almost the full extent of the lords' achievement in this parliament. There was one other: it appears that it was the lords who introduced the first public health statute. 'So much dung, filth, and entrails of dead beasts and other corruptions is cast into ditches, rivers and other waterways, and many other places, within about and near to the cities, boroughs and towns of the realm . . . that the air is greatly corrupted and infected and many maladies and other intolerable diseases do daily happen . . .'[64] They ordered fines of £20 to be levied on all those who had not remedied the situation within a year, and passed the responsibility for keeping the streets clean to local officers. Apart from this, there was no significant agenda for reform. The Appellants as a group seem to have opted to sink back into the mass, as if the rebellion had never happened. They had been a single-cause party, and after the removal of Richard's friends (and the reason for their opposition) they had little in common. An interesting footnote to this lack of lordly engagement is that, in the absence of a lordly legislative programme, the commons put forward an exceedingly detailed and comprehensive petition regarding the labour system. It resulted in the statute which made communities responsible for providing for poor people and itinerant labour-seekers, and so established the precedent which remained the basis for the poor law until the nineteenth century.

*

Henry probably left the Cambridge parliament early, judging from the fact that his third son must have been conceived midway through the parliament.[65] He returned to Kenilworth to his wife and children and remained with them intermittently into the New Year.[66] He and the other Appellants were no doubt hoping that a quieter, less contentious stance would allow a new normality to develop. But in the fourteenth century, when opposition lords lessened their pressure on the king, they became vulnerable. At Christmas, when most of Richard's opponents returned to their own castles, the king told some of his friends who had escaped the carnage of the Merciless Parliament that now things were safe enough for them to return to court. Sir John Golafre – whose possessions had been distributed to Henry and others – returned openly. So did Sir John Lovell and Sir Thomas Blount, both of whom had fled from the Appellants. A banished clerk, Richard Medford, now resumed his post as Richard's secretary.[67]

In February 1389, the three senior Appellants – the duke of Gloucester and the earls of Arundel and Warwick – gathered again in London. There is no indication that Henry was with them. But then, on 13 February, the king wrote to Henry Reede, armourer of London, ordering him to deliver a breastplate to Henry as a gift from the king.[68] Was this a sign of reconciliation? Or was it something else, a warning perhaps?

Given that Richard invited Henry on to his council shortly afterwards, this gift has come to be seen as a sign of peace. One leading historian of the period has taken it as an indication that Richard was 'cultivating' Henry.[69] Another has gone further and stated that it 'marked the growth of a warmer and more intimate relationship between them'.[70] But there may have been more to this gift than meets the eye. For a start, there is nothing to suggest that this breastplate was an unusually expensive item; the breastplate which Henry bought in 1388 cost him £1 6s 8d, and it would have taken a far more substantial present than this to make Henry believe that Richard genuinely valued him. And there are good reasons to suspect that this 'gift' was not really a gift at all. The day it was given – 13 February – was the anniversary of the judgement on de Vere, de la Pole, Tresilian and Archbishop Neville. The person who had originally owned it, Sir John Beauchamp of Holt, was a man whom Richard had admired so much that he raised him to the rank of baron in a letter patent (the first time this had ever been done) and stood as godfather to his son.

Beauchamp had never taken his seat in parliament because he had been executed by Henry and the other Appellants as a traitor. So for Richard to give Henry this particular breastplate on this particular day was an exceptionally loaded present. It reminds us of John of Gaunt going to see Richard in 1385, wearing a breastplate under his gown. Richard may well have been telling Henry that, whatever had been agreed in the Tower in December 1387, he would not forgive him for the proceedings of the subsequent parliament.

Henry attended the council meeting in the Palace of Westminster on 3 May 1389.[71] He was the only one of the Lords Appellant present. Thus he was the only Appellant sympathiser there to see the pro-Appellant chancellor and treasurer sacked, the justices replaced, and the duke of Gloucester and the earl of Arundel removed from the royal council. Henry was appointed to the council in their place, possibly in recognition of the fact that his superior royal status had been the key factor in preventing Gloucester from seizing the throne. Henry can have taken little pleasure in his new position, however, for Richard publicly announced that he would now take responsibility for government on himself once again. He would end the war with France quickly and peacefully. He would justify this to the people through reduced taxation: half the grant for the war was to be returned. In furtherance of this, he immediately despatched a peace delegation; a truce was agreed within six weeks. To Henry it looked very much as though he would never emulate his grandfather, never lead an army in France, never be more than a jousting puppet at the court of King Richard.

As he rode back to Kenilworth a few days later (where his wife was about to give birth to their third son), he must have been torn.[72] On the one hand, Richard had successfully dislodged him from his kinsmen and fellow Appellants. He had also removed Henry's chances of winning glory in the war. On the other, Henry had apparently managed the transition from Appellant to the royal council. He had prevented Gloucester from seizing the throne, and had prevented Richard carrying out his threat to make Roger Mortimer his official heir. He had survived these problems amazingly well, considering he was still only twenty-two. The problem was that his success was so fragile. As it happened, Richard would never forgive him for riding against de Vere, nor for sanctioning the deaths of so many of his friends.[73] His political survival was a delicate balancing act, not a solid achievement. Perhaps he would have need of that breastplate sooner rather than later.

FOUR

Iron Wars

In thy faint slumbers I by thee have watch'd,
And heard thee murmur tales of iron wars.
Henry IV Part One, Act II, Scene 3

Battles, plots and parliamentary storms are all exciting and undoubtedly important but they tend to overshadow less dramatic events of equal political significance. While Henry had been arguing with Richard, and tentatively searching for a middle way between the senior Appellants and the king, his father had been seeking his fortune in Spain. After landing in Galicia in the autumn of 1386, John had brought the region under control, albeit with heavy losses. He had then concluded an agreement with João I of Portugal, reinforcing the alliance of 1373 between Portugal and England (which, incidentally, is still in force today: the longest lasting peace treaty in the world). As part of this agreement, his daughter Philippa had married João, and the combined Anglo-Portuguese army had invaded Castile. John, having taken a leaf out of his father's book and adopted the title of 'king' of the kingdom he claimed, seized on the offer of a favourable peace settlement. As part of the deal he gave his daughter Catalina in marriage to the grandson and heir of Enrique de Trastámara, the usurper who had murdered her grandfather. By this John prevented his wife from avenging her father's death but brought peace to Castile and the guarantee that her family would once again rule. It also brought him a lot of money: one hundred thousand pounds in cash and a valuable pension of ten thousand marks (£6,666) per year. He had been by far the richest man in England before this; now his income had almost doubled. Money, he must have felt, would never again be a worry for the dukes of Lancaster.

John landed at Plymouth on 19 November 1389, and straightaway travelled towards London. Henry had been intermittently at court that autumn, attending council meetings, and probably rode westwards to join his father as soon as he heard the news.[1] As John approached Reading the king went to meet him, a mark of exceptional honour. Richard embraced his uncle, and kissed him, and took the livery collar from John's neck and put it around his own, saying that he wanted to show 'the good love felt heartfully between them'.[2] Many of those present must have wondered at this; it was quite a turnaround from the days when Richard plotted to have his uncle murdered. But Richard had clearly made up his mind to honour John, just as he had made up his mind that – whatever he thought of Henry personally – it was better to have him on his side rather than against him. As Richard knew, with Lancastrian support he could rule England without worrying that the duke of Gloucester would try to depose him.

After this show of reconciliation, Henry and his father withdrew to Hertford Castle for Christmas and the New Year.[3] They returned to Westminster in January 1390 to attend parliament. The main business on the agenda was the second Statute of Provisors, which sought to strengthen the legislation stopping the pope providing clerics to English benefices. The labour legislation of the Cambridge parliament was confirmed and reinforced, and the anti-livery petition of 1388 was enacted, although much watered down from the commons' original demands. On 16 February Richard confirmed the palatinate duchy of Lancaster as an inheritable possession of the Lancastrian house, probably in response to John's request, with an assumed long-term benefit to Henry. Nine days later, Henry's cousin, Edward of York, was created earl of Rutland. Henry witnessed the confirmation of this grant on the last day of the parliament, 3 March, perhaps a little suspicious of Richard's motives.

A few days later, Henry left the country, to take part in a tournament in France. It was perhaps the easiest way to remove himself from the court intrigues. When his father had been threatened by Richard in 1385, he had responded by planning an overseas trip. He had returned to a royal embrace. Maybe the magic of an overseas trip would work for Henry too? Even before the end of the parliament, Henry was packing his bags.[4]

*

The jousts at St Inglevert are among the most famous of the entire middle ages. The renowned French knight Sir Jean le Maingre, or 'Boucicaut' as he was better known, had challenged all comers to joust in March 1389.[5] He and two other famous French knights – Renaud de Roye and Jean de Saimpy – proposed that the three of them would encamp at St Inglevert and would ride five strokes, or courses, against anyone who cared to challenge them in the space of thirty days. And if one of them was badly injured or killed, the remaining two would take on the responsibility of fighting all challengers, down to the last survivor.

John of Gaunt – who had seen Boucicaut joust in Gascony – was impressed and ordered his own herald to carry news of the challenge throughout England. Of course John exhorted his chivalric son and heir to take part. Henry and a large number of English lords and esquires departed some time after 13 March.[6] Thomas Mowbray, Henry's fellow Appellant, went with him. So too did his violent brother-in-law, John Holland, a number of very experienced knights, including Lord Beaumont, Thomas Clifford and Sir Peter Courtenay, and a vast crowd of patriotic noncombatants.

It is not difficult to see the reason for the excitement. The three French protagonists had offered all their opponents the opportunity to fight with uncapped steel lances. These 'jousts of war', as they were called, were exceptionally dangerous. As a result, they were very rare events. So all attention at St Inglevert was fixed on a fine spruce tree which stood beside the jousting field. Two shields hung from its lowest bows. Each challenger was expected to strike one of the two shields with a wand, in true Arthurian fashion. One shield meant a joust of peace, with lances capped. The other meant a joust of war, with sharpened steel lances, which often resulted in severe injury and death. A herald sat in the tree from sunrise to sunset each day, and recorded the name, title and nationality of each challenger.[7]

The most accurate details of the jousts are preserved in the monastic chronicle of Saint-Denis. The lists of contenders recorded therein seem to be based on the lists composed by the heralds sitting in the spruce tree. The monk of Saint-Denis, however, was not particularly interested in which knight did what; he only made special note of the deeds of the three Frenchmen and one group of Englishmen. It is Froissart's chronicle which provides the most detail with regard to the actual strokes. Froissart was not an eyewitness of events himself, and unfortunately his source only stayed for the first week, so we do not have an eyewitness account of Henry's feats of arms; but nevertheless from other accounts we can see that Henry acquitted himself very well indeed.[8]

The great event began with three days' feasting, from Friday 18 March to Sunday the 20th. The next day, the first day of combat, John Holland, earl of Huntingdon, rode up to the shields, determined to prove himself. He took the wand and struck the shield demanding a joust of war. As Boucicaut strode out of his pavilion, he was sporting a new motto emblazoned on his arms: 'whatever you want'. Holland mounted his horse. With his minstrels playing behind him, he rode to the end of the lists. Crowds gathered around, and he stood there, said the chronicler, 'in a very exalted manner' and waited while his esquires fastened his helmet. Boucicaut and the earl then faced each other, with the crowd chanting their names. They began to gallop. Froissart and the biographer of Boucicaut differ as to which lance strike it was exactly when Holland's shield was broken in half by Boucicaut's lance, and which strokes he rode against Boucicaut and which against de Saimpy; but clearly the earl sustained a series of blows. Sparks flew from their helmets as the steel lance tips struck them. At one point Holland's helmet came off. At another, their war horses collided. But at the end of the five strokes, Boucicaut was still unbeaten.

The next knight to try his luck was Thomas Mowbray, who also struck the shield for the joust of war. His opponent was Renaud de Roye. At the first stroke their horses shied away from each other. At the second, de Roye's lance broke, and Mowbray caught his opponent, but not hard enough to unseat him. At the third, de Roye struck Mowbray so hard on the helmet that he broke the straps and left Mowbray stunned, reeling. Mowbray had done well, but he could not complete his five strokes of war against the Frenchman.

So it continued. That day, eight more men jousted against the French: Thomas Clifford, Lord Beaumont, Sir Peter Courtenay, John Golafre, John Russell and Thomas Swinburn.[9] The three Frenchmen outlasted all of them. The next day, after hearing Mass and sharing a cup of wine, they survived ten or eleven more challengers, all of whom demanded jousts of war.[10] By this time, no one could ask for a joust of peace, with capped lance tips. To do so would seem cowardly. On the Wednesday, the three Frenchmen rode against thirteen challengers, and apparently wounded all of them.[11] On the Thursday they fought against at least seven more.[12] By the evening of that fourth day, they were exhausted. There followed four days of feasting and pleasant pastimes, and honourable receptions for those who were just arriving from England, Hainault, Lorraine and further afield: Germany and Bohemia.

Henry was in his element. His new friend, Boucicaut, was just seven months older than him. The Frenchman was charming, affable and hugely talented. He had good stories to tell of his father and his own deeds of valour. Henry might have been jousting in public from the age of fourteen, but Boucicaut had been fighting since he was a page, taken on his first campaign at the age of twelve. He had been knighted on the eve of his first battle, at the age of sixteen. He had twice fought with the Teutonic Knights in the crusades against the Lithuanians. In addition he had fought in Spain, the Balkans and the Middle East. But as they feasted together, Henry would have realised that there was more to the man than that. As Boucicaut's chronicler noted, he was abstemious, and did not revel in food and drink, but rather concentrated on what was good for his fighting skills. Moreover, he was as pious as he was single-minded in his pursuit of martial glory. He had even been to the Holy Land. To Henry he was a kindred spirit, and Henry lavished gifts on him and his companions. Only one shadow crossed his mind: he would yet have to ride against him, and with uncapped steel lances. Henry could not be seen to be the first one to strike the shield for the joust of peace.

The fifth day of jousting saw John Holland return to the lists, and Thomas Mowbray too. Boucicaut and Renaud de Roye dealt with them and nine more men, but they were both so badly injured by the end of the afternoon that they had to be taken to their beds for medical help. Their challenge now rested entirely on the one remaining knight, Jean de Saimpy. Fortunately for him, he did not have to joust all nine days; Maundy Thursday, Good Friday and the Easter weekend and Easter Monday intervened, and as these were religious feasts, no jousting took place. Jean de Saimpy had to hold his own for just two days, but even that meant facing a further fifteen men single-handed. He did so, and remained undefeated, to the ecstatic applause of the Frenchmen in the crowd. The challenge was still on. Thursday 7 April saw Boucicaut and de Roye back to full strength. Eight men from Germany and Bohemia clashed with them that day. The next day was a Friday, so was spent feasting and dancing. Then came the weekend, with religious observances on the Sunday. The next strokes would take place on Monday 11 April. It was Henry's turn.[13]

John of Gaunt had written in advance to Boucicaut asking him to show his son a lesson or two; would he therefore do Henry the honour of riding not five strokes with him but ten? This may have been meant literally, but Henry was the same age as Boucicaut and an experienced jouster; he did not need tuition. John was probably teasing his son.[14] Boucicaut could not refuse such a request from the duke of Lancaster, whether in jest or not. With Henry were his second cousin, Henry 'Hotspur' Percy, John Beaufort (Henry's half-brother), John Courtenay, Thomas Swynford, and five other men. With all of them in armour, and the flags flying around the lists, and the crowds chanting his name, Henry closed the visor on his war helm and spurred his war horse forward, hooves thudding into the turf. He rode all ten strokes with Boucicaut, to great cheers.

At the end of the day the three Frenchmen were still alive, and so was their challenge, and great was their honour indeed. But they had very nearly come to grief. Jean de Saimpy could not take a further part in the competition; Henry afterwards gave him a new saddle, presumably having destroyed the old one with his lance.[15] Not even John Holland had given the Frenchmen such a hard time. At the end of the tournament, on or about 13 April, after two more days' jousting, the Frenchmen judged Henry and his companions the most praiseworthy of all those who had challenged them.[16] How much of an impact Henry made may be seen in that one French chronicle names him alone out of all the knights – more than a hundred – who attended.[17] Boucicaut was profoundly impressed. Would Henry care to join him on the duke of Bourbon's forthcoming crusade to Tunis? Then they could travel together to the crusade in Prussia. Henry must have felt the golden path to glory had suddenly been revealed.

Henry returned to England and probably went directly to Windsor to attend the Order of the Garter ceremony on St George's Day. Two weeks later, on 6 May, using his full string of honorific titles 'Henry of Lancaster, earl of Derby, Hereford and Northampton, lord of Brecon', he appointed Richard Kingston his treasurer for war.[18] Kingston set about purchasing horses and stores with which to join the crusade assembling at Marseilles on 1 July. Henry crossed to Calais, where he and his knights awaited their letters of safe-conduct. Their wait was in vain. It is normally presumed that Richard wrote to the French king asking him not to allow Henry to go on the crusade. Whether this is correct or not, Henry's representatives were unable to obtain permission for him to travel through France.[19] His half-brother John Beaufort had to go on to Marseilles without him. Henry knew that if he wanted to prove himself in arms, there was only one option left: Lithuania.

*

The fourteenth-century crusades in Lithuania are not as well known as those of the twelfth century in the Holy Land or the *Reconquista* in Spain. The days of long campaigns in the Middle East were practically over, and although there were two or three military expeditions against Mediterranean Turks and Arabs at the end of the fourteenth century, these were relatively rare. Those who took part sought not to gain great territorial empires but rather strategic victories on behalf of Christendom. Lithuania remained practically the sole arena for crusades of conquest, for one region, Samogitia, was still pagan, and it was there that the Teutonic Knights held the frontier.[20]

The Teutonic Knights had been founded in 1128. Like other military orders, such as the Hospitallers and the Templars, they undertook to protect the Christian pilgrims travelling to Jerusalem. After the fall of Jerusalem in 1187, they refounded themselves as a monastic brotherhood at Acre. After forty years of protecting pilgrims, they set out to fight pagans in Prussia, and merged in 1237 with the Brothers of the Sword, an order which held various Prussian lands, including Livonia. The fall of Acre in 1290 again left them homeless; another period of uncertainty followed, and it was not until 1309 that they established themselves at Marienberg. From then on, their expansion was at the cost of the pagan Lithuanians. In 1386, the conversion of Lithuania began, with the baptism of the king,

Jagiello. By 1390 the Teutonic Knights were hardly crusaders at all; they were more like a militant Christian state in their own right, making alliances with their neighbours and fighting enemies of various faiths, including fellow Christians.

It might seem a little extreme to us that a young man such as Henry, eager to prove himself in arms, should venture to the far edge of Europe. It would not have appeared that strange in 1390. From London, Lithuania is only about half as far as Jerusalem and although geographical features inhibited travel by land or water in a straight line, the most substantial detour was the need to sail around Denmark, which meant the onus fell on the sailors. Besides, it is probable that the real reason for our surprise is our comparative ignorance about medieval Lithuania and our presumption that our medieval ancestors knew very little about the world. Because of its crusades, Lithuania probably figured more prominently in the medieval English conscience that it does in the modern English mind. A number of English knights had made the journey there to fight with the Teutonic Knights. Sir Robert Morley had died there, Sir John Breux had served there with Lord Lovell, Sir Hugh Hastings had been there, as had Sir William Scrope of Bolton and three of his cousins, one of whom died there in 1362. And this is just to quote a handful of examples known from evidence given in heraldic lawsuits; it is probable that most knights and lords in England knew someone who had served in Prussia on the *reyse* (as the annual expeditions were called). Henry would have known more than most. In addition to his new friend, Boucicaut, there was his own grandfather the great duke of Lancaster, who had travelled to Germany with the intention of fighting on a *reyse* in 1352. His deceased father-in-law, the earl of Hereford, had campaigned in Prussia, as had the sons of the earl of Devon, and Thomas Holland, earl of Kent. The Ufford family had been campaigning in Lithuania since at least 1331, with one son, Thomas, taking part in three crusades, in 1348, 1361 and 1365. Another veteran of the Prussian crusades was Henry's fellow Appellant, Thomas Beauchamp, earl of Warwick, who had set out for Lithuania with his younger brothers, William and Roger, in 1367. The earl's late father had left a particularly inspiring story, as he had returned from Lithuania in 1364 with a pagan prince, whom he had had baptised in London. Last and most importantly there was Henry's own jousting companion and cousin, Hotspur, who had been to Lithuania in 1383. It was by no means an easy way of winning glory – memorial panes of heraldic glass to dead English knights were to be seen in many churches in Eastern Europe – but it was a well-established route to the combined heights of spiritual salvation and fame in arms.[21]

Henry returned from Calais by 28 May.[22] He did not try to persuade the French king to change his mind about the safe-conduct but instead set about organising everything he would need for the forthcoming expedition. The intense excitement is vividly preserved in the enrolled accounts, which testify to his men rushing here and there, buying necessities or having them made, arranging for carriage of some items and the repair of others. Money was clearly no worry to the young man who intended to travel in the highest luxury. A sum of about 24,000 Aragonese florins – about £2,700 – was given to him by his father from his Spanish treasure, and this was followed in early June with a further thousand marks. John was enormously generous and clearly supportive of his son's venture.

The list of items which Henry obtained is an excellent source for the lifestyle of the very richest men of the English court. The range of foodstuffs is particularly striking. At one point in the account the reader is left with the distinct impression that Henry must have raided a sweetshop. Just one bill to a London confectioner, amounting to £4 16s 8d, paid on 4 July 1390, included:

> 7 lb. of ginger
> 11 lb. of quince jam
> 4 lb. of a conserve of pine nuts
> 2 lb. of caraway seeds
> 2 lb. of ginger sweets
> 2 lb. of preserved cloves
> 3 lb. of *citronade* [a lemon marmalade?]
> 2 lb. of 'royal sweets'
> 4 lb. of red and white 'flat sugars' [sugar loaves]
> 6 lb. of 'sugar candy'
> 3 lb. of 'royal paste' [made of flour and sugar]
> 2 lb. of aniseed sweets
> 2 lb. of sunflower seeds
> 2 lb. of mapled ginger
> 2 lb. of barley sugar
> 2 lb. of digestive sweetmeats
> 1 lb. of nutmeg
> 2 lb. of red wax
> and two quires of paper.[23]

And this was just one bill. On another occasion the clerk of the spicery had to pay out £10 6s 7d for four-and-a-half hundredweight (506 lb., or 230kg.) of almonds, a hundredweight (112 lb.) of rice, 14 lb. ginger, 14 lb.

pepper, 14 lb. cinnamon, 10 lb. of sugar syrup, 7 lb. 12 oz. 'sugar caffetin' (loaves of sugar), six gallons of honey, 1 lb. of saffron, ½ lb. of mace, ½ lb. of cloves, ½ lb. of cubebs, 1 lb. of sandalwood (a food colouring), forty gallons of strained verjuice (a sour liquor for cooking), 1 lb. of cumin and 6 lb. of ground rice.[24] Beyond this, the same clerk had to account for other quantities of the same foodstuffs, and many other exotica, including quantities of dates, currants, liquorice, figs, raisins, saffron, caraway seeds, aniseed, alkanet (a red food colouring), galingale (warm spice powder), and pistachios.

In addition to the spicery there were purchases for the kitchen, the saucery, the poultry, the scullery, the chaundry (cleaning), the buttery and the pantry. The clerk of the saucery entered one bill 'for thirty-six gallons of vinegar'. Similarly large orders were noted for the buttery. Very large quantities of ale were obtained, normally at a cost of 1½d or 2d per gallon (so for £1 he could buy 960 pints of the best ale). It arrived in barrels of twenty-four gallons. Large quantities of Gascon wine were also purchased, and huge quantities of meat. No individual provider was able to supply the amounts which Henry desired, and so the accounts are peppered with payments, for example, for ten flitches of bacon bought at Bolingbroke (12s 6d), or forty sheep bought at Boston (72s). Henry seems to have been just as keen on fish as his maternal grandfather, whose favourite food was salmon.[25] At most places where Henry stopped, we read of payments for fish. He ate many more varieties than the average modern consumer, the range of fish eaten on Fridays (a non-meat day in the Catholic Church) being a sign of high status. His accounts record payments for a vast array including salt fish, whale (oil?), herring, cod, conger eels, many sticks of freshwater eels (twenty-five eels per stick), flat fish, sturgeon (by the barrel), pike, whelks and porpoise (which was considered a fish in medieval times). In Prussia he was to pay for bream, lampreys, roach, tench, ray, crabs, lobsters, thornbacks, plaice, flounder and trout. Later, when he visited the Mediterranean, he regularly ate many more kinds. Eating fish remained a lifelong passion: in later years, when he was king, magnates gave him presents of fresh fish.[26]

As Henry made his way north with Mary (five months' pregnant with their fourth child), he assembled the other necessities for his journey. Ten cauldrons, six spits and two pairs of racks for hanging cauldrons. A frying pan. A new tapestry, and cords to hang it in his dining hall. His armour. Repairs to his favourite sword. Even canvas aprons for the cooks. His horses had to be taken to Boston, if they were going on the crusade, or back to Bolingbroke if they were remaining in England.

Henry also sent a clock to Bolingbroke. This is a detail which seems not to have sparked much attention, but it deserves particular notice if only for the fact that it was portable. The entry reads 'to John the Clockmaker for a *pannier* bought from him for the transportation of one clock from London to Bolingbroke 8d'.[27] This was presumably a clock which Henry already owned, for there is no payment for the making of the said clock to John or anyone else. The extraordinary thing is that clocks at this period were all turret clocks, and not remotely portable: they were constructed *in situ*. No portable clocks are known to have existed for another half-century, when the spring mechanism was developed which permitted table-top clocks to be designed and built. But here we have a reference to a clock small enough that it could be carried. Moreover, Henry was not prepared to leave it in his London house while he was away. Given what has previously been said about Henry's logical mind, with all the implications for his attitude to time-keeping and the structure of the day, it is not surprising to know that he was one of the very few fourteenth-century individuals who personally owned a clock. But if he owned a *portable* timepiece in 1390 – the earliest recorded such item – that would be extraordinary.

At Boston, eleven days were spent fitting out the ship. Although we have no record of what sort of ship this was, the largest vessels of the day are estimated to have been little more than 100 feet (30m.) in length; and given Henry's purpose, status and retinue, it is unlikely that he had requisitioned a much smaller vessel. Carpenters were sent aboard with timber and wains-cot to provide Henry and his knights with cabins in the vessel, each neatly done with wood panelling and fitted with a hammock. In Henry's cabin there was also a lamp. Extensive repairs were carried out to the boat, both carpentry and tarring, to ensure its seaworthiness. Cages were built on deck for the large numbers of live chickens they were taking. A stall was built for the cow they were taking to provide them with fresh milk. Cases were carried on board with the 3,400 eggs required for the voyage. Henry's armour, flags, tents, horses, chests of clothes and all the cooking equip-ment and supplies were carried aboard. Finally, on 19 or 20 July, everything was ready. Henry said goodbye to Mary and his three sons at Lincoln, and returned to Boston.[28] A flotilla of smaller vessels towed the great ship and three hundred men, dozens of horses, three hundred and sixty chickens and one cow away from the dock and out into the open waters of the North Sea.[29]

Now it becomes clear where all those sweets and sweetmeats went, and all that ale and wine. There was little to do on board for the next three weeks except eat, drink, pray and tell stories. It was summer, so we may suppose that the weather was fine, but even so, cramped on board for three weeks, the voyage cannot have been pleasant for Henry and his men.

Perhaps they practised their swordsmanship on deck as the boat rocked its way across the North Sea and then the Baltic. There were about two dozen knights and esquires with him, including Thomas Erpingham, Thomas Swynford, Peter Bucton, Thomas Rempston (his standard-bearer), John Clifton, Richard Goldsborough, John Loveyn, Sir John Dalyngrigge, John Norbury, John and Robert Waterton, Ralph Rochford, Richard Dancaster and Hugh Waterton (his long-serving chamberlain). At least five of these men had taken part in the jousts of war at St Inglevert (Swynford, Bucton, Rochford, Dalyngrigge and Dancaster).[30] No doubt they also joined with Henry in gambling on throws of the dice (to which he was addicted, like most of the medieval royal family) and board games, such as chess and draughts, and ball games, such as fives (*jeu de paume*).[31] Henry also had an altar set up in his cabin, and his chaplain Hugh Herle was on board, so prayer would have occupied more of his time. Finally, he had also brought his falconer with him, so no doubt he and his men had fun sending up their birds of prey to pursue the smaller sea birds.

On 8 August Henry landed at Rixhöft, in Poland, and disembarked with a few of his men. He spent the night in a mill near Putzig before riding to the port of Danzig (modern Gdansk), where the ship docked. From there he sent his heralds out to announce his arrival and to offer his assistance to the marshal of the Teutonic Knights, Engelhard Rabe. While he waited for his messenger, he whiled away a few hours jousting, and managed to injure himself, so that a doctor was urgently required to staunch the bleeding.[32] On hearing that Marshal Rabe was already in arms, and that the *reyse* was underway, Henry gathered his fighting men and chased after him, through Elbing and Braniewo, Brandenburg and Königsberg. He arrived at Insterberg Castle – a fortress of the Teutonic Knights – on the 21st. The following day he finally met Marshal Rabe, on the banks of the River Memel, near Ragnit.

Henry probably did not fully understand the nature of the war in which he now found himself. It had changed since the days of his grandfather and the earl of Warwick. The key change was the baptism of King Jagiello, in 1386. In theory this meant that all of Lithuania was now Christian, which would have left the Teutonic Knights with no pagans to fight. However, although the conversion of Lithuania was almost complete, there were still substantial elements of paganism left to stamp out in 'the Wilderness', as the north of medieval Lithuania was called (roughly the same area as modern Lithuania). That was where the knights were about to campaign now. It was a vast tract of marshy land, the paths slippery with mud and blocked by fallen trees.

That was not the whole story. A fuller picture has to take account of the political machinations of Vitold, or Vytautas, cousin of Jagiello. Vitold was an ambitious man who, in the 1380s, had converted to Christianity and allied with the Teutonic Knights against Jagiello. He had betrayed them, and made peace with Jagiello, but in 1389 he had decided to grasp another opportunity to make himself king of Lithuania and had renewed his alliance with the Teutonic Knights. His vision of a united Lithuania under his rule was very different from Jagiello's Polish–Lithuanian empire. The campaign which Vitold was now waging, and which Henry was supporting, was directed against Jagiello's brothers, Skirgiello and Karigal. These men had also been baptised. Thus it could be said that Henry was taking part in a crusade against fellow Christians as well as pagans. Although he believed he was fighting for the glory of God and the Teutonic Knights, it would be more accurate to say he was fighting in the name of Vitold, a man of questionable loyalty to the Christian cause, against the subjects and allies of a Christian king.

A week later, coming to the River Wilia, the Anglo-Teutonic army and their allies (the Livonians and Vitold's Lithuanians) saw Skirgiello's Russo-Lithuanian army on the other side. A battle ensued, in which the archers with Henry played a key part.[33] The cover of arrow fire permitted the knights to advance and engage the enemy on the far bank. One of Henry's knights, Sir John Loudham, was killed here. Enemy losses amounted to three hundred dead. Three Russian leaders ('dukes') and eleven other lords (boyars) were captured. After a night's rest on the battlefield, Henry sent Loudham's body back to Königsberg for burial. The rest of the army pushed on through the mud towards Vilnius.

Vilnius was a wooden city, protected by a strong castle, filled with archers. Henry led the first attack on the walls on 4 September, using English gunners as well as his knights. According to both German and English sources, it was the valiant attacks of the English which allowed a flag bearing the cross of St George – the patron saint of the Teutonic Knights as well as the English – to be raised above the town parapet.[34] Contemporary English reports put the number of dead after this onslaught at around four thousand, although this is surely an exaggeration.[35] But the castle protecting the town held out. Three weeks later, Henry was still ensconced in a waterlogged camp of cold, disease-ridden, despondent men. All the edible luxuries he had obtained in England had been consumed. He was now dependent on Vitold for supplies. After a month, he and his fellow soldiers had had enough. The gunpowder had been used up. Men were dying of the inevitable diseases to be found in temporary army camps. Two of Henry's men (Thomas Rempston and John Clifton) had been captured by the enemy. Henry made an attempt to secure their release –

we do not know whether he was immediately successful – and then marched back towards Insterberg.[36] From there he took his men to Königsberg, where he set up his winter quarters.

*

There were several reasons why Henry did not return to England directly after his return from the *reyse*. It was so late in the year that storms could be expected on the long voyage, which meant it would be both miserable and dangerous at sea. Two of his men were probably still held captive, and to leave them behind would be dishonourable. Henry himself was ill, and needed the attentions of a physician from Marienberg.[37] And he had no wish to return and have to put up with the bitterness of the English court. Although Henry learned on 1 November 1390 that he now had a fourth son, Humphrey (named after Mary's father), that in itself was insufficient to tempt him to return. He was independent on his travels, and that independence suited him.[38] Besides, he liked these German knights with whom he had been fighting and bonding. Like Boucicaut, they had both spiritual virtue and martial skill. They had pride in themselves, as men and as fighters. They thought of themselves as soldiers of Christ. They were dedicated. They knew how to enjoy themselves too, with their hunting and jousting.[39] They espoused all the virtues in which Henry also believed.

At Königsberg Henry listened to music, feasted, prayed and attended the funeral of one of his esquires. He had captured some pagan boys on the *reyse*, and now had them baptised and installed them in his own household for their education. His accounts note payments for carrying his hunting gear – two cartloads of it – to go hunting with Marshal Rabe. He wrote letters home, and sent them via his esquires, paying each time twenty marks (£13 6s 8d) for their delivery.[40] The noblemen sent their entertainers and musicians to each other, and in this way Henry and his six minstrels – his trumpeters, pipers and a percussionist – would have been exposed to different tunes and rhythms.[41] One Hans the Hornpiper seems to have gone down very well, for Henry gave him several large payments.[42] Although foreign beers had been imported into England before this time, now Henry was able to sup continental beverages in quantity.[43] He also saw the horses of Eastern Europe, and came face to face with Russian troops. Presents given to him, for his amusement, sport or curiosity, include three bears, hawks, a wild bull and an elk.[44] It is not clear what he did with all these animals, least of all the elk.

Henry remained at Königsberg from November until 9 February, when he removed his household to Danzig. Arriving there on 15 February, he lodged at the house of one Klaus Gottesknight, while his retinue lodged at a bishop's house in the town. A group of clerics gathered to sing to him.[45] Three fiddlers came to play to him in Lent, receiving a whole mark (13s 4d) as a reward.[46] On 5 January he doled out many gifts to his minstrels, knights, esquires, grooms, valets and servants, giving most of them a warm fur gown against the bitter cold of the winter. Another of his servants died, and he paid for a tomb to be built for him at Königsberg. A series of pilgrimages occupied him in Holy Week: he visited at least four churches each day, and gave alms to the poor wherever he went. On Maundy Thursday (23 March) he gave alms, clothes and shoes to twenty-four paupers (that being the day he entered his twenty-fourth year).[47] Finally, at the end of the month, after a deluge of gifts, alms and goodbyes, he stepped on board his ship again and set sail for England. With him went John Ralph and Ingelard of Prussia, two of the several boys he had converted to Christianity.[48] It took his pilot four weeks to guide the ship across the twelve hundred miles home.[49]

*

Henry's first voyage overseas magnified his reputation in England in every possible way. Not even his glorious grandfather, Edward III, had actually taken part in a crusade. His other grandfather had reached Stettin (eighty miles north-east of Berlin) on his 1352 expedition, but if he actually joined the *reyse* that year, his exploits were neither notable nor memorable. As far as anyone in England was aware, Henry was the first member of the English royal family to take part in a holy war since Prince Edward (later Edward I), more than a hundred years earlier.

A more subtle aspect, of which everyone would have been keenly aware at the time, was that Henry had been representing England. Some writers in the past have called Henry's expedition 'semi-diplomatic', even though there was no specific foreign-relations purpose to Henry's voyage.[50] But there was one sense in which Henry's journey did have a diplomatic dimension: he was a walking advertisement for England, with regard to his appearance and largesse, and his men were an advertisement for the supremacy of the English longbow over all other weapons of war. This is an important fact to bear in mind, for when Englishmen heard that Henry had won a river battle against the pagan Russians, and when they heard that it was an Englishman in Henry's entourage who first placed the flag of St George on the walls of Vilnius, they understood these as *English* victories. They knew also that these acts had been witnessed by men from many other countries: from Germany, Hungary, Poland, France and Italy. Henry had been exporting the idea that the English royal family still bred warriors of the stature of Edward III and Duke Henry.

We get a real sense of this inspiration and national pride from reading the chronicle of the monk of Westminster. In a very telling passage, the monk wrote that Henry landed on 8 August 1390 at Danzig. This is actually wrong – Henry landed, as we have seen, at Rixhöft – but in that very error we have good evidence that the chronicler received his information from one of the men who sailed with Henry, for most of them did disembark at Danzig. It is not hard to picture an esquire from Henry's retinue sitting down with a cup of wine in the hearing of a number of clerics at Westminster, and telling them the story of how Henry had marched to join the marshal of Prussia against the king of Lithuania at the head of fifty lances and sixty bowmen, and how, on the banks of the River Memel, Marshal Rabe had ridden forth to greet Henry with 'his face wreathed in a smile of pleasure'. The esquire went on to say that at the battle to cross the river three Russian 'dukes' were captured by the 'Christians' and three others killed, and three hundred men were left for dead, with Skirgiello fleeing for his life. Of course there was no reference to the fact that Skirgiello himself was a Christian. In his version of this story, 'the king of Lithuania' fled from Henry and holed himself up in the citadel of Vilnius. Although the siege was ultimately unsuccessful, in the conquest of the town the Prussian marshal seized 8,000 prisoners for conversion, and the master of the Livonians took a further 3,500. And, of course, the man who first planted the flag of St George on the walls of Vilnius became not one of Henry's men but Henry himself.[51] Such is the nature of story telling, especially stories about deeds of valour.

Henry did everything he could to live up to this reputation. The news of his crusading success followed on from that of his prowess against Boucicaut at St Inglevert, and Henry was keen to demonstrate his fighting skills on English soil. He set about amassing new armour: jousting helmets and visors, bascinets for war, bascinets with aventails (hanging mail collars), vambraces, rerebraces, manifers (gauntlets), breastplates, lances of steel and wood, mail coverings and swords. On 24 June, Henry was supplied with new armour and eighteen lances for a tournament.[52] Shortly afterwards, he went up to London, from which he travelled by barge to Lambeth, and then on to Kennington, where another joust was to take place.[53] For this he bought another eighteen lances, and dressed in spangles, as he had done at his earliest recorded tournament.[54] In September, at Hertford, Henry started planning for the next tournament, this one to be at Waltham on 6 October.[55] These were all supposedly jousts of peace, but even so Henry obtained new steel lances, just in case he would be challenged to the ultimate test.

In this way Henry can be seen to have returned from his expedition much more confident and self-assured than before. So inspiring were the tales of adventure from the east that a number of lords set off to take part in the 1391 *reyse*, including Lords Despenser, Beaumont, Clifford and Bourchier (who set off in May). Henry's uncle, the duke of Gloucester, also set off for Lithuania, but was caught in a storm, lost his ship and was washed ashore at Bamburgh.[56] Henry's time abroad had also taught him how to live and behave like a prince. The enormous wealth bestowed on him by his father, combined with his own independence, gave him the chance to buy what he wanted and give lavishly. The serious student of piety and the lance had blossomed into a champion with depth of character: an affable, knowledgeable and likeable young man.

Despite all this glory and affability, the fact remained that he was now back in England, and that was where his real problems lay. He did not attend court. He probably saw Richard at the Kennington tournament in July, at which time the king gave him a couple of pieces of plate armour, but the Lancastrians kept themselves to themselves, just as Richard kept his court tightly around him. Not surprisingly, Henry preferred to be with his family than with the king. Mary was pregnant again, with their fifth child. They indulged themselves in their love of music together: at Peterborough they were entertained by two minstrels accompanying each other on the lute and fiddle.[57] When Henry went to London for the parliament on 3 November, he sent Mary a present of a hundred apples ('costardes'), and a hundred and fifty pears ('wardens').[58] All this homely fireside love and music is of an altogether different character from Henry's position at court. In public he and Richard wore thin-lipped smiles for the sake of politeness and exchanged formal presents; privately they kept apart, and only came together when Richard needed the support of the Lancastrians.

A third faction was developing around the young earl of March, whom Richard had once rashly declared to be his heir. Although he had no intention now of ratifying this, the announcement had given Hotspur – who was married to the earl's sister – good reason to hope that March would succeed Richard. There was no getting away from the fact that Richard had now been married for nearly ten years and Anne had not once become pregnant, let alone given birth. Thus, when the earl of March's wife gave birth to a son, Edmund Mortimer, in early November 1391, no one could have ignored the implications for the succession. The earl of March had a responsibility to try to preserve the inheritance for his son, just as John had ambitions for Henry.

The parliament of November 1391 itself raised further questions. The chancellor declared in his opening speech that one of the purposes of the meeting was again to discuss the issue of maintenance, with connotations for those wearing livery collars. The repeal of the Statute of Provisors was discussed, with a firm anti-papal statement coming from the commons. The wool trade was debated, especially the problems arising from a collapse in wool prices, which in turn were perhaps a consequence of the plague that ravaged the north that summer.[59] Further reforms were enacted relating to the administration of admirals, the duties of Justices of the Peace to prevent forced entry on to another man's property, the removal of the tin staple (official trading post) from Cornwall to Calais, and the alienation of land to religious institutions. But most importantly, on the last day of the parliament the commons presented a petition to the committee appointed for the purpose (which, for the first time, included Henry), demanding that Richard should be 'as free in his regality, liberty and royal dignity as any of his predecessors', and that he should not be restrained by any statute or ordinance, including those passed in the reign of Edward II. Richard had been clever. If the Appellants could use parliament to limit the power of the king, then he could use it to bolster his authority. Henry and the rest of the committee had no choice but to assent to such a petition, even though it clearly originated with the king himself. So they passed it on for the king to ratify, which he did, declaring himself 'well-pleased' with the commons' request.[60]

The very next day, Henry removed himself from court.[61]

FIVE

As Far as to the Sepulchre of Christ

Therefore, friends,
As far as to the sepulchre of Christ –
whose soldier now, under whose blessed cross
we are impressed and engaged to fight –
forthwith a power of English we shall levy;
Henry IV Part One, Act 1, Scene 1

Henry spent Christmas 1391 at Hertford with his father, wife and children. He took part in a tournament, his fourth since returning to England. On Christmas Day a dolphin was seen in the Thames, which prompted one chronicler to write a short passage all about dolphins for those of his readers who had never seen these marvellous creatures which 'generally, as they leap, fly across the sails of ships'. Notwithstanding this wonderful monastic exaggeration, from his reference to the dolphin's appearance foretelling the bad storms the following week we may be sure that the season was stormy.[1] Heralds arrived from France in the rain to invite Henry to take part in jousts with French knights the following year.[2] In the fire-lit evenings, Henry's and John's musicians entertained the gathering, Henry further showing his appreciation of their contribution with large rewards.[3]

Then came the giving of traditional New Year presents.[4] To the king Henry sent a gold brooch in the style of a panther with sapphires and pearls, costing £7. To his father he gave a golden swan with a ruby and pearls, costing £12 17s 4d. To Mary he gave a golden hind covered in white enamel with a golden collar around its neck, at a cost of £9.[5] This reference in particular has interested art historians over the years, as white enamel is a rare refinement of the jeweller's art and one exquisitely displayed in the famous Dunstable swan jewel: a tiny gold swan in white enamel which also has a golden collar around its neck. In fact, there is a reference in this same account to Henry paying Ludwig the Goldsmith for 'mending and enamelling a golden swan' of Henry's own, which he had broken, which probably relates to something very similar to the Dunstable swan jewel.[6] Other presents of jewels were given out to the duchess of Lancaster (Henry's stepmother), the duchess of Gloucester (Mary's sister), the countess of Huntingdon (Henry's sister), Thomas Mowbray, earl of Nottingham, Katherine Swynford, Joan Beaufort (Henry's half-sister), and the principal officers of his and his father's households. One of the pagan boys he had brought back from his crusade also received a present of a golden brooch with a diamond, worth £1 10s. Henry received presents in return from the king and queen, his father, the duchess of Lancaster, the duke and duchess of Gloucester, the countess of Hereford, the countess of Huntingdon, Katherine Swynford and Thomas Mowbray.[7]

Apart from his uncle, the duke of York, with whom Henry never exchanged presents, two names are conspicuous by their absence from this list. Warwick and Arundel had been fellow Appellants, and in 1388 they had both been high on Henry's New Year presents list. Yet now they had dropped off. The splits between the Lords Appellant had become so wide that the king could turn them against one another. He could also start to undo the work they had done. In presenting that petition on the last day of the last parliament, he had already secured his freedom from councils being brought against him. Now he sought to accomplish the final stage of his rehabilitation as king, the return of his banished friends.

At the beginning of February Henry and John were summoned to a royal council at Westminster to discuss the forthcoming negotiations for peace with France. Henry was present on the 12th when it was decided that the embassy should be led by John of Gaunt, and that John should be accompanied by the bishop of Durham, the earl of Huntingdon, Lord Cobham and Thomas Percy.[8] Although Henry was planning to accompany his father, no mention was made of him having an official capacity, even though he was of considerably higher status than either Percy or Cobham. Henry did not attend the king for the following two days. Then on the 15th he took part in the discussions about the last two surviving men who had been sentenced to death for high treason in the Merciless Parliament. This was how Richard hoped finally to reverse the processes by which Henry and the other Appellants had sought to restrain his authority in 1388. Richard probably thought it not too much to ask; Tresilian and Brembre had been executed at the time, and de la Pole had died in exile in Paris the year after the trial, so he was only asking for two men to be restored to him (Archbishop Neville and de Vere). Four years had now passed since they had fled: might they now be allowed to return? With emphasis, the lords present, including Henry and John, rejected this supplication.[9] They urged Richard to recognise that the banishment was permanent. Richard had no option but to accept this, at least for the time being.

Henry, his father and the other emissaries left London on 25 February. They travelled slowly down to Dover and sent their possessions ahead to

Calais, following on afterwards and arriving on 11 March.[10] When assembled, the retinue consisted of more than two hundred mounted men. The king of France had undertaken to pay the expenses of the ambassadors once they crossed the Channel, and sent four dukes to receive them. The royal uncles – the dukes of Berry and Burgundy – rode ceremonially on either side of John of Gaunt on the way to Amiens, exactly keeping pace with him. When they arrived, John repaid the courtesy by going directly to the bishop's palace to pay his respects to King Charles, bowing three times before him. Everything was designed to make this a most impressive event, even down to the security arrangements. Frenchmen were warned that those involved in a fight with any member of the English party would be summarily executed. English arms and bows did not have to be deposited with innkeepers, and there were four thousand Frenchmen on guard at the corners of the town, as well as specially detailed brigades to cope with any fires which might break out.[11]

Negotiations went on for fifteen days. The English had the outline of a treaty, and so did the French. Unfortunately, these outlines had nothing in common. Each thought the other wanted a permanent peace far more desperately than the other, and that the other side was prepared to make significant compromises. The English wanted a return to the terms won by Edward III in 1360, with the payment of the rest of the ransom of the late King John, who had died in 1364: an unrealistic proposal. The French wanted the English to surrender Calais and recognise French sovereignty over the whole of Gascony, with Aquitaine being given to the duke of Berry for his lifetime and thereafter to John of Gaunt and his heirs: an equally unrealistic proposition. So no agreement was possible. All that this ostentatious meeting managed to secure was a truce for a further year, which was agreed on 8 April. Then, with as much ceremony as they had received on arrival, the English were escorted back to Calais. A few days later, Henry and his father were back in England and riding towards Eltham Palace, to report to the king.[12]

Richard was not happy. He gave the order that the peace was to be discussed at a forthcoming council at Stamford, in May.[13] As everyone there heard, the French had wanted the English king to give up his claim to the throne of France and to drop the fleur-de-lys from his arms. Those demands were acceptable. But to allow Gascony to pass for his lifetime to the duke of Berry was not. For Gascony to become an inheritance of the house of Lancaster under French sovereignty was a nonstarter. To whom would the duke owe allegiance in a war? And for Richard, the idea of giving away a princedom which had been enjoyed by his own father – and which was his own birthplace – was unthinkable.

No sooner had it been decided to reject the French treaty proposals than Richard found another outlet for his royal frustrations: the mayor and aldermen of the city of London. According to one chronicler, the writ he sent against them on 29 May was 'so fearsome and utterly hair-raising as to cause the ears of whosoever heard it to tingle'.[14] This also had the potential to draw Henry into a dispute with the king. Both John and Henry were patrons of several of the implicated London merchants. In particular, Henry had close links with Richard Whittington – the famous lord mayor – and John Woodcock.[15] This new dispute, together with the French demand that Henry should inherit Gascony, and the ever-present problem of the succession, probably made Henry wistful for the freedom of the Teutonic Knights, fighting their *reyse* in 'the Wilderness' of Lithuania.

*

On 27 June 1392, Henry received letters of protection for his second voyage to Prussia. Four days later his father granted him two thousand marks per year to supplement his income, and agreed to advance the whole first year's allowance for his forthcoming voyage.[16] Henry appointed Richard Kingston, archdeacon of Hereford, to be his war treasurer again, and immediately set about gathering in all the provisions he would need. The scale was even greater than before. He requisitioned three ships at Lynn, on the north coast of Norfolk, and over the month of July these were packed with such items as thirty-seven empty barrels to contain fresh water, two hundred and seven crabs and lobsters (presumably kept alive on board), three hundred stockfish, 20 lb. pears, 20 lb. ginger, 3 lb. saffron, 20 lb. cinnamon, 12 sugar loaves weighing a total of 36 lb., 6 lb. mace, 1 lb. galingale, 336 lb. almonds, 23 lb. soap, 8 lb. currants, 2 lb. cubebs, 3 lb. nutmeg, 6 lb. liquorice, 4 lb. caraway, 4 lb. aniseed, 6 lb. alkanet, one ream of paper, 3lb. red wax and 3lb. sunflower seeds. Henry took English brewed beer as well as ale, a banner bearing the arms of St George, six dozen plates and a newly painted tapestry. A vivid image of all this being loaded is provided by references to the barrels being carted to the crane on the dock at Lynn to winch them on board.[17] When all was ready, the three vessels were towed the fourteen miles along the coast to Heacham by ten smaller ships. There Henry waited for a favourable wind, playing dice to while away the time.

Many of those travelling with Henry had been on his previous expedition. Hugh Waterton (his chamberlain) and Hugh Herle (chaplain) were nearly always with him, so their attendance is no surprise. Peter Bucton and Ralph Rochford were two knights who took advantage of this chance to return to Prussia. Eighty-seven men in all are named in his accounts, including ten knights and officers, fifteen esquires and forty-nine valets. The chroniclers estimated his total retinue at three hundred, as before, suggesting that there were many unnamed men besides these.

The vessels set sail on 24 July, and the wind remained in their favour all the way to Prussia. They landed at Putzig on 10 August, after only eighteen days at sea. But then their luck ran out. On reaching Danzig they learned that Vitold had made peace with Jagiello, and was now in effect his lieutenant in Lithuania. Vitold had no further need of the Teutonic Knights, nor of Henry or any other Christian warriors. Henry and his men had sailed more than a thousand miles, at great expense and some discomfort to themselves, prepared to fight to the death, only to find that their services were not wanted.

This was a curious situation: to be a crusader without a cause. What was Henry supposed to do? Having left in the usual blaze of promise and glory, with a military and jousting reputation to live up to, he could not return home straight away without losing face. He lingered at Danzig for two weeks, during which time his restless soldiers killed two men in a brawl. Henry quickly made reparations through the intercession of his chaplain, Hugh Herle, and paid for the burials. Then he set out to Königsberg where he met with Marshal Rabe, who seems to have been deeply apologetic about the lack of a *reyse* that year.[18] Rabe explained the delicate situation to Henry and gave him the substantial sum of £400 towards his expenses. This still did not resolve Henry's problem. Having set out to show himself a soldier of Christ, he needed to achieve something honourable before he could return to England.

Henry went back to Danzig and pondered his next move. He did not have many options. He could have travelled back to England by land, which would have taken time and been unexciting and expensive. He could in theory have pushed on eastwards, through Lithuania, to encounter the Tartars in Russia, but that would have been dangerous to the point of suicidal with only three hundred men. He could in theory have sailed around to the Mediterranean and fought against the Moors in Spain and northern Africa, but he had insufficient supplies for such a long voyage. Besides, the ships in which he had sailed were manned by men who knew the Baltic, not the Atlantic. Thus he decided to do what very few Englishmen had done before him: a pilgrimage though Poland, Bohemia, Austria and Italy, and then across the sea to the Holy Land. He would go to Jerusalem.

*

Even today people think twice before undertaking a journey of two thousand miles. In the fourteenth century it was a considerable psychological challenge. For a start, Henry knew he would be heading through Pomerania (the north of Poland), which was intermittently fighting the Teutonic Knights. Then there was the obvious vulnerability which any gold-laden traveller needs to consider, including pirates in the Mediterranean. On the other hand, Henry did have money, an armed retinue and the prestige of both his grandfathers' names. Everywhere he went he would be seen by the leading families as a curiosity – the grandson of the great King Edward III and his most famous warrior, Lancaster – for although English people were not very familiar with Eastern Europe, the fame of the English warriors had spread across the whole of the Christian world. Moreover, Henry was King Richard's cousin, and even though he and the king did not get on, the connection opened doors for him. Richard's queen, for example, was the sister of both King Wenceslas of Bohemia and King Sigismund of Hungary. In addition, because Henry was descended from Edward II's queen, Isabella of France, and Henry III's queen, Eleanor of Provence, he had distant cousins in many of the ruling houses of Europe. Wenceslas's eldest half-sisters, for example, were his second cousins twice removed.[19] As Henry sat in the hall of Klaus Gottesknight's house in Danzig, the idea of the long pilgrimage to Jerusalem dawned on him. Once it had dawned, it rose like a fiery sun of ambition.

Henry sent a knight, Otto Grandison, to the duke of Stolp to obtain letters of safe-conduct under his seal. These arrived, and Henry set out on 22 September 1392. The following day, at Schonec, an old friend caught up with him: Sir Thomas Erpingham, who had travelled with Henry on his first expedition to Lithuania. Henry spent two days at Schonec celebrating with Erpingham before passing through the vineyards of the region and making his next stop at Hammerstein.

Each morning his valets and heralds rode ahead with banners of his arms to announce his approach and to arrange accommodation for him and his men in the most suitable house. In this fashion he entered Polschken, Schievelbein, Dramberg, Arneswald, Landsberg and Drossen (to use their German names; today these places lie in Poland). Twelve days and 250 miles after leaving Danzig he rode across the long wooden bridge over the River Oder and entered Frankfurt an der Oder, fifty miles to the east of Berlin. As soon as he entered the town his men set about obtaining quantities of wine, beer and good white bread. A cart which had been damaged on the way was mended. Henry had a good look at the prosperous town – a member of the Hanseatic League, whose trading boats sailed up and down the Oder, between Stettin and Breslau – and set off again the next day. A local guide was paid to show them the way, along the road by the wide, meadow-banked Oder, to the point at which it met its tributary, the Neisse.[20]

The next town on the Neisse was Gubin. Each day a separate guide was taken on to lead the party along the safest path beside the slow-flowing river. On 7 October they came to Görlitz, and entered the lands ruled by King Wenceslas of Bohemia. Like the other towns along the Neisse and the Oder rivers, Görlitz was a major trading town. Henry's spicery clerks were able to buy ginger, pepper and wax candles. Henry gave alms to three lepers he met here; and some of his horses were reshod before the party continued on their way, following another guide down the river towards Zittau, and from there down to Prague, which Henry entered on 13 October.

Prague was already ancient. On the summit of the hill overlooking the city, the tenth-century castle had seen royal palaces and chapels come and go within the circuit of its walls. The basilica of St George stood there; so did the old convent associated with it, where the relics of St Ludmilla were revered. The new cathedral of St Vitus towered high above everything else, including the royal palace, its steeple dominating the skyline. It was the coronation place of the kings of Bohemia, their capital and their seat of power. It was also a thrusting and progressive modern city, boasting a new royal palace, an international market and a university, founded about forty-five years earlier.

Henry was greeted with honour by King Wenceslas. His fame had preceded him: in addition to his connection to the English royal family, several Bohemian knights who had been at St Inglevert were able to testify to his martial skill. The king treated Henry not as a mere earl but as a prince in his own right, and invited him to join him at his hunting lodge. For three days Henry feasted and hunted with Wenceslas. When he returned to the city he visited the shrines and churches within the precincts of the castle, giving alms and oblations at each one, honouring the Bohemian royal family and the queen of England's ancestors.[21]

Elsewhere in the city, Henry's men were preparing for the next stage of their journey. In the hall of Henry's house his heralds were busy painting more coats of arms on paper and wood. Henry set great store by parading his coat of arms wherever he went. Here too his clerks were able to obtain for him local souvenirs of his trip – two painted altarpieces – as well as the more usual necessities of supply, including food, drink and provisions for the horses. On the 26th he set out on the next stage of his journey, 160 miles to Vienna, where he arrived on 4 November.

Henry's expedition was beginning to acquire some of the characteristics of the Grand Tour of the eighteenth century, when young aristocratic men completed their education by visiting the great cities and ruling families of Europe. Henry crossed the River Danube and travelled to meet

King Sigismund of Hungary, another of Queen Anne's brothers.[22] In Vienna, the capital of Austria, he met Duke Albert III, who welcomed him and paid his expenses while he stayed in the city. The duke was both a soldier and a man who could appreciate scholarship. He had taken part in the *reyse* of 1377 and had expanded the University of Vienna, which his late brother had founded in the 1360s. Henry could see for himself how the whole region was locked in a cultural battle, with the universities of Prague and Vienna vying for pre-eminence, and the Viennese planning to rebuild their cathedral even taller than that of St Vitus in Prague. Like the young lords on their European tours three or four hundred years later, simply visiting these places was an education. The key difference between Henry's journey and the Grand Tour is that, in the eighteenth century, it was the educational value of the travelling and meeting people which was the main purpose. For Henry, these were just by-products of the ultimate aim: to pay homage to God in Jerusalem, at the Holy Sepulchre.

While he stayed in Vienna, Henry sent Sir Peter Bucton ahead to Venice with a small party of knights and heralds to make arrangements for a galley to take him across the Mediterranean. On 7 November he said his farewells to Duke Albert and took the road which followed the River Murz south from Vienna through Carinthia. The harsh winter was setting in; the uneven roads were rutted with frozen mud. Henry was riding towards the foothills of the Alps with his one remaining carriage. On 9 November he was at Neukirchen, on the 12th at Leoben. Somewhere on the road between the two, Henry met a dwarf and gave him alms. A week later he rode into Klagenfurt, which had supposedly been founded where once a dragon had lived and been slain by a brave St George-like warrior. Here he stayed the night before riding along the north side of the blue-green waters of the Wörthersee up the steep road towards Villach.

A lot of grease had to be used on the rough axles of his carriage, but even this was insufficient, for the paths were too narrow for such a large, heavy vehicle. Eventually he abandoned it altogether and bought two smaller carts. Whether he paid any attention to the blue-green waters of the lake as he struggled towards the snow-capped mountains in the distance is open to doubt. For men of his day, the beauties of nature were not a great attraction. Surrounded by unspoilt countryside and greenery all the time, it was great buildings which especially excited the fourteenth-century traveller. For Henry and his men, they had the towns and churches of Italy ahead of them, which they were looking forward to seeing far more than the steep slopes of the Alps in the bitter cold.

On 17 November Henry reached Arnoldstein, on the border between

Austria and Italy. The following day he began the slow descent to San Daniele, Spilimberg and the ancient city of Treviso, where he arrived on the evening of the 22nd. A multitude of tall, thin towers bristled above the walls of the town, and the cathedral and churches sat hunched over their small piazzas. The Roman walls still stood, enclosing the many municipal buildings of the bustling old town. This was the first Mediterranean city Henry had seen, and here he must have felt that he was at last nearing his destination, for Treviso had recently come under the dominion of Venice itself, and the winged lion of St Mark was carved in several prominent places. Henry rested for several days. He sent his baggage carts out to the small city of Portogruaro on the coast of the Adriatic, where he established his winter quarters. From here he could be rowed down the coast to Venice and back in hired barges. The bitterly cold winter, however, meant that even the salt waters of the Adriatic impeded him. On one occasion nine men were paid for breaking the ice so that the barge could pass.[23]

At Venice Henry came face to face with a huge city, far larger than anything he had previously seen. At this time London probably had fewer than thirty thousand inhabitants. No other English cities were even half this size, and all but a handful had populations under five thousand. At Venice he found himself surrounded by about sixty or seventy thousand souls, all packed tightly into the overpopulated, overdeveloped islands. The display of wealth was astonishing, from the citizens' dress and the palaces of the merchants to the relics in each of the churches. The goods in the markets were greater in range and variety than the produce available anywhere else in Europe. Indeed, many of the spices he bought in markets in London had come through Venice. From the Eastern-inspired quixotic architecture to the boats in the lagoon, from the exotica available in the markets to the three thousand sea-going ships that the Republic could boast, there was no doubt that Venice was the key to unlock the known world.

The senate of the Venetian Republic had, of course, heard of Henry's arrival. Sir Peter Bucton had arrived two weeks earlier, and had brought letters from Henry and from the duke of Austria. It was rare for an important member of the English royal family to visit Venice, and accordingly the senate had voted by a margin of forty-two to four to grant him a galley to take him and his men to the Holy Land. They also declined any payment for this honour. On 30 November, hearing that he had settled his household at Portogruaro for the winter, they spent 360 ducats (about £60) on a reception in his honour.[24] On 1 December he arrived at the house prepared for him on the Isle of St George, and the following day he met the doge and senate, and joined with them in a service at St Mark's Cathedral.

The next three weeks must have been a constant delight to Henry, waking every morning to see the wide Mediterranean dawn, the ice on the frozen canals being broken by the boatmen, the colourful eastern cloths and the aromatic spices in the markets. He spent three weeks visiting the churches and listening to the music. He was shown around much of the city by the doge himself.[25] Besides his donations at St Mark's (which he visited more than once), he gave alms at the churches of St Lucy, St Nicholas, St Agnes, St Anthony, St George, the Innocents and St Christopher. These churches were filled with relics, many of them removed from Constantinople in 1204 by the mercenaries of the Fourth Crusade. Like everything else in Venice, these were not just buried in stone, they were dazzling: encased in gold and jewelled reliquaries.

In the markets Henry's clerks were able to obtain whatever their lord desired. Fish of all sorts were bought in large quantities, including eel, pike, tench, crabs, plaice, trout, crayfish, barbutt, mullet, shrimps, oysters, cockles, greenback, perch, chub, pimpernel, carp and flounder. Pigs, hens, eggs, chickens and ducks were all laid on for the journey to the Holy Land, as well as all the saffron, mace, sugar candy, and other sweets which Henry liked to have on a long journey. Here he was able to obtain gingerbread and *citronade* (probably a sort of lemon preserve). Huge amounts of food were provided. Two thousand dates were loaded on board, and 2,250 eggs. One thousand pounds of almonds were taken: that equates to a hundred-weight for every week of the voyage (most to be used as almond milk in the cooking). And to pay for it all, Henry secured a money transfer from his father in England, through the services of the bankers, the Albertini. Medieval Venice was unrivalled for its financial facilities as well as its range of things to buy.

*

On 22 or 23 December 1392, Henry finally set sail. The route was a prescribed one, followed by Venetian ship captains for centuries as they plied the pilgrim trade. They followed the coast of Croatia and stopped at the Venetian city of Zara (now Zadar) on Christmas Day. Then they sailed down the Dalmatian coast to the island of Lissa (Vis), and south-wards, to the island of Corfu, around the Peloponnese to Rhodes and possibly Cyprus. Excluding Zara, these stops seem to have been roughly at 250-mile intervals, and probably represent a full six days at sea.[26] At each place the men disembarked and had the tablecloths and communal linen taken ashore and washed. At a port on the Peloponnese clerks were sent ashore to buy wine, lemons, fish, bread, herbs, olive oil, milk and oranges; on the island of Rhodes they obtained a thousand eggs, six partridges, oil, bread and herbs. By the time they reached the shore of the Holy Land, they had been at sea for about five weeks.

We know very little of what happened to Henry in the Holy Land. His accounts become minimal, recording only bare essentials, as if he walked around and bought nothing but just stood and gawped. In fact one of the most telling lines about his experience comes from a letter written many years later, when he was king, to the emperor of Abyssinia. In this letter he expresses his intention to revisit Jerusalem, but he stresses with great pride that he had *already* been to the Holy Sepulchre, in person.[27] And he may well have been proud: the only other members of the English royal family who had set their eyes on the Holy Land were Richard I and Edward I, and neither of them had entered the Holy City itself. When he saw land that day in late January 1393 it must have seemed to Henry that he would soon tread in the footsteps of Jesus Christ.

This is the important thing to understand about Henry's voyage to the Holy Land. A cynic might say that he only went on his pilgrimage because he had nothing better to do, and his greatest hardship along the way was the chill as he rode through the Alps in winter. But such a judgement would be wrong, for it ignores the all-important element of motive. The reasons why medieval men travelled all the way to Jerusalem go far beyond cynicism. Henry certainly had a more luxurious time travelling than his non-royal contemporaries, but it cannot be denied that what had pushed him all that way was the zeal of the pilgrim. When Englishmen making the pilgrimage to Canterbury saw the cathedral before them, they started to run as fast as they could towards it, unable to stop themselves, so powerful was the grip of the impending spiritual fulfilment of their journey. For the few Englishmen who made the journey all the way to the Holy Land, how much greater their excitement must have been. For Henry, who had come via Poland, Prussia, Bohemia, Austria and Italy, travelling almost constantly for nearly seven months, the sight of the intended destination must have sent more than a slight shiver of excitement running down his spine.

Jaffa itself stirred deep feelings of pride, for this was where King Richard had fought his two battles with Saladin in the summer of 1192, two hundred years before. From the boat, Henry would have seen where King Richard had waded ashore with a handful of knights, his sword above his head, to inspire the garrison of the citadel to resume fighting. Outside the town itself he saw the place where Richard had fought a great pitched battle, commanding fifty-four knights and two thousand infantrymen against seven thousand Saracens. But then, turning his sight towards the east, he would have been aware that the real goal for which he had come was not this pleasant port, nor these historical distractions, but the shimmering city that lay just thirty miles away.

Henry hired one horse to carry the food supplies for him and his men and then started to walk towards Jerusalem.[28] For the Christian pilgrim, every step of the way was imbued with symbolism and meaning. The landscape was one vast holy relic. Just to be at Jaffa, 'where Peter was raised from death to life', earned the pilgrim absolution from seven years' worth of sins.[29] Leaving the town they came to a stone: the very stone upon which Peter was standing when Jesus called to him to follow him.

From that stone to Jerusalem, the experience for the pilgrim grew more and more intense with every step. If Henry followed the usual pilgrim trail, he would have gone to Ramah and then Lydda, where St George was martyred. He would have seen the tomb of Samuel the prophet, and the house where the Last Supper was held. As he entered Jerusalem, the drama grew even greater as he saw the Roman gate where Pilate proclaimed 'Ecce Homo' ('Behold the man'), and started to walk in the footsteps of Christ himself towards Calvary. His guide pointed out to him and his companions the stone where Christ rested with his cross, the chapel on the site where Christ appeared to his mother after the Crucifixion, the pillar to which Christ was bound and then beaten with scourges, and the place where Christ was crowned with thorns. Slowly, story by story, the pilgrim approached the culmination of the journey: the Holy Sepulchre itself, on the site of where the angels said to the three Marys, 'whom do you seek?' and in the choir of the same church the chamber where Christ was laid to rest, and where he rose again from the dead.

At the Holy Sepulchre Henry gave his six gold ducats (£1), the standard amount. The donation was less important than the spirit of the offering, and the *being* there, the believing. Henry had adopted the path of the crusader and pilgrim, and followed God. Everything we have been able to determine about his character to this point in his life – from his logical mind to his courage, his conventional attitude to religion, his self-confidence and his intellectual ability – leads us to believe that the pilgrimage to Jerusalem was the most intense confirmation of his spiritual belief. He may have travelled the long journey in comparative luxury, but having been in the Holy City he had achieved a status which could never be taken away from him. It made him more than just a prince among men.

*

Henry's return from Jerusalem was a slow business. He had accomplished his journey's great purpose; there was no rush to get home. Indeed, he preferred this independent life – travelling as a prince, meeting foreign

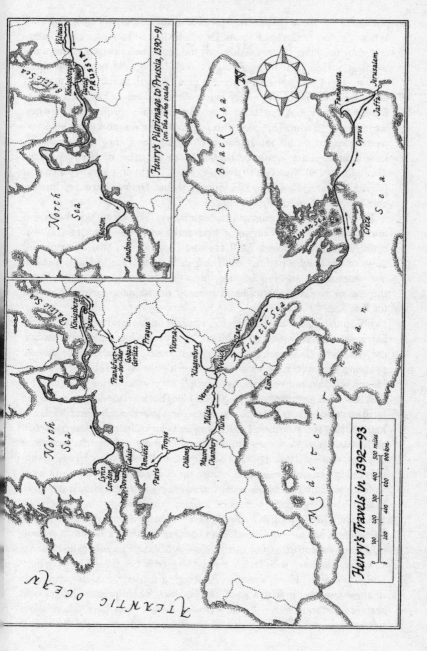

Henry's Pilgrimage to Prussia, 1390–91 (on the same scale)

Henry's Travels in 1392–93

potentates – to the undemanding role of an underemployed heir in England. When the ship docked at Cyprus, he was invited to Famagusta and entertained by the king, James I. Although the island was ravaged at that time by plague, Henry, in his spiritually touched state, did not worry about disease. The king gave him a present of a leopard, for which a cage had to be built on board the galley before he could set sail again. Later, in England, Henry took care of his leopard, purchasing medicines for it when it grew sick.[30] Somewhere along his pilgrimage he was also given a parrot, which escaped on his return journey. At Rhodes Henry took under his wing a Saracen boy, whom he baptised with the name of Henry, perhaps as tangible proof of his visit to the Holy Land. Normally pilgrims purchased pilgrim badges to show they had visited a shrine. Henry went a step further, and bought captured infidel children.

Henry returned to Venice on 20 March 1393. The senate voted to spend one hundred ducats in honour of his return, 'so he may return to his own country well pleased with us'.[31] He had copies of his coat of arms and those of his knights painted and hung in St Mark's Cathedral to remind the Venetians of the English pilgrims who had visited their city.[32] After three more weeks in the trading capital of the Mediterranean, he set out for England.

Of all the places at which Henry stopped on his return journey, one in particular deserves mention. At Milan, Henry met Gian Galeazzo Visconti, the duke who had recently overthrown his uncle Bernabo and was now planning to conquer the whole of northern Italy. As in Poland-Lithuania, Henry was confronted with the example of a ruler being challenged – and, in Milan, overthrown – by a rival heir. Their relationship was helped by the fact that Gian Galeazzo was in a sense a kinsman. His sister, Violante, had married Henry's uncle Lionel in 1368. Gian Galeazzo charmed Henry, and took him to see Lionel's tomb as well as those of Boethius (author of *The Consolation of Philosophy*) and St Augustine. In later years Henry always referred to him by his most poetic title, 'the count of Virtue', and continued to write to him. The Milanese in turn were charmed by Henry, the archbishop being especially impressed by this crusading prince.[33] The duke invited him to arbitrate in a dispute between himself and a house of friars. Someone in Milan – probably Gian Galeazzo himself – gave him a present of a set of cups made out of ostrich eggs. A Milanese esquire called Francis Court was so taken with Henry that he begged to be allowed to serve him, and thus entered Henry's service. Another particularly smitten companion of these few days in Milan was Gian Galeazzo's own twenty-one-year-old sister-in-law and cousin, Lucia Visconti. Seven years later, when asked whom she would like to marry, she replied that if she could be sure of marrying Henry, she would wait for him forever, even if she were to die three days after the wedding. This was solemnly recorded by the clerk for posterity in the same document in which she gave her assent to an alternative marriage proposal. Even a desirable and acceptable candidate was second best when compared with the twenty-six-year-old Henry.[34]

Henry proceeded through France at a stately pace, arriving in Paris on 22 June and landing at Dover on the 30th. He had been away from England for almost a year. In that time his experiences had tempered him: the passionate crusader had absorbed the responsibility of having been a pilgrim in the Holy City of Jerusalem. Many lessons remained to be learned: he had hardly come to terms with the financial implications of living such a lavish lifestyle. But at the end of the journey, as he rode into London, no one could say that he had not put his family advantage to good effect or his father's wealth to good use. When people thought of Henry of Lancaster now, they did not just picture a rich heir but a conscientious and brave soldier, a pious and judicious man, who had looked into the eyes of the pagan warrior and braved the lance of Boucicaut. It is not surprising that Lucia Visconti fell for him. Considering his crusading, his pilgrimage and his jousting, it is not going too far to say that he had made himself into an exemplary knight, combining the spiritual and chivalric values of his age more completely perhaps than any other Englishman of the late fourteenth century.

SIX

Curst Melancholy

Why hast thou lost the fresh blood in thy cheeks
And given my treasures and my rights of thee
To thick-eyed musing and curst meancholy?
Henry IV Part One, Act II, Scene 3

Imagine Henry, on the deck of his ship, the day he returned to England. There he stands, looking at the chalk cliffs of the south coast as the ship rolls over the waves. Ahead of him lies the road back to London, through Canterbury and Sittingbourne. Ahead of him too lies the meeting with his family, his wife, Mary, and his four sons and a baby daughter, Blanche, named after the mother he never knew. No doubt he is looking forward to meeting his father too, and telling him about Prague, Vienna, Venice and, above all else, Jerusalem. He is brimful of confidence that the story of his travels is one worth telling everywhere. And yet there is something more in his mind. As he stands on the deck, looking at England, he knows that this is the one place in Europe where he will not be respected as a visiting prince. In England he is merely a vassal, and treated with less respect than he had received in the courts of Europe.

Henry could not but have cast his mind ahead to the reception that awaited him in his home country. The last time he had returned, from his crusade, he had been fêted as a hero. This time he had completed a journey every bit as remarkable, yet he had no way of knowing the political climate in England, with the exception of rumours he had picked up in Paris. There he had arrived just after his father's departure with a draft agreement for a permanent peace between England and France. With his father's apparent success, and the tale of his own adventures to tell, Henry may have expected his homecoming to be as much of an excited celebration as his last, two years earlier.

It was not. The country was uneasy. The draft treaty which John and his brother, the duke of Gloucester, had negotiated was not to the liking of the English court. Some lords were positively hostile to the idea of giving up the claim to the sovereignty of France. Elements of the commons too were deeply suspicious of the motives for peace. Even before Henry had arrived back in England a great number of men had gathered in Cheshire and Lancashire intent on killing him, his father and his uncle Gloucester. They accused them of plotting to deprive the king of England of his sovereignty for their own personal benefit, and openly declared their ambition of assassinating all three men. The rebels gathered in unlawful assemblies under the leadership of Thomas Talbot, their ranks swelled by those who saw the likelihood of mayhem and the opportunity for plunder. The earl of Arundel, equally angry at the likely turn of peace, did nothing to put down the revolt. As for the king, although he did belatedly send representatives to calm the insurgents, he was suspected of turning a blind eye.[1]

When Henry rode into London on 5 July 1393 he must have been worried. His own name was linked with this unpopular peace, even though he had had no part in forming the draft treaty. Moreover, he must have wondered why his father had agreed to such unpopular terms. Was this the logical and inevitable outcome of all those years of talks, patiently seeking a path between the warmongers and the mercenary captains? If so, it meant that John had come to prefer the kingship of Richard II to that of Edward III, if only for the pragmatic reason that Richard was incapable of leading an army in battle. But that was not the case. The reason why John was following the king's bidding in seeking peace at any price was because Richard had no heir. John was putting all his efforts into supporting Richard's ambition for peace so that Richard would acknowledge Henry as his successor. John had set himself on the narrow path of absolute loyalty, with his son's eventual succession as his ultimate goal. He would do nothing to discourage Richard from recognising the Lancastrians as the rightful heirs to the throne.

Henry seems to have gone directly to his father on his return to England, who was marching north to confront the rebels.[2] John was at Lancaster on 10 and 14 August, and it is likely that Henry was with him. Thomas Talbot admitted his misdeeds before Henry and Lord Lovell, who perhaps had gone as representatives to negotiate with him.[3] Following the break-up of the revolt, John went to Beverley and Henry went south, to join his wife at Peterborough.[4] A few weeks later, Mary was pregnant again. Henry remained with her there until December, when they both joined his father at Hertford, and Henry took part in the traditional Christmas tournament. Happy to be back with his family, he paid for a new suit of armour for his half-brother, Thomas Beaufort, so he also could take part in the festive joust.[5] The king of France's own jester joined them, and was rewarded by Henry with a gift of forty shillings.[6] New Year's presents were received from the king and queen, his father and stepmother, the duke and duchess of Gloucester, his mother-in-law the countess of Hereford, Thomas Mowbray, the countess of Norfolk (Mowbray's grandmother), the bishop of Salisbury and Lady Audley.[7] Those to whom Henry gave presents included his old governess, Katherine Swynford, his heralds, his loyal friend, Thomas Erpingham, Katherine Waterton (the wife of his chamberlain, Hugh Waterton), and Sir John Bussy, Speaker of the House of Commons.

*

Henry remained at Hertford with Mary in January 1394, delaying setting off for parliament until the end of the month.[8] When he finally departed, he sent her a present of oysters, mussels and sprats.[9] It was just like the last time he had left her in mid-pregnancy to attend parliament, when he had sent her a present of apples and pears. As before, the gift marked a contrast between his happy, homely life with his wife and children, and the harsh exposure of politics at Westminster. At about this time he purchased a brooch for his own use which bore the motto *sanz mal penser* ('think no evil'), along with elaborate prayer books and crucifixes.[10] It smacks of apprehensiveness, echoing the Garter motto, '*honi soit qui mal y pense* (shame on him who thinks it evil)'.

Parliament met on 27 January. Almost immediately, John of Gaunt and the earl of Arundel were at loggerheads. The chancellor declared that one of the reasons for the parliament was the peace of the kingdom, following the Cheshire uprising. John bitterly accused Arundel of doing nothing to control the revolt, even though the rebels' declared intention was to kill him and Henry, and despite the fact that Arundel had been encamped in Cheshire with an army at the time. Arundel retorted with a stinging attack on John, accusing him of being too friendly with the king. The parliament roll (which offers the most precise account of the argument) omits John's accusations against Arundel, and states that Arundel decided to unburden himself of matters on his conscience, namely that it was not to the king's honour to spend so much time with his uncle, nor that he should wear the livery of the Lancastrians. Why did he not treat his other uncles with similar favour? Why had John benefited so much from the money for his Spanish campaign, which had ultimately achieved nothing more than the enrichment of the Lancastrians? And what right did John have to give up the king of England's authority to the French throne?[11]

Richard placated the earl of Arundel. He explained it was only natural that there should be affection between nephew and uncle, and he was not aware of treating John differently from his brothers. As to the Spanish money, Richard pointed out sensibly that it was parliament's wish that John undertake his Spanish campaign, and in France he had simply negotiated a draft agreement, as he was charged to do as an English ambassador. Nothing yet was set in stone on that matter. So there was no damage either to the king's honour or to John's. Arundel was forced to apologise publicly to the duke for his accusations. [12]

But the uneasiness did not end there. Despite his crusade and pilgrimage, Henry had been overlooked by the king when it had come to appointing receivers of petitions in parliament. In the last two parliaments at which he had been present – those of 1390 and 1391 – he *had* been appointed, along with the earls of Kent, Salisbury, Arundel and Warwick. In January 1394, all four of these earls were reappointed; not Henry, though. This may have been a further cause of upset for John. His son and heir was now approaching the age of twenty-seven, and had every right to be regarded as one of the most important men in the country. It was a clear slight to him that he was not. As a result, when Richard declared that he intended to lead an expedition to Ireland, the question arose as to who should be keeper of the realm in his absence overseas. Normally the next in line to the throne was appointed keeper.[13] John understood that he was next in line, as his father had stipulated, but he was aware that he would have to go to Gascony. So he formally asked that Henry be appointed. In effect this was asking Richard to recognise that Henry was the heir apparent, in line with Edward III's settlement. The twenty-year-old Roger Mortimer, earl of March, heard this and was outraged. He believed that he was the heir apparent, not Henry: the king had declared as much in 1386. Richard did not want to deal with such issues then and there, where he might provoke uproar. So he commanded both John and the young earl of March to be silent. He himself said nothing more on the subject.

For Henry, the parliament of 1394 amounted to another grinding disappointment, in which nothing of substance was resolved to his benefit. Even if his father was not politically damaged by Arundel's stinging criticisms, Henry himself was. There was now a serious rift between the house of Lancaster and the earl of Arundel, a kinsman and a fellow Appellant. That, coupled with a property dispute, led to a further rift between Henry and the earl of Warwick.[14] After all the honour foreign princes had afforded him, and after his journey to the Holy Land, it must have seemed incredible to Henry that he should be so disregarded by the king and members of the English court. Why were the earls of Arundel, Warwick and Kent appointed to be receivers of petitions, when Henry was now the best-known Englishman in wider Christendom, with the exception of his father and the king? And to whom was the king planning to entrust the realm if not to him? As for his feelings towards the earl of Arundel, it was unbecoming for that man to lecture his father on honour and loyalty. Had not John striven hard all these years to do the king's bidding? Had he not forgiven the king for trying to murder him, and trying to undermine his authority, as well as accusing him of treachery without good reason? What more did John have to do to prove himself a loyal servant of the king?

Such arguments had damaging consequences outside parliament too. With the king planning an expedition to Ireland, further taxation was required. For many people this represented a dangerous precedent: direct taxation was supposedly only levied in wartime. But this was the third instance of Richard demanding subsidies while pursuing a peace-making policy. And still he was unable to make ends meet. Many believed that the ills which had caused the Lords Appellant to take action were still with them, and yet those one-time champions of the people were now accusing each other of dishonour and selfishness. Only the younger Appellants, Henry and Thomas Mowbray, remained outside this criticism. The poet John Gower, having concluded the first draft of his great work, *Confessio Amantis*, in 1390 with passages praising the king, was sickened. He now deleted his lines in favour of Richard and dedicated the entire work to Henry. In return Henry gave him a Lancastrian livery collar, which the poet wore with pride until his death.[15]

*

As Henry and his father rode back from Westminster to Hertford Castle following the conclusion of the parliament, they both had reason to be disappointed.[16] All John's hard negotiations had ended in his draft treaty being rejected by parliament. Henry had simply been ignored. But perhaps the most worrying consequence of the session was the realisation that the king did not need either of them any more. Richard had defended John against Arundel's accusations, not vice versa. And when it had come to clearing up the question of the succession, Richard had refused to recognise Henry's claim. He no longer needed John's help to fend off the royal uncles or the troublesome senior Appellants. John was still a dignified royal uncle and ambassador but the idea that he represented the rightful line of inheritance, as Henry had insisted in 1387, had dissolved in the turbulent waters of Richard's personal kingship.

Unfortunately Henry's accounts for the spring of 1394 do not survive, so it is not possible to determine where he was between March and June of that year. He may have accompanied his father and uncle Gloucester on their expedition back to Leulinghen to let the French ambassadors know the English answer to the proposed treaty. It is equally likely that he stayed at Hertford with his wife. Either way, a few days after his father set out, Henry heard the sad news that his stepmother, the duchess Constanza, was dead. She had died unexpectedly, probably after a short illness, on 24 March.[17]

For Henry, Constanza's death came as a shock. Although he had lost many members of his family in his youth, nobody close to him had died in recent years. Unusually (for late medieval England), all five of Henry's children were alive and well; his father had passed fifty years of age, and he himself was healthy and fit, to judge from his regular jousting. He had grown close to his stepmother since she had come to England and he had entered her household, at the age of four. She had never been as close to John as Henry's mother had been; nevertheless she had won much affection from the Lancastrian entourage. She was always high on Henry's list of New Year presents. Hearing of her death, John decided that she should be laid to rest at Leicester, in the Lancastrian collegiate church there, but that the funeral should wait until he had returned to England. He wanted to attend. In the elaborate and expensive burial arrangements he demonstrated that he too had grown much fonder of his Castilian princess than he had anticipated on her arrival in England in 1371.[18]

The news of the duchess's death was thus a tragedy such as Henry had not previously known. But it was nothing compared to the next news which reached him. His own wife, Mary, was dead.[19]

Her death left him devastated. It was her sixth confinement, and all the previous children had been born safely. There was no reason to suspect anything different would happen this time. But Philippa, in being born, had joined her siblings in motherlessness. Henry knew all about that; he and his sisters had been in the same position twenty-five years earlier. His eldest son, Henry of Monmouth, was nearly eight: almost the same age as Henry's elder sister had been when their mother had died. Little Blanche was just two.[20]

If Henry was with his father in France at the time, news of this death must have made both men regard each other with the utmost sympathy. John had been twenty-eight – only a year older than Henry now – when Blanche had died. Henry no doubt cast his mind back over his days with his wife: the musical interests they shared, their fine books, praying together, discussing matters of state together – even down to little aspects of daily life, such as the meals they shared. It comes as no surprise to read that Henry went into mourning for a whole year.[21]

As if these deaths were not tragedy enough, on 7 June, at Sheen, Queen Anne died. Richard too was utterly distraught. He ordered the entire palace to be destroyed. He demanded that her funeral be the most lavish ever held. The court around him held its breath, quaking at his fearful anger. Away from the court, the nation was deeply troubled. This run of royal deaths was surely ominous for the country. Walsingham referred to the period in his chronicle as 'the Death of Ladies'. For Richard it marked a personal tragedy as great as Henry's, for Richard had genuinely loved his wife. At her magnificent funeral on 3 August, the earl of Arundel turned up late. He then made his excuses and asked permission to leave early. Hearing this disrespectful request, the grieving king lost control of himself. He took a rod from one of his attendants and beat the earl so hard about the head that the earl bled profusely over the floor of the church. The result was confusion, fear and delay, as Arundel was arrested and dragged away to the Tower. It was nightfall before the ceremony was over.

The funerals of the duchess Constanza and the countess Mary took place in a much more sober atmosphere, at Leicester, on consecutive days at the beginning of July. Black cloth in huge quantities adorned the church of St Mary. Henry and his father attended, joining in the procession with other members of the family and the Lancastrian retainers. First, on Sunday 5 July, Constanza was buried. Mary was laid to rest in the Lady Chapel on the following day. Interestingly, Henry never commissioned an effigy of her. Although Richard commissioned two men to make images for the queen's tomb the following April, and the work was finished by July 1397, it was not until after Henry's death that a likeness was constructed for his wife.[22] The most likely explanation is that he initially wanted a double effigy to be made for them both when he himself died, so that they would lie together (a plan changed by his accession to the throne and the necessity of him having an altogether grander place of burial).

*

In August 1394, seven weeks after the funerals of the Lancastrian ladies, John of Gaunt held a meeting at Pontefract Castle. The principal male representatives of the dynasty were present: Edmund, duke of York; his son, Edward, earl of Rutland; and Thomas, duke of Gloucester. It is very likely that Henry was there too. The outcome of this meeting was a letter to the king stressing that, although a person of low estate had entered the palace and uttered things to dishonour John, 'touching the royal estate', John had always worked for the benefit of the king and the realm.[23] It seems that someone had accused him of plotting to obtain the crown for himself or his son, for this was an assembly of the male heirs of Edward III. If Henry was present at that meeting at Pontefract, then the first, second, third, fourth and sixth in line to the throne were all there, according to the entail, and if Edmund's younger son, Richard, was also present then that would mean every potential beneficiary of Edward's entail attended that meeting.[24]

As soon as the letter was despatched, John started preparing for his trip to Gascony. Shocked by French proposals that the duchy of Aquitaine should eventually be held by the dukes of Lancaster and not the more prestigious and powerful king of England, a number of Gascon lords had refused to accept John's lordship. It now fell to him to reassert English control of the duchy. His departure left Henry once more in charge of Lancastrian affairs in England, and once more vulnerable.

At the end of September, when John set sail, Richard appointed his uncle Edmund, duke of York, keeper of the realm. It was the betrayal which both Henry and John had long been expecting. Since 1331 the keeper of the realm had been the member of the royal family foremost in the order of succession, regardless of how old or young he was. Whenever a non-royal regent had been selected in the distant past, it was either because the heir to the throne was himself abroad, under-age or in custody. Henry was none of those things. Thus for Richard to appoint Edmund was not just a prevarication – a temporary refusal to decide between the claims of March and Lancaster – it was a public refutation of the pre-eminence of the Lancastrian claim.[25]

Richard had timed this insult to perfection. John was sailing away, and would be gone for a year. Henry was left standing, publicly stripped of his position in the order of succession. At the same time, Thomas Talbot – the leader of the Cheshire uprising against John of Gaunt, Henry and the duke of Gloucester – was transferred from the Tower of London to the more comfortable surroundings of Windsor Castle, and quietly permitted to escape. All proceedings against him were dropped, by order of the king.[26] Even though he had openly accused John of treason, and had confessed that he had roused the Cheshire men to kill three senior members of the royal family, he went unpunished. Three years later, when John specifically demanded that Talbot be brought to justice, Richard did nothing.

This raises another spectre which must have haunted Henry in the autumn of 1394. Talbot had been recruited as one of the king's personal knights in 1392.[27] Cheshire was ardently royalist, the earldom of Chester being an ancestral title of the eldest son of the king. Why would the men of Cheshire have risen up in arms against their beloved king? Explanations in the past have centred on the war providing employment for the king's archers in Cheshire, and that their protest was against the peace, not against the king. That may be correct as far as the rebels themselves were concerned. But it does not explain why this loyal knight led the rebellion, nor why he went unpunished if he was acting against the king's wishes, nor why one of his stated ambitions was to kill Henry. Talbot's second-in-command during the rising was Nicholas Clifton; he was not punished either, and in 1396 he too was recruited by Richard, despite his actions in 1393 being clearly treasonable. Furthermore, when Talbot surrendered, proceedings against him were dropped after only three days.[28] This does not suggest the man was acting as the leader of a local rabble but one who knew he was protected at the highest level. Despite the king's public statements against Talbot in the parliament of 1394, it is very difficult to avoid the conclusion that Richard was protecting him, and that Talbot believed he spoke honestly for Richard in wishing that Henry was dead.

This flies in the face of most historical writing about the relationship between Henry and Richard. Most scholars are of the opinion that Richard and Henry were friendly to one another in the 1390s. According to one leading writer, Henry was 'in favour with Richard' at this time.[29] According to another, 'Richard . . . now did his best to win over to his side this young and popular kinsman [Henry] . . . from now onwards Derby became a member of a new and differently constituted court group'.[30] Such views – especially the last – are mistaken. Henry had just been dismissed by Richard as a receiver of petitions. His status as second in line to the throne had just been publicly denied. The king patently bore no ill will to two men who had called for Henry and his father to be murdered. These are hardly grounds for close friendship between men of great pride.

Similarly, we may ask how often Henry was with the king? The usual way of assessing this is the proportion of royal charters which a magnate witnessed. In the years 1393–7 Henry witnessed fourteen out of forty-two royal charters.[31] Not a small number, it would appear, but three of those were in early 1395 when Richard was out of the country. Three were during or just after parliaments, when Henry was at Westminster anyway. The others point to about five dates when Henry met the king, over the course of four years. Although we know that Henry visited court more often than this, the charters do not show him becoming a member of a 'court group', still less of him being 'in favour'.

This use of negative evidence – the measurable *absence* of evidence which we might reasonably expect to exist had the friendship been genuine – can be pushed further. How many diplomatic missions was Henry appointed to in these years? None. How many royal castles was he given custody of, together with the incomes attached to them? None. How often did he attend court when parliament was not sitting? Hardly ever. Compare this with the pile of honours and favours heaped upon Henry's younger cousin, Edward of York. Edward had been given the stewardship of Bury St Edmunds in 1390, and the keepership of the castle of Oakham, together with the forest of Rutland and the shrievalty of the same county. In 1391 he had been given the joint keepership of the forest of Bradon, had been appointed an admiral, and had been given the important captaincy of the town and castle of Calais. The following year he was empowered to negotiate a truce with France. He accompanied Richard on his Irish visit in 1394–5, was given a second earldom (Cork). On his return to England he was made a feoffee of the lands of the late queen. He was then given the keepership of Brigstock Park and sent to France to negotiate another peace treaty and to arrange the royal marriage, being permitted to secure his own marriage to a member of the French royal family at the same time. And so it went on. Every year, those in favour with Richard received lucrative grants, honours and positions of responsibility. And what did Henry receive in these years? Nothing. When Richard had wanted to open up a diplomatic channel with King Sigismund of Hungary in January 1394, the obvious person to send was Henry, who had already met Sigismund, and had received gifts from him on his travels. Instead, Richard sent his half-brother, the earl of Huntingdon. Coming in the same month as Henry's dismissal as a receiver of petitions and Richard's refusal to acknowledge him as his heir, this amounted to a third instance of Richard simply ignoring Henry. And what had Henry done to deserve being ignored? He had won fame, gone on crusade, sired sons, visited Jerusalem, and proved himself pre-eminent as a tournament fighter. Each of these was a significant achievement in the chivalric world of 1394 and each one marked another of Richard's failings. Looking at the situation from Henry's point of view, we can only see Richard's behaviour towards him as being driven by jealousy and characterised by spite.

For these reasons, we should view the appointment of Edmund of Langley to be keeper of the realm in 1394 as the moment when Richard's previously subtle attempts to undermine Henry became public. Far from being a favourite, Henry was denied any of the usual marks of royal dignity. Shortly before leaving for Ireland, Richard appointed ambassadors to treat with Scotland. Henry was not one of them. We cannot say that such a task was below him – it was not below the dignity of the earl of Northumberland or the bishop of Durham – but Henry was never appointed to such a position of responsibility, or any similar position for that matter. In July 1395, when the touchy question of a royal marriage with the French royal family had to be discussed, and while John of Gaunt was still in Gascony, Richard had to appoint a member of the English royal family to represent him. Henry, aged twenty-eight, would have been the ideal choice. Instead, Richard chose Edward of York. By then it was abundantly clear to Henry that the king had not forgiven him for joining the Appellants in 1387, and would never forgive him. Instead Richard wanted his uncle Edmund of York to be his heir, with the idea that Edmund's son Edward would succeed him. All John's hopes, as well as Henry's own, looked like being dashed by Richard.

*

If Henry could draw any hope from his situation, then it was through his father's example of how to behave when out of favour with the king. On every occasion when Richard had either accused John of treason, or tried to murder him, John had resolutely and firmly responded with a declaration of his unfailing loyalty. Indeed, he was so adamant and consistent that we can hardly doubt that he was genuinely loyal, even if his motive was increasingly to secure the succession of his son. Henry now followed his father's example. If he had objected to Richard's treatment of him he would only have made matters worse.

Parliament was summoned by the duke of York to meet at Westminster at the end of January 1395. With so many lords in Ireland with the king, or in Gascony with John, only thirty-seven peers were summoned, about two-thirds of the total.[32] Henry was restored to his place among the lords appointed to receive petitions, but few were presented. Nor were any statutes enrolled. The only important business of the parliament was granting yet another subsidy to cover the king's expenses in Ireland and discussing a curious document which appeared one day nailed to the door of Westminster Abbey. This was the famous Twelve Conclusions of the Lollards, the followers of the church reformer John Wycliffe. The document, written in English, put forward ten statements of faith. Among these were the idea that faith, hope and charity were driven out of the church through the possession of worldly wealth by the clergy; that priestly celibacy encouraged unnatural levels of lust, and should not be imposed; that nuns' vows of celibacy led pregnant nuns to kill their children at birth; that modern priesthood bore little or no resemblance to that espoused by Christ; that confession led to arrogance among the clergy; that transubstantiation was a lie; and that all warfare was against the teaching of the New Testament. Although later generations of Englishmen shared several of these views, they were shocking in 1395, and to present them in this fashion was even more disturbing. The lords and prelates present at the parliament gathered together in two groups on 13 February and sealed two letters to the king asking him to return to England to attend to the threat to the church posed by these heresies. Henry was among those who set his seal to the letter from the lords, his first recorded action against heretics.[33]

When parliament broke up two days later, Henry lingered in London. With his wife dead and his father in Gascony, there was little reason to return to Hertford, and probably a great deal of heartache in revisiting

Peterborough, where he had spent so much time with his wife. Instead he spent his time at court with his uncle the duke of York and listening to music and poetry.[34] Four of the six musicians who had accompanied him on his pilgrimage were still in his household, and three others had joined them, so that now his retained performers included four pipers, a trumpeter and two 'minstrels'.[35] As for poetry, Geoffrey Chaucer had joined Henry, temporarily at least. Like other members of Henry's household, Chaucer received a furred robe for Christmas 1395, and a present of £10 from Henry's own hands.[36] It is not hard to picture the wizened poet, a sparkle in his eye, engaging the wistful Henry with his *Canterbury Tales*, alluding to the 'parfit' and 'gentil' soldier of Christ who had fought in Prussia, Lithuania, Russia, Granada, Algezir and other such places.

Six weeks later, at the beginning of April, Henry left London. Tracing his movements is not easy; his accounts give very few direct references to his whereabouts. Instead we have to build up a picture of where he was by payments which correspond with his lifestyle. For example, as saddles were repaired for him at Leicester, we may presume that he had passed that way, if only briefly. Likewise, when he was paying the expenses of his London bargemen, it is likely that he was travelling up and down the Thames. However, even these payments do not give us sufficient information. In order to get a more complete picture, we need to consider payments such as those for his 'cotton'. The section of his accounts entitled *Necessaria* includes many miscellaneous payments, including several for quantities of cotton together with disposable glass urinals. That Henry used cotton as toilet paper is suggested by the *Boke of Nurture* written by John Russell, servant to one of Henry's sons, who states that the chamber attendant should make sure that 'there be blanket [undyed woollen cloth], cotyn or lynyn to wipe the nethur ende' for the lord in the privy.[37] Cotton, however, was expensive – at 4½d or 5d per pound too expensive for common men to use for wiping the 'nether end' – so where we find payments for 'cotton for the lords stool', or 'cotton and urinals', it indicates that Henry was present (or expected soon to arrive) at the places where the cotton was bought. It means that we end up tracing the movements of the future king in the most undignified way – like an animal, by his droppings – but biographers must sometimes stoop to such levels.

From London, Henry went to Gloucester, where he was in early April. He did not stay long, for he was at Tutbury (eight miles south-west of Derby), on Maundy Thursday, when he distributed alms and clothes to the poor, and washed their feet with his own hands, marking the religious feast which was also his birthday.[38] He seems then to have gone north to Pontefract (where cotton was unavailable; he had to make do with wool) and returned south to Leicester, where his two older sons were staying. The eldest, Henry, had in fact been ill in March, and Henry had sent an express messenger from London to see him, probably carrying medicines.[39] Taking leave of his sons, he returned to London via Higham Ferrers and St Albans, arriving at the end of May. On the anniversary of Queen Anne's death, he gave a cloth of gold at Westminster, and on the anniversary of his own wife's death he sent as many of her gowns as accorded with her age at death – twenty-four – to Leicester, where she was buried.[40]

In London we have a few further insights into Henry's surroundings. Black mourning curtains and two hundred curtain rings were purchased for his bed, which thus appears to have been a four-poster.[41] Two books of his, which had been damaged, were rebound. He paid 33s 4d for 'four *tapetis*, called carpets'. Rose water from Damascus – sometimes mixed with wine – was purchased for him, and a pewter bottle was bought specially to take the said rose water to Hertford Castle, to which he seems to have withdrawn for a few days. Interestingly, we read also of a 'stool of iron in store for the lord's chamber' being mended and newly covered (probably in velvet) at a cost of 7s 6d. Its meaning and high value become clear when we read in the next entry of a payment for a new brass basin to put in it, and three pounds of cotton bought at the same time. This is the earliest known entry to a portable close-stool, of the type which became very popular among the upper classes a century later.[42]

Richard returned from Ireland in May 1395 and went to Leeds Castle in Kent. He summoned Henry to a royal council at Eltham on 22 July. Henry accordingly took his barge from the city down the Thames.[43] At Eltham he met the ageing chronicler Jean Froissart, who had returned to England to present a book of his poems to the king. The purpose of the council meeting, however, was serious. The lords of Gascony had objected to the king granting Gascony to John of Gaunt. It was an unalienable inheritance of the king of England, they claimed. Their view was supported by the legal opinions voiced at that time, that Edward III had guaranteed that Bordeaux would never be granted to any but the eldest son of the king of England. Thomas, duke of Gloucester, broke from this consensus and insisted that John's two Gascon representatives should speak. They declined. Silence fell. The bishops present decided that the matter should be referred to the two royal dukes. Thomas declared that it would be a 'strong measure' for the king to revoke his grant, which had been made with the unanimous assent of the council. Henry dutifully supported his father's interest, saying 'good uncle, you have spoken well and justly explained the matter, and I support what you have said'. Froissart adds that three-quarters of the council there gathered was against them. So

Thomas and Henry left the king's chamber, went into the hall and demanded food, and sat down to eat by themselves.[44]

Henry did not stay with the king much longer. Even before the council meeting he had once more been very obviously ignored as a potential leader of the embassy to France. He was still at Eltham on 26 July but left shortly afterwards. He seems to have travelled to Hertford, Coventry and Nuneaton, and only in September appeared again at court, witnessing royal charters on the 11th, 22nd and 26th.[45] His purpose in attending Richard at that time was at least in part his own business: to secure for his son part of his mother's inheritance.[46] Having done so, he wandered off again, the lack of coordination in his household being notable by a payment to a servant sent from London with two horses and new clothes to 'look for Henry at Salisbury, then at Kingston [Lacy] in Dorset' before finding him at Plympton in Devon.[47] On 16 October he was at Plymouth.[48] It seems Henry had travelled down to the West Country port through which he could expect his father to return. He remained there for some weeks. At the end of October he was still at Exeter. Not until the end of November did he return to London.[49]

It is difficult to avoid connecting this wandering with a certain lack of direction in Henry's personal life. It is of course entirely possible that he visited these places – as far north as Pontefract and as far west as Plympton – on official business. He was, after all, head of the family in his father's absence. But it is equally possible that this travelling represents a wish to be away from court, and away from places reminiscent of his life with Mary. Although Henry attended the annual tournament at Hertford to celebrate Christmas, this period of uncertainty seems only to have come properly to an end when he heard that his father was returning by land, and hurried to the south-east to welcome him.[50] On or just before 1 January 1396 father and son were reunited at Canterbury, and no doubt unburdened each other of their respective woes. For John there was the double disappointment of being both unsuccessful in Gascony and failing in health. For Henry there was the double disappointment of grief and being ignored by his cousin. Music, reading and jousting in themselves were not enough.

*

When John met the king in early 1396, he saw for himself why Henry had avoided court for much of the last year. Despite the fact that he (John) made a special visit to see Richard at King's Langley, there was no great welcome. The king did not take the Lancastrian livery collar and put it around his own neck as he had done before. His reception was cold, and obviously so to all present. Walsingham noted that it was 'without love' that the king acknowledged his uncle's return.[51] John left court immediately, and went to Lincoln, where Katherine Swynford was staying. There he did the unthinkable. He proposed to her, his mistress, a commoner. In February they married.[52]

The romantic shimmer which distorts our view of the age of chivalry has inclined many people to see this as the zenith of a great romance: that despite their social inequality, John threw everything aside to marry the love of his life. Although he certainly loved Katherine, this is a misrepresentation of the facts.[53] Katherine was now approaching fifty – old for a woman in medieval England – and she was not even the 'love of his life'; in his will he requested to be buried with his first wife, Henry's mother. Nor can we say he married her so that she would be well treated after his death; she was never likely to end up destitute and cast aside – Henry would always take care of his mother's maidservant and his own nanny. Rather we should bear in mind that a medieval marriage was above all else a political union, not a romantic one, and that it was impossible for John to marry Katherine without creating uproar, and making life exceedingly difficult for her. As a duke's mistress, Katherine was acceptable in society. As a duchess, she was not. Two noblewomen who were particularly hostile to her after her marriage were Eleanor Bohun – Henry's sister-in-law – and the countess of Arundel. They declared that their hearts would burst with grief if they had to acknowledge Katherine's precedence.[54] This was not just selfish pride; it was pride in their fathers' and ancestors' brave achievements. Their families had won their titles and lands through loyal service in battle, and these women perpetuated the memory of their families in their own high status. For them to see their ancestors' honour relegated below that of a foreign-born commoner was contrary to their view of the whole of society.

The real reason for the marriage – and the reason why it is important in a biography of Henry – is the effect it would have on the inheritance of the house of Lancaster. By marrying Katherine, John could make his sons by her legitimate. This not only enabled them to advance to higher status on their own account, it also put them in a position to inherit the Lancastrian estates if Henry died or was outlawed. Even more importantly, Edward III's entail settled the throne on John's legitimate sons. If Henry died or was killed – by a man like Thomas Talbot – John's other children would have no claim. The Lancastrian claim to the throne would depend wholly on Henry's young sons, the eldest of whom (Henry of Monmouth) was not yet eight. He would be no match for the duke of York, nor his heir, the earl of Rutland.

In keeping with past policy, Richard ignored Henry when he appointed ambassadors to treat with France in early 1396. Again, it was the earl of Rutland who led that embassy, supported by Thomas Mowbray, earl of Nottingham. Rutland's success in agreeing a twenty-eight-year truce and arranging a royal marriage between Richard (now twenty-nine years old) and the eight-year-old princess Isabella de Valois meant that the king increasingly regarded John of Gaunt as a great but ageing magnate, of little or no further political use to him. Rutland now lived permanently at court. Likewise Mowbray and Richard's violent half-brother, John Holland, earl of Huntingdon, were in almost constant attendance on the king. Henry was entirely superfluous to Richard's social and political requirements.

It is not clear where Henry was for much of 1396. His father was with the king at Windsor on 1 May 1396, when the three royal uncles promised to return the French princess to her father in case of Richard's death. The following month John secured a charter of liberties for his duchy.[55] But Henry did not witness the royal charters granted on 8 July and 24 September, even though John was present on both occasions.[56] It seems that Henry did not spend that summer living with his father.[57] He seems to have attended court only once between September 1395 and November 1396 (on 25 July).[58] Thus, it would appear that while his father followed Richard's court, and laboured to win back the king's approval in the summer of 1396, Henry kept himself out of sight.

Wherever he was, Henry was preparing for war. Not a war in England but on the Continent. King Sigismund of Hungary had proclaimed a crusade against the Ottoman Empire, whose sultan, Bayezid, was threatening 'to feed his horses on the altar of St Peter's Basilica' in Rome. This was an insult to all of Christendom. John of Burgundy was appointed to lead a French army to help the Hungarians. Among his companions were Boucicaut, Renaud de Roye and Jean de Saimpy: the three champions against whom Henry had jousted at St Inglevert in 1390. The temptation for Henry to join this expedition must have been great; he would probably have undertaken any challenge to get him out of England and back in arms, out on the open road, where people of consequence respected him. But his desire to go on the Nicopolis Crusade was stifled, which was lucky, for it ended in a catastrophic disaster.[59]

With this ambition thwarted, Henry seems to have turned his thoughts instead to the count of Ostrevant's campaign in Friesland. In June the count sent a squire, Fier-a-Bras de Vertain, to England to seek out Henry and ask him whether he would take part. Henry was both flattered and keen, and asked his father for permission to go. John was inclined to agree, but before he did so he asked the duke of Guelderland (who was then visiting the English court) for advice. The duke replied that the expedition would be highly dangerous, for the land was not easily conquered and the territory marshy and surrounded by the sea, and full of bogs and islands which only the Frieslanders knew well. Moreover, the natives were so lacking in honour that they paid no respect to any lord they captured in battle but executed them all. The duke told John that he himself had been asked to go on the campaign but would never set foot in that country. Now he strongly urged John to prevent Henry from doing so. Immediately John sent a messenger to Henry telling him to give up all thought of going to Friesland. Henry probably came to court to see his father to discuss this matter at the end of July.[60] But John was adamant.

Henry did not go to Friesland.

SEVEN

By Envy's Hand and Murder's Bloody Axe

One vial full of Edward's sacred blood,
One flourishing branch of his most royal root,
Is crack'd and all the precious liquor spilt,
Is hack'd down and his summer-leaves all faded,
by envy's hand and murder's bloody axe.
Richard II, Act 1, Scene 2

John's policy of staying with Richard and talking up the usefulness of all his sons was moderately successful. The letter he sent to the pope asking for the Beaufort children to be legitimised met with Richard's approval as well as the pope's. Richard also agreed that Henry should accompany the royal family when they went to France to witness his wedding to the French princess. Thus it was that Henry found himself travelling south from Kenilworth to sail across to Calais in early October 1396. Although Froissart asserts that Henry was left behind with the duke of York 'to guard England', this is certainly wrong. Payments for Henry's requisites and luxuries – including candle wax, beer, soap and a chicken for his favourite falcon – were made in Calais, Guines and Saint-Omer.[1]

The meeting of the kings of England and France, preceding the wedding, was one of the spectacles of the age, foreshadowing the later Field of the Cloth of Gold.[2] Both kings brought enormous retinues. Huge quantities of food and drink were sailed by barge to Calais for the occasion. New clothes were made for all, and gifts liberally dispensed by the monarchs on both sides. Even though the French king had begun to be afflicted by the madness which would characterise his reign – Charles VI suffered intermittently from the delusion that he was made of glass and about to shatter into pieces – it was very important for his people that he was seen to be as magnificent as the king of England. Charles sent the count of St Pol to Calais to greet Richard. When the count returned to Saint-Omer, he was accompanied by most of the English royal family, including Henry, John and Katherine.[3] At Saint-Omer they were joined by the duke of Brittany and his duchess, Joan (Henry's future wife). A magnificent banquet was held by the duchess of Burgundy at which every effort was made to delight the English lords, through wine, food and flattery. The English then escorted the dukes of Berry, Bourbon and Burgundy to a similar reception near Calais.

On 26 October, the two kings and their thousands of companions and retainers assembled in a huge encampment at Ardres. The whole plain was covered with brightly coloured tents and pavilions. Next day the kings met, surrounded by their dukes, knights and guards, and talked while they ate sweetmeats. Richard agreed to support the king of France in his quarrel with the duke of Milan, and to pursue a common policy towards the Church, which was then split between two popes. The following day they met again, and the princess was handed over to the English. Henry attended the royal wedding at Calais on 4 November and a few days later took ship back to Dover.[4] Then the various parties split up, Richard going via Rochester to Kennington, Henry travelling via Dartford to London.[5]

Henry left London on 23 December and spent Christmas at Hertford.[6] He was back in London by 6 January 1397. He departed again on the 13th to take part in a joust, probably at Hertford, following which his horses needed medical treatment. He was back in London on 19 January, at 'the time of the parliament', as the treasurer of his household noted.[7] After his father's constant efforts to talk up Henry's usefulness to the king, Henry was once more appointed a receiver of petitions. So he was present at parliament from its opening, on 22 January. But trouble was brewing. Several other lords stayed away.

Henry would have had a lot of sympathy with those who absented themselves. Their reasons concerned Henry's friend Gian Galeazzo Visconti, the duke of Milan. When Richard had agreed at Ardres to support the king of France in a war against Gian Galeazzo, he had not properly thought through the implications. Now, in parliament, those implications became clear. Richard proposed to demand a full measure of war taxation to pay for an expedition which could do the English no good at all. On 23 January, members of the commons elected Sir John Bussy as their Speaker and he immediately asked for clarification of certain points mentioned in the chancellor's address. Bussy also asked that those lords who had stayed away from this parliament should now appear. The next day, the king's officers openly explained that taxation was necessary to finance a war against Milan. The commons were not happy about this, and refused. The next day an irate Richard demanded they reassure him they would not try to resist his war plans.

Henry was deeply concerned. He had kept in touch with Gian Galeazzo by letters and gifts since he had met him in 1393, affectionately addressing him as 'the count of Virtue'.[8] He still had not forgotten Lucia Visconti, and would in due course discuss marrying her.[9] To him, Richard's plan to raise an army to fight Gian Galeazzo was absurd. It was unwarranted, a sign of Richard's weakness for all things French. After all, the reasons for the hatred between Milan and France were hardly any more reasonable than the French king himself when in one of his fits. Gian Galeazzo's daughter, Valentina, was married to Louis, duke of Orléans, brother of King Charles. One day in 1395, while she was looking after the three-year-old dauphin and her own four-year-old son, a poisoned apple had been slipped through the open window of the chamber, in the hope that the dauphin would eat it. Instead, her own son saw it, ran to it and bit it; he died shortly afterwards. The story sounds like a vicious slander, but the idea that she herself had tried to give the apple to the dauphin in the hope that her own son would succeed, and that he had died out of divine punishment for such an evil act, caught the public mood in France. Despite Valentina's extreme distress – this boy was her fourth child to die in infancy – she was castigated as a traitor and an enemy of France. So terrible was her treatment that Gian Galeazzo had to demand action to restore her status and honour. He was ignored. This made Gian Galeazzo even angrier, and to spite France he supposedly informed the sultan Bayezid that the Nicopolis Crusade was on its way, giving warning of the French army's strength and movements. When this became known, the French felt Gian Galeazzo had betrayed them spiritually as well as politically, and there was bitter enmity between Milan and Paris.

Even though there was probably more to the dispute than this account reveals, Froissart's story shows that it was widely circulated.[10] Hence, for the English to set out to fight for the king of France against the duke of Milan was a ridiculous waste of taxpayers' money. Henry knew it, so did the commons. But Richard would not be argued with. He had given his word to the French king that he would help him. He had also promised some of his magnates that he would pay for their expenses in going to fight Milan.[11] His third reason for insisting on attacking Milan was that Gian Galeazzo was a tyrant, and an unjust ruler (having usurped his uncle's throne), and an enemy of Christian people everywhere, and it behoved the English to eradicate such an upstart. His fourth reason was that he wished to be 'at liberty to command his people, to send them to aid his friends, and to dispose of his own goods at his will, where and whensoever he chose'.[12]

Henry seems to have suffered this outburst in silence. His father had requested that Thomas Talbot be brought to justice and that his Beaufort children be recognised as legitimate by the king. These things had yet to happen. So, although Richard had just outlined the basis for his absolutism,

Henry said nothing. But he must have thought hard. He would have thought even harder a few days later, when Richard seized upon a petition presented by one Thomas Haxey. This had been passed by the receivers of petitions in this parliament, including Henry, but the king was infuriated by one clause, which stated that the expenses of his household should be reduced. He demanded that the author of the petition be brought before parliament. On 7 February Haxey was taken before the king and condemned to death as a traitor. Alarmed, the archbishop of Canterbury, Thomas Arundel, immediately stepped forward to plead mercy for Haxey. He also asked that, as a cleric, Haxey be handed over to the archbishop for custody. Richard assented. But the message was clear: to deny the king his unfettered right to rule was punishable by death.

*

Historians have argued for many years over whether Richard went mad in 1397. In the mid-twentieth century it was thought that he had indeed lost his mind, and the death of Queen Anne was identified as one of the catalysts. But really this is a modern myth: there is no evidence of madness in the king, just an ever-increasing tendency to rule his subjects through the medium of terror. In explaining their actions in 1397–8, the lords who were later arraigned for treason all pleaded that they had been frightened of the king. It was a genuine excuse; anyone in their position would have been scared. Even those intimate and trusted friends of the king, who were given high titles and extensive lands, were only favoured so long as they followed the king's orders. Modern scholars now see Richard as essentially narcissistic, convinced of his own perfection, and yet deeply insecure. We might elaborate on this slightly and say that he was exceptionally self-conscious: so much so that his own identity, royal personage, ideas, rivalries and feelings formed not only the core but the limit of his entire world. As a result, with no real balance or objective view of himself and his kingdom, he suffered from a chronic lack of self-confidence, which made him by turns unreasonably angry and vengeful, as well as unreasonably generous, unjustifiably kind and increasingly paranoid. Moreover, these characteristics were noticeable from an early age: in his sacking of the chancellor for disagreeing with him, for example. When he rode out in front of the crowd during the Peasants' Revolt, aged fourteen, he may have been very brave in the eyes of the expectant public, but he was driven by his own narcissistic obsession with himself and his powers as a monarch. Now, sixteen years later, he was wiser and more artful, but no one now believed he was a great leader. He was a thirty-year-old who still had something about him of the boy who pulls the legs off spiders – not because he is interested in insects or likes causing pain but because he has an unending fascination with the contrast between his inner fear and his apparent power.[13]

While we may have some sympathy for Richard, his psychological problems had a disastrous effect on the political situation in England. Haxey's plight was just the tip of a very big iceberg. The Nicopolis Crusade (in which Bayezid defeated and massacred a Franco-Hungarian army) had plunged all France into grief, so they cancelled the intended expedition against Milan. Richard's response was to follow their lead and reverse his declaration of war. Even though he had justified his bellicosity towards Milan in terms of his moral responsibility to remove Gian Galeazzo from power, he now justified his change of mind by saying he had always sought peace. Such a mercurial ruler could hardly be an inspiration to his people. Wise men do not follow leaders whom they suspect might later reproach them for their loyalty.

Following the parliament, Richard summoned a meeting of the royal council. He had decided to change his mind on another issue: the pursuit of a single policy towards the Church of Rome. Richard had recently decided his priority was to be elected Holy Roman Emperor, and this required some diplomatic shifting.[14] Both the duke of Gloucester and the earl of Arundel refused to attend the council meeting, both claiming they were ill.[15] Richard was furious, and sought a means whereby he could stop his regal authority being treated with such disdain. He fixed on the fact that his uncle and the earl of Arundel had been Appellants. Richard now sought to be revenged on the Lords Appellant, to make them an example to anyone who would question his authority, as he had done with Haxey.

Henry, as a former Appellant, had every reason to be afraid. Even though he had been pardoned for any action against the king in 1388, he knew that it would not take much for Richard to reverse all the pardons he had granted and to sentence all five Lords Appellant to death. Besides, his alienation from Richard was growing more serious. In February 1397 Richard adopted his cousin, Edward, earl of Rutland, as his 'brother'.[16] This was perhaps in emulation of Edward II's adoption of Piers Gaveston as his brother.[17] The implications of Richard actually having a brother would have been enormous – a real brother would automatically have become heir to the throne – and it is surprising that historians have tended to overlook this formal adoption.[18] With Richard making Rutland's father keeper of the realm in 1394 and 1396, the adoption was the clearest indicator yet that Richard wanted the succession to the throne to pass to the house of York, not the Lancastrians or the Mortimers.

Wisely, Henry disappeared off to the Lancastrian estates in the Midlands after the council meeting. He went to Leicester in March, then moved to

Tutbury at the end of the month, and returned to Leicester at the beginning of May.[19] These cannot have been happy days. Indeed, one of the reasons why he did not marry at this time may have been his pre-occupation with his own fate. Even though Edward 'the king's brother' was commissioned to negotiate a marriage between Henry and the daughter of the king of Navarre, and there were rumours of his marrying Lucia Visconti (which Henry himself may have started), he stayed single.[20] No doubt at Leicester he reflected sadly on the tomb of his dead wife. In June he returned south to Hertford, to discuss the looming crisis with his father.[21] Within two weeks they were both summoned to Westminster. Richard wanted to know exactly where their loyalties lay. In this dispute between the king and the leaders of magnate opposition, would John and Henry defend the duke of Gloucester? Or would they remain dutifully quiet?

For John there was no question. He was loyal through and through, in both policy and instinct. He had not joined the Appellants in 1387, having been out of the country, and even though he had protested his loyalty on every occasion it had been called into doubt. Moreover, he hated the earl of Arundel. His only predicament concerned his son, Henry. If Richard revoked the pardons granted to the senior Appellants, then what was to stop him revoking the one granted to Henry too? What was there to stop Richard from accusing Henry of treason at a later date? If Henry did anything to incur Richard's wrath, then he too would find himself on the wrong end of the executioner's axe.[22]

Henry had even less choice. When Richard outlined his plans to him in the summer of 1397, he made it quite clear that he could either support the impeachment or be impeached along with the others. Eight lords would appeal the three senior Lords Appellant of treason. Henry did not join these Counter-Appellants, but was with the king at Westminster on 5 July and stayed for the next month in his household.[23] Thus we may be sure that he had prior knowledge of the king's actions on 10 July. That night Richard and a contingent of men-at-arms left Westminster and went to Pleshey Castle in Essex, where his uncle Duke Thomas was staying, and dragged him out of bed. Those at Pleshey, seeing the king there in the middle of the night, immediately knew that this was no ordinary arrest. The duchess, Lady Eleanor, wept copiously, and pleaded with the king to be merciful. Richard declared – whether to her or not is unclear – that he would show him as much mercy as the duke had shown Simon Burley nine years earlier.[24] He took him to Tillingbourne, and handed him over the next day to Thomas Mowbray, constable of Calais, with orders to take the duke across the Channel.

It seemed that Richard had successfully carried out a coup against the

Appellants. Henry was utterly disempowered. When announcing to the Londoners that he had arrested the duke of Gloucester, and the earls of Arundel and Warwick, Richard could say that not only had he the approval of the eight Counter-Appellants but also John, Henry and the duke of York (even though these three did not join the appeal).[25] Henry's acquiescence to the arrests, and his subsequent elevation to a dukedom, have led a number of historians to think that in 1397 Henry was again in favour with the king. However, there was still no amicable grounding to their relationship. Henry's loyalty to Richard at this time was simply life-preserving, not approving, as can be seen by his refusal to join the Counter-Appellants. Richard's lack of action against him was, rather, a matter of expediency. Had Richard threatened Henry and Mowbray as well as the leading Appellants in July 1397, he would have forced John also into revolt, and with him the entire Lancastrian confederacy. As it was, Richard broke the opposition by dividing Thomas and Henry from the other Appellants.

Everyone was nervous. No one knew what was going to happen. Even with their accord with the king worked out, Henry and his father were in danger. With the duke of York, they raised a large body of men which they brought to Dale Abbey for five days while the king was at Nottingham.[26] That this was with the king's approval is shown by various payments in Henry's accounts and by the king's later explicit instructions.[27] However, the raising of a Lancastrian army was a sure sign of uncertain times. On 28 August, Richard issued a letter patent specifically ordering John and Henry to bring an army to the next parliament 'for the king's protection'.[28] John was to raise three hundred men-at-arms and six hundred archers; the duke of York one hundred men-at-arms and two hundred archers; and Henry was to assemble two hundred men-at-arms and four hundred archers. These forces, plus another two thousand of the king's Cheshire archers, effectively destroyed any chance of men rallying to defend the accused lords.[29]

Then came the shocking news. The duke of Gloucester was dead. He had died, it was said, of natural causes in Calais.[30] That sounded suspicious, coming so soon after his arrest. What were John and Henry to think? If Thomas was really dead, there was nothing they could do now to save him. If he was being kept alive – as, in fact, he was – the best they could do was to persuade Richard of his loyalty.[31]

*

On St Lambert's Day, 17 September 1397, parliament assembled in a great marquee which had been set up in the yard of Westminster Palace. The old hall was being refashioned and rebuilt, so it was not possible to gather in the usual place. Outside there were many ranks of armed men. The two thousand Cheshire archers held their bows ready, arrows notched.

With the empty throne towering above them at one end, the members stood and waited. Then the king entered. The chancellor began to explain why parliament had been summoned. It was, he said, 'to the honour and reverence of God and the salvation and correction of the realm'. If anyone there thought that it sounded like a crusade, they were not far wrong. 'One king shall be king to them all', declared the chancellor, 'and they shall be no more two nations, neither shall they be divided into two kingdoms any more.'[32]

The atmosphere was tense. There were many new faces, many men appointed by Richard. The rumours went around among the older hands that the king had arranged the return of as many pro-royalist members as possible.[33] Rumours of the duke of Gloucester's survival circulated too, as did speculation as to the earl of Arundel's fate. More certain was the tension throughout the city. Thousands of archers and men-at-arms created an atmosphere of nervous hostility. The inns in the city had been overrun, with many of the Cheshire archers getting drunk and violent, and taking advantage of their favoured position as the king's men.

The chancellor continued. 'Our lord the king – considering how many high offences and misdeeds have been committed by the people of his kingdom against their allegiance and the estate of our lord the king and the law of his land in the past . . . and willing in his royal benignity to show and do grace to his said people, so that they should have greater courage and will to do good, and bear themselves the better towards the king in time to come – so he wills and agrees to make . . . a general pardon to his lieges . . . excepting fifty persons whom it would please the king to name, and all those who will be impeached in the present parliament.'

The king refused to name the fifty. Fear struck all those present.

It intensified the following day.

'My lord king', said Sir John Bussy, after the commons had re-elected him Speaker, 'since we are bound by your command to tell your royal highness who undermined your power and transgressed against your regality, we tell you that Thomas, duke of Gloucester, and Richard, earl of Arundel, in the tenth year of your reign, with the assistance of Thomas Arundel, then chancellor of England and now archbishop of Canterbury, compelled you to concede a commission touching the government and state of your kingdom which was to the prejudice of your regality and majesty, whereby they did you great injury.'[34]

With that, the king demanded the commission of 1386 be read out. When everyone had heard it, the king declared in cold anger that it was hereby revoked, repealed and perpetually annulled, and so was every single Act which had been passed as a consequence.

Next the king demanded that the pardons against those who had risen in revolt in 1387 be read out aloud. When they had been heard, these were all revoked also. So too was the special pardon granted to the earl of Arundel in 1394. The pro-royalist commons, through Bussy, demanded that Richard be informed that the archbishop of Canterbury had advised the granting of this pardon to his brother, the earl, and so he too should be declared a traitor. Immediately the archbishop rose to his feet and began to speak. But Richard silenced him, declaring he could answer tomorrow. He never had the chance. As Bussy had said to the king, the archbishop was too clever; he should not be allowed to speak.

What Henry thought of this can be seen in the charges he later brought against Richard. But for the moment he kept quiet. He had to. His own pardon had just been revoked, and although Richard was prepared to forgive him on the grounds that he had tried to restrain the others, this provided him with little reassurance. In this mood of terror, it would take barely a word against Richard to incur the penalty of death. When the chancellor went on to announce that the matters that were about to be discussed were criminal offences, and that the prelates need not be present, it was clear that someone was going to die. The bishops and abbots withdrew. Outside the Cheshire archers were nervous. Someone spread the word that the king was under attack. Shouts went up, bows were drawn. Some arrows may even have been let fly. Not until the king himself appeared did the Cheshire men settle down.

On the third day, Wednesday 19 September, the tension rose higher still. The clergy were ordered to put their authority into the hands of a lay representative. They chose Sir Thomas Percy. Satisfied, the king turned to the Speaker and stated that, although certain people had asked to know who were the fifty men to be impeached, he refused to say. Moreover, anyone even asking for such information was a traitor and would be sentenced to death. The guilty men would take flight, the king explained, and men who were not on the list might also flee.[35] In fact there was no list of fifty names, or, if there was, it was never produced. The king was purposefully creating the maximum amount of fear. In Richard's mind, the fear of his subjects equated to his own sense of power.

On Thursday the 20th the terrified archbishop of Canterbury returned to parliament, prepared to speak against the accusations of treason and defend his life. The last two days must have been an ordeal for him, no less than they had been for his brother, the earl, locked in the Tower. But when he appeared at his seat in the parliamentary marquee, the king ordered him to leave. This was shocking: the king was acting as if he really was going to impeach the archbishop of Canterbury. Yet what had the archbishop done? He had acted as the spokesman for parliament in 1387. He had not ridden in arms against the king or de Vere or anyone else. He had been sent by parliament, along with the duke of Gloucester, to speak on their behalf when it had emerged that Richard was planning to waylay and murder the parliamentary embassy. He had dutifully served as chancellor for seven of the last ten years. How could this man be called a traitor?

Nevertheless, the trial went ahead. No one dared speak up for the archbishop. Bussy, speaking on behalf of the commons, in accordance with instructions given to him by the king, accused the archbishop of high treason.[36] Following the recital of his actions in 1386, the proctor acting on behalf of the clergy was required to speak on their behalf. Sir Thomas Percy had no option but to do as the terrified clergy told him, and declared that the archbishop was a traitor. Richard then announced that he would take advice on how to punish the archbishop. A few days later he announced that he had decided to confiscate all of his lands, chattels, income and other possessions, and banish him from the kingdom for life.

On Friday 21 September Richard's adopted brother, the earl of Rutland, entered parliament with the king's half-brother, the earl of Huntingdon, the earls of Kent, Nottingham, Somerset and Salisbury, and Lord Despenser and William Scrope. They were all dressed in red silk robes banded with white silk, which was powdered with letters of gold. These men were the Counter-Appellants, and now they appealed six men of treason in direct emulation of the Merciless Parliament of 1388.

The six accused men were the archbishop of Canterbury, the duke of Gloucester, the earls of Arundel and Warwick, Lord Cobham and Thomas Mortimer.[37] The last of these, although he was not one of the Lords Appellant, had slain Thomas Molyneux at Radcot Bridge. Henry had been there too. There was no doubt now that he was on very dangerous ground indeed. When the king ordered Roger Mortimer, earl of March and lieutenant of Ireland, to arrest Thomas – the uncle who had raised him from infancy – and to surrender him as a traitor, Henry could see that the king was prepared to test to destruction the loyalty of everyone whose past was questionable. The earl of March had three months to give up his uncle or be declared a traitor himself. The Mortimers were doomed. Henry must have known then that it was only a matter of time before he too would be forced into a similarly impossible situation.

Thomas Mowbray was equally nervous. On the face of it, as one of the Counter-Appellants, he was firmly and safely in the king's camp. But he, like Henry, was one of the original Lords Appellant, and if the original three were guilty of treason, then he and Henry were too. Moreover, Mowbray had been entrusted with the custody of the duke of Gloucester. This had also entailed him supposedly murdering the duke on Richard's orders. As Mowbray confessed to William Bagot a month later, he had never been so scared in his life as the day he had returned to England from Calais having received the order to murder the king's uncle, and having failed to carry it out.[38]

When the earl of Arundel was dragged before parliament that Friday, he had heard nothing of the earlier proceedings. As far as he was concerned, he was an innocent man wrongfully arrested. Nevertheless, he knew he had many enemies, and since he had failed to do anything to stop Thomas Talbot from plotting the assassination of John and Henry, the Lancastrians were among them. Knowing this, Richard now looked to John, as hereditary high steward of England, to accuse the earl formally. The ensuing argument was recorded by the author of the anonymous but contemporary *Historia Vitae et Regni Ricardi Secundi*.[39] When the appeal had been read out, Arundel insisted that he had been pardoned for any wrongdoing in 1388, and again in 1394.

'Those pardons have been revoked, traitor', John responded.

'Truly, you lie', replied the earl. 'I was never a traitor.'

'Then why did you seek a pardon?' asked John.

'To silence the tongues of my enemies, of whom you are one', replied the earl. 'And to be sure, when it comes to treason, you are in greater need of a pardon than I am.'

'Answer the appeal', interrupted the king angrily.

The earl now realised he was alone. Far from being pardoned, he was already a condemned man. He looked around him. He – unlike everyone else there – had nothing to lose.

'I see it clearly now', he said. 'All those who accuse me of treason, you are all liars. Never was I a traitor.' Then he faced the king. 'I still claim the benefit of my pardon, which you, within these last six years, when you were of full age and free to act as you wished, granted to me of your own volition.'

Richard was in no mood for bargaining. 'I granted it provided that it were not to my prejudice', he said coldly.

'Therefore the grant is worthless', added John.

The earl could not believe what was happening to him. 'In truth', he said to John, 'I was as ignorant about that pardon as you were – and you were abroad at the time – until it was willingly granted to me by the king.'

This was true. John could say nothing. But Bussy could. 'That pardon has already been revoked by the king, the lords and us, the faithful commons.'

The earl shook his head. 'Where are those faithful commons?' Turning to them, he exclaimed, 'You are not here to act faithfully. You are here to shed my blood. If the faithful commons were here they would without doubt be on my side, trying to help me from falling into your clutches. They, I know, are grieving greatly for me while you, I know, have always been false.'

Bussy, seeing the earl running away with the debate, and knowing he did indeed have sympathisers among the terrorised commons, and more sympathisers outside among the Londoners, interjected hurriedly. 'Look, lord king, how this traitor is trying to stir up dissent between us and the commons who stayed at home.'

'Liars, all of you!' shouted back the earl. 'I am no traitor.'

At this point Henry rose to his feet. 'Did you not say to me at Huntingdon, when we first gathered in revolt, that before doing anything else it would be better to seize the king?'

The earl glared at his erstwhile comrade-in-arms. This was betrayal. 'You, Henry, earl of Derby, you lie in your teeth! I never said anything to you or to anyone else about my lord king, except what was to his welfare and honour.'

But this reply only gave the king himself the opportunity to testify. 'Did you not say to me at the time of your parliament, in the bath behind the White Hall, that Simon Burley was worthy of death? And I replied that I neither knew nor could discover any reason for his death. And even though the queen, my wife, and I interceded tirelessly on his behalf, yet you and your accomplices, ignoring our pleas, traitorously put him to death.'

To this the earl had no answer. Henry had asked him a question to which he obviously knew the answer. The king had then asked him another, to which there was no answer.

'Pass judgement on him', snapped the king.

Then the earl heard John, in his capacity of steward of England, sentence him to be drawn to the gallows, hanged, beheaded and quartered. To which the king added that, out of regard for his rank, he need only be beheaded.

The earl did not flinch. He walked to his death, smiling at those who lined the streets to see him go.

With the earl of Arundel executed, Thomas Arundel banished, and Thomas Mortimer in exile in Ireland, only the duke of Gloucester, the earl of Warwick and Lord Cobham were left for Richard to deal with.

Cobham, who had been a commissioner in 1386, was accused on the same day as Arundel, but his trial was postponed. The earl of Warwick was led into parliament and broke down in tears, weeping and wailing. He was a sixty-year-old man, and unable to function in the atmosphere of terror which Richard had created. So much did he confess, and so many tears did he shed, and so abject was his apology, that, although he was sentenced to death by John, as was required, the king granted him his life, and only ordered that he spend it on the Isle of Man.

That left Thomas of Woodstock, duke of Gloucester. The king had announced his death in late August or early September, after ordering Mowbray to murder him, but Mowbray had not been able to do the deed, and had returned to England. On being told this, Richard had insisted that Mowbray had to kill the duke. To make sure, Richard sent his own chamber valet, William Serle, with Mowbray to Calais. Just before the parliament began, having made a confession on 9 September, Thomas of Woodstock was smothered to death under a featherbed in the back room of an inn in Calais. Although the duke had been kept secretly alive, he was dead by 21 September, when Richard ordered Mowbray to bring him to parliament. Three days later, Mowbray announced that the duke had died in custody in Calais. This time it was true.

In return for his loyalty during this parliament, and in return for his and his father's cooperation in the lead up to it, Henry was raised to a dukedom. On the last day of parliament, 29 September, he became the duke of Hereford, in recognition of his late wife's inheritance of the title of Hereford. He was also permitted to bear the arms of St Edward the Confessor, along with certain other men of royal descent. At the same time seven of the eight Counter-Appellants were given new titles. The king's adopted brother, Edward, was made duke of Aumale; Mowbray became duke of Norfolk, and the king's half-brother, John Holland, became duke of Exeter. Richard's nephew, Thomas Holland, son of his recently deceased half-brother of the same name, became duke of Surrey. The earl of Somerset became the marquis of Dorset, Lord Despenser became the earl of Gloucester, and William Scrope became the earl of Wiltshire. In return for doing Richard's bidding, these men were well rewarded. But even now Henry could not feel at ease. On the very day that he was raised to a dukedom, one of his men, William Laken, was murdered by Sir John Hawkston, one of Richard's Cheshire knights, in Fleet Street. In fact, Laken was killed while he was waiting to meet Henry, and if Henry believed that the king was secretly plotting against his own life at this time, he would have been correct.[40]

After years of rivalry and jealousy, Richard could at last feel that he had brought Henry to heel. Richard had always lived in the shadow of his cousin's achievements. Henry had sired sons, was a jousting champion, had been on a crusade, led an army and travelled to Jerusalem. It had taken many years, but at last Richard had proved to himself that he could master him. As far as Richard was concerned, he had finally achieved the sort of power which he believed a king ought to wield over his subjects.

For Henry the parliament of September 1397, and the lead up to it, had been like nothing he had ever known. He had seen the workings of his cousin's mind finally revealed in all their terrifying selfishness and cruelty. The duplicity which Richard had demonstrated was anathema to a logical, honest man like Henry. But more than anything else, it was the murder of his uncle that stuck in his mind. This time, Richard had not just threatened to kill a member of the royal family. He had actually done it.

EIGHT

The Breath of Kings

> How long a time lies in one little word!
> Four lagging winters and four wanton springs
> End in a word: such is the breath of kings!
> *Richard II*, Act III, Scene 3

At some point between February 1397 and January 1398, Henry paid his goldsmith to make a gold chain for a 'medicinal stone' to protect him against poison.[1] This was probably a bezoar, from the Middle East, which the owner dunked into a wine goblet to nullify the harmful effects of the potion.[2] For such a payment to appear in Henry's accounts in this year is a telling fact. He was in fear of his life, and one of the forms of attack he feared was poison.

To judge from Henry's recorded public behaviour, he was unconcerned by any of the intrigues of the court, and as confident as ever. He gave the appearance of being utterly loyal. His dukedom even suggests that he and Richard were getting on well at this time. Yet the wearing of jewellery containing stones to protect him from poison gives a very different impression. The fear prevalent in Richard's 'Revenge Parliament' and the murder of Henry's man, William Laken, on the day of his elevation similarly alerts us to the fears concealed behind his courtly smiles.

One day in December 1397 Henry was riding on the road between London and Brentford in the company of his household staff and knights. Towards him came the party of Thomas Mowbray, the newly created duke of Norfolk. According to Henry's own testimony, given later under oath in parliament, Mowbray told him 'We are about to be undone.'[3]

'Why?' asked Henry.

'Because of what was done at Radcot Bridge.'

Henry, aware that Mowbray had close links at court, was alarmed. 'But the king has given us a pardon, and declared his will to uphold that pardon in parliament. He even said that we had been true and loyal to him.'

Even as he said these words, Henry must have known what was going on. To get rid of the senior Lords Appellant, Richard had not taken action against Henry and Mowbray, saying they had deserved their pardons for they had restrained the others, and had tried to prevent them from killing Burley. But now the senior Appellants had been dealt with, Richard could turn his thoughts to them.

'He will do with us what he has done with the others', replied Mowbray. 'He wants to wipe clean any trace of our opposition.'

Henry was aghast. 'It would be a great wonder', he said, 'if the king went back on what he said in parliament.'

'It is a wondrous world, and a false one', Mowbray agreed. And then his nerve broke. Maybe he should have stopped there, and not said what he said next. But what followed changed the political state of England forever. 'It is a false world indeed', he declared, 'for I know well, that, had several of us not taken action, you and your father would have been murdered on the way to Windsor after the parliament. But Edward, duke of Aumale, John Holland, duke of Exeter, Thomas Percy, earl of Worcester and I all swore that we would never agree to destroy a lord without a just and reasonable cause . . .'

Henry suspected that Mowbray had already killed his uncle 'without a just and reasonable cause', but for the moment he let that matter lie as he listened to this stunning revelation. Who were those behind this plot?

'The duke of Surrey, the earl of Wiltshire and the earl of Salisbury were against us. They persuaded the earl of Gloucester to join them. They mean to destroy all of us, including you and me, your father, John Holland, John Beaufort and the duke of Aumale. They mean to reverse the pardon of Earl Thomas of Lancaster, for this would be to the disinheritance of us all.'[4]

'God forbid!' Henry exclaimed, 'it would be a great wonder if the king agreed to that, after promising to be a good lord to us, and even swearing so by St Edward the Confessor.'

'He has often sworn – even on the Holy Sacrament – to be a good king to me, but I no longer trust him', said Mowbray, adding that the king had decided to lure the earl of March back from Ireland to join the others in their plot.

'We will never be able to trust them again', Henry said.

'Certainly not', agreed Mowbray. 'Even if we succeed in thwarting them now, they will still be intent on destroying us in ten years' time.'

*

Stunned by Mowbray's revelations, Henry went to see his father.[5] Under such pressure, he could hardly not tell him that there was a plot against them. It was not just the threat to their lives either; the dignity of Henry's ancestors on his mother's side was under attack, and that meant the dignity of his grandfather, the great duke of Lancaster. If Thomas, earl of Lancaster, had been a traitor, then it followed that the Lancastrian titles and estates should not have passed to his brother Henry, the father of Duke Henry. That meant that no one but the king should have enjoyed the benefit of the Lancastrian titles and estates since 1322. If the Lancastrians still carried any hope that Edward III's entail would place Henry or his eldest son on the throne after Richard's death, then that hope was about to be extinguished.

John must have been furious when heard the news. He was angry with Mowbray for killing his brother. Now to hear from Henry that Mowbray believed 'they were about to be undone' made him reflect not only on Mowbray's responsibility for Gloucester's murder but also Mowbray's own actions in February 1385, when he and de Vere had sought to murder him (John). With this new information, it was obvious to John what he needed to do. Rather than allow both his son and Mowbray to be 'undone', he would make sure it was just Mowbray. He went to see the king.[6]

Richard's state of mind in the days after the parliament was not steady. He was feeling more vulnerable than ever. It was said that the earl of Arundel's head had miraculously reattached itself to his body. Hundreds were congregating around the tomb, to demonstrate their opposition to the king through fidelity to a man who was deemed to have given his life resisting Richard's tyranny. Most kings would have tried to weather such demonstrations, but not the insecure Richard. He demanded John come with him to the church where the earl was buried. Under the cover of night, they watched as workmen dug up the earl's decomposing body and carted it away.[7]

When Mowbray discovered that John had reported his words to the increasingly paranoid king, he was terrified. He probably went to the king and threw himself on his mercy. According to the later testimony of the duke of Exeter (Richard's half-brother), a plot was now made between Richard, Mowbray and William Bagot to kill John before he reached Shrewsbury.[8] With John out of the way, Richard would be free to act against Henry and the Lancastrians (by reversing the pardon on Thomas of Lancaster), and Mowbray could hope to be forgiven for his indiscretion.

Mowbray's plot to kill John failed. Although the details are not clear, it seems likely that Bagot betrayed him. Although Bagot served Mowbray, his loyalties were changeable: he had once been a Lancastrian retainer. He had served Henry at the time of Radcot Bridge.[9] He must have been worried that Richard was looking not only for Henry's and Mowbray's destruction in revenge for 1387 but his too. Later, Henry went to some lengths to save Bagot's life after he was accused of treason, and he may have done so in return for Bagot betraying Mowbray in January 1398. Either way, Bagot was discovered, forced to confess his crimes and to swear that he would never again try to murder John or any of his family, nor to try and disinherit him or them. So routine had murder plots become at the court of Richard II that Bagot sealed two official documents promising not to murder or disinherit the duke of Lancaster and had them enrolled in chancery as if they were the usual business of the day.[10]

It was in this atmosphere that Henry proceeded with his father to Shrewsbury. Between 18 and 23 January 1398, at Great Haywood in Staffordshire, Henry entered Richard's presence. Richard announced that he had heard that Henry had accused Mowbray of slandering the king. Henry boldly repeated what Mowbray had said to him, and was told to draw up his accusations in writing. Henry probably delivered his testimony to Richard at Lilleshall Abbey on 25 January, when he received a renewed pardon for anything that he had done against the king in the past.[11]

On Monday 28 January, Henry and his father entered the thronged hall at Shrewsbury and listened to the chancellor remind them of the proceedings of the previous sitting of parliament, including a strict exhortation that there should be no more than one ruler in the realm.[12] The chancellor announced that further taxation for the defence of the realm would be required. After a few further preliminaries, all the proceedings of the Merciless Parliament were revoked, and the questions to the judges of the preceding year were reinstated. The crushing wheel of Richard's will had begun to turn once more.

On Tuesday 29 January, the newly created earl of Wiltshire, William Scrope, was appointed proctor for the clergy, so that parliament could proceed to try Lord Cobham for treason, or, more particularly, to sentence him to death for participating in the commission of 1386. Richard played the part of a merciful monarch and granted him his life. As in the previous session of parliament, the trial was a show trial, and the death sentence and its revocation a publicity stunt. No one was left in any doubt about Richard's deadly form of justice.

On Wednesday 30 January, the Speaker Sir John Bussy announced that, although in the past many parliamentary decisions had been reversed and revoked, this should not happen to any Act of this present parliament, and if anyone in any way sought to reverse, repeal, invalidate or annul any of the judgements, he would be guilty of treason and punished as a traitor. Parliament was sober and wary. Certain prelates explained to the king that he could not oblige his successors as kings of England to abide by his will. To this Richard replied coldly that he would write to the pope and ask him to excommunicate those who sought to repeal any Act of this parliament. In this chill atmosphere, Henry was called to present his bill against Mowbray. Standing before the throne, he resolutely repeated the words which had passed between them on the road between Brentford and London.

Everyone was aware of the seriousness of the libel. Henry was accusing Mowbray of saying that the king himself was involved in a plot to destroy the Lancastrians. Even if this were absolutely true, Richard could not acknowledge it had anything to do with him, and so he had no option but to present it as a slander against him by Mowbray. Mowbray was so terrified of being impeached in parliament and summarily executed that he did not even turn up to defend himself. The best Richard could do to protect the instrument of his scheming was to delay matters. The following day, with the assent of parliament, Richard declared

> that the matters contained in the said writing should be determined and finally considered by the good advice and discretion of our lord the king and the advice and discretion of certain commissioners appointed in the matter by authority of parliament; namely, the duke of Lancaster, the duke of York, the duke of Aumale, the duke of Surrey, the duke of Exeter, the marquis of Dorset, the earl of March, the earl of Salisbury, the earl of Northumberland, the earl of Gloucester, or six of them, the earl of Worcester and the earl of Wiltshire, the proctors of the clergy, or one of them, and John Bussy, Henry Green, John Russell, Richard Chelmeswyk, Robert Teye, John Golafre, knights, coming for the parliament, or three or four of them.[13]

Extraordinarily, as soon as he had referred this 'slander' to himself and the commissioners, Richard did something to support the truth of Mowbray's statements. He reversed all the judgements passed against Hugh Despenser and his father in 1326. At a stroke, the enemies of Thomas of Lancaster were vindicated. It follows that Richard believed they had been correct to advise Edward II to march against the Lancastrians, and that the 1320s condemnations of Thomas and Henry of Lancaster as traitors should be upheld. There can be little doubt that, had Henry not produced his bill and upset proceedings, the Lancastrian pardons of 1327 would have been repealed, if not at this parliament, then soon afterwards.

With such accusations looming, and deep discontent in the air, Richard brought the parliament to a sudden end. Henry went down on his knees and confessed that he had taken part in the 'uprisings and troubles' of 1387, and pleaded that he had done so with no intent of harming the king.

Richard pardoned him again, and added that he would offer a general pardon to everyone throughout the realm who had taken part in the troubles. In return he demanded that he should be able to levy the wool subsidy for life, plus one and a half subsidies of 'a tenth and a fifteenth' of people's goods. (This was the usual means of levying extraordinary taxation: a tenth of the value of the moveable goods of townsmen and a fifteenth of the value of country dwellers' goods.) Such requests were shocking in themselves; a life grant of the wool subsidy – about £30,000 per annum – effectively meant that, as long as he did not go to war, he could rule without having to summon parliament. In reality, he was not so foolish as to announce his intention of ruling alone, but the political bond between king and people – forged over the last century in the furnace of parliament – had been weakened. In future, petitions could be presented to the commissioners. No more would the king need to consent to the wishes of his people. No more would they be able to hold his ministers and favourites to account. The king's rule was now, in theory, absolute.

*

Although Henry was pardoned for his acts in 1387–8, Richard nonetheless had him arrested. The reason was that the matter of the 'slander' had yet to be resolved. As far as Richard was concerned, the question was this: had Mowbray slandered the king? Or was Henry slandering Mowbray? On 4 February, Richard demanded that Mowbray appear before him within two weeks. Mowbray did so, and was stripped of his office of Earl Marshal and lost his lands. On 23 February, at Oswestry, Richard made an attempt to reconcile the two dukes. He asked Henry if he stood by his accusations. Henry removed his black hood. 'My lord', he said, 'as the petition I have given you makes clear, I declare that Thomas Mowbray, duke of Norfolk, such as he is, is a traitor, false and recreant towards you and your royal majesty, to your crown, to the nobles and to all the people of your realm.' When asked to reply, Mowbray declared that 'Henry of Lancaster, duke of Hereford, has lied in what he has said and wishes to insinuate against me, like a false traitor and disloyal subject that he is'. 'Ho!' said the king, 'we've heard enough of that', and he promptly gave orders for both of them to be arrested.[14] Three days later the constable of Windsor Castle was ordered to take both men into custody.[15] In Henry's case, four dukes – his father and uncle, his cousin Edward and Thomas Holland – stood bail for him. He remained free, for the moment at least.[16]

The level of dissembling around the court now reached its most extreme. Here was Henry, in fear of his life, pretending loyalty to the king. Here was Mowbray, murderer of one of the king's uncles, who had twice now attempted to kill another (John), protesting that he was not a traitor. And here was John of Gaunt pretending that nothing was wrong, despite two attempts to murder him in the last six months. When Roger Mortimer, the earl of March, had arrived at parliament in January, he had apprehended that he too was vulnerable, and had professed his loyalty even though he detested the form of rule which Richard had assumed. He swiftly realised that Richard was plotting against him, and, far from drawing him over to support the anti-Lancastrian cause, was planning to arrest him.[17] Although March's only crime was to protect his ageing uncle, Thomas Mortimer, whom the Counter-Appellants had accused in 1397, Richard deprived him of office and sent the duke of Surrey to Ireland to arrest him. March never knew that his suspicions of Richard were well founded, for by the time his arrest was ordered he was dead. At Kells, on 20 July 1398, he fell fighting bravely in the vanguard of his army against the Irish. Any claim to the throne through him – denied by Richard – now passed to his sons, Edmund and Roger, aged seven and five. Their claim was practically unenforceable, throwing Henry even more clearly into the position of heir apparent.

For Henry, however, inheritance required staying alive, and that was looking a less likely prospect by the day. His argument with Mowbray was considered by the parliamentary commission at Bristol on 19 March 1398. It was decided then that the matter would be put to the Court of Chivalry, unless Henry could prove the slander or Mowbray could prove his innocence. That meant a duel. Henry returned with his father and the king to London at the beginning of April, and remained in the city until setting out for the Order of the Garter feast at Windsor.[18] Shortly afterwards, on 28 April, he faced the parliamentary commissioners once again. This time he openly accused Mowbray of embezzling funds for the protection of Calais and, astoundingly, of murdering the duke of Gloucester.[19]

This new accusation was extremely dangerous. Froissart records that Richard had announced that anyone even mentioning the deaths of the duke of Gloucester and the earl of Arundel would be deemed a traitor.[20] Mowbray had been acting on Richard's orders. Would he now betray the king? Henry hoped perhaps to present Mowbray with such a difficult situation that he confessed to some lesser element of his crime and was judged the culprit. But Henry had struck a raw nerve: the king was incandescent with rage. Richard demanded an explanation from Mowbray. One of Mowbray's knights answered for him, and accused Henry of lying. Richard directly asked Mowbray himself if these were his own words, and Mowbray answered that he had accepted money for the defence of Calais, but had never misappropriated any. He also admitted trying to kill John of Gaunt, and claimed he had been forgiven. That was all he wished to say. Richard did not press him on the matter of the murder. Instead he asked whether either of them would withdraw their accusations. They could not; as Mowbray said, honour was too deeply involved. Richard dismissed them. The following day they were told that their dispute would be settled by a duel to be fought at Coventry in the autumn.[21]

Each man must have felt betrayed. In return for warning Henry of a murder plot against him and the disinheritance of his entire family, Mowbray was now in prison, in disgrace, had lost his position as Earl Marshal, and would have to fight for his life. He had been openly accused of murder, which he had committed out of loyalty to the king. Henry, having reported to his father what had been said about a plot to kill them both, was now being treated as if *he* was the traitor. These two men were now to fight a duel, a joust of war. The lances would not be capped.

Henry's physical state seems now to have taken a turn for the worse. Payments appear in his accounts for mending his brass astrolabe on 17 May and again on 8 July.[22] They do not necessarily indicate that Henry was intent on having his future told, for the position of the stars was a factor taken into consideration by physicians when deciding the most propitious time to use medicine, or to let blood; but it is good evidence that he was either ill or consulting the stars for some other purpose. In support of the illness interpretation, medicines were bought for him in London on the last day of May.[23] Other medicines were transported to him at Hertford in the summer.[24] It is likely that the stress of the situation was making him ill. Another example of his concern might be a payment for a figure of St Christopher – the protector of travellers – which he bought for one of his messengers, John Elys, when he sent him to the king.[25] On Maundy Thursday in this year (4 April) he gave alms to as many paupers as were in his age not *next* birthday but the year after that: thirty-three paupers, although he was only thirty-one.[26] In later years, the payment by the king of an extra year's alms was described as 'the Year of Grace', that is, the next year which the king hoped that by God's grace he would live to see.[27] Henry's example in 1398 might be the first instance of such a hopeful donation.

We may ask why Henry was so worried, given that he was one of the most proficient jousters in the realm, and had done nothing wrong. Mowbray was hardly any less a jousting champion than Henry.[28] At St Inglevert, eight years earlier, Mowbray had dared to ride one of the first jousts of war against Renaud de Roye, and had broken one of the Frenchman's lances. Thus the forthcoming duel was not only the first in England between two dukes, it was between two of the best jousting champions in the kingdom. Another reason for Henry to be worried was Richard's reaction. If he survived, he would be the last of the Appellants whom Richard had sworn to destroy, and more vulnerable than ever. If he lost this joust, he would be either dead or guilty of slander, and thus ruined.

For the forthcoming duel, Henry understandably wanted nothing but the very best military hardware. Thus he sent to his old friend Gian Galeazzo Visconti, duke of Milan. The Italian esquire Francis Court, who had devoted himself to Henry's service since 1393, was now sent back to his old master to request the finest Italian armour available.[29] Later that summer a group of Italians from Duke Gian Galeazzo arrived, and were entertained at Henry's expense, probably bearing the equipment.[30] At the same time, Mowbray was soliciting the help of the best German armourers. The forthcoming duel was set to be the greatest chivalric event of the age: two dukes, two jousting champions, the two leading manufacturers of armour, and a fight to the death over a matter of honour.

Over the next five months Henry travelled around the country. Froissart states that both his father and the king kept their distance from him at this time.[31] However, Henry was with the king in London in April, and with John at Pontefract on 9 July.[32] A month later he was in London, presumably at his house in Bishopsgate Street.[33] On 22 July he was ordered, on pain of death, to present himself to the king in person on 2 August at Shrewsbury, with no more than twenty men in his company. Mowbray – still in custody – received the same order.[34] It is not known what happened at that meeting. Perhaps it marked a last attempt to reconcile the two men. Writs to attend the duel had yet to be sent out, and it seems that Richard understood that Henry's charge against Mowbray's misuse of the Calais money was provable.[35] He may have asked that Henry withdraw the accusation of murder against Mowbray in return for Mowbray admitting he had misappropriated the Calais money. If this was the case, then Henry refused. There was nothing for it now but to do battle.

*

Henry arrived at Coventry on 15 September, the day before the duel.[36] He stayed in a large house just within the town gates. The excited towns-people craned to see in but could only catch a glimpse of the wooden pavilion sited in its grounds, not those coming and going. Many lords and knights had come to witness the fight, and many others had come from overseas with entreaties to stop it. The count of St Pol had come from France for just such a purpose. French feelings were mixed. On the one hand, a fight between two dukes was too much of a horror to be contem-plated, for it threatened to divide two major families of the realm, so

Richard was a fool to let them fight. On the other, there was the view that it did not matter if they fought, on account of the English being 'the most perverse and proud people on Earth'.[37] Opinion was divided in England too, for different reasons. The mass of the people, who had come to regard Henry as a hero, were of the opinion that he should avenge the death of his uncle on the murderer Mowbray. Others, who realised the risk to themselves of Henry being killed in such a fight, and the possible disinheritance of the Lancastrians, were of the contrary view.

On the morning of Monday 16 September, Henry's esquires strapped him into his Italian armour. Mowbray set out at eight o'clock to say farewell to the king, who was lodging at Baginton, William Bagot's house, just outside the town. Henry had performed the same duty the previous evening. Thus it was Mowbray whom the crowds saw first: splendidly arrayed in his German steel, his war horse covered with crimson velvet embroidered with silver and mulberry trees. An hour later Henry appeared, even more spectacularly armed, on a white war horse, draped in a livery of blue and green velvet embroidered with gold swans and antelopes.[38] Behind him followed six other war horses with various exotic trappings.[39] The crowd was ecstatic, and the popular support behind Henry immediately became apparent.

The lists themselves were set up in an area sixty paces long by forty wide, with a central barrier seven feet high. There stood the constable of England (the duke of Aumale) and the marshal of England (the duke of Surrey). They and their sergeants-at-arms and heralds were all dressed in red Kendal cloth, with belts embroidered with a near-quotation of the motto of the Order of the Garter, *Honniz soit celluy qui mal pense* ('shame on him who thinks evil'). First they addressed Henry, as he rode up on his white charger. The constable and marshal demanded that he show his face and announce himself. With the visor of his helmet open, Henry declared in a loud voice, 'I am Henry of Lancaster, duke of Hereford, and I have come here to prosecute my appeal in combating Thomas Mowbray, duke of Norfolk, who is a traitor, false and recreant to God, the king, his realm and me.' Henry then swore that his bill was true in all respects, and that he had no other weapons but those allowed, and that he would either kill his adversary or force him to surrender. Having sworn these oaths, he was asked to present his arms. He lifted his shield arm, bearing not the royal arms but those of St George: a red cross on a white background. He was fighting in the arms of the martial saint, under whose banner Edward III had fought. There could be no surer sign of his belief that he was in the right.

With his arms acknowledged, Henry entered the lists and rode straight for his pavilion, a huge tent decorated with red roses (later to become the most potent Lancastrian symbol of them all). There he awaited the arrival of his adversary. With the king and thousands of people watching, Mowbray rode up and announced himself. He uncovered his face and swore his oaths. The herald in charge then proclaimed from the heralds' stand that it was the king's will that anyone who touched the lists should forfeit his hand, and anyone who entered the lists should be hanged. Mowbray then shouted 'God speed the right!' and rode to his pavilion, dismounted and hung his shield up. The constable and marshal measured the lances of each combatant, to make sure they were the same length. This done, Henry rode to the end of the lists.

Henry's war horse had only advanced seven or eight paces, and Mowbray had not yet moved at all, when suddenly a shout went up. 'Ho! Ho!' called the king from his seat, rising to his feet. Henry came to a halt. Incredibly, Richard was ordering the fight to be stopped.

Henry sat there, shocked, as the king gestured for his lance to be taken away from him, and for him to be conducted to his pavilion. With thousands of onlookers wondering what was going on, the pair of them had been made to look like fools.

The morning drew on. Noon came, and nothing happened.

After two hours of waiting, the herald of the duke of Brittany mounted the heralds' stand with a long roll of parchment in his hand. He began to read, as follows:

Listen! My lords, I inform you by order of the king and council, the constable and the marshal, that Henry of Lancaster, duke of Hereford, Appellant, and Thomas Mowbray, duke of Norfolk, defendant, have both appeared here valiantly and that each was and is ready to do his duty like a brave knight. Nevertheless, our lord the king, considering the reason for the battle is so high, that is to say treason determined by parliament, and the dukes of Hereford and Norfolk being so close in blood to the king and of his arms, our lord the king, as one who has always trusted in the worth and honour of all those of his blood and of his arms, and grieving in his heart, as a good and gracious lord ... to avoid complete dishonour befalling one of the said dukes ... of his special grace has taken the battle into his own hand. And our said lord the king, with the full advice, authority, and assent of parliament, wills ... that the said Henry of Lancaster duke of Hereford should quit his realm for ten years. And that he should be outside the said realm before the day of the octave of St Edward the Confessor, upon pain of incurring the penalty for treason by authority of parliament.[40]

It is difficult for a biographer to reflect the full crushing weight of this announcement. As Henry's reactions are not recorded, it is difficult to say anything certain about how it affected him. Certainly we cannot say that it unleashed a burst of violence; with two thousand Cheshire archers present, he could hardly attack the king. But nor would it be right to say that he accepted this judgement, or his banishment, with equanimity. What had just happened was one of the grossest acts of tyranny in English history. Richard was not going to let him fight for the justice of his case. Instead, the king was apportioning blame for the slander, as if both men were partly responsible. Thus Henry shared a fate which carried all the stigma of treason, loss of royal favour and dishonour. All for mentioning another man's accusations against the king.[41]

In the heat of the moment it is unlikely that Henry fully comprehended what had happened. The injustice, we may imagine, consumed him too much. But if Henry was astonished, his father must have been astounded. John had only told the king of Mowbray's indiscretion in order to focus the king's retribution on the real culprit, Mowbray, the murderer of the duke of Gloucester. John's strategy was in tatters. Moreover, his long-term policy of remaining absolutely faithful to the king, so that Richard would never have any reason not to recognise Henry as heir to the throne, had been wrecked. His life's work was about to be undone. He had often petitioned Richard in council to recognise Henry as his heir, but Richard had always fobbed him off with some excuse.[42] Now everything was laid bare. Richard never meant to acknowledge Henry, rather he intended to get rid of him; and he did not care if he had to commit a gross injustice to do so.

Henry went with his father to Nuneaton, where the king was staying, but soon after their arrival the king departed for Leicester.[43] It seems probable that they tried to convince Richard that he was being unjust, that Henry did not deserve to be banished, but Richard refused to change his mind. Perhaps he believed John had only reported the conversation between Mowbray and Henry in order to stir up trouble, and, by apportioning the treason, sought to answer John's implied criticism that he, Richard, had ordered the death of Gloucester. Either way, he stuck to his decision. Nor was Henry's sentence commuted from ten years to six, as Shakespeare claims.[44] Henry and Mowbray were told to say farewell to the court at Windsor on 3 October, and then to depart, Henry to go via Dover to France or Spain for ten years, and Mowbray from an east coast port, to Germany or the Mediterranean, for life.

It is in the length of time that the desperation of Henry's situation becomes clear. Some writers have suggested that he did not mind being banished, as it allowed him to get out of England again and visit people, as he had so enjoyed doing in the early 1390s. Such writers are lacking in sensitivity to the facts and sympathy for the man. Ten years was ten times the duration of his journey to Jerusalem via Prussia and back again. It was more time than he could have spent constructively travelling, especially as he had a reduced income of just £2,000 to spend (less than half of his expenditure on his travels in 1392–3). More importantly, it meant that he would never see his beloved father again. He would not see his children grow up. They had already lost their mother; it seemed they were now to lose their father too. Richard, who had himself lost his father at a young age, and who had no children of his own, had no regard for such things. Henry, it seems, did. We may read of him buying two ABC grammar books for his daughters in this year, a sure sign that he wanted them to learn to read and eventually to be as well educated as their mother had been.[45] Looking through his most recent New Year present lists, we may read the name of one of his sons, Thomas, high up in the list of recipients.[46] There too we may read of Henry's presents for his beloved father, stepmother and sister, the duchess of Exeter. Henry was losing not only his immediate family but a great number of supportive kin, and many more friends, many of whom would be dead within ten years.

Another point we need to remember is that the very fact of banishment would have wholly changed Henry's attitude to travel. How could he show his face in a foreign court, after he had been banished for a supposedly traitorous act? Richard claimed this had been agreed in parliament, and even though this was a lie, foreign potentates were going to judge Henry's character by the favour his king showed him, not the justness of his case. The more he thought about his position, the more awful it must have seemed. All he had was £2,000 a year and the prospect of living in exile in France, at his half-sister's court in Castile, or his eldest sister's court in Portugal.

Henry and his father travelled to Windsor to see the king on 3 October. There he received a direct promise from the king that, when his father died, his representatives would be able to take possession of his inheritance on his behalf.[47] Then he and his father went on to London. Henry spent a week there making arrangements, paying rewards and giving presents to his faithful followers and friends. He appointed his attorneys on 8 October, and witnessed two of his father's charters on 9 and 10 October.[48] Then it was time to go.

On the day of his departure, he could not but have realised how he had become a hero. Crowds gathered and cheered him: it was said that forty thousand people lined the streets of London when he departed, and the citizens declared that the nation would not be safe until he returned from exile.[49] This was in marked contrast to the king, who was detested in the south-east. Even before the duel, there had been a peasant uprising in Oxfordshire aimed directly at ambushing the king, who was seen as a tyrant and an arch-traitor to the realm.[50] By his own admission, Richard was unable to ride around his own realm because of the enmity of the people of London and all the south-eastern counties. Consequently, he had excluded the people of London and sixteen other counties from the general pardon of 1398, and demanded that they each pay large sums to regain his favour.[51] The fact that they had already paid for this pardon through the lifelong grant of a wool subsidy was of no concern to Richard. If forty thousand is an exaggeration of the number who actually turned out to see Henry go, it is not an exaggeration of the number who despised the king for exiling him.

*

Henry said farewell to his father for the last time on 13 October, at Dover.[52] That day he embarked with his most faithful followers and servants, including the knights Thomas Rempston, John d'Aubridgecourt, Thomas Erpingham, John Tuchet and John Norbury, and his other lifelong followers, Henry Bowet, William Loveney and Robert Challoners.[53] No doubt he had many more men with him than this – the king authorised him to take 'no more than two hundred persons' – but few of them could have been of knightly status. His permission to stay in the castle at Calais allowed him to be accompanied by no more than twelve men, and then they could stay there only for a week. His whole company was allowed to stay no more than six weeks at Sangatte.[54] Then he was on his own.

According to Froissart, Henry had sent envoys to the French king in Paris before leaving England. King Charles in response sent a messenger saying that he sympathised with Henry's present disgrace, and invited him to Paris. The count of Ostrevant heard Henry was heading to Paris and sent Fier-a-Bras de Vertain to invite Henry to Hainault. Henry, however, felt an obligation to go to Paris. The dukes of Orléans and Berry met him as he approached the city, and accompanied him a little distance, and then the dukes of Burgundy and Bourbon did the same, and a great number of prelates and barons. The brilliant array accompanied Henry to the Hôtel de St Pol, where he was favourably received by King Charles. So impressed was the king with his charming manners that he allowed Henry to wear the livery of his order, and gave him the use of a house, the Hôtel de Clisson, and offered him financial support.[55] But despite this magnificent reception, Froissart notes that Henry was at times very melancholy, and not without reason, on thus being separated from his family. He was impatient to return, and much vexed that for such a frivolous cause he should be banished from England, and from his four promising sons and two daughters. [He] frequently dined with the king, the duke of Orléans and other great lords, who did everything they could to make his time pass agreeably.[56]

One of the ways in which the French royal family helped him 'pass the time agreeably' was to involve him in their attempt to heal the schism in the Church. At that time there were two popes trying to exercise authority. England supported one, France the other. The issue had exercised the greatest minds since the schism had first occurred in 1378. The French royal family joined in the debates, and Henry did too, attending discussions at the University of Paris. Philip, duke of Burgundy, was particularly impressed with Henry's ability to weigh the theological arguments he heard. 'Though we have clerics in England who are more subtle in their imaginative suggestions, these here in Paris have the true and sound theology', Henry remarked to Duke Philip, who afterwards repeated it as if, coming from Henry, the dictum carried special weight.[57]

The French also tried to brighten Henry's mood with discussions of his possible marriage to a member of the French royal family. Mary of Berry was proposed, the daughter of the duke of Berry, in whom Henry is supposed to have placed special trust.[58] Henry seems to have been very positive about the match. Mary was the same age as him, an attractive widow and of royal blood.[59] Her father was the duke who commissioned *Les Très Riches Heures de duc de Berri*, probably the most famous illuminated manuscript of the late middle ages. He was also the younger son of King John II. From the duke's point of view, the match was an excellent one: his proposed son-in-law or his eldest son was likely to succeed to the throne of England in the event of Richard dying without a male heir. But when Richard heard about the proposed marriage, and was made aware of how favourably Henry was being treated, he instructed John Montagu, earl of Salisbury, to speak to the French king. At Christmas, the earl presented his letters of credence to Charles and spoke to him privately, referring to Henry as a traitor, and urging that no marriage should be contemplated. He then delivered the same message to the duke of Berry. When he had received assurances that the French council had decided to break off the marriage, he hastily returned to England, without seeing Henry.[60]

According to Froissart, no one broke the news to Henry for a month. It was only when Henry himself sought to proceed with the arrangements that he was told what had happened. Philip, duke of Burgundy, uncle to the king of France, was charged with delivering the news to him. He chose an unfortunate way to express himself. In the presence of the court, he declared, 'we cannot think of marrying our cousin to a traitor'.

Henry was appalled. 'Sir, I am in the presence of my lord the king, and must interrupt your speech, to answer your accusation. I never was, nor ever thought of being, a traitor; and if anyone dares to charge me with treason, I am ready to answer him now, or at whatever time the king may appoint.'

'No, cousin', replied the king himself. 'I do not believe you will find a man in all of France who will challenge your honour. The expression my uncle has used comes from England.'

At this Henry is supposed to have sunk down on his knees and exclaimed, 'My lord, I believe you. May God preserve all my friends and confound my enemies!'

The king then made Henry rise, 'Sir, be appeased; this matter will end well. And when you are on good terms with everyone, then we will talk of marriage. But first you must obtain your inheritance, for it will be necessary for you to make provision for your wife.'[61]

Henry, on returning to the Hôtel de Clisson, was exceedingly angry. He was furious with the duplicity of the whole business, and the false charge of treason, and the stain on his character implied by his banishment. The undeserved shame of his exile was appalling and distressing. No one at the French court knew how to treat him. Normally medieval kings did not banish great lords for no reason. Henry was an anomaly in being exiled, and pitiable as a political liability.

It was probably as a result of this humiliation that Henry decided to leave Paris.[62] His friend Boucicaut was planning to undertake another crusade, to help the king of Hungary in his fight against Bayezid. He wrote to his father asking for permission to go with Boucicaut, but John suggested it would be better for him to visit either his sister Philippa, queen of Portugal, or his half-sister, Catalina, queen of Castile.[63] The letters from his father concerned Henry so much that he read them twice over. The knight who had brought them from England watched him, and told him that he should prepare himself for bad news. The physicians and surgeons attending his father had told the knight that John had only a matter of weeks to live.

John fell grievously ill over Christmas, at Leicester Castle. Richard was at Lichfield, a day and a half away. A massive feast was in progress, and jousts continued day and night, culminating on the king's birthday, Twelfth Night. Richard declared to William Bagot at this time that he would never allow Henry to return to England.[64] But despite this bitterness towards Henry, it seems Richard paid a visit to John on his deathbed.

Richard probably saw John in early January.[65] In fact, he gave out advance news of his burial between 8 and 19 January, while John was still alive.[66] The most likely explanation for this seems to be that it was at John's own request. The announcement of his forthcoming burial would have been outrageous and pointlessly antagonistic if it had been made without his permission, and John's generous personal bequests to the king are confirmation that he was not angered by it. In addition, the long period of time before the date for the funeral – about two months – and the place of burial would suggest that Richard had prior knowledge of John's funeral instructions: namely, that his body should remain unembalmed for forty days and that he wanted to be buried in St Paul's Cathedral, London, alongside his first wife.[67] John's motive in having his funeral announced by the king so far in advance was probably his hope that Henry would be able to make peace with Richard and return from France to attend. Unfortunately, it was not to be.

John of Gaunt died on 3 February 1399, surviving just long enough to force the delay of his funeral by a couple of days, to Saturday 15 March.[68] Henry did not attend the ceremony.[69] By then he had received a message from William Bagot informing him that 'the king was his sworn enemy, and that Henry must help himself by force'.[70] Receiving this sort of information is unlikely to have tempted Henry to return to England to attend his father's funeral, in the king's presence. Froissart notes that Richard wrote an account of John's death 'with a sort of joy' and that, when he sent a messenger to announce it to the French court, the messenger did not let Henry know the news.[71]

The entire French royal family joined with Henry in attending a Mass to pray for his father's soul. They pitied him, but they could hardly have comforted him. Their real interests lay in supporting Richard, the rightful king, whose queen was the daughter of the king of France. Justice had to take second place to political expediency. Thus, although we have no written record of Henry's feelings at that moment in March 1399 when he received news from Bagot, we can have little doubt that he was torn between emotions: grief for his father and anger at the way Richard had treated him, together with a sense of frustration at being stuck in Paris.

He had lost everything because of Richard. He had been kept back from having a prominent position as an international diplomat, which he could have reasonably expected. He had been prevented from winning as much fame in arms as he could have achieved. He had had to put up with plots against him and his father, constant worry, and seeing his uncle murdered and his friends summarily executed. He had been banished from his estates and separated from his father and children. And yet he had been wholly loyal to the king for ten years. What did he have to show for such loyalty? A ducal coronet and ten years in exile. It was a poor return for a man who was so highly educated, well-travelled, pious and militarily skilled.

And therein lies the explanation of 1399, one of the most momentous years in English history. Richard personally hated Henry. According to a French contemporary, he felt 'an implacable hatred' for him.[72] According to an English contemporary, he 'vehemently hated' him.[73] Reflecting on their lives from their first meeting, it is obvious that their characters were totally conflicting: Henry was so dutiful, almost ploddingly obedient to his father, Richard so mercurial. Henry was so logical and self-disciplined, Richard so flighty. Henry was so physically confident, Richard so insecure, needing to cocoon himself within his royal self-righteousness. But beyond these reflections, we have to suspect that the very root of Richard's active hatred (as opposed to passive dislike) was his own fear. He was afraid of Henry as the hero of the joust. He was afraid of his confidence, his affable nature, his logical mind and his strength. And he was afraid of his royalty, and the prophecies concerning the two of them. To impress his fellow men, and to get their obedience, Richard had to terrorise and cheat, to push himself forward and demand obedience. Henry was quite the opposite. It had been that way ever since they were children.

Thus it was a long-lasting hatred which brought the crisis to a head now. On 18 March 1399, twenty-eight years after he had first come to England, Richard sat on the throne, glowering at his subjects, and ordering them to address him in no other fashion but as 'your majesty', terrifying those around him, and demanding that his close friends be addressed as 'magnificent' and that the duke of Aumale should be referred to as his 'brother'.[74] At the same time, Henry sat in his chamber in a borrowed house in Paris, having been unable even to attend his father's funeral. And as they sat in their respective states – one haughty, the other reduced to waiting modestly on a foreign king – Richard announced that Henry's pardons were all revoked. The entire Lancastrian inheritance was confiscated. Everything Henry possessed was forfeit. And Henry himself was to be regarded as a traitor, and banished from England for the rest of his life.

NINE

The Virtue of Necessity

> All places that the eye of heaven visits
> Are to a wise man ports and happy havens.
> Teach thy necessity to reason thus;
> There is no virtue like necessity.
> *Richard II*, Act 1, Scene 3

This biography began by referring to the character portraits of Henry IV and Richard II with which we are most familiar, namely those conveyed by Shakespeare's plays. It has to be said that Shakespeare sympathises more with Richard, portraying him as unable to come to terms with the fragility of his power and the failure of his identity as a king. Shakespeare's Henry – or, more accurately, his *Henrys* – are never in need of our sympathy, even when (as duke or king) they are politically weak. Rather it is Harry Hotspur with whom Shakespeare sympathises in *Henry IV Part One*: a rebellious but doomed subject. In *Henry IV Part Two* it is the prince. In *Henry V*, the king becomes the object of Shakespeare's sympathy because of the weight of responsibility he has to bear. Shakespeare focused on the key problems facing his historical characters to create a sense of sympathy for them. In other words, he explores them through the struggles they faced, and we have come to see Richard as one such struggling man: a victim of his rebellious subjects' oppression, worthy of our sympathy.

In ignoring Henry at this point in time, Shakespeare missed a great opportunity. Had he construed the beginning of this series of four history plays differently, and written *Richard II* from Henry's point of view, as a preliminary 'Henry IV Part One' (of three parts), we would see Henry and Richard in a very different light. Henry would be the wronged man, the 'struggling man', and Richard a detestable tyrant. The four plays would then have had a dynastic unity, charting the rise of Lancastrian fortunes from their nadir of 1399 to culminate in the victory at Agincourt, the climactic point of the fourth and final play of the sequence, *Henry V*. Such a progression would have truly glorified the Lancastrians. It would also have been closer to the truth.

Consider Henry's thoughts in the long nights of March 1399. He had been robbed of everything. Knights, tradesmen and clerks in England could rely on the king's protection and some level of justice, but not Henry. What could he do about it? Nothing. His enemy was above the law. But nor could he accept his disinheritance. He knew well that to live under a sentence of perpetual banishment and forfeiture – however unjust – was an admission of guilt. He could not journey around the courts of Europe for the rest of his life, saying how wronged he had been, if he meant to do nothing about it. His personal capital would be worthless. He would lose the one thing he had left, his dignity.

Yet what should he do? Invade England? Presuming he could raise an army – which in itself was open to doubt – what could he hope to achieve? If he was successful, and forced Richard to restore his Lancastrian inheritance, Richard would only hate him more intensely. One day the king would seek revenge, just as Edward II had done against Thomas of Lancaster. Few would dare to fight against the royal banner if the king was in command. As we picture Henry in the long nights of March 1399, in the Hôtel de Clisson, we must picture a man in this plight. He knew that he *had* to dethrone Richard. He had no choice; it was either an end to Richard's rule or an end to everything Henry held dear: his royalty, family dignity, status and self-respect. But the means at his disposal were negligible. Assassination was out of the question; the risks were too great, and in any case it would simply confirm Henry as a traitor, no better than the murderer Richard himself. So he had no choice but to try and provoke a revolution, and for that there was no guarantee of success.

The English were not particularly given over to revolution. Only once since the Conquest had anyone dethroned a king of England. In 1327 Roger Mortimer had overseen the parliamentary deposition and enforced abdication of Edward II. But Mortimer, political genius though he was, had been unable to do more than put Edward II's legitimate heir on the throne. If Henry was successful in provoking a revolution, would he be accepted as Richard's heir? Richard had always refused publicly to accept him as such, despite the agreement they may have reached in the Tower at the end of 1387. Indeed, Richard had for several years now given preference to his last surviving uncle, Edmund of Langley, duke of York, with the idea that his son Edward, duke of Aumale (Richard's adopted brother), would eventually succeed.[1]

Herein lies another aspect of Henry's plight. Even though he had been brought up to believe that he would be the heir of a childless King Richard, he could not produce Edward III's entail, let alone enforce it. As Richard had never acknowledged that such a document existed, and had probably

destroyed the original, the potency of Edward III's wishes was hugely lessened. Moreover, King Edward's intentions now had to be set against King
Richard's. When Richard drew up his will on 17 April 1399, he did not
name his successor but indicated whom it should be (his uncle, the duke
of York) in a separate settlement of his own.[2] In addition, Richard tried
to impose a condition on his successor: that he should uphold the sentences
of the 1397–8 parliament and the later meetings of the commissioners,
including the decision by which Henry was declared a traitor and banished
forever. Richard did not just demote Henry in the order of succession, he
removed his right even to have a place in it.

Here, then, was a wonderful opportunity for Shakespeare to champion
the cause of an oppressed man. Rather than the 'king unking'd' we would
have had the banished heir fighting for his right. Instead of the downfall of
an autocratic king we would have had the victory of natural justice. What
great speeches Shakespeare could have made of that! But Shakespeare
refrained from taking Henry's side. He ignored him in his plight. Even
though it would have given the four plays a better structural unity, been
more accurate and allowed him to contrast the champion of justice against
the tyrant, he could not do so. The reason becomes clear when we realise
the enormity of the task facing Henry in March 1399. To dethrone an
anointed king he had to destroy part of the very fabric of society. Fundamental
ideas of loyalty, service and divine right would have to be overturned if
Richard were to be disempowered. It could be done – Roger Mortimer had
done it – but it could only be done by setting the will of the people against
the laws of God and the kingdom. Had Shakespeare written such a play,
championing a man who was prepared to do such things, it would have
been banned immediately, and the author would have been arrested. Even
as it was, *Richard II* caused great uneasiness, often being played without the
deposition scene, and being performed on the eve of attempted rebellions
(such as that of the earl of Essex). If that play had been written from the
point of view of the 'traitor' defeating the legitimate government of the realm,
it could not have been performed in England until the mid-seventeenth
century, as it would have been a justification of armed rebellion against a
divinely anointed monarch. In 1599 the publication of John Hayward's prose
history of Henry's life and reign resulted in the author being thrown in the
Tower and the burning of all the unsold copies.[3] Thus the task now facing
Henry was something which people could not even *write* about two hundred
years later. What Henry himself was thinking in those long nights in the
Hôtel de Clisson was such a fundamental break with the world in which he
lived, it was almost beyond his comprehension. It was only through reflecting
on those resolute leaders he had met in his long travels, such as Vitold of

Lithuania and Gian Galeazzo Visconti of Milan, and the example of Roger Mortimer, seventy years before, that he had any grasp of what was needed to accomplish such a task.

*

Henry was fortunate in one respect. His adversary was not only personally insecure and politically unreliable, he was a poor strategist. Nor was he willing to take advice from others. At the same time as he banished Henry for life and revoked his pardons – a decision which outraged and further alienated Henry's many supporters across the country – he summoned a prestigious army with which to invade Ireland and bring the rebellious Irish lord Art McMurrough to heel. In so doing he created his own two-front war. On the one hand he took a number of his most loyal fighting men to Ireland, and on the other he left England angry and sympathetic to Henry, whom he had now given no option but to return and start a revolution.

Richard did take some precautions. He drew up a set of 'blank charters' for London and the sixteen counties which he had decided to remove from the provisions of the general pardon.[4] Representatives of these places were required to set their seals to these blanks charters, so if Richard required more money, or wanted to punish or threaten these counties, all he had to do was to fill in the details of what he decided they should give him. Another precaution was to take hostages from families whose lords might rise against him. Henry's own son and heir, Henry of Monmouth (now aged twelve), and seventeen-year-old Humphrey, son of the late Thomas of Woodstock, were taken into Richard's household. There was a blanket prohibition on sending letters abroad unless they had first been vetted by the privy council.[5] Despite this last precaution, it is still likely that Henry and members of his household were fed information from those remaining in England. Moreover, because Richard's Irish plans had been in progress from before the death of John, there can be little doubt that Henry knew at the time of his disinheritance that Richard was about to leave the country. Richard's precautions were thus too slight to pose any significant disincentive to Henry, who could see his opportunity.

Thomas of Arundel, the exiled archbishop of Canterbury, was staying in Utrecht on the day that John died. That night he had a vision of John apologising for his harsh treatment of him in 1397.[6] Hearing of Henry's disinheritance, he travelled to Paris to find his cousin. He arrived there at roughly the same time as the message from William Bagot stating 'that Henry must help himself by force'. Thomas Arundel agreed with that advice, fully sympathising with Henry. They were in similar situations: Arundel's 'crimes' amounted to representing the views of parliament to the king in 1386 and taking an active part in the trials of Richard's friends in 1388. Like Henry he had been forbidden from trying to clear his name. He had lost his position as archbishop, had all his worldly possessions confiscated, and had been banished for life. He now was prepared to say openly to Henry that Bagot was right. Something had to be done.

With Thomas Arundel came another lord: his nephew, Thomas Fitzalan. He was the son and heir of Richard Fitzalan, earl of Arundel, whom Richard had had beheaded during the Revenge Parliament. Henry and his father had, of course, been instrumental in bringing him to his fate, and it is fair to say that Henry had acted without dignity in turning on the earl, his kinsman. But there had been mitigating circumstances – namely, Richard's tyranny – and that was what now brought these three men together. They had all lost their lands and honour due to Richard's willingness to destroy anyone and everyone who challenged his authority. These three also were innocent of any blame in the public mind. Henry had never been charged with any crime. Nor had Thomas Fitzalan; instead he had been prevented from inheriting his ancestral title and had been imprisoned in Reigate Castle (from which he had escaped). And Thomas Arundel had been wrongfully removed from his see.

However much these three might have been in the right, they were all dissidents from the legitimate English regime as far as the French were concerned. Herein lies the first major difference between their situation and that in which Roger Mortimer and Queen Isabella had found themselves in 1326. The French royal family in 1399 had every intention of supporting the king of England, who was married to their own Princess Isabella. In 1326, Queen Isabella had been one of the dissidents from the rule of her husband Edward II, and the French royal family had done nothing to stop her taking an army against the king of England. After all, Edward II had been at war with them at the time. Richard, in contrast, promised peace between the English and the French. Henry showed some of the letters smuggled out of England to the duke of Berry, but the duke was horrified to read them, as they implored Henry to return and depose Richard. The duke urged him to do nothing of the sort, and told him that 'brave souls do not allow themselves to be downhearted by reversals of fortune, but resign themselves to waiting for better times'.[7]

There was one notable exception to this collective French stance. Louis, duke of Orléans, entered into a secret pact with Henry. This at first seems very strange: Louis was the brother of the king of France. But Louis and Henry got on well in Paris. Perhaps Louis could sympathise with Henry's plight, himself having little or no respite from the rule of an unstable king who was also a close kinsman. He and Henry had Milanese sympathies in common too. They were both friends of Gian Galeazzo Visconti, Louis being married to his daughter (she of the poisoned apple incident). However, it is far from clear that Louis fully appreciated in 1399 that Henry might put himself forward for the throne. Their formal 'treaty and alliance', which the two men sealed on 17 June 1399 stated only that they promised to love and help one another, and to defend each other against their enemies, with certain exceptions, including the kings of England and France.[8] Thus the agreement did not imply that Henry expected Louis to help him attack Richard, even if he did make clear his plans to him, as he later claimed.[9] Nor did the exception clauses imply that Henry would not attack Richard himself. Given Louis' altercations with the duke of Burgundy over the regency, the 'treaty and alliance' probably had more to do with French politics than Henry's plans (as Henry later pointed out).[10] Thus it would appear less of an immediate strategic alliance for Henry's benefit than a pact for mutual support at some date in the future when things had settled down.

If Louis knew that Henry was returning to England, he was one of very few. Henry had no option but to conceal his real plans from the French. On announcing his departure from Paris, he stated that he intended to go to Spain, and in this way obtained the king's leave. Froissart's story that he departed by way of Brittany, and sailed in Breton ships to Plymouth, is incorrect, and cannot have any more truth to it than an echo of a visit by Henry to Brittany earlier in 1399, if that.[11] Rather he seems to have sailed in a small fleet gathering near Boulogne. Before leaving Paris, he first stopped at the abbey of Saint-Denis. There the abbot asked him to help the abbey to recover the Gloucestershire priory of Deerhurst, which had been taken into lay hands. Henry agreed 'to do what he could', and later, as king, was as good as his word.[12] Then he set out for Boulogne, and his ships.

*

Few writers who have described the events of 1399 mention the key attribute which was all-important to the success of Henry's expedition, namely his personal courage. This is strange, for it contrasts so completely with Richard. The king may have had moral courage in abundance but there was nothing physically brave about him. The sheer audacity of Henry returning to England at this point is impressive, and it impressed contemporaries too. That he did so in the wake of Mortimer, risking not just his life but the danger of being labelled a traitor, is particularly striking. Yes, he had seen the crowds lining the streets as he left London to go into exile. Yes, he probably had assurances from the earls of Westmorland and

Northumberland that they would support him. But he had no guarantee that those crowds would risk their lives for him now. Nor could he be certain that the earls of Westmorland and Northumberland would raise an army larger than that of the duke of York, the guardian of the realm. And what if Richard returned from Ireland? No Englishman had marched against the king on English soil and won a full-scale battle for more than 130 years.[13] Henry could not even be sure that he could disembark in safety. The first town he came to after landing – Kingston upon Hull – refused him admittance. Added to these problems, he was risking the king killing his eldest son, Henry. He might have been taking action to put an end to Richard's systematic destruction of him, his family and his estate, but action in itself increased his vulnerability.

This point about his courage alerts us to its corollary, his resolution. When Henry went into exile, he was followed by a loyal band of men who had been with him for years. At least three men – Thomas Rempston, John Norbury and Thomas Erpingham – were old comrades-in-arms, having accompanied Henry on his crusade in 1390. But would those who had followed him into exile now follow him into revolution? The answer was not in doubt as long as Henry was fully resolved to go through with what he planned. For that, courage alone would not be enough. At Vilnius in 1391, Henry had shown courage, leading his men to capture the citadel. But then, six weeks later, he and the army had withdrawn to the comparative refinement of Königsberg. Determination to see the job through to the end was lacking then. No half-measures would be adequate now.

For this reason, if we want a picture of Henry as he was on the ship that brought him to England in July 1399, we should envisage him not as the frustrated and submissive heir of John of Gaunt, obediently following his father's command to do nothing contrary to his oaths of loyalty. Nor should we see him as the brow-beaten character delicately treading on eggshells as Richard revenged himself on the senior Lords Appellant in 1397. Instead we should recall the terrifying determination of his grandfather, Edward III, in the campaign of 1346, which culminated in the battle of Crécy; and the resolve of his other grandfather, the duke of Lancaster, as he refused to give up the siege of Rennes before he had fulfilled his oath to place his standard on the battlements. Henry was of a similar disposition now: a man fully resolved to save England from its misfit king or die in the attempt.

*

Henry landed 'where the town of Ravenspur once stood', now Spurn Head (at the mouth of the Humber), on or about 4 July 1399.[14] Intelligence that he was gathering men in Picardy had reached the duke of York at Westminster by 28 June, for on that day the duke sent out letters warning the sheriffs that Henry was likely to invade, and ordering them to muster at Ware, in Hertfordshire.[15] According to Walsingham, Henry had spent some days sailing up and down the coast, searching for undefended landing places. On the south coast, a group of men under Sir John Pelham seized Pevensey Castle in Henry's name, probably to divert attention away from the north until Henry had managed to make contact with his supporters there. Henry's ships put in at Cromer too, to buy provisions, but also to create false news of his landing.[16] He had to depend on such ruses; he had very few knights – Walsingham estimates no more than fifteen – and in total he had no more than three hundred companions.[17] With so few soldiers, a single lord could have stopped and overpowered him immediately, had he known when and where Henry would come ashore.

As it was, Henry's strategy was good. Edmund, duke of York, had no idea where he was intending to land, and the information he received from various places only confused him. He may have actually set off westwards at one stage, completely in the wrong direction. When Henry did land, it was on a beach between two and three days' hard ride from London.[18] This gave him time to meet up with the northern lords, at least some of whom had been primed by letters sent from France, and then to ride to the comparative safety of the Lancastrian heartlands.[19] He probably went north first to Bridlington Priory, then to Pickering Castle, which opened its gates to him without resistance. At Knaresborough Castle he had more difficulty gaining access – the castle was held against him for a short while – but he prevailed, and left his own garrison there before marching on. He arrived at the great Lancastrian fortress palace of Pontefract Castle on 13 or 14 July.[20]

By this time, a large number of men had rallied to his cause. His loyal knight Robert Waterton had joined him very soon after landing, and it is possible that he met the earl of Northumberland and his son, Hotspur, at Bridlington.[21] At Pontefract itself, 'crowds of gentlemen, knights and esquires from Yorkshire and Lancashire flocked to join him with their retinues', so many that, when he left Pontefract and marched south to Doncaster, it was said he had thirty thousand with him.[22] Although this is an exaggeration, there is no doubt that thousands of men did muster under his banner.[23] Another chronicler wrote, 'so many retainers who had served his father flocked to join him, that within a short time he was in command of an almost invincible army'.[24]

It was almost certainly at Doncaster, on 15 or 16 July, that Henry was forced to face the key question about the revolution. Now it was clear that he had the support of the country, what exactly did he hope to achieve? The Percys – the earl of Northumberland and his son Hotspur – demanded an answer. They were in a particularly ambiguous situation. Being of Lancastrian descent, they had felt directly threatened by Richard's plans to reverse the pardons granted in the 1320s to the Lancastrians, for they, like Henry, would have been rendered the descendants of a traitor. Richard also threatened their political domination of the north of England.[25] Hence they were keen to put an end to Richard's prejudicial form of government. On the other hand, Hotspur's wife was Elizabeth Mortimer, aunt of the eight-year-old Edmund Mortimer, the Mortimer claimant to the throne. With Henry's army gathered around him at Doncaster, and growing larger every day, both the earl and his son must have begun to realise that soon they would be in no position to restrain Henry from taking the throne himself. Thus they came up with the idea of asking him to swear an oath.

No one knows exactly what Henry swore at Doncaster, or even if he swore his oath only there and not elsewhere. One source states he swore 'on the relics of Bridlington that he would never try to seize the throne, and that if anyone could be found who was more worthy of the crown than he was, he would willingly stand down for him; the duchy of Lancaster was all that he wished for'.[26] Another source states that he swore an oath at Knaresborough never to levy lay or clerical taxation in his lifetime.[27] The Percy manifesto recorded by Hardyng strongly supports the idea that Henry swore an oath of some sort in the house of the White Friars at Doncaster but it is highly dubious with regard to the wording.[28] It claims on the one hand that Henry personally held and kissed the holy gospels and swore that Richard would remain king for the duration of his life under the direction of the lords spiritual and temporal. On the other it states that Henry promised to reform the royal household and not to levy taxes upon the people without the assent of parliament, thus according him quasi-regal status.[29]

Putting these sources together, there is no doubt that some sort of oath was sworn by Henry concerning both his claim to the throne and his liberty to tax the people. The same oath (or different versions) may have been sworn more than once, at Bridlington and Knaresborough as well as Doncaster. But we can be confident of just two of the terms, and these only in outline. Clearly he promised not to take the throne by force. Secondly, whatever he swore to do or not to do with regard to Richard, it involved the complete disempowerment of the king. From now on, Henry had 'sovereign' power: literally, authority *above* that of the king.[30] Beyond these two points it is possible only to see a correlation between later events and the testimony of the Dieulacres chronicle: that Henry would not 'seize' the throne but would stand aside for anyone 'more worthy of the crown'. This is what happened. When Richard resigned, Henry did not seize the throne, he claimed it as the 'nearest male relative and *worthiest* blood-descendant of Henry III'.[31] That he did all he possibly could to influence the decision to make his claim appear 'the worthiest' suggests that the Dieulacres chronicler was exactly right: he had sworn to lay aside his claim if there was someone 'more worthy' to be king. Worthiness, of course, was an ill-defined concept, relating to character and experience as well as birth. At the time of swearing the oath, however, that ambiguity was left unexplored. It suited both the Percy family and Henry to carry on as before, without exploring their differences too closely until Richard's authority was overthrown.

Whatever fractures there were in Henry's army at the time of the oath, they remained hidden. Indeed, just swearing the oath reinforced Henry's position. It confirmed him as the leader of the revolution. Rarely have historians ever felt the need to say why it was Henry who led the opposition to Richard in 1399. But as earlier chapters have shown, there was much more to Henry than a disaffected duke. Contemporaries would have recognised his double royal inheritance, his seniority in the male line of the royal family, the prophecies that the line of Lancaster would inherit the throne, and his experience as a battle leader and a crusader. The crowds which turned out on the day of his departure from London must have confirmed in many people's minds that Henry was the natural leader of opposition even before he went into exile. That he had been wrongly disinherited by Richard the following March simply reinforced this position. No one else could easily have assumed it.

The other important point about this oath, or series of oaths, was that it gave Henry a platform on which to present himself, to state clearly what he stood for. Henceforth he was not simply reclaiming his patrimony; he was championing the restitution of lands for all the disinherited. He stood for a non-taxing or low-taxing government. He stood for the reform of the royal household, and the disbandment of the bands of Cheshire archers, Richard's enforcers. And most of all he stood for an end to tyranny. If Richard was permitted to reign any longer, it would be in name alone. Royal authority would be vested in the person of Henry of Lancaster.

*

Henry moved further south, arriving at his own castle of Leicester about 20 July. His army was growing larger every day, but in order to use it effectively he had to move quickly. Given enough time, the men would lose interest and return home, especially as it was very difficult to feed so many of them. He wisely capitalised on rumours of the forces attending him by sending out persuasive letters to lords, abbots and mayors, telling the Londoners in particular that they could only expect Richard's rule to grow worse.[32] But his real strategic options were limited to marching on the capital and seat of government at London and Westminster or against the regent and council. He decided on the latter, to make straight for the regent, his uncle.

Duke Edmund was still with his army at Ware, in Hertfordshire. Initially he set out north-west, to Bedford, but then on 13 or 14 July, while Henry was at Pontefract, he had turned south-west to take the road through Oxford to Gloucester. It is probable that his plan – seeing as he had not mustered a large enough army to crush the forces which he now heard were gathering to Henry's banner – was to meet with Richard on his return from Ireland. He had no will to fight Henry. Not only was he a very reluctant military commander, he was also an invalid, suffering from an extreme arthritic condition which had left five of his lower dorsal vertebrae fused together.[33] He arrived in Oxford on the 16th and spent four days discussing the situation with the rest of the council. Edmund by now wanted to disassociate himself from them. He despatched them to Bristol, perhaps to await the king's return. Edmund himself headed to Berkeley Castle.

Had Edmund wanted to maintain a united front against Henry, he should have remained with the other members of the council. But he did not. Moreover, his choice of Berkeley was significant. To the English royal family, Berkeley Castle was synonymous with the captivity and reputed murder of Edward II, the king with whom Richard most identified. Now Duke Edmund chose to await his nephew's arrival in that same castle, along with Lord Berkeley and other men who refused to join the royal council at Bristol. There was no strategic advantage to this; rather it was a sign of Duke Edmund's willingness to acknowledge the wrong which had been done to Henry. From the 24th he waited at Berkeley. Henry rapidly advanced through Coventry, Warwick, Evesham and Gloucester. Edmund did nothing.

On Sunday 27 July, in the church which stands just outside the walls of Berkeley Castle, Henry met his aged uncle. Standing among the silent tombs of the Berkeley family, they came to an agreement. What Henry said we cannot know for certain, but the result of the meeting was that Edmund agreed to let Henry proceed against Richard. This had been in his mind from the moment he divided his forces and those of the rest of the council at Oxford. In fact, he may have been considering his position even before this, when at Bedford he realised that most of the country was prepared to join Henry. According to one chronicler, he had already declared that he believed Henry's attempt to reclaim his inheritance was just and right. According to another, his army was breaking up. On top of these problems, it would have been obvious by mid-July that defending the king would have led to civil war.[34] Edmund was not prepared to go that far to defend his tyrannical nephew.

After the meeting at Berkeley, Henry despatched his uncle to take custody of Richard's young queen. He himself marched towards Bristol. His half-brother, John Beaufort, marquis of Dorset, who had travelled westwards with the duke, came to him and begged forgiveness. The earl of Northumberland and his son Hotspur both wanted John put to death immediately but Henry stayed their hand. Pulling a letter out of his blue velvet pouch, he said to them, 'Harm him not, I beseech you; for he is my brother and has always been my friend. Look at the letter which I received from him in France.' Then Henry embraced his half-brother. If he was going to win this fight against Richard, he needed to make sure no potential ally shunned him out of fear of retribution.[35]

The following day Henry's army encircled Bristol Castle. Those inside could see the standards and heraldic banners of the duke of Lancaster and the earls of Northumberland and Westmorland and knew that there was no escape. There were four thousand English archers in the army.[36] But when Henry demanded that the castle be surrendered, the castellan, Peter Courtenay, refused. The earl of Northumberland proclaimed outside the walls that anyone who wished to surrender now would be allowed to go free; anyone who did not would be beheaded. A few men let themselves down on ropes from the castle ramparts. Moments later, others began to make their escape from windows, and soon the entire garrison was in flight, leaving the castle by any means they could. The gates were flung open. Courtenay gave himself up. Henry's men entered and arrested William Scrope, earl of Wiltshire, John Bussy and Henry Green and the few friends who had remained with them. On the 29th they were all brought before Henry. They could expect no mercy: they all had witnessed and thus approved of the deeds whereby Richard had confiscated Henry's inheritance and banished him for life. In addition, Scrope had accepted Henry's castle and honour of Pickering, and Bussy, who had once been close to Henry, had proved himself personally untrustworthy. All three men were executed as traitors, their severed heads displayed at York, London and Bristol.

*

Just as Richard's accession in 1377 had been compared to the coming of Christ, now Henry was himself compared to the Saviour. His arrival was

Henry's maternal grandfather and namesake, Henry of Lancaster. He was the epitome of the aristocratic warrior: brave, talented, rich, literate, pious and dutiful. This image, drawn about 1440, shows him in the robes of the Order of the Garter.

Henry's paternal grandfather, Edward III, the hero-king of England. He knighted Henry at Windsor on St George's Day, 1377. Here he is shown with his eldest son, the Black Prince.

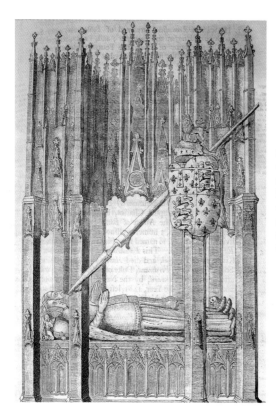

Henry's father, John of Gaunt, was buried in St Paul's Cathedral alongside his beloved first wife, Blanche of Lancaster. The tomb, with John's lance and shield, stood to the north of the high altar until it was destroyed in the Great Fire of 1666.

Only the foundations now survive of Henry's birthplace, Bolingbroke Castle, in Lincolnshire. The King's Tower, shown here, was remodelled about 1450 as a stately polygonal structure. It is possible that the remodelling was a public commemoration of Henry's birthplace.

Edward, the Black Prince, was Henry's uncle. His chivalrous deeds of arms and devotion to the Trinity were followed by Henry, who chose to be buried in the same chapel, in Canterbury Cathedral.

Mary Bohun was ten or eleven when she was depicted with her mother,
the countess of Hereford, in this psalter. It was probably commissioned to mark
her wedding to Henry in early 1381.

This is by far the most famous image of Henry IV. Unfortunately it is not actually him. In the late sixteenth century, when series of English royal portraits were in demand, no portrait of Henry was known, and so this was concocted from a suitable French original and widely copied.

Henry's actual appearance is best revealed by several miniatures and his funeral effigy. This fine example appears in the Great Cowcher, a cartulary of the dukes of Lancaster, made in about 1402.

Richard II. Deeply insecure, his struggle to reign with a strong hand was a tragedy both for himself and his subjects. His bitter hatred of Henry directly led to his own downfall and ultimately his death.

Henry's uncle, Edmund, duke of York, came to regret his support for Richard II, despite Richard making him his heir. His change of allegiance in 1399 ensured that Henry's revolution was almost bloodless.

Jean Creton's chronicle contains a number of contemporary illustrations of the events of 1399. Here he shows Henry (in the black hat) presenting the captive Richard to the citizens of London.

Pontefract was one of the greatest castles in the kingdom and an important base for the Lancastrians. It was also the place where Richard II was finally imprisoned, and where he was killed on Henry's orders, almost certainly by enforced starvation.

The spectacular ruins of Conway Castle still brood over the town as they did at the end of the fourteenth century. It was here in August 1399 that Northumberland persuaded Richard to meet Henry, taking him prisoner soon after he left the castle.

described as 'miraculous'. Crowds shouted 'blessed is he who comes in the name of the Lord, our king of England!'.[37] Poets compared him to the Emperor Augustus. Chaucer in particular wrote about how he had come 'to mend all harm'.[38] The poet Gower – who was an ardent Lancastrian even before Henry landed – recorded how, on his landing at Ravenspur, Henry had knelt and kissed the ground.[39] Prophecies were searched out in old chronicles and reinterpreted to show that it was God's will that Henry should put an end to Richard's rule. He was universally regarded as the champion of the Church and the people, a rescuer of good government and a promise of better times to come.

Yet Henry's position was far from safe. He had not faced the king, and thus the kingdom had not yet had to choose between the good government he promised and the legitimate government represented by Richard. The crucial question was this: when the king returned, would the army surrounding Henry march in defiance of the royal standard? To do so would be treason – there was no doubt on that score. So it was now, at the very end of July 1399, that the battle lines were drawn. The king had landed in the far south-west of Wales, at Milford Haven, and was marching to Carmarthen. Which path would the kingdom choose: tyranny in the name of loyalty? Or treason in the name of justice?

As it happened, the kingdom would not fight the battle implied in this choice. Extraordinarily, Richard abandoned his army at Carmarthen. He fled north with about two dozen men, including the dukes of Exeter and Surrey, the earl of Gloucester and three bishops (Carlisle, St David's and Lincoln). That was all. He had no army. At the very point when he was required to show resolve and determination, he ran.

This decision proved fatal for Richard's cause, and it is tempting to rank it among the greatest failures of royal judgement in the middle ages. But it is very likely that there was more to it than a complete failure of nerve. For a start, there was some logic to his destination: North Wales was not far from Chester, the administrative centre of his Cheshire archers and arguably the most loyal region in the realm. More significantly, by fleeing he narrowly escaped a plot to seize him in Carmarthen.[40] The key agent in this plot was probably none other than Richard's own adoptive brother, Edward, duke of Aumale, acting with the support of Thomas Percy, earl of Worcester.[41] What is not in doubt is that these two men rode to join Henry soon after Richard had fled. Men whom Richard had regarded as loyal were now deserting his cause and supporting Henry, regardless of their oaths of loyalty.

Richard's attempts to raise a force in North Wales were in vain, his strategy hopeless. He rushed between the empty shadows of Edward I's great castles, desperately searching for the core of an army. Meanwhile Henry began to head north, through Ross-on-Wye, Hereford, Leominster and Ludlow. On 2 August, Henry appointed the earl of Northumberland as warden of the Marches of Scotland. What capacity he was acting in when he did this is not clear. He may have done so as hereditary steward of England, with a responsibility to maintain the safety of the realm in times of crisis.[42] However, it is more likely that he made this appointment in the capacity of holding 'sovereign' power. By 31 July he was using a seal which had the motto 'sovereign' engraved on it.[43] He may only have claimed to be 'duke of Hereford, earl of Derby and Northampton and Lord of Brecon' on this seal, but the motto suggests that sovereign power was now vested in him (as it probably had been since swearing the oath at Doncaster).

The stress and strain were already beginning to tell on Richard. He was waiting for the net to close in, and fearing it, knowing there was nothing he could do. At Conway Castle, pale and barely himself, he implored his half-brother, the duke of Exeter, to advise him. They agreed that Richard would send two negotiators to Henry. Richard sent Exeter and his nephew, the duke of Surrey. Then he departed for Beaumaris Castle. Feeling too vulnerable there, he went on to the great fortress of Carnarvon. He was on the run. There was no furniture in these castles; they were little more than empty shells. The handful of men still with Richard slept on straw, anticipating a cold and bloody end. After a few days Richard returned to Conway, and waited for news.

The dukes of Exeter and Surrey met Henry at Chester. He had marched up the Welsh border to Shrewsbury, where he was when the citizens of Chester saw fit to surrender their town to him before he took it by force. The two dukes met him in the castle. He greeted them cordially, and asked Exeter the reason for his visit. Exeter told Henry that the king was prepared to forgive him this outrage against his royal authority, and to restore his lands and titles to him, if he would do his duty, disband his army and submit to the king. Henry of course did not believe a word. He had every reason to distrust Richard. Rather than reply to the duke, he detained him. Surrey was arrested and locked up in the castle. Exeter was taken to witness the removal of the king's enormous treasure of £40,000, which had been hidden in Holt Castle.

All the cards were now in Henry's hands. Richard had nothing left with which to bargain. He did not even have the means with which to approach Henry, for Henry could just as easily imprison the next man Richard sent, and then the next. It was down to Henry to make the decisive move. A siege of Conway could take some time, and his army was so unwieldy and expensive that already he had had to send some men home. So he decided to lure Richard out into the open. On or about 15 August he sent the earl of Northumberland to the king at Conway with a large force of men with orders to arrest him.

Northumberland had a plan, devised by Thomas Arundel (according to Jean Creton, a Frenchman staying with Richard).[44] He concealed the bulk of his forces at the foot of a mountain, guarding a pass. Then he went ahead to the castle with only five men, and asked to see the king. When admitted to the royal presence he promised Richard that all Henry wanted was his inheritance and that justice be meted out to the five men who had procured the death of his uncle, Thomas of Woodstock. The earl proposed that Henry and Richard would ride together and hold a parliament at London at which Henry would be reinstated as duke of Lancaster and Hereford, and steward of England, and the criminals would be punished. To impress Richard with the sincerity of this offer, Northumberland swore upon some relics that Henry would honour these terms to the letter.[45]

Richard had little choice. The alternative was flight, but he knew he was unlikely to be able to escape Henry that way for long. So he decided to go along with the earl's suggestion, thereby luring Henry into a false sense of security. According to Jean Creton, Richard said to the earl of Salisbury, after Northumberland had withdrawn, that he would persuade Henry to take the route south through Wales. Then, at his order, certain Welshmen would rise and capture him. 'I swear to you', he said to Salisbury, 'that whatever assurances I may give him [Henry], he shall surely be put to a bitter death for this outrage and injury that he has done to us. Doubt it not, there shall be no parliament held at Westminster on this matter.'[46] But Richard spoke too soon. Soon after setting out, he found himself surrounded by Northumberland's men, who now formed his escort. He had fallen into the trap.

Henry received news of Richard's capture via a messenger who had travelled through the night, reaching Chester at daybreak on the 16th. He summoned his lords and captains and set out shortly afterwards, following the coastal road towards Flint Castle, to which Richard had been taken. The army which accompanied him that morning was overjoyed at the news. They set out in ordered columns, playing horns and trumpets as they marched. Richard heard the noise, and watched them approaching from the top of the castle. He now had visible proof that it was all over. There were no bushes or trees to obscure his view: he could see for himself the substantial forces Henry had at his command. The realisation that the nation had deserted him affected him deeply. As he watched the army surrounding the castle, he began to pray, according to Creton. 'Good Lord God! I commend myself into your holy keeping, and cry you mercy, that you may pardon all my sins; since it is your pleasure that I should be delivered into the hands of my enemies; and if they cause me to die, I will take death patiently as you took it for us all.'[47]

Richard at this point declined to take food. He had been reluctant to eat at Rhuddlan (where he had stopped briefly on the way to Flint), perhaps for fear of being poisoned, and had only accepted bread and wine when Northumberland himself had offered it to him. Now again he chose to fast. Northumberland reported this to Henry, and Henry decided to wait outside the castle until Richard had eaten. So Richard was forced to sit down and dine. Fearing the worst, he bade his fellow prisoners sit down with him, and eat. The king sat at the table solemnly. But still he did not eat. Eventually Henry went to the gate of the castle and sent his herald in to fetch out the unimportant men with the king. Creton was one of them. By his own admission, he was more frightened than he had ever been in his life. The herald announced to Henry in English that these men were French. Henry spoke to them in their own language, and assured them that their lives would be spared. Then he went into the chamber in which the king was sitting at the table.

Henry bowed low before the king, and approached. He bowed low again, sweeping his cap to the floor.

Richard took off his own hat. 'Cousin of Lancaster, you are right welcome', he declared.

Henry bowed again, and addressed the king in English. 'I have come without being summoned by you for the following reason. The common report of your people is that you have for the last twenty or twenty-two years governed them very badly and very rigorously, and they are not content with this. But if it please the Lord, I will help you to govern them better than they have hitherto been governed.'

In the words of Jean Creton Richard responded, 'fair cousin, since it pleases you, it pleases us as well'.

Then Henry spoke to everyone else there individually, including the bishop of Carlisle. There was only one person to whom he refused to speak. He told an elderly knight of his to pass a message to the earl of Salisbury. The knight announced that the earl should not expect to be spoken to any more than he had spoken to Henry when he had been in Paris. Reference to that event, when Salisbury had told the French king that Henry was a traitor, and asked him to refuse to let Henry marry Mary of Berry, caused the earl to be silent and afraid.

Henry led Richard to Chester, and had him secured in the castle keep.

The royal party remained there for three days, agreeing that parliament should be summoned, as the earl of Northumberland had promised the king. The notice required to hold a parliament was forty days; writs of summons dated 19 August were sent out announcing a parliament would be held on 30 September, the day after Michaelmas. With that important element of government again in place, the bureaucracy which had stopped functioning since 9 August started slowly to regain its usual efficiency. The civil servants knew who and where their king was, and they knew in whom sovereign power lay. That these two facts were not embodied in the same man was not essential for them to do their work.

Henry, his companions and the remainder of the army took Richard and headed towards London on the 20th. The first night after leaving Chester there was an unsuccessful attempt to liberate the king. At Lichfield, on or about 23 August, Richard himself made an attempt to get away, lowering himself from a window. After that there were no more chances. The king was placed under a twenty-four-hour armed guard, with ten or twelve men detailed to watch him closely. In this state he was conducted to London.

On the last day of August, two miles out of the city, Henry was met by the mayor and aldermen. He presented Richard to them. 'What would you have me do with him?' he asked, probably referring to the request of an earlier embassy asking him to have the king beheaded.[48] 'Take him to Westminster', they replied. So Richard was conducted to the Palace of Westminster and lodged there for the night. The following day he was led to the Tower, with a mass of people surrounding him at a distance and jeering. Men-at-arms kept the space around him clear, so that everyone could see his face. The hatred of the crowd was bitter. They called him a 'little bastard', or a 'wicked bastard'.[49] An attempt to murder him as he was paraded through the city was narrowly averted by the mayor and aldermen.

While Richard was being taken to Westminster, Henry entered the city of London in triumph. He rode around to the principal gate of the city, Aldgate, in order for his procession to be seen to best effect. 'Long live the good duke of Lancaster!' shouted the rapturous crowds, 'God bless Henry of Lancaster!' Jean Creton, who recorded the procession, declared in dismay: 'had the Lord Jesus Christ himself arrived, he could not have been greeted with more pleasure by the citizens'.

With the crowds' shouts and blessings ringing in his ears, Henry rode to St Paul's Cathedral and dismounted. He entered the old cathedral in full armour and walked solemnly towards the high altar, where he knelt and prayed. Then, rising, he turned to his left. There stood a stone tomb.

Nearby hung a lance and a shield. The shield bore the royal coat of arms. In this tomb his father had finally been reunited with his much-loved mother. Henry looked at it, and remembered his father, and perhaps recalled Chaucer's stories of his mother's dancing and singing. At that point the tension gave way, and all the stress and fears poured out of him in tears and uncontrollable emotion. With all the crowd watching, Henry wept.[50]

*

The months of July and August 1399 rank as the most important yet in the life of Henry of Lancaster. Through deliberate and well-planned action he had transformed himself from an exiled traitor into a national hero. He had been acknowledged as the sole and undisputed leader of the popular movement for justice, and he had been recognised as the man who would wield royal power when (and not if) Richard's ability to rule was officially terminated. Finally, he had received the king as his prisoner and placed him under guard in the Tower of London. They had been the most extraordinary two months.

Nevertheless, September was to be even more important, for it was now that Henry had to reckon the full weight of what he had achieved. That meant not just taking stock of the situation but identifying what to do next. Some things were clear. The king's position had to be diminished, so that he would never again be able to exert his personal form of government. Henry had to be restored to all his titles and estates, as did the other disinherited lords, including Thomas Arundel, who had to be reinstated as the archbishop of Canterbury. But what of the future? Indeed, the one question which mattered above all others – the defining question of the rest of Henry's life – now had to be addressed. What were his own intentions with regard to the throne?

This is a hugely difficult question. Paradoxically, this is not because it is difficult to come up with an answer; it is because there are so many answers. For a start, we could say simply that the strength of support he had received since marching south from Pontefract had convinced him that he could and should make himself king in place of Richard. But this does not mean that he had always intended to supplant him. If we ask ourselves the question *when* Henry decided to make himself king, the complexity of the question is revealed. It is not hard to envisage Henry as a boy dreaming of taking his cousin's place and leading a chivalric nation in war, like his grandfather Edward III. Likewise there is no reason to doubt that his grandfather's entailment persuaded him absolutely that he was Richard's legitimate heir. A man who grows up believing he is the heir to the throne is unlikely ever to be able to let go of such an idea. As the years passed, and Richard showed no sign of producing a child, Henry's awareness of his position and responsibility as the heir must have grown stronger. But desire, belief and duty are not the same as intention, and even an intention needs the context of a particular set of circumstances in order to be understood. Although one popular historian has claimed that Henry's promise to the abbot of Saint-Denis to help him recover Deerhurst Priory was a clear indication of his intention to take the throne, these two things cannot be directly connected; Henry only promised to 'do what he could', and this may have related to his future status as a duke rather than as a king.[51] Had the huge army which had gathered around him at Doncaster sought the coronation of the eight-year-old earl of March, he would have had difficulty in resisting such demands. As a result it is fair to say that, while he had hoped since childhood that he would one day become king, and had every intention of ascending the throne if he could, he was not a conqueror in the sense that he would now make himself king against the will of the governing classes. It was, rather, their support which convinced him that it was the best course of action both for him and them.

It is this combination of the necessity of removing Richard from power and the widespread support for Henry as a leader that best answers our question about his intentions towards the throne in September 1399. The people had not called for another boy-king like Richard, nor for an old man like Duke Edmund; they wanted a responsible warrior-leader like Edward III had been in his thirties and forties. Given the death of the popular earl of March in 1398, Henry (aged thirty-two) was the obvious candidate. Thus it is likely that Henry swore the Doncaster oath on the basis that, while he had promised not to *seize* the throne, he knew that once Richard had abdicated, the way would be clear for him to inherit it. If parliament accepted the king's abdication, Henry would become king.

It all sounds perfectly straightforward. But there was a problem. Despite everything he had been told all his life, and despite his personal conviction that he was next in line for the throne, it now emerged that Henry was not Richard's legal heir.

This statement needs some explanation, for, by the terms of Edward III's entail, Henry *was* the heir, without any doubt. The reason we can be so categorical in saying that circumstances had changed is because, when it came to actually claiming the throne, he did not use this document. In fact, he did not even mention it. He claimed the throne not as the heir of his grandfather, Edward III, but as the heir of Henry III, his double great-great-great-grandfather, who had died in 1272.[52]

Many writers down the years have puzzled over the problem of Henry's succession. Some have suggested that Henry wanted to draw attention to his double royal descent from Henry III, through both his father and his mother, in contrast to the single royal descent of Edmund Mortimer (which was through his grandmother). This is very doubtful. If Henry claimed a right of inheritance through his mother, he would only add strength to Mortimer's claim to the throne, which rested entirely on a woman's ability to convey a right of succession. Thus any reference to a claim through a woman rendered Henry lower in the order of succession than all the Mortimers. For this reason it is not possible to accept that Henry's claim to the throne through descent from Henry III was due to a wish simply to demonstrate his mother's as well as his father's royal ancestry.

The other most frequently cited explanation is equally problematic. Three chronicles – the continuation of the *Eulogium Historiarum* and the chronicles of John Hardyng and Adam Usk – refer to a Lancastrian belief that Edmund Crouchback, earl of Lancaster, was not the second son of Henry III but the first, and that because of his supposed imbecility he was set aside for the inheritance of the throne, and his brother, Edward I, was made king instead.[53] But as contemporaries knew, Edward I was definitely the elder of the two boys. In early September Henry called together a team of lawyers and clergymen to investigate two questions: how to depose Richard and how Henry might claim his inheritance. One of the above-mentioned chroniclers, Adam Usk, was among them. As Usk made clear, there were many chronicles and other documents which showed that the Edmund Crouchback story was false.[54] In addition, there was the unequivocal evidence of Henry III's will, a copy of which remained on hand in the exchequer.[55] Henry would have been left in no doubt that this claim was without foundation. So why did he stake his claim on descent from Henry III and not Edward III? Did he present a flawed claim to the throne?

The answer to this last question is not a straight yes or no, but it is much more of a yes than a no. Clearly there was an overriding reason why Henry could not claim the throne as the heir male of Edward III, in line with the settlement of 1376. We might speculate that he did not have the original document (which Richard had probably destroyed) but even if he did not, this cannot be the full answer because the official order of precedence in the royal charters of 1394 recognised Henry and all the male heirs of Edward III taking precedence over the Mortimers. In addition, one or two of those who had witnessed Edward III's entail were still alive.[56] There was a far simpler and stronger reason why Henry had to forget about Edward III's entail. It was legally invalid.

This point has not been made in the historical literature before, and so it needs to be explained carefully. In 1290 Edward I had made a settlement of the Crown in which he had stipulated that the throne should pass to his son Edward *and his heirs* – not necessarily just male heirs – in preference to any younger sons whom the king himself might yet sire.[57] Furthermore, he clearly stipulated that his own daughters *and their heirs* should inherit in preference to his brother, Edmund Crouchback, and his sons. This could have been considered a legal precedent, so that not only would female heirs thereafter have been able to be queens in their own right, but a daughter of an elder son would have taken precedence over the son of a younger son. John of Gaunt had himself admitted as much in 1376 when he petitioned first parliament and then the council to decree that women could not transfer a right to the throne.[58] By this reckoning, Edmund Mortimer should have taken precedence over Henry until Edward III drew up his entail in late 1376. However, if Edward I's settlement of 1290 could have been legally supplanted by Edward III's of 1376, it followed that it would in turn have been supplanted by any subsequent settlement made by Richard II. It is highly probable that, by April 1399, Richard had indeed made a settlement of his own.[59] In such circumstances, Henry's chief legal adviser – Justice William Thirning – would have strongly advised Henry against depending on Edward III's entail for his claim to the throne.

The only legal avenue open to Henry was to question whether English kings had the right to appoint their successors. If they did, then Richard II's settlement took precedence over Edward III's, and Duke Edmund was the legal heir. If they did not, all of these settlements were irrelevant. In these circumstances, and with little time to spare, Henry cut the Gordian knot and opted for the latter interpretation of the law. He claimed the throne as the heir male of Henry III on the grounds that all subsequent settlements had been without a legal foundation, and that the original male-only law of inheritance prior to the reign of Edward I should be restored. It was the only way in which he could claim to be next in line to the throne.[60]

As a result of this, we can be sure that Henry's claim was not wholly lawful, for it depended on the dubious assumption that kings had never had the right to entail the throne away from their male line of descent.[61] That is not to say it was *unlawful* – the subject was far beyond being legally black and white in 1399 – but it was a fudge at best, for never before had a king's right to settle the throne on a specific line of the royal family been questioned. It is hugely ironic that, although Henry had believed all his life that he and his father were Richard's legitimate heirs – and, in doing so, had trusted a king's right to appoint his successor – when it actually came to claiming the throne he was forced to do so in defiance of this very principle.

*

In all this business Henry was heavily reliant on legal advice, especially that of Justice Thirning. According to one account, when Henry suggested that he could solve the technical problem concerning his inheritance by claiming the kingdom by right of conquest, Thirning warned him that 'this would arouse the anger of the entire population . . .' because 'it would appear to the people that he had the power to disinherit anybody at will, and to change the laws, establishing new ones and revoking old ones, as a result of which no one would be secure in his possessions'.[62] He might have added that Henry would be guilty of perjury too, for he had sworn at Doncaster not to seize the throne by force.

Thus it was the lawyers who guided Henry's actions over the course of September 1399. There may have been a meeting at the Tower between Henry and Richard on 3 September, at which Richard railed bitterly against Henry and the dukes of York and Aumale, declaring them all to be traitors and asking to be brought to trial.[63] Certainly Henry summoned the royal council in order to discuss how to deal with Richard.[64] The question of a trial was a moot one. Could a king be tried for treason? No, for the king was above the law, as the law proceeded from the king. But Richard was clearly too fickle to be allowed to keep the title of king. By 10 September it had been decided that he would be deposed.[65] This decision raised another problem. Parliament was due to assemble on 30 September. When it did, the king's presence was necessary to give it the status and power of a parliament. Obviously no one would allow Richard to take the throne when it assembled. But if the king did not attend, there was nothing to stop Henry's enemies – or more particularly, supporters of the Mortimer claim to the throne – from leaving. Therefore, instead of following the precedent of 1327, and using parliament to force the king to resign, the council (led no doubt by Henry) decided to do the reverse. The king would be required to resign first, before parliament even assembled, nullifying the writs which had been sent out in his name. And then he would be deposed by a 'parliament', or representatives of the estates, acting in their own name.

On the evening of 28 September a delegation led by the earls of Northumberland and Westmorland and the archbishop of York, and including representatives of the barons, clergy, knights and gentlemen of the realm, entered the Tower in the company of two lawyers and two notaries. They asked the king whether he would resign the throne. Richard's response was measured; he wanted to see a copy of the terms first. The lawyers with the delegation produced the document and presented it to him. He said he wished to study it, and would give them a reply in the morning. The delegation departed, promising to return the following day.

The following morning they found Richard in an angry mood. He refused to abdicate. Exactly why should he, a king, resign his throne? And to whom? Should he resign it to his designated heir – Edmund of Langley – or to Henry, his conqueror? The lords presented him with further arguments. The chronicler who recorded the details of Richard's outburst unfortunately did not record what these were, but it is possible that they threatened him with being declared illegitimate, either on the grounds that there were irregularities in the permission for his father and mother to marry or (more probably) because his mother was a woman easily linked with adulterous liaisons because of her first two marriages.[66] Faced with some such dire prospect, Richard began to waver, and after a time asked the delegation to bring Henry to him, stating that he was willing, upon certain conditions which he would explain to him, to give up the throne.

Henry arrived in a large cavalcade that evening. The archbishops of Canterbury and York were with him, along with the bishop of Hereford, Justice Thirning, and many other abbots, priors, lords and lawyers. With this assembly watching him, Richard repeated that he would resign the throne if Henry agreed to observe certain conditions. Henry immediately replied that he would accept no conditions. Richard had to abdicate simply, and without argument.

The pressure on Richard was tremendous. He tried to put a brave face on his plight and assumed a cheerful countenance. He read aloud the whole of the abdication document. Certain passages must have caused him to feel angry and perhaps remorseful, such as 'I confess, acknowledge and recognise and from my own certain knowledge truly admit that I have been and am entirely inadequate and unequal to the task of ruling and governing the kingdom . . .' But he read it to the end. Then he assented, and signed the document, stipulating that he reserved the right to withhold from the grant certain lands he had purchased with which to endow a priest to pray for him at Westminster after his death.

Immediately clerks were brought forward to record the names of the witnesses. As this was done, Richard spoke again. It was impossible for him to renounce those special dignities of a spiritual nature which had been bestowed upon him at his coronation, he explained. For example, he could not renounce his anointment. Justice Thirning answered, firmly stating that Richard had himself admitted in the renunciation to which he had just assented that he was not worthy or adequate of government. Richard, now a pathetic figure, replied that this was not true; it was just that he was not loved by the people. Justice Thirning reiterated the absoluteness of the renunciation. Richard smiled, and said nothing more on the subject. He simply asked to be allowed sufficient income to maintain himself honourably.

In that solemn, shattering act, a king was unmade. Henry left the Tower that night. He never saw his cousin alive again.

*

The following morning, between noon and one o'clock on Tuesday 30 September, Henry took his place in the great hall of the Palace of Westminster. It was the seat reserved for him as the duke of Lancaster, which his father had always occupied. But he did not do this humbly, as a mere duke; it was important for him to appear like a king if he wished to be accepted as one. The monks of Westminster had come out to meet him as he had arrived at Westminster that morning. They had sung responses as they accompanied him into the church to hear Mass. After the service, Henry was led in procession to Westminster Hall by the two archbishops, his own four sons and Sir Thomas Erpingham carrying a magnificent jewelled sword before him. This sword was 'Lancaster Sword', a new sword of state, being the one Henry himself had carried at Ravenspur. Behind him came the three Counter-Appellant dukes: Exeter, Surrey and Aumale. The whole of the yard outside was filled with people, thronging to catch a glimpse of Henry as he entered the hall.

The throne, draped in cloth of gold, stood vacant. Everyone present knew what was happening; the writs to this parliament had been withdrawn, on account of the king's resignation. They were all aware that this was not a parliament but an assembly, and its sole purpose was the ratification of the old king's deposition and the confirmation of the inheritance of his successor.

The atmosphere was exhilarating; a 'frenzy' gripped Westminster.[67] As Thomas Arundel had not formally been reinstated as archbishop of Canterbury, it fell to the archbishop of York to open proceedings. He took his theme from Isaiah 51: 16 – 'He has put his words into my mouth' – and charged the assembly with a sense of divine responsibility as well as political momentousness. The lawyer John Burbach solemnly read out Richard's renunciation of the throne. He explained that Richard had resigned 'cheerfully' – no mention was made of the king's initial refusal to abdicate – and stated that Richard had expressed a wish that Henry be his successor. Whether or not this was the case, there was no doubt that it was the will of almost everyone present that Henry be crowned. At that moment it did not matter whether he was first, second or tenth in line to the throne: he was the leader of the opposition and the hero of the hour. When Thomas Arundel stepped forward, and dramatically asked them whether they assented to the king's resignation, he was merely giving the people the chance to express the mood of the whole country. 'Yes! Yes! Yes!' they all shouted, in loud and excited voices.[68]

When the calls for the king's resignation to be accepted had died down, Thomas Arundel declared that, for the benefit and advantage of the realm, the specific wrongdoings and shortcomings of Richard's government should be clearly set down and confirmed. Although it might be said that deposition was unnecessary in the light of Richard's resignation, there was an awareness that Richard might at some point in the future claim he had acted under duress, and change his mind. He had revoked pardons to others; there was a good likelihood he would revoke his own resignation if he got the chance. So the lawyer John Ferriby stepped forward to read out a list of thirty-three charges against the king.

Although the charges were framed by lawyers, and not written up by Henry himself, there is no doubt that Henry was involved in the discussions leading to their creation. So it is interesting that the first three all relate to the events of 1386–7. Just as Richard had never forgiven those who had taken action against him in parliament in 1386, so Henry too was still motivated by the events of that year. Whatever deals Henry and his father might have tried to negotiate along the way, whatever compromises had been sorted out, these were nothing more than rope bridges over deep chasms in the relationship between the king and the nobility. The events leading up to Radcot Bridge, which had taken place when both Richard and Henry were under age, were now among the principal reasons for deposing the king.

The next charges against Richard concerned his treatment of the Lords Appellant since 1387. The unlawful seizure and murder of the duke of Gloucester was mentioned, as well as the imprisonment of the earl of Warwick and Lord Cobham. The impeachment of the earls of Arundel and Warwick after they had received pardons was denounced, and so too was Richard's use of Cheshire archers to threaten people attending parliament and as instruments of his terror elsewhere in the kingdom. The seventh charge drew attention to other communities which had paid for letters of pardon, in compliance with the king's demands, only to find that they could not benefit from such pardons until they had paid the king yet more money. The eighth pointed out that Richard had falsified the rolls of parliament in order to give his actions in this regard greater authority.

Three of the charges related to crimes committed by Richard against Henry himself. Contrary to his coronation oath, the king had decreed that no one should intercede with him to try and obtain a pardon for Henry in his exile. Clause eleven stated that Richard 'without any legitimate cause, ordered the said duke of Lancaster to be banished for ten years, contrary to all justice'. Doing this against the law of arms – refusing to allow Henry to fight his duel – was construed as an act of perjury as well. Clause twelve was similarly phrased as an act of perjury: although Richard had given Henry letters guaranteeing that he could receive his inheritance through his attorneys, these had been revoked, contrary to the law.

The language of the charges against Richard is certainly legalistic but the message overall was clearly Henry's. On many matters of justice, Richard had acted in a selfish and arbitrary way, like a spoilt child. After thirty-three counts of tyranny, perjury, misappropriation of funds, murder, harassment, maintenance, toleration of violence and rape committed by his Cheshire archers, deception, dishonesty, theft, wrongful imprisonment (contrary to the terms of Magna Carta) and the removal from office and exile of the archbishop of Canterbury without trial – nearly all of which are supported by damning evidence extant today – there was no doubt in anyone's mind that the man they were removing was one of the worst rulers England had ever known.

It is in this light of popular exuberance that we should see Henry stepping forward to claim the throne. Rarely has parliament been so charged with energy. Henry was not only the foremost living victim of Richard's tyranny, he was the leader who had put an end to it. His reputation as the deliverer of England, which had been growing since he had reached Doncaster, was now at its absolute height. Thus, as much as Richard was now openly derided, Henry was championed. When the bishop of St Asaph declared on the behalf of the representatives of the estates that the throne of England was now vacant, Henry rose from his seat. Standing before the assembly, he made the sign of the cross on his forehead and on his breast, and made a speech in English. The officially enrolled version of this is as follows:

In the name of the Father, Son and Holy Ghost, I, Henry of Lancaster claim this realm of England, and the Crown with all its members and appurtenances, as I am descended by right line of the blood coming from the good lord King Henry the Third, and through that right, God of his grace has sent me, with the help of my kin and my friends, to recover it; the which realm was at the point of ruin for the default of governance and the undoing of good laws.

Henry's exact words are open to question. He probably claimed to be the 'nearest male heir and worthiest blood-descendant of Henry III, son of King John'.[69] He may also have displayed a copy of his own descent from Henry III. But whatever he actually said, the essence of his claim is clear. So too is the approbation with which it was received. He was not only king by strict male inheritance, he was king by election too.[70] When the members of parliament were collectively called upon to deliver their judgement as to Henry's right to be king, they responded with shouts of 'Yes! Yes! Yes!' as enthusiastically as they had done when asked whether they assented to the old king's resignation.

Even that collective vote of confidence in him was not enough for those orchestrating this transition of power. Henry's advisers sought to capitalise on the spirit of the moment by asking for everyone present to affirm their support for the new regime. According to Creton, each man was asked in turn whether he would have the duke of York for his king, or whether the duke of Aumale, or York's younger son, Richard. To all these alternatives the people said 'no': to Henry, they said 'Yes, we will have no other'.[71] Henry seems to have been embarrassed by this demand for such personal demonstrations of loyalty.[72] 'We beg you not simply to speak these words with your mouths if they do not come from your hearts, but to agree to them with your hearts as well as your mouths', said Henry, adding 'should it happen that some of you do not in your hearts assent to this, it would be of no surprise to me'. Nevertheless the prelates were all asked by John Norbury whether they agreed with Henry's claim and, with the possible exception of the bishop of Carlisle, each of them said yes.[73] The earl of Northumberland asked the same question of the secular lords, with the same unanimous response.

There could be no doubt now. The climactic moment had come. The duke of York, the archbishop of York and Thomas Arundel (shortly to be restored as the archbishop of Canterbury) went to Henry, kissed his hands, and led him up to the throne. Standing there, before the gold-covered seat, Henry bent his knee and said a prayer. Rising, he made the sign of the cross on both the front and back of the throne, and then, flanked by the two archbishops, he sat down. It was the visual signal the crowd were looking for, the culmination of the revolution. Inside the hall and out, the people were jubilant, those inside cheering enthusiastically and those outside adding a massive crescendo of support which Henry could not have failed to hear. There was clapping and throwing of hoods in the air. Thomas Arundel, ready with his sermon on God's approval of Henry's accession, tried to quieten the crowd but they would not have it. The applause was an outpouring of relief. If this was 'usurpation' – as it is usually described – it was the most popular usurpation in English history.

Arundel finally called for silence, and began to preach his sermon. A flood of biblical lines poured forth, all delivered by a confident and conscientious prelate to an assembly which was awestruck by the events of the day. Significantly, the key theme of the sermon was of the preference for a nation to be ruled by a man and not a boy. 'It is certain that a child is inconstant in speaking, he easily speaks the truth, easily tells lies; he easily promises with a word but that word he quickly forgets. These things are inappropriate and extremely damaging to a kingdom . . .' Perhaps the most telling lines were, 'When therefore a boy reigns, will alone reigns, and reason is exiled . . . From this danger we have been freed because a man rules, who rules not as a child but as one perfect in reason.' No one present could have failed to recognise what Arundel was saying. Richard had been a child when he had acceded to the throne and his rule had been one of will over reason. Edmund Mortimer was also still a child, younger even than Richard had been when he had inherited. The sermon was principally a justification of the pragmatic decision to have Henry as king rather than to follow the common law (allowing female inheritance) or royal successor-designation, and risk another turbulent reign.

Following Arundel's sermon, Henry thanked the assembly, and promised them that 'it is not my will that any man should think that by way of conquest I would disinherit him from his inheritance, his franchise, or any other rights that he ought to have, nor would I put him out of that which he has and has had by the good laws and customs of the realm'. Those who had been office holders under Richard surrendered their marks of office and received them back from Henry, their positions confirmed. Finally Arundel announced that Henry's first parliament would sit on 6 October, and his coronation would take place on the 13th.

After years of living in Richard's shadow – after years of trying to prove himself with a lance, or in crusades and pilgrimages – Henry was king of England. The prophecy which Froissart had heard in 1361 – that the house of Lancaster would inherit the throne – had come true. And more than that, Henry had lived up to his father's expectations. Looking down from the throne at the empty seat of the dukes of Lancaster, he no doubt realised that a chapter in English history had come to an end. What he could not possibly have realised was what the new chapter would hold. No one had ever done what he had accomplished, so he had no idea what the terrible consequences would be for him and his family. He would have to learn for himself what it was to be a hostage to the mood of the people, especially a people who now knew they had the power to dethrone a king.

TEN

High Sparks of Honour

For though mine enemy thou hast ever been,
High sparks of honour in thee have I seen.
Richard II, Act 5, Scene 6

The day on which Henry was crowned – 13 October 1399 – was one of special significance. It was exactly a year since he had said goodbye to his father for the last time at Dover, and had stepped on board the boat taking him into exile. It also marked the feast of St Edward the Confessor, the saint-king with whom Richard had repeatedly tried to associate himself. It was thus a statement of regal as well as personal importance, and an invocation of the saint's protection of Henry and his dynasty in the years to come.

Henry and his advisers knew exactly what they were doing when it came to making him a king. He himself had been close to the ceremonies of royalty all his life, and understood them. In addition, his had been a most unorthodox accession, and so every symbol of kingship – both secular and divine – was employed to underline the correctness of the ceremony. He wore cloth of gold, and made the traditional procession from the Tower to Westminster Abbey on the day of his coronation. He went bareheaded as custom dictated, despite the autumn rain. Six thousand men followed him, it was said, and nine water fountains were made to run with red wine in Cheapside. In Westminster Abbey, seated on the throne, he received the insignia and swore the same four-part coronation oath as Richard had done. It was all scrupulously correct, in line with parliament's advice that 'nothing which ought to be done should be left undone'.[1]

The ceremony was not without innovation. Four swords of state were employed, rather than the traditional three. The two swords of justice, 'wrapped in red and bound with gold straps', were carried by the earls of Somerset and Warwick. Curtana, the blunt sword of mercy, was held by Henry's eldest son, Henry.[2] But before them all went Lancaster Sword, borne by the earl of Northumberland. Another innovation took place on the eve of the coronation. Henry knighted about fifty men, creating a second royal order of knighthood, the Order of the Bath, in emulation of

Edward III's Order of the Garter, created fifty years earlier.[3] To add weight to his family's royalty, three of the first knights were his younger sons, Thomas, John and Humphrey.

In the most famous of all these innovations, Henry was anointed with a sacred oil, the oil of St Thomas. Almost a century earlier, the duke of Brabant had brought this oil to England, with the intention that it would be used at Edward II's coronation. It had supposedly been given to St Thomas Becket by the Virgin, who appeared to him in a dream. She had told Becket that it was for the benefit of the fifth king of England after St Thomas's time (Edward II) *and his successors*, to help them fight for God's Church and recover the Holy Land.[4] Despite the duke of Brabant's good intentions, Edward II had not been anointed with the oil. Instead it had been given to the Black Prince, then sealed in a chest in the Tower and forgotten. It had eventually been rediscovered by Richard II himself. Richard had asked the then archbishop of Canterbury, Thomas Arundel, to anoint him with it. Arundel had refused, but Richard had kept the oil with him nonetheless and had only parted with it after his capture. That Henry now became the first king to be anointed with this holy oil – lying down in front of the high altar, his clothes being opened in four places to receive it – added divine sanction to his regal promotion.[5]

The feast which followed the coronation was a grand affair. The four sword-bearers stood around the king throughout.[6] Lord Latimer stood alongside them holding the sceptre; the earl of Westmorland held the rod. Every bow of ceremonial etiquette was rigidly observed. One took place even though it was unplanned. As the duke of Aumale and the young earl of Arundel were dispensing wine to the king, there was an almighty crash and much shouting as a knight rode into the hall in full armour. He was arrayed as if for war, and his horse too was in armour. His name, he announced to all present, was Sir Thomas Dymocke, and he claimed the right by inheritance of his mother, the lady of the manor of Scrivelsby, to challenge to a duel anyone who doubted the king's right to the throne. No one spoke, even though Sir Thomas rode around the hall several times looking for an opponent. It was Henry himself who brought this display of chivalric fervour to an end, saying, 'if need be, Sir Thomas, I shall personally relieve you of this duty'.[7]

*

Parliament resumed its session on the day after the coronation. It had previously met on 6 October, when the restored archbishop of Canterbury, Thomas Arundel, had delivered the opening speech. Henry was a 'wise and prudent man', the archbishop had declared. He had been 'sent by

God through his great grace and mercy to govern the realm . . . and wished to be ruled and advised by the wise men and elders of the realm, for his own advantage and assistance and that of all his realm'.[8] These were high ideals indeed, especially as Henry was about to preside over a parliament which included men who had plotted against his life. Therefore it is important to ask what Henry's intentions as king actually were. How far did he wish to be ruled by the 'wise men and elders'? What was his vision of his kingship?

The most important element of Henry's kingship was his intention to end his cousin's experiment in autocratic rule. It comes as no surprise to see that one of Henry's first acts as king was to repeal the proceedings of the Revenge Parliament. This of course reduced the power of the monarch, for it wiped out Richard's perpetual grant of the wool subsidy. Henry also repealed the judgements on those who had been condemned in the Revenge Parliament, and reinstated the decisions of the Merciless Parliament as lawful and correct, even though he himself had not agreed with all of the verdicts at the time. He annulled the blank charters by which Richard had sought to control the sixteen counties and London, and had them publicly destroyed by the chancellor. All this was expected of him: it was the understanding upon which he had been welcomed back to England.

Henry's plans for governing in future (as opposed to undoing the wrongs of the past) may be connected back to the oath he swore at Doncaster, and in particular his policy of not levying direct taxation in peacetime. Through Sir Thomas Erpingham and the earl of Northumberland, he assured the prelates of his intention not to levy taxes except in times of war. Unlike Richard, Henry would 'live off his own', as he put it: from the revenue of customs duties, the royal estates, the royal treasury and his own great Lancastrian inheritance.

At the same time as promising the prelates that he would not levy taxes, he promised them that he would not tolerate heresy. This religious dimension to his vision of kingship is in keeping with everything we know about his religious orthodoxy prior to his accession: from his washing paupers' feet on Maundy Thursday to his journey to Jerusalem. But his very accession enlarged his spiritual conviction. As Arundel had proclaimed, it had been by God's grace that he had redeemed England from Richard's rule. In fact, his personal crisis in 1398–9 seems to have brought out the sense of the divine particularly strongly in him, marked by a number of references to the Trinity. The peace treaty he had sealed with the duke of Orléans in France earlier in the year had been agreed 'in the name of the Almighty and the most holy Trinity'.[9] The motto he gave to his new order of chivalry – *Tria juncto in uno* ('the three joined in one') – was a direct reference to the Holy Trinity. Occasionally he ended his letters not with a wish that the Almighty would keep the recipient in good health but that 'the Blessed Trinity would grant you joy and health always'.[10] Others wrote to him with this same salutation, including his lifelong friend Richard Kingston, his sons Henry and John, his half-sister Catalina, and his future wife, Joan of Navarre.[11] Later in life he continued to make his devotions to the Trinity, and to incorporate images of the Trinity into his buildings. Parliamentary petitions were offered to him 'in honour of the Trinity'.[12] Most significantly of all, he requested to be buried at Canterbury Cathedral and was laid to rest alongside his uncle and fellow Trinity follower, the Black Prince, in the Trinity Chapel. Indeed, he may have originally been attracted to the Trinity precisely because it had been famously sponsored by the Black Prince, a chivalric hero.[13] Whatever the reason for it, such particular and consistent devotion to the Trinity points to a firm and pious outlook, underlined by his declaration against heresy.

These elements of Henry's kingship – the determination to rule in conjunction with the great men of the realm, taxation only in wartime, religious orthodoxy, and the establishment of a chivalric order – are all reminiscent of Edward III's kingship. Even the language in which he made his speeches – English – harks back to Edward III's use of English to stir up nationalist sentiment. These parallels between Henry in October 1399 and Edward III are not a coincidence. By 1399, Edward III's reign had come to be seen as a golden age, being peaceful at home and glorious abroad: everything which Richard II's reign was not.[14] Hence we find Henry likened to his grandfather out of hope as well as the obvious parallel between their knightly virtues. Edward III's epitaph in Westminster Abbey recorded that he was 'the undefeated warrior, a second Maccabeus'. When Arundel preached Henry's virtues to the people, he described him also as 'another Maccabeus'.[15] Similarly, Edward III's epitaph states he was 'a merciful king, the bringer of peace to his people'. On the day of the coronation, Adam Usk overheard Henry promising Archbishop Arundel that he would 'strive to rule his people with mercy and truthfulness in all matters'.[16] As will be seen, mercy was perhaps the most pronounced of all the elements of Edward III's kingship which Henry now adopted for his own, and it was present from the start.

In this light of modelling his reign on that of Edward III, it is no surprise to see that Henry's vision of kingship included warfare. Just as Edward III had won great victories in France and Scotland, so Henry promised to win them too. As it happened, the Scots attacked Wark Castle during the parliament, taking advantage of the fact that the wardens of the Marches (the earls of Northumberland and Westmorland) were both at Westminster.

The Scots seized the wife and family of Thomas Grey and held them to ransom, and destroyed Wark, in contravention of the truce. Shortly after this, on 10 November, Henry received a letter from the king of Scotland, Robert III, refusing to acknowledge him as king and loftily declaring that past breaches of the truce should be discussed at Haddenstank, a point well within English territory, as if that was now the official border.[17] Henry's reaction was uncompromising. In an emotional speech to the lords on 10 November, Henry declared his intention to lead an army against the Scots.[18] As for the war with France, although his initial move was to make peace, and to secure that peace through a marriage between one of his sons and Isabella, when that hope foundered he stated his warlike intentions in a speech during a procession through London. 'I swear and promise to you that neither his highness my grandfather King Edward, nor my uncle the prince of Wales, ever went so far forward in France as I will do, if it please God and St George, or I will die in the attempt.'[19]

As a result of all this, we have a clear picture of Henry's vision of his kingship at the outset of his reign as that of a pious and conservative leader, merciful to his people, leading them in victorious battles overseas, maintaining peace at home, working with parliament and facilitating the economic prosperity of the nation. This innate conservatism goes a long way to explain why Henry was so popular at his coronation, in the wake of the radically individual Richard. His ideas about kingship were familiar to all: reminiscent not only of Edward III but also of the Old Testament kings: 'merciful to their people and terrifying to their enemies'. Yet this was a form of kingship whose most vivid colours had already begun to fade. An early fifteenth-century king could not hope to impose spiritual orthodoxy on his people and avoid controversy. Lollardy had affected the religious outlook of the Church in England too much for there to be complete unity ever again. Similarly, it was increasingly hard to equate overseas warfare with economic prosperity at home. Overseas wars cost a lot of money, and that meant direct taxation. Victories over the French, Scots and Spanish still had their place (as shown at Agincourt in 1415), but such conflicts were difficult to justify economically. The mechanics of war were changing too, with guns and longbows replacing the massed charge of knights, so that chivalry had lost much of its purpose. Lastly, the relationship between king and parliament had changed. Whereas Edward III had been forced to work closely with parliament, Henry unwittingly compromised himself at the outset, in declaring his objective of cooperating with parliament as a matter of principle (a position from which he later had to withdraw). Therefore, although Henry's vision reflected the greatest form of kingship then known, it was already out of date. Even if he managed to satisfy a few or all of his competing priorities for a short while, he could not continue to do so for long. It sounded magnificent to his people, and resounded in parliament, but it was much easier to announce than to perform.

*

Henry's principal aims in his first parliament were to make his dynasty secure and to administer justice for those who had benefited from, or been victimised by, the old regime. In line with the first of these, he created his eldest son prince of Wales, duke of Aquitaine and earl of Chester – the traditional titles for the king's son to bear – and had him recognised in parliament as heir to the throne. He also gave him the title of duke of Lancaster. All four of his sons were nominated as Knights of the Garter. No matter what happened to Henry himself, his dynasty was as safe as he could reasonably make it.

Justice was a much more complicated issue. Many people at that parliament wanted Richard to be put to death. Many more wanted those who had benefited from his reign to be punished as traitors. Part of the problem was that the very concept of treason had been greatly enlarged by Richard to encompass anyone who dared disagree with him: in Richard's own words 'he is a child of death who offends the king'.[20] Thus the first step towards re-establishing justice in such matters was to reaffirm Edward III's Statute of Treasons as the proper measure by which traitors should be judged. This was done on 15 October.

Nothing, however, could entirely smooth the path which Henry and those at that parliament had now to tread. When the Speaker, John Doreward, asked that all of Richard II's 'evil counsellors' be arrested, many saw an opportunity to revenge themselves on Richard's companions. William Bagot, who had been captured in Ireland and brought back in chains by Peter Bucton, was the first 'evil counsellor' summoned before parliament, on 16 October.[21] He had already submitted a bill to Henry which outlined a defence of sorts, based partly on his alerting Henry to Richard's ill will in March 1399. But the main thrust of his defence was that the duke of Aumale had been the principal 'evil counsellor'. He directly accused the duke of at least two treasonable acts (being an accessory to the murder of the duke of Gloucester and expressing a desire that Henry himself might be killed). He was asked whether he stood by the terms of his bill, and he swore that he did. 'It was you', he said to the duke in person, 'who said that if the duke of Gloucester, and the earls of Arundel and Warwick, and others were not killed, the king would never be able to exercise his regal power to the full.' In addition, he stated that

Mowbray and himself had urged Richard to resign in favour of Henry. Richard had retorted that he would never do so on account of his belief that Henry 'is a worthless man at heart, and will always remain so. Besides, if he were to rule the kingdom, he would want to destroy the whole of God's Holy Church.'[22]

Henry felt the need to defend himself on this point. 'With the grace of God, I will show such a prediction to be quite false', he declared, adding that he had taken a vow to uphold, protect and support God's Church with as much zeal as any of his predecessors. 'But I hope to see men appointed to churches who are worthy of their position, unlike many of those who were appointed in Richard's reign.'[23]

Meanwhile Edward, duke of Aumale, was seething with fury at Bagot's accusations. He knew he was now on trial for his life. 'If the duke of Norfolk maintains that I sent two yeomen to Calais to see to the duke of Gloucester's death', he bellowed, referring to Bagot's informant, 'then I say that he lies falsely, and I shall prove it with my body!'[24] And with that he flung his hood at the feet of Bagot in the middle of the hall, challenging him to a duel.

Henry was in a difficult position. Both men were guilty. But Bagot had probably saved Henry's father from being murdered in January 1398 and had subsequently been a useful informer. As for the duke of Aumale, despite being Richard II's adopted brother, he had been part of the plot to arrest the king in July, triggering his flight to North Wales. His father, the duke of York, had practically acted as kingmaker at Berkeley. Despite their guilt, Henry could not afford to punish either man severely. He ordered the duke to pick up his hood and return to his seat.

Bagot was asked why he had consented to so much of the bad advice which the king had received. His reply is revealing of the fear which had prevailed at court during the last days of Richard's rule. 'Is there any one among you all who, if King Richard had demanded a certain thing from you, would have dared to disagree with him, or not have complied with his order?'

John Norbury, whom Henry had appointed treasurer, stepped forward and claimed that he for one would have refused. But Norbury was a mere esquire, and protected by Henry. It was hardly fair to compare him in his current safe position with the dukes and earls in Richard's line of sight a year earlier. Henry himself had been forced to accede to the proceedings of the Revenge Parliament. He knew that Bagot was speaking the truth.

Bagot went on to incriminate other great lords present, especially those who had been among the Counter-Appellants. The dukes of Surrey and Exeter threw down their hoods, challenging him for accusing them of being complicit in the murder of the duke of Gloucester. Again, Henry ordered them to step forward and pick up their hoods themselves. Bagot saw that he had an opportunity to prove the substance of what he was saying. 'If you really want to know who was responsible for the murder, then you ought to question a valet named John Hall, who is now in prison in Newgate', he said. Hearing this, Henry gave instructions to his clerk, James Billingford, to interrogate Hall.

The following day, while Hall was being questioned, Henry summoned all the lords with the exception of the three dukes whom Bagot had accused (Aumale, Surrey and Exeter). He wanted to know whether these three should be arrested or not. Lord Cobham, a victim of the Revenge Parliament, was firmly of the opinion that they should. Those who had incited or encouraged the king in his malice should be punished too. They had referred to themselves as the 'foster-children' of Richard, and, Cobham claimed, 'as the foster-parent is, so shall the foster-children be'. He added that he said this not for the sake of revenge but for common justice. The other lords unanimously agreed.[25]

Henry was picking his way shrewdly between the potential pitfalls of royal judgement. After the discussion about the dukes, he considered a petition of the earl of Warwick to delete the record of his shameful confession in the Revenge Parliament. He refused, on the grounds that he could not justify obliterating the record of what so many knew to have taken place. Next he showed similar wisdom in responding to the commons' calls for *all* the evil counsellors who had advised Richard to be brought to justice. He replied that some were already in custody, and others could be arrested at short notice, if the commons would be more explicit as to whom they suspected. That silenced the commons, who realised that there would be no general blood-letting by the new king to purge the country of his predecessor's crimes.

Bagot appeared again on 18 October and was questioned further by Thomas Percy, earl of Worcester. He resorted to a defence based on letters of pardon he had received, which were then at Chester. Henry ordered that he be held in custody while parliament attended to its next item of business: the confession of John Hall.

Poor John Hall was one of the most unfortunate men of the fourteenth century. He was not only in the wrong place at the wrong time but also in the service of the wrong man, Thomas Mowbray, who ordered him to do a very wrong thing. Hall had been asleep in his house at Calais when Mowbray came to him and demanded to know what he had heard of the duke of Gloucester. Hall replied that he had heard that he was dead. Mowbray then told him that he was not, but the king and the duke of

Aumale had sent men to kill him. Hall was one of six valets who would represent Mowbray at the murder, along with two valets of the duke of Aumale and William Serle, Richard II's man. Hall was horrified, and prayed that he might be forgiven for not doing this, even to the loss of all his goods, but Mowbray struck him hard and ordered him to obey. Hall himself played no part in the actual killing (or so he claimed). But he stood by with the others as William Serle and one of the duke of Aumale's valets named Frauncis smothered the king's uncle.

Hall's confession was deeply shocking. The mismatch between the royal status of the victim and his lowly murderers was deeply troubling to the lords present. As he waited there in shackles and manacles, not knowing his fate, Hall saw the bitter recriminations fly. The duke of Aumale tried to exonerate himself, but Lord Fitzwalter launched into a tirade. 'It was you who appealed him of treason', he shouted at Aumale, 'you who brought accusations against him, and you who made the king hate him; and for all these reasons it was you who brought about his death, which I shall prove in battle.'

At this the duke of Surrey, realising that the Counter-Appellants' only hope was to stick together, defended Aumale. 'You are always interfering', he snapped at Lord Fitzwalter, 'you talk too much. Why are you so eager to accuse us on the grounds of this appeal when in fact there was no way that we could have avoided doing what we did at the time? When we were so much in the king's power, and in so many ways under his authority, how could we dare disobey any command that he gave us?' Then the duke accused Fitzwalter of also acquiescing to the appeal against Thomas of Woodstock. There he fell into a trap, as Fitzwalter was able to claim he had not been present at the time. So Surrey was forced to sit down.

Lord Fitzwalter resumed his attack on Aumale. 'You were cause of the duke of Gloucester's death. You were midwife to his murder. And this I shall prove by battle!' he declared, throwing down his hood. Aumale, angered and fearful, responded by throwing down his own hood. But even without Hall's testimony, many lords there believed that he had indeed countenanced the royal murder. A wave of outrage and shouting rose through the hall. The earl of Warwick, Lord Morley and Lord Beauchamp were just three of the lords who threw down their hoods, and the commons roared like men so angry that it seemed as if a battle would break out there and then, if justice was not done.

Amid this, Henry called for silence. He stood up. First he begged them not to do anything that was against the law. Then, with a growing sternness, he warned them of the consequences if they lynched the duke of Aumale or anyone else in parliament. Finally he ordered them to act legally and to restrain themselves until proper discussions had taken place. It was an impressive speech, and it stopped all those who had been about to seize the duke of Aumale. Unfortunately for John Hall, it focused attention back on him. When Henry called for judgement by the lords upon the wretch, there was only one fate suitable to the moment. Despite having done nothing but witness the murder – and that against his will – Hall was ordered to be drawn to Tyburn, hanged and then cut down and disembowelled alive, with his entrails being burned in front of him. Then he was to be beheaded and cut into quarters, and the parts of his body publicly displayed, with his head being sent to Calais, where the murder had taken place. It was the full traitor's death, the disembowelling being a particularly harsh treatment reserved for those of the worst kind.[26] The sentence was carried out immediately.

The next day was Sunday, and so parliament did not sit. On the Monday the king's ceremonial bath took place, it being a week since his coronation. No parliamentary business was conducted that day, but Henry had all six surviving Counter-Appellants arrested: the dukes of Aumale, Exeter and Surrey, John Beaufort, marquis of Dorset, Thomas Despenser, earl of Gloucester, and John Montagu, earl of Salisbury. They were questioned over the following week.

Meanwhile parliament deliberated the future of Richard II. The commons wanted him brought into parliament to be tried, but Henry did not agree. Instead he replied that he wished to consult with the prelates before making a decision. The commons responded by asking Henry to assign legal advisers to help them deliberate further on the matter. Henry did so, and for three days they debated the ex-king's fate. Henry in the meantime asked the earl of Northumberland to consult the lords about the same issue. In particular the lords were asked how the ex-king 'should be kept in safekeeping, saving his life, which the king wished to be preserved to him in all events'.[27] They were not at liberty to demand the death penalty. Archbishop Arundel made a preliminary address, requiring them all to keep their advice secret.

On 27 October parliament met again – lords, prelates and commons together – to hear the judgement on Richard II. The lords had come to an opinion, to which all fifty-eight of them had set their names: two archbishops, thirteen bishops, seven abbots, Prince Henry, the duke of York, six earls, twenty-four lords and four knights. In their view, Richard should be 'kept under safe and close guard, in some place where there was no coming and going of people; and that he should be guarded by reliable and competent men'; and that none of his previous companions should be allowed to come into his presence; and that everything concerning his keeping 'should be done in the most secret manner possible'.[28] The commons unanimously agreed. Richard would be confined in isolation in perpetuity. Two days later, in accordance with parliament's wishes, the ex-king was secretly removed from the Tower by night and taken via various castles to Knaresborough, and finally to the great Lancastrian stronghold of Pontefract, to be guarded by Henry's trusted friends, Robert Waterton and Thomas Swynford.[29]

With Richard's sentence agreed, the trial of the Counter-Appellants could go ahead. A good deal of hood-throwing ensued, as several men challenged each other to mortal combat. Each of the accused lords claimed that they had never consented to, nor known about, the murder of the duke of Gloucester, and that they had only participated in the Revenge Parliament out of fear of the king. Henry asked the lords to deliver judgement; but they declined, and passed the problem back to him. They only stipulated that the security of the kingdom should be his top priority. The prelates added that they hoped the men's lives would be spared. On 3 November, Chief Justice Thirning delivered judgement on them. They were to lose all their new titles acquired in September 1397, and any grants of land they had received since then. Otherwise they were to retain their old titles and inherited lands, and go free.

It was an incredibly lenient sentence, so much so that it needed an official explanation. Three key points were made: (1) that the foremost consideration had been the security of the realm, as the lords had requested, for leniency would incline these men to support the new king; and besides, it was specifically laid down that any attempt by the Counter-Appellant lords to restore Richard would be regarded as treason; (2) that the commons had intended that the evils of the Revenge Parliament 'should be reversed and amended in this parliament', which had been done; and (3) that, if these men were traitors, then the full penalty of the law should also be meted out on others not yet accused. On this point, Henry explained that he did not want to threaten the people 'but should make his judgements in righteousness and truth, with mercy and grace'.

The key in all this seems to be Henry's understanding that a great king should be merciful. Indeed, one might go so far as to call it the 'Merciful Parliament'. He had promised mercy, and he had delivered it. This is most clearly revealed in his treatment of Richard's closest advisers. Six prelates and five secular lords had witnessed Richard II's last charter (dated 23 June 1399), and these same eleven men had witnessed most of Richard's charters during the period of his tyranny.[30] Of the prelates, four – the archbishop of York and the bishops of London, Winchester and Exeter – continued to witness Henry's charters as if there had been no change of regime. The other two were dealt with very leniently: Roger Walden, who had presumed to take Archbishop Arundel's place in his exile, was only temporarily arrested, and four years later was nominated by Henry for a bishopric. Guy Mone, bishop of St Asaph, suffered no loss of status or property and was reappointed as treasurer by Henry in 1402. As for the secular lords, only one (William Scrope, executed for armed resistance) had been killed in the course of the revolution. The Counter-Appellants John Beaufort and John Montagu, earl of Salisbury, were dealt with very leniently, as mentioned above. John Beaufort was actually given the office of royal chamberlain, despite being stripped of his marquisate. The last two – Thomas Percy, earl of Worcester, and Richard Clifford, keeper of the privy seal – were also given royal appointments by Henry. Percy was chosen to lead an embassy to France to negotiate a marriage between the French royal family and Henry's own children, and Clifford remained in post as keeper of the privy seal. Thus of the ten surviving charter witnesses none suffered a dire punishment. They were all treated leniently, even though they were among Richard's closest companions and supporters. Bagot too was spared the axe. Most significantly, Richard II himself was allowed to live, at Henry's personal command. In fact, Henry was thought to have been too merciful. A number of those present in the parliament accused him of accepting bribes to save these men's lives, and an anonymous letter was found not long after in the king's chamber, threatening him with deposition for treating Richard's supporters so leniently.

At the end of his first parliament, on 19 November 1399, Henry could feel very satisfied with his performance. He had shown great tact in dealing with tricky matters, such as the earl of Warwick's repeated requests to erase the official record of his confession, and the calls for the duke of Aumale to be executed. In matters of judgement, no victim had been dealt with harshly except John Hall, whose bloody fate met with universal approval. Thomas Haxey at last received a full pardon for presenting his petition for reforming the royal household, and William Rickhill was exonerated for obtaining the confession of the duke of Gloucester. Henry had also shown he had personal authority too. When parliament had almost collapsed in disarray, he had taken control of proceedings in person and impressed the assembly with an impromptu speech. And he had proved himself a man as good as his word in living up to his oaths not to levy direct taxes except in wartime. The only significant shadows in his first parliament were an awareness voiced by the commons that he was rewarding those who had supported him with more than he could afford, and an unease that he might have been too merciful in dealing with the Counter-Appellants.

*

On 17 December a group of men secretly met in a chamber of the abbot's lodging at Westminster Abbey. They included five of the six Counter-Appellants who had been tried in the parliament and who had forfeited their titles. Only John Beaufort, Henry's half-brother, was not there. With these five were the abbot of Westminster, the ousted archbishop of Canterbury, Roger Walden (who was being looked after by the abbot), the bishop of Carlisle, Master Pol (Richard's physician), Sir Thomas Blount and Richard Maudeleyn, an esquire.[31]

The reason why lowly Maudeleyn was present in such noble company was that he looked very like King Richard – so much so that he could impersonate the ex-king. Hence he was essential to the plan which these men now discussed. On 6 January 1400, Epiphany, Henry was planning to hold a great tournament at Windsor. The lords had been invited to attend. They planned to assemble their forces quietly at Kingston from 1 January. The lords themselves would go to Windsor on the evening of the 4th to assassinate Henry, the archbishop of Canterbury, and all four of Henry's sons, and give the signal for their armies to advance and seize several leading towns. Richard Maudeleyn's role was to dress in armour and act the part of the king so that Londoners would gather to the royal banner and march against anyone who continued to support Henry, until they could recover the real Richard from his place of imprisonment.

What happened on 4 January is not exactly clear. According to one chronicle, the former duke of Aumale, Edward, dined with his father, the duke of York, on the evening of the 3rd and left an indenture of his confederacy confirming his involvement in the plot on the table, where his father could see it, prompting father and son to agree to betray the plot.[32] According to another, a royal man-at-arms spent that night with a London prostitute and heard of the plot from her, she having slept the night before with a man in the service of one of the rebel lords.[33] There are problems with both stories. With regard to the first, which is a deeply biased French source, it is extremely unlikely that men plotting treason would seal indentures of confederacy, for to do so would be an unnecessary security risk; it would be enough for them all to swear a solemn oath together. Rather this seems to be a literary device introduced by the chronicler to explain why it was that Edward betrayed the conspiracy and brought the news of the plot to the king. What is certain is that Edward was the only one of the lords gathered at that meeting on the 17th who was never punished by Henry. In fact he was not even charged with having been part of the conspiracy.[34] Thus we may be confident that he broke the news to the king, as at least two other chronicles state.[35] This might explain the second story, which seems to be a smokescreen to conceal the identity of Henry's informant. It is very possible that Henry did not want anyone to know that Edward had betrayed his co-conspirators because he wished to continue to use him as a spy (which is what he did).

Henry took action immediately on hearing the news. He sent a messenger directly to find Archbishop Arundel and to warn him of the likely attempt on his life. Then, taking his sons and Edward with him, he rode hard for London. The rebel lords set out at dusk with the intention of arriving at Windsor that night; Henry rode through the darkness by a long, circuitous route, to avoid them. On the road near the city he met the mayor of London, who was travelling with four attendants to inform the king that the rebel lords had six thousand men in the field. Henry and the mayor rode through the gates of London at nine o'clock that night, and roused the citizens. Henry ordered his sons to be safely lodged in the Tower and all the ports to be closed. He issued writs for the arrest of the rebel lords. Then he ordered a proclamation to be made, throughout the city, that whoever would ride with him on the following day would be well paid: eighteen pence per day for a mounted man with a lance, nine pence for an archer. The Londoners responded with determination. By the morning, Henry had an army.

Henry marched out of London on 5 January. He sent Edward to meet the conspirators, to find out what their plans were by pretending to remain faithful to them. After him he sent two vanguards, one commanded by his half-brother, John Beaufort, and the other commanded by Sir Thomas Erpingham. The remainder of his army was ordered to follow him. No one was to ride ahead of the king's horse on pain of death, he announced, for he himself wished to be the first man to engage the rebel army in battle. Edward told the rebel lords that two vanguards of the royal army were approaching and behind them was a huge force of men. Thomas Holland resolved to hold the bridge at Maidenhead as long as he could, but after darkness that evening, before Henry's full army arrived, he fled towards Oxford.

The rebels had badly miscalculated. They had believed that the whole country felt as aggrieved at Richard's deposition as they did, and thus they convinced themselves that the people would rise in their favour. The opposite happened: the people rose in favour of King Henry. Henry's quick thinking and strong leadership was crucial, but the real force to defeat the rebels came from the people. In Cheshire, the heartland of Ricardian support, the rebels took arms on 10 January and were in flight by the 12th.[36] Thomas Despenser tried to flee from Cardiff by ship but the crew had no wish to help a traitor, and took him instead to Bristol, where the citizens beheaded him. In London, Richard Maudeleyn and a few other conspirators were rounded up by the authorities and hanged. In Devon, the forces of John Holland (formerly duke of Exeter) failed to rouse the people. Holland himself, who had remained in London, fled in a small boat hoping to reach the Continent but was twice blown back on the Essex coast. Deserted by his men, he tried first of all to find refuge with the earl of Oxford at Hadley Castle, but was fearful of being betrayed and so sought refuge in the house of the Ricardian sympathiser John Prittlewell. There he was arrested. He was placed in the custody of Joan, dowager countess of Hereford, Henry's mother-in-law and mother-in-law of the murdered duke of Gloucester. She was in no mood for mercy. She had him dragged to Pleshey Castle, where Gloucester had been arrested, and assembled a mob to cut off his head. Thus died Richard's half-brother. His nephew, Thomas Holland, earl of Kent and formerly duke of Surrey, died in Cirencester with the earl of Salisbury. The inn in which they were staying was surrounded by the townsfolk during the night. In the morning the two earls were arrested and handed over to Thomas Berkeley, but a fire started in the town. One story goes that the townsmen were afraid that the rebel lords' servants were trying to burn down their houses to distract them and facilitate their lords' escape, so they took the precautionary measure of beheading them. Whether true or not, their ultimate fate is not in doubt. The heads were sent to Henry in a basket.

The failure of the Epiphany Rising, or the Revolt of the Earls (both names are regularly used to describe the rebellion), was predictable from the moment Henry heard that his life was in danger. If the rebels had succeeded in killing Henry and his four sons, they might have stood a chance of success. But even then it would only have been a slim chance. So fervent had been the public in support of Henry since his landing that not even the law and the idea of divine legitimacy had been sufficient to preserve Richard. To murder the man commonly seen as the saviour of England, especially after he had been so merciful to the Counter-Appellants, would have resulted in civil war. The cold-blooded murder of four innocent boys of the royal blood – aged fourteen, thirteen, eleven and ten – would have caused widespread revulsion. And the majority of the fifty-eight lords who had attested to the sentence of perpetual imprisonment on Richard would not have acquiesced in Richard's restoration but would have fought against him in the name of either the aged duke of York or the earl of March, Edmund Mortimer, if only to avoid Richard's retribution.

Rebels from Cirencester and other places were brought to Henry at Oxford Castle on 13 January. He personally sat in judgement. One of the captives deserved special attention. He was John Ferrour, the man who had saved Henry's life in the Tower during the Peasants' Revolt. We do not know whether he entreated the king to save him, reminding him of his earlier duty, or whether Henry recognised him. All we know is that Henry now repaid his debt, and ordered him to be released and pardoned.

It is interesting that, despite the man's change of allegiance, Henry's loyalty and indebtedness after nineteen years remained paramount.

In all twenty-six men were beheaded. Many more were pardoned. The clergymen involved (the abbot of Westminster, the bishop of Carlisle and Roger Walden) were arrested and tried in the Tower of London on 4 February. Walden and the abbot were released soon afterwards without charge; the bishop was condemned to death – despite his clerical status – but was kept in the Tower for a while and eventually pardoned. Nicholas Slake, who had been arrested by the Lords Appellant in 1388, then again in 1399, and yet again now, found himself forgiven a third time by Henry. As one modern commentator has written, it is difficult to account for this except by pointing to Henry's consistent magnanimity.[37] Only six men, including Sir Thomas Blount, received the full traitor's death of being drawn, hanged, disembowelled, and forced to watch their own entrails burned before being beheaded and quartered. Blount's execution resulted in one of the greatest displays of wit in the face of adversity ever recorded. As he was sitting down watching his extracted entrails being burned in front of him, he was asked if he would like a drink. 'No, for I do not know where I should put it', he replied.[38]

ELEVEN

A Deed Chronicled in Hell

> For now the devil that told me I did well,
> Says that this deed is chronicled in hell.
> *Richard II*, Act 5, Scene 6

Henry rode back into London to rapturous applause, and shouts of 'God preserve our lord King Henry and our lord the Prince!'[1] But the Epiphany Rising had been deeply damaging. It had also been a distraction. His priority in January 1400 should have been the defence of the realm. Charles VI of France had refused to recognise him as king, and had refused even to meet his ambassadors, Thomas Percy, earl of Worcester, and Walter Skirlaw, bishop of Durham. Nor would he confirm the truce. Instead he had strengthened the castles on the borders of Picardy, forbidden all trade with Englishmen, and had gathered a fleet at Harfleur ready to invade South Wales and take possession of Pembroke and Tenby castles. Thus, when Henry processed into London and made his speech about taking an army further into France than even his grandfather and uncle had done, it was not a sudden whim.

On 9 February 1400, Henry held a council meeting at Westminster. One William Faryngton was admitted into the royal presence: an envoy from Henry's ambassadors in France. He brought with him letters of credence from the ambassadors with their seals attached, supporting the authenticity of the copy of a letter they had received from Charles VI.[2] Extraordinarily, this letter was a confirmation of the truce which Henry had offered to renew at the end of the previous year. It had been sealed by Charles in Paris twelve days earlier, on 29 January.[3] The ambassadors did not know what to make of such a sudden reversal of French policy. They did not believe that it boded well for peace. As they made clear through Faryngton, they still had not received safe-conducts to meet Charles. The council concluded that 'it was more reasonable to expect war than a truce'.[4]

It was not just the sudden unilateral acceptance of the truce which troubled the ambassadors. In Charles's letter, the name of Richard II was followed by the expression 'on whose soul God have mercy', implying that he was dead. Their confusion is not surprising: exactly how did the French king, their enemy, know of Richard's death before they did? Was it a mistake? They had no way of knowing. But with the benefit of access to the French records, we know that Charles had instructed his representative, Pierre Blanchet (by letters also dated 29 January), to tell the English ambassadors 'that he had been advised of the death of King Richard'.[5] Three other letters dated that day also show that Charles was disseminating news of the death to others. This was intentional; there had been no mistake.

This brings us to the problem of Richard's death, for about this time he did indeed die. There is no doubt about this; there is no possibility that he escaped or was rescued from Pontefract and went to live in Scotland, as was later claimed.[6] But most historians rely on timing and motive in deciding whether Henry was guilty of murder or not. This is unfortunate, for motive is not the same as evidence, and to pretend it is is to risk introducing modern prejudices into a historical argument. While it is obvious that Henry had a motive to kill Richard – if Richard was dead, no one would be able to restore him – we can equally find motives for Henry *not* to kill Richard at this time. Henry was no fool, and he and his advisers would have been aware that to kill the ex-king immediately after the Epiphany Rising might prove counter-productive, for it might make people suspicious and perhaps even sympathetic for Richard's cause. In particular, Henry would have been suspected of the same sort of arbitrary killing as Richard, who had murdered his uncle Gloucester. Thus there were good political reasons why Henry should not have killed Richard. This is not to say that he did *not* give the order, only to remind us that one cannot judge innocence or guilt on the strength of motive alone.

The leading scholars in late fourteenth-century studies are, at the time of writing, quietly at variance over the issue of Richard's death, one writing that he died 'almost certainly on Henry's orders', another stating that it was the council's direction that 'Richard was to be disposed of', another that 'it is possible that Richard died a natural death'.[7] The authors of his entry in the *Oxford Dictionary of National Biography* state that 'there is no evidence that he was murdered and his skeleton showed no sign of violence. He could have been starved to death or even starved himself.' Notwithstanding this scholarly caution, there is hardly any subject more important in a study of Henry IV's life than whether he murdered his cousin or not. Therefore the question must be dealt with in greater detail and with a sterner methodology than simply presenting a range of options.

To begin with, it is necessary to stress that no chronicler was familiar with the details of the death at first hand. What each man wrote depended on his own point of view and what he had heard, and these things depended

very much on what milieu he was part of. The pro-Ricardian French chroniclers, for example, were anxious to present Henry as a murderous usurper,
and so they claimed that Richard had been killed on Henry's orders. In
the story circulated by the French author of *The Betrayal and Death of Richard
II*, Henry sent one 'Sir Piers Exton' on 6 January to the castle in Kent
where Richard was being kept, with instructions to kill him. When told
that Richard was waiting for his dinner, Exton announced that the ex-king
'should never eat again'. After a fight, in which the ex-king valiantly wres-
tled an axe from one of the seven men who now set about him, Sir Piers
gave him repeated blows to the head, from which he died. This chronicle
goes on to state that Richard was buried at Pontefract. In other French
accounts, the killing took place not in Kent but at the Tower of London.
But whatever the variations, the stories of violent death have long been
recognised as propaganda.[8] There was no knight called Piers Exton. It is
exceptionally unlikely that a Ricardian sympathiser was allowed to witness
the murder. And a forensic examination of Richard's skeleton and skull
revealed no sign of violence.[9] The murder story was derived from a few
circumstantial details and concocted for a French audience, in order to
strengthen popular feeling against Henry.[10] Unfortunately for Henry's reputation, the same story served as excellent propaganda against his dynasty
in England seventy years later, and thus it eventually found its way into
sixteenth-century English historical works, and Shakespeare's *Richard II*,
whence it passed into popular currency.

The information circulated in England in the immediate aftermath
was that Richard voluntarily went without food and water, and died on
14 February 1400. Even the French chronicles which refer to the violent
murder include some reference to starvation, such as that Richard 'will
never eat again'.[11] Most chroniclers referred to his self-starvation, including
those who did not believe it. The author of the *Historia Vitae et Regni Ricardi
Secundi* stated that he 'declined into such grief, langour and weakness that
he took to his bed and refused any food, drink or other sustenance. Thus
on 14 February . . . he died there [Pontefract] in prison. Others say, however,
and with greater truth that he was miserably put to death by starvation
there.'[12] The *Brut* notes that he was 'enfammed unto the death by his
keeper', dying after four or five days.[13] Jean Creton wrote that, after the
Epiphany Rising, Richard 'was so vexed at heart by this evil news that
from that time onwards he neither ate nor drank and thus, so they say, it
came to pass that he died'.[14] Similarly, a contemporary Londoner wrote
that 'for sorrow and hunger he died in the castle of Pontefract', and the
Dieulacres chronicler said that he died on 14 February, after twelve days
without food and drink.[15] Adam Usk also had him dying of hunger, partly

out of sorrow and partly due to the tormenting of his keeper.[16] Thomas Walsingham stated that he starved himself so that 'the orifice leading to his stomach closed up . . . and he wasted away through natural debility, and finally died at the aforesaid castle [Pontefract] on 14 February'.[17]

But did Richard really starve himself? Or was he killed on Henry's orders? And how can the official version of his death on 14 February be squared with the French king's statement that he had heard of the death by 29 January?

The council debated the death in early February. Astoundingly, Henry neither confirmed nor denied the French message that Richard was dead. Our evidence for this is the minutes of a council meeting, which was held on or after 3 February 1400.[18] It contains two relevant entries. The first reads 'if Richard, former king, still be living as some suppose [or 'as may be supposed'], then it is ordered that he be well and securely guarded for the safety of the estate of the king and of his realm'.[19] That such doubts about Richard's survival were entertained by the councillors themselves (and not just by people outside the council) is shown by an even more illuminating passage on the other side of the folio, which states that: 'it seems to the council necessary to speak to the king that, in case Richard [the] former king etcetera is still living, he should be kept in security agreeable to the lords of the realm and if he be gone from life then he should be shown openly to the people at the end so that they may recognise him'.[20]

This raises the question of why the council did not seek further information from Henry as to what had happened to Richard. The council's order that 'he should be kept in security' shows that their doubt was not due to his escape (otherwise we would read of orders for his recapture). We might conclude that Richard had indeed taken the initiative and started to starve himself to death (and, of course, the council may have been told this, whether true or not). But the key phrase here is 'it seems to the council necessary to speak to the king'. This shows that the council considered Richard's fate separately, without Henry being present.[21] It demonstrates a possible difference between the information communicated to the council and that available to the king. It follows that either the whole council, including Henry, did not know for certain whether Richard was dead or not, because the matter was beyond Henry's control and *could not* be clarified; or knowledge that Richard was already dead was known only to Henry and those members of the council who were privy to his secrets, who *would not* clarify the matter to the others.

Let us now consider the instructions issued by Charles VI to his ambassador Pierre Blanchet on 29 January, particularly 'that he had been advised of the death of King Richard'. How did Charles know this? Firstly, and most probably, there may have been a French spy in contact with someone connected with Richard's killing. There are very few alternatives. It is possible that Henry secretly informed the French king, in order to restart peace negotiations. But why then did his messenger not inform his own ambassadors on the way, especially as Charles was on the verge of invading England? He would have been undermining his own diplomatic position by giving this information to the French. Thus this explanation is hardly credible. Even more difficult to accept is that the French acted on an unsubstantiated rumour.[22] Although Charles was periodically mad, the rest of the French royal family – who ruled in his name when he was unwell – would not have accepted a mere rumour unquestioningly. There is no sign of any doubt on the part of the French government of the veracity of the information. They certainly would not have reversed their entire policy to England, confirmed the truce and initiated negotiations unless they were confident that their information about Richard's death was shared by Henry.

Scholars have traditionally referred to the French information as a mere rumour, and presumed that we cannot connect it with the actual death. But though the French information may have prompted a rumour, in itself it was more reliable than hearsay, for the originator triggered an entire reversal of French royal policy. It is important to remember this when considering the alternative narratives of Richard's death. Let us suppose for the sake of argument that Richard *did* starve himself in Pontefract on hearing of the news of the failure of the Epiphany Rising. This would tally with Richard's reaction on his arrest – he refused to eat – and so would be believable. It would explain the council's doubt about whether he was alive or not in February 1400, because no one at that council meeting – at least three days' ride from Pontefract – knew whether he would go through with his self-starvation. However, the theory that Richard starved himself cannot be reconciled with the French king confidently circulating news of his death on 29 January. It would imply that it was a complete coincidence that, within a few days of Richard choosing to starve himself to death at Pontefract, someone close to the French royal family invented a spurious story that he had died and persuaded the French king to circulate the news without first checking it. This is simply not credible, especially in the light of their reversal of policy in the wake of the report. The French must have had some intelligence which they considered trustworthy, and that cannot have originated with Richard or his guards in the dungeons of Pontefract.

With this in mind, we can return to the question of why the English council was uncertain whether Richard was alive or dead at the time of their early February meeting. It is very difficult to accept that the reason was because the matter *could not* be clarified, for the French already had information which they considered reliable. Henry's closest friends on the council must have claimed that they had no certain knowledge of it, or simply said nothing. Why? If Richard was already dead, and the French were circulating the information, why did Henry not confirm or deny his death to the council? The could not/would not question above would appear thus to be answered. The matter was left in doubt because those in the know *would not* clarify it. For this reason, the minutes of the council meeting, coupled with the French evidence, are very suspicious, if not damning.

Now let us tighten the final screws in this investigation. In searching for a source for the French information about Richard's death, we have no option but to return to the contemporary French chronicles mentioned above, for they alone give an early January date for Henry ordering Richard's death. According to the original of all of these French texts – preserved in *The Betrayal and Death of Richard II* – the name of the man whom Henry ordered to do the killing was Sir Piers (or Peter) Exton. As mentioned above, no man of this name is known, but it bears resemblance to that of Sir Peter Bucton (or Buxton), Henry's old friend, fellow crusader and erstwhile steward. This is important for Bucton was one of the very few men who knew where Richard was secretly being held.[23] The specific entry reads 'on the day of Kings (6 January), when Henry had taken the field, outside London, with all his people who were about to fight the lords who had risen to support King Richard, he commanded a knight called Sir Piers Exton to go and deliver [Richard] straightaway from this world'.[24] The man who recorded that command was a Frenchman who was in London at the time, and whose source was with Henry in person on that day.[25] Furthermore, the Frenchman in question had excellent connections with the highest-ranking members of the English court. If he or one of his French contacts sent word of Henry's order to France, this could have been the source of Charles VI's knowledge that Richard was dead. In other words, it might not have been news of the death itself which persuaded the French king, it might have been trustworthy intelligence that Henry had issued an order for Richard to be killed. Certainly in *The Betrayal and Death of Richard II* we have evidence that the French had intelligence of such an order being issued in early January. Furthermore, if the French king knew that Henry had given this order, then presumably some members of the English court – and some members of Henry's council – knew too. Hence the doubt in early February about whether Richard was dead. The royal council needed clarification as to whether Henry's order had been carried out. The French presumed that the order had already resulted in Richard's murder.

We cannot be certain that this is the true basis for the French information, but it would explain a great deal, including the otherwise intractable problem of the timing of the French announcement. It also allows us to reconstruct in outline the circumstances leading to Richard's death. On or about 6 January, while riding against the rebels during the Epiphany Rising, Henry ordered Bucton to go to Pontefract and kill Richard, or at least to be prepared to kill him if the rebellion got out of hand. The essence of this order was overheard by the French agent in London, and the news was sent to Paris that Henry had secretly ordered Richard's death. The French king, having no regard for the sensitivity of the matter in England, used the information to try to persuade Henry to return his daughter, Isabella, on the grounds that she was now a widow. He sent his messages to Henry's ambassadors via his own representatives on 29 January. The French king's letter would have been received by the English delegation at Calais on or about 1 February, and they lost no time in sending a copy to Westminster with William Faryngton. Henry, seeing the French king's statement that Richard was dead, allowed the question to be discussed by the council at the early February meeting, to determine what they believed should be done with the king in the event of his death. Having no clarification of the matter, the council responded as best they could, providing for each eventuality.

The remainder of the story is evidenced in the Issue Rolls. About this time Henry sent William Loveney to Pontefract and back 'on the king's secret business' with a small company of men.[26] Loveney was the keeper of the great wardrobe, a faithful Lancastrian, who had been in Henry's service since 1381.[27] The task Henry now gave him was either to organise the process of announcing the death to the council (if Bucton had already killed Richard) or to outline to Thomas Swynford what to do about the ex-king (if he was still alive). On 14 February, Swynford sent a valet from Pontefract to 'certify' to the council that Richard was dead. He arrived in Westminster three days later, on 17 February. That same day Henry authorised the payment of one hundred marks to bring the body to London.

Taking all this evidence into account, two narratives are possible. Henry's order to Bucton may have been simply to go to Pontefract and *be ready* to kill Richard if the Epiphany Rising looked like freeing him, this order being misinterpreted by the French agent in London. When news of this led the French king to infer that Richard was dead, and to offer a renewal of the peace, Henry realised the opportunity to avert both a war and the risk of Richard being rescued, and sent Loveney to Pontefract to arrange

Richard's final demise. Alternatively, Richard may have been killed by Bucton on or shortly after 9 January, as a direct consequence of Henry's first order, issued on or about the 6th. Following that, Henry may have delayed announcing the death until it was safe for him to do so, after the heat of the Epiphany Rising had died down.

In determining which of these narratives is most likely to be correct, we have two final pieces of evidence to consider. First, there is the text of the Percy family manifesto.[28] This was written in 1403, after the Percy family declared their hostility to Henry. In it the earl of Northumberland – a member of the king's council and one of Henry's strongest supporters in 1400 – stated that Henry ordered Richard to be killed by starvation, and that the ex-king lingered for fifteen days before he died. It goes without saying that the manifesto is an inherently biased document; nevertheless, if Bucton had killed Richard suddenly on Henry's orders, Northumberland could have said so, rather than falsely claiming that Henry had starved Richard to death, for he was in a very good position in February 1400 to know the truth.[29] The second piece of evidence tallies with this. When Thomas Swynford's valet came south to confirm to the council that Richard was dead, he hired an extra horse 'for speed'.[30] Why would there be a need for extra speed if this was simply a ruse to cover up a death which had happened a month earlier? The council would not have known how many horses Swynford's valet had used on the journey.

In conclusion, it appears that Richard did die on 14 February, and that Henry's order to Bucton on 6 January was a precaution, to kill him *only* if it looked like he might fall into rebel hands.[31] It would follow that the French agent misinterpreted this order, and that Henry did not issue the command actually to kill him until later, probably after 3 February (the earliest possible date for William Faryngton's arrival at Westminster). That the order was taken north by Loveney, and yet news of the death did not come south until brought by Swynford's valet, suggests that there was a period of delay between the receipt of the order and the death, and this correlates with the starvation story as officially announced and as claimed by the Percy family. More than this it is not possible to say. But whatever other details we might wish to know, and whatever clarifications of the foregoing conclusion are desirable, there can be no doubt about one thing. Richard II did not starve himself to death in Pontefract Castle; he was killed on Henry IV's instructions.

*

How do we account for this? A man who was a pious believer in the Trinity, who enjoyed discussing morality, who went on crusades and even made a pilgrimage to Jerusalem – how come he turned into a murderer? What drove him to it? This question takes us right into the heart of what Henry was, or rather what he had become by January 1400. It is thus one of the most interesting aspects of his life.

Richard's hatred of Henry in the past was not a critical factor in determining his death. If Henry had wanted Richard killed for past grudges, insults and attempts on his and his father's lives, he had every opportunity to bring this about in the parliament of 1399. Indeed, it would have been far easier to let parliament execute Richard than to murder him secretly a few weeks later. Thus we may be sure that it was not a personal vendetta but a political assassination. On 4 January Henry finally realised that the die-hard Ricardian faction would never accept him as their monarch. Worse, they were prepared to murder all four of his sons to achieve their aim. Henry's children were a part of his political world: they embodied his hope of founding a dynasty. So, now he was king, he had a duty to maintain stability and the political order, and that meant his own personal wishes were subsumed within the interests of the Crown. He had no choice but to do all he possibly could to preserve himself and the royal family, and that included eradicating the destabilising threat which was Richard II.

In this light it is striking that Richard was probably not killed on a whim, but only after the precaution of sending Bucton to Pontefract. Even if one takes the Percy manifesto literally, so that Henry starved Richard for fifteen days, he did not issue the command to begin the starvation until 27 or 28 January. The precautionary order may be seen as a strategic move, that of a general on the field of battle, which is indeed what Henry was on 6 January. The order actually to starve Richard – issued probably in early February – was more considered, after the immediate danger had passed, to make safe his position. The immediate advantages of the assassination were obvious, the long-term disadvantages less so. When news arrived of the French king's understanding that Richard was already dead, and that Charles was now more concerned with his daughter's return than with invading England, the opportunity to make peace with France and at the same time safeguard his throne from pro-Ricardian fanatics persuaded Henry that bringing about Richard's death 'by natural causes' was the best course of action.

Although the killing of Richard was actuated by political necessity rather than personal hatred, that necessity in itself points to a profound change in Henry. To most critics, Henry weathered the Epiphany Rising with relative ease: the support of the country was never seriously in doubt, and support for Richard withered quickly. But the rising itself shattered Henry's image of himself as a universally popular king, and seriously ruptured his faith in the value of mercy. It forced him to see political reality: that he might be required to stoop to underhand methods for the sake of the safety of the realm, including the assassination of a kinsman. Far from being the new Edward III, he was vulnerable. Of course, kings do not write letters revealing their weaknesses, so there is no overt evidence of his fear; but there can be no doubt that in Henry's case his vulnerability was suddenly and violently exposed. The attempted revolt cannot but have raised the question in his mind of another attack. When might it come? And would the next attacker seek also to kill all his sons?

Unsurprisingly, Henry did not lament Richard's passing. He ordered the body to be brought to London with its face exposed, so that all who saw it could recognise the ex-king, in accordance with the council's directions. The face was exhibited from the forehead down to the neck.[32] The corpse was taken first to St Paul's, where it arrived on 12 March.[33] A Mass was sung there for the dead king's soul, which Henry respectfully attended, bearing the pall himself. After two days on open display at St Paul's, the body was taken through the main street, Cheapside, where it was left on its carriage for all to see it for two hours. Following that it was conducted to Westminster Abbey, where another Mass was sung for the late king, before being taken for burial at King's Langley.

Henry's refusal to allow Richard to be interred in the tomb in Westminster Abbey which he (Richard) had constructed for himself and his first wife has occasioned much debate and speculation among historians.[34] One view is that Henry did not believe Richard was worthy to lie in the special circle of tombs around the shrine of the Confessor. The other Plantagenet kings there – Henry III, Edward I and Edward III – were all more deserving monarchs than Richard (the weakest of them, Henry III, had rebuilt the entire abbey church). But debate on this point has overlooked the fact that Henry did not remove Richard's tomb, which he would have done if he had meant Richard *never* to lie in it. It lay half-empty, housing only the body of Richard's queen, Anne of Bohemia, until Henry himself was dead. Moreover, Henry did not even move it from the innermost ring of royal tombs, where it filled the last of the six places of honour around the royal saint's shrine.[35] He was not at all averse to moving tombs: at about this time he shifted the duke of Gloucester's body to a place more in keeping with his royal status.[36] So it appears that he meant Richard only temporarily to lie at Langley. He also paid for a thousand masses to be said at Langley for the salvation of Richard's soul, a number fully in keeping with his kingly status.[37] It is therefore unlikely that the explanation for Richard's burial at Langley was his unworthiness and far more probable that Henry simply did not wish Westminster Abbey to become a focus for political supporters of the late king. Richard had rebuilt the hall of the Palace of Westminster in a very impressive fashion, and filled it with kingly statues. He had also been a patron of the abbey, and installed his huge gilt portrait there. Thus for Henry to separate Richard's body and the physical remains of his kingship was – like the murder itself – a political act. His successors could rebury Richard where they liked in due course, but Henry himself was not going to risk adding to Richard's potency in death by allowing his royal body to lie at the centre of his self-glorifying art and architecture.

*

In the spring of 1400, Henry moved to Eltham Palace, which now became his favourite residence.[38] The accommodation and facilities had been extensively remodelled and extended by Edward III and Richard II, so that it was already one of the most comfortable royal houses in England. Henry improved it still further. He added a large study and a great chamber for himself, above a cloister leading to the chapel, together with a kitchen, a buttery, a larder and a parlour. These were all built of timber with stone chimney stacks. The parlour had six stained-glass windows decorated with birds and 'baboons' or grotesques. The great chamber was heated by two fireplaces and lit with three bay windows, the middle one bearing stained-glass emblems of his kingship and the Lancastrion motto, *Souveignez vous de moi* ('remember me' or 'will you remember me?'). A window beside the door was decorated with figures of the Trinity and the Salutation. More Trinity and Salutation figures gazed down at him from the seven windows of his study, along with four saints. He had two desks constructed to furnish the study, one specifically for him 'to keep his books in'. He also had a small private oratory built, with a rood-loft (for musicians to perform) and a spiral staircase for ease of access from his chamber.[39] Such additions are reminiscent of Henry as he appears in the accounts of his youth: bookish, pious, conscientious, musical and a relatively private man for a medieval king.

How much quiet time he had in which to enjoy his study and private quarters was a different matter. He had an armed expedition to Scotland to organise. His resolution to carry through this plan was hardened when his second offer to open negotiations with the Scots was ignored in early January.[40] The Epiphany Rising, the threat of war with France and the burial of Richard then distracted him, but by May he was again thinking that he should demonstrate in Scotland that he was worthy of the crown of England, and capable of living up to the high standards which he had publicly set himself at his coronation.

Two pieces of good fortune in the spring assisted him in organising this campaign. The first was a letter from the Scottish earl of March, George Dunbar, which he received at the beginning of March.[41] Dunbar had fallen out with the duke of Rothesay, son and heir of Robert III, on account of the duke's rejection of his daughter as a prospective bride. In his letter he offered to switch his loyalty from the king of Scotland to Henry. Dunbar was clearly a valuable ally, being a sound military commander and in possession of secret information of particular importance to Henry.[42] Seeing a great opportunity, Henry wrote back warmly, issuing a safe-conduct for him to come to England. The other piece of good fortune was that Henry's negotiators in France managed to bring about a mutual confirmation of the twenty-eight-year truce, which still had twenty-four years left to run. With this finally agreed on 18 May, Henry could march north without fear of leaving England open to a French invasion.[43]

Despite these turns of events, Henry still had a significant problem to overcome. He had no means to pay for an army. This perhaps explains why, on 24 May, he offered Robert III a third opportunity to renew the peace between England and Scotland, as the French had just done. Once more King Robert ignored him. In theory Henry could have solved his financial predicament by summoning a parliament and asking the commons for a grant, but in practice that would take far too long. Just to summon parliament required forty days' notice, and, presuming there was a grant, it would take time for the money to be gathered. So he decided to use a different method for organising the defence of the realm. Summoning an army to muster at York on 24 June, he asked the magnates to supply men for his expedition directly. All those lords who had received a grant from Henry himself or his predecessors (Edward III, the Black Prince, John of Gaunt, or Richard II) would lose their lands if they refused to fight in Scotland. It was a clever way of testing loyalty and raising a cheap army at the same time. But it also had the side effect of putting Henry's popularity to the test. It became essential that all those participating should gain in some way from the expedition. If they did not, Henry would have lost a measure of their loyalty, as well as their respect.

The army was large. A total of 13,085 fighting men attended, not including the mariners and other support staff who kept the forces supplied.[44] Of these, 1,771 were men-at-arms; the remaining 11,314 were archers. Henry's two eldest sons – Henry (aged thirteen) and Thomas (twelve) – also travelled with the army, as part of their military education. They took eight single and six double cannons (the latter having two barrels) and eight hundred pounds of gunpowder.[45] Such was the size and scale of the force that the Scottish king sent negotiators at the last moment; but their instructions were to try and delay the army's progress rather than to present realistic terms. They offered a perpetual peace along the lines agreed by Edward III and Robert Bruce in 1328.[46] Henry naïvely believed that Robert III was in earnest, and wrote to the council asking for further details of the treaty in question. That meant a long delay. Jousts were held to keep the men occupied, and Sir John Cornwaille performed so impressively that Henry awarded him the hand in marriage of his own sister, the recently widowed Elizabeth.[47] All the while his army was eating up its supplies, and the wages he had promised the men were depleting his small reserves. Henry had to ask for loans from the bishops and his trusted Lancastrian supporters. And the waiting was all in vain. The treaty of 1328 was unworkable – it had not been called the 'Shameful Treaty of Northampton' for nothing – and Henry could hardly use it as the basis for further negotiations. Realising he had been fooled, he demanded that Robert III do homage to him for Scotland in Edinburgh on 23 August, and gave the order to march north.

Henry crossed the border on 14 August and advanced to Leith. The duke of Rothesay offered 'to avoid Christian bloodshed' in the traditional way by fighting him in person with one, two or three hundred supporters, but Henry did not take him up on his offer. Instead, he merely reissued his demand that the king of Scotland perform homage. Henry approached Edinburgh, expecting obeisance. The king of Scotland stayed away. The Scots reverted instead to their time-honoured tactic of withdrawing in the face of an English army. They knew from centuries of experience that no English force could stay in the north perpetually; there was a limit to their patience as well as to the king's purse and their food supplies. Seeing Edinburgh Castle fully garrisoned by the duke of Rothesay himself, and knowing his small financial resources were all but exhausted, Henry realised the extent of his strategic predicament, and agreed to talks at the cross between Edinburgh and Leith.

Henry had already shown himself to be naïve in two respects: believing that the Scottish emissaries were sincere in seeking peace and expecting the Scots would do battle against his eleven thousand archers. Now he showed his lack of kingly experience a third time. Despite never having led a diplomatic embassy before, he took charge of the English negotiations in person. The Scots ambassadors tricked him. Two years later, when one of them, Sir Adam Forrester, was brought to him in chains at Westminster, Henry stated that Forrester, 'by many white lies and subtle promises, had suddenly caused the king to leave the land of Scotland' in 1400.[48] What these 'subtle promises' were may be deduced from matters arising from the colloquium between Edinburgh and Leith issued to a later set of English negotiators. The principal question was whether the king of Scotland owed homage and service to the king of England, and, if so, whether he should be summoned to attend parliament in England.[49] Forrester seems to have argued to Henry that the king of Scotland had assumed that he was not a subject of the king of England as he had not been summoned to parliament. Maybe he promised Henry that Robert III would obey a future summons? Either way, Forrester must have offered some form of political bait. And Henry fell for it. He returned to England almost immediately, recrossing the border with his army on 29 August.

Henry had failed. There is no other way to look at this expedition. There were some slight advantages – at St Albans, the chronicler Thomas Walsingham was left with the impression that he had ravaged the north, and there were some naval successes during the campaign – but otherwise all Henry had achieved was to demonstrate that the English still had the ability and will to muster a large, well-equipped army.[50] All those whose loyalty he had drawn on had nothing to show for their efforts. There was no glory, no strategic victory, not even a diplomatic settlement. Why? After all, it was not yet a year since the commons and lords had collectively cheered him at his coronation. And it had been a huge army. Henry was not a rash man; how could he have miscalculated so badly?

For a start he probably ran short of provisions.[51] His Lancastrian officers were not used to supplying armies on this scale. For this Henry himself must take the blame; great war leaders make sure they delegate to officers who will not fail to supply the army in the field. But there were other reasons for the failure. Henry was primarily a tournament fighter – an individualist – and had some way to go before he could be considered a fully-fledged general. This is not to say that he was weak tactically; later events would prove that he had lost none of the sharp battlefield thinking he showed at Radcot Bridge. But on the broader strategic front he had much yet to learn. Had he known about his grandfather's continual warfare strategy, he would not have withdrawn entirely from Scotland but would have kept up the pressure on the Scots, to make sure they made good their promises. Similarly, he overestimated his skills in taking on the negotiating role personally. However clever he was, he simply did not have the experience. The Scottish negotiators ran rings around him.

To add to these problems, he had difficulty coming to terms with money. His attitude was that financial matters were beneath him. 'Kings are not wont to render account', he later declared.[52] We can understand where this attitude came from: he had grown up as the son and heir of the richest man in England, and had never had to shuffle his funds to make ends meet, let alone go without. So he had no way of realising at the time how his promises not to levy taxation would tie his hands as king. Not only could he not raise further money for his campaign, what money *was* coming in was still being diverted to pay for his own invasion. Grants to his supporters had already exceeded £22,000, and the duchy of Lancaster itself was in debt.[53] The customs revenues were in free-fall, and the harvest of 1400 had not been good.[54] If Henry had not had his loyal Lancastrian supporters to call upon, and substantial loans from the prelates, he would have found it difficult to keep the army in the field as long as he did.

But probably the most important reason for Henry's failure in Scotland was the man himself. His character was not what men expected in a warrior-king; he was just too serious. Henry was never 'a blithe hero', as some historians have suggested; he was logical, scrupulous and fervent, and (at this juncture) sincere to the point of naïvety. However much he had studied kingship, he was no Edward III. His grandfather had understood the value of books but he never built himself a study. Rather Edward built halls and roasting houses, hunting lodges and dancing chambers, and spent his time with his companions feasting, jousting, hunting and planning the next campaign. Then he delegated to his leading lords missions in which they could compete for glory. Henry's friends were fewer in number, and many of those who pretended to be his friends were untrustworthy, and he knew it. His companions did not want to serve him; they wanted to control him, or even remove him. How could Henry display an ease of manner with his subjects, and inspire them to feats of glory, when he was waiting for one of them to stab him in the back?

No English king ever again led an army into Scotland. The age of asserting English sovereignty (as opposed to merely claiming it) was over. The claim itself was not dropped until the sixteenth century, but from now on the kings of England had to prioritise domestic security over the sovereignty of Scotland. Partly this was a result of Henry's actions: having destabilised the realm by dethroning a monarch, no English king for the next hundred years felt sufficiently secure at home to mount a northern expedition on the scale required. By then Scotland was firmly established in its independence, and English sovereignty of Scotland was as unrealistic as English sovereignty of France.

Henry was back at Newcastle by 2 September. He was at Durham for the next two days, and at Northallerton for the next two. By then his army had disbanded, each group of men wending their ways over the rain-soaked roads to their villages. As they retreated, a large number of Scotsmen gathered to inflict a massacre, but they were met in Redesdale by Sir Robert Umfraville on 29 September, who routed them, killing two hundred men and taking many prisoners. Henry issued writs from Pontefract summoning a parliament to meet at York on 27 October, perhaps hoping to resolve his failure in Scotland. Then he rode further south. At Northampton on 19 September, he stopped. Urgent messages had reached him, about a rising in Wales.[55] A gentleman of Welsh birth had defiantly claimed the title 'prince of Wales' three days earlier, and had sworn to kill him and his eldest son. That man was now marching with nearly three hundred followers to burn the town of Ruthin.

Such an insurrection could not be ignored. Nor could its charismatic leader. His name was Owen Glendower.

TWELVE

The Great Magician

Against the great magician, damn'd Glendower.
Henry IV Part One, Act III, Scene 1

Owen Glendower – or Owain Glyn Dŵr, as he is called in Wales – was descended from the ancient princes of Wales on both his mother's and father's sides. His inheritance from his father included the lordship of Glyndyfrdwy, or Glyn Dŵr, in North Wales, after which he was named. Despite his lineage, he was not a natural rebel, or even a natural Welsh partisan. He was in his early forties, and had spent much time in England. He had trained as a lawyer at the inns of court in London, and his wife was English, a daughter of the lawyer Sir David Hanmer. He had served as an esquire of the earl of Arundel – Henry's kinsman and fellow Appellant – and he and his brother Tudor had fought for the English at Berwick against the Scots in 1384. His grandmother was an Englishwoman and his sister married an Englishman. Nevertheless, despite all these English connections, on 16 September 1400 Owen was proclaimed prince of an independent Wales and swore enmity to Henry and his eldest son.

It was an extraordinary act for a man who had previously been loyal to the English Crown. The reason is often said to have been an argument between him and Lord Grey of Ruthin over a piece of land, but this hardly explains why his revolt assumed the aspect of a nationalist uprising from the outset. The extant correspondence between Lord Grey and Glendower suggests a longer, more complicated story.[1] Glendower had been led to believe in early 1400 that he would receive a charter from King Henry making him the master forester and warden of Chirkland, a marcher lordship in North Wales. In this he was deceived. Moreover, a friend warned him that Grey had sworn 'to burn and slay in whatever part of the country which he [Glendower] was secured in'. Glendower replied in a belligerent letter on 11 June 1400. He boasted that he had stolen some of Grey's horses and declared, 'as many men that you slay and as many houses that you burn for my sake, as many will I burn and slay for your sake, and doubt not that I will have bread and ale of the best that is in your lordship'. Grey replied shortly afterwards, denying that he had said these things about burning and slaying, and insisting that Glendower had heard false reports of this matter. Grey added that he would make all the details known to the king and his council, and that, because of the treason and theft confessed in his letter, he would obtain for him 'a rope, a ladder and a ring, high on a gallows for to hang; and thus shall be your ending'.

Such tensions meant that Henry was aware of the danger of a rebellion in North Wales long before the September proclamation. But he urged Grey and the other local landowners to follow a policy of conciliation.[2] No doubt he felt that, until actual hostilities broke out, there was nothing to be gained from direct intervention, and there was a risk that a strong hand might exacerbate the crisis. As it was, enough Welshmen took up arms for Glendower to destroy several towns in the region. From Glyndyfrdwy he and about 270 men – including his brother Tudor, his two English brothers-in-law and his son – set off for Ruthin, which they plundered and burned on 18 September 1400. Over subsequent days they destroyed the other regional towns one by one: Denbigh, Rhuddlan, Flint, Hawarden, Holt, Oswestry and Welshpool.[3] Had Sir Hugh Burnell not met Glendower in battle on 24 September, the Welsh revolt would have spread across North Wales. But that day Burnell, leading the men of Shropshire, Staffordshire and Warwickshire, defeated Glendower on the bank of the River Severn, not far from Welshpool. Glendower fled from the battlefield. Eight days after being proclaimed prince of Wales, he was a fugitive.

Henry was travelling westwards from Lichfield on the 24th and would have heard news of Burnell's victory as he approached Shrewsbury. It meant that he could afford to pause there to deliberate his next move carefully. He had already decided to put off the forthcoming parliament until November; now he prorogued it until the New Year. A Welshman who had espoused Glendower's cause was brought to him and executed as a traitor, the four corners of his body being sent to Bristol, London, Chester and Hereford. After this the king set out with his knights, archers and cannon, riding north to Chester and then westwards through North Wales along the coast road. Everywhere the Welsh forces followed the example of the Scots and withdrew into the mountains. On 7 October Henry was at Bangor. Two days later he entered Carnarvon Castle.[4] A week later he was back in England, riding to London. He granted Glendower's confiscated estates to John Beaufort, earl of Somerset. Glendower himself and seven companions hid all winter in the woods of North Wales.

On the face of it, Henry's campaign in Wales had much in common with his unsuccessful campaign in Scotland. In both countries he failed to bring the enemy to battle, and in neither place was the nationalist leader brought to the diplomatic table. In both cases there were victories – Hugh Burnell's against Glendower and Richard Umfraville's against the Scots – but these were won by the king's officers, not by the king himself. Yet the Welsh and Scottish campaigns of 1400 were very different. Henry went to Scotland with a huge army and the clear aim of making the Scots pay for breaking the truce the previous year. He failed completely. In Wales, on the other hand, he reacted quickly and decisively to news of a revolt. Although no English king had led an army through North Wales for more than a century, he speedily gathered sufficient force to make a show of strength there within a month of Glendower's proclamation. That in itself was enough to quieten the rebels, and to stifle declarations of Welsh independence. Following Burnell's victory, Henry himself had no need to bring Glendower to battle. If the self-proclaimed Welsh prince had had several thousand men at his command, it would have been a different matter; but, with a handful of outlaws in his entourage, there was no enemy force to be destroyed. In October 1400 it was reasonable to suppose that the Welsh rising had been nipped in the bud. Time would prove it had not, of course, but it certainly would have been unwise for Henry to spend weeks or months hunting down the fugitive. Likewise it would have been undignified for him to seek to address Glendower's grievances – as some historians have suggested he should have done – after the Welshman had confessed himself to be a thief and had proved himself guilty of treason.[5] Just as modern governments cannot be seen to negotiate with terrorists, neither could medieval kings be seen to deal with traitors, especially not those whose methods included armed insurrection.

Henry could thus be satisfied that he had done well in North Wales. Nevertheless, it is unlikely that he was complacent. There had been two full-scale revolts against his kingship in the first year of his reign – one of which had nearly resulted in his assassination – and he had been diplomatically forced to withdraw from Scotland. He had also been forced to order Richard's starvation and to execute a number of traitors. What a contrast from the enthusiasm and the declarations of justice and mercy at his coronation! What a blow to his hopes of being a magnanimous and victorious warrior-king. The distrust and disappointment were driven home to him with further force the following month when he was the subject of a second assassination attempt. A plot was uncovered to smear the saddle of his horse with a poisonous ointment which would have caused him to swell up and die before he had ridden ten miles.[6] The implication for

Henry's supporters was that their king was under threat. For the rest of the country, it meant that Henry's very survival was open to question.

*

Still the deadlock with France continued. King Charles demanded that his daughter Isabella be returned. Henry detained her at Havering, a victim of the slow diplomatic process and a hostage against French aggression. He had agreed in March to the principle of her return, but many questions remained, including whether she could keep the jewels and gifts which she had received as queen since arriving in England. There was also the question of her dowry. Apart from the 300,000 francs which Charles had paid at the time of her wedding, his officers had handed over two further instalments of 100,000 francs which were repayable in the event of Richard's death. Henry could not afford to repay such sums – he was dangerously short of money – and so his negotiators argued that, as there were still sums outstanding from the ransom of King John II of France, who had been captured by the Black Prince in 1356, the 200,000 francs should be written off against that debt.

To counter this hardening diplomatic position, on 6 September Charles despatched two of his negotiators to England in person to tell Isabella that under no circumstances should she agree to marry without her father's permission, and to try to arrange her return as soon as possible. Henry's campaign in North Wales prevented the Frenchmen from approaching him directly, and in the intervening period one of the diplomats died. The other, Jean de Hangest, went to Windsor in October. He was honourably lodged in the keep, and invited to enter Henry's presence after dinner. But the French king had still not recognised Henry as king of England. Hangest was not so foolish as to pretend that he could insult the English king by failing to acknowledge him, so he made a bow and presented himself as a private citizen of France. Henry asked to see his letters of authority. On hearing that he had none, he was told to withdraw. After discussing the problem with members of his council, Henry readmitted him and said that if he came as a representative of a man who refused to recognise him as king, he could not listen to him; but if he had anything to say as Jean de Hangest, lord of Hugueville, he could speak. Hangest must have felt as if the floor of Windsor Castle was about to swallow him up, but he stood his ground and stated that he represented the king of France, and if Henry would not listen to him in that capacity, he would have to return home. At that Henry became angry, and spoke in a fierce and proud manner, and told the Frenchman to withdraw again.[7]

Henry had good reason to be angry. Charles could not have it both

ways; he could not refuse to recognise Henry as king and at the same time
expect him to listen to his requests. But Henry was not an unreasonable
man, and what happened next offers us a small but telling insight into his
character. He readmitted Hangest and told the experienced diplomat that
it was extraordinary that the king of France could have expected him to
do his bidding in this manner. Hangest was left in no doubt that he did
not deserve to have an audience. Nevertheless, when the time came for
him to speak, he resolutely announced Charles's demand that Isabella be
returned by 1 November. Henry was astounded, and asked whether this
message was supposed to be good for their two nations. Hangest affirmed
that it was, and explained that it was because of a promise Henry had
himself made – to return Isabella – and added that 'there is no greater
good for a prince or anyone than to be faithful to his promises'.[8]

Henry might have reacted badly to having this philosophy flung in his
face. Instead he invited the Frenchman to dine with him the following
evening. The two men ate together again the evening after that, and were
able to have a long conversation. On the second evening, when Henry
had discussed the matter with his council, it was announced by Thomas
Percy that the king had decided to keep his promise to return Isabella. He
would also keep the 200,000 francs. Hangest then found himself shaking
hands with the king, something he could hardly have expected on first
being admitted into his presence. In the event, Isabella was not returned
to France until the following year, but the episode is a rare detailed example
of Henry in action, and reveals a streak of pragmatism in him, and even
forbearance, despite his injured pride.

*

Henry's problems were growing. Men who had served on his abortive
Scottish mission were aware both of its failure and the slowness to pay
them their wages for serving. Those with interests in Wales were concerned
that they were prey to Welsh outlaws and insurgents. In England, clergymen
were mindful that heresy was on the increase, despite Henry's promises to
defend the Church. The most important problem facing him – his financial chaos – was far from being solved. As the second parliament of the
reign approached, people began to look at the Lancastrian servants whom
Henry had brought into government and to question whether they were
the right men to occupy high office.

Henry was thus on the political back foot when he received a visit from
a man who had travelled several thousand miles to see him. This was the
emperor of Byzantium, Manuel II, whom he met on Blackheath, just south
of London, on 21 December 1400. Manuel's hope was that Henry would

live up to his chivalric reputation and lead an army to Constantinople to defend the eastern half of Christendom against the sultan, Bayezid. Reports of Henry's chivalric deeds in his youth had no doubt reached the emperor from King Sigismund of Hungary and King Wenceslas of Bohemia. Boucicaut had gone to Constantinople the previous year (1399) and had accompanied Manuel to Paris to beg the help of the French.[9] Manuel broached the idea of travelling to England in the summer of 1400, but his visit was deferred on account of Henry's campaigns in Scotland and Wales.

The visit of an emperor was an exceptionally rare occasion; there were only two 'emperors' in medieval Europe (the Holy Roman Emperor being the other one). Never before had the emperor of Byzantium visited England. Crowds gathered to see the strange potentate and his companions, all dressed in long white tabards, almost puritan by comparison with the colourful, extravagant clothes of the English court.[10] The long-haired and bearded Eastern priests contrasted sharply with the tonsured English clerics. Prayers were said daily by the Byzantines, and the English witnesses paid due attention to their strange rites. In an effort to please the English, the Byzantines declared that three British princes, Trehern, Llywelyn and Meric – uncles of the Emperor Constantine, founder of Constantinople – were among the common ancestors of the Byzantine nobility, and thus there was a distant bond of kinship between the people of the East and those of Britain. Notwithstanding the unlikelihood of this, Henry entered the city of London in a procession along with the emperor, and led him to Eltham to spend the Christmas season.

For Henry, the emperor's visit presented an opportunity to promote himself as a splendid king, worthy of his guest. At Eltham, in the outer court of the palace, tournaments, hunts and plays were held to entertain the imperial company. Pennons and standards bearing the royal arms were painted for the occasion, and the emperor was maintained in the highest standards of luxury. Twelve aldermen of London performed as mummers. Henry's eight-year-old daughter, Blanche, presided over the thirteen jousts (which took place on 1 January, with blunt lances). All the ladies represented by their challengers took honourable and romantic names – Venus, Virtue, Nature, Penelope, Delilah and Cleopatra – and the knights who took part similarly drew their names from chivalric literature, such as Ardent Desirous, Lancelot, Ferombras and Lost Wisdom.[11] Henry himself was variously described as 'the king of Albion', 'the lord of the land of wonders' or 'the king of Great Britain'. English witnesses declared Henry to be a deserving successor to Charlemagne and Arthur, and the 'worthy successor of King Saint Louis' (from whom he was descended). The emperor himself wrote that Henry was the smartest man in his dress, and witty too.[12] He added that Henry outdid all other men in personal strength (presumably in the jousting), and made many friends through his good sense. He was 'the one man of all the company who blushed at not doing enough for his guests – good at the start, good at the finish, and getting better every day'. For visiting emperors, Henry could be the very embodiment of chivalric courtesy.

Whatever the appearances of his court, and however many compliments were paid to him, Henry was in dire financial difficulties. He could barely afford to pay for the emperor's visit, let alone finance an expensive overseas war. Besides, with men prepared to assassinate him in England, an insecure Scottish border and a rebellion in Wales, he could not afford to leave his realm. It would be too easy for a Ricardian sympathiser or a supporter of the Mortimers to oust him, just as he himself had removed Richard. He made arrangements for the emperor to stay at Eltham until February, and gave him £2,000 towards fighting the Turks.[13] But that was all he could do – that and make his apologies.

*

Henry's second parliament met at Westminster on 20 January 1401. He knew it was going to be a bruising occasion. Certain representatives had approached him privately in advance with requests for his attention, which had irritated him. But there was a deeper unease. Throughout all the estates of the realm – nobility, clergy and commons – there was growing concern that he had promised everything and delivered nothing but large debts.

Chief Justice Thirning delivered the opening address. Wishing to put a positive gloss on the reasons for calling the parliament, he declared that its prime purpose was the maintenance and support of the Church. He followed it with a declaration that the king was determined to see that the law should apply equally to the rich as well as the poor, as he had sworn at his coronation. Then came the sting. Thirning recounted the many reasons for the king's impoverishment, namely his campaign to save the realm from Richard's tyranny, the costs of putting down the Epiphany Rising, the campaigns in Scotland and Wales, the necessity of returning Princess Isabella, the defence of Calais, and the likelihood of war in Gascony. The commons would be required to pay for all these, and to reimburse the loans which Henry had had to take out. It marked the failure of his promise not to levy taxation except in wartime, after only fifteen months of his reign.

The elected Speaker, Sir Arnold Savage, was an experienced representative from Kent. In a bold move, Savage declared that the commons should not be burdened by taxes and tallages, such as Henry now proposed.

Savage's speech was the first of a number of such confrontations. Over the next six weeks the commons adopted the most flattering, polite language and yet demanded reforms far beyond those which Henry himself would have wanted to grant. Several times Savage was required, or felt it necessary, to apologise for the commons' presumption. The commons even requested that in future the king should address their petitions *before* they agreed to render the taxation demanded. From Henry's point of view, this was tantamount to holding him to ransom.

Henry was alarmed. He was facing a crisis, and it showed every sign of worsening. In explaining why he needed more money he could not help but draw attention to his failure in Scotland and his unpopularity in Wales. The four offices of his household (wardrobe, great wardrobe, privy wardrobe and chamber) had spent a total of nearly £60,000 over the first year of his reign, and much of this had been in Wales and Scotland.[14] The commons saw an opportunity to take the initiative. With regard to Wales, they submitted no fewer than eleven petitions for action. These included such measures as barring Welshmen from buying land in England, from holding public office in the border towns and from prosecuting an Englishman in Wales. Although Henry tried to minimise the extent of the anti-Welsh legislation, and refused to rule out granting a general pardon for those involved in Glendower's rising, he could not resist the swell of anti-Welsh sentiment around him, and was forced to agree to most of the commons' demands.

Such were the circumstances when, on 26 February, Henry was presented with a petition on behalf of the prelates, proposed by Thomas Arundel, archbishop of Canterbury. A relapsed heretic, William Sawtre, had been tried in convocation and deemed guilty, whereupon the clergy demanded the 'customary' death sentence of burning at the stake. This was unusual; it certainly was not customary in England to burn people for lapsing into heretical ways. It *was* customary to burn women for petty treason – attempting to kill their husbands or lords – but burning heretics had previously only been known on the Continent and in Ireland.[15] Nevertheless, on 26 February Henry issued the order for the mayor of London to burn Sawtre in a public place in the city. The horrific sentence was carried out on 2 March. Sawtre thus became the first man in England officially to suffer death by burning for heresy, being packed into a barrel and set upon a great fire.[16]

At the end of February the commons tackled Henry over the key issue of the parliament. His officers were nearly all friends from the Lancastrian household, with little or no experience of national government. Henry was trying to run the country as if it was a large extension of the duchy of Lancaster. Henry's view was that he had appointed officers whom he could trust absolutely: men who had already shown they were prepared to follow him on crusades, into exile and even into a revolution. But that was just the point: they served Henry, not England. It made his kingship resemble Richard's in that it was a personal form of government. Over the subsequent days he was forced to remove his faithful Lancastrian officers, including Thomas Rempston, Thomas Tutbury, Thomas Erpingham and John Scarle, and replace them with men who had gained their experience under Richard II. None of these men fell from favour; all remained close to Henry and were found other positions in the royal household. Nevertheless, the key positions of government were now vested in men who were of sufficient experience to manage affairs of state and of sufficient rank to resist Henry's personal commands.[17]

The new chancellor was Edmund Stafford, bishop of Exeter, who had served as chancellor to Richard II. Thomas Percy, earl of Worcester, became the new royal steward, just as he had been under Richard II. Thomas More and Thomas Brounflete, respectively treasurer and controller of the royal household, had also been civil servants in Richard II's reign. Such appointments were a severe correction to Henry's government. Yet the commons went even further, and presented a petition that the king should name his officers in parliament, and define their duties, and not replace them before the following parliament. In addition, they requested that he should do the same with the royal council.[18] It was a sharp attack on Henry's authority, being an attempt by the commons to hold Henry's officers and the council to account. Although their petition was not granted, Henry's new officers were indeed sworn in before the king in parliament. As for the council, the more powerful magnates began to take a greater role, at the cost of Henry's Lancastrian officers.[19] The encroachment on the royal prerogative was obvious, and there was nothing Henry could do.

By the second week in March Henry had been forced into a number of tight corners. He had been forced to agree to almost all the anti-Welsh legislation.[20] His obedient household officers had been replaced with magnates strong enough to question his rule. His financial embarrassment had been exposed. He had agreed to make concessions regarding immediate payment for items purveyed to the royal household. His council had been altered at the commons' request. Yet despite all this, he still had not received his grant of taxation. This did not come until 10 March. Afterwards he declared his refusal to accept the principle that the king should answer the commons' petitions before they had made their grant, but in reality he had been forced to do so already. It was a turning point in the relationship between the king and the commons.

It was also on 10 March, the last day of the parliament, that Henry gave his assent to the most famous piece of legislation of perhaps his whole reign. It arose from a petition put forward by the prelates, supported by a commons' petition against the Lollards. The prelates asked that no one in England 'should presume to preach publicly or secretly without first having sought and obtained a diocesan licence' and that no one 'should teach, hold or instruct anything, secretly or openly, or produce or write a book, contrary to the Catholic faith'. Judgement was to follow within three months of the arrest. The petition ended by specifying that if the wrong-doers refused to abjure their heretical faith, then royal officers should be assigned by the king to carry out the sentences 'lest these wicked doctrines and heretical and erroneous opinions, or their authors or supporters in the said kingdom, be maintained or in any way increased, which God forbid'.[21]

In theory, this amounted to something not far short of the state per-secution of heretics. Henry, 'with the consent of the magnates and other nobles of his kingdom present at this parliament', granted the petition in full. And he added certain further clauses; for example: that heretics shall pay a fine to the king in proportion to the magnitude of their crime. With regard to heretical books, Henry declared that they should be delivered to diocesan officials within forty days of the proclamation of the statute. And then – to make matters absolutely clear – it was pronounced that such persons found guilty and refusing to abjure their heresy, or being pronounced relapsing after abjuring, should 'be publicly burned in a high place . . .' to 'strike fear into the minds of others'.

De heretico comburendo (about the burning of a heretic), as the statute became known, did indeed strike fear into the minds of others, being the most stringent and terrifying religious legislation ever enacted in England and the legal basis for Mary I's burnings in the sixteenth century. But why did Henry, who had placed such emphasis on mercy at the outset of his reign, not only support the petition but even enlarge upon it? Can this be reconciled with what we know of Henry's character and personal priorities?

At fifteen, Henry had been conventionally religious. By thirty-three, he was spiritually more sophisticated. The process was one of constant develop-ment, from his crusade and pilgrimage to the emergence of his personal spirituality, reflected in his worship of the Trinity. In his anointment with the oil of St Thomas at his coronation we can see how religious symbols had increased in importance as he himself had assumed a greater polit-ical role. That he should have acquiesced to requests for a tightening up of religious control, in line with the demands of both the commons and the prelates (led by his close friend Thomas Arundel) is hardly surprising. For a king wishing to be seen as absolutely devout, the enshrinement of Sawtre's punishment in statute law was a test easily passed.

But beyond this, it is possible to see other, more personal factors at work, such as Henry's own seriousness, his individualism and his conservatism. The evidence of this parliament shows Henry trying to manage the realm in an authoritarian fashion, trusting his obedient household staff rather than the magnates, who might hold him to account. It indicates a strong desire to retain control, and this in turn reveals a personal commitment to government. This explains why it was that a would-be merciful king enacted *de heretico comburendo*. It was meant to be the ultimate threat – and indeed only once more in his reign was a man burned for relapsing into heresy – but it was also meant to show that Henry was as firmly committed to stamping out religious dissent as he was to eradicating its political equivalent, treason. Mercy was all very well in theory, but, as he had learnt from the Epiphany Rising, there were limits to how merciful a king really could be.

*

Henry was stung by the intensity of the criticism in the 1401 parliament but it was not without justification. Across the kingdom, officers of the king were attacked as they tried to gather taxes. The women of Bristol fought a battle with the tax collectors, shouting that the king had promised not to demand a subsidy so they would not pay. The townspeople of Dartmouth in Devon chased a royal tax collector to the quay and forced him to flee for his life in a rowing boat. In the small Somerset town of Norton St Philip, a tax collector and his servant were killed. Local support for the murderers – who had inflicted more than a hundred wounds on their victims – prevented them from being brought to justice. At Abergavenny three thieves were freed from the gallows, Robin Hood-style, by archers who killed Sir William Lucy, the officer responsible for carrying out the executions.[22] Law and order was collapsing, and Henry was unsure how to respond.

Part of Henry's problem was that he was removed from the actual events on the ground. There being no equivalent of a 'news service', he only heard about such failures when someone told him. Fearing his reaction at such implicit criticism, few men were so bold. One who was able to speak plainly to him was his confessor, Philip Repingdon. Repingdon was about twenty years older than Henry, and had known him nearly all his life. He was the abbot of Leicester and chancellor of the University of Oxford, and had been present in the parliament of 1401. When he spoke to Henry about the lawlessness of the realm, Henry listened. Indeed, the king was so shocked that he asked Repingdon to write down his comments in a letter.[23]

The text of the long letter which Repingdon eventually wrote on 4 May (three days after the murders at Norton St Philip) is still extant.[24] 'Most illustrious prince and lord', he began, 'may it please your most gracious highness to look with your customary consideration upon me, your majesty's most humble servant, who prostrates himself at your feet quite desolate with grief ... Never since my youth do I recall hearing such foreboding in wise men's hearts, because of the disorder and unrest which they fear will shortly befall this kingdom. For law and justice are exiles from the kingdom; robbery, killing, adultery, fornication, persecution of the poor, injury, injustice and outrages of all kinds abound, and instead of the rule of law, the will of the tyrant now suffices.' Repingdon did not pull any punches. 'Now widows, the fatherless and orphans wring their hands and tears flow down their cheeks, whereas recently, at the time of your entry into the kingdom of England, all the people were clapping their hands and praising God with one voice, and going forth, as did the sons of Israel to meet Christ on Palm Sunday, crying out to heaven for you, their anointed king, as if you were a second Christ, "Blessed is he that cometh in the name of the Lord", our king of England.' Repingdon concluded that perhaps twenty thousand people in England deserved execution because of the collapse of law and order.

The combination of the 1401 parliament, Repingdon's report and the murder of royal officials shocked Henry into action. No one could accuse him of being lazy before this date but henceforth he began to apply extra-ordinary energy to the business of running the realm. His claims to be a new warrior-king in the image of his grandfather, he now realised, were inappropriate and inadequate to guarantee justice and safety from attack. Consequently he tried to involve himself personally at almost every level of government. According to Adam Usk, he went to Norton St Philip to remedy the problems there. On the financial front, he dutifully removed Norbury as treasurer and appointed the experienced official Laurence Allerthorpe in his place. Nor did he shirk international diplomacy: he issued new commissions for a new round of discussions with the French and personally received ambassadors from the duke of Milan, the king of Sweden and Denmark, and Count Rupert, the new Holy Roman Emperor.[25] Similarly he personally received information about the treaty with the Scots. Diplomatic papers concerning the duke of Guelderland were brought to him for his consideration. And all the while he was personally receiving almost all the petitions presented to the government, dealing with as many as forty per week and delegating barely a handful to the council.[26] Somehow, despite this wholehearted involvement in domestic and foreign business, he still managed to find time to enjoy himself. A payment was made about this time for compensation to a knight who had fought with the long sword against the king and been wounded in the neck.[27] And Henry found the time to indulge himself in physical love too. Edmund Lebourde, his only illegitimate child, was born in this year.[28]

*

Henry's personal involvement in so many aspects of government inevitably meant that he was overstretching himself. While he concentrated on the internal workings of the government he was prevented from being in Ireland, or patrolling the seas, or campaigning in Wales. The solution was to delegate responsibility, but that raised the question of who was sufficiently trustworthy. The northern lords were employed in maintaining the Scottish border or commanding the forces at Chester. The other obvious candidates were his sons. Their loyalty to the Lancastrian regime was guaranteed but the eldest was not yet fifteen. Nevertheless, Henry firmly believed that they had a duty to do, despite their youth. He also believed that early experience in a position of responsibility would be to their advantage. Prince Henry was already at Chester with Hotspur, providing effective leadership to the troops in North Wales. His success was a model for his younger brothers' education.

Ireland was to be the destination for Henry's second son, Thomas. The situation there was not dissimilar to that in England and Wales. The key issue was a chronic lack of government money, resulting in a decline of law and order. By the beginning of 1401, Sir John Stanley, the King's Lieutenant in Ireland, had no reserves left on which to call, and the attack on Ulster that year by the Scots exposed the weakness of English rule further. So on 18 May, Henry decided to demonstrate his commitment to the Irish problem by appointing Thomas to be lieutenant of Ireland.[29] Measures were accordingly made to secure his passage. Sir Thomas Rempston was given command of the fleet, and the new constable of Dublin, Janico Dartasso, was made his deputy, to rout out any piracy in the Irish Sea.

Henry knew he would be giving Thomas a hard education. In July 1401 the archbishops of Dublin and Armagh told him exactly what to expect. The king's authority had no power in Ireland, they said, due to the number of people with commissions exempting them from local jurisdiction. The mercenaries were acting like an occupying army, taking what land and property they wanted. Gangs roamed the countryside, stealing money and food. In addition the royal castles were crumbling.[30] Nevertheless, Henry entrusted his son to his faithful old retainers, Sir Thomas Erpingham and Sir Hugh Waterton, and planned his departure in November, after Thomas had turned fourteen. If Ireland was in such a bad way, then there was all the more reason to despatch a royal lieutenant there sooner rather than later.

To give an impression of Thomas's first year in Ireland, it is worth referring to a letter written by the archbishop of Dublin in August 1402. The tone is similar to Repingdon's letter: humble but at the same time critical. 'Most excellent, most dread and sovereign lord, with the greatest humility, and with all the obeisance that we know how', the archbishop began,

> we recently wrote to your high nobleness concerning the great inconvenience and danger which our most honoured lord, your son, and all his people and soldiers at that time were under, through nonpayment from England . . . We testify anew that our said lord, your son, is so destitute of money that he has not a penny in the world, nor can borrow a single penny because all his jewels and his plate [silver] that he can spare are spent and sunk in wages. And also his soldiers are departed from him, and members of his household are on the point of deserting.[31]

The archbishop went on to say how he felt that, properly, he or one of his companions should have laid all these things before the king in person. However, so great was the danger they were facing that they did not dare leave the security of Naas, where the prince was practically besieged. The prince himself wrote at the end of the year, stating that many of his soldiers had deserted on account of his failure to pay their wages. Despite this, it was not until 1 September 1403 that Henry authorised his son's return to England. Indeed, he had initially appointed Thomas – to whom he was as close as any of his sons – to stay in Ireland for a full six years, until he was twenty. Few monarchs have expected so much of their sons or placed them in so much danger at such a young age. Had Richard put a fourteen-year-old boy in such a position, he would have been castigated as callous or irresponsible. But in Henry's case it is evident that he was neither. It was simply a matter of duty.

*

No one took the business of royal duty as seriously as the king himself. From his abundant energy in running the government to his willingness to encounter risks in the course of defending the realm, he was absolutely committed. Unlike a king who had passively inherited the throne, Henry had to prove himself worthy of his title. This is particularly clear in his policy towards Wales, which now returned to the top of the political agenda. Although Prince Henry and Hotspur were already engaged in manoeuvres restricting the spread of Welsh nationalism, Henry was determined to be seen in Wales by his people, and to demonstrate his preparedness to defend the region. Again, it was something he had to do in person.

It could be said that the renewal of Welsh nationalism was as much a product of the anti-Welsh legislation of the 1401 parliament as Glendower's renewed efforts. Henry had been wise to try and limit it. It was one thing to lead a campaign attacking an insurgency and quite another to authorise a repressive series of laws against the entire Welsh people, including those who had remained loyal.[32] Rumours spread through Wales that the Welsh people and their way of life were under attack, even to the extent of abolishing the Welsh language. It seemed to the Welsh that they would henceforth be regarded as second-class citizens, prohibited even from intermarrying with the English.

On Good Friday 1401 (1 April), William ap Tudor and about forty Welsh rebels murdered a couple of guards and marched into the near-impregnable Conway Castle while the rest of the garrison was at mass. It was a dramatic gesture but without a general Welsh rising to support them their position was hopeless. They realised this and began negotiations with Hotspur, lieutenant of North Wales, on 13 April. A week later Hotspur agreed in principle that they might be pardoned. After handing over nine of their companions to be executed as traitors – whom they reputedly seized and bound while they were asleep – the Tudors were permitted to relinquish the castle without penalty.[33] Hotspur duly took the nine and hanged, eviscerated and quartered them. No one gained much honour from the incident but it was further evidence of discontent in Wales, and discontent which was growing more severe, not less.

Glendower was raising another army. In May he won a minor battle against an English force at Mount Hyddgen near Cardigan, and in the wake of this had written to several Welsh landowners urging them to join his revolt.[34] Hearing this, Henry immediately left Wallingford Castle and marched to Worcester. On the way he received a letter from his council directing him not to go to Wales in person, on account of the danger. But Henry had heard reports of very large numbers of men joining Glendower, and deemed it necessary to go in person precisely because of the danger – not to himself but because of the likelihood of the revolt spreading. However, arriving in Worcester he received news of an English victory, won by Lord Charlton. Many Welshmen had been captured and many more had fled.[35] It gave him sufficient breathing space to return to London and consult with his council in person.

Henry was back in London by 27 June. On that day he saw Princess Isabella, whom he was finally sending back to her father. He also intervened in the case of Hugh Blowet, a Scots herald, who had been seized and tried for uttering deprecating remarks in France about Henry. The Court of Chivalry had sentenced him to be forced to ride on his horse through London, facing its tail, and to have his tongue cut out. Henry pardoned him – before he lost his tongue – and sent him to the king of Scotland with letters detailing his offence and his pardon. But small acts of mercy could not divert attention from the financial and strategic problems now facing him. A few days later he received a letter from Hotspur complaining about the lack of financial support he had received for maintaining peace in North Wales.

Hotspur had previously written requesting sums of money on 10 April, 3 May, 17 May, 25 May and 4 June. On one of these occasions (17 May) he had threatened to resign if he was not reimbursed for his expenses. Henry may have thought that the ample rewards which Hotspur had received, plus his salary as lieutenant of North Wales, were sufficient to cover his costs. Besides, as Henry pointed out in a letter to his son, Hotspur was at least partly responsible for Conway Castle falling in the first place.[36] Now Hotspur stated that he had been to London to seek reimbursement from the treasurer, and had not been satisfied. Moreover, he boldly accused Henry in his letter of underestimating the costs of keeping the Marches in check, and prayed that if the town again fell due to lack of money, those who refused to pay him should be blamed, not him. It was not the kind of support which Henry needed from one of his most important and active officers.

*

The issues facing Henry in the late summer of 1401 were beginning to overwhelm him. Despite his own huge efforts to maintain control of the government, he was increasingly unable to cope. On 20 July, while at Selborne Priory in Hampshire, he assented to the council's request that he hold a great council to discuss 'certain weighty matters'. Still determined to control business himself as far as possible, Henry dictated a list of those who should be summoned and handed it to his clerk, Henry Bowet, to take to Westminster. The total – almost three hundred men – amounted to practically a full parliament.[37]

The great council assembled at Westminster on 16 August and heard the catalogue of threats to the kingdom. In Scotland, overtures of peace had been rejected. In France, King Charles had created his son duke of Aquitaine and was threatening to invade Gascony. The count of Périgord himself arrived to tell Henry that over recent months not only Périgord itself had fallen to the French but a total of thirty castles.[38] If there was to be war with France, then Calais too needed defending. The coasts required stronger defences. The Welsh rebellion was patently not over. In England purveyors were continuing not to pay for goods simply because they had no money. Putting together all the problems into one sum, it was calculated that the government's required expenditure amounted to £130,000 for the year.[39] Some prioritising was needed urgently.

The range and the seriousness of the threats meant that none of them could be ignored. Rather it was a case of calmly arranging who was to lead which army, and what forces could be allocated to each field of action. Further negotiations with the Scots and French were authorised. The earl of Rutland was appointed lieutenant of Gascony.[40] An embassy, including Hotspur, was appointed to negotiate with the Scots. Money was allocated to the defence of Calais, Ireland, Wales and Gascony, as well as the costs of returning Princess Isabella and paying annuities. Henry's direct responsibility, with the council's assent, was to be the defence of Wales. Accordingly, on 18 September he gave the order to muster at Worcester on 1 October.

Henry rode into Worcester on the appointed day amid the crowds of men-at-arms, archers and knights gathering for the campaign. On the 10th the army set out, marching quickly through South Wales down into Cardigan.[41] As with all his campaigns, we know very few of the details. On 14 October he was at Llandovery, from which he wrote to the treasurer demanding a thousand marks to be sent to him. He witnessed the drawing, hanging and quartering of Llywelyn ap Griffith Vaughan there, a rebel lord, who had promised to take him to Glendower and who then had led him into a trap. Proceeding to the monastery of Strata Florida, he ordered his army to destroy everything in the region. The abbey itself was stripped of its plate and horses were lodged in the church.[42]

It was another very short campaign, barely two weeks. Like its predecessor, the principal objects were for Henry to be seen in person and for him to see with his own eyes the character of the terrain and the rebels he was facing. Back at Hereford he ordered the safekeeping of a number of Welsh castles, and then progressed via Worcester and Woodstock to London, in order to meet his council. But this time his failure to engage Glendower had left him exposed. As Henry marched towards London, Glendower saw an opportunity and sacked Welshpool for a second time. Immediately after this success, he attacked Carnarvon Castle in the north. Even though his men were driven off with heavy losses, he effectively demonstrated his defiance of Henry's short campaign. He built on this in November, when he wrote to the king of Scotland and various Irish lords.[43] He called upon them to join him in his struggle to throw off the oppression of the English, and to send him as many men-at-arms and foot soldiers as they could spare. In his letter to the king of Scotland he went so far as to promise to 'serve and obey' him, offering to transfer his allegiance to Robert III.

The vultures perched on the Welsh and Scottish borders could see the king of England ailing, and were preparing to swoop down for the kill.

THIRTEEN

Uneasy Lies the Head

Canst thou, O partial sleep, give thy repose
To the wet sea-boy in an hour so rude;
And in the calmest and most stillest night
With all appliances and means to boot,
Deny it to a king? Then, happy low, lie down!
Uneasy lies the head which wears a crown.
Henry IV Part Two, Act 3, Scene 1

By Christmas 1401, Henry's hopes of reviving the glorious kingship of
Edward III had been destroyed. Only two years after his triumphant
coronation, he was under pressure in almost every area of his responsibility. Bitter feelings against him were spreading as food became increasingly scarce and purveyors continued to requisition food for the royal
household.[1] Thomas Walsingham recorded a story about a new attempt
on the king's life. A vicious three-toothed iron implement was concealed
in his bedstraw, which would have skewered him when he lay down on
it.[2] Such a story is almost certainly untrue.[3] Nevertheless, it illustrates
how unpopular Henry had become in certain quarters. Facing a three-
pronged barbarous instrument of torture was not an edifying image for
a pious warrior-king.

Part of the reason for his declining popularity, and a fundamental reason
for the lawlessness of the country, was the soaring price of corn. The
harvest of 1400 had been bad; now that of 1401 failed too, so that wheat
had doubled in price.[4] This coincided with a dramatic drop in revenue
from wool exports. These had once benefited Richard II to the tune of
£47,000 per year but now barely reached £39,000.[5] Thus, just as Henry
had greater need to call for money from the wool merchants, they had
less ability to pay. Similarly, as his purveyors came under heavier pressure
to find food for men in royal service, those from whom they were taking
the food had less to give. The result was that they themselves ended up
contributing to the breakdown of law and order. It was a vicious circle,
and one which could not be ended simply by dropping the import duties
on corn until midsummer the following year, as the council suggested.

Circumstances such as these made it very difficult for Henry to act in what he would have considered a kingly way. He might have considered matters of finance beneath his dignity but he could hardly ignore the weight of loans under which the exchequer was operating. At the same time he could hardly put all royal business on hold until his finances were more securely established. This extended far beyond his need to maintain law and order. The marriage of his daughters to potentially important allies was another very expensive royal responsibility. There was a solution to this problem: the old feudal responsibility for every knight's fee to pay an aid of twenty shillings on the marriage of the king's eldest daughter. But levying such an aid for the first time in living memory was not likely to soothe the anger of those who had felt betrayed by the demand for taxation in the last parliament. Lords of manors would simply pass on the expense to the tenants. As Adam Usk later put it: 'the king imposed a tax on the whole kingdom in order to marry his daughters'.[6] But if Henry wanted Blanche to marry the heir of the Holy Roman Emperor, he had little choice. Besides, he knew there would be another expensive royal wedding before long. His own.

Henry's relationship with the widow Joan of Navarre was one of the real surprises of his reign. She was the same age as him, the daughter of Charles the Bad, king of Navarre, and Joan de Valois, daughter of King John II of France. Thus she was Henry's third cousin twice over. By her previous husband, the duke of Brittany, she had eight children. Following the duke's death, she had acted as regent in Brittany during the minority of her eldest son. She was not just a Navarrese princess, she was an important member of the French royal family.

Such a match was bound to cause shock waves in society, on both sides of the Channel. England was on the verge of war with France, and had been since the revolution. As recently as November 1401 the council was considering the question of how 'to counter the malice of those of France who wanted war'.[7] Such was the fear that it was deemed necessary to summon a great council to discuss the matter in January. Henry accordingly kept his discussions about the marriage secret. Nevertheless, he could hardly conceal the presence of Navarrese ambassadors at his court. When his council asked what the ambassadors had come to talk about, he would say only that they would be told in due course.[8]

Although it is not known when Henry and Joan first met, they were probably already acquainted when Henry travelled to France for the celebrated meeting at Ardres in 1396 and the subsequent royal wedding at Calais. On that occasion he stayed almost a month in France, and had several opportunities to see her. They would have met again at the Garter feast at Windsor in April 1398, which Joan attended with her husband.[9] It is likely that they met again during Henry's exile, when his marriage to Mary of Berry was being discussed.[10] No marriage at this stage was possible, of course, as the duke of Brittany was still alive. But after the old duke's death in November 1399 it seems that the idea swiftly entered Joan's mind, if not Henry's too. Within three months she sent ambassadors to Henry, and on 15 February 1400 wrote him a letter which is almost intimate in its expression of good wishes:

My most dear and honoured lord and cousin,
Forasmuch as I am eager to hear of your good estate – which may our Lord make as good as your noble heart can desire, and as good as I could wish for you – I pray you, my most dear and most honoured lord and cousin, that you would tell me often of the certainty of it, for the great comfort and gladness of my heart. For whenever I am able to hear a good account of you, my heart rejoices exceedingly. And if, of your courtesy, you would like to hear the same from over here – thank you – at the time of writing my children and I are all in good health (thanks be to God, and may He grant the same to you) as Joanna de Bavelen, who is bringing these letters to you, can explain more plainly . . . And if anything will please you that I am able to do over here, I pray you to let me know; and I will accomplish it with a very good heart according to my power. My most dear and honoured lord and cousin, I pray the Holy Ghost that He will have you in his keeping.
Written at Vannes, 15 February, the duchess of Brittany.[11]

The tone of this letter leaves no doubt that there was a genuine closeness between Henry and Joan. It goes far beyond the usual politeness between a member of the French royal family and the king of England, especially considering that it was written a few days after the English ambassadors at Calais had warned Henry that war with France was more likely than peace. But there is more here to suggest a genuine closeness. Intimacy is the sole purpose of the letter: apart from its kind thoughts, it says nothing of consequence.[12] It implies – in Joan's thanks to Henry for asking after her health – that he had already written a letter to her. And it reveals that Joan, like Henry himself, was a believer in the power of the Trinity (as shown by the reference to the Holy Ghost). They were more than just friends; they shared a spiritual outlook.

Their courtship was conducted in secret and from afar. Ambassadors conveyed their communications to each other, never putting anything in writing as sensitive as the above letter. The obstacles to their relationship were not just limited to the likelihood of war between their countries and the disapproval of the French Crown. France recognised the pope at Avignon, Benedict XIII; the English recognised the Roman pontiff, Boniface IX. In order for Henry and Joan to marry, they had to obtain a dispensation, as they were related within the degrees of consanguinity prohibited by the Church. Not until 20 March 1402 did Joan obtain a bull from Pope Benedict allowing her to marry Henry. Immediately she empowered her ambassadors, Antony and John Rhys, to arrange the ceremony. They did so with great speed. She was married to Henry by proxy just two weeks later, at Eltham, on 2 April 1402. Present to witness proceedings were Henry's half-brother, John Beaufort, and several of his closest friends, including the archbishop of Canterbury and all three Percys, namely the earls of Northumberland and Worcester, and Hotspur.[13] The form of words used on this occasion included 'thereto I plight thee my troth', the first recorded appearance of the well-known phrase.[14]

Marriage was just the beginning of the struggle. As soon as the deed was done, Henry had to explain to his kingdom why he was marrying a Frenchwoman at this particular time. The English people were astonished. For her part, Joan had to persuade the rest of the French royal family that she could marry their enemy: the man who had ousted King Charles's son-in-law and thus deprived his daughter of the throne of England. She also had to persuade Benedict XIII to grant her permission to live among schismatics (those who supported his papal rival). But Joan was a resourceful and determined woman. Henry too had made up his mind.

These problems show that this was far from being a marriage of convenience. So it is likely that it was yet another royal love affair, like so many royal partnerships in the late middle ages.[15] Yet all royal marriages have a political dimension, however emotionally and spiritually close the couple may have been. In Henry's case this is made clear by simultaneously arranging his two daughters' marriages as well as his own. Blanche was already betrothed to the son of the Holy Roman Emperor, and was about to set out for the Rhineland; and Philippa's hand was the subject of discussion between Henry and the king of Denmark. These multiple negotiations indicate that Henry was looking at connections with ruling houses not just to cement alliances with other countries but in order to achieve a wider recognition of his dynasty. If he could persuade everyone else in Europe to accept him as the rightful king of England, and if he himself could marry a French duchess, how much longer could the French refuse to recognise him as king of England?

With his lofty ideas of kingship sinking like a ship beneath the choppy waves of insolvency, rebellion and revolt, he needed every bit of recognition he could get.

*

Henry's marriage was almost the only happy development in his life. In February 1402 he received a letter from his fourteen-year-old son Thomas, in Ireland, saying that several royal officers had deserted because he had been unable to pay them. The treasurer of England proved unable to balance the books, and was replaced by Henry's faithful clerk, Henry Bowet (now the bishop of Bath and Wells). In March the earl of Crawford, a Scottish admiral in the pay of Louis d'Orléans (who had turned against Henry along with the rest of the French royal family), began to harass English shipping.[16] In April Glendower ambushed and captured his archenemy Lord Grey of Ruthin and carried him off gleefully into the mountains, demanding an exorbitant ransom. The council advised Henry against permitting his daughter Philippa to marry King Eric of Denmark, much to Henry's annoyance. But by far the most worrying development was the discovery of a new threat to the Lancastrian dynasty. Rumours were circulating that Richard II was still alive.

Whether the Ricardian rumours of March–June 1402 count as the third revolt against Henry's rule is difficult to say. Certainly men were accused of attempting to overthrow Henry, and to kill him and his sons, and to reinstate Richard as king, and so there is no doubt that it constituted a serious threat.[17] But the means by which they hoped to achieve these things are unclear. It is hard now to discern any coordination of the various strands of discontent, beyond the fact that many of the dissidents were friars. It is possible that there were no actual plots at all, just widespread sedition. Considering the people's proven ability to dethrone a king, popular rumour could easily result in a real plot if left unchecked. The line between rumour and rebellion was not as clear as it had once been.

The discontented were united in one respect: they believed that, if Richard II was still alive, he should be restored to the throne. By that reckoning, strangely, it did not matter if he was actually dead. Those disaffected with Henry's kingship could take up arms in the name of Richard II and fight for his right still to be king *if* he was still alive. Whom they would actually crown if they were successful was a minor detail. The main objective was removing Henry, not restoring Richard.

The plot was first discovered in early May, when a priest was arrested at Ware in Hertfordshire. Before he was executed, he named many collaborators. Already the rumours about Richard's survival had spread abroad.

In April Jean Creton was sent by the French king to Scotland to discover whether the man there who claimed to be Richard was genuinely him. Although Creton quickly discovered – to his great disappointment – that the Scottish Richard was an impostor, he obviously did not circulate such information in England. On 9 May Henry issued an order to the sheriffs to take action against those who said Richard was alive. Two days later he wrote to the master of the Dominicans at Oxford warning him to keep his preachers under control. His words had little effect. A few days later, the prior of Launde was arrested and executed for treason.[18] On 27 May the prior of the Dominicans at Winchester was seized, as was the rector of Horsmonden (Kent). The head of the Cambridge Dominican house was taken into custody, along with one of his brethren. They and several other clergymen were committed to the Tower on 3 June.[19] A further proclamation had to be issued two days later against seditious preaching 'in taverns and other places where people gather'.

A friar from the Franciscan house at Aylesbury (Buckinghamshire) was arrested and brought before the king.

'You have heard that King Richard is alive, and you are glad?' Henry asked him.

'I am as glad as a man is glad of the life of his friend, for I am in his debt, as are all my kin, for he was our patron and promoter', answered the friar boldly.

'You have said openly that he lives, and so you have excited and stirred the people against me.'

'No.'

'Tell the truth as it is in your heart', insisted Henry. 'If you saw King Richard and me fighting on the battlefield together, with whom would you fight?'

'In truth, with him, for I am more beholden to him.'

'Do you wish that I and all the lords of the realm were dead?'

'No', replied the friar.

'What would you do if you had the victory over me?'

'I would make you duke of Lancaster', replied the friar.

'Then you are not my friend', declared Henry angrily.[20]

At his trial in June, John Bernard of Offley (Hertfordshire) claimed that he had been ploughing near his home when William Balshalf of Lancaster told him that Richard was alive and well and living in Scotland, and would return to England to meet his loyal supporters near Merevale Abbey (Warwickshire) on 24 June.[21] The recipient of this news promptly gathered more supporters, showing just how dangerous unsubstantiated rumours could be.

Henry continued to question the friars in person. One told him to his face that Richard would return and fight Henry 'as it is prophesied'.[22] Henry did not need to be reminded that the Prophecy of the Six Kings declared that the fifth king – Richard, the lamb – would lose his kingdom to a 'hideous wolf'; but he would fight back and recover his lands. Unlike the friar in this case, Henry knew for certain that Richard was dead, and that the prophecy could not come true. Even so, it was plain that those who hated him would just say that he was the sixth king – the mole or 'moldewarp' – under whom (according to the prophecy) the kingdom would be wrenched apart in three warring factions. He could not win.

Henry kept in mind his coronation oath to rule justly for all. He took pains to stress that he did not wish to punish men for being simple or naïve. He wrote to the sheriffs commanding them to announce that the king would not punish those who repeated the rumour, only those who started it.[23] He was as good as his word. He pardoned one Robert Westbroom of Bury St Edmunds for circulating rumours of Richard's survival because he had merely heard 'such lies and innocently repeated the same'.[24] John Bernard of Offley was likewise pardoned (after he had defeated Balshalf in judicial combat).[25] Other men were more dangerous. Sir Roger Clarendon was the illegitimate son of the Black Prince, and thus a half-brother of Richard II. Outlawed for murder in 1398, he had never been entertained at court by Henry.[26] He therefore had nothing to lose from opposing the regime, and may have been expected to take a leadership role during the hoped-for uprising. In the event, he was eliminated at an early stage. On 19 May Henry ordered him to be arrested, as well as a clerk, John Calf. Four days later, Clarendon, his esquire and valet were imprisoned in the Tower. They all protested their innocence but were found guilty of treason, and hanged.[27]

On 1 June, Henry held another revealing interview.[28] A Franciscan had betrayed a fellow friar of Leicester, who was planning to meet ten of his companions near Oxford on Midsummer's Eve and to go in search of Richard. One of these was an older man, Roger Frisby, a master of divinity. On investigation, two of the friars could not be found, but the remaining eight and Frisby were brought bound to London. When presented to him, Henry saw that some of them were young and illiterate. 'These are uncouth men, without understanding', he observed. Then, turning to Frisby, he said, 'you ought to be a wise man. Do you say that King Richard is alive?'

Frisby gave a straight reply. 'I do not say he is alive, but I say that if he is alive, he is the true king of England.'

'He resigned', retorted Henry.

'He resigned against his will, in prison, which is against the law.'

'He resigned with good will', Henry insisted.

But Frisby remained firm. 'He would not have resigned had he been free, and a resignation in prison is not free.'

'He was deposed', said Henry.

'When he was king, he was taken by force and put into prison, and despoiled of his realm, and you have usurped the crown.'

Henry must have been startled at Frisby's effrontery, but still he continued the debate. 'I have not usurped the crown, I was chosen by election.'

'The election is nothing, if the true and lawful possessor be alive', said Frisby. Then he added the words guaranteed to anger the king. 'And if he be dead, then he is dead by you, and if that be so, you have lost all right and title that you might have had to the crown.'

Shocked, Henry roared back, 'By my head, I shall have your head!'

'You never loved the Church', declared Frisby as Henry's men set hands on him, 'but always slandered it before you were king and now you shall destroy it.'

'You lie', Henry replied, as his men dragged the priest away to the confines of the Tower.

'We shall never cease to hear this clamour of King Richard until the friars are destroyed', said a knight at Henry's shoulder as the master was removed.

Henry seems to have agreed. When the master of the Franciscans came before him to plead mercy for those of his order, and assured Henry that he had directed his brethren not to speak ill of the king, Henry did not trust him. Referring to the eight friars – who were repeatedly tried until a jury could be found to condemn them – he replied in memorably chilling words: 'They will not be chastised by thee, and therefore they will be chastised by me.'[29]

*

Glendower had been greatly heartened by the capture of Lord Grey of Ruthin. In June he led a strike into the heart of the Mortimer lordship of Maelienydd. On 22 June 1402 at Bryn Glas, a hill near Pilleth, he defeated an army led by Sir Edmund Mortimer, uncle of the earl of March.[30] After the battle the Welsh women had gone to the dead bodies of the English and cut off their genitals, stuffing them into the dead men's mouths, and they cut off their noses and shoved them up their anuses.[31] Even worse (in the eyes of Henry's contemporaries), the corpses were not given a Christian burial. Henry had little choice but to do what he had already done twice: to take an English army and impose his authority where it mattered most, in Wales itself.

To his credit, he did not delay. On 25 June he wrote to the council telling them of Mortimer's capture and his determination to lead an army in person. The same day he issued an order summoning forces to assemble at Lichfield. Five days later he wrote another letter announcing the defeat of four hundred Scotsmen by George Dunbar and Hotspur at Nesbit Moor, but requiring that the council attend to the threat of twelve thousand Scotsmen now massing on the border, near Carlisle. By 5 July he was at Lichfield, coordinating preparations. He ordered Hereford, Ludlow and Chester castles to be fully provisioned, and Leominster to be fortified. In the course of planning he seemed to have decided to enhance his campaign and to invade with three armies, his largest offensive yet.

The plan was for the three armies to set out on 27 August and spend two weeks ravaging Wales.[32] One was to muster at Chester (led by the sixteen-year-old prince of Wales), one at Hereford (led by the earl of Stafford) and one at Shrewsbury (led by Henry in person). Henry did all he could to ensure that this campaign would end the Welsh revolt. He toured the Midlands rapidly, issuing orders and trying personally to direct as many things as he could.[33] No arms were to be transported into Wales, under pain of death. Command of the Southern Marches – from Wigmore – was entrusted to the earl of Stafford. The Marches north of Wigmore were placed in the keeping of the earl of Arundel, and the towns most vulnerable to a Welsh attack, such as Welshpool and Ludlow, were properly defended.

It was said that Henry had more than one hundred thousand men under orders that September.[34] Although contemporaries were very poor at assessing such large numbers, this exaggeration in proportion to their usual figures suggests that it was far larger than any army hitherto seen in the region. The village of Llanrwst was destroyed by Henry's forces. Yet still he failed to bring Glendower to heel. In fact, Henry's third campaign was less successful than both of his earlier ones. As before, when the English approached, the Welsh disappeared into the mountains. It was rumoured that Glendower had a magical stone, coughed up by a raven, that allowed him to become invisible. The reality was that the Welsh forces had the advantage of knowing the terrain, and were able to withdraw and disband long before the English scouts could find them. The local men and women fled, unwilling to be pressed into serving as guides for the English. One William Withiford, who did serve, was murdered by Glendower as soon as the English withdrew. Still the campaign might have served as a demonstration of English force, like Henry's earlier marches, had not the weather intervened. On 7 September torrential rain began to lash down, threatening to sweep the army away. The winds were so strong that men despaired of their lives. Henry himself, sheltering in his tent one night, was almost killed as the whole structure, poles and all, was blown down on top of him. Walsingham commented that, if he had not been sleeping in his armour, he would have been crushed. Several days of rain and gales disheartened the men and made further military progress impossible. Henry had also to bear in mind that he had summoned a parliament to meet at Westminster on 30 September, and his presence there was essential, for he desperately needed more money. So, when the two weeks of the campaign were up, the English returned to England, to dry their wet clothes and bathe their armour-chafed arms and legs.

It was a dismal moment, coming on top of so many other disappointments. But as Henry rode back to London to attend parliament, he heard great news from the north. The Scots had attacked, as he had expected, and had met an English army in battle at Homildon Hill on 14 September. The English commanders that day had been the earl of Northumberland, Hotspur and the Scottish earl of March (George Dunbar). The English archers had done their worst, and volley after volley of arrows had ripped apart the Scottish army. The remainder either fled, were captured or slaughtered by hand. Among the prisoners were eighty Scottish lords and knights, including the earl of Douglas and Lord Murdoch Stewart, son of the duke of Albany. In addition, thirty French knights had been fighting with the Scots, and were captured or killed. Last but by no means least, among the prisoners was Sir Adam Forrester, the Scottish negotiator who had tricked Henry into leaving Scotland in 1400, an act of duplicity which the king had not forgotten.[35] Henry ordered that no prisoners should be ransomed without his permission but should instead be brought to him at Westminster.

*

When Henry's third parliament gathered on 30 September, it was without his uncle, Edmund, duke of York. Edmund had died, at the age of sixty-two, on 1 August. He had not been close to Henry during Richard's reign, but he seems to have reassessed his position after Richard murdered his brother in 1397. From then on he seems to have been increasingly sympathetic to Henry, eventually playing a major role in undermining resistance in 1399. As the most senior of all the magnates, he had subsequently provided an important stabilising element in the establishment of Henry's regime. Thus there was a political as well as a personal loss for Henry, who had few close friends among the higher nobility.

The chancellor opened proceedings on 2 October. He reminded people of how God had sent Henry for the salvation and recovery of the realm, and how He had miraculously delivered their Scottish enemies to them as prisoners. He spoke about the schism in the Church and how the Holy Roman Emperor himself had written to Henry 'as to the most powerful king in the world' to heal the discord between Rome and Avignon. He outlined the challenges facing the government in respect of the Scottish war, the rebellion in Wales, the conflicts in Ireland, and the safe-keeping of Calais and Gascony. Henry was left facing the irony of being compared to 'the most powerful king in the world' on the one hand and having all his strategic shortcomings listed on the other.

Henry's problems largely stemmed – as before – from his financial situation. The treasury was empty and the loans he had taken out recently were larger than ever. With this in mind he deputed officers to explain to the commons how much taxation he required. The commons warily replied with a request that they might consult a committee of lords. Henry agreed, equally warily stating that he did not intend to set a precedent. The committee he named included his most trusted friends: the archbishop of Canterbury, the bishops of London, Lincoln and St David's, the earls of Somerset, Westmorland, Worcester and Northumberland, and the lords Roos, Berkeley, Bergavenny and Lovell. It is not difficult to gauge his priorities: on the one hand he desperately needed cash but, on the other, he could not afford to grant too many liberties.

The only good news Henry had to celebrate was the arrival of the Scottish prisoners. On 20 October the earl of Northumberland led Lord Murdoch Stewart and the other captives, including Adam Forrester, into the White Chamber, where Henry was enthroned. At the door to the chamber they were forced to kneel. Halfway across the room they were forced to kneel again. They had to kneel a third time as they approached the king. With Forrester cowering before him, Henry could afford to remind the Scotsman of the trick he had played on him two years earlier. In the course of the conversation Forrester suggested that Henry might now arrange a final peace. Henry responded calmly that 'the last time he had been in Scotland, the said Sir Adam, by many white lies and subtle promises, had suddenly caused him to leave'. If he had known Forrester then as well as he knew him now, he declared, 'he would not have left Scotland so readily'. He left Forrester and the other Scotsmen sweating on their knees for a few moments more. Then he told them that he would spare their lives, and invited them all to dinner. He had not forgotten the benefits of mercy.

One Scottish prisoner, the earl of Douglas, was noticeable by his absence. He had been wounded in five places and had lost an eye at Homildon Hill, but he did not die of his injuries, and was fit enough to fight another battle within the year, so it was probably not his physical health which kept him away from Westminster. The most likely explanation for the earl's absence lies in Hotspur's attitude towards Henry. Hotspur was increasingly resentful towards the king for not reimbursing him his expenses upon demand. His letters had assumed an increasingly arrogant tone over the last eighteen months, and the lucrative offices which Henry had given him and his family had not soothed his temper. Most of all, his brother-in-law, Sir Edmund Mortimer, had been a prisoner in the mountains of Wales for the last six months, and Henry had not even tried to ransom him. Henry had agreed to help raise the ransom for Lord Grey of Ruthin, but not Mortimer. Perhaps he suspected that Mortimer might have given himself up too easily into the clutches of the Welshman. Either way, it did not bode well for the restoration of good relations with Hotspur.

The parliament of 1402 was not nearly so bruising as that of 1401. All the same, some hard questions were raised about finance. The commons asked where Richard's great treasure had gone: John Ikelington, Richard II's clerk and the custodian of £44,000 of the hoard, was examined and acquitted. The money, it turned out, had all been given to the Percy family to defend the Scottish border. Another tough question was why Henry had appointed his personal friend, Henry Bowet, as treasurer. Was this not a return to his personal style of government, exercised through personal friends, about which parliament had warned him the previous year? Henry managed to resist a demand to examine his officers, but was forced to sack Bowet and replace him with a more experienced man.[36] Guy Mone, bishop of St David's and Richard II's treasurer in 1398, was given the unenviable task of righting the royal finances. Only after this, and after agreeing to a large number of petitions against the Welsh, against the friars and against the foreign priories, was the tax granted on the last day of the parliament (25 November 1402).

*

In late August, while he had been dashing around the Midlands, preparing to lead his three armies into Wales, Henry had received a letter from his estranged friend, Louis, duke of Orléans, the brother of the French king. It was stupefying.

> I, Louis . . . am writing to tell you that, with the aid of God and the blessed Trinity, in the desire which I have to gain renown, which you in like manner should feel, considering idleness the bane of lords of high birth who do not employ themselves in arms . . . I propose that we should meet at an appointed place, each of us accompanied by one hundred knights and esquires . . . there to fight each other until one of us surrenders, and the victorious man may do with his prisoners as he pleases

... I propose (after hearing your intentions) to be at my town of Angoulême, accompanied by the aforesaid number of knights and esquires. Now, if your courage be such as I think it is, for the fulfilment of this deed of arms, you may come to Bordeaux, when we may depute properly qualified persons to fix on a spot for the combat . . .[37]

Not surprisingly, Henry did not immediately respond. After all, what was Louis thinking of, challenging a king to a duel? But – as with his interrogations of the friars – Henry was unable to ignore a good argument; he was determined to have the final word. And where a point of honour was concerned, Henry knew that it had to be the one whose honour was impugned who answered the challenge. Ten days after parliament broke up, he sent a reply:

We write to inform you that we have seen your letter, containing a request to perform a deed of arms, and from the expressions contained therein, we understand that it is addressed to us, which has caused us no small surprise for the following reasons. First, on account of the truce . . . in which you yourself are a party. Second, on account of the alliance that was made between us at Paris, which you swore to uphold in the presence of our well-beloved knights and esquires, Sir Thomas Erpingham, Sir Thomas Rempston and John Norbury, to whom you gave letters, sealed with your great seal, reciting this treaty of alliance . . .

Since you have seen fit, without any cause, to act contrary to this treaty . . . we therefore inform you that we have annulled the letter of alliance received from you, and henceforth throw aside all love and affection towards you, for it seems to us that no prince, lord, knight or any person whatsoever ought to demand a combat from him with whom a treaty of friendship exists. In reply to your letter, we add that considering the very high rank in which it has pleased God to place us, we are not bound to answer any such demands unless made by persons of equal rank with ourselves. With regard to what you say, that we ought to accept your proposal to avoid idleness, it is true that we are not as often employed in arms and honourable exploits as our noble predecessors have been; but all-powerful God may, when he pleases, make us follow their steps, and we, through the indulgence of his grace, have not been so idle but have used our time to defend our honour . . .[38]

He finished off with a threat to invade the French-occupied parts of Gascony, at a time and place of his own choosing, and he urged Louis to be more circumspect in his letters in the future.

Politicking though these letters are, they reveal another dimension of Henry's perseverance: an adamant streak that prevented him from letting go of any question of his kingly status. No Welsh rebels were allowed to go unchecked, no friars were allowed to get away with sedition, and certainly no French prince could be permitted to deny him his title. He was a king, and that very fact had become the most important thing in his life. If anyone doubted it, he would answer them personally, defending his character and his royal status to the last.

Louis was of a similar proud disposition, and scorned Henry's reply in his next letter. He described it as 'a New Year's gift' and added:

In regard to your ignorance, or pretended ignorance, whether my letter could have been addressed to you, your name was on it, such as you received at the font, and by which you were always called by your parents when they were alive. I did not give you your new titles because I do not approve of the manner in which you attained them . . .[39]

And his justification for going against his own treaty of peace – a copy of which Henry had sent him – was that he 'never conceived it possible you could have done against your king what it is well known you have done'.

This was the crux of the matter. Few Frenchmen could understand why Henry had removed Richard from the throne, and even fewer approved of it. As they probably believed that Henry had violently killed Richard through the offices of 'Sir Piers Exton', there was an extra shock associated with this story, similar to that felt in England when it emerged that Richard had had his own uncle murdered. Thus Louis would have felt deeply embarrassed by the fact that he had promised to support Henry, and had agreed a treaty with him. So he felt obliged to defend his honour, and the only way he could do that was by challenging Henry to combat. That Henry would probably make mincemeat of Louis in the lists was neither here nor there; kings did not accept challenges, so it went without saying that there would be no duel. Louis was seeking to defend his dignity just by issuing the challenge. Henry should simply have ignored it.

But Henry could not ignore it. He sent another, even longer letter back to the duke, stating that 'we ought not to reply to your request [for the duel] nor to your accusations . . . however, as you attack our honour, we send you this letter . . .'. He turned Louis' pretended eagerness for combat in his first letter into the hot-headedness of youth, which then he claimed had taken 'a frivolous turn'. But the most interesting lines in all this sword-rattling concerned Richard's death. Henry wrote:

In regard to that passage in your letter, where you speak of the decease of our very dear cousin and lord, on whose soul God have mercy, adding 'God knows how it happened, and by whom caused', we do not know what you mean by this; but if you mean, or dare to say, that his death was caused by our order or consent, that is a lie, and will be a lie every time you say it, and this we are ready to prove, through the grace of God, in personal combat, if you be willing and have the courage to dare it . . . As to your saying that . . . 'at the time you made the alliance with us, you never imagined that we should have acted against our very dear lord and cousin, as is publicly known to have been done by us' we reply we have done nothing against him but what we would have dared to do before God and the whole world . . . By the honour of God, of our Lady, and of my lord St George, when you say [that Henry had less regard for Richard's life than the French royal family] you lie falsely and wickedly, for we hold his blood dearer to us than the blood of those on your side . . . and if you say that his blood was not dear to us in his life-time, we tell you that you lie . . . This is known to God to whom we appeal, offering our body to combat against yours, in our defence as a loyal prince should do, if you be willing or dare to prove it.[40]

In these letters, Henry seems to have been genuinely and deeply moved to defend himself. The matter of dethroning Richard is dealt with simply and confidently: he had done nothing which he need be ashamed of 'before God and the whole world'. But the accusation that he had murdered Richard clearly troubled him. He could not have protested his innocence more fervently. This is fascinating, for, as we have seen, Henry *did* issue an order for Richard to be killed or deprived of sustenance. Was his denial anything more than perjury, deceit and blasphemy?

On the face of it the answer to this is no. Yet that inflexible negative implies a character totally contrary to the serious, spiritual, conscientious Henry we know from other sources. So it is hardly satisfactory in a biography simply to say he was lying and leave it at that. Let us consider the lie from his point of view.

Henry's letter denying his involvement was very probably worded in conjunction with members of his council, in which forum it was necessary to maintain that Richard had starved himself to death. Nevertheless, Henry's appeals to God and the Virgin suggest that he had convinced himself that the death had been predicated by matters beyond his control. The explanation for this is a question of fault. For example, Froissart records that Henry had promised to preserve Richard's life *unless* he took part in a plot against him. Henry may thus have believed that Richard's death was an inevitable consequence of the Epiphany Rising, and thus the fault of those who had sought his (Henry's) own death. This is illustrated when we consider the references in this last letter to 'his [Richard's] blood' for this would include Richard's half-brother and nephew. They had also been killed, *but not by Henry*. It had been the people of Cirencester and Pleshey who had destroyed Thomas and John Holland. Likewise, it had not been Henry but a judge who had sentenced Richard's illegitimate half-brother, Sir Roger Clarendon. This is how Henry could have convinced himself that he was innocent of the murder in the eyes of God. Others had 'executed' him, his death being a consequence of the plot to free him. Thus Henry was able to deny his guilt by refusing to accept personal responsibility for what had been a political act carried out for the security of the kingdom. Politicians in all ages have felt similarly inclined to draw a line between public expediency and personal conscience.

*

Henry spent Christmas 1402 at Windsor, preparing to go to Southampton to meet his bride. The formal arrangements had taken a long time to sort out. The Navarrese themselves had presented no difficulty; Charles III of Navarre referred to Henry as 'our most dear brother' before the end of the year. But the French put up a stiff resistance. This included not only the French royal family but Joan's Breton vassals, who were opposed to the marriage. The Bretons sought the intervention of the duke of Burgundy. The royal duke went to see Joan at Nantes in October 1402. She would have to surrender control of Brittany, he told her, and custody of her male children. To marry Henry, Joan would have to give up her sons (the youngest of whom was just seven), her friends, her title and her home for the past sixteen years. It cannot have been an easy decision.

Nevertheless Joan departed from Nantes on 26 December, accompanied by her two young daughters (Blanche and Margaret). Henry had sent his half-brothers, John and Henry Beaufort (the earl of Somerset and the bishop of Lincoln respectively), and the earl of Worcester to accompany her on the voyage. She boarded on 13 January and spent the next five days being thrown about on wintry seas. The rough weather meant that the ships had to put in at Falmouth on 19 January 1403.[41]

Three days later, Henry was at Farnham in Surrey, probably still unaware that Joan had landed.[42] But as soon as he heard, he gave orders to head westwards. Joan was taken slowly from Falmouth via Bodmin to Okehampton, twenty-two miles from Exeter, where she was on 27 January.[43] By the 28th Henry was at Clarendon Palace, in Wiltshire, fifty miles from Exeter. With Joan travelling slowly from the west, and Henry rapidly from the east, they were on course to meet near Exeter. On the 30th they were entertained in that city, amid much celebration, together at last.

From Exeter the royal party made its way via Bridport and Salisbury to Winchester Cathedral, where they were married on 7 February by Henry's half-brother, Bishop Beaufort. The old bishop of Winchester, William Wykeham, was too ill to preside (he died the following year), but it may have been as a special favour to him – foremost of the prelates in lending Henry money – that Henry chose his church for the wedding. The newly rebuilt nave was truly splendid. The king's younger sons, John and Humphrey, were in attendance, as was most of the English aristocracy, and a lavish feast was held, costing £522 12s.[44] The menu for this survives, showing that Henry and his bride were treated to roast cygnets, 'capons of high grease', venison, griskins, rabbits, bitterns, stuffed pullets, partridges, kid (as in young goat), woodcock, plover, quails, snipe, fieldfares, cream of almonds, pears in syrup, custards, fritters and subtleties decorated with crowns and eagles. One of the highlights was a cake in the shape of crowned panthers, each panther having flames issuing from his mouth and ears. Henry's wedding present to Joan was a fantastic jewelled collar costing £385, 'with the motto *Soveignez* and the letter "S", ten amulets garnished with nine pearls, twelve large diamonds, eight rubies, eight sapphires, with a great clasp in the shape of a triangle with a great ruby set in the same and garnished with four great pearls'.[45] Following the wedding, the royal party returned to London, and were received by the citizens on Blackheath. They processed into the city, to Cheapside, and from there to Westminster, where the queen was crowned on 26 February, with more feasting and jousting. Following the festivities, Henry took Joan to Eltham, and toured Kent, returning to his favourite palace, Eltham, for Easter.

Henry had at last found in his new wife the sort of companionship he had lost with Mary's death, nearly nine years before. In the early years of his reign we find occasional references to his pastimes – swordfighting and hunting, and even an idiot or fool – but otherwise his time was heavily employed in the relentless business of state.[46] There was precious little time for enjoyment, and only a handful of trusted old friends with whom to spend it. Now he had a constant, intelligent and trustworthy companion. She was passionate and determinedly loyal.[47] She was also a woman with whom Henry could discuss business. Joan had, after all, managed the affairs of the duchy of Brittany. The following year Henry granted her a tower at Westminster in which to maintain an office. The business she took on included holding councils, handling and auditing accounts, and keeping charters and similar documents.[48] She was clearly a hands-on sort of woman, more inclined to administrative duties than needlework. In that, too, she seems to have been a good match for the king.

Unfortunately her arrival did not end Henry's seemingly endless run of ill fortune. Joan herself cost the public purse an extra ten thousand marks (£6,666 13s 8d) per year from the day of her marriage, adding to Henry's financial problems. The marriage of young Blanche to Count Rupert's son was even more expensive, the dowry amounting to twenty thousand marks, half of which was due immediately.[49] The exchequer was under greater pressure than ever, and not even the experienced Guy Mone was able to make the royal accounts balance. In February, Henry sacked Bishop Stafford and appointed Henry Beaufort chancellor of England. Glendower's operations started again, and the prince of Wales – now formally appointed King's Lieutenant in Wales – was forced to begin a campaign against him in North Wales, which cost more money. Then on 10 May Henry's kind stepmother, Katherine Swynford, died. It cannot have been an easy honeymoon.

But all Henry's problems to date were as mere whispers compared to what happened next. In July 1403 Henry heard that the whole Percy family – including the earls of Northumberland and Worcester, and Hotspur – had taken up arms against him. They had joined forces with Glendower and his prisoner, their kinsman Sir Edmund Mortimer.

Henry had a civil war on his hands.

FOURTEEN

A Bloody Field by Shrewsbury

> I run before King Harry's victory;
> Who, in a bloody field by Shrewsbury,
> Hath beaten down young Hotspur and his troops,
> Quenching the flame of bold rebellion
> Even with the rebels' blood.
>
> *Henry IV Part Two*, Act 1, Scene 1

The betrayal and treason of the Percys must have shocked Henry even more than the Epiphany Rising. It had been their support which had allowed him to gather enough troops at Doncaster in 1399 to seize power, and it had been the earl of Northumberland himself who had taken Richard captive. Subsequently Northumberland had been the leading statesman in Henry's councils and parliament. He and Hotspur had defended the north of England and worked alongside the prince in maintaining control in North Wales. Hotspur was the sole survivor of all those young men and boys who had been knighted with Henry in 1377. He too had been at St Inglevert and had fought with the Teutonic Knights. Thomas Percy, earl of Worcester, was even closer to Henry. He had been his principal representative in negotiations with France, and a leading member of the royal council. Like his brother, he had been a witness at Henry's wedding, and, even more significantly, Thomas had been the man entrusted with the guardianship of Henry's eldest son. Just a few months earlier Henry had chosen him to join his half-brothers in accompanying his new wife on her voyage to England. So what occasioned this rebellion against Henry? Was Henry even remotely aware of the impending danger to his regime?

The answer to these questions lies in the expectations of the Percy family. One of the reasons why they had wanted Richard II disempowered in 1399 was because he had sought to reduce their authority in the north. They had supported Henry in the hope that he would reverse Richard's policy and provide 'good government' for the realm, where 'good government' meant a form of rule favourable to them. However, Henry had proved not to be their pawn. He had acknowledged his indebtedness to them with many grants in 1399–1401. But the positions he awarded them transferred greater responsibilities, as well as power. What the Percys could not have foreseen was the strength with which the Scots and Welsh reacted to Henry's insecure rule; their incursions and rebellions forced them to fulfil the responsibilities of their newly secured offices, and to fight expensive border wars in Scotland and Wales. Therefore they did not benefit financially from their positions as much as they had expected, but were more fully occupied than before in the defence of the realm. When they sought reimbursement of their expenses, the money was not forthcoming, because of the impoverishment of the treasury. This in turn was connected to Henry's promises not to raise taxation. Ironically, it had been the Percys themselves who had forced him to make such promises, at Doncaster in 1399. The Percy family plan of having a tame monarch who would appoint them each to positions of power and levy no taxes turned into a nightmare scenario in which they themselves were responsible for the defence of a realm whose king was unable to meet their costs. Of course, they blamed Henry, not themselves.

Another irony underlying the revolt of 1403 is the Percys' king-maker status. The very fact that they had been the principal actors in the elevation of Henry as a prospective leader in 1399 was one of the reasons why they now rebelled.[1] To understand this, we need to remember that certain positions in medieval society conveyed an informal responsibility to act as a check on the king's rule. The archbishops and some of the bishops took this responsibility very seriously. Thomas Becket is the most famous example, but throughout the fourteenth century there had been many others.[2] It was possible for the great magnates to feel the same political obligation, especially the northern and marcher lords. The Lords Appellant – the heirs of the rebel earls of 1312 – themselves had taken on such a role in 1387. Hence the Percys felt obliged to act as an opposition. Richard had failed them, and had had to be deposed. Now Henry was failing them too. It was their responsibility, they felt, to act as a corrective force.

The problem for the Percys was that their idea of correction was totally out of line with the ideas of duty and homage which governed medieval society. Therefore Henry felt he could chastise them for stepping out of line, and he did. The first we read of this is Henry's comment in his letter to his son – who was then with Hotspur – that Hotspur's negligence was partly the reason for the fall of Conway Castle on 1 April 1401. Over the next eighteen months the relationship with Hotspur went from bad to worse. After the battle of Homildon Hill, Henry openly berated Northumberland for Hotspur's failure to bring the captured earl of Douglas into parliament.[3] According to the *Brut*, Hotspur went to see Henry in person to demand more money for his defence of the Marches. Henry, having nothing in his treasury, tried to brush him off. Hotspur declared that he would not accept such an answer. In the ensuing argument, Henry punched Hotspur in the face.[4] According to another chronicle, Henry drew a dagger and threatened Hotspur, who retorted with the challenge 'Not here but in the field'.[5] Whichever version is preferred, by the end of 1402 the friendship between the two had come to an end.

The breakdown of the relationship with Hotspur was not the sole reason for the rebellion. There were three other important factors. One was a growing friendship between the Percys and Glendower. Sir Edmund Mortimer's decision to marry one of Glendower's daughters and to side with the Welsh rebel – publicly announced in December 1402 – meant that Hotspur's brother-in-law was in arms against Henry.[6] A dialogue between the Percys and Glendower now opened up, acknowledging a common enemy in Henry. The second reason was that in Hotspur's and Mortimer's nephew, the twelve-year-old earl of March, they had a valid hereditary candidate for the throne, and one too young to resist their control. The third reason was the declining position of the Percy family in the north. Henry increasingly gave positions and incomes which the Percys had come to think of as their own to his brother-in-law, Ralph Neville, earl of Westmorland. Similarly, the justiciarship of Wales – which had been split between the earl of Northumberland and Hotspur – was given to Prince Henry in March 1403. Hotspur was not recompensed for his loss. Northumberland was, but the lands Henry allocated to him were those of the earl of Douglas, in Scotland, which had not yet been conquered. Furthermore, on the same day as Henry made his son King's Lieutenant in Wales, he issued a commission for an enquiry into the prisoners taken at Homildon Hill. The reason he gave for placing the prisoners in the hands of a commission was that 'they [the earl of Northumberland and Hotspur] cannot act honestly because of their interests'.[7] It is not wholly surprising that the man who requested this commission was their rival, the earl of Westmorland.

Henry only vaguely anticipated the Percy rebellion; he could not possibly have seen what form it would take. He knew that his friendship with Hotspur was a thing of the past, but he remained confident that the senior members of the family would keep Hotspur in check. In May 1403 the earl of Northumberland wrote to the council reminding them that he and Hotspur were bound to be at Ormiston Castle in Scotland on 1 August to accept its surrender, and asking for payment of arrears for financial support.[8] Henry had no reason to be perturbed by this letter; it was typical of those he had received over the last two years. The earl wrote again on 26 June. He stated that Henry had ordered him to receive Ormiston Castle, and that in order to do so he needed money quickly. He claimed that Henry had promised him a sum but had not stated how much it would be or when it would be delivered. There may have been a veiled threat in the earl's phrase that 'the good reputation of the chivalry of your realm will not be kept in that place [Ormiston], resulting in dishonour and disaster to myself and my son who are your loyal lieges . . .'. There was a real concern in his refutation of the rumour that he and Hotspur had received £60,000 since Henry had come to England; the earl protested that they were still owed £20,000. He now urged Henry to command his treasurer to pay this sum for the safety of the kingdom. He signed the letter 'Your Mathathias'.[9]

Henry was at Kennington when he received this letter. It greatly alarmed him. The demand from the earl for £20,000 for the safety of the realm had a double meaning: was it to protect England from the Scots or to protect him – Henry – from Hotspur? The signature 'Your Mathathias', in the earl's own hand, emphasised the seriousness of the revolt. Mathathias was the father of Judas Maccabeus. The epithet 'second Maccabeus' in England referred to an ideal king; it had been applied to Edward III in his epitaph and had been associated with Henry on his return to England in 1399, when he had received the support of Northumberland. Thus, for Northumberland to claim to be 'your Mathathias' was for him to point out he was like a father to Henry. It had been Mathathias who had begun the resistance to King Antiochus's tyranny, thus making Judas Maccabeus's victories possible. 'Your Mathathias' was a reminder to Henry of just how much he owed Henry Percy, earl of Northumberland.[10]

Henry set off three days later, on 4 July.[11] On 7 July he arrived at Newenham Priory in Bedfordshire, and spent two days there, moving to Higham Ferrers, in Northamptonshire, on the 9th. The next morning he wrote to the council, telling them that the prince had been successful in North Wales (he had destroyed Glendower's manors of Sycharth and Glyndyfrdwy in May, and had recently relieved the siege of Harlech Castle). He asked the council to send the prince a thousand pounds immediately so he might keep up the good work.[12] He added that it was now his intention to go towards Scotland 'to give aid and comfort to our very dear and loyal cousins the earl of Northumberland and his son Henry in the fight honourably undertaken between them and the Scots'. On this basis historians have generally said that he had no notion of the approaching rebellion. But at the very end of the letter, there is a note to the council to give credence to what the bearer, Elmyn Leget, would say to them on Henry's behalf. This was a common way of sending secret information: an oral message backed up by a letter of credence. Henry's journey to see Northumberland and Hotspur almost immediately after receiving the Mathathias letter, when his relationship with Hotspur was one of enmity, leaves little room for doubt that the secret message carried by Leget conveyed his suspicions about the Percys' loyalty.

From Higham Ferrers, Henry went north, covering the sixty-two miles to Nottingham by the evening of 12 July. There he stopped, having heard rumours of Hotspur gathering the men of Cheshire. He wrote a brief letter to the council ordering them to close all the ports, and went southwest next morning, through Derby and Burton-on-Trent, reaching Lichfield on the 16th. All the Midlands counties' sheriffs were ordered to send men immediately. The following morning he wrote an urgent letter to the council, the tone of which resembles that of a man in turmoil. Hotspur was in open revolt, proclaiming 'King Richard is alive', the rallying cry for those in opposition to the Lancastrians. Henry commanded all the members of his council to come to his aid immediately, with the sole exception of the treasurer, who was ordered to raise all the loans he could.

This could very easily have become a last, pitiful letter from a beleaguered and betrayed king. It was not that he was isolated – Edward, duke of York, and the earl of Dunbar were with him, and so were perhaps two thousand men – but the forces gathering against him were numerous, skilled and motivated.[13] Hotspur was at Chester, gathering the best archers England had to offer. The earl of Northumberland was gathering another army in the north, ready to march south and join Hotspur in the Welsh Marches. Glendower was gathering an army in South Wales, preparing to join the Percys at Shrewsbury. There they would meet, seize the prince and march against Henry.

Immediate action was necessary. Henry could not afford to wait for the men of the Midlands counties. He summoned the earl of Stafford to come as quickly as he could and set out with what men he had for Shrewsbury. His only hope was to combine his forces with those of the prince, and to engage Hotspur in battle before the armies of Glendower and Northumberland could arrive. He had to reach Shrewsbury first. On that day, 17 July, Hotspur was gathering his men at Sandiway, about thirty-eight miles from Shrewsbury. Henry was at Lichfield, thirty-nine miles from the town.

In working out what happened next we have a range of sources, the fullest of which are perhaps the least accurate.[14] What is clear is that when Hotspur arrived at the gates of Shrewsbury on Friday the 20th, he found the town and its bridges held against him. Lack of battlefield experience over the years had not dulled the king's strategic thinking. That almost bloodless engagement at Radcot Bridge in 1387 had been won by his bold use of a rapid advance to cut off the enemy's line of retreat; that was exactly what he did now. He sent a contingent of men ahead to meet with the prince and to defend the town.[15] He did not need to get his entire army to Shrewsbury to secure the town and the bridges; indeed, trying to do so would delay him. But sending a smaller force to meet with the prince allowed him to seize the initiative.

It was a brilliant move. By holding Shrewsbury he not only cut off Hotspur from the possibility of meeting up with Glendower's army, he also trapped him. When Hotspur arrived before the walls of Shrewsbury, he did not just find the town held against him and his plan in jeopardy, he found the king approaching from the east. Hotspur was caught between the town, the river and a royal army. There was nothing he could do but choose the site on which to do battle.

*

In the twenty-first century it is difficult to convey what 'doing battle' meant to Englishmen in 1403. We think of battles as fought by professional, trained soldiers, following strict orders. We think of structured formations and clear lines of command. And we tend to think of medieval people as constantly fighting. These images are misleading. Most of the men with Henry had been pressed to serve their king by the sheriffs of the counties. Apart from a few dozen knights and men-at-arms who lived, ate and slept border warfare with Hotspur, few had actually fought a full-scale pitched battle. More importantly, they had never faced fellow Englishmen in war. The English archers had shredded the tapestry of French chivalry at Crécy in 1346, and since then had dominated large-scale warfare in the same way that machine guns later dominated at the battle of the Somme. Never before had two armies of archers with longbows faced each other. Each man could shoot up to ten or twelve arrows a minute, with an effective killing range of half a mile. At short range their arrows could penetrate the strongest plate armour. To fight a thousand of them meant advancing into a rapid rain of sharp iron, so dense that it darkened the sky. These armies were both equipped with weapons which – to the medieval mind – were capable of mass destruction, and the result of the forthcoming battle was to change perceptions of warfare in England forever.[16]

There were other reasons to fear the approaching clash of arms. In Anglo-French or Anglo-Scottish conflicts there was a respect for those high-status opponents who fought valiantly. If a man was unfortunate enough to be captured, he could normally expect his captor to ransom him. In civil wars these chivalrous niceties were dispensed with. Hotspur and all his followers were traitors to their king. The king, in their eyes, was a murderer and a usurper. There would be no hostage-taking; this was a conflict of absolute right against absolute wrong. Prisoners could expect to be executed, regardless of how valiantly they had fought or how wealthy they were. This disregard of rank, coupled with the fact that arrows do not distinguish between rich and poor, forced the leaders to anticipate an unprecedented deadliness to proceedings. The king and his son were as likely to be killed as their men-at-arms. Unless Hotspur could be persuaded to give himself up, what would follow would be the bloodiest, most horrific battle yet fought on English soil.

Henry stayed at Haughmond Abbey on the night of Friday 20 July, four miles north-east of Shrewsbury.[17] That evening he sent out spies and runners to ascertain the numbers of men with Hotspur and their location.[18] They found Hotspur encamped with his men in Berwick Field, two miles outside the town. The chronicle of Jean de Waurin states that Henry was facing eighty thousand men; the Dieulacres chronicle gives sixty thousand. Both are wild exaggerations; John Capgrave states that Hotspur had fourteen thousand men with him, and this is more likely to have been the intelligence Henry received. Thomas Walsingham states that the king had fourteen thousand also.[19] Whatever the true numbers, the detail Henry would have most wanted to know was how many Cheshire longbowmen were with Hotspur. Five thousand archers would have been comparable to Edward III's archery strength at Crécy, easily capable of destroying an army six times its own size, if they had enough arrows. Hotspur had at least a thousand archers, perhaps more.

That night, as Henry consulted with his fellow leaders, he must have realised that the defining moment of his kingship had arrived. This battle was not about two nations fighting over borders. This battle was about him. In many ways it was the battle of conquest which he had not had to fight in 1399, his own battle of Hastings, in which the one question to be resolved was whether he had the right to be king. If what he had done in 1399 and afterwards had been against God's will – if he had broken the laws of God in dethroning Richard and starving him in prison – then he could expect an arrow to find him out. Being Henry, he took the canny precaution of asking two of his knights to wear his livery. Since it would be the sole purpose of the enemy army to kill him, he would confuse them.

Next morning the runners reported that Hotspur had drawn his army up on a low hill in Berwick Field, a wide-open area sown with peas. The southern approach to this was difficult, being wet ground. The peas' stems had been wound together, to trip up charging horses and advancing men. The weather was fine, the morning giving way to a hot July day. The earl of Dunbar urged Henry to start the battle as soon as possible. Henry agreed. He heard Mass, took a draught of wine, mounted his horse and gave the order to his marshal to advance.

The king's men were divided into two battalions, with the prince's men providing a third force issuing from the town to the south. The vanguard, including the archers, was headed by the earl of Stafford. Henry himself took charge of the main army. In this formation they marched south from Haughmond along the Shrewsbury road, until they were due south-east of the enemy, who were drawn up on a low ridge.[20] Hotspur had chosen his spot well, to force the king to attack him by riding up a gradual incline and into the sights of his archers, the classic defensive arrangement employed by English archer-dominated armies for the last seventy years. To advance against Hotspur in that position would be like throwing oneself into the embrace of several thousand murderous arrows. It was obvious that there was going to be a bloodbath.

Henry spent the whole morning trying to avoid the need for battle. He sent the abbots of Shrewsbury and Haughmond to Hotspur, offering a safe-conduct to him if he wished to negotiate, or to send a representative if he wished to present a statement of grievances. Hotspur refused to come in person, but sent his uncle, the earl of Worcester. It seems likely that Worcester carried the Percys' manifesto, a defence of their rebellion. It outlined Henry's supposed acts of perjury and openly accused him of ordering Richard to be starved to death.[21] Worcester repeated the old complaint about Henry's inability to maintain a solvent exchequer, or to pay his debts. Henry acknowledged his financial problems, but, with regard to his supposed usurpation, pointed out that he had been elected king. He urged the Percys to put themselves on his grace. 'I do not trust your grace', Worcester replied. 'Then on you lies the responsibility for the blood that will be shed this day', replied the king.[22] Another account states that Henry gave Worcester sufficient assurances that he believed he had done enough to avert the battle, but when Worcester returned to Hotspur he told him that Henry had refused to negotiate. Either way, the talks broke down. Henry decided he had done all he could. There was nothing left to do but attack.

Going among the ranks of men, he urged them that day to fight well. He had been chosen to be king, he insisted to his men, and they would be doing God's work if they would defend him. Victory would be to the common profit of the realm, he declared. The banners of St Edward and St George were fluttering above him, and the royal standard was beside him in the hands of Sir Walter Blount, one of the men he had asked to wear the royal livery. Henry appointed the earl of Stafford constable of England, and ordered him to lead the advance. The earl, thus honoured, gave the command for the vanguard to march forward. It was by this stage early afternoon.[23]

Stafford was a brave man. He cannot have doubted that the Cheshire archers were capable of inflicting massive casualties on the vanguard. He would have known that the longbows were at their deadliest when facing an oncoming charge. Thus his force was doubly disadvantaged. He and his men would come within range of the Cheshire archers on the incline before they were able to shoot their own arrows, for stationary men on higher ground have more time to aim and can shoot further than those below them. As a result, Stafford needed his men to advance rapidly. But running forward through a murderous barrage of thousands of deadly arrows only made the task of shooting up a slope – albeit a gentle one – more difficult. Not only that, the Cheshire archers were entrenched, and they had shields to protect them. Nevertheless, shouting and hollering abuse at the Percys, the royal vanguard marched forward. With trumpets and clarions sounding and bows at the ready, Stafford led them into the battle. At a thousand yards from the hill, the first arrows may have reached them. A minute later the sky began to grow dark, as if a cloud was passing over them. Dust began to swirl around the advancing army, but it was not dust that blotted out the sun, it was a volley of arrows. In the words of Thomas Walsingham, 'the king's men fell as fast as leaves fall in autumn after the hoar frost'.

No scholar sitting in his study surrounded by old chronicles can do justice to the feelings which now swept across that battlefield. No amount of analysis of the sources – even if the path of truth could be tracked through all the conflicting accounts – could summon up the fear, or the desperate fury of the combatants. Obscured by dust, with trumpets blaring, men screaming in agony and horses whinnying, Henry's vanguard was cut to pieces. For the men in the front line, the terror must have been beyond anything any of them had ever experienced. But there were enough of them that they kept going, and pressed on towards the rebels. In the words of Jean de Waurin,

> after the arrows were exhausted, they put their hands to swords and axes with which they began to slay each other. And the men and horses were slain in such wise that it was pitiable to see. None spared his fellow, mercy had no place, each one tried only to escape and put himself at the head of his party, for there was no friend or relation but each man thought only of himself, so they fought with such equality of bitterness that it was a long time before one could conjecture to whom would remain the day and the victory. But at length, by the prowess of the earl of Douglas and his companions, the king's vanguard was overwhelmed.[24]

The first words of this passage probably contain the key to understanding the battle. Although the Cheshire archers killed a great many men in the vanguard, they began to run out of arrows, allowing the vanguard directly to engage the rebel army's position. It was the earl of Douglas who defeated them, and forced them back, not the rebel archers themselves.[25] Thus it seems that, although the king's vanguard under Stafford lost the initial stage of the battle, they performed the all-important task of sapping the strength of the Cheshire archers.

It was at this stage in the battle that the earl of Stafford was killed.[26] All resistance to Douglas now gave way. The king's vanguard ran back in terror. Walsingham states that four thousand of Henry's men fled.[27] In the meantime the Cheshire archers ran down the slope and ripped their arrows out of the dead and dying bodies of the king's vanguard, and started shooting again. Seeing his vanguard in flight, Stafford's banner down, and the enemy charging towards him, Henry knew that it fell to him to show leadership, to stop the fleeing men. Regardless of how many knights were wearing royal armour, there was only one genuine king, and only he could give the decisive order to advance. Having sent a message to the prince to attack Hotspur's army on the flank, thus further diverting the archers, Henry commanded his trumpeters to give the signal for the main body of the army to charge.

The two armies clashed at the foot of the slope, near where Battlefield church stands today. Almost every chronicler stresses how bitter the fighting was. It was 'the heaviest, and unkindest, and sorest battle that had ever taken place in England', wrote the author of the *Brut*, 'for there was the son against the father, and the brother against the brother, and kin against kin'.[28] According to Waurin, the rebels were encouraged by the appearance of victory, and charged into the fray 'where the cry and noise were loudest on all sides, trumpets and clarions made a marvellous clamour'. Waurin continues with the most evocative descriptions of the fighting:

and it was horrible to hear the groans of the wounded, who ended their lives miserably beneath the hooves of the horses. There was such slaughter of men whose bodies lay soulless that the like had not been seen in England for a long time . . . for as I have heard tell by word of mouth and by writing it is not found in any book of this chronicle that there was ever in the kingdom of England since the conquest of Duke William so horrible a battle or so much Christian blood spilled as in this one . . . King Henry who was concerned in this matter more than any man, disturbed by the defeat of his vanguard, which was destroyed, with a loud voice began to exhort his men to do well, and throwing himself into the battle did many a fine feat of arms so that on both sides he was held to be the most valiant knight, and it was said for certain that on that day with his own hand he slew thirty of his enemies . . .[29]

Even allowing for exaggeration, there is no doubt that Henry himself led his men straight into the thick of the fighting. The king's presence only exacerbated the viciousness of the situation, for the strategic aim of both sides was to kill the enemy leader. Those Cheshire archers who still had arrows now aimed through the swirling dust cloud at the king. Those who were fighting the prince on the flank aimed at him. One arrow flew from the bow of a Cheshire archer straight into the prince's face while the visor of his war helmet was raised, penetrating into his skull just below his left eye. Despite this, as the hand-to-hand fighting raged, Hotspur saw his position weakening. His archers were all but a spent force, and his men-at-arms and infantry were being overwhelmed by Henry's. The situation was growing desperate. Something had to be done.

What happened next is one of those moments when history itself turns to watch in solemn admiration at the courage of men. Hotspur decided to stake everything on one great charge straight towards the king. Gathering thirty of his most trusted supporters, including the earl of Douglas and his uncle, the earl of Worcester, he urged them all to couch their lances together in preparation.[30] Henry himself was still in the thick of the fighting, oblivious of the impending force of thirty knights about to smash their way through to him. But the earl of Dunbar saw what was happening, and immediately understood that the king was in great danger. A group of charging mounted knights with lances could suddenly smash their way through a mass of infantry and motionless cavalry, scything through the battle. Dunbar shouted to Henry, urging him to withdraw. Henry seems to have been reluctant; if anyone saw his banner leaving the battlefield they would presume that all was lost. But there was simply no time to lose. As Hotspur and his fellow knights charged through the fighting infantry, Dunbar persuaded Henry to fall back. In so doing the oncoming knights were drawn further and deeper into the killing mass. If Henry had looked back he would have seen the brave Sir Walter Blount, still holding the royal standard, struck down.[31] He would have seen several of his other knights slain. But he would also have seen Hotspur's charge fail as the thirty were caught on the swords of the royal men-at-arms, their horses' legs broken by the axes of the infantry who, unable to flee, stood and fought for their lives.

No one knows who wielded the blow which stopped Hotspur. But gradually the charge of the thirty knights slowed to a halt, and the royal soldiers in their fury rushed in and cut him down. On seeing Sir Walter Blount killed as he wore Henry's spare royal armour, the rebels sent up the shout that 'King Henry' was dead, and started yelling 'Harry Percy King'. Encouraged, the rebel army renewed their efforts. Astounded, Henry raised his visor and yelled back, 'Harry Percy is dead!' Again he roared it, 'Harry Percy is dead!' That was it; the challenge was over. In his own mind, and in his own conscience, God had spoken. It had not been an unequivocal judgement in his favour, as the wound his son had received was so grave it was unlikely that he would live, but Henry had been given the victory.

The rest of the battle was a foregone conclusion from that moment on. The rebels, seeing their beloved Hotspur dead, and the earls of Worcester and Douglas and several other knights being led from the battlefield as prisoners of the king, knew they were defeated. One instant they had been fighters for justice, striving to rid England of an unjust ruler; the next they were traitors, fugitives from justice. There could be no mercy for them. They would be chased down and slaughtered unless they fled. In a very short time the battlefield was cleared of all those who could run, leaving the king's men to cut the throats of those who could not, as twilight settled down across the field of bloody corpses and trampled peas.

*

We tend to judge battles historically by how famous they are today. By that reckoning, Shrewsbury barely ranks in the top twenty. It was not like the great battles of the previous century, all of which had been gloriously won or lost against the Scots or the French. It had much more in common with the inglorious civil wars of the later fifteenth century. Indeed, it is possible to describe it as the first battle of the Wars of the Roses, the series of conflicts between the houses of Lancaster and Mortimer or York for the throne. Yet even that comparison is misleading, for it was followed by fifty years of domestic peace. If it was the first 'War of the Roses', then it is a strange episode, for it started on about 9 July 1403 and was over within a fortnight. That is hardly the pattern of a dynastic struggle.

But therein lies the importance of Shrewsbury. By his timely and decisive action, Henry prevented Hotspur's rising from becoming a full-blown dynastic conflict. It was a very serious rising – it had three earls among its leaders and a suitable hereditary candidate for the throne in the form of the young Edmund Mortimer – and it could easily have led to a more general civil war. It is thus valid to pose the question, what if Henry had lost? What was really at stake that day?

If Henry had been killed at Shrewsbury, the royal army would have fled and the wounded prince would probably have been captured. Power in the north would have shifted back decisively in favour of the Percys. The Lancastrian claim to the throne would have been left between the captive ailing prince and his brother, Thomas of Lancaster, who was still in Ireland. The Lancastrians would have been ousted. Hotspur, being a rash fellow, may well have tried to claim the throne for himself, by right of conquest, but it is unlikely he would have achieved widespread support outside the north, and so we can see him being forced to accept the young Edmund Mortimer, his wife's nephew, as king. How different English history would have been if Edmund Mortimer – a weak, unconfident character with no aptitude for war or even kingship – had succeeded to the throne instead of the victor of Agincourt! And how differently Henry IV would be viewed now if he had lost at Shrewsbury. What would he have been to the intervening centuries but an example of God's judgement on a man who dared to overthrow and murder a divinely anointed king?

The course of English history teetered on this confrontation. Never before had a Plantagenet king led his men to victory in a pitched battle on English soil, and yet Henry had now done so, by showing chivalric leadership of the highest order. The significance of divine retribution on Hotspur, and *not* Henry, was powerfully felt throughout the realm. In symbolic terms, it was of profound importance. Hotspur's body was initially carried off to Whitchurch for burial, but that night Henry gave orders for it to be brought back to Shrewsbury. The hero's corpse was placed in a sitting position and propped against an axe stuck between two great millstones, so everyone could see he was dead.[32] Later the head was cut off and sent to be displayed in York. The battlefield too acquired a symbolic status. Although only about two thousand men had died, more than half of those present had either fled in fear or had been badly wounded or killed.[33] A large number of the dead – between 1,100 and 1,800 – were placed in a mass grave. Certainly a large number of men had died in a relatively small space.[34] The king's vanguard had been torn apart by the arrows of the Cheshire archers. Many of the wounded had been trampled to death in the same place. Dozens of Hotspur's men had perished there too, overwhelmed by the king's army. Building a church on the battlefield was not only respectful to the dead, it was a powerful statement. The church told people that they could expect a similar fate to Hotspur if they defied the king. The message equally applied to Glendower's Welsh rebels, just across the border.[35]

It would have been easy, in such victorious circumstances, to have lapsed into complacency. At this point in his chronicle, Jean de Waurin launches into a paean of honour to Henry (extraordinarily, for a Frenchman).[36] But, contrary to Waurin's assumption that he returned in triumph to Westminster,

Henry neither went to Westminster nor lapsed into self-congratulatory inactivity. The men he had just crushed had once been his ardent supporters, not his enemies. Killing Hotspur had not reversed any of their complaints against his rule. Most significantly, Hotspur's father was still at liberty, with an army, and Glendower was likewise in the field. To return to Westminster and pretend a triumph would have been foolish.

Henry wrote to the earl of Westmorland on 22 July, the day after the battle, ordering him to take immediate action against Northumberland, and to arrest him if possible. On the 23rd he showed the earl of Worcester Hotspur's dead body, and let him weep over the corpse. When that lachrymose ceremony was complete, he had the earl beheaded for treason along with two other knights captured in the battle, Sir Richard Vernon and Sir Richard Venables. Then he set off to the north in pursuit of Northumberland. He was at Nottingham at the end of the month and reached his great fortress of Pontefract by 4 August.[37]

There was no doubt as to the earl of Northumberland's complicity in the Percy revolt. Their manifesto had borne his name as well as those of Worcester and Hotspur, and the number of men whom he had gathered at Tadcaster showed that he had every intention of marching against the king. When he learned of the defeat at Shrewsbury and his son's death, he retreated to Newcastle upon Tyne. With Westmorland advancing to intercept him, and Robert Waterton in the field preparing to cut off his retreat, Northumberland had little room for manoeuvre. Unfortunately for him, the loyal men of Newcastle had also heard of Hotspur's defeat. They refused to admit his army and would only allow him within the walls with a small retinue. For some reason Northumberland decided this was still a suitable course of action and entered the town, leaving his army outside. Outraged at being abandoned, with Waterton and Westmorland in the field, Northumberland's men attacked the town. Hastily Northumberland disbanded the army and slipped away, taking refuge in Warkworth Castle. He was still there when Henry wrote to him demanding that he come to York and make his submission.

There were several gates to the city of York, and over one of them the head of Hotspur was placed. Perhaps Northumberland was made to enter the city by that same gate, and to look up and see the face of his dead son, drained of blood and with sunken eyes. Even if he did not, the symbolism of having to make his obeisance to Henry in the same city must have been crushing. Henry had promised in his letter that he would spare the earl's life, but with betrayal on this scale there was absolutely no hope of any real reconciliation.

In order to save his life, the earl subjected himself utterly. He denied any knowledge of the rising and pretended that his son had acted without consulting him. Henry heard these pleadings and told the earl he would be allowed to address parliament. He took him to Pontefract and made him seal documents directing his officers to surrender all the castles held for him. When that task was done, he ordered all the knights and esquires in the county of Northumberland to swear an oath of loyalty to him: a forerunner of the general oaths of loyalty and allegiance which were to become so regular a feature of political control in the wake of rebellions in Tudor and Stuart times. The earl himself was despatched to Baginton, near Coventry, to wait for the next parliament. As a final precaution, Henry executed a hermit for threatening him with his false prophecies.[38] Only then could he feel he had neutralised the rebellion.

*

On the same day as Henry concluded his arrangements with Northumberland at Pontefract, he ordered the sheriffs to send men to meet him at Worcester, ready to make another foray into Wales. The date he set was 3 September; it only gave him eighteen days to make the necessary preparations with his fellow leaders. Nevertheless, he was there on the day. The momentum was with him. Unfortunately his old money problems were with him too, and he was delayed for a week at Worcester. There he held a council and commanded all his leading magnates to reaffirm their oaths of loyalty. At the same time he was receiving letters from his old friend Richard Kingston, archdeacon of Hereford, telling him that Herefordshire was on the verge of attack, and if Henry did not send help soon the local gentry would desert him to make their own peace with Glendower. Henry went to Hereford as soon as he could, and stayed there from 11 to 15 September, ordering the provisioning and garrisoning of the castles in the area. When he was satisfied, he took his army into Wales again, on the long road to Carmarthen.

Henry's fourth campaign in Wales followed the pattern of his second, that of 1401, being a short military dash to south-west Wales. He was at Michaelchurch on 19 September and at Devynock, on the road to Carmarthen, on the 21st. Three days later he rode into Carmarthen itself and immediately set about ordering the reinforcement of the local garrisons, the repair of strategic walls and the provisioning of the castles. Then he promptly turned around and headed back to England, returning to Hereford by 3 October. Perhaps he believed that Wales was essentially secure as long as the castle garrisons remained in place. In that he was not wrong, not in the long term at least, so it is unfair to accuse him of not being thorough enough in his suppression of the Welsh people (as some historians have done). As we have seen, he was willing to be more lenient towards the loyal Welsh than many members of parliament, who saw persecution as a sign of strength.

Another complication in the Welsh situation was developing at this same time. The 'pirate war' with France had been going on for nearly two years, since the duke of Orléans had commissioned the earl of Crawford to start attacking English shipping in early 1402. Henry had responded by tacitly encouraging the English pirates to respond by attacking French ships. The famous John Hawley of Dartmouth was just one of many wealthy mariner-merchants who jumped at the chance to supplement his legal trade with stolen French goods. Gradually the whole conflict had assumed a broader, more vigorous form. In August 1403 Plymouth was sacked. But on 4 October 1403 a force of French and Bretons landed in South Wales and began to attack Kidwelly Castle and the area around it. Coupled with Glendower's attack on Cardiff, which was launched just after Henry withdrew into England, this presented an altogether new combination of threats. At Bristol on 23 October he wrote to the council urgently asking that they give letters of safe-conduct to men serving with the earl of Warwick in Brecon. 'Necessitas non habet legem' ('necessity has no law') he wrote in his own hand on the letter. The phrase sums up Henry's kingship: neither legally correct, nor wholly lawful, but done anyway, because the safety of the nation is more important than the law.

Thus the year 1403 drew to a close. The great danger of the Percys' rebellion had been faced and defeated but otherwise Henry was beleaguered. His money problems were as bad as ever, Glendower was stronger than ever, and now Henry had further French hostility to deal with. On 14 October the duke of Orléans sent his third and final insult to Henry.[39] In November he received another challenge from the count of St Pol, and in December that count attacked the Isle of Wight. At Carnarvon in January, the besieged constable could not spare a single man to take a letter requesting a relief force because he had only twenty-eight men to hold the castle against Glendower.[40] All Henry could do was to despatch men to face the worst threats, and borrow what money he could to pay them. A contingent of Devonians was ordered to assemble to defend Cardiff; another was gathered at Dunster to sail to Carmarthen. It all added up to an extremely stressful situation. As Henry and his wife travelled to Abingdon to spend their first Christmas together, they could have been forgiven for wanting to turn their backs on the problems of the realm. But if they enjoyed a break for a few days, it was a short relief. By 14 January 1404 the king was back at Westminster preparing for a meeting with an angry parliament. And the next plot to remove him from the throne was quietly being hatched.

FIFTEEN

Treason's True Bed

Some guard these traitors to the block of death,
Treason's true bed, and yielder-up of breath
Henry IV Part Two, Act IV, Scene 2

Today we are familiar with the image of an embattled political leader chairing a round of meetings with his cabinet in order to stave off opposition within parliament. In January 1404 this was unusual. Negotiations about finance clashed with the very dignity and majesty of kingship. But the last four years had taught Henry that he needed to play the political game in order to maintain the confidence of the people. Thus he decided to pre-empt the likely complaints about another request for taxation by summoning a meeting of the council to Sutton on Friday 11 January, three days before parliament was due to meet. Among other things he probably outlined the amount of money he required and the novel way in which he intended to raise it, through a form of land-based income tax. A shilling on every pound of annual income was to be levied – a rate of five per cent – with each holder of a knight's fee being liable for £1. Those without a land estate were to be taxed at five per cent on the value of their goods and chattels. In order to get all the possible opponents on board from the start, the Speaker of the 1401 parliament, Sir Arnold Savage, who had been so harsh in his criticism of Henry's requests for money, was also invited to attend the council meeting.

On Monday the 14th parliament assembled at Westminster. Henry's half-brother, Henry Beaufort, delivered the opening speech. After his initial sermon, he listed the reasons for summoning the parliament. According to a newsletter preserved in Durham, the first reason he gave was that Henry had received further challenges from the duke of Orléans and the count of St Pol, which were 'a great outrage and disgrace to our lord the king, and a shame and offence to the whole realm'. Other issues included the defence of three regions – Gascony, the south coast of England and the Scottish Marches – the government of Ireland (following the return to England of Prince Thomas), the ordinances for Wales, the reimbursement of costs incurred in the suppression of the Percy revolt, and the trial of the earl of Northumberland. Sir Arnold Savage was elected Speaker the following day.

Henry may have thought that such a long list of threats to the safety of the realm should have been sufficient to consolidate the varying interests in parliament. He was in for a shock. Savage, far from taking the king's message to the commons, now took it upon himself again to lead them in defying royal policy. When the royal council requested a grant of money in order to meet all these needs, Savage turned against Henry. 'The king has sufficient wealth to support and provide for all these policies, if he would be well-guided', he declared, 'and for this reason do not trust in having any subsidy from the commons until we know how the king's wealth has been spent, and in what manner.' He proceeded to demand information about grants to various ladies amounting to £50,000 per year and a single grant to Francis the Lombard of £8,000 per year, through his letters patent. Speaking directly to the king, he said, 'you should be well advised by your high council on these aforesaid matters, because your commons have no wish to bear as much as they have previously'.

Henry must have been dismayed, and searched for a response. 'It would be a great shame and disgrace to repeal and annul our letters patent', he said, not very convincingly.

Savage did not back down. The matter could easily be amended, he said, without annulling the letters, by paying recipients of £100 annuities just £10. 'And therefore you should be advised by your council to make the best ordinances that you can for the aforesaid matters, because your commons are very discontented that the goods of the realm are in such a way given to those who will never bring it honour or profit.'

Henry's powers of argument seem to have deserted him. All he could do was express his 'amazement that the commons were so ill-disposed towards him'.

'It is nothing to wonder at', Savage replied, 'because the whole realm knows that every year you have had a tenth and a fifteenth from your lieges. In addition, they are often harassed and compelled to take part in expeditions in Wales and elsewhere without any wage, but at their own expense. Besides, your ministers and purveyors do not pay anything for the provisions taken for your use, to such an extent that one of your ministers owes various people £6,000 or more for provisions, and this is a key reason why the commons are not as well-disposed towards you as they were previously. There are also certain lords of your council who lead and advise you with a very evil intention, against the honour of your person and the profit of the realm, and of this you will be informed more fully later; and for this reason may it please you to discuss all the aforesaid matters with your wise council, and also to order your affairs in the way that your commons outline to your council, and then you will enjoy peace and quiet within your realm. And if not, we do not see how your realm will be well-governed.'[1]

This stunning rebuke, coming from a man he had been hoping would help him, left Henry speechless. It was a direct threat to royal government, questioning his fitness for the throne. Appalled, Henry rose and left the chamber, just as Richard II had done when his fitness to rule had been similarly attacked in 1386.

Henry, however, was a different shape of character from Richard. Rather than smoulder in ire at Eltham, waiting for a grovelling apology for the insult to his royal dignity, he sent his chancellor, Henry Beaufort, and the treasurer, Lord Roos, back to parliament to explain in more detail the reasons why he needed this grant. Savage, having attacked royal policy in the king's presence, had no compunction about speaking his mind to the chancellor and treasurer. He demanded that the royal accounts be subjected to public scrutiny and asked again that a committee of commons should be appointed to discuss business in conjunction with the lords.

Over the course of five or six days, Henry came to terms with this new wave of parliamentary opposition, and decided to deal with the matter personally. He came back into parliament on 28 January only to hear Savage demand that the lords should voice openly their views on the state of the king and the realm. This was a tacit reference to the rumours that other lords besides the Percys were of the opinion that Henry was guilty of murder and perjury. Immediately Archbishop Arundel sternly rebuked Savage. Savage had his answer ready. 'It would be more honourable for these lords to make clear their wills at this point than to be found disloyal afterwards.' But Henry had recovered from his shock and was prepared to argue his case.

'As regards my person', said Henry, 'it is known to the whole realm that I am the true heir of Lancaster. It is also known how I was driven out of the realm, and how I was returned to it, and how afterwards I was chosen by all the lords of the realm to be its governor and king; and for those reasons it seems to me that I have a good right.'

Savage realised he had been neatly side-stepped. If he wished to urge the disloyalty of some lords further, he would end up speaking on their behalf, leaving himself open to accusations of treason. All he could do was to request that the champion of royal opposition, the earl of Northumberland, be brought into the parliament to plead his case, 'and if it were found that he had trespassed in any way against the Crown, that

Henry should, of his special grace, grant him a charter of pardon, and if no fault should be found in him, that it should then please him to cause him to be restored to all his lands just as he had been before'.

Northumberland had already been granted his life; Savage's request was tantamount to letting him go unpunished for impugning Henry's character and title and plotting rebellion. Henry immediately replied that he did not want to grant such a request before he had had a chance to consult his council on the matter. He adjourned the meeting.

It was the right move at the right time. It calmed the situation. Pardoning Northumberland was no longer the outright demand of a hostile commons, it became a matter of royal grace. Henry rode to Windsor, where the earl was being held, and told him to present a petition seeking a pardon. He also invited the earl to ride with him to London, to present his petition in parliament. There the lords heard the earl's case, and conveniently deemed him guilty of trespass but not treason, and sentenced him to be fined. Henry gracefully forgave the earl the fine, and formally accepted his renewed allegiance. With that, there was no further questioning of Henry's royal dignity. The figurehead of opposition was humbled before Henry. At last, three weeks after parliament had opened, the commons could now be expected to discuss the key issue, Henry's new tax.

It was not an easy discussion. The commons wanted concessions on a scale personally humiliating to Henry. They demanded that four members of his household, including his confessor, be sacked. Henry objected that they had done nothing wrong, but right or wrong had nothing to do with it; the commons were principally interested in exploring their ability to control the king. They demanded that all foreigners be excluded from the royal household, with the exception of a very few personal assistants to Queen Joan. They demanded a limit on royal expenditure through the household, slashing its budget from £42,000 per year to £12,100.[2] They demanded that Henry name his council in parliament. To all these measures Henry had to agree, in order to get his grant of taxation. When, finally, the tax was granted, the commons insisted that four war treasurers should receive the money and that they would ensure it was only used to fight Glendower and to defend the coasts and the Scottish Marches. Furthermore, all reference to this tax was to be wiped entirely from the written records of government, including even the parliament roll.

In the midst of these discussions a letter arrived, purporting to be from Richard II in Scotland. So popular had the rallying cry 'King Richard is alive' become that it had become expedient to put forward a living ex-king to be a focus for the dissent. The man chosen, Thomas Ward of Trumpington, was welcomed at the Scottish court. Jean Creton went to visit him there in 1402, believing at the outset that he was genuinely Richard II, only to find later that year that the man was an impostor. Nevertheless, the false Richard did not actually need to do anything in order to satisfy his supporters; he had merely to exist as a rival king in order to sap the strength of Henry's kingship. The letters now received in parliament were sealed with Richard's privy seal, which had been removed in 1399 by William Serle. With such letters in circulation Henry could do nothing but summon Richard's erstwhile keeper into parliament and ask him what he thought of them. The man declared he would fight a duel with anyone who declared Richard II was alive.[3] It was only superficially a solution to the problem. As Henry was well aware, his real enemy in this debate could not be harmed, being less substantial and more popular than a ghost.

The parliament of January 1404 was humiliating from beginning to end. Ironically, the commons were only further weakening Henry's kingship by placing such fetters on his expenditure. For the new tax was very far from being sufficient to solve Henry's problems; it probably raised no more than £10,000.[4] As a consequence many annuities of loyal crown servants could not be paid, and the officers responsible for the financial administration of the kingdom were faced with ever-increasing debts. Quite what the new queen must have thought on learning that the majority of her servants had to leave the country we can only guess, but it is likely that Henry bore that shame particularly heavily, especially considering his comments to Savage about the shame in annulling the 'grants to ladies' in the early days of the parliament.

Was it all worth it? No doubt Henry would have said yes, it was, for the simple reason that he had survived. He had been drawn into a political situation similar to Richard II's in 1386, and yet he had managed to avert a rising similar to that of the Lords Appellant which followed that assembly. He had stooped so far and compromised his royal dignity far more than Richard would have done. And whatever humiliations he had had to endure, he was the stronger for surviving them. He was learning new political lessons with every blow struck at him. The most telling sign of this is the list of councillors which he was forced to announce in parliament. It included the usual intimates, namely two of his half-brothers (Henry and John Beaufort), his brother-in-law Westmorland and his close friend Archbishop Arundel. But it also included Lancastrian retainers of the sort who had come in for so much criticism in the parliament of 1401, such as Hugh Waterton and John Norbury. Similarly, the Lancastrian Sir Thomas Erpingham had quietly been reappointed steward of the household the previous November. The council and household were packed with his supporters. And, most interestingly, among all these Lancastrians and old friends there was the lone critical figure of Sir Arnold Savage. Far from holding a grudge against him, Henry sought to put his critical faculties to constructive use. Where Richard would have held a grudge, and looked for a chance to execute a man who dared to speak so harshly against him, Henry sought an opportunity to accommodate the man's skills within the government. That difference, the ability of the tree to bend and sway in the storm, was one of the key reasons why Henry survived and Richard did not.

*

Henry went down to Eltham for Easter (30 March) 1404, but was back at Westminster shortly afterwards. On 15 April – his thirty-seventh birthday – the French invaded Dartmouth. The following day, the duke of Burgundy, who had hitherto restrained his nephew, the duke of Orléans, from taking France into war against England, fell mortally ill. The day after that, Henry learned that a new plot was being hatched against him. Out of the frying pan of parliament and into the fires of invasion and rebellion: the spring of 1404 was shaping up to be a sequence of renewed challenges.

The plot of Margaret, countess of Oxford, was the sixth against Henry in four years.[5] In some ways it was the strangest of them all. It involved a series of local prelates and the countess inviting the duke of Orléans and the count of St Pol to invade England by a certain route in Essex the previous December, and to march on Henry in the name of King Richard.[6] That had not happened, of course, but still the plot developed as the plotters involved more and more people, shifting their expectations to a projected meeting between the supposedly living Richard II and Owen Glendower at Northampton on Midsummer's Day 1404. The first Henry seems to have known of it was on 17 April, when he despatched his loyal esquire Elmyn Leget and Sir William Coggeshall to Essex to arrest three men: John Staunton, a servant of the countess of Oxford; John Fowler, a canon of St Osyth; and John Nele, a goldsmith. At the same time he ordered a precautionary fleet to assemble at Sandwich.

By any reckoning, it was a half-baked plan. The plotters themselves seem to have been very patient in their plotting, and we have to suspect that there was a certain degree of catharsis for the countess in the whole process. She was not only the mother of Richard's favourite, Robert de Vere, but a first cousin of the Percys. Discussing ways to bring down Henry's government seems to have occupied her agreeably in the wake of Shrewsbury and the loss of her kin. In reality, a French invasion was never likely to rouse the people into deposing Henry; more probably it would have been seen as a threat. If the attack on Dartmouth at this time was anything to go by, the French were not welcome. A well-organised series of defensive measures forced the invaders to fight immediately on landing there. Even the women of Dartmouth joined in the resistance. The French lord of Château Neuf – a man who had been vociferously against Henry – was killed, and many prisoners taken, including the lord's brothers. Another attack by the count of St Pol on the Isle of Wight similarly met with stiff resistance. Regardless of what the people of Essex might have thought of the idea of an invasion in the name of Richard II, the French parties to the countess's plot had no illusions about being greeted as a relieving army on landing in southern England.

Henry himself seems to have given little time to the plot. Long before the first confessions came – Staunton made his at the end of May – he had departed for the north. He wrote to the mayor of Dartmouth from Nottingham on 25 May asking him to bring five of his prisoners for questioning about the French plans.[7] Perhaps it was in this way that he learned of the secret negotiations between the French and Glendower, which resulted in a treaty sealed the following month. His enemies were massing against him, and increasingly acting in conjunction with each other. In June the Cistercian abbot of Revesby Abbey (Lincolnshire) preached a sermon claiming that there were ten thousand men in England who believed 'King Richard is alive'.[8] With East Anglia seething with treason, and the Percy castles in the north holding out against Henry (despite the earl of Northumberland's surrender), and the enmity of the Welsh, French and Scots, Henry was under attack on all the points of the compass.

Henry's motive for moving north had nothing to do with any of these outward pressures. By June he was aware that his resources were woefully inadequate. The January 1404 parliament had practically disempowered him. He thus retreated to his own estates, and tried to live more like a Lancastrian magnate, using the wherewithal of his own manors. By 21 June he was at his castle of Pontefract; after that he kept close to Lancastrian lands for several months, spending almost all of September, for example, at Tutbury Castle. Even this measure did not save sufficient money to alleviate the situation. It was for want of men and money that two of the most important castles in North Wales – Harlech and Aberystwyth – now fell to Glendower. Harlech had been defended by just five Englishmen and sixteen Welshmen.[9] They had successfully held the immensely strong castle against Glendower and had even locked up their castellan who had been on the verge of surrendering, but in the end they opted for a peaceful surrender. Henry must have cursed; it would be very difficult to win it back again.

Henry did have one piece of good luck at this time. William Clifford, a retainer of the earl of Northumberland, brought William Serle to him in June.[10] Henry could take a particular satisfaction in administering justice to the man who had personally killed his uncle. More importantly, Serle's capture was a dramatic propaganda coup. He confessed he had stolen Richard's signet ring in 1399, and that he had used it to seal the letters from the false Richard in Scotland. He also confessed that he knew the Scottish Richard to be an impostor.[11] There was no doubt as to his sentence: he was to be drawn, hanged, disembowelled with his intestines being burnt before him, beheaded and quartered. It was the same full traitor's death as that suffered by John Hall five years earlier, with one dramatic refinement. He was to be drawn through the streets of all the towns through which he passed on the way to London, going the long way, through East Anglia. Furthermore, he was hanged in each place and cut down while still alive, before being drawn on to the next town.[12] In this way, over the next six weeks he was drawn through the streets of Pontefract, Lincoln, Norwich and many towns in Suffolk, Essex and Hertfordshire. Those ten thousand who said 'King Richard is alive' were now shown the man who had created the lie. This demonstration went a long way to persuading the clergy and commoners that it would be useless from now on to campaign against Henry in the name of Richard II. Combined with the betrothal of Richard's widow, Princess Isabella of France, to her cousin Charles, son of the duke of Orléans – by which the French royal family demonstrated that they believed Richard truly to be dead – the name of Richard II was stripped of its political potency. For many years men continued to profess faith in the Scottish impostor but only on an individual basis. Never again was there a serious rebellion in the name of the murdered king.

*

In normal circumstances the loss of Harlech would have resulted in Henry leading a short, punitive expedition. He had led such a campaign every year of his reign to date. But this time there was no money. The cash in the hands of the war treasurers was consumed in paying for the defence of the seas and for the troops with the prince. So, when Glendower held his first 'parliament' at Machynlleth that summer, and had himself crowned Owen IV, prince of Wales, there was nothing Henry could do to stop him. There was no money even to pay the wages of the troops already stationed in South Wales. Predictably, Prince Owen took advantage of this English inaction. The villages around Shrewsbury were attacked. On 20 August the town of Kidwelly was captured and burned by the Welsh. Rumours reached the English court of a substantial French fleet gathering at Harfleur to support Glendower. It was becoming apparent that the January 1404 parliament had made a grave mistake in trying to improve government by financially tying the king's hands.

Henry was in a very difficult position. He could simply have sacrificed Wales, and done nothing, blaming parliament for everything. But that would have been breaking his coronation vows, and counter to everything for which he had returned in 1399. It would have done nothing to encourage his son, the prince, who was pawning his own goods in order to keep an army in the field to defend Herefordshire.[13] Henry had to do something, even if it involved summoning another parliament and going through the whole damaging process again. On 26 August that was precisely what he decided to do, issuing writs on that day for parliament to assemble at Coventry in October. No lawyers were to be summoned this time, because it was said they spent too much time dealing with their own business and not enough with the more important matters of state. It has thus been known historically as the Unlearned Parliament.[14] That is a misnomer; it was a more serious assembly than many others of the reign, for it was concerned exclusively with meeting the threats from France and Wales. Lawyers who wanted to present their own petitions could wait until the dangers had passed.

On 29 August Henry held a meeting of his council at Lichfield.[15] The French fleet gathering at Harfleur was discussed, and letters were sent out to the leading maritime men of Devon, including John Hawley of Dartmouth, Philip Courtenay of Powderham, Peter Courtenay (the earl of Devon's son) and Henry Pay (another notorious Devon privateer), instructing them to resist the expected armada. The council confirmed that, as Henry could not afford to raise an army to defend Wales, he should not attempt a campaign. Until parliament gave him enough money to do otherwise, he himself was to remain on his estates at Tutbury.

Meeting in such circumstances, the leaders of the commons might have been expected to acknowledge the deep flaws in their experiment in royal control and readily grant the necessary taxation. They did no such thing. A bitter dispute ensued, in which two forms of raising money were discussed at length. The first involved the confiscation of the temporalities – the secular income – of the entire Church. Needless to say, the commons were more than happy to think that the clergy could be forced to give up a proportion of their wealth to dig the nation out of a financial hole. But equally unsurprisingly the proposal gave rise to several sharp and impassioned speeches from Archbishop Arundel, who persuaded the commons at length to give up on the plan. Instead a petition was put forward whereby Henry would rebuild the ancient inheritance of the Crown, taking back into his hands everything – annuities, fees, castles and lands – that had been granted since the fortieth year of Edward III's reign, which ended on 24 January 1367. To this Henry replied in person, in English – the first time a king is recorded as replying to a parliamentary petition in English. He thanked the commons for their proposal, and agreed to put it into practice as soon as practicable. He promised that a commission would be set up to examine which grants made since January 1367 should be confirmed and which should be revoked. He did not agree to the resumption of annuities, but with regard to lands, fees and castles, he ordered that those with grants since 1367 should present their documents for inspection to the commission by 2 February 1405.[16]

To the commons it seemed at last that the king was taking action to increase royal income, and on this basis they agreed to an exceptionally generous tax. This amounted to *two* tenths and fifteenths, as well as a renewal of the wool subsidies for two years, and a five per cent income tax on the lords with annual incomes over five hundred marks (£333 6s 8d). Three weeks later, the convocation of the clergy in the province of Canterbury agreed to a subsidy of one and a half tenths, a generous grant which no doubt reflected Archbishop Arundel's relief at the Church not having its temporalities confiscated. By the end of November, Henry could be confident that he had the means to do what he considered to be his main responsibility as king: to defend the realm.

*

As Christmas 1404 approached, it seemed that the tide had turned. At last Henry had the money for the military expeditions which parliament felt were necessary and which he himself felt obliged to lead. Although the cash was in the hands of two war treasurers, Sir John Pelham and Lord Furnival, both men were Henry's friends.[17] Henry himself was happily married again, one daughter was married and the other betrothed; his elder sons were performing well in their respective duties, and his half-brothers John and Henry Beaufort were providing a sound base for his kingship among the magnates and prelates. His brother-in-law Ralph Neville, earl of Westmorland, had a firm grip on the north of England and was siring nephews and nieces for Henry by the dozen (literally). To cap it all his sister Elizabeth was pregnant with a child by her new husband, Sir John Cornwaille, Henry's jousting friend. But the fundamental problem had not gone away. Indeed, it could be said that Henry had made a grave mistake in the parliament of October 1404. The promise he had made to the commons – to resume control of the ancient royal inheritance – was one he could not keep without alienating the recipients of these grants. These included many of the supporters on whom he relied, especially those Lancastrian retainers who held his head above water in parliament. In short, Henry had made a promise he could not keep. When political leaders start to break their promises, they very quickly destroy any trust the political classes have in them.

Nor was that the limit of Henry's problems. As he and Joan spent Christmas 1404 at Eltham Palace, he may have been the subject of yet another assassination attempt. It is difficult to be certain of the details, but two months later Lady Constance Despenser (the widow of the earl of Gloucester killed during the Epiphany Rising) accused her brother, the duke of York, of attempting to assassinate Henry at Eltham. She claimed that the duke's assassins were planning to scale the walls of Eltham Palace, or would ambush him on the road.[18] What is not in doubt is that, shortly afterwards, the duke was complicit in a plot to seize Edmund and Roger Mortimer, the two heirs to the Mortimer claim to the throne. Henry certainly blamed him, as he imprisoned him for ten months. Thus, even if the Eltham assassination attempt was a complete fiction invented by Lady Despenser, we now come to the seventh plot against Henry in just over five years.

When Henry had come to the throne in 1399, he had wisely taken the precaution of securing the two young Mortimer boys, and placing them in royal custody at Windsor. Their claim to the throne, through Edward III's son Lionel, was arguably superior to his own, as was that of their uncle (the Edmund Mortimer who had married Glendower's daughter in late 1402). Although it would have been difficult to resurrect it after Henry's accession, particularly because of their youth (they were born in 1391 and 1393 respectively), they remained the most potent dynastic rivals to Henry. In fact their potency was enhanced by their youth; they might yet turn out to be good leaders, and so their cause was worth championing. Although Henry had had Richard II starved, he was never going to have two innocent boys murdered in cold blood simply on account of their claim to the throne. But he could not afford to let them fall into the wrong hands.[19] With their uncle Edmund in support of Glendower, the potential for another plot against him on behalf of the Mortimers was something of which he was acutely aware.

In February 1405 the Mortimer boys were still at Windsor, in the care of Lady Despenser. With her assistance, a locksmith made duplicate copies of the keys to their chamber. At midnight, on or about 13 February, one Richard Milton took the duplicate keys and led them from the chamber in which they were sleeping.[20] He was joined by Lady Despenser, her eight-year-old son, Richard, and an esquire called Morgan. Together they fled into the night, riding westwards for Abingdon and then South Wales, where her tenants were already in arms.

Parliament assembled around the empty throne shortly after noon on Tuesday 30 September 1399. Henry (in the tall black hat) sits in the seat of the dukes of Lancaster, with his eldest son, Henry, beside him.

Henry and his eldest son, as king of England and prince of Wales respectively, from the Great Cowcher of the dukes of Lancaster, painted about 1402.

Thomas of Lancaster, duke of Clarence, was Henry's second - and probably favourite - son. Governor of Ireland at the age of fourteen, he became the epitome of a royal warrior. He married his uncle's widow, died in battle in 1421, and was buried near Henry at Canterbury.

Ralph Neville, earl of Westmorland, was Henry's right-hand man in the north. The effigy of his second wife, Joan Beaufort (Henry's half-sister) lies nearest the camera. Note their Lancastrian livery collars, and those of Thomas (*above*) and John (*facing page, top*).

John Beaufort, earl of Somerset, was Henry's eldest half-brother. Although favoured by Richard, he surrendered to Henry in 1399, and thereafter remained unswervingly loyal. He now lies with his widow and her second husband, Thomas, his nephew (*facing page*, *top*), in Canterbury Cathedral.

Henry Beaufort, bishop of Winchester, was the second of Henry's three half-brothers. His arguments with his nephew Thomas (*facing page*, *top*) and Archbishop Arundel proved extremely divisive. His effigy in Winchester Cathedral shows him in a cardinal's red hat, which he was awarded in 1426.

Henry's seal as duke of Hereford (*left*) was based on earlier royal seals, such as that of the Black Prince (*right*). Note, however, that Henry's seal bears the motto 'so/ve/rey/ne' on the feathers. It is possible that the motto was added in July 1399 and relates to his assumption of *sovereign* power, or regency, at that time.

Henry's second great seal is acknowledged as one of the two most magnificent royal seals from medieval England (the other being Edward III's Brétigny seal).

This exquisite enamelled gold swan livery badge was found in Dunstable in 1965. Henry's own accounts for 1391-2 mention him having just such an enamelled gold swan of his own.

This spectacular crown was originally made in Paris about 1380. It probably came to England with Anne of Bohemia, on her marriage to Richard II. Henry gave it to his daughter, Blanche, when she left England to marry Louis of the Rhine in 1402.

Dere ſhewe holwe dan fane Duches of Breteyn dougter of the kyng

The coronation of Henry's queen, Joan of Navarre, in Westminster Abbey
on 26 February 1403.

Henry's effigy, in Canterbury Cathedral, is the best likeness we have of him, and the benchmark for assessing all other representations shown of the king. His widow, Queen Joan, lies beside him.

Thomas Arundel, archbishop of Canterbury, shown here preaching in 1400, was Henry's cousin, lifelong supporter and probably his closest friend.

Battlefield Church, near Shrewsbury, marks the site of Henry's great victory of 1403. The figure above the chancel window represents Henry in armour.

Lancaster Castle gatehouse was Henry's sole major secular building project. Ironically, today it is named after his father, John of Gaunt.

That night the king had been at Kennington, twenty-three miles away from Windsor. The disappearance of the Mortimer boys was discovered early in the morning of the 14th. The king set off immediately, sending his half-brother John Beaufort and a small group of men ahead to ride through the night. He reached Windsor that same evening. The following morning, before he left the castle, he dictated a letter to his secretary with news for the council:

> At six o'clock this morning the king's half-brother and others who rode before the king met a man who said that Lady Despenser and the March children have fled by Abingdon. The king's men are going after them, but if they can escape they will take the road to Glamorgan and Cardiff. They have with them an esquire called Morgan, who according to his wife, is going to Flanders and France as part of the plot. If he is in London, try to capture him; also send to all the ports to prevent him getting a passage. Written in haste on Sunday morning at Windsor Castle.[21]

Henry himself added the words at the bottom of the page, 'we pray you to think of the sea', and signed it with his initials, 'HR'. So rapid had been his reaction since learning of the Mortimers' escape at Kennington that he had abandoned almost all his household, even his signet ring. It was the only time in his entire reign that he acted without his personal seal.

Henry was lucky. His advance party was able to ride ahead along the Cardiff road at breakneck speed and catch up with Lady Despenser and her young charges. They caught sight of them in a wood near Cheltenham and launched themselves into an attack. Several of Lady Despenser's men were killed and the rest fled. Lady Despenser herself was arrested, and the precious Mortimer boys were taken back into custody. Lady Despenser was sent to Westminster immediately, where she accused her brother of treason before the royal council. She challenged him to a duel, hoping that someone would fight for her. One William Maidstone offered to do so, but the duke was not given the chance to respond. Instead he was arrested and imprisoned in the Tower.[22] As for the locksmith who had made the keys, he was made an example to others. First his hand was cut off, and then his head.

*

Although Henry did not realise it at the time, the escape of the Mortimer boys was potentially more dangerous than the mere escape of rival heirs to the throne. Two weeks after the failure of the plot to seize the Mortimers, their uncle negotiated an agreement with Owen Glendower and the earl of Northumberland. This was straightforward in one respect: each man promised to defend the others and to give them warning of any impending dangers. But then it added, 'if it appears to the three lords with the passage of time that they are indeed the persons of whom the prophet speaks, between whom the government of Great Britain ought to be divided and partitioned, then they will strive ... to ensure that this is effected'.[23]

There is no doubt what this means. The Prophecy of the Six Kings states that the sixth king after John (i.e. Henry IV) would be the last. He would be a 'moldewarp' (a mole) and he would have a rough skin like a goat. Early in his reign,

> a dragon shall rise up in the north which shall be full fierce, and shall move war against the moldewarp, and shall give him battle upon a stone. This dragon shall gather again into his company a wolf that shall come out of the west, that shall begin war against the moldewarp on his side, and so shall the dragon and he bind their tails together. Then shall come a lion out of Ireland that shall fall in company with them, and then shall England tremble ... the moldewarp shall flee for dread, and the dragon, the lion and the wolf shall drive him away ... and the land shall be partitioned in three parts: to the wolf, to the dragon and to the lion, and so it shall be for evermore.[24]

Clearly, the earl of Northumberland saw himself as the dragon from the north, Glendower as the wolf from the west and Edmund Mortimer the lion out of Ireland. Edmund was the grandson of Lionel, Edward III's third son and for several years governor of Ireland, and the Mortimer family were among the largest English landowners in Ireland. If they could drive away Henry, the land would be theirs to divide between them. They even made an arrangement as to where the borders were to run. Northumberland was to have twelve northern counties, Glendower all of Wales and a fair portion of the Midlands (the area bounded by the rivers Severn, Trent and Mersey). Edmund Mortimer was to have the rest of England.[25] Edmund's own claim to any form of kingship was, of course, subsidiary to that of his nephews; and it is unlikely a man who was a mere knight by birth could ever have been accepted as a king of southern England, especially when he himself was not the heir. His nephew, on the other hand, had a genuine claim to the throne and was an earl twice over, being the earl of March and Ulster. It goes to show how important the recapture of the elder Mortimer boy was in February 1405. If he had escaped, the ground would have been clear for the Glendower-led rising to have been accompanied with a revolt in southern England in the young earl's name and a Percy-led revolt in the north. The last of these was already in the planning; the Mortimers' claim on the south was the one piece of the jigsaw missing.

For Glendower, this agreement (known as 'the Tripartite Indenture') was a means to an end, a bargaining chip. Much of the English land he supposedly coveted in this agreement had been threatened or actually destroyed by his forces, especially parts of Herefordshire and Shropshire. He could always give up his claim to these at a later stage, if such a negotiated settlement with the Mortimers was required. His principal interest remained Wales, and there he seemed stronger than ever. Two of the four Welsh bishops – St Asaph and Bangor – now joined his cause. He planned to hold his second parliament that August at the mighty Harlech Castle, a fitting surrounding to his emerging court, to which representatives from France and Scotland were again invited.

As Glendower's boldness grew, so too did Henry's resolve. It is interesting to see these two leaders battling independently for their respective causes. As individuals they had much in common. Neither man was born to rule, yet both had glorious ancestries and were connected to prophecies of greatness. Both were intelligent and had a much higher standard of education than most of their contemporaries. Both were spiritually devout and yet prepared to manipulate the Church to suit their political aims.[26] Both were fervent nationalists and believed force should be used to advance the nationalist cause. Both courted foreign approval for their novel forms of government, and both were the subject of assassination attempts.[27] But, most strikingly, both were incredibly resilient, able to weather defeat and opposition and to come back, time and time again, pressing for the higher goal. They each had their difficulties, the waves of good and bad luck, popular appeal, widespread criticism and distrust, but their determination was similarly absolute. Now, as Glendower raised the bar of resistance, Henry leaped to the challenge. And this time he had the funds to take an army into Wales and hammer the Welsh harder than ever.

Directly after the recapture of the Mortimer boys, Henry had returned to Westminster. From there he went to Berkhamsted, where he received a letter from his eldest son, dated 11 March 1405, announcing that he had that day defeated a force of eight thousand Welsh rebels who had burned part of the town of Grosmont.[28] Exultant, Henry went to St Albans and announced to a great council his intention to ride against the Welsh the following month. Provision was made for reinforcing the castles in Wales with two thousand men. Plans were made for a double attack on Wales, with the prince leading an army of five hundred men-at-arms and three thousand archers into North Wales while Henry led a similar army into South Wales.[29] It was reminiscent of the three-pronged attack planned against Glendower in 1402, and designed to end the Welsh rebellion once and for all.

As soon as the 1405 Garter feast had been held at Windsor, Henry rushed towards the mustering point, reaching Worcester on 3 May. There he waited a week, before moving on to Hereford. News was coming in from all over his dominions. The troublesome count of St Pol had attacked the English-held town of Marck, near Calais, with several thousand French, Genoese and Flemish troops on 12 May. The small garrison abandoned the town and retreated into the castle, which the count then proceeded to besiege. At Calais, the English saw the chance of a quick expedition to relieve the garrison. On 15 March, Sir Richard Aston took a force of seven hundred men, including two hundred archers, against the assailants, backed up with twelve cartloads of arrows.[30] Once again, English archery proved devastating; fifteen French knights were killed, nine hundred prisoners were taken, and the count of St Pol fled to Saint-Omer without his armour.[31] When Henry heard the news of the relief of Marck, he declared it a miracle and ordered all the bishops in England to give thanks for the victory.[32]

The news followed hard on the heels of a Welsh attack, also in early May, on Usk Castle. The assault was led in person by Glendower's son, Gruffydd.[33] The castle, defended by its captain Sir John Greyndour and Lord Grey of Codnor, had recently been strengthened with more royal soldiers. They not only beat off the attack but made a sortie, pursuing the Welsh through Monkswood, killing many and capturing more at Pwll Melyn. So bitter was the hatred of the Welsh at this juncture – two years after the town of Usk had been burned by Glendower's forces – that three hundred Welsh prisoners were beheaded. But the real victory lay in the symbolic defeat of Glendower's family. His son and heir Gruffydd was captured and sent in chains to Henry. On the battlefield, among the dead, the English found a body that resembled Glendower himself. It turned out to be his brother, Tudor, but nevertheless the Great Magician who had once been so elusive, and who had caused Englishmen to believe he could make himself invisible, had lost his son and his brother. Even if he claimed to be prince of Wales, his dynasty was hanging by a thread. Only one son, Maredudd, now remained at his side.

*

As has already been seen, Henry had high expectations of his sons. Considering he himself had been jousting in public at the age of fourteen, it is perhaps not surprising that he should have regarded them as competent for military command at the same age. At fourteen, the prince had been entrusted with an army in North Wales; Thomas had been sent to Ireland at the same age. Since then both boys had proved their worth; the eldest had led a battalion at the battle of Shrewsbury and defeated the rebels at Grosmont, and Thomas had shown himself to be similarly courageous. In May 1405 Henry made Thomas an admiral, although he was not yet seventeen, and directed him to lead a naval attack on the French coast. Henry's third son, John, had also been fourteen when his father had made him constable of England and appointed him Warden of the East March. In the wake of the Percy revolt, this had been a heavy responsibility. Now, two years on, John too was about to repay his father's confidence.

While Henry was at Hereford planning his Welsh campaign he received a letter from the council. They acknowledged a letter he had sent on 8 May from Worcester, and answered most of the points he mentioned, providing money for various forces. They also mentioned that Henry's son John had relayed some important intelligence. Lord Bardolph had recently left Westminster, unexpectedly, and John had learned that he had secretly made his way into the north. Lord Bardolph was a close ally of the earl of Northumberland. John had the presence of mind to inform the council immediately of this news, and the council in turn at once informed Henry, sending him a thousand marks in case prompt action was required.

Henry realised the danger of leading the campaign into Wales while the earl of Northumberland and Lord Bardolph were conspiring. The intelligence he received from his son confirmed a number of suspicions. It followed an attempt by the earl of Northumberland to ambush Westmorland.[34] In the wake of this attempt, Henry had sent Sir Robert Waterton to the earl at Warkworth, to interrogate him. Northumberland had responded in a high-handed fashion, imprisoning Waterton. News of Lord Bardolph's secret trip finally confirmed to Henry that trouble was brewing in the north. They were waiting for him to ride into Wales so they could take advantage of his absence to proclaim the renewal of their rebellion.

On 23 May Henry rode to Worcester, to call off the Welsh campaign. On the 26th he began a rapid journey north, hoping to surprise any would-be rebels as they gathered. On the 28th he was at Derby, from where he wrote to the council, stating that he expected they had heard by now that the earls of Northumberland and Norfolk, and Lord Bardolph, had raised an army against him.[35] He urged the council to bring men to meet him at Pontefract for the safe-keeping of the realm. Then he rode on to

Nottingham, receiving regular updates as the situation developed. He heard that Northumberland had ordered his castles to be defended against the king. The earl of Westmorland and John of Lancaster, the king's son, were marching together to confront a rebel army gathered at Topcliffe. And at York, Richard Scrope, the archbishop of York, had led an armed mass of citizens on to Shipton Moor, six miles from the city.

Archbishop Scrope's armed mass demonstration followed so soon after Northumberland's seizure of Waterton that it appears impossible it was mere coincidence. Too many men joined in the rising at almost the same time for it to have been a series of separate conspiracies which all just happened to be in full swing on 26 May 1405.[36] Nevertheless, there were many different agendas, and many different forms of protest. What seems to have happened is that, after the earl of Northumberland's rising began to take shape, the northern gentry assembled at Topcliffe, Allerton and Cleveland, led by Sir John Fauconberg, Sir Ralph Hastings, Sir John fitz Randolph and Sir John Colville.[37] At the same time or very shortly afterwards, Archbishop Scrope, Thomas Mowbray, earl of Norfolk, Sir William Plumpton, Sir Robert Lamplugh and Sir Robert Persay sought to bring the city of York and its environs out in sympathy, raising a manifesto which their supporters pinned to church doors and city gates, and in the streets and alleys. The clergy were stirred by the archbishop's sermons against clerical taxation.[38] The merchants and people of the city were only too pleased to follow the archbishop's lead in complaining against taxes. When it became clear that Northumberland, Lord Bardolph and Sir William Clifford had risen in arms against Henry, the archbishop's word ignited an explosion of pent-up anger within the city. Eight or nine thousand men followed him and the earl of Norfolk out on to Shipton Moor.[39]

Coming so soon after the sealing of the Tripartite Indenture, there can be little doubt that the earl of Northumberland's ambition was to drive Henry from the realm. The gentry who raised their standards at Topcliffe sought to correct faults in the government of the kingdom and to remove certain individuals who were advising the king. The archbishop's demands were similar: a general reform of the government, the reversal of clerical taxation and the reorganisation of government expenditure for the purposes of resisting foreign enemies and to protect trade. His manifesto added that if these reforms were carried out, the rebels in Wales would lay down their arms and submit to English rule.[40] While this seems preposterous, it perhaps reflects Northumberland's hope that, somehow, the combination of forces would drive Henry from the kingdom, according to the old prophecy, and bring peace to all Britain.

The Yorkshire Rising was doomed from the outset. The various leaders seem to have operated on the basis that numbers alone would lead to success. There was no real strategy. Perhaps the failure lay in the very first act of the rebellion, the failure to seize Westmorland. Had that move succeeded, the gentry might have been able to move south with greater force, under Northumberland's leadership, linking up with the citizens of York. As it was, Westmorland and John of Lancaster were at liberty to drive the earl of Northumberland and Lord Bardolph north to Berwick, and then to disperse the army gathered at Topcliffe. Following those successes, the king's brother-in-law and son rode for York, where they met the archbishop and the earl of Norfolk. They pitched camp a little way off, and persuaded the archbishop and the earl to leave their citizen army in order to discuss their grievances. At the meeting Westmorland pretended to be most convivial, drinking with the archbishop and earl and assuring them that they had now done their part in raising these matters about the government of the realm.[41] He gave them assurances that he would put their complaints forward for discussion by the king. As he spoke, the armed citizens were being persuaded to return to the city. Archbishop Scrope and the earl of Norfolk were then discreetly arrested. By the end of the month, Westmorland and John had destroyed the entire rising.

Henry had sent reinforcements during the disturbances but had himself stayed clear of the trouble, at Nottingham.[42] After the arrest of Scrope, Mowbray and Plumpton, he moved north via Doncaster to Pontefract, where Westmorland brought the three arrested men. Henry took them to Bishopthorpe, the archbishop's castle, three miles south of York. The news he heard of their wrongdoings only confirmed the fate he had in mind. They complained of poor government: as far as Henry was concerned, displays like theirs were the cause of his government's failings. At the very moment he had been about to lead a double attack to end the Welsh revolt, their disturbance had forced him to call off the expedition, wasting large amounts of money in the process. Nor was this the first time; regularly the archbishop had persuaded the northern province not to grant money for the defence of the realm. Since 1401, they had granted only half the taxation of their brother clergy in the south. When the archbishop of York sought an interview with the king, he was refused. Instead Henry sent his half-brother, Thomas Beaufort, to take away Scrope's crozier. It was an ominous sign.

Archbishop Arundel knew Henry well and realised what the likely outcome would be. As soon as he heard that his fellow archbishop had been arrested for treason, he set off from London, hoping to catch Henry before he could sentence the archbishop. On the way he learned that Henry was intending to teach the northerners a lesson by executing their rebellious archbishop at his own castle.[43] Arundel pushed on, riding day and night. On 6 June, as Henry and his prisoners arrived at Bishopthorpe, the fifty-one-year-old Arundel was still some way south. It was not until late the following night that he rode into the courtyard of the castle, and asked to see the king. He was told Henry was in his chamber. Arundel, believing that he was the only man who could persuade Henry not to take the drastic action of executing the archbishop, burst in and pleaded with Henry for Archbishop Scrope's life. What would people think if he, Henry, were to kill an archbishop? Look what people said about the last King Henry who had killed an archbishop, Thomas Becket! Could he really be willing to bring such disaster upon himself? He was widely rumoured to have killed his cousin, an anointed king; was he now going to compound his sins by killing a religious leader? He told Henry in no uncertain terms that, as archbishop of Canterbury and the king's spiritual father, and the 'second man in the realm' after the king, he should leave any sentencing of the archbishop to the pope. Either that or let the man be judged in parliament.[44]

Henry listened to his old friend, but he did not agree with him. He had been down each of these roads before. He had let judgement on the bishop of Carlisle pass to the pope after the Epiphany Rising. There had been a long delay and eventually the man had been acquitted. He had let judgement on the earl of Northumberland pass to parliament the previous year. They had celebrated his opposition to Henry and had irresponsibly let him keep his castles and lands. Such a decision was one of the reasons he was facing this plot now and not fighting Glendower. The time had come to show absolute resolve, to show that the stability of the realm was more important than respect to a man of the cloth who was prepared to commit acts of treason in the name of God.

Henry, of course, did not say these things directly to his friend. Instead he said 'I cannot [agree], on account of the masses'. He urged his friend to go to bed, as he was tired after his long ride. In the morning they would have breakfast together and discuss the matter further. Nothing would be done without Arundel's advice, he said. Exhausted, Arundel retired for the night, but not before he had summoned a notary to the chamber and had him record exactly what the king had said to him. The two men then bade each other good night. But Henry did not go to bed. As soon as the arch-bishop had left he ordered a court to be summoned. He called together the earl of Arundel (nephew of the archbishop) and his own half-brother, Thomas Beaufort, and several lawyers. They tried the archbishop, the earl of Norfolk and Sir William Plumpton that same night, and found all three of them guilty of treason. As Thomas Arundel went down to breakfast next morning, he did not know that the prisoners were being sentenced elsewhere in the castle. About midday, all three were led out to a field nearby and beheaded.

*

The execution of an archbishop stunned all of Christendom, not just England, and it demands that we stare hard at Henry, who was solely responsible. No one else can be apportioned a part of the blame. Henry had taken the archbishop to his own castle deliberately, and had forcibly removed his crozier before his trial. When Justice William Gascoigne declined to pass the sentence of death on an archbishop, Henry set about finding a lawyer who would, even though Gascoigne was a man in whom he had 'a special confidence'.[45] So why did Henry kill the archbishop? And what does it say about Henry himself, the only Englishman ever to authorise the killing of an archbishop as well as a king?

It is necessary to look at this question from various points of view. Take Archbishop Arundel's position, for example. As we have seen, he was still one of Henry's staunchest supporters, and widely known to be his close friend and adviser. Arundel's close association with the first king to order the death of an archbishop since Henry II killed Becket made him look a fool. The alternative was that Arundel could be seen to be complicit in the death. Hence Arundel could only see the death as deeply damaging to himself, and a slap in the face for his friendship over all the years. It is hardly surprising that he collapsed shortly after being told about the execution.[46]

The public were similarly shocked. Killing an archbishop deeply damaged the king's popularity. Whether justifiable or not, it was evidence of a disregard for holy office which was simply un-Christian. Unsurprisingly, it was not long before men were reporting miracles at the tomb of Archbishop Scrope. Those disposed to give Henry the benefit of the doubt could only say that he had snapped under pressure, that his temper had momentarily given way. Even his supporters would probably have said that he had committed a grave mistake. Any rebels who wished to use a dead man's name for a rallying cry against the king now had an alternative to 'King Richard is alive'. They could cry with far greater conviction 'Archbishop Scrope is dead'. He was a second Thomas Becket, murdered by the king for daring to question royal policy. This last aspect – the martyrdom of Archbishop Scrope as a spokesman against royal tyranny – would have been the most worrying aspect of the whole episode in the eyes of Henry's secular supporters.

But what about Henry himself? What was going through his mind in the early hours of 8 June 1405? Herein lies an opportunity to view him at his most exposed: reacting violently, under great pressure. And the more we concentrate on him at that moment, the more it appears that there is a character here who is determined – desperate, yes, but acting in full awareness of what he was doing. This is the crucial point: Henry refused the advice of the men he most trusted. In addition, he planned the killing before the sentence was delivered, as can be seen in the way he fobbed off Archbishop Arundel. He clearly believed that he knew better than anyone else – better than the lawyers and the prelates – what was good for him and England. It shows incredible self-confidence after at least eight attempts to dethrone or kill him and uncounted numbers of protests against his rule, both in and outside parliament. Any normal person by this stage would have wanted to take a back seat and let others take the responsibility, but not Henry. He went all the way, and killed an archbishop, at the very moment it was guaranteed to make him exceedingly unpopular.

For this reason we may be sure that, contrary to what many people thought at the time, the killing of Archbishop Scrope was not a mistake. This is not to say it was the right thing to do, just that Henry knew the likely consequences and did what he personally felt was right. The bitterness he felt towards Scrope set the context, especially his anger at the timing of the revolt to coincide with his great Welsh campaign. But the real reason why Scrope's execution stunned people was because of his religious high office, not Henry's antipathy. Henry had no respect for high office, be it religious or secular. Richard II had been a divinely anointed king and that had not saved him. Besides, it was a kingly thing to do, to execute a traitor who occupied high office. Peasants might *murder* an archbishop, as they had done during the Peasants' Revolt, but only kings could authorise an archbishop's execution. The killing of Archbishop Scrope thus sent a political message throughout the kingdom. No matter who you were, whether archbishop or earl, you could be killed in order to preserve order.

The man who had come to the throne vowing to be merciful had been forced once again to display ruthless force, to demonstrate to his people that they could not presume upon his mercy. Ever since the Epiphany Rising, Henry had been learning this lesson. It would appear that he now fully understood how naïve this promise had been. The experience of government had changed him. His promise to rule with the advice of the great men of the realm had similarly turned sour: any leader who felt ignored could accuse him of breaking his word. Henry seems now to have decided that what England needed was not a compromised, listening, merciful king who consulted his advisers on every important matter of state, but a man of spiritual confidence and political determination. He would not be taken for granted any more. From now on, when necessary, he would rule with an iron fist.

SIXTEEN

Smooth Comforts False

They bring smooth comforts false, worse than true wrongs.
Henry IV Part Two, Act 1, Scene 1

On 8 June 1405, the day of Archbishop Scrope's execution, Henry rode into York. Having conducted his business – arranging for the administration of the diocese and granting several pardons – he set out for the north. Notwithstanding that a summer storm was brewing, he wanted to attack the earl of Northumberland's castles as soon as possible. The wind turned to a gale, the rain grew heavier, and Henry directed his companions to seek shelter at the nearby manor of Green Hammerton. Later that night, as he slept at the manor, Henry started screaming. 'Traitors! Traitors!' he yelled, 'you have thrown fire over me!' When his servants reached him they found him complaining that his skin was burning. They gave him wine and tried to soothe his fears that this was yet another assassination attempt, but with little success. He was clearly ill. According to one account, his face was covered in red pustules.

For those who were with him, the king's sickness was shocking. For the rest of the country, coming on the very day of the archbishop's execution, it could be nothing other than an act of divine vengeance. Within a short while it was being reported that God had smitten him with leprosy.[1] The use of the emotive biblical word is anti-Lancastrian propaganda; the rumourmongers may as well have said that Henry had the 'elderlich skin of a goat' which the last of the prophesied six kings, the moldewarp, was supposed to have. Henry did not have leprosy (not as we understand it, anyway), as proved by an examination of his corpse in the nineteenth century.[2] But only in this respect was his illness a fiction. Having been taken to more suitable accommodation at Ripon, he spent a full week convalescing. Shortly afterwards he wrote to the council reassuring them of his good health, and thanking God for it.[3]

This brings us to perhaps the knottiest problem in the life of Henry IV: how ill was he, and did he ever recover? Did his illnesses have significant consequences for his mental state? Was he able to travel? At what point did people start to look more to his successor as the key to future preferment? All these questions suddenly become relevant. And they all require a degree of precision in their answering. Edward III, for instance, had probably been physically weak and 'ill' for at least ten years before he died in 1377, but he continued to transact a significant level of royal business until the mid-1370s and even attempted to lead an expedition to France in 1372.[4] As we shall see, even when Henry was undoubtedly ill, he still declared that he would lead armies against his enemies. It is thus one of those areas of biography in which we cannot 'err on the side of caution' for no side is safer than another. The dangers of overstating the effects of Henry's illness are every bit as great as those of ignoring them.

The traditional way of approaching the illness of a historical individual is to act as a sort of bedside consultant across the centuries, and try to determine what was wrong with him. The idea is that by identifying the illness, we may understand what was happening to the sufferer. However, as medical historians are quick to point out, this is nigh on impossible in the case of a medieval king. All we have to go on are a few symptoms reported by chroniclers who probably never met Henry at all, let alone met him at the time of his suffering. Henry himself never publicly gave out any details about his health; it was not becoming for a king to reveal his weaknesses.[5] But lack of knowledge of the symptoms is just the tip of the problem. We do not know what diseases were suffered in the early fifteenth century which are not suffered now. Some diseases (Sweating Sickness, for example) have come and gone since Henry's time. Similarly, it is not possible to assume that all modern diseases which fit the pattern of Henry's illness were around in fifteenth-century England. Nor can we assume that the same diseases were suffered in the same way; for example, plague in 1348 and syphilis in 1500 manifested themselves very differently from the equivalent diseases in later centuries. Even if we could say that Henry suffered from a specific illness, there is the problem that we do not know which complications attended his suffering. He could have had a skin disease and heart disease at the same time, and then suffered a stroke or heart attack, or both consecutively. Alternatively, the cause of his suffering might have been a hereditary weakness, such as the inability to produce an enzyme, leading to the gradual degradation of the body. In short, acting as Henry's bedside consultant is a parlour game for medical antiquaries.

The starting point for considering Henry's medical condition historically has to be his health before this: how well he was before this new ailment struck. To this question we might reply that Henry had fought at Shrewsbury two years earlier and been very active both before and after the battle, and so we should presume he was in good health at least at that time. However, it has to be added that there are signs that he was never a well man, in the sense of being in good health for long periods of time. From as early as 1387, when he and two of his servants contracted 'the pox' (meaning a skin disease of some sort), he was troubled by skin problems. He had been ill on the *reyse* at Königsberg in 1391, and had purchased medicines in 1395, 1397 (a plaster for his back) and 1398.[6] These payments, like the pox, might indicate skin complaints long before 1405. According to Adam Usk, shortly after his coronation his hair fell out, supposedly a result of lice.[7] Two images of Henry from the Great Cowcher of the duchy of Lancaster, made about 1402, show him with a full head of hair and a forked beard, but his portrait effigy at Canterbury, probably made from a death mask, shows him as completely bald; only the forked beard remains. Thus Usk (who was in exile at the time) might be right in stating that he lost his hair, although his timing is probably awry and a skin disease is a more likely cause than lice. In 1403 his surgeon purchased medicines for him, and admitted to the Holy Roman Emperor the following year that Henry had been ill.[8] About the same time Henry was employing an extra surgeon. In Henry's accounts we read of so many glass urinals that it would appear that he regularly sent samples of his urine to his physician, for inspection as to colour and consistency, from which his general state of health could be determined (according to medieval ideas of medicine). In this light it is particularly interesting that he commissioned a treatise on uroscopy – the examination of urine by physicians – to be written.[9] When we add the purchase of the bezoar stone to protect against poison and the repair of astrolabes to work out the positions of the stars for determining when to let blood and take medicines, what emerges is a picture of a man who was not only regularly ill but fearful of ill health. He even seems to have had problems with his teeth.[10] This morbidity allows us to say with conviction that Henry paid particular attention to his physical condition, and was aware of the implications of being seen to be ill. It also means that he was used to coping with sickness. So when he was afflicted suddenly at Green Hammerton, it was not just a minor irritation which caused him to suspend his journey north and spend a week recovering at Ripon.

To go beyond this we need to concentrate not on the king's incapacity, but on his health. This paradox may most easily be explained by referring to Henry's mental state. Henry took part in at least fifty jousting competitions before he became king. If he rode just ten strokes in each tournament, that still amounts to at least five hundred occasions when, in full armour and mounted on a war horse, he charged straight into another object of a similar weight (the man, armour and horse combined weighing more than half a ton), with all the pressure of the charge focused on the point of the lance, at a closing speed of more than forty miles per hour. The strain on the body, including the brain, of such an impact would have been considerable, way in excess of the being-hit-by-a-twenty-pound-hammer effect which modern boxers experience. It is therefore reasonable to wonder whether he suffered from the condition which affects some boxers in retirement, known as 'punch-drunk'. Alternatively, it has been suggested that during the storm on 8 June 1405, Henry had a stroke, for one account of his illness says he fell suddenly ill, having felt a blow during the storm.[11] However, if we look at the extant examples of his handwriting, we can see that his pen control in 1409 was almost as good as it had been in 1403.[12] Hence we may be confident that Henry's sickness was not a brain condition resulting from his years of martial practice, nor was it a stroke which affected the writing-hand side of his body. In the summer of 1406 he was able to ride eighteen miles in a day and is described walking around the cloisters of Bardney Abbey, and these at a time when he seems to have been particularly determined to find a religious cure for his suffering. So we may rule out the idea that he suffered a severe stroke or apoplexy. His handwriting suggests that he retained his mental faculties even after the very severe attacks which left him apparently dead in 1408 and 1409. Until the last year of his life, his mind remained sharp, as is clear in his behaviour in later parliaments, especially that of 1411, and his other activities (for example, personally designing a large cannon in 1408). Therefore, whatever he was struck with in June 1405, his mind was not affected. It is unlikely that he ever fully recovered from his skin affliction, and his eventual baldness is probably to be connected with this ailment, but he remained sane. The more profound consequences of his illness would only became apparent the following year.

*

A week after his burning skin experience at Green Hammerton, he was back on the road, heading north. Good news spurred him on. In Wales, Glendower's brother-in-law, John Hanmer, had been captured. The earl of Northumberland's castles of Langley, Prudhoe and Cockermouth had capitulated without a fight. Warkworth Castle initially defied Henry, even though he appeared in person before the walls, but submitted after one of his great cannon had blasted it seven times. These cannon were far advanced on the guns of the fourteenth century. They could weigh up to two tons and were specially designed to shoot very large balls of stone at high velocity into castle walls.[13] Such weapons gave Henry a great advantage in tackling the strongholds of those who chose to rebel. They proved decisive again a few days later at Berwick, one of only two castles still holding out for the rebel earl. First, small cannon were used to demolish part of the walls of Berwick Castle; then a single stone from a larger cannon brought down a large portion of the Constable Tower, entirely removing a staircase and killing a man who was climbing it at the time.[14] With such firepower ranged against them, the garrison despaired. By 12 July Berwick Castle was in Henry's hands. Any men of high rank who had remained loyal to Northumberland were beheaded within the walls. Mercy was shown only to the common soldiers.

Henry did not waste time celebrating. As soon as Berwick had fallen he led his army along the coast road to Alnwick, twenty-seven miles to the south. He was there within two days. As soon as he appeared, the earl of Northumberland's grandson capitulated, and marched out of the castle to surrender. Within two months of hearing of the earl of Northumberland's plot, Henry had subdued every last fortress which had been held against him. In every respect it had been a ruthlessly efficient operation, despite his illness.

Nevertheless, two days' rest was all Henry allowed himself at Newcastle. On 18 July he set out for the Lancastrian heartlands, to deal with the legal and bureaucratic fall-out from the rebellion. Enquiries had to be made, fines exacted and executions carried out. Many pardons had to be granted too, to those who did not deserve to die. Lands belonging to the discredited lords had to be taken into the king's hands. Some of Mowbray's estates went to Henry's brother-in-law, Sir John Cornwaille. Lord Bardolph's properties were largely given to his son John as a reward for his good service. Other lands were distributed around the royal family to help them with the shortfalls in their income following the restrictions imposed by parliament.

At the same time Henry attempted to relaunch his campaign against Glendower. This was never going to be easy: the opportune moment had passed. Had he been able to advance with two armies and ten thousand men in the immediate aftermath of the victories at Grosmont and Usk, he might have completely undermined Glendower's position. Instead, the Yorkshire uprising had given Glendower the chance to regroup and reorganise. It had also allowed him to enlist the help of his French allies. Worst of all, it had depleted Henry's reserves. Treasury clerks were ordered to raise advances to pay the troops for the forthcoming campaign on 20 July, while Henry was still at Durham. The money granted in 1404 had already been spent – on repaying old debts, the defence of the coasts, the defence of the Welsh castles, the aborted Welsh campaign, and financing his campaign against the earl of Northumberland. Henry was once again facing the problem of fighting a war with an empty treasury.

In these circumstances, it is hardly surprising that Henry's fifth Welsh campaign was very much like its four precursors: short and inconclusive. The principal difference was that a French force under the command of the lord of Hugueville had landed in Milford Haven in early August. Joining forces with Glendower, they had burned the towns of Haverfordwest, Tenby and Carmarthen. They then proceeded eastwards, and were within ten miles of Worcester when Henry arrived in the city. Seeing the enemy so near at hand, Henry led what forces were at his disposal out to meet them on Woodbury Hill. It was a courageous move; for eight days there was a stand-off, as the more numerous Franco-Welsh army hesitated to attack the English, and Henry did not dare risk leading his men against the Franco-Welsh without reinforcements. On the eighth day the assailants gave way, running short of supplies, and they retreated, leaving Henry free to ride to Hereford and assemble a larger force.

Henry's 1405 campaign eventually set out from Hereford on 10 September. His purpose was, as always, to be seen by the people at the head of an army. This time he also had the specific war aim of relieving Coity Castle, in Glamorgan, which was then being besieged by the Welsh. This was quickly accomplished; the garrison was supplied with victuals and reinforced. On his return, however, Henry's luck ran out, as it had so often in Wales, and he lost men and part of his baggage train in flash floods. Forty or fifty carts had to be abandoned to the swollen rivers and the impassable roads. By the end of the month, when Henry's bedraggled army staggered back into Hereford, his frustration must have been immense. Having had such grand plans of crushing Glendower in May, all he had managed four months later was to relieve one castle. Despondent, he returned to Kenilworth.

The remainder of 1405 was a relatively inactive time for Henry. Perhaps his skin disease was still a problem, preventing him from travelling easily. In terms of bureaucratic business, of course, he was anything but inactive. He continued to receive petitions and sent out hundreds of letters.[15] But there were no more military activities that year. After a month at Kenilworth Castle with his family, he slowly returned to London, staying at the Tower until about 22 November, when he shifted to the Palace of Westminster, ready to attend the betrothal of his eleven-year-old daughter Philippa to the king of Denmark.[16] He was still at Westminster on 7 December, when the council agreed to free the duke of York and restore all his estates to him (after almost a year in prison), but shortly afterwards he departed for Hertford. From there he wrote to the council on the 11th stating that they needed to fund the fleet which had been assembled to take him to Gascony, and promising that he or some other suitable person would go there soon. But as he well knew, the money to undertake such an expedition was not available. Ten days later he returned to London and issued writs for a new parliament. Immediately he departed to spend Christmas at Eltham, and to spend a few days with his queen, his sons, and his friends Thomas Langley and the earl of Westmorland before preparing to face his next battle with the commons.

*

The 'Long Parliament' which met on 1 March 1406 at Westminster was, as its name suggests, the longest single parliament of the middle ages. For historians it is also one of the most important and problematic. Usually it is portrayed as a classic *Rex vs commons* contest, in which both sides badly bruised the other, and Henry came off worst, his royal power subjected to the supervision of a council and his income drastically diminished. Recently it has been suggested that parliament was not trying to limit Henry's authority but to safeguard it at a time when he was very ill, and perhaps likely to die.[17] What is not in doubt is that Henry's power as a king was severely curtailed. So extreme were the limitations placed upon him that we have to ask what caused them: were they implemented for his benefit or in spite of him?

The argument that the restrictions on royal authority were done to benefit Henry and safeguard his regime stems from the fact that more than half of the representatives of the counties in the commons were Lancastrian supporters. If parliament was functioning as 'a Lancastrian forum', so the argument goes, how come it was so determined to diminish the power of a Lancastrian king? Given that during the course of the parliament Henry wrote to the council saying he was not well enough to attend, there seems to be a good case for seeing parliament's attempts to regulate royal authority as a means of coping with a head of state who was seriously ill and absent for much of the time. This is all the more so as measures were taken during the parliament to clarify the succession, further suggesting an expectation that the king would die. But significant problems remain. Even though more than half of the county members were Lancastrian retainers, these men were hugely outnumbered by the members of the boroughs, over whom the king had much less control.[18] Nor can we ignore the complete lack of evidence connecting the most severe limitations on royal authority and the king's physical incapacity.[19] Had he been mentally unwell, we could understand why severe checks were placed upon his actions, but there is no evidence of any mental instability – quite the opposite – though he does seem to have experienced some form of depression.

The first session of the parliament began on 1 March with the customary speech from the chancellor, Thomas Langley. Langley gave the reasons for summoning the parliament as the need to counter the Welsh rebels, and to provide for the defence of Gascony, Calais, Ireland and the Scottish marches. No reference was made to the king's health. The following day, the twenty-eight-year-old Lancastrian retainer Sir John Tiptoft was elected Speaker. Routine business followed for several days. On 23 March the criticisms of the king's government started, with demands from the Speaker for ordinances for the defence of the seas, Wales and Gascony. The first of these was set in motion straightaway, but the criticisms seem to have intensified. On 3 April the commons reiterated their demands for the expulsion of various foreigners in the queen's household. They were also forced to apologise for 'speaking of the royal person of our lord the king other than they should have', on which account the king was angry. Henry excused them, and accepted their apology, but the damage was done. He adjourned parliament the same day.

On the political front, Henry now experienced an amazing piece of luck. On 22 March the eleven-year-old James Stewart, son and heir of the king of Scotland, had been captured in a boat off the coast of Norfolk. Two weeks later, the boy's father, King Robert III, died. That meant the new king of Scotland was in Henry's custody at the Tower (along with Glendower's son). Not surprisingly, Scottish politics fell into disarray.

On the personal front, however, Henry's luck dissolved, for his health collapsed. After the end of the first session, he took the royal barge down the river to Eltham, where he celebrated Easter (11 April).[20] Two days later he made a grant to his physician, Louis Recoches.[21] He stayed at Eltham as long as possible before leaving for the Garter festivities, only embarking at Greenwich on the 22nd.[22] His bargemen transported him as far as Kingston upon Thames, where he stayed the night, being conveyed the rest of the way to Windsor the next day, St George's Day itself.[23] At Windsor his health rapidly deteriorated. On 28 April, two days after parliament was meant to have resumed sitting, he wrote to the council from a lodge in the park, saying that a sudden illness had attacked his leg, and his doctors had advised him not to travel by horse, in order 'to avoid the grave peril'. He added that he hoped to be at Staines by the evening and to travel by water to London, arriving in three or four days. Later that same day he wrote saying that his leg was now so bad that he could not travel at all. He directed parliament to discuss the safety of Gascony and to make arrangements for conducting his daughter Philippa to Denmark, as he had agreed she should be married there in early May.[24]

It is unlikely that Henry reached London until 4 May. When he did arrive, he stayed at the hostel of Thomas Langley, at Dowgate (at the bottom of what is known today as Dowgate Hill), and not at Westminster. From Dowgate he could easily travel the short distance to Westminster by boat, and at the same time keep his distance from the parliament. There is no doubt that this was due to his continuing illness. In his letter to the council he describes the ailment as 'une grande accesse', which relates to a sudden illness in general, a fit or an ague (intermittent fever), correlating with his inability to ride a horse, and reminding us of his burning skin complaint of the previous summer.[25] Given Henry's long stay at Kenilworth after the Welsh campaign of 1405, and his continued presence near the river after his return to London, it is likely that his skin problem had never entirely gone away.[26] The references to his 'uncurable' skin disease in the chronicles (albeit misinterpreted as leprosy) further support the idea that this was an ongoing illness. So too does the reference to 'his physicians' (in the plural). The royal household ordinances made provision for just one physician and one surgeon.[27] All this paints a picture of Henry quietly fighting both his own body as well as his enemies.

Henry attended the second session of parliament on at least nine occasions.[28] The rest of the time he stayed at Thomas Langley's house. He communicated with his council through letters sealed with his privy seal, and did little in person. On the days when he attended parliament he seems to have stayed a short while and then returned to Dowgate. The pattern is so unlike his usual behaviour that we can only conclude that his illness had become his preoccupation. Indeed, his physical illness and the increased stress of running the government in such circumstances together seem to have led to a sudden crisis of confidence. On 22 May he appeared in parliament and directed that a bill he had drawn up should be read out on his behalf. In it he asked to be relieved of certain aspects of government 'because he alone would not be able fully to devote his attentions to the same as much as he would like'.[29] His bill went on to name his council, hoping that thereby 'he might be further relieved in his royal person of the aforesaid concerns'. Most significantly, the council was given the power to endorse or refuse bills issued by the king's officers, acting almost as a collective regent. On 7 June, Henry attended parliament to hear the magnates and prelates acknowledge his son Henry as the heir apparent, with his male heirs succeeding after him. In the context of his illness and the fact that the prince had already been recognised as heir apparent (in the first parliament of his reign), the reason would appear to have been Henry's own anticipation that he might not live to see his fortieth birthday.

The initiative in this second session of parliament clearly lay with the king, or, rather, the king's illness and stress. The measures of 22 May were not a parliamentary solution to the king's problem but his own suggestion, as recorded on the roll. He still had not received the grant of taxation for which he had originally summoned parliament, even though three months had passed. In that time he had heard the commons speak of their wish that he should deliver them good government, and had heard them speak disparagingly of him personally. He had largely resigned his authority, putting the government into the hands of the council. If the 22 May bill had been an attempt to appease the commons, Henry's agreement should have been sufficient to unlock the taxation he required. But the commons were still not satisfied. All they granted was an extra shilling in the pound on the duty on foreign merchants' goods for the defence of the realm. According to an oblique reference in one chronicle, they were angry that, despite their large grant of taxation in the October 1404 parliament, Henry had failed to take back all the royal grants made since 1367.[30] On 19 June, Sir John Tiptoft delivered the commons' demand that they should be permitted to audit the accounts of the two war treasurers appointed in October 1404. This is the occasion when Henry is said to have tersely replied, 'kings are not wont to render account'. Nevertheless, the commons insisted that he allow them to appoint a committee of enquiry. Henry had to give in. With no taxation forthcoming, he adjourned the parliament until 13 October.

*

As the members of parliament returned to their homes to oversee the harvest, Henry set about preparing to accompany his daughter, Philippa, to Lynn, from where she would sail to Denmark. Although she should have been there two months earlier, he did not rush. However, it is very interesting that he did not sail to King's Lynn; he went by road. Had his legs been as sore as they were in April, when the short trip from Windsor to Staines was beyond him, he would not have been able to undertake such a journey. As it was, he not only undertook it, he rode or was carried at nearly the same speed as he had travelled when fully fit.[31]

Yet something was profoundly wrong with Henry. On the way to King's Lynn he made a sudden trip to Walsingham, where there were two holy wells capable of effecting miraculous cures. Very shortly afterwards, having said goodbye to his daughter for the last time, he swiftly travelled to Bardney Abbey, near Lincoln, where he locked himself away in the abbey library. Not only that, he actually kissed the relics kept in the church there, to receive their full healing power.[32] Bardney Abbey held the tomb of St Oswald, a northern Christian king killed in battle whose bones had effected many cures. In the library Henry could have read about St Oswald's shrine curing children of fevers, and driving devils out of frenzied men, and even bringing men back from the point of death.[33] After this trip Henry returned south: he made no move towards Wales, even though Lord Bardolph and the earl of Northumberland were known to be consorting in arms with Glendower. The clergy had agreed to a grant in Henry's favour, and a substantial loan had been raised too, but Henry himself seems to have lost the will to fight.

The evidence suggests that in 1406 Henry was coming to terms with the fact that he would never be well again. All his life he had been very active, a jouster, a crusader, a soldier and a man who liked to take charge of things personally. Now his entire world had been thrown apart by his illness. If we are right in interpreting this as having been ongoing and worsening since 1405, a temporary abatement in the symptoms (allowing him to ride) would not necessarily have led to restored confidence and vigour. It was the future which mattered, and the future looked bleak. Never would he do what his grandfather and uncle had done, and ride at the head of an army into France. Never would he defeat Glendower on the battlefield. And it was all due to an illness, God's will and divine punishment. With the deaths of Richard II and an archbishop on his conscience, Henry may well have feared that he deserved such affliction. As we shall see, the language of his last will (written just over two years later) strongly repeats how sinful he was, and how he had misspent his life, at a time when such sentiments were anything but orthodox. It would thus seem that almost every aspect of his life was in turmoil – his identity as a man of action, his outlook on government and his relationship with God – and he had little to look forward to but pain, death and damnation.

This defeatism was very much in evidence when he returned to parliament in October. He was late in arriving. When he did turn up, news came of an attack by the duke of Burgundy on Calais, and it would appear that Henry postponed parliament to allow his council to deal with that threat.[34] When they reassembled on 18 November, the commons immediately launched a bitter series of criticisms of the king. They accused him of trying to divert the money intended for the defence of the seas into the exchequer. The Speaker asked him to force the lords to explain how 'evil governance' had been allowed to prevail. The lords and commons were both adamant that he should change his settlement of the Crown to allow daughters to inherit the throne. The discussions grew more and more bitter. The commons were deeply unhappy at the thought that Henry was proposing to resign power to a council composed of his friends and relations, over whom they had even less control than they did over the king. Henry was asked to reappoint his council, and he did so on 27 November, in an almost unchanged format.[35] That was not good enough. Over the following days the commons forced him to sack the faithful Hugh Waterton, as well as Sir John Cheyne and Sir Arnold Savage. They also sacked Henry's old friend Richard Kingston as treasurer of the household and brought in Tiptoft to replace him. And they started to rewrite the clauses governing Henry's resignation of his administrative duties. What they proposed was so radical that Henry lost his temper and threatened them with a trial of strength. But strength was the one thing he no longer had, and he was left isolated, weak and unable to resist their will.

The 'Thirty-One Articles', to which he eventually agreed, was not his own solution to the problem of his illness but that of parliament. Henry would have to devote two days a week (Wednesdays and Fridays) to seeing his council and receiving petitions. He was to intervene in no quarrels, even those of his own household, but was to submit them to the arbitration of the council. The council was to take over the administration of Henry's household, chamber and wardrobe offices. He was not allowed to make gifts to anyone. He was given just £6,000 to cover his household expenses (half the drastically reduced allowance stipulated in the January 1404 parliament). He was not to intervene in any disputes which could be dealt with by the common law. The queen was to pay a sum out of her allowance for the time she spent with the king in his household. Henry was to be subjected to the sort of supervision given to Richard II as a ten-year-old boy. And all he could do was to assent, for the sake of obtaining the essential tax. On 22 December the commons agreed to a single tenth and fifteenth. An Act was passed against religious and political sedition, and parliament began to disperse, leaving only a committee of members to oversee the accurate enrolment of proceedings.

Henry went to Eltham to spend Christmas with his queen. He was physically weak and despondent. He had let his and his family's royal authority be trampled by parliament. Nor had it resulted in unlocking sufficient funds for the exchequer: the grant of taxation had not been that generous, and the long sitting had been very costly. The expenses of the seventy-four county members alone came to more than £2,500; those of the burgesses may have amounted to considerably more.[36] The chronicler Walsingham suggested that the total cost amounted to the whole value of the tax, which, though an exaggeration, makes a point.[37] The disputations had added nothing to the standing of the royal family. The council instructed Henry that, as soon as Christmas was out of the way, he should take himself off into the country somewhere, and live quietly and cheaply.

*

Ironically, at the moment when Henry's reputation was at its lowest, a figure from his glorious heyday came to England. Lucia Visconti arrived to marry the earl of Kent at Southwark on 24 January. Henry gave her away at the church door.[38] He could hardly have avoided reflecting on how much had happened in the fourteen years since they had last met. Then he had been the chivalric hero in his mid-twenties, an earl in the prime of life, and she, at twenty-one, had swooned. Now she was in her mid-thirties and past her prime, and he was an incapacitated king heavily reliant on his second wife and his council, with more problems than he could have believed he would ever have had to face in 1393. If she did not avert her eyes from his out of respect for his royal dignity, what did she see? That through this man she might have been a queen? Or that she could have been married to a majestic invalid? Whatever her thoughts, Henry must have silently asked himself which of the two was uppermost in her mind.

After the wedding Henry returned to Westminster. In the royal chapel on 30 January he directed Thomas Langley to relinquish the great seal to his old friend Archbishop Arundel. Arundel thereby became not only the most prominent member of the council but chancellor too. It heralded the height of his political career: for the next few months he was effectively the ruler of England, a sort of prime minister. Together with the prince, who now attended the royal council, he set about reforming the government. Money from direct taxation – the tenths and the fifteenths – could henceforth be directed to pay for the expenses of the royal household.[39] Revenues which had in the past been paid in cash to the household were now required to be paid directly to the exchequer. Payments from the treasury were to be authorised more regularly. The budget was subjected to a process of prioritisation, with defence being given top priority. And through Sir John Tiptoft, treasurer of the royal household, he managed to reduce Henry's household expenses by ten per cent. In this way, the government's finances were gradually brought under control.[40]

The employment of Archbishop Arundel was a pragmatic move on Henry's part. It marks a point of realisation that he could not govern personally, however well-meaning he was. He could not control all the departments of the household, nor could he dictate national priorities and expect his treasurer to meet all the expenses. Most of all, he realised that his very attempt to govern in this manner allowed his critics to attack him. Had he been successful and glorious in his military expeditions he might have been forgiven, but by 1406 it was impossible to ignore that he had failed to deliver on a number of his own policies, most notably Wales. The Thirty-One Articles, coupled with his physical weakness, seem finally to have shocked Henry into doing what he had always publicly promised to do – to rule with the advice of the great men of the realm – and in the way that the commons expected him to do it: by openly subjecting himself to their counsel. To oppose such measures would only result in more criticism, whereas, by giving up control and working with those who sought to rebuild the royal finances and restore trust in the government, he might yet recover the dignity of the Crown.

In this way, Henry came to rely more closely than ever on Archbishop Arundel, whose political fortunes had been intertwined with his own now for twenty years. As chancellor, the archbishop dominated the council, both intellectually and politically, as evidenced in a number of council proceedings.[41] Such pre-eminence led to clashes between him and the twenty-year-old prince, Henry of Monmouth. Young Henry may have seen the limitations placed on his father as a dangerous precedent for controls which might one day be placed upon him. In addition, it was almost inevitable that questions would arise over whether or not a chancellor-archbishop had authority to direct a prince. In February 1407 Arundel confirmed the Act legitimising the Beauforts, Henry's half-brothers, but he introduced a clause which barred them from the throne. The Beauforts, thus slighted, seem to have taken against the archbishop, and supported the prince against him.[42]

This shift of the political initiative to the archbishop and prince, coupled with his illness, meant that the year 1407 was not one of great activity for Henry. Abiding by the council's direction that he should reside cheaply away from London, he stayed at Hertford Castle for much of February and March. Although he stated in a letter dated 5 February that he wished to lead a military campaign against the French, either from Calais or in Gascony, this was quickly scotched by the council.[43] In April he went to Windsor for the Garter feast, and stayed there a month. Affairs of state – dealing with the mutiny of the Calais garrison, for example, who seized the wool of English merchants in lieu of their unpaid wages – were mainly handled by the council in his absence. It would appear that when he did try to act in defiance of the Thirty-One Articles, Archbishop Arundel took measures to undermine him. On 20 April a writ was sent to the exchequer 'from the king' – for which read 'from Arundel' – demanding that the Articles be properly observed by officers even if the king were to issue a writ to the contrary.[44] Arundel was determined that Henry would swallow his reforming medicine, every last drop.

The council sat continually for nine weeks, during which time Henry remained in the Thames area, presumably receiving petitions on Wednesdays and Fridays, as he had promised to do. After this period, in June, he travelled north to the Lancastrian estates, keeping in touch with the archbishop by letter. Despite the distance, the archbishop continued to rule him. On 1 June Henry declared that he would lead an army into Wales; nine days later he retracted this, probably on the advice of the archbishop, who knew that Henry was neither physically nor politically strong enough to lead a campaign. When Henry's old comrade-in-arms Sir Thomas Rempston drowned in the Thames, and the duke of York was appointed by the council to replace him as constable of the Tower, Henry ordered his most important prisoners (namely the young king of Scotland and Glendower's son) to be taken from the Tower to Nottingham Castle, indicating that he remained uncertain about the duke's loyalty. Again, he was overruled by the council. A third example of Henry's plans being thwarted came after the archbishop had already summoned the next parliament to meet, at Gloucester. Although the writs for this had been despatched on 26 August, Henry declared on 22 September that he would lead a force to help the prince in the siege of Aberystwyth.[45] There is no doubt that he was ardent for glory, and longed to be present at the surrender of Aberystwyth Castle, but equally there is no doubt that he was financially and politically ill equipped to take arms in person. He might have been motivated by a wish to be seen leading his men even at the point of death, like his great-great-grandfather, King Edward I, exactly a century earlier. But in 1407 there was no room for such chivalric histrionics, and Archbishop Arundel was quick to make sure the council's careful financial measures were not all blown in a rash campaign.

*

Henry spent the summer in the north, travelling by boat between his castles and pilgrimage sites.[46] The long stays at Lancastrian castles might have been part of a money-saving measure but just as probably they were due to the difficulties he was now experiencing when travelling by road. The man who once jousted along with the best of them, and had won praise from Boucicaut, now rode on a brass saddle, or possibly a form of litter.[47] Although this meant that his speeds on occasion were as fast as they had been in 1403 (fifteen or sixteen miles per day), there were protracted periods of rest between these journeys. In order to be at Gloucester on 20 October, for the next sitting of parliament, he set out from York on 21 September, giving himself a full month to cover a journey of less than two hundred miles. Some of that was probably undertaken by river: from Bishopthorpe along the River Ouse to Cawood, for example, and along the River Trent from Nottingham to Repton.[48] At Evesham Abbey, on the River Avon, he rested for six days. From there he could have been rowed the rest of the way to Gloucester.

The 1407 parliament, which opened on 24 October in Gloucester Abbey (now the cathedral), was orchestrated by Archbishop Arundel from the moment it opened. As chancellor, it was Arundel who delivered the opening speech. The purpose of the parliament, he announced, was nothing less than that they should 'honour the king'.[49] He then outlined three reasons. First they should honour him because Henry had upheld the liberties of the cities and boroughs of the kingdom – a direct appeal to the representatives of the boroughs who had given him such a hard time in the previous parliament. They should honour him because of his maintenance of the law and in particular his own personal efforts to defend the realm in war. And thirdly, they should honour him because 'he had shown such great compassion and clemency that, in the case of anyone who had offended against him . . . who had been willing humbly to acknowledge his offence and beg for grace and mercy for it, the king had been so full of compassion that he had been quicker to show mercy than the person who had committed the offence had been to request it'.[50]

Henry was not present to hear this parade of his cardinal virtues. This was undoubtedly by design, as he could easily have come down the river from Evesham in time for the parliament.[51] Nevertheless, it was very unusual. It was even more unusual for the *purpose* of the parliament to be that of honouring the king. When he did arrive, on the second day, Henry kept silent, only speaking (so far as we can tell from the parliament roll) when told to do so by Archbishop Arundel. After the commons had chosen their Speaker to be Thomas Chaucer (son of the poet Geoffrey Chaucer), the discussions started. At the first plenary session, on 9 November, the crucial debate was held concerning the Thirty-One Articles. Arundel managed it perfectly. The commons pressed their usual request for 'good government' and reminded the king that they had made their grant in the previous parliament with high expectations upon the performance of the council. To this Arundel deftly replied that he had already spoken to them about this matter, and had provided them with a written schedule of the council's actions. Then he added that many members of the council had, over and above the call of duty, made good the shortcomings of the commons' finance through loans from their own estates. Since the commons had not seen to offer any reward or gratitude for this, or for the council's labours in running the affairs of state, the councillors no longer wished to be bound by their oaths to observe the Thirty-One Articles.

The commons were taken by surprise. They had no response. Rather lamely, Thomas Chaucer changed the subject and presented the commons' complaint against royal purveyors. Tiptoft gave them as sharp a rebuke as Arundel had dealt: if there was a purveyor who was breaking the law, then he should be reported to the sheriff in the same way as any other law-breaker, and he would be tried. On Tuesday 14 November the commons asked that a committee of lords be appointed to discuss matters of state with them; Arundel of course put himself at the head of the list of the six lords appointed by the king. But this was nothing compared to his strategy for extricating sufficient taxation out of the commons. On 21 October, the lords met in the abbey council chamber. There Arundel put to them the question of how much taxation would be needed to defend the realm adequately. No doubt he produced his defence budget, worked out in council earlier in the year. The lords agreed that what was required was nothing less than one and a half tenths and fifteenths, plus a contin-uation of the wool subsidy for three years. Arundel then asked that a committee of twelve commoners be appointed to attend a meeting of the lords. The members of the committee appointed were astounded when it emerged that they were to take back the details of the sum they were required to grant. The rest of the commons were outraged, but the alter-native was to be held responsible for the inadequate defence of the realm and for failing to 'honour the king'. They were mollified by Henry's declar-ation that he would not again levy direct taxation for two and half years – until March 1410, a promise he put in writing to each of them, and kept – and they were pleased with his grant that the commons in future could have the right to discuss the state of the realm in his absence. But otherwise the commons had been forced to confront a stark reality: they could not continue to blame the king for the problems of the realm. He had been nearly a year out of power, and yet their complaints had not abated. The solution to their demands lay in a combination of adequate finance through taxation, to be spent on properly costed priorities, with tight financial controls and competent military leadership. It was not the continual denigration of the king.

The parliament of 1407 was thus something of a lesson in medieval governance to all participants. The commons were used to seeing the throne as the centre of their political battleground. Henry too had always believed that it fell to him personally to deal with the issues of govern-ment. But as a result of his illness, and the collapse of royal authority in the Long Parliament, the battleground had shifted away from the throne.

Of course Arundel had help in his restoration of Henry's royal power, especially from Henry's half-brothers, John and Henry Beaufort and Thomas Langley, all of whom were on the committee to the commons in November 1407; but otherwise Arundel must be given the credit.[52] And so too must Henry, for appointing Arundel in the first place. It had taken just a year to halt the decline of the royal fortunes, and the process marked a watershed in Henry's government.

*

Henry remained for some days at Gloucester. He was still there when he received news of an extraordinary story unfolding in France, which was to have the most profound implications for England. Henry's sworn enemy, the duke of Orléans, had been making himself increasingly unpopular amongst the French nobility, partly for his philandering and raping of noblewomen (including his sister-in-law, the queen of France) and partly because of his rivalry with his cousin, the duke of Burgundy.[53] On Wednesday 23 November he had attended a reception in Paris for the recovery of the queen from the birth of her twelfth child, who had died after only a day. As the duke joined the other guests in trying to rouse the queen's spirits, a messenger entered with a summons: the king wished to see him immediately at the Hôtel de St Pol. The duke politely left, and set out into the cold winter evening with five attendants. As he rode past an empty house on the rue Barbette, seven or eight masked men rushed out and attacked him. They dragged him from his horse, hacking off the hand with which he clung to the saddle, and stabbed him repeatedly in the face and body as he lay on the ground, eventually smashing open his skull to finish him off.

When Henry first heard about the murder, he was told that it was the work of a lord whose wife had been seduced by the duke.[54] But over subsequent days it emerged that, far from being a crime of passion, it was a cold-blooded political assassination. The duke of Burgundy had suspiciously fled Paris. Later he would return at the head of an army and admit his guilt.

Regardless of who was responsible, the duke's death immediately changed the political landscape. Orléans had been the most important manipulator of power in the French council since the death of the old duke of Burgundy in 1404. He was also the principal member of the royal family agitating for war with England. Ever since 1399 he had been at pains to show that he felt Henry had betrayed him with his revolution, and his three bellicose letters to Henry in 1402–3 had merely been the written expositions of his anger. In September 1406, he personally led an army to attack English castles in Gascony at Bourg and Blaye, and had kept up the siege of Bourg until January 1407. There was no doubting his resolve to continue with such hostilities, especially since Charles had supported him by creating the dauphin nominal duke of Aquitaine. Thus his death immediately relieved the anxiety in Gascony. It also scotched any possibility that he would fulfil his offer to the earl of Northumberland in 1405 to assist him in attacking Henry in England.[55]

When it emerged that the duke had been assassinated by his own cousin, however, the crime assumed a wholly new complexion. Hatred of Henry in France had been particularly stirred up by the rumours that he, a member of the English royal family, had ordered his own cousin, Richard, to be murdered. The horror Frenchmen felt at this injustice was now transferred to their own royal family. They could hardly maintain that the crime of cousin murder barred Henry from the throne of England when members of their own royal family were busy hacking each other to pieces for similar political motives. Worse, the various plotters began to appeal to King Henry, the enemy of France, for protection and help. As France slipped towards civil war, the protagonists of the various factions each sought help from Henry. As for Glendower, he could no longer pretend to his fellow Welshmen that the French would offer them military assistance.

For the moment all these military implications were far off, and the first thought in Henry's mind was that the duke's death allowed the truce with France to be finalised. As it happened, news of the murder arrived at Gloucester at the very time the French ambassadors were present for the truce. On the penultimate day of the parliament, Henry renewed his commission to his own ambassadors – Thomas Langley, Sir Thomas Erpingham, Sir Hugh Mortimer and John Catterick – and the following day added his second son, Thomas, to the team. With the assassination of the key French agent for war, the way to peace in Gascony was clear, and it took the negotiators just six days to reach a settlement. The truce was concluded on 7 December and ratified by the council in the king's name on the 10th.[56]

By then Henry himself was on his way back to Eltham, travelling slowly by way of Cirencester to Windsor and probably from there along the Thames. At Eltham he spent Christmas, free from the worries of both government and disempowerment. With the prince making headway against Glendower, the Scots king in his custody, his French adversary dead, his finances improving and the truce proclaimed in Gascony, it was the easiest Christmas of his reign. There were only two black clouds in the otherwise relatively clear winter sky. One was his worsening health. The other was the earl of Northumberland's last stand.

SEVENTEEN

Golden Care

Why doth the crown lie there upon his pillow,
Being so troublesome a bedfellow?
O polish'd perturbation! Golden care!
Henry IV Part Two, Act 4, Scene 4

In France they called it 'the big winter', in England 'the strong winter' or 'the great frost and ice'. Animals died in their thousands, rivers froze – even the Baltic Sea froze. Clerks picked up their pens to write only to find the ink frozen in their inkwells.[1] Nevertheless, at the depth of this cold, the earl of Northumberland and Lord Bardolph decided to enact their latest plot to dethrone Henry. Perhaps they had had enough of flight, having gone from England to Scotland, to Wales and finally to France in their hope of finding a sympathetic lord who would give them an army. Or maybe they thought that they would have the advantage of surprise, the winter being so severe that the normally muddy roads were frozen solid, allowing them a faster advance. Either way, in January 1408 the rebel lords crossed once more into England and attempted to rally their supporters with the old cry, 'King Richard is alive'.

Henry himself was designing artillery at the time, or to be specific 'a large cannon . . . newly invented by the king himself'.[2] Guns had always interested him. Gunners travelled with him to Lithuania in 1390, and he had taken several cannon into Scotland in 1400. His accounts reveal that he had thirty-nine guns and cannon stored at the Tower.[3] In 1401 he had equipped the prince with six artillery pieces, including 'two large double cannon' with which to attack Conway Castle, and had taken cannon into Wales on his own expeditions.[4] In 1405 the big guns proved their worth in action against the earl of Northumberland's castles. When Henry wished to help his eldest son in the siege of Aberystwyth, he sent him 'our great cannon' and a quarter of a ton of gunpowder from Nottingham. This may have been the two-ton giant 'The Messenger' which blew up during the siege. Notwithstanding this setback, powerful guns had clearly become a lasting feature of the English military scene, and Henry wanted to do his part in improving them. We do not know how successful his own design of 1408 was, but the payment of more than £210 to the same man the following year for iron and coal to make more cannon suggests that the project was not unsuccessful. The general idea seems to have been to manufacture an unrivalled series of large iron bombards with which to smash down the castle walls of his potential enemies.[5]

There had been signs before January 1408 that the earl of Northumberland and Lord Bardolph would raise the cry of rebellion again. In July 1407 one of Lord Bardolph's servants was captured carrying seditious letters and imprisoned in Nottingham Castle. In August a letter from the earl of Northumberland to the constable of Warkworth Castle led to the discovery of a plot to stage a rising in the north. But nothing can have prepared Henry for the surprise advance in January. It came just when he was finally free from widespread criticism. News of his illness and discomfort inclined many lords to believe that God was punishing Henry for his misdeeds. Therefore they did not need to bother holding him to account. It is ironic, but the more people who believed that Henry's illness was divine retribution for his sins, the less justification there was for taking up arms against him.

Henry heard of the rebels' incursion on 15 February 1408.[6] That day he ordered forces to be raised against Northumberland and Bardolph and prepared to set out for the north. But before the month was out, news reached him that the rebellion was over. Sir Thomas Rokeby had led a small force north to meet the rebels at Grimbald Bridge, near Knaresborough. Having pursued the earl and his troops to Tadcaster, Rokeby set men along all the roads to the town, not allowing them to escape undetected. Realising that the hour had come, the earl drew up his forces on Bramham Moor, on 19 February. Rokeby's men attacked with fury, charging beneath the banner of St George.[7] Northumberland himself was their first target. He was killed on the battlefield. The prelates who had thrown in their lot with him were all captured, including the bishop of Bangor, the prior of Hexham and the abbot of Halesowen. Lord Bardolph fled but was chased and forced to turn and fight. In the ensuing conflict in the snow he was so badly hacked about that, when he was finally overpowered, he was fatally wounded. He died that night. The rebellion was over before it had properly begun.

Despite this relieving news, Henry decided he would press on to the north. He was at St Albans on 2 March and Leicester on the 12th. There he paused for three or four days before moving to Nottingham.[8] His journey from there was at least partly by boat, for several places at which he is known to have stayed were on the River Ouse.[9] From 26 March to 6 April he stayed at Wheelhall, seeing to the punishments and rewards due as a result of Bramham Moor. The abbot of Halesowen was executed. The others were treated more leniently. The bishop of Bangor was sent to be imprisoned in Windsor Castle. The prior of Hexham was tried for treason and later pardoned. Of course, Rokeby and his friends were well rewarded, Rokeby himself receiving several of the late earl's manors. As for the earl of Northumberland, his body was cut up and exhibited around the realm, at Berwick, Lincoln, Newcastle and York. His grey-haired head was set on a pike on London Bridge. Thus ended the life of the man who had been instrumental in raising Henry to the throne, and had betrayed him.

*

Henry spent Easter 1408 at Pontefract Castle. He remained there for the feast of St George; it was the first time in his reign that he was not at Windsor to oversee the Garter festivities in person. His illness was impinging more and more on his freedom of movement and his ability to govern. On 25 April he delegated to the earl of Westmorland the right to pardon or punish six captured rebels. Leaving Pontefract on the 30th he made his way to Leicester by road, and there rested. He did not stay at the castle. Instead, from the quiet sanctuary of Birdsnest Lodge two miles outside the town, he wrote a note in English and in his own hand to Archbishop Arundel, thanking him heartily for 'the great business that you do for me and for my realm, and trusting plainly in your good counsel, and hoping to God to speak to you hastily and thank you with good heart'. He signed the letter 'Your true friend and child in God, H[enry] R[ex]'.[10]

Well might Henry have wanted to see Arundel and to thank him for his work. From now on he would be dependent on him. On his return from the north, Henry's health had completely collapsed. He spent four days in Leicester, and the next nine on the road to Windsor. He rested there for several days at a lodge within the park. By boat he travelled to London, but even that journey was slow. He met Arundel at the end of the month, and took a barge up the river to the archbishop's manor of Mortlake. There in late June he fell into a coma. Those about him could not determine whether he was alive or dead.[11]

Henry's disease or diseases had gone far beyond being just a skin ailment. Adam Usk later dated the onset of the illness which killed him to about this time. Indeed, Usk's testimony is the best evidence we have as to what was actually wrong with Henry, for Usk was on good terms with the archbishop, who gave him several benefices after 1411.[12] Not only did this attack happen at the archbishop's house, in later years the king and the archbishop spent much time together, and the king often stayed at Lambeth Palace with his old friend. So if anyone knew what was wrong with Henry, Archbishop Arundel did. According to Usk, from this time to the end of his life, Henry suffered 'an infection' which resulted in 'festering of the flesh, dehydration of the eyes, and rupture of the internal organs'.[13] This is as close as we are likely to get to the archbishop's own understanding of what was wrong with the king. In this 'festering of the flesh' it would appear likely that Henry's skin disease had grown progressively worse, from his burning skin at Green Hammerton in the summer of 1405 to the great 'accesse' he suffered in April 1406 to a more general degradation of his lower body. Such a wasting disease is reminiscent of the condition which affected the Black Prince from 1367 to 1376. His illness also started with an inability to ride a horse, then stopped him from walking, and finally killed him nine years after his first infection. Henry died eight years after his burning skin experience.[14] Both men remained sane to the ends of their lives. Whether or not they suffered the same problem, there can be no doubt that Henry in 1408 was as incapacitated as the Black Prince had been in his last years. He was an invalid, dependent on others and in agony as his lower body, quite simply, rotted away beneath him.[15]

Henry recovered consciousness after a few hours but spent several weeks recuperating at Mortlake. He now felt it necessary to apply to a physician of European renown. This was David Nigarellis of Lucca, who had arrived by the end of September.[16] In the intervening time he had a two-volume book of hours specially illuminated for his own use in his private prayers.[17] In late July he was persuaded to come to London to take part in the debate in the cathedral chapter house about the schism which continued to divide the Catholic Church. Later he made a pilgrimage to Waltham Abbey, probably by litter. No signet letters from this period are extant. A measure of his state of health is that for the rest of the year he avoided residing at the royal palaces, staying instead at the private houses of his family and close friends. These included Southwark Palace (belonging to Henry Beaufort), Hugh Waterton's London house, and Lambeth Palace (belonging to Archbishop Arundel). All of these places could be reached by river. He also made a short visit to King's Langley, the place where Richard II was buried, perhaps a result of increasing feelings of guilt for ordering his death.

Thus the second half of 1408 is little more than a hollow period in the life of Henry IV. He was expected to die. His eldest son, Henry, was recalled to be with him in December, and so too was his second son, Thomas, even though he was in Ireland. On Christmas Eve the king's barge docked at Lambeth Palace, so he could visit Thomas Arundel on the way back to Eltham for Christmas. The magnates and prelates of England braced themselves for the worst.

*

On 21 January 1409, Henry made his will. It is without doubt an extraordinary document. Most surprising is the language in which it was written. It is the first royal will written in English, even though his own first language was French. Normally Henry reserved English for public statements of national importance, such as his claim to the throne, and it is possible that 'national importance' was the reason he dictated in English now. An alternative explanation lies in his close friendship with Thomas Arundel. His handwritten manuscript notes to Arundel in 1408 and 1409 were also in English, and the two men were close spiritually as well as politically. This is revealed very clearly in the most extraordinary aspect of the document: the way in which Henry talks of himself. It begins as follows:

> In the name of God, Father and Son, and Holy Ghost, three persons and one God. I Henry sinful wretch, by the grace of God, king of England and of France, and lord of Ireland, being in my whole mind, make my testament in the manner and form following: First I bequeath to Almighty God my sinful soul, which has never been worthy to be [a] man but through his mercy and his grace; which life I have misspent, wherefore I put myself wholly in his grace and mercy, with all my heart. And when it pleases him of his mercy to take me to him, my body [is] to be buried in the church at Canterbury, at the discretion of my cousin the archbishop of Canterbury.[18]

Here we see an invocation of the Trinity, in line with Henry's spiritual preference for the cult. But then follow three strikingly harsh, self-recriminating phrases: 'sinful wretch', 'sinful soul' and 'never worthy to be a man'. Testamentary sentiments like this generally only appear in Lollard wills of the period. Only two other contemporary non-Lollard wills are known to have similar self-abasing lines: those of Philip Repingdon, bishop of Lincoln, and Archbishop Arundel himself, both of whom died after Henry. Thus Henry's was the first supposedly orthodox will to contain such extreme statements of unworthiness.[19]

It seems extraordinary, paradoxical even, to find such spiritual conscientiousness in someone who had executed an archbishop. But Henry was a sincere man, like Arundel and Repingdon, and all three were sufficiently conscientious in life to project their guilt beyond the moment of death. It seems that these three were linked in a spiritual conversation which touched all their lives. Repingdon served as Henry's confessor for several years before being promoted to Lincoln, and he remained in close touch with Henry in 1408.[20] In fact we could say he is a religious shadow in the background through Henry's life. He had been the abbot of Leicester, an abbey patronised by the Lancastrians, before Henry's accession. He wrote the humble yet harshly critical letter to Henry about the failings of his government in 1401. It was to him that Henry sent his ring after winning the battle of Shrewsbury.[21] He accompanied Henry on his pilgrimage to Bardney Abbey when he kissed the relics there in 1406, seeking a miracle cure. This makes us take notice of the fact that he was a former supporter of the Lollard, John Wycliffe, and had preached in support of Wycliffe at Oxford in the early 1380s. As for Arundel, Henry described him as his 'father in God' in his letters at this time. This spiritual conversation is the best evidence we have that when men such as Richard II accused Henry of being 'against the church', they were mindful that his approach to religion was personal and unconventional, and not remotely obsequious. Henry was dangerous because he did not blindly accept the Church as an institution but could decide on spiritual matters for himself (as he did when commenting on the theologians at the University of Paris). That independent intellectual approach to spirituality now led him to reflect Repingdon's post-Wycliffite ideas about unworthiness and the decay of his flesh. When Repingdon wrote in his will that, on account of his sin, he willingly consigned his putrid body to be food for worms, he could well have been reflecting ideas which Henry had about his own body. By January 1409 he had come to hate it, and its decay, and he was willing to believe he would soon be rid of it.

Henry's will continued with an expression of thanks to 'all my lords and true people' for their service. He begged their pardon if he had mistreated them in any way. Bearing in mind his declaration that 'kings are not wont to render account' this seems surprisingly humble. He continued with a bequest to found a chantry for twenty priests at Canterbury, and promised special rewards to the grooms of his chamber, as well as the payment of all sums owed to his household servants. He asked that the queen be endowed from the estates of the duchy of Lancaster, his personal inheritance. He appointed the prince his executor. The will was witnessed by Archbishop Arundel, Bishop Langley, Edward, duke of York, Lord Grey (Henry's chamberlain), John Tiptoft (treasurer), John Prophet (keeper of the privy seal) and three of the faithful Lancastrian retainers who had been with him all his life: Sir Thomas Erpingham, Sir Robert Waterton and Sir John Norbury.[22]

In the late middle ages only those who expected to die in the near future made wills. Thus we may be confident that, having abased himself before his fellow men and before God, Henry was preparing to meet his maker. But his maker did not reciprocate. Henry was left lying in his bed at Greenwich, day after day, his body an increasingly great embarrassment to himself and those around him.

A month passed. Improving a little, he began to take a role in government again. He had his secretary write to the council expressing his satisfaction with the work they had done in drafting diplomatic replies to the merchants of the Hanseatic League and the grand master of the Teutonic Knights.[23] On 12 March, still at Greenwich, he chose to complete the foundation of the collegiate chapel marking the site of the battle of Shrewsbury.[24] It was one of Henry's three religious foundations, chantry chapels at St Paul's for his father and mother, and at Canterbury Cathedral for himself being the others. Considering he had so little control over his own finances and was hardly able to travel to Shrewsbury to oversee the foundation in person, it is hardly surprising that his collegiate foundation is a small matter by comparison with the great Lancastrian foundations of Henry VI, his grandson.[25] Nevertheless the chapel still stands, although the college buildings have long since disappeared, and it still holds a statue of the victorious king in a niche above the east window.

In mid-March, Henry was well enough to travel the short distance to Eltham Palace. On 20 March he started to undertake royal business on a regular basis again. At least five letters sealed with his signet ring were sent out to the council over the next four days, concerning such matters as the general council of the Church at Pisa, the grant of a Windsor prebend to his old physician, John Malvern, and pardons to eight men from Sowerby, Yorkshire. On 31 March, he wrote to Archbishop Arundel and assured him firmly that he was 'in good health'.[26] The following week, he sent another letter to the archbishop asking that letters patent be granted to the queen, confirming her income in the event of his death. By this stage he was well enough to add in his own hand the following note to the archbishop:

> With all my true heart, worshipful and well-beloved cousin, I greet you well and next to God I thank you for the good health that I am in, for so I may well without saying so. Reverend and well-beloved cousin, I send you a bill for the queen touching her dower, which I pray you might speed, and you shall do us both great ease therein, wherefore we will thank you with all our heart. Your true son, Henry.[27]

Making provision for the eventuality that Joan might soon become a widow suggests that Henry's health was actually far from normal; nevertheless, it was improving. Not long afterwards he took his barge up the river to Windsor to attend the Garter festivities at the castle. He went on a slow but steady tour of the area, taking in small places like Easthampstead, Swallowfield, Henley-on-the-Heath and Chertsey, and returned to London in June to join his son, Prince Henry, in watching a four day-long enactment of the Creation story at Clerkenwell. Then, from an unexpected quarter, tragedy struck. He received a letter from Germany. His daughter Blanche was dead.

The first Henry would have known of her death was seeing the sealed letter from Count Rupert, father of Blanche's husband, Louis. The text survives. Whoever had the unfortunate duty of reading the letter to Henry would have had to utter the count's words on how their two houses were bound together in happiness and sadness. 'It weighs heavily with us, the tearful case of your illustrious daughter, our late daughter-in-law . . .' From the moment of hearing those words, Henry would have known that his daughter was no more. She had died in childbirth on 22 May.[28]

The count's letter contained many further lines of consolation and spiritual platitudes, but Henry probably heard none of them. Just as his own mother had died in her youth, and just as his own wife had died when his sons and daughters were in infancy, so too now had his seventeen-year-old daughter died, leaving an infant boy, a grandson whom Henry was destined never to see. At the same time Henry received a letter from Blanche's husband, Louis, who spoke of his grief at losing his 'most loved and sweetest wife', and how all the delights and joys of his life were gone as he stood looking at her grave.[29] It was a passionate letter for a prince, and expressive of a genuine feeling of loss. The young man did not marry again for another eight years.

Henry's reply to the count was measured and formal, and yet at the same time tinged with sadness. 'Excellent prince, very dear brother, having read your letters our mind is filled with sorrow', he began, 'for in the beginning of those accounts as well as at the end, one senses her extraordinary beauty and a bitter sadness mixed with consolation.'[30] The consolation to which he was referring was twofold: the birth of her son and the fact that she had received the holy sacrament before she died. But beyond phrases designed to alleviate the grief of others, there was little more than measured politeness. What more could he say? How could a king express his feelings? And what was the point of doing so in a letter to a distant ruler? Indeed, what should the dying say about the dead?

Henry did not shut himself away after hearing of Blanche's death and burial; he had practically already done that. But he appeared in public towards the end of July, in order to attend a great tournament at Smithfield in honour of the steward of Hainault. This was the social event of the year. The steward himself fought with Henry's half-brother, John Beaufort, who 'put his adversary to the worse in all points and won himself great worship and degree of the field'.[31] Although Sir Richard Arundel lost to his challenger, the king's brother-in-law, Sir John Cornwaille, defeated his. Sir John Cheyne's son did so well that Henry knighted him on the spot. But for the forty-two-year-old king it must have been another reminder of his former glory. He and John Beaufort had both jousted at St Inglevert in 1390. Now he could only look on – a cloud of royal greatness – just as he could only look on as Archbishop Arundel and the council governed the country in his name.

*

In modern times if a political leader is critically ill then he or she simply steps down and hands power to a colleague. In the late middle ages, when political power was vested in a hereditary monarch, that was only possible through the king's abdication. Having fought so hard to maintain his position, Henry was not going to abdicate now. Thus there was a power vacuum developing in 1409, and it increasingly sucked in the leading members of the royal council.

When the rule of the council had been set up in 1406 it had been a temporary measure, only to last until the next parliament. In 1408, owing to his declining health, Henry continued to delegate most business to his council and especially to the chancellor, Arundel. As already mentioned, tensions arose between Arundel and the prince. For a start, there was the question of who was ultimately responsible for the war expenses in Wales. Since control of the money – which was in Arundel's hands – ultimately governed policy, it was inevitable that the twenty-two-year-old prince would run into difficulties with the fifty-five-year-old archbishop. Arundel did not help matters by banning the Beauforts from the succession. The prince increasingly promoted his Beaufort uncles, and they increasingly sided with him against Arundel.[32] Tiptoft, who had been treasurer since July 1408, was on the side of the archbishop in maintaining strict control of the royal finances. In this way the council became divided. No one was an enemy of the king – all these men were Lancastrians through and through – but they jostled for influence as the king's authority waned and the council's increased.

There was another dimension to this development of factions, namely sibling rivalry. Several writers have suggested over the years that Thomas was the king's favourite son.[33] In support of this, in his will Thomas asked to be buried at the foot of his father's grave in Canterbury Cathedral, unlike his elder brother. When Henry was thought to be dying in late 1408,

Thomas returned straightaway from Ireland. The prince also attended his father's bedside, but the latter came with the expectation of his coronation. In reality, Henry and his eldest son did not see eye to eye on a number of issues, with the result that Thomas stood higher in his affections. The king and the prince had differing views on Richard II, who had been far kinder to the prince than his father.[34] Second, the prince never much liked his stepmother, Queen Joan, whom he later falsely accused of sorcery so he could confiscate her income.[35] Third, the king and the prince did not agree about the developing situation in France.[36] But perhaps the most striking evidence of the king's favouritism to Thomas is his attempt to entail the throne upon his male descendants only in 1406. This would have had very little effect on the succession, but with one important exception. In the absence of the prince having a son, the throne would pass to Thomas.[37] It is not surprising that the prince was keen to see this altered, so any daughters of his would inherit before his brother.

These differences between the king's two eldest sons became even more marked in the autumn of 1409, when the prince expected shortly to inherit. He had completed his duties in Wales, having recaptured Aberystwyth Castle in September 1408 and Harlech in February 1409, thereby leaving Glendower a helpless outlaw. Such success gained him praise and left him free to engage more directly with the council. But as his father's health improved it became apparent to the prince and his Beaufort uncles that royal power might remain vested in Archbishop Arundel for many years to come. They began to speak of Henry abdicating.[38] Naturally, they were opposed by the archbishop and Thomas of Lancaster.[39] In August 1409 Thomas returned to his father's household and demanded payment from the council for his service in Ireland.[40] His elder brother tried to get him to resign his position. Thomas refused. Both parties were aware that the money from the 1407 parliament had run out, but bankruptcy only made agreement between the two factions more difficult. On 26 October Arundel persuaded the king to summon another parliament to meet at the end of January at Bristol. It looked as if the government would fail in its promise not to call for further taxation before March 1410.

Henry had been largely absent during this worsening of relations between his chief councillors, sons and half-brothers. In July 1409 he stayed in private houses in London, and in the late summer and autumn he went on a pilgrimage tour, taking in the abbeys of Romsey and St Albans.[41] He dined with the prince on 20 November at Berkhamsted, apparently unaware of the crisis unfolding, and then headed north by road to visit Leicester. In the meantime the council tore itself to pieces. The very next day – 21 November – Henry Beaufort declared himself to be in support of the prince.[42] Over the next two weeks Tiptoft and Arundel found their positions on the council unworkable. On 11 December Tiptoft resigned.[43] On the 18th Arundel was forced to agree that parliament should be summoned to London, not Bristol (where he would have been able to control proceedings more easily). Three days later he too resigned, in the presence of the king, who had hurried back as quickly as he could to attend to the crisis.[44] At the same time he resigned from the council. The king's ministers had been forced to yield to the prince. The king's authority was being usurped by his own family.

*

Henry spent Christmas 1409 at Eltham, as usual. He did not immediately appoint new ministers; instead, he kept the great seals of the chancellor and treasurer himself. On 6 January 1410 the prince persuaded him to give that of the treasurer to one of his own supporters: Henry, Lord Scrope of Masham. As for the chancellorship, Henry declined to appoint anyone, probably hoping that he could persuade Arundel to change his mind when parliament began.[45] If so, Arundel steadfastly stood by his resignation. The obvious alternative candidate was Henry Beaufort, but the king was reluctant to appoint him. He seems to have become a little suspicious of his half-brother.[46] There is no direct evidence of a rift between them at this time, but Beaufort's rivalry with Thomas Arundel was probably sufficient to bar him from high office.[47] The king could not appoint Beaufort without betraying the archbishop, who had now become his closest friend.

When parliament opened at Westminster on 27 January, Bishop Beaufort performed the role of the chancellor in delivering the opening speech. He explained that parliament had been summoned for the good government of the realm and its defence, and, in particular, that the duke of Burgundy was now planning an attack on Calais. If the town were not strengthened immediately, it would be vulnerable to attack. Having made these points, Beaufort continued with a matter of his own interest: an exposition on two forms of government, 'one by right of government, and the other by right of subjugation'. As Aristotle had informed Alexander the Great, the love of the people was a stronger means of protecting a city than any walls. Bishop Beaufort's ideas may have been governed by a belief in the merits of a constitutional monarchy, or they may have simply been a way of bringing to an end the dissent in the council. Either way, making this speech was as close as he came to being chancellor. Four days later the office was given to his more acceptable younger brother, Thomas Beaufort.[48] In this way the king prevented Henry Beaufort from being seen to triumph over his rival, Arundel, but the compromise marked another advance for the prince, who was on equally good terms with Thomas.

What did Henry make of this attempt by his son to obtain control over the council? This is an interesting question, and it is insufficient just to point to the disagreements between him and the prince as an indicator that he resented his son's ambition. It was hardly surprising that the young man was impatient to rule. After all, it was his birthright, so this attempt to take royal power was an encouraging sign of his son's enthusiasm to perform his royal duties. After his successes in Wales, he deserved a chance to prove himself. However, there were many dangers, not least to Archbishop Arundel. Henry was not unaware of these, as shown by his reaction when Thomas Chaucer (the Beauforts' first cousin) was again elected by the commons to be Speaker. Henry warned Chaucer that he was free to speak only as far as tradition allowed. The king obviously feared for his prerogatives, and the most likely explanation is that he suspected he might be asked to abdicate. As things turned out, the situation did not arise. There were radical developments in the air of a very different and far more horrific kind.

Lollardy was a subject of debate from the outset. The commons presented an extraordinary petition to disendow the Church, taking away the entire worldly wealth of the diocesan clergy and paying them each a subsistence allowance of £2 per year. In this way, it was argued, the king would be able 'to support fifteen new earls, 1,500 knights, 6,200 esquires and 100 new almshouses, and still be left with an annual income of £20,000'.[49] Moreover, by taking away the temporalities of 'worldly clerks', fifteen new universities could be founded, each educating one thousand scholars. That the sums did not add up was only the first problem with such a radical proposal.[50] The political obstacles were insurmountable. The whole scheme was bound to anger Archbishop Arundel who had fought long and hard against such ideas, most notably in the parliament of October 1404. As on that occasion, he received Henry's full support. The king went so far as to prohibit such proposals ever being put to him again, and the petition was not included on the parliament roll.

Probably because of this reaction (which was supported by the prince) the commons asked on 8 February that a petition they had submitted 'concerning the statute formerly made about the Lollards' might be withdrawn from consideration in parliament. The king agreed. Another petition was resubmitted in the hope of lessening the powers of local ecclesiastical officials to imprison Lollards. Even this was too much for Henry, who retorted that he would rather the heresy statute was made stricter than more lenient.[51]

It was while these Lollard debates were echoing around the chambers of Westminster that Archbishop Arundel decided to make a show
of religious orthodoxy. A craftsman, John Badby, had been arrested early
in 1409 for uttering heretical ideas. Upon examination by the bishop of
Worcester, he had declared that he did not believe a priest could turn
a piece of bread into the body of Christ. Not only did he deny the
possibility as well as the reality of transubstantiation, he insisted that a
priest had no more power to effect this miracle than 'John Rakyer of
Bristol', probably referring to a 'raker', or cleaner, of refuse and animal
excrement from the town streets. This was not just heresy, it was a brutal
attack by a layman on the dignity of the Church. The case had
confounded the bishop of Worcester. How could this man, who had no
religious credentials or qualifications, question the orthodox outlook of
the whole Catholic Church? And what should he do with him? He could
hardly excommunicate him, for, by definition, this man would not care
whether he was excommunicated or not. He decided to refer the matter
to his superior, Archbishop Arundel.

On 1 March Badby was brought into a hall in the London house of the
Dominican friars. Never before in his life could he have been confronted
by so many great men of the realm. Both archbishops – Arundel and
Henry's old friend, Henry Bowet, now archbishop of York – were present.
So were the duke of York, Bishop Henry Beaufort, Thomas Beaufort and
the bishops of London, Exeter, Norwich, Bath and Wells, St David's, Bangor
and Salisbury. Arundel, of course, took the lead in examining the prisoner.
What he hoped for is not clear: he said he would 'offer his soul' for Badby
at the Last Judgement if Badby would only recant. Badby had no intention of doing any such thing. It was not that he was irreligious – he stated
he wished to believe in an omnipotent divine Trinity, and that the bread
and wine left on the table after a priest had failed to turn it into the body
and blood of Christ was still symbolic of God – but his certainty that the
clergy were powerless was unshakeable. If each consecrated host was really
the body of Christ, he said, then there must be twenty thousand gods in
England, but he believed only in one. That was it. In the eyes of everyone
present, he was damned.

Badby was locked up in another part of the friars' house to await
sentencing. Arundel himself kept the key. By this stage Arundel would have
known that he had an extraordinary man to deal with, and to show the
would-be reformers in the commons that they could expect harsh treatment for heresy he decided that the sentence upon Badby should be passed
by the whole of convocation (all the prelates of England and Wales). On
5 March convocation assembled in St Paul's Cathedral, together with several

prominent laymen: the duke of York, the earl of Westmorland, Lord Beaumont and the chancellor, Thomas Beaufort. Before them all Badby declared that he would not renounce any of his beliefs, and further declared that the holy sacrament was 'less than a toad or a spider', because these were at least living things. Anything created by God, he said, was more worthy of worship than a man-made image.[52] Having heard him utter these abominations against the tenets of the Church, Arundel confirmed the bishop of Worcester's verdict of heresy and handed Badby over to the secular authorities for punishment under the law, expressing his wish that he should not suffer death by burning.

Did Arundel really want the man spared the flames? Or was his intention all along that he would be burned to death, like William Sawtre, a terrible example to the faction in parliament which had dared to suggest the disendowment of the Church? We cannot know. Nevertheless, the warrant for his execution by burning alive was obtained very rapidly, so fast in fact that we must suspect it had already been written. Such a warrant had to come from the office of the chancellor, Thomas Beaufort, who was present at the final examination at St Paul's. It is unlikely to have been at Beaufort's own instigation that the warrant was issued; rather, it is more probable that it was done on Henry's instructions or those of the prince and the bishops on the council. It was certainly an ominous sign that the prince suddenly arrived to witness the spectacle, presumably having prior knowledge of the sentence. There was no going back now.

If anyone thinks of English history as one long, great progression of social improvement, they should ponder on what happened next. Until 1410 no layman in England had been burned simply for stating what he believed, and Sawtre had been the only priest. But now men-at-arms forced Badby into a barrel, and placed it in the middle of a heap of faggots. As the condemned man waited, chained inside his barrel, the prince approached the pyre and called to him to renounce his heresy. Badby refused. So the faggots were lit, and in a short while the barrel began to burn. Badby began to scream in pain. All the bishops who had attended his last interrogation – including the three who were members of the council – stood watching. As his screams intensified, the horror-struck prince gave the order for the man to be taken off the pyre. This was impossible, for the heat was already too intense. Instead, the burning faggots were pulled away. When the barrel was cool enough to approach, the prince went up to the scorched and sweating man and offered him a pardon and three pence a day for life if he would only renounce his heresy. The prior of St Bartholomew's was standing by with the Holy Sacrament should he agree, but still Badby refused. So the faggots were pushed back around the smouldering barrel, and the man was burned to ashes.

There was no more talk of disendowment or heresy in the parliament of 1410.

*

Parliament was suspended for Easter on 15 March. The following day, at the hospital of St Katherine by the Tower, John Beaufort uttered his last will at about 9 a.m., in the hearing of his assembled household servants.[53] Later that day he died. John had been the eldest of Henry's half-brothers, and thus the closest in age when they were growing up. In their jousting and travelling, John was the one with whom he had the most in common. In 1399, Henry had produced letters to save John's life when the earl of Northumberland and Hotspur had demanded that he be executed. From that moment on he had remained absolutely loyal. With his death, Henry lost a strong supporter and a close companion. In line with Henry's own intention (already made explicit in his will of 1409), John desired to be buried in Canterbury Cathedral.

In the wake of John's death, Henry withdrew even more from the business of government. He stayed with Archbishop Arundel at Lambeth. Neither attended meetings of the royal council. Instead the council met at the prince's house. Its membership was reduced to the bare minimum. On some occasions, only the prince himself, the chancellor and the treasurer were present.[54] The prince's preference was for a smaller council than his father, who had hitherto appointed twelve or fourteen men to advise him.

Parliament reassembled on 7 April, and the prince's influence was soon felt. On 23 April the commons presented eighteen articles to the king. This seems to have been a recapitulation of matters discussed over the previous two weeks and was presented in the form of a petition to Henry, who had probably been absent throughout. He spent three days considering the articles, and replied to them all in writing. One, the fifteenth, concerning the bribing of royal officials, was taken in hand by the prince and the council even though the king had assented to it. In other words, the king was overruled by his son. This is interesting, for about this time parliament agreed to another mysterious article, the terms of which are not known but which severely curtailed the king's authority. It probably rendered the king's judgement subject to the approval of the council in some way, and the prince and council taking this fifteenth article into their own hands might be evidence of it working.[55]

On 2 May the commons asked that the royal council be announced in parliament; the chancellor read out just seven names: the prince, Henry Beaufort, Thomas Langley, Nicholas Bubwith (the bishops of Winchester, Durham and Bath and Wells respectively), the earls of Arundel and Westmorland and Lord Burnell. To these should be added the chancellor himself, the treasurer and the keeper of the privy seal. Thus the council consisted largely of the prince's friends. The absence of other prominent men – Arundel and Tiptoft – was explained by a statement that they had 'reasonable causes' to be excused. At the end of the parliament the prince strengthened his hand still further by asking that two more of his friends, Bishop Henry Chichele (bishop of St David's) and the earl of Warwick, should also be appointed to the council, as the earl of Westmorland and Bishop Langley (the members most friendly with the king) could be expected to be regularly absent in the north. When parliament broke up on 9 May, the transferral of power appeared to be complete.

Henry withdrew from the parliament a sick, redundant man. He must have known he had surrendered power to his son, and that he was back where he had been after the 1406 parliament, when the council had told him to go off somewhere and live quietly and inexpensively. He now did the same again. He spent the next month at Lambeth Palace and Windsor Castle. As June turned to July, he headed off for Woodstock, where he stayed for five weeks. He spent more than three months shuffling between Leicester and Groby (five miles from Leicester) in the autumn and early winter. There were no more pilgrimages to health-giving shrines; he had stopped searching for a miracle cure. That December he did not venture south to spend Christmas at Eltham, as was his custom, but travelled the far shorter distance to spend it at Kenilworth Castle. There he remained for another two months, his inactivity undoubtedly a symptom of his illness. For all this time there are just two or three signet letters extant.[56] As for the royal charters, they were all granted in the king's absence.[57] Henry simply did not involve himself in royal business. He had retired.

For a short time it looked as if the king really had retired. But in one very important respect he could never relinquish power. He was unable to give up his concern with that royal identity which governed his entire life. Just as Richard had claimed he could never abdicate the divine anointment he had received at his coronation, so too Henry could not relinquish sovereignty, even in his invalid state. So, as the events of 1411 unfolded, he roused himself for one last time, and set about reasserting himself. It was not for the sake of personal power, not now; it was for something more. Or, rather, two last things: royal dignity and spiritual duty.

EIGHTEEN

In That Jerusalem

> It hath been prophesied to me many years
> I should not die but in Jerusalem;
> Which vainly I suppos'd the Holy Land: –
> But bear me to that chamber; there I'll lie;
> In that Jerusalem shall Harry die.
>
> *Henry IV Part Two*, Act 4, Scene 4

Most men in Henry's position in 1411 would have relaxed a little, confident that power had now been transferred safely to the next generation. Not Henry. Despite his physical incapacity, he continued to pay close attention to events within his realm. He was following Archbishop Arundel's attempts to root out heresy at the University of Oxford. He was alert to the prince's negotiations with the duke of Burgundy concerning English involvement in the French civil war. And he could hardly ignore the state of the treasury. That summer, his supporters found the payment of their annuities suspended again, by order of the council. Henry's own friends and servants were left without their reward for their years of royal service. They, of course, complained to him. And Henry found himself powerless to help them.

We do not have to look far to see why the council made this decision. When the commons in the 1410 parliament had granted one and a half tenths and fifteenths, they had stipulated that this tax was to be spread over three years, thus amounting annually to just half of a tenth and fifteenth (normally about £18,500). Such a modest grant could not meet the costs of an expedition to France, which was looking increasingly likely. So the prince's council decided to save money by suspending the payment of royal annuities.

Henry had always been against letting down his supporters in this way. It is true that in 1404 he himself had suspended payments, under pressure from parliament, but Arundel's skilful chancellorship had reversed this, so that annuitants in 1409 received arrears of the sums due to them.[1] For the prince and his council now to fail to do something which Arundel had succeeded in doing was a grave mistake. The prince and his council might have claimed that they had insufficient funds but their excuse would have fallen on deaf ears. Never had Henry considered his resources adequate for government.

In February 1411 he left Kenilworth Castle and proceeded slowly towards London. On Sunday 15 March he was with Archbishop Arundel at Lambeth, and there, four days later, a great council was held in his presence. The prince's small council was outnumbered: both archbishops, ten bishops and two abbots were present, along with the duke of York, four earls and ten other lords.[2] The business was almost entirely financial. The surviving set of accounts are incomplete but they indicate the council demonstrated how the wool subsidy of £30,000 and other income, including a tenth from the clergy, would be insufficient to meet the expenses of the royal household (£22,811) and the defence of the realm (£42,115).[3] No mention was made of the direct taxation which should have been collected the previous November, with which it would have been possible to balance the books. A budget which takes into consideration the king's expenditure survives from shortly after this, and it is noticeable that it allows £23,333 for the king's household and chamber, far more than the £13,000 laid down by parliament. It would appear that Henry was beginning to reassert himself.

Henry went to Windsor for April and was there for the Garter feast of 1411. For the rest of the spring he remained in the south-east, being rowed along the Thames between Windsor Castle, Lambeth Palace, Westminster and his house at Rotherhithe. In June and July he spent time at Stratford Abbey, and he was there when Archbishop Arundel's attempts to eradicate heresy at Oxford ran into difficulties. This also forced him to involve himself in the business of government.

Several years earlier Arundel had formulated a series of thirteen constitutions against Lollardy. Among other things, these laid down that disputes about the worship of the cross were forbidden, as were arguments about the nature of the Mass, marriage, confession and any other article of faith. No scriptures were to be translated into English except in an authorised version. And none of Wycliffe's writings were to be circulated in schools, halls, hostels or anywhere else unless sanctioned by twelve theologians appointed by the universities of Oxford and Cambridge. Two years later these constitutions were promulgated in a convocation at St Paul's. The twelve theologians subsequently read all of Wycliffe's works and published a list of the parts which they found heretical; for example the references to the pope as 'the Head Vicar of the Devil' or 'a sinful idiot'.[4] One of these theologians was an Oxford master of arts called Richard Fleming. He poured scorn on the whole process and appealed to Congregation (the governing body of the university) against Arundel's constitutions. He was supported by four other members of the university. Arundel railed furiously against them all, and decided to make a visitation of the institution, to root out the abuses. But when he arrived on 7 July 1411, he was refused admittance. He placed the university under an interdict, forbidding them from celebrating Mass. Two Oriel fellows broke open the church in the night and celebrated Mass anyway. Arundel spent two days at Oxford trying to bring the rebellious university to heel. But all the miscreants were protected by the chancellor of the university, Richard Courtenay, who maintained that the university was exempt from the archbishop's jurisdiction.

Henry had taken an interest in Richard Fleming ever since his objections had been made known to him in December 1409. Henry initially intervened on Fleming's behalf, making sure that a committee was appointed to reconsider his doctrines, which had been declared erroneous.[5] But by October 1410, the refusal of 'certain members of the university' to obey the archbishop's constitutions had assumed a higher priority, and he ordered the arrest of all such persons. The university wrote to the king stating that, if their liberties were infringed, according to their oaths they would have to disband the university. Henry curtly told them that the exemption which the pope had granted them from ecclesiastical jurisdiction in England had never been ratified by Richard II or himself. On 9 September 1411, at Lambeth, Henry delivered judgement unequivocally in favour of Archbishop Arundel and his jurisdiction over the university.[6]

By this time Henry was also heavily involved in discussions concerning an expedition to France. Negotiations at the end of 1410 had progressed, so that in 1411 the prince and his council expected an agreement with the duke of Burgundy. But there is evidence that this was never to Henry's liking.[7] A London chronicle sheds further light on this.[8] It states that the duke of Burgundy approached the king of England with a view to obtaining English help in his fight against the dukes of Orléans and Berry and their supporters, collectively known as the Armagnacs.[9] The duke offered to hand over four Flemish towns to the English, plus the hand of his daughter as a bride for the prince of Wales. Henry was cautious of the proposal, and remained so throughout the first half of 1411. On 14 August, he ordered the sheriffs of thirty-five counties to proclaim that he would shortly be sailing to Calais to defend the town, and summoned troops to be in London ready to sail on 23 September.[10] On 28 August he assigned one thousand marks for the expenses of his journey, calling the council to meet him on 9 September to discuss the expedition. Pennons were painted for the voyage, standards embroidered and the king's bed was made ready for transportation.

Then something snapped. Suddenly Henry changed his mind, and instead of sailing to the defence of Calais, he started to make plans for another parliament, even though the existing grant of taxation had two years left to run. The reason is often said to have been his ill health, but for once this was not behind his change of plans.[11] The real cause was his disapproval of the prince's government, and his decision to bring his son to heel. Henry was still planning to sail on 3 September, when ships were ordered to be made ready for him, but he changed his mind sometime before 21 September, when the parliament was summoned.[12] It is possible that it was the prince's support of the chancellor of Oxford which was the catalyst.[13] Alternatively, it could have been the bitter argument which broke out at this time between Henry Beaufort and Thomas of Lancaster. Thomas wanted to marry the widow of John Beaufort, his uncle, and the king supported him in this; but Henry Beaufort was bitterly opposed to the match.[14] A third possibility is the growing disagreement between himself and the prince about which side to support in the French civil war. However, this too is unlikely to have been the key reason for such drastic action, for on 1 September the king licensed the prince to send ambassadors to the duke of Burgundy and empowered his own ambassadors to negotiate the marriage of the prince and the duke's daughter if all went well. Clearly there was still room for negotiation and compromise in foreign relations.

The most likely reason why Henry summoned parliament, and thus the most likely reason for calling off the French expedition, was an attempt by the council to depose him. There are two sources for this; one places the event in 1413 and explicitly states that the prince, Henry Beaufort and many other lords asked him to resign the throne and let the prince be crowned.[15] The other places the event in the parliament of 1411, and states that the prince personally approached his father and told him he should abdicate 'because he could no longer apply himself to the honour and profit of the realm'.[16] It is possible that there was more than one attempt to get Henry to abdicate in the period after he made his will; indeed, it would have been strange if it had not been raised several times in council. Either way, the circumstances of the forthcoming parliament leave very little room for doubt that, by 21 September, either the prince or Henry Beaufort had made the suggestion to the king that he should abdicate. It was a bad move. As already mentioned, nothing was more important to Henry than his regal identity. After seeing off so many attempts to wrest the throne from him, he was not going to let anyone do so now, not even a member of his own family.

*

When parliament gathered at Westminster on the appointed day, 2 November, they were told by the chancellor that he had received a writ witnessed by the king himself putting off the parliament to the following day 'for certain reasons'. The writ was dated at Westminster, so it was not distance which kept the king away. It may have been ill health or it may have been trouble with the prince. Ten days earlier the king had arrested six of the prince's household knights and sent them to the Tower, including his steward, Sir Roger Leche. When the king and parliament did assemble on 3 November, the chancellor declared that the reasons for summoning the assembly were 'the good governance of the realm, the due execution of the law, the defence of the kingdom and overseas territories, and the safeguard of the sea'. He elaborated on each of these, emphasising the need for 'loyal counsel without wilful bias' and for men to show 'due obedience and honour to their liege lord'. Few present would have understood the full meaning of these objectives, but when the Speaker – Thomas Chaucer again – made his protest that nothing he said on behalf of the commons should be held against him, Henry made his position clear. As in the previous parliament the Speaker could speak only as far as his predecessors had done; Henry wanted 'no novelties'. In other words, he wanted no talk of deposition.

The early sessions were taken up with an abuse of the law – the wrongful doings of a royal justice, Sir Robert Tirwhit – and the official enrolment of the authority of the archbishop of Canterbury over the University of Oxford. The decisive political move did not come until 30 November. At the suggestion of the Speaker, Henry addressed the members of the council, who all came forward and knelt before the throne. He thanked them for performing their duties in a true and loyal fashion over the past eighteen months. The prince sourly responded that they could have done more if they had been given more money. Henry no doubt sympathised with such a view. But he said nothing about reappointing him or any other members of the council. Indeed, he did not name a council in this parliament at all. The whole council got up and returned to their allotted seats. With a growing awareness, they began to suspect the reality of what Henry had just done. He had sacked them all. With a polite word of thanks, he had resumed complete control of the government.

On the last day of the parliament, 19 December, Henry reinforced his position. He directed the chancellor to remind parliament about the article limiting his power enacted in the previous parliament. Thomas Chaucer asked Henry to explain his intentions concerning this. 'To which our lord the king replied by saying that he wished to have and preserve his liberties and prerogatives in all respects, as wholly as any of his noble progenitors had done.'[17] Chaucer voiced the approbation of the commons, and Henry politely thanked them. The article limiting his power was annulled.

Perhaps the most telling sign of Henry's return to power was a petition submitted immediately afterwards. Addressed 'to our most dread and most sovereign lord king' it stated that 'a great rumour has arisen among your people that you harbour in your heart ill-will towards various of your lieges who have come and are present by your summons at this your present parliament'. It begged him 'to declare it as your noble intention in this present parliament that you think, maintain and consider all the estates ... to be your faithful and loyal lieges and subjects, and regard them as people who have been, are, and will always be your faithful lieges and humble subjects'.[18] Henry, of course, agreed, and ordered a general pardon to be granted as soon as parliament ended for all crimes, even treason, committed before that date.[19] The commons assented to a modest land tax, a statute was agreed regarding the devaluation of the currency and parliament was dissolved. The following day Thomas Beaufort and Henry Scrope were sacked as chancellor and treasurer, and the king's resumption of power was complete.

Henry's seizure of authority in 1411 was extraordinary by any reckoning. For a man who had been so regularly attacked in parliament, how on earth did he so easily resume power? Considering the popularity and success of the prince, how come he so easily gave it up? And as for the ambitious bishop, Henry Beaufort, why did he acquiesce so completely?

The answer has to lie within a combination of the character and the condition of the king himself. It must have been apparent to all those concerned that Henry would never give up the throne. In the 1411 parliament, if not before, he made his determination to remain king absolutely clear. The parliament roll suggests no hard bargaining over this matter, and it is likely that in fact there were few objections; the magnates had already been silenced. What kept them quiet was the physical condition of the king. Henry may even have given the impression of having only a few more weeks to live. Also there remained the unassailable fact that Henry was an anointed king. That had not saved Richard but Henry was a different calibre of man. To depose him would be far harder than it had been to depose Richard. Henry was no longer seen as a failing king; the rebels were all defeated. Glendower was a vanquished fugitive, the Scottish king was an English prisoner, the French were fighting a civil war in the power vacuum created by their own king's sickness, and England was more secure than it had been at any time since the reign of King Edward III. Besides, Henry still had his stable of strong Lancastrian supporters in the commons: men like the faithful Sir Robert Waterton, Thomas Erpingham and John Norbury. Thus, ironically, in Henry's very physical weakness lay a new, indomitable strength. It was easier by far for the prince and the Beauforts to bide their time than challenge this man whose determination to remain king proceeded not just from his mind but his heart and soul.

*

On 23 December 1411, Henry handed over the seal of the exchequer to his new treasurer, Sir John Pelham. After Christmas at Eltham, he persuaded Archbishop Arundel to accept the great seal of the realm as chancellor for a fifth and final time. His new council – appointed that same month – consisted of these two officers and his faithful keeper of the privy seal, John Prophet, and four others. Apart from two bishops who had served the prince, Thomas Langley of Durham and Nicholas Bubwith of Bath and Wells, all the old councillors were passed over. Instead he appointed Archbishop Bowet of York, who had proved unswervingly loyal, along with Lord Roos.[20] It was an even smaller council than that with which the prince had governed. Henry had learned something from his son's short administration.

Henry's resumption of power, of course, implied taking responsibility for war policy, and that was by no means an easy matter. His inclination to support the Armagnacs in the French civil war, though described by one modern historian as 'backing the wrong horse', was entirely understandable at the time.[21] His Gascon subjects were in alliance with the Armagnacs, and so to support Burgundy against them would have been to risk war between his English and his Gascon subjects. Similarly his relations with Aragon, Navarre and Brittany would have been strained by English intervention on the Burgundian side in the war.[22] His choice may also have been governed by the way the Burgundians had treated him, for they still refused to acknowledge him as king of England. Their pride may have been no worse than his own but, in this instance, they were the ones who needed help.

Matters were complicated, however, as a consequence of the prince's eagerness to entertain Burgundian ambassadors in 1411. Henry had been equally eager to make sure that it was the prince, and not he himself, who was associated with such approaches, but that had not prevented an Anglo-Burgundian alliance. An English expedition had set out in September 1411, commanded by the earl of Arundel, to supply the duke of Burgundy with an English military force of eight hundred men-at-arms and two thousand archers. In November, at St-Cloud, near Paris, the Anglo-Burgundian army won a significant victory over the Armagnacs. It was clear to all parties that the English archers were a major asset. In February 1412 both sides sent representatives to try and forge closer links with England.

For Henry, the maximum political gain lay in exploiting these divisions in France. The best way to achieve this was through supporting those who opposed the French king and the duke of Burgundy. Henry remained convinced therefore that he should be supporting the Armagnacs. However, the prince's negotiations for the hand in marriage of Anne of Burgundy had progressed too far to be ignored.[23] The Armagnacs knew this, and started a bidding war for English help. As rebels to their king, their cause was the more desperate, and so they offered more. They acknowledged Henry as king of England and promised him eventual sovereignty of all of Aquitaine, as well as suitable marriages with girls of the royal blood. Although the Burgundian negotiators had arrived first, in Henry's eyes there was simply no contest.

Henry went down to Canterbury soon after the Armagnac envoys arrived. He heard how they had been intercepted on leaving France by agents of the duke of Burgundy, and had had their bags searched. Letters from the Armagnac lords recognising Henry as king of England had been confiscated. The duke of Burgundy himself hypocritically accused the Armagnac lords of treason for consorting with the king of England, and quietly recalled his own unsuccessful ambassadors from Westminster. The Armagnac negotiators were aware that their lords wanted an English alliance quickly, and on 6 April they concluded one. Fired up, Henry once again declared his intention of leading a force to Gascony in person, but the sad reality was that, just at this point, when it would have been politically feasible for him to lead an overseas expedition, his body was incapable of the task. According to Walsingham, he could not even walk without pain, let alone ride a horse.[24] Henry maintained his resolve for a few days – on 18 April he gave orders to enlist mariners for his forthcoming expedition – but soon afterwards he came to accept that he would never lead an army again.

Throughout this period he was attended by members of the council. Interestingly the prince was also with him, together with other key members of the previous council. A charter granted by the king in person was witnessed at Canterbury on 30 March by the prince, Henry Beaufort, the duke of York, and the earls of Arundel and Warwick, as well as members of the new council.[25] Henry seems to have been making an effort to remain on favourable terms with those he had sacked the previous December. He even went so far as to reward some of them for their service, including the earls mentioned above.[26] All these men presumably accompanied Henry back to Windsor for the Garter celebrations on 23 April, for they were all still with him to witness royal charters at Westminster on 12 May and 1 June.[27] Thus the prince and Henry Beaufort

– the architects of the pro-Burgundian alliance – were with Henry when he agreed to help the Armagnacs.

This shift of English policy, from the Burgundians to their enemies, confused many contemporaries in England as well as France. It also threatened to humiliate the prince and Henry Beaufort. It meant that they had opened negotiations with the king's enemies: men who were about to invade Gascony.[28] In this light, it would have been inappropriate to entrust command of the English army to the prince, and it is likely that Henry only considered giving his eldest son a role while he (the king) was intending to command the expedition in person.[29] When this proved impossible, the king decided to give overall command to his second son, Thomas. The appointment doubled the tension in the royal family, for not only had the prince been passed over, he was not on good terms with Thomas. Nor was Henry Beaufort. They were infuriated even further when Henry reinforced Thomas's position by conferring on him the title which Edward III had given to his second son: duke of Clarence. Perhaps to calm their anxieties, Henry also named Thomas Beaufort as a co-leader of the expedition, and promised to create him earl of Dorset. But if by this he hoped to sweeten their mood, he failed. Neither the prince nor Henry Beaufort was at Rotherhithe to see the king gird Thomas Beaufort with the belt of an earl.[30]

The prince and Henry Beaufort angrily left court shortly after 1 June. By then Henry had summoned all the council to him, including the archbishop of York and the earl of Westmorland.[31] But it was too late to hold things together. At Coventry on 17 June the prince issued a public letter, which was – and still is – astonishing for its fulminations against those who advised the king, and, by implication, against the king himself. In his letter the prince drew attention to the king's plans to go to Gascony and claimed that Henry had named the prince as one of the leaders. The prince explained that he had subsequently declined to go because he had been offered so few men. Instead, he went on to say, he had withdrawn from court and travelled to Coventry to raise stronger forces but then:

> Some sons of iniquity, nurselings of dissent, schism fomenters, sowers of anger and agents of discord . . . desiring with a serpentine cunning to upset the ordered succession to [the] throne . . . wickedly suggested to my most revered father and lord . . . that I was affected with a bloody desire for the crown of England, that I was planning an unbelievably horrible crime and would rise up against my own father at the head of a popular outbreak of violence, and that in this way I would seize his

sceptre and other royal insignia on the grounds that my father and liege lord was living a life to which he had no proper title and which relied on tyrannical persuasion.[32]

What is astounding about this letter is that the prince felt bound to repeat such accusations. He would not have taken arms publicly against his own father; it would have been greatly to his dishonour and the destruction of his future authority. So the fact that he felt it necessary publicly to refute such allegations proves that men of consequence were publicly saying such things, and it follows that the prince must have behaved in such a way that these things were believable. Similarly, in the second half of the letter the prince defends himself against the accusation of trying to disrupt the expedition to Gascony. Again, the necessity to defend himself reveals that others were accusing him of exactly this, so he can have done nothing or very little to promote the king's expedition, and his refusal to serve must be interpreted in this light. Indeed, the fact that Henry forced all his sons to swear an oath to observe the terms of the agreement with the Armagnacs on 20 May strongly suggests that one of them – the prince – was threatening to lay aside the treaty and disregard his father's policy altogether.

For these reasons, the months of May and June 1412 mark the nadir in the relationship between Henry and his eldest son. The near-collapse had been due to a number of factors: rivalry between the prince and Thomas, rivalry between Henry Beaufort and Archbishop Arundel, differing views on France, and perhaps the prince's own youthful lasciviousness.[33] It was also partly due to their similar dispositions. Neither man was likely to admit he was wrong; neither was likely to back down. Both men were spiritual – both faithful believers in the Trinity – and both were royal soldiers through and through. Both were conservative, intelligent, well-educated, determined and eloquent. They were both committed to the principle of serving the realm. But Henry was still the king, and he felt it was his son's duty to be as loyal to him as he had been to his father. This is an important point in understanding the relationship between father and son. The prince was not just younger – and thus healthier and more ambitious – than his father; his upbringing was different from his father's in that he had grown up with the expectation of exercising power. Henry's upbringing had been one of duty throughout, of service and loyalty to the Crown. Thus, although his obedience to his own father may have given Henry an idea of how a son should behave, he could hardly expect the prince to do likewise. The prince's very ambition was evidence of Henry's success in transforming his family from a ducal one into the royal one.

The split did not last long. On or shortly after 29 June, the prince returned to Westminster, attended by a huge crowd of supporters.[34] According to the earl of Ormond (who claimed to be an eyewitness), the meeting took place at Westminster.[35] The prince arrived dressed splendidly in blue satin with the Lancastrian 'esses' livery design emblazoned in gold on one arm. He told his followers to remain in the lower part of the hall while he alone proceeded to the dais to address the king. Henry then

> caused himself to be borne in his chair (because he was diseased and could not walk) into his secret chamber, where in the presence of three or four persons in whom he had most confidence, he commanded the prince to speak his mind. The prince knelt before his father and said to him: 'Most redoubted lord and father, I have come as your liegeman and as your true son, in all things to obey your grace as my sovereign lord and father. And whereas I understand that you suspect me of acting against your grace, and that you fear I would usurp your crown against the pleasure of your highness ... how much I ought rather to suffer death to relieve your grace ... of that fear that you have of me, who am your true son and liegeman. And to that end I have this day by confession, and by receiving my Maker, prepared myself. And therefore most redoubted lord and father, I desire you in your honour of God, for the easing of your heart, here before your knees to slay me with this dagger'. And at that word, with all reverence, he passed the king his dagger, saying, 'My lord and father, my life is not so dear to me that I would live one day that I should be to your displeasure ... I forgive you my death'.[36]

Henry's reaction at this solemn show of loyalty from his son was an emotional one. He wept openly. He took the dagger and flung it across the room, and tearfully embraced his son, and kissed him, and said to him,

> My right dear and heartily beloved son, it is true that I partly suspected you, and as I now perceive, undeservedly on your part. But seeing your humility and faithfulness, I shall neither slay you nor henceforth any more have you in distrust for any report that shall be made to me. And therefore I raise you upon my honour.[37]

From this moment on, Henry was as good as his word. And the prince was as good as his. There were no further attempts to force the king to abdicate.

*

In France, despite Henry's treaty with the Armagnacs, the civil war was shifting into an Anglo-French conflict, with an English attack on Berck and a French one on Guines.[38] The Armagnac city of Bourges was already being besieged by the duke of Burgundy. On 8 July 1412 Henry agreed the financial arrangements for his son's campaign. On the 11th he formally appointed his son Thomas, duke of Clarence, as lieutenant of Aquitaine and instructed four knights to survey the thousand men-at-arms and three thousand archers mustering at Southampton to accompany Clarence to France.[39] Soon afterwards the ailing king bade farewell to his dear son for what he must have known would be the last time.

Although he had no way of knowing it, Henry had sent Clarence into a trap. In August, news reached him that the Armagnacs had betrayed him. The dukes of Burgundy and Berry had met and resolved their differences, in a show of peace, on 8 August, probably while Clarence was still at sea. A fortnight later the duke of Orléans was publicly reconciled with his father's murderer, with the English being identified as the common enemy. Thus, when Clarence arrived in France, he found his army not just unwanted but resented as an invading force. On 16 September, Clarence wrote to the Armagnac leaders refusing to accept their peace agreement, and declaring war on them in return for their betrayal. Three days later he sacked the town of Meung and crossed the Loire into the lands of the duke of Berry, demanding compensation for the sudden reversal of Armagnac policy. Thomas was clearly able to handle himself; Henry's policy of placing his son in command in a war zone at the age of fourteen was yielding benefits.

As Thomas led this unplanned, destructive march through France, Henry was carried to and fro between the bishop of London's house at Fulham and Archbishop Arundel's mansion at Croydon, growing increasingly ill. In September he took a boat down the Thames from Fulham via London and the Tower to Canterbury, where he met Archbishop Arundel. He stayed there for a few days before being brought back to Westminster. On 23 September, the prince came to see him with a large following, as he had at the end of June. Again the prince complained about rumours spread about him, this time that he had been accused of sequestrating money entrusted to him for the defence of Calais. He drew two rolls of accounts from his robe and showed how the money had been spent on wages.[40] As

Henry read through them, the prince demanded that those who had slandered him – almost certainly meaning Archbishop Arundel – should be tried.[41] The tired king assented, but insisted that such a trial should take place in parliament. He knew, perhaps, that he would not live to see it take place.

Henry spent most of October at Merton Priory. The council met in his absence at Westminster on 20 October and drew up a list of matters for his consideration, including the repair of the walls of Berwick Castle, the defence of Calais and Wales, and the government of Ireland.[42] The list was presented to the king the next day, who dictated his answers. It was the last documented business he conducted with his council. Even now, in his final days, he retained his love of music, one of his last known orders being to arrange for a new suit of clothes for his minstrel, William Bingley, on 23 November 1412.[43]

On 1 December parliament was summoned for the last time in the name of King Henry IV. It was Henry's wish to hold one final, farewell meeting. The date was set for the anniversary of Henry's father's death, 3 February 1413. The strategic purpose of the parliament was undoubtedly financial but the money may not have been intended solely for war. Some of it may have been intended to fund a voyage to the Holy Land. According to one chronicle, on 20 November 1412 the council had agreed to construct galleys to transport the king to Jerusalem, where he hoped to die.[44] There is no extant independent record of this decision but in January 1413 the long-serving William Loveney organised the cutting of timbers to make three such galleys.[45] Henry himself had expressed the wish several years earlier of visiting the Holy Land again, and it seems that his vision of his own death was a farewell parliament followed by him and his closest friends sailing off into the east in three ships. It did not turn out that way. He was simply too ill to choose the manner of his departure.

Henry spent his last Christmas with his much-loved wife at Eltham Palace. He remained there for a full month, until 25 January, when Archbishop Arundel took him up the river by barge to Mortlake. He returned to Eltham once more, at the end of January, and tried to attend parliament on 3 February, staying at Lambeth shortly afterwards. The members had dutifully assembled on the specified day but Henry himself was too sick to attend. He was drifting in and out of consciousness, unable to stand or to speak, a dying man. The members lingered in and around Westminster. They knew they were experiencing one of the rarest and strangest moments in the life of a kingdom. For only the fourth time since 1216, the realm was pausing, waiting for its sovereign lord to die of natural causes, and for the government to pass to his heir. In all the chambers of the palace, across Westminster and London, the officers of the household waited quietly for the end. The bureaucracy was at a standstill. The last letters in the name of Henry IV had already been written. The clock of government had come to a stop and was waiting for a new hand to set it going again.

By 21 February 1413 Henry had been ferried back from Lambeth to Westminster, but he was destined never to leave nor to set foot on one of the galleys he had commissioned to return him to the Holy Land. While he was in the abbey making an offering at the shrine of St Edward the Confessor – on whose feast day he had been exiled in 1398 and crowned in 1399 – he lost consciousness. He was carried through the church to the abbot's lodging. When he recovered his senses, he found himself lying by a fire in a chamber which he did not recognise. He turned to his chamberlain and asked in a whisper where he was.

'The Jerusalem Chamber', said his chamberlain.[46]

'Praise be to the Father of Heaven', said Henry, 'for now I know I shall die in this chamber, according to the prophecy told of me, that I should die in the Holy Land.'[47] The release from his physical torment which he craved was finally at hand.

Henry spent his last hours in that chamber, in great pain, laying by the fire. If then he had reflected on what he had achieved in his life, it would have appeared to him as one of the most extraordinary stories ever told. That he should have visited such faraway places as Vilnius and Jerusalem, then seen his long years of loyal service to his cousin turn to bitter rivalry, and emerge as nothing less than king of England, must have still seemed the most remarkable twisting and turning of fortune, like no other king's fate known to him. And yet, the real battles of his life had then only just begun. How many rebellions had he faced? The Epiphany Rising in 1400, the revolt of Glendower, the poisoned saddle, the friars' conspiracy, the Percy revolt, the conspiracy of the countess of Oxford, the kidnapping of the Mortimer boys, the rebellion of Archbishop Scrope, Northumberland's and Bardolph's last stand, perhaps a barbed contraption left in his bed, and even an attempt by the prince and the Beauforts to force him from the throne. Add to those the hostility of the French and Scots, and five campaigns against the Welsh, surely he had faced more opposition than any king of England? And that did not even begin to touch on his battles in parliament. It is somehow appropriate that, even as he lay dying, a man called Richard Whytlock had taken sanctuary in the abbey and there had raised the old rallying cry 'King Richard is alive!'. If Henry was told this, it would not have mattered greatly to him. All the force had gone from those words. Henry had defeated all his enemies. His life's work was done.

Henry's deathbed has left us with several stories. The most famous of all is that as he lay, apparently dead, his son Henry picked up the crown from the cushion where it lay beside his bed and took it away, only to be summoned back by his indignant father. This is unlikely to have been based on an eyewitness account. No English chronicles mention it. It only appears in the French chronicles of Enguerrand de Monstrelet and Jean de Waurin (the latter copying the former).[48] Their account says that after the crown had been returned, Henry confessed that he had no right to the kingdom, so the prince had even less. In Monstrelet's words, the prince replied, 'my lord, as you have held it by right of your sword, it is my intent to hold and defend it in the same way during my life'. Henry replied, 'Well, act as you see best. I leave all things to God and pray that He will have mercy on me', after which he died. These last words conflict with those given in the English accounts. The story seems to have been circulated in France to discredit the new king personally (through his presumptious behaviour) and dynastically (though the dying king's confession).

A more reliable account of Henry's deathbed confession was repeated some years later by John Capgrave, the mid-fifteenth-century prior of Lynn, who wrote works for Henry's son Humphrey (among others).[49] He wrote two different accounts of Henry's deathbed confession. One was included in his book *The Illustrious Henrys*, written for Henry's grandson, King Henry VI. The other was written later, for Edward IV. In the first, the dying king sent for the prince and said to him,

Consider, my son, and behold thy father, who once was strenuous in arms but now is adorned only with bones and nerves. His bodily strength is gone but by the grace of God, spiritual strength has come to him. For even this sickness, which I certainly believe will prove fatal, renders my soul braver and more devoted than before ... My son, pay faithfully your father's debts, that you may enjoy the blessing of the Most High, and may the God of our fathers, the God of Abraham, Isaac and Jacob, give thee his blessing, laden with all good things, that so may you live blessed, for ever and ever, amen.[50]

These were supposed by Capgrave to be Henry's last words. When he rewrote the death of Henry IV in his *Chronicle of England*, he was far less polite. Just as Edward IV maintained his right to the throne on the grounds that the Lancastrians were usurpers, Capgrave cut the above scene and, instead of the prince, had the lords at court persuade Henry's confessor, John Tille, to go to the king on his deathbed and try to extract a confession from him for three things: for the death of Richard II, the execution of Archbishop Scrope and the usurpation of the realm. Capgrave claims that Henry's response was to say that he had letters of absolution on account of the first two sins, and had performed his penance for them, and, with regard to the usurpation, he would not make any remedy, for his sons 'would not permit the throne to go out of our lineage'.[51]

Capgrave's willingness to change his narrative according to his patron's preferences is a worrying trait, and would leave us uncertain as to the king's final days if it were not for another account which supports the earlier of these narratives. This was written by Thomas Elmham, whom Henry V described in a letter the following year as 'our chaplain'. Elmham was thus close to the royal family and – as modern examination of his work on the early history of St Augustine's Canterbury has proved – a discerning man. He also wrote a life of Henry V. Both he and Capgrave were clergymen, and thus both had a reason to stress Henry's religious exhortations at the end of his life, but otherwise there is no reason to doubt that, on his deathbed, Henry exhorted his son to follow a life of righteousness and piety, compared his sickness with his former strength, and asked the prince to pay all his debts.[52]

Henry's last request probably formed a nuncupative will (one given verbally and recorded by witnesses). The terms are not known in detail but he left directions for his goods and chattels to be sold and for the sums raised to be put to pious uses.[53] He named Henry V and Archbishop Arundel as supervisors, but they both declined to act, leaving as executors the archbishop of York, Bishop Langley of Durham, Sir John Pelham, Sir Robert Waterton and Sir John Leventhorpe. It is likely that all these men were with him when he died. His wife and at least two of his sons, Henry and Humphrey, were also present. Thus Henry – the revolutionary king – died peacefully, surrounded by friends. He breathed his last on 20 March 1413, three and a half weeks short of his forty-sixth birthday.

*

Henry's body was embalmed and wrapped in cerecloth and laid in state in Westminster Abbey. His final instructions had probably included the direction that he was to be buried on Trinity Sunday (18 June) in the Trinity Chapel at Canterbury, which not only was in line with his personal faith but gave his son Thomas sufficient time to return from France to attend. Thus it was not until two months after his death that his corpse was placed in a lead coffin and an elm chest and rowed down the river to Gravesend in a torch-lit barge. It was then taken by carriage to Faversham, and finally to Canterbury, where it was placed on an iron-framed hearse draped in black cloth and covered in candles and torches. Thomas – who had marched all the way across France to Gascony – returned to England in time, and was present with his three brothers at the funeral. The rivalry between him and the prince, now King Henry V, dissolved into an acknowledgement of brotherly respect and loyal service.

The house of Lancaster was united once more. A golden age had begun.

NINETEEN

That I and Greatness were Compelled to Kiss

Necessity so bow'd the state
That I and greatness were compelled to kiss . . .
Henry IV Part Two, Act 2, Scene 1

This book began with a note stressing how Shakespeare used the historical Henry as a sort of dressmaker's dummy over which to sew two very different characters: the cold usurper, Bolingbroke, and the aloof, regal father of England's hero, Henry V. Occasionally in the plays there is a flash of poetic understanding which accords with the historical Henry's situation – for example, the speech which ends 'uneasy lies the head that wears a crown' – but otherwise Shakespeare's Henry is just an archetypal king, lacking a distinctive personality. As any ardent Shakespeare reader will have realised, although the nineteen chapter titles in this book have all been drawn from the three plays in which Henry appears, only five have been used in context. 'The Summons of the Appellant's Trumpet', for example, relates to the events of 1397, not the Appellants' rising in 1387, and 'The Virtue of Necessity' comes from a speech in which John of Gaunt tries to persuade Henry to see the positive aspects of exile, and has nothing to do with his return to England in 1399. Such words were drawn from the stardust cloud of poetic truths which turns slowly around the historical Richard II and Henry IV, sometimes shedding light but more often obscuring the characters.

In one respect, though – the title of this final chapter – Shakespeare was absolutely correct. Henry and greatness were *compelled* to kiss. Henry was kept distant from greatness all through his youth. Richard appointed him to lead no embassies, and gave him no military command. His visits to Lithuania and Jerusalem were remarkable but they were not the stuff of greatness. His patience and forbearance in the 1390s were equally remarkable but again, silence is not greatness. Then came the moment of compulsion, the kiss. To think that Henry could have done anything other than to return to England in 1399 is to misunderstand both the man and his times. He could not have remained a knight, stripped of his titles, in exile; it would not have been good enough for his family or his retainers – the hundreds of people who depended on him – let alone for himself and the dignity of his position. Moreover, he was a fighting man, the sole man to be the grandson of the two greatest war leaders of the fourteenth century. He was the *ultimate* thoroughbred warrior. The very fact that Richard tried to dishonour and destroy such a man showed contemporaries that their king was acting without thought for the consequences of his actions, and that in itself was dangerous for the realm. Henry was compelled by circumstances to return to England in 1399. And that implied either a kiss with greatness or the more permanent embrace with failure and a traitor's death.

A kiss is a fleeting thing, but once it has taken place it cannot be undone. Henry's kiss with greatness was similar. In 1399 he was called upon to act in an extraordinary manner and he did not shrink from the heavy responsibility placed upon his shoulders. What he did – against all the social conventions of his time – was astounding. His manner of assuming the crown was not that of a usurper but more like the winner of an election, a point he recognised himself in his arguments with the friars in 1402. That he did not go on to be a great king does not detract from the courage, initiative and consideration of his actions in 1399. There is almost no sense in which his reign can be considered great; it was dogged by financial problems and rebellion, so that defeating or outlasting all his enemies is his sole claim to greatness as a ruler. But in terms of his stature as a man, those judgements do not apply. His rule may have been characterised by crisis and opposition, but he was one of the most courageous, conscientious, personally committed and energetic men ever to rule England. It is unfortunate that he has historically been judged solely as a king and not as a man.

The purpose of this final chapter is therefore to correct this imbalance, or rather more fairly to appraise the character and achievements of Henry of Lancaster. In doing this, it hardly needs to be repeated that we need to break up the old frames through which we see the kings and queens of England. The idea that we can look down the list of monarchs and compare them all is a facile one, for each man and woman faced his or her own unique problems, and, as we have seen, no one had previously had to face the range of difficulties which confronted Henry. But it is valid to ask how well he personally coped with his particular set of problems, and (to repeat a question posed in the introductory note) why he survived as a king and Richard did not. And the starting point for any such reckoning has to be the personality of Henry himself.

There is no getting away from the fact that Henry was a complex character. Logical, conservative, intelligent, articulate, eager to engage in dispute, militarily minded, energetic, a creature of routine . . . Already we have some obvious contradictions, for how could Henry have been both 'conservative' and the leader of the most far-reaching revolution in England before the seventeenth century? How can he have been so argumentative, in his disputes with the friars, and so fond of routine (in his itinerary, spending virtually every Christmas at Eltham, for instance)? This point is an important one, for it is arguably the key to understanding any historical person. In the course of writing *The Perfect King: the life of Edward III*, it was impossible to avoid the realisation that Edward III was also a mass of apparent contradictions: romantic yet hard-headed, pious yet ruthless, faithful to his wife yet encouraging of sexual adventure.[1] As that study showed, it is only when we tease out and juxtapose the apparent contradictions of a lord or king that we obtain an in-depth view of his character. In fact, apparent contradictions such as these very rarely represent real aberrations but rather are different viewpoints from which to see a multi-dimensional character.

To show how this affects our interpretation of Henry, consider his spirituality. There is no doubt that Henry's devotion to the Trinity was sincere and unfaltering. There are far too many references in his life for his adherence to the cult to be considered any less sincere than the devotion of his uncle (the Black Prince) and Henry V, both of whom were fervent believers in the Trinity. Yet Henry executed an archbishop. He also executed the abbot of Halesowen, the prior of Launde and a whole host of friars. He had the bishop of Carlisle tried for treason, and was accused by Richard II of being an enemy to the Church. These details prevent us from interpreting his religious views as traditional and straightforward. Knowing that he had no respect for opponents who held high office in the Church allows us to contextualise his piety and see a direct link between his God and himself, thereby largely circumventing the role of the clergy. His attitude towards the prelates he executed was that they deserved no special treatment if they stood in the way of God's will that Henry should rule England. Hence the apparent contradiction of a pious king who executed an archbishop is explained, and a much fuller picture of his religious conscience obtained.

So, what was Henry really like? Having started with his spirituality, it seems appropriate to continue with that theme. Very clearly, Henry cared more for God than for the Church, and more for the Church than for some of the men who exercised office within it. Indeed, his relationship with God was one of the most powerful drivers in his life. This is not reflected in great buildings and worthy foundations like those of Henry III or Henry VI; Henry simply did not have the time or the money to build on a lavish scale, nor did he have the need to make a show of his religion. But there is plentiful evidence for his zeal. Although there were already two chapels at Eltham, he built another for his own personal use, connected by a staircase from his own bed chamber. In decorating the windows of his private rooms within the palace, he chose figures of saints and the Trinity. Similarly, when prevented from going on crusade in 1392, his alternative was a protracted pilgrimage. Throughout his life we may notice this tendency to opt for the religious path, even celebrating his birthday through Maundy alms-giving. As mentioned in the text, Richard and others feared this personal religious confidence in Henry. Those who have seen Scrope's execution as evidence that Henry was irreligious are missing the key point: Henry's spiritual strength was so great that not even an archbishop could stand in the way of him performing what he believed was right. This spiritual conviction – so dramatically reflected in his will of 1409 – must be considered to have been a solid foundation for his outlook on life and a reassurance in dealing with the vicissitudes of his reign.

This personal religion – Henry's 'direct link' with God – is closely connected to the private side of his life, and his preference for the company of his household staff and family, not a great mass of courtiers and magnates. It is this respect in which he differs most markedly from his grandfather, Edward III. Although he was extraordinarily courageous, confident and militarily accomplished, he did not have his grandfather's ability to bring together a large number of knights and bind them in a quasi-Arthurian thirst for collective glory. The Arthurian renaissance was not yet over in 1399 but Henry was unable to capitalise on it. Similarly, the Welsh expeditions in which he took part were all short forays, with the prime purpose of demonstrating that the king of England could march through Wales at will. We do not sense any great collective enthusiasm for glory in the company around Henry on these expeditions. He was just too serious. His nature did not prevent him being one of the greatest knights of his age, and a good battle commander, but it did make his court less exuberant, less romantic, less fun and less united than that of his male-bonding grandfather.

From this we can begin to see the makings of an individualist, and this accords with other aspects of Henry's character. The serious, logical underpinning of many of his interests was outlined early on in this book; for example, his love of music, jousting and disputation. To these we might add his preference for archery and cannon: highly efficient means of fighting with projectile weapons, not hand-to-hand gallantry. This logical way of thinking, combined with his high level of education and a natural intelligence, gave him an intellectual self-confidence matched by very few of his contemporaries. Hence his ability to comment constructively on theological disputes at the University of Paris, and his readiness to engage in arguments with the friars about their perverse loyalty to a discredited and deceased ex-king. Such argumentativeness is supported by Capgrave's line about Henry's tendency to discuss moral issues at length. It is further supported by Jean de Waurin, who recorded that 'his good sense, and his prudence extended into many lands and divers countries. He maintained and loved justice above all things, and besides was a very handsome prince, learned, and eloquent, courteous, valiant and brave in arms . . .'[2] It is no surprise that he continued arguing with the duke of Orléans far beyond the point of regal dignity.

Henry was unswervingly loyal to his friends and loved ones. His loyalty to his father was exceptional: as far as we can see, he never went against his father's directions, even though such obedience risked humiliation at court. That instinctive loyalty and fidelity is noticeable through his entire life: from his relationships with his wives, both of whom he loved dearly, to his children and his Lancastrian retainers. His only known illegitimate child was conceived and born between his marriages. His support of Thomas Arundel was unflinching, even on those occasions when it was contrary to his own interests. Naturally, for a man with a logical mind, this was part of a *quid pro quo* agreement, and his loyalty to his friends was only half the story. Just as important was his appreciation of the loyalty of others, and his ability to encourage and retain that loyalty even in the face of adversity was crucial. The betrayal of the Percys, for example, proved less significant than the loyalty of those who stood by the king in 1403. Henry's relationships with his sons, and his ability to retain their devotion, and to forgive Prince Henry in 1412, is similarly striking. When we recall the Lancastrian retainers who had supported him all his life – for example, John Norbury, Thomas Erpingham and Hugh and Robert Waterton – the importance of these personal ties is revealed. He did all he could to keep his promises to them – resisting the commons' demands in 1404 for their pensions and gifts to be cut – and they stuck by him with an equal loyalty.

Beyond this we can see another sort of loyalty in Henry: loyalty to his kingdom. There is no doubt that Henry's responsibility to the realm was of an altogether different nature to Richard's. Part of this is due to the fact that Henry could not take his status as king for granted. Not only was it constantly under threat, he himself had been a subject – a vassal – for most of his life. His outlook as a subject of the king became transposed, on his accession, to becoming a subject of the kingdom. In parliament this allowed him to be far more tolerant of opposition than any previous king. It can also be seen in his readiness to accept responsibility for the defence of the realm, especially Wales. In neither arena did he shirk his responsibilities. Henry's loyalty to individuals and his sense of obligation to the kingdom are factors which cannot be ignored in assessing his character.

Loyalty? In Henry IV, the man who rebelled against his liege lord and usurped his throne? We have another apparent contradiction here. But it is not hard to find an answer; it is a matter of to whom or to what he was loyal. Henry was loyal to his friends, not to Richard II. Readers of *The Greatest Traitor* might have recalled the first line of the opening chapter of that book when reading this one: 'the roots of betrayal lie in friendship; those of treason lie in loyalty'. It is a truism which may be repeated over and over again for the later middle ages, for the causes of rebellion are normally to be found in an undiminished loyalty to another cause. It was the Counter-Appellants' loyalty to Richard II which led to the Epiphany Rising. The reason Glendower took arms was not just hatred of Lord Grey but his loyalty to the idea of an independent Welsh nation. Even the Percy rebellion was partly actuated by loyalty to the Mortimer claim to the throne. Similarly Henry, in returning to England in 1399, was acting in accordance with a combination of Lancastrian and national loyalties which went over and above his obligations to an unworthy king.

The above parade of Henry's characteristics makes him appear a model medieval magnate. Spiritually motivated, intellectual, conscientious, courageous, loyal to his friends, family and kingdom: all these – coupled with his education and his military skill – make him appear too good to be true. Add to these his wit (remarked on by the emperor of Byzantium) and his charming manners (noticed on his pilgrimage as well as in Paris during his exile) and we may begin to wonder was there no downside to him as a man. The answer to that question, of course, lies in the ultimate testing of his character, following his accession. Yes, he was a virtuous man, but virtue is not necessarily the most suitable characteristic in a king, especially if the kingdom's highest priority is to stamp out opposition at home and to win overseas victories. As a king, under pressure, the potential weaknesses in his character became clearer and clearer. His concept of mercy was pushed to the limit, and then beyond, with the inevitable result that he was forced to take more direct action against unrepentant rebels, making his initial promises of mercy appear false. His own standards of duty and loyalty were so high that he expected more of his leading subjects than they were able to give. A few lived up to his expectations – such as the earl of Westmorland – but others did not, and broke from him. Most of all, he wanted so much to be a good king – attempting to please everyone all the time – that he inevitably displeased some. In no aspect of his rule is this clearer than his failure to cope financially. His natural generosity and his loyalty to his friends meant that, after 1399, he became generous to a fault, giving away far more than he could afford. When the implications of this were made clear in parliament, he was reluctant to do anything to remedy the situation. He would rather tax the anonymous masses than take away a grant from a loyal supporter. In this way the strains of kingship almost proved Henry's undoing.

Almost, but not quite. For in the foregoing list of Henry's qualities and characteristics we have not mentioned the most important two. First of these is his tenacity. With the exception of his expedition to Scotland, it is difficult to think of anything on which Henry gave up. Surely Glendower cannot have expected in 1400 that the king of England would personally lead expeditions against him every year for the next five years? And that he would delegate to his son the responsibility to continue the fight for another four years? As reflected in his propensity to argue points of honour, he was determined to have the final word in everything. On matters of loyalty, duty and almost every aspect of his royal prerogative, he *did* have the last word, dying peacefully with his royal power intact and the word 'Jerusalem' on his lips. Even his illness did not overwhelm this tenacity; it is wholly remarkable that a man whose flesh was rotting, who could not walk and who had twice been in a coma should stage a comeback and resume power as he did in the parliament of 1411. If he did indeed suffer from the same disease as the Black Prince in the last eight years of his life, then his achievements in his time of illness outstrip the prince's by a very great margin, and that is due wholly to his determination to see things to an end.

This brings us to the last and by far the most important characteristic of Henry IV. Without it, none of the above would have happened, and this book would not have been written, for Henry himself would not have survived. It is, of course, his pragmatism. It runs like a golden thread of self-preservation throughout his life. Without it, he would have seen his uncle Thomas seize the throne from Richard in the last days of 1387. He would have buckled under the weight of Richard's antipathy, forced into an open and treasonable revolt in 1385, when Richard tried to murder his father, or in 1394, when Richard appointed his uncle to be keeper of the realm, ignoring Henry's claim to the throne. Or in 1397 when Richard murdered his uncle. As for how he managed to contain himself in 1398, after learning that Richard had planned to murder his father and was yet planning to destroy the Lancastrians, we can only guess. By the time of the duel with Mowbray, Henry must have been on the point of lynching Richard. But he did not. His pragmatism during his revolution was a clear factor in his success, and it is repeatedly in evidence, from his oath-swearing to his claiming the throne by inheritance from Henry III, and his precaution of being confirmed as king in parliament. Afterwards, his pragmatism proved his saving grace. His order to have Richard killed – a reversal of his earlier decision – is perhaps the best example. All those thousands who rallied to the cry 'King Richard is alive' would have been able to cause a great deal more trouble if Richard had been languishing in some dungeon, or able to return from Scotland and lead an army in person. And most of all, Henry's pragmatism in standing back from the most intense criticisms and demands of his kingship allowed him to weather the worst political storms. Whereas Richard's attitude towards political opponents was summed up in his phrase that 'he is a child of death who offends the king', Henry accommodated his opponents' skills within his government. It has been said once already but it is worth saying again that *that* quality – the ability of the tree to bend and sway in the storm and not to snap – was the key reason why Henry survived and Richard did not.

*

If you go looking for the visual reminders of Henry IV today, you will find very few. Nothing at all remains of his palace at Eltham: the surviving hall was built for Edward IV. The gatehouse at Lancaster Castle is Henry's only significant secular structure, and the church at Battlefield, near Shrewsbury, and the chapel of St Edward the Confessor at Canterbury are his only religious foundations visible today. Given his shortage of money and the need to prioritise what gold there was for the defence of the realm, it is not surprising that Henry did not build on a large scale. It is also important to remember that in his reign, most of Edward III's great buildings were still standing, and thus he did not need to build huge palaces to celebrate his kingship. Thus the physical impact of Henry's reign on the landscape was, and is, minimal.

Much the same can be said about other artworks and items of patronage. You will find little to do with Henry IV in any museum. Coins from the reign are relatively rare, because Henry was able to depend on the specie in circulation from the long reign of his grandfather. No textiles have survived. The Dunstable swan jewel may or may not have passed through his hands. The crown of his daughter, Blanche, survives in Munich, but it was inherited with the treasure of Richard II, and was probably made for Queen Anne in Paris in about 1380. A few livery collars survive; none, however, can be associated with Henry himself. Some early fifteenth-century cannon survive but there is no evidence that they were based on Henry's designs. Even the two extant pieces of music probably by him are often attributed to his eldest son, and are very rarely sung. To see physical evidence of Henry's existence we must either go to Canterbury Cathedral to see his tomb, with the effigy of him placed there after his death by his widow, or we must go to The National Archives to see his accounts, a few letters bearing his handwriting, and images of him in manuscript.

For these reasons, it could be said that Henry hardly made a mark on England. With few visual reminders, he just does not crop up in conversation or feature on the tourist trail. Even the custom of the sovereign giving an age-related amount of money to an age-related number of recipients has lost its connection with Henry. Ask the man in the street which English crusader king entered Jerusalem, and the chances are that he will answer Richard I (who never set foot in the holy city), not Henry IV. Henry's life, of course, saw a golden age of literature, and he had an indirect legacy in the work of the poets Chaucer, Hoccleve and Gower, all of whom he patronised or employed. But if our purpose in searching for antiquities and literary remains is to establish what difference Henry made to England, we are setting about answering it in wholly the wrong way. The Roman Emperor Claudius never came to England but he has a good claim to be named one of the most important men in the history of the country, for it was his invasion which brought the country within the Roman Empire. Likewise Henry's importance is not to be found in any physical manifestation of royal power, such as a great palace or a widely read book. It lies in the fact that Henry forced all of England and much of the rest of Christendom to consider the nature of the accepted social order in relation to God. If the king ruled badly, broke his promises and murdered his subjects, could it be lawful for a man to depose him and take the throne in his place? Could it be justified in the eyes of God? These questions would continue to tear society apart for the next two hundred and fifty years, and would only be finally answered when England deposed its king in 1649 and killed him, not secretly by starvation but with an axe, in public.

This challenge to the social order is undoubtedly Henry's lasting legacy. It is ironic that it was accidental; he himself was very conservative in his determination to preserve the royal prerogative. But there is no avoiding the fact that he dealt a colossal blow to the prerogatives of the English throne. Not only did he force the king to abdicate, he used parliament to introduce and confirm a new royal legitimacy, scrubbing the lawbooks clean in order to facilitate his 'inheritance'. Thus the precedent was created that parliament had the *de facto* authority to choose a new king as well as to depose one. If we take the view that Henry was not Richard II's legal heir (and the claim from Henry III seems to indicate that he was not), then it follows that he was the first elected ruler of England since William the Conqueror, who was 'chosen' to be king by the Saxon Witan following the battle of Hastings.

That empowerment of parliament was, of course, where many of his problems started. A parliament which had ratified a king's claim to the throne was always going to have a high opinion of its own importance and authority. From 1401 we get the impression that, in parliament, Henry was like a wounded mammoth, surrounded by scavengers scenting that the great animal was weak, although it was still strong enough to lash out with its great tusks and defend itself. In that he was unfortunate. Indeed, luck was rarely on his side. He was fortunate to have the king of Scotland fall into his hands but unlucky that the Scottish and French kings chose not to recognise him in the first place. He was financially unlucky too. He could hardly help the terrible harvests and high food prices early in the reign, or the simultaneous collapse of the revenue from the wool trade, but they both caused enormous hardship, fuelling discontent against him and his government. Similarly he was unlucky to have prophecies stacked against him, foretelling his doom and encouraging opposition. People did not have to believe in prophecy to see that such calamities might well come true.

Considering these misfortunes, it was no small achievement for Henry to retain the throne. But the reign was not without its political achievements. First and foremost there is the stabilising effect of his ability to see off all attempts to dethrone him. Then there was the stability of his form of kingship. In the 1407 parliament Thomas Arundel listed the reasons why he thought the people should 'honour the king': because Henry had preserved the liberties of towns and religious institutions; because he had showed himself unstinting in his efforts to defend the realm; and because he had showed mercy to his adversaries. All of these were matters of maintaining the status quo; nothing here was a new development. This points to the very success of his conservative policy. If a revolution is to be wholly successful, all the counter-revolutions must be defeated. That Henry did so while showing mercy and preserving existing liberties is to his credit.

Historians of parliament of course can (and do) list many other developments in this reign. To what extent they were due to Henry himself, and to what extent they can be classed his achievements, are quite different questions. Perhaps Henry deserves some credit for his flexibility and initiative in proposing new forms of taxation, such as the land tax. The promise of low taxation was very clearly unsustainable but it did result in the acceptance of the principle that extraordinary taxation could be used to repay the government's debts. On the other hand, the confirmation of the right to discuss matters of state without the king being present was a step forward for the commons. Both sides of the parliamentary lobby thus gained from the reign. That is hardly surprising, but if Henry can be credited with these developments it is only on account of his successful management of change. As stated at the outset, most of the developments in parliament were in spite of his involvement, not because of it.

On this basis, we have to conclude that Henry has been unfortunate in the way he has been treated historically, and to have had his reputation stamped with the superficial judgement of 'usurper'. At the time, men called him a saviour, not a usurper, and it was largely the ambitions of subsequent aspiring usurpers and the vulnerability of subsequent rulers which has maintained the 'usurper' tag. Another blow to Henry's reputation came with the success of his son. Given that Henry IV's reign was a struggle to stabilise the realm, the subsequent one seemed glorious by comparison. The contrast was exaggerated by polemicists wishing to create a warrior-hero out of Henry V. To make the younger Henry's achievements seem even greater, they compared his victories to his father's frustrations. And Henry IV's successes, such as the victory of Shrewsbury and the defeat of Glendower, were associated with the hero-son, not the usurper-father, as if it was only due to Prince Henry's presence that Henry IV survived at all. There is a clear mismatch of condemnation and praise.

How then should we see Henry today? In chapter fifteen it was observed that he and Glendower had a number of points in common; for example, their high level of education, justification for revolution, aspirations for international recognition, military skill and political resilience. In terms of reputation, they cannot be compared. Not only was their struggle an unequal one; there is still today a cultural need in Wales to celebrate Glendower as a national hero, whereas in England there is no equivalent need to view Henry in a positive light. Historical judgement is cruel; most historical reputations develop in an arbitrary way. In fact, to see just how unfair historical judgement can be, consider Henry's life in relation to that of a later ruler of England, Oliver Cromwell. Neither Henry nor Cromwell was born to be head of state. Both men deposed and (reluctantly) killed their lawful king. Both were soldiers, both achieved power through a military campaign and parliamentary acclamation. Both were serious, spiritually motivated, private men, and both attempted to rule through God's direction. Neither man was educated in governance but did so in good faith, and both had to face a series of economic disasters. Both died of natural causes, still in power but exhausted and gravely sick, after little more than a decade of rule. Of course there are significant differences – Henry was a nobleman, Cromwell was a commoner, and the country deserted Richard II whereas many stood by Charles I – but the point is clear. Cromwell is judged a great man and a great leader; today there are statues to him, and he is a household name. There is only one commemorative statue to Henry IV, on the east end of Battlefield Church, near Shrewsbury. He is still labelled a usurper because that is the way subsequent monarchs wanted people to think of him, and the way their subjects (including Shakespeare) agreed to present him.

Thus we come to the end of this study of the life of Henry IV. And what more appropriate image is there with which to end but that final moment his life. Picture him lying on that low bed in the Jerusalem Chamber of the abbot's house at Westminster. He is lying by the fire, covered in blankets, dying. He is in great pain. But as he lies there, who can doubt that his career has been the most phenomenal success. What has he *not* achieved? The king of Scotland is his prisoner. The Welsh revolt is crushed. The French are in disarray as Clarence rides at the head of an army all the way to Gascony. Henry's throne now will pass unopposed to his eldest son, Henry of Monmouth, who is at his bedside, reconciled to him. Despite all Henry's fears, despite Richard's bitter hatred, despite all those rebellions, plots, and arguments in parliament and in the council chamber, he will die in peace, a respected man and an unvanquished king.

Few men confront the basic tenets of the society in which they live and try to change them. Very few of those are successful. And even fewer survive to reflect on their success. Henry IV was one of these very few.

APPENDIX ONE

Henry's Date of Birth and the Royal Maundy

When I began the research for this book, Henry was the only Plantagenet king whose date of birth was in doubt.[1] As a consequence, and because of the importance of ascertaining his age in relation to Richard II, a considerable amount of time was devoted to this problem at the outset. The result is a short essay entitled 'Henry IV's date of birth and the royal Maundy' which will appear in the journal *Historical Research*. Readers wishing to check the methodology and sources used should refer to that article. What follows here is simply an explanatory note on the complications of the date of birth itself and the establishment of the part of the royal Maundy custom which relates to the sovereign's age.

Henry was almost certainly born on Maundy Thursday 1367. Because it was such an important day in the Christian calendar, he commemorated his birthday on Maundy Thursday, not on the calendar day (15 April). In itself there was nothing unusual in this, for medieval people expressed their birthdays in terms of a saint's feast day (i.e. Edward II spoke of his birthday as St Mark's Day, not 25 April, and Edward III spoke of his as St Brice's Day, not 13 November). What is unusual in Henry's case was that the feast on which he was born was a moveable one. Thus he celebrated his birthday on a different day each year. This seems very strange to us, but it was not that uncommon in the middles ages; King John even started his regnal year on a different day each year (having been crowned on Ascension Day), with the result that his administrative or financial years were all of different lengths.

As a result of this, it is likely that Henry did not know the calendar date of his birth. If he had asked to know the exact date, he may have been told that no significant saint was celebrated on that day. So there was a good reason to continue celebrating it on Maundy Thursday. In addition, Richard II was very proud of his birth on the Epiphany; so Henry, by drawing attention to the fact that he was born on Maundy Thursday, could demonstrate that Richard was not the only member of the royal family to be so favoured by God. Indeed, by performing the traditional *pedilavium* (feet-washing) ritual, Henry was able to contrast his own royal humility with Richard's style of self-interested absolutism.

An interesting by-product of this research has been the identification of the origin of the current Maundy tradition of giving alms according to the sovereign's age next birthday. Henry himself started this tradition, on Maundy Thursday 1382, which he celebrated as his fifteenth birthday. Previously kings and other members of the royal family had made Maundy Thursday donations to thirteen, fifty or two hundred paupers (thirteen being the number of men present at the Last Supper). But in 1382, when his father gave him the money to make the usual donations of alms to thirteen paupers, Henry added the money to spread his donations among fifteen, the same number as years in his age. In later years he gave money, clothes and shoes, but the number always corresponded with either his age last birthday or his age next birthday. By 1388 the tradition had been taken up by his wife, Mary, who made a donation that year relating to her own age (eighteen), and his sons did likewise. Thus, when Henry V ascended the throne, Maundy Thursday became a sort of 'official birthday' for the king. The Yorkist kings dropped this custom, perhaps remembering it as Henry IV's birthday, but even if its origins had been forgotten, it had already become a potent Lancastrian custom. Henry VII resurrected it shortly after his accession, and there is plenty of evidence that it was being adopted by many Lancastrian sympathisers in the early sixteenth century (following a similar pattern to the wearing of Lancastrian livery collars). The later Tudor monarchs perpetuated the ceremony and added to it, and thus handed it down to modern times.[2]

It is somewhat ironic that the one royal date of birth which has been unknown to historians for so many years is actually the one still commemorated by the sovereign to this day.

The Succession to the Crown, 1386–99

Many writers have considered the question of the succession in the reign of Richard II. Few, however, have considered it in the light of Edward III's 1376 entailment of the Crown upon his male descendants. Even fewer have considered the question from Henry's point of view, and no one (as far as I know) has fully considered the implications of Richard II making his own entailment in early 1399. As research on this book progressed it became clear that this was a significant problem, and so time was taken to examine the question in depth, attempting to ascertain how Richard's fickle attitude to the succession affected Henry. The result, published as 'Richard II and the Succession to the Throne' in the July 2006 issue of the journal *History*, reveals several deliberate moves by Richard to eliminate Henry from the order of succession, the first dating back to the parliament of 1386. Readers who want an in-depth understanding of the matter prior to 1399 should refer to that article. What follows is a summary of the key turning points in Richard's attitude to Henry as his potential heir.

Perhaps the most confusing aspect of the discussion is a single entry in the continuation of the *Eulogium Historiarum* that Richard II declared the Mortimer boys to be his heirs presumptive in the parliament of 1385. Many writers have taken this at face value. Many others have dismissed it as unsupported nonsense, asking why no other chroniclers and no official sources record such an important announcement. Richard certainly believed he had the right to appoint his successor, and there is some corroborative evidence in the *Westminster Chronicle* in an entry relating to the year 1387. However, if we check the text, a startling point emerges, previously unnoticed. There are at least two layers to the continuation of this chronicle. A lost original, written before 1404, was copied and substantially altered by one or more later writers, the last of whom was definitely writing after 1428 (as shown by his reference to the exhumation of Wycliffe in that year). If we examine the part relating to the announcement concerning the Mortimer boys, it turns out to have been made in the parliament of October 1386, not 1385, and to have been the work of the original pre-1404 chronicler. The writer of the original (lost) chronicle had made a mistake in placing the creation of the earl of Suffolk in the October 1386 parliament. The copyist corrected this by adding a new phrase of his own, which reads 'however in the ninth year of Richard's reign [June 1385–June 1386], the king held a great parliament at Westminster in which . . . Michael de la Pole was made earl of Suffolk'. With the use of the word 'however' (*autem*) and his reference back to the 1385 parliament, there is no doubt that this is a later interpolation, included to correct the pre-1404 continuator's dating of Suffolk's creation. But by inserting this detail, the later writer has dislodged the next entry from the original chronicler's account of the 1386 parliament and inadvertently associated it with the 1385 one, for it states that 'it was in this parliament' that Roger Mortimer was declared the heir to the throne. Thus it can be seen that the original pre-1404 included the entry that Mortimer was declared the heir in the parliament of 1386, not that of 1385.

Redating Richard's declaration to the parliament of 1386 explains many things. Obviously it is clear why Gaunt (Richard's heir, according to Edward III's entail) and Richard did not fall out over this matter: Gaunt was not at the October 1386 parliament, being in Castile. Henry was present, and reacted by joining the Appellants the following year. In addition, he was both a blood relation and a close ally of the two men who went to the king from the 1386 parliament to threaten him with deposition, namely Thomas of Woodstock and Thomas Arundel. This gives a context to the declaration, for the accepted process of deposition was to force the king to abdicate in favour of an heir. Richard was hardly likely to acknowledge Henry as his heir if he had an alternative. Thus there were good reasons for Richard to declare publicly that his successor would be Roger Mortimer, a twelve-year-old boy. It was a swiping blow to Henry's kinsmen and allies and a sharp reminder to parliament that his youthful successor's ruling abilities might be no greater than his own.

Following the success of the Appellants in 1387, Richard was forced to accept the terms of Edward III's entail. Evidence from the charter rolls' witness lists for 1394 shows that Richard gave precedence to the heirs male of Edward III's fourth and fifth sons (John of Gaunt and Edmund of Langley) over the heir general of his third son (Lionel of Antwerp). However, in that same year Richard resisted John of Gaunt's request to recognise Henry as heir presumptive by appointing him keeper of the realm. Instead he appointed his uncle, Edmund of Langley. That he continued to regard Edmund as his heir is shown by three pieces of evidence. The first is Edmund's precedence over Henry in late 1397 and early 1398 (when they were both dukes and so precedence can be compared). The second is Richard's will (April 1399), which does not name Edmund as his successor but indicates him by default, for it includes a phrase about who was to act if his successor refused the throne, and the men who were next in the order of precedence after Edmund were all named in this capacity. The third is a petition submitted by Bagot in 1399 in which he described a discussion between him and Richard in 1398 in which Richard spoke of one day resigning in favour of Edward, duke of Aumale, Edmund's son and heir. Crucially this discussion took place before the death of Roger Mortimer was known and before Henry's own exile; it thus is further evidence of Richard's propensity to favour the line of York over the lines of March and Lancaster.

As a result of all this there were three clear turning points in Richard's view of the succession. The first was his declaration in favour of Roger Mortimer, expressed in the parliament of 1386. The second was his decision in December 1387 – at the persuasion of the Appellants – to acknowledge Gaunt as his heir, in line with Edward III's entail. The third was his decision to subvert the entail and elevate Edmund of Langley over Henry in 1394. This remained his preferred order of succession thereafter, during which years he was probably planning to charge Henry with treason (for joining the Appellants) as soon as John of Gaunt died. When this happened, Richard very probably destroyed the original of Edward III's entail. Either way, Henry was finally removed from the order of succession on 18 March 1399 by being branded a traitor and exiled for life.

The foregoing is the substance of the article in *History*. Unfortunately it was not until later, after this article had been published, that I realised that one very important piece of the jigsaw was missing. This only emerged in reconsidering Henry's inheritance claim from Henry III. As the Crouchback legend was known at the time not to be correct (and thus a weak basis for establishing a dynasty), and as Henry's claim from Henry III could not relate to his maternal descent (which would have implied the Mortimer family were the legal heirs), there had to be some other reason for the reference back to Henry III (who died in 1272). It is now known that in 1290 Edward I made a settlement which permitted females to inherit the throne, so Henry's concentration on his status as the male heir seems to have been the key to understanding his claim all the way back to Henry III (as one contemporary source specifies).[1] But Edward III's settlement of 1376 would have supplanted that of 1290, and restored the male-only line of succession, so again we have to ask why Henry did not even mention it. Even if he did not have the original document, Richard II had himself observed its contents in the early 1390s. What should have been spelled out was the implication of Richard II's recognition of the duke of York as his heir. If Richard *officially* settled the throne on Edmund and his family in 1399, Edward III's entail would have been supplanted, and thus rendered void, even if Henry had had possession of the original.

Although no settlement by Richard exists today, this does not mean one never existed, especially as we should expect it to have been destroyed by Henry. (The originals of both Edward I's settlement of 1290 and Edward III's of 1376 have been lost, almost certainly destroyed by those who did not agree with them.) In Richard's case we may be reasonably confident that he did draw up a settlement of the throne, for two reasons. One is the logical argument outlined above: Henry's failure to use Edward III's settlement suggests it had been rendered void by a later royal decree. The second reason is that Richard's will of 16 April 1399 – through not naming a 'successor' but implying his identity – suggests that the succession was clarified by a separate document. The reason for a separate document in 1399 was not just to supplant the 1376 entail; there was a real risk that the ageing and arthritic duke of York might die while Richard was in Ireland, so there was a need for the succession beyond him to be clearly delineated. This was especially the case as the next in line after the duke was his eldest son Edward, who was with Richard in Ireland.

Given these circumstances, it is likely that Richard drew up a settlement of the throne in conjunction with his will in April 1399, in much the same way as Edward III had drawn up his entail in conjunction with *his* will in October 1376. Richard's settlement apparently threw out the Lancastrian claim altogether (Henry had been declared a traitor by this time) and designated Edmund of York as the heir apparent, followed by Edward, duke of Aumale (Richard II's adopted brother). Edward's younger brother, Richard of Conisburgh, was probably named as well, as third in line and a potential keeper of the realm in case Edward became king while still in Ireland. Evidence that such a settlement was widely known in September 1399 and that it named all three of these men is to be found in the chronicle of Jean Creton, who noted that the assembly of 30 September 1399 was asked whether they would prefer any of these three – Edmund, Edward or Richard of Conisburgh – to be king instead of Henry. The gathering preferred Henry, of course, and in so doing they set aside the king's right to appoint his successor. In line with this, when Henry himself made provision for the succession in the summer and autumn of 1406, it was done on both occasions in parliament. This, then, was the basis of the Lancastrian claim in 1399: that only males could inherit the throne and all attempts by previous kings to settle the inheritance without consulting parliament were without any basis in law and thus void.

APPENDIX THREE

Henry's Children

Henry and Mary were married on or about 5 February 1381. For the early years of their marriage, they lived apart. Mary remained with her mother, the countess of Hereford, who was paid for her upkeep.[1] Despite this, McFarlane declared that 'they must have met occasionally, for on 16 April 1382 the countess of Derby gave birth to her first child, a son who not unnaturally failed to live; his father was sixteen, his mother thirteen'.[2] This statement is wrong: the child failed to live because he never existed. The source for McFarlane's statement was Wylie's *Reign of Henry IV*, but this was based on a misreading of the original Lancastrian account book in The National Archives (DL 28/1/1). Wylie noted this as:

Data uni armigero voc' Westcombe de dna' mea' Princessa de Bokyngham portanti domino meo nova quod domina sua erat deliberata de puero Apr. 16th, 1382, by order of Duke of Lancaster (66/8).[3] [*Given to an esquire called Westcombe of my Lady the Princess of Buckingham for bringing to my lord news that his lady was delivered of a boy . . . £3 6s 8d*].

And the next entry reads:

Ap. 18th 1382 at Retheford [Rochford?] magistre pueri predicti (40/-) nurse pueri predicti (26/8).[4] [*. . . to the master of the aforesaid boy £2, [to the] nurse of the aforesaid boy £1 6s 8d*].

Given the entry relating to the master and nurse, which seems to be a payment made on Henry's orders, Wylie has presumed that the earlier entry relates to a son of Henry's by Mary, and that Henry is confirmed as the father by the following entry, in which Henry clearly paid for the nurse. This in turn misled McFarlane and many others less discerning. One recent compilation has given this boy a name, 'Edward', and states that he lived for only four days.[5]

The original document reads as follows:

Et dat[a] uni armigero qui attulit d[omin]o suu[m] annidonu[m] de domina mea Princessa xiijs iiijd . . . Et dat[a] uni armigero voc[atur]

Westcombe d[omi]ni de Bokyngham portanti d[omi]no meo nova quod
d[omi]na sua erat deliberat[a] de pu[er]o per mandat[um] d[omi]ni mei
Lanc[astrie] xvj die Aprilis lxvjs viijd.[6] [*And given to an esquire who brought
to the lord his New-Year gift from my lady the princess [of Wales] 13s 4d . . . And
given to an esquire called Westcombe of Lord Buckingham for carrying to my lord
news that his lady was delivered of a boy, by the order of my lord of Lancaster
[dated] 16 April £3 6s 8d*].

This shows that the messenger was not Henry's own but in the service of
his uncle Thomas of Woodstock, earl of Buckingham, and that the lady
who had given birth to a son was not Henry's wife but his (i.e. the
messenger's) mistress. This was Henry's sister-in-law, Eleanor Bohun,
countess of Buckingham. The boy was Humphrey, known as Humphrey
Bohun, who became duke of Gloucester on Thomas's death in 1397.
Confirmation of this is to be found in Thomas's Inquisitions Post Mortem,
most of which refer to his son as being '15 and more' (i.e. in his sixteenth
year) in October–December 1397, and so born in the year October
1381–October 1382.[7] The reason for the payment being ordered by John
of Gaunt (as duke of Lancaster) to be paid by Henry's treasurer was that
John was with Henry at the time the news arrived. It was also by John's
order (not Henry's), on 18 April, that the payments were made to the
master and nurse of the infant.

Henry's first son was Henry of Monmouth, later Henry V, who was
born in Monmouth Castle on 16 September 1386.[8] Until recently this date
has been open to question, for other sources record his date of birth as 9
August 1387.[9] In Monmouth itself all the public commemorations of the
birth of the town's most famous son are proudly marked '1387'. However,
Henry IV's accounts as earl of Derby for 1387–8 clearly show that Thomas,
his second son, was born before Christmas 1387, as Christmas livery was
purchased for his nurse in that year.[10] If Thomas was born before Christmas
1387, his older brother cannot have been born later than the winter of
1386–7. Thus the date of 16 September 1386 must be preferred over 9
August 1387, not as a matter of likelihood but due to the impossibility of
the later date applying to Henry. Tallying with this is the fact that Henry
IV's household was at Monmouth in September 1386 and was not there
in August 1387.[11] In 1403 Henry V made a Maundy payment to seventeen
paupers, indicating that he was then in his seventeenth year (following his
father's example), and so born before Maundy Thursday 1387.[12] On the
strength of this and evidence cited by Christopher Allmand, Henry V's
date of birth is as certain as that of any late medieval king, and the references to his birth in 1387 are incorrect.[13]

Henry's second son, Thomas, was born in the autumn of 1387, as stated above. It is possible that the date of 9 August 1387 wrongly assigned to Henry V is in fact the date of Thomas's birth. It would appear that he was born in London, for Henry made a gift to the midwife who had assisted at the birth in London on 25 November 1387.[14] A London birth would also explain why Thomas is never given a topographical surname, except in relation to his family (Thomas of Lancaster).

Henry's third son, John, was born on 20 June 1389.[15] His fourth son, Humphrey, was born in the autumn of 1390. Henry received news of Humphrey's birth on or about 1 November 1390 at Königsberg, from an English sailor.[16] It appears likely therefore that he was born in mid-to-late September 1390.

Henry's elder daughter, Blanche, was born in the spring of 1392 at Walmsford, near Peterborough.[17] Henry's account for 1391–2 refers to payments for gowns for his sons and Blanche's nurse in May 1392. No payments for her appear in relation to Christmas 1391, so she was not born before the end of that year.

It was in the summer of 1394 that Mary (Henry's wife) died, giving birth to their youngest daughter, Philippa. Given that the child survived, Mary probably died after the actual birth rather than during it. Thus the date of her death is the nearest we can get to a reliable date of birth for Philippa. We currently cannot be more precise than a little before 6 July, the day Mary was buried at Leicester.[18] The *ODNB* gives 4 July as the date of her death.

In 1401 Henry had an illegitimate son, Edmund Lebourde, by an unknown woman. The boy was raised in England and educated in London. Henry wrote to Pope John XXIII to grant a dispensation for him to enter the Church in late 1411, and this was granted on 15 January 1412. Nothing more is known of him.[19]

Henry had no children by his second wife, Joan of Navarre.

APPENDIX FOUR

Casualties at the Battle of Shrewsbury

As noted in the text, some rather fanciful figures are quoted by the chroniclers for the number of participants in the battle of Shrewsbury. Jean de Waurin in particular stretches belief far beyond breaking point by stating that eighty thousand men were in the host which faced Henry.[1] The modern guide to Battlefield church is hardly more restrained in suggesting there were thirty thousand royal troops and twenty thousand rebels. Even some usually reliable contemporary writers, such as Thomas Walsingham and the author of the Dieulacres chronicle, say that there were fourteen thousand men in each army, with the implication that there were twenty-eight thousand men present on 21 July 1403. Against this, the number of slain is in several cases said to be under two thousand. If this was the case, and only one in twenty men perished, why do all the chroniclers agree that it was one of the bloodiest battles ever fought on English soil?

The key problem in assessing the scale of the battle is this tendency of chroniclers to exaggerate numbers. Armies are enlarged to biblical proportions as well-educated, cloistered writers wrote their dramatic accounts in the only language of battle they knew: a mixture of Old Testament stories, classical history and earlier chronicles. In general, unless they could talk up a skirmish to sound like the great battles of the past, it would hardly merit inclusion in a book. But from the mid-fourteenth century there was an increasing desire to know accurate casualty figures, at least with regard to men of quality. After Crécy, the victors collected the heraldic surcoats of the dead, thereby accounting for the knights and esquires killed. As a result, casualty figures (as opposed to the total numbers involved) *can* be a more accurate way to approach the scale of a battle. Of course casualty figures are often exaggerated too. Adam Usk states that sixteen thousand men died at Shrewsbury, and the Scottish chronicler Wyntoun suggests seven or eight thousand.[2] Nevertheless, correlating the various lower figures allows us a greater degree of reliability, if only for the reason that the smaller a number is, the easier it is for contemporaries to count, or estimate, accurately.

The starting point has to be the mass grave. Several chroniclers mention this, and interestingly they give different figures for the number of bodies in it. This suggests they were not all using the same source. The Dieulacres chronicle, which gives the total number of dead as between five and six thousand, states that the mass grave contained the suspiciously precise figure of 1,847 bodies.[3] The *Brut* states 1,100 bodies.[4] Other accounts mention the mass grave but give no number of corpses.[5] There can be little doubt therefore that a mass grave of some sort existed. It is also worth noting that the narrative of the battle implies that many men died in the same space, with the wounded royal vanguard dying under the hooves of charging horses. A mass grave would have been a sensible solution to the problem of burying all these bodies quickly.

This brings us to the well-known set of dimensions given to the grave: apparently it was 159 x 60 feet, and 60 feet deep. Leaving aside the incredible depth, which may be a mistranscription of IX (nine) for LX (sixty), there are reasons to doubt these dimensions. Allowing six square feet for each corpse, this would equate to a burial of 1,802 bodies. However, medieval burials were not so regular (bodies were often piled on top of one another), and we have to suspect that the dimensions were based by the writer on the reported number of dead, not an observation of the grave itself. In addition, a grave of that area with a depth of just nine feet – let alone sixty – would be very difficult to back-fill evenly, and we would expect considerable subsidence on the site. None is to be seen, except the sunken and overgrown area associated with the fishponds of the collegiate buildings. Although large numbers of bones have reportedly turned up near the battlefield church in the past, archaeologists today have great difficulty finding any, even though thousands of decaying corpses would not have been carried very far. Given that the church was constructed within six years of the battle, it is unrealistic to suggest the mass grave lies very far from the site. The lack of subsidence in the vicinity and the paucity of bones on archaeologists' spades allows us to infer we are looking for a relatively small number of corpses, not seven or eight thousand.[6]

The figures in the Dieulacres chronicle, given above, imply that only a third of the dead were buried in the mass grave. The *Brut* suggests only the 1,100 who were buried in the mass grave were killed. The continuation of the *Eulogium Historiarum* has a total of just 1,600 men dead.[7] On this basis, it would seem unreasonable to suggest that more than three thousand men were killed, and perhaps as few as 1,600 died on the battlefield, with several hundred of those not being buried in the mass grave (being of higher status). This causes us to address the main question again: why was it universally described as such a bloody battle?

Consider the number of men of quality killed. Capgrave and Walsingham both mention a total of two hundred Cheshire knights and esquires, plus an unknown number of common men.[8] This is likely to be a reasonably accurate figure, for the surcoats could easily have been counted. This many men of quality is not a high proportion of the dead when compared to battles like Crécy or any other battle in which the English archers took part, but it is a high figure for a hand-to-hand battle, and it is a very high figure for *English* losses. Traditionally men of quality were ransomed, not killed. Archers do not take hostages, however, and herein we probably have the real reason for the horrific descriptions of the battle. The Dieulacres chronicle gives the figures of twenty-eight knights dead on the king's side and eight on Hotspur's. Many of these knights can be identified from the various chronicle accounts.[9] The total – thirty-six dead knights – bears comparison with the forty or so knights killed at Towton (1461), which is usually described as the bloodiest battle of the Wars of the Roses. It was not so much the numbers killed that made reports of the battle so deadly, it was the indiscriminate method of killing. If we consider the likelihood that the people who would have spread the story of the battle to the chroniclers were among the 'knights and esquires', we can immediately see why they were horrified by what they had seen.

The figure of fourteen thousand in the king's army may be a little exaggerated, but it is unlikely that Henry would have fought a battle with many fewer, and to his forces we must add those guarding the prince. That his vanguard was defeated by the Cheshire archers despite this, and yet Hotspur's army fought on until the evening, suggests that Hotspur had a force which, if smaller, was not negligible. If Henry had fourteen thousand men, and if four thousand of those were in the royal vanguard which fled during the battle, and three thousand of the royal army were badly wounded and died later (as Walsingham states), and about half those actually slain on the battlefield were in the royal army, then maybe as many as eight thousand men (considerably more than half the royal army) either fled during the battle, were badly injured or killed. Furthermore, if one-third of the injured whom Walsingham describes later died of their wounds, then one in seven men in the royal army did not survive the encounter. And this was the *winning* side. Similarly, if Hotspur had a force of about ten thousand – easily enough to overwhelm Henry's vanguard – and if one thousand of those were killed on the battlefield and a similar number were wounded as on the royal side, we can understand why the battle was shocking despite there being fewer than two thousand corpses in the mass grave. At the start of the day there had been twenty-four thousand men; at the end there were just six thousand royal troops standing, surrounded by two thousand corpses and between three and four thousand injured and dying men. The rest had fled. For the knights and esquires who circulated accounts of the conflict, it was especially shocking to see several hundred heraldic surcoats in the dust. It is not going too far to say that it was at Shrewsbury that the northern English gentry was forced to realise that loyal service in a fifteenth-century civil war necessitated facing the risk of an indiscriminate and ignoble death, whichever side they were on.

Henry's Speed of Travel in 1406 and 1407

As the text makes clear, Henry's physical health in the summer of 1406 is of crucial importance to understanding the Long Parliament, and in particular whether it was a confrontation between king and commons (as it is usually portrayed) or an attempt by the commons to protect the king in his illness by placing a number of royal duties in the hands of the council. One tool used to determine Henry's health at this time is his speed of travel. For example, it has been suggested that a journey of 355 miles over 98 days – an average of 3.62 miles per day – is very slow, and indicates ill health.[1] This may be the case, but this analysis does not allow for the fact that much of the time the king needed to be stationary in order to perform royal business, even after the arrangements of 22 May 1406. The average of 3.62 miles thus includes a lot of time spent in one place, when Henry cannot be said to have been 'travelling' at all. In order to examine this more closely, his journeys in the summer of 1406 have been assessed according to the actual days on which he was travelling, to get a more accurate estimate of his speed, and by implication, his ability to ride. The results are as follows:[2]

Date (1406)	Journey	Route	Approx. distance (miles)	Daily mileage
20 July	Hertford to Barley	direct	18	18
21–24 July ((3/4) days)	Barley to Bury St Edmunds	via Babraham & Newmarket	37	9–12
25 July – 1 August (7/8 days)	Bury St Edmunds to Walsingham	via Thetford, Wymondham & Norwich	70	9–10
2–4 August ((2/3) days)	Walsingham to Castle Rising	direct	23	8–12
16–21 August (5/6 days)	King's Lynn to Bardney Abbey	via Spalding & Horncastle	76	13–15

Date (1406)	Journey	Route	Approx. distance (miles)	Daily mileage
25–29 August (4/5 days)	Lincoln to Leicester	direct (Fosse Way)	51	10–13
6–15 September (9/10 days)	Leicester to Smithfield	via Northampton, Huntingdon & St Albans	132	13–15
Total for 31/37 travelling days			407	11–13

This results in an approximate rate of 12 miles per travelling day during the summer of 1406. This does not sound very much by the standards possible at the time: royal messengers could travel at four or five times this speed, and although this is not representative of a king's rate of progress, 30 miles per day was attainable for a fit king. Therefore in order to see how it compares to Henry at his fittest, a check has been made on his progress in the summer of 1403. This period has been chosen because (a) it was also summer, and the roads may be presumed to have been more or less in the same state of dryness; (b) Henry was at least reasonably fit, as he was about to fight in person at the battle of Shrewsbury; and (c) he was travelling north with a specific purpose, to face the Percy revolt. The results are as follows:[3]

Before the battle of Shrewsbury (1403):

Date	Journey	Route	Approx. distance (miles)	Daily mileage
4–7 July (3/4 days)	Kennington to Newenham Priory	via Waltham, Hertford & Hitchin	64	16–21
9 July	Newenham Priory to Higham Ferrers	direct	14	14
10 July	Higham Ferrers to Market Harborough	direct	21	21
11–13 July (2/3 days)	Market Harborough to Derby	via Leicester & Nottingham	54	18–27
14–16 July (2/3 days)	Derby to Lichfield	via Burton-on-Trent	25	8–13
19–20 July (1/2 days)	Lichfield to near Shrewsbury[4]	[via 'St Thomas Abbey', which is unidentified, so presume direct]	c. 39	c. 20–39
Total for 10/14 travelling days			217	16–22

After the battle:

Date	Journey	Route	Approx. distance (miles)	Daily mileage
22–24 July (2/3 days)	Shrewsbury to Stafford	via Lilleshall Abbey	31	10–16
25–29 July (4/5 days)	Stafford to Nottingham	via Lichfield, Burton-on-Trent & Derby	56	11–14
30 July– 3 August (4/5 days)	Nottingham to Pontefract	via Mansfield, Blyth & Doncaster	57	11–15
6–8 August (2/3 days)	Pontefract to York	via Rothwellhaigh and Tadcaster	24	8–12
13 August	York to Pontefract	direct?	24	24
15–17 August (2/3 days)	Pontefract to Worksop	via Doncaster	31	10–16
18–23 August (5/6 days)	Worksop to Woodstock	via Nottingham, Leicester, Lutterworth and Daventry	114	19–23
Total 20/26 travelling days			337	13–17

As is evident from a comparison of the above tables, when Henry was fit and well and in a hurry he could cover more than twenty miles in a day. In a similar state of good health, but with less urgency, the distance he covered was less, around fifteen miles per day. Thus, unless he was being carried in a litter or a carriage, the twelve miles per day recorded in the summer of 1406 does not indicate *chronic* ill health, being four-fifths of his usual healthy travelling speed.

Henry's speed of travel in 1407 has also been described as slow and 'leisurely' and has consequently been associated with a pilgrimage.[5] For this year it is harder to use the above method, as we have fewer details about Henry's itinerary. However, it is possible to make a few observations on account of some specific journeys in the summer months:[6]

Date	Journey	Route	Approx. distance (miles)	Daily mileage
16–19 August (3/4 days)	Nottingham to Pontefract	via Newstead and Worksop	57	14–19
13–16 September (3/4 days)	Beverley to Bishopthorpe	via Bridlington (by boat?) and Kilham (by road)	69	18–23
16–17 September (1/2 days)	Bishopthorpe to Doncaster[7]	unknown (by boat?)	31	16–31
29–30 September (1/2 days)	Worksop[8] to Nottingham	direct	27	14–27
4–10 October (6/7 days)	Repton to Evesham	unknown	68	10–11
Total 14/19 travelling days			252	13–18

The distances in the above table all presume Henry travelled by road, and it needs to be stressed that some of the journeys were probably by water. In fact, Douglas Biggs has suggested that Henry moved mostly by water in 1407.[9] With regard to his journey from York (5 September 1407) to Beverley (11 September): he sailed down the River Ouse, pausing at Faxfleet, and up the River Hull to Beverley. Similarly Henry could have travelled by water from Nottingham to Pontefract (via the rivers Trent and Calder), and from Bishopthorpe to Cawood (via the Ouse). However, he did not always move by water. His journey from Nottingham to Pontefract via Newstead and Worksop in the above table must have been by road, and his presence at Kilham indicates that, although he probably sailed from Beverley to Bridlington, he returned to Bishopthorpe by road. Thus it is very interesting that for these short periods at least, his speeds were as high as they had been immediately after the battle of Shrewsbury in 1403. It is possible that he had recovered his health. An alternative explanation is to be inferred from a payment for two metal saddles made for him in this year.[10] Quite what these were is unclear; they were not the first brass saddles made for him (he had had 'leather and brass' saddles made for his own use in 1392), and so were probably not specially designed to cope with his ailment.[11] They may have been some form of litter. Either way, his speeds suggest they helped considerably.

Few periods of sustained travel can be so precisely measured in later years, largely because Henry confined himself to the Thames area. One of the few which can is his return from seeing to the punishments and rewards following Bramham Moor in 1408: he left Pontefract on 30 April and travelled the 52 miles by road to Newstead Priory, arriving on 4 May (10–13 miles per day). Another is his pilgrimage to Leicester in the winter of 1409. He left Berkhamsted on or after 20 November 1409 and was at Stony Stratford (26 miles) and Northampton (another 13 miles) on the 23rd.[12] Hence on the 23rd he must have covered at least 13 miles by road, if not more, and kept up a rate of 9–13 miles per day over the previous two or three days. However these are rare examples. There are no indications that Henry travelled by road at a rate in excess of 13 miles per day after September 1407.

On the basis of these figures one may tentatively conclude that Henry was in discomfort when he travelled to East Anglia in 1406, but not chronically unwell. The irreversible collapse of his health – to the point of being an invalid – probably did not occur until some time after the autumn of 1407. This would accord with Adam Usk's evidence that the disease which killed him could be dated to the early summer of 1408, when he lapsed into a coma for the first time.

Henry's Physicians and Surgeons

Henry was often in poor health. We first find him ill with the pox in 1387 at the age of twenty, when the king's physician, John Middleton (d. 1429) was summoned to assist him.[1] This was not a permanent employment. The following year he employed Geoffrey Melton, an Oxford physician, to come to Kenilworth to attend his wife.[2] Melton was not retained either. When Henry was ill on the *reyse* in Lithuania, he was given the services of the physician of the Master of the Order of the Teutonic Knights.[3] On the same trip he paid a 'leech' in Danzig for staunching a wound, perhaps obtained while jousting.[4] It was only after his return from his pilgrimage, in 1393, that Henry began to retain a personal physician, Dr John Malvern (d. 1422).[5] It was presumably under Malvern's care that medicines were bought for him in 1395, 1397 and 1398. Malvern continued to appear in Henry's company for the rest of his life but seems not to have followed Henry into exile in 1398.[6]

Henry took on his late father's French physician, Master Louis Recoches, when he returned in 1399. From 22 February 1400 to 13 April 1406 Recoches is described as 'the king's physician' in grants to him, receiving the office of the keeper of the Royal Mint in the Tower on 24 January 1404.[7] In Henry's extant wardrobe account book for 1403, Recoches is the only king's physician mentioned.[8] However, in April 1402 there is a reference to one Richard Grisby, 'king's physician', being given a general safe-conduct.[9] The safe-conduct suggests that this was a one-off appointment, an impression made all the more likely by the absence of any other reference to Grisby serving the king in a medical capacity.[10] Nevertheless, this is the first indication that the king was enlisting additional medical help. As mentioned in the text, medicines were bought for him the following year, and there is evidence in a letter written by his surgeon that Henry had been ill before 1404.

Recoches was replaced as 'the king's physician' by David Nigarellis of Lucca before 17 November 1408.[11] On that day Nigarellis received the keepership of the Royal Mint with which Henry had previously paid Recoches. By 2 February 1412 his salary amounted to eighty marks per annum.[12] He and his heirs became subjects of the king of England that same month but Nigarellis himself died very shortly afterwards, at Easter 1412.[13] Henry also benefited from the ministrations of two other Italian physicians at the end of his life: Elias de Sabato, a Jewish doctor from Bologna, who was given permission to come to England and practise in December 1410, and Pietro D'Alcobasso, or Alto Bosco, who was in royal service in 1412.[14]

It is interesting that, after his accession, Henry preferred foreign physicians whereas prior to his coronation he had been attended by English medics. Two of the three identified foreigners employed after 1407 were Jews and all three were from Italy. Although we have no names regarding the identity of the 'physicians' (plural) who were with him at Windsor in April 1406, thereafter Henry's attempts to find a medical solution to his problem became more intense. There may be many more physicians as yet unidentified whose names have still to be pulled from the official documents of the period. One historian has gone so far as to suggest that he may have been attended in 1405 by as many as five.[15]

With regard to surgeons, the name of John Bradmore (d. 1412) is pre-eminent. He was connected with the royal household from 1399 and acted as an official surgeon to the king from at least 1402 to at least 1406, if not until the end of his life.[16] He is most famous for his surgical treatise which details his most notable cases and which is now in the British Library. This is the source for the description of how he managed to save the life of the prince of Wales after the battle of Shrewsbury, by extracting the arrow from his face, when many other physicians had failed to do so. He was also a founder member of the Fraternity of the Trinity in the parish of St Botolph, Aldersgate, and master of the fraternity in 1409, and bequeathed the fraternity its first property.[17] This gives him a religious link to Henry as well. In 1403 he was one of two surgeons to receive robes in an official capacity (the other being John Justel).[18]

The final medical reference for Henry which is worth noting is one dating to 5 April 1400. On that day Henry gave a generous allowance of sixpence per day to Matthew Flynt, a toothdrawer of London so he would pull the teeth of 'any poor lieges of the king who may need it in the future, without receiving anything from them'.[19] One cannot help but feel that this is evidence of Henry himself experiencing toothache in early 1400, and wishing to reward the man who helped him in his plight. That he did so by helping the poor of London at the same time is to his credit.

The Lancastrian Esses Collar

Most readers will have at some point come across a Lancastrian livery collar of esses. Whether an original in a museum, a representation on a church effigy, or a detail in a fifteenth-century painting, it is recognisable as a distinctive chain consisting of interlinked metal esses (letters 's'). It was of great significance to the Lancastrians, like the celebration of Maundy Thursday donations (see Appendix One), and thus it has received much attention regarding its origin and significance, including what the esses stand for. However, this attention has not always been based on the best evidence. Nor has every commentator on this arcane subject considered the logical implications of their suggestions. Therefore this appendix has been drawn up to bring together some new evidence and a few common-sense suggestions to illustrate what the 'esses' collar meant to Henry, and to refer to an important possibility connected with this interpretation.

The earliest references to livery collars in Henry's accounts are those for the year 1387–8, distributed to his supporters, Lord Darcy, William Bagot and John Stanley.[1] On John of Gaunt's return from Castile in 1389, it is noted that Richard II took John's livery collar and put it around his own neck. This would place the origin of the Lancastrian livery collar in or before 1386, the year in which John departed for Castile. There is no reason to doubt that this collar was composed of a series of esses: all the representations of Lancastrian collars from this time onwards show a form of esses, and Henry himself was known as 'the one who wears the S'.[2] Certainly by the early 1390s the collar assumed this esses form, as proved by the many references in Henry's accounts. As for the earliest possible date for its use, it is highly likely that the Lancastrian collar postdates the first known reference to a livery collar, which is the king of France's grant to his chamberlain of the right of wearing a livery collar in 1378.[3] This would date the invention of the Lancastrian livery collar to the time of Henry's youth.

Many antiquaries have speculated on the meaning of the esses. The author of the brief description of an example included in the catalogue of the *Gothic* exhibition at the V&A Museum quotes the work of R. W. Lightbown, who suggests *soverayne* (sovereign), *souveignez* (remember) or a combination of *sainteté, sagesse, sapience* and *seigneurie* (sanctity, wisdom, learning and lordship).[4] Other suggestions have included St Simplicius.[5] Only two of these are supported by the extant evidence: sovereign and *souveignez*. Of these two, it is 'sovereign' which has received the most support. The key evidence amounts to the following three facts: that Henry's tomb at Canterbury has a carving of an 'esses' collar around the royal arms which bears the motto *Soverayne*; that the motto *Soverayne* appears on the scabbard of the ceremonial sword he presented to the mayor of Dublin in 1403; and that the motto *Sovereigne* was used by Henry's son, John.[6] However, all these references date from after he became king, when he was indeed the 'sovereign' lord of England. It would have been treasonable for Henry and his father to use such a motto during Richard's lifetime. Every secular appearance of the word 'sovereign' relating to an individual on the parliament rolls relates to the sovereign power of the king, or the king himself, and no other member of the royal family.[7] When Henry used a motto incorporating the word 'sovereign' before 1399 (as on his seal as earl of Derby), it was in the qualified form *ma souveroine* ('my sovereign'), in the feminine, a motto alluding to the 'sovereign' power of a lady.[8] It has been suggested that 'sovereign' was adopted as a motto by John of Gaunt because of his claim to be king of Castile. This is demonstrably incorrect. John sold his claim on Castile in 1389. Even more significantly, Henry's accounts mention many esses collars in the 1390s although he himself had no claim on Castile at all.[9] Consequently, we may be confident that the esses cannot stand for 'sovereign' as this would imply John and Henry were claiming a share in the sovereignty of the realm from at least 1391 and probably before 1386, which would have been tantamount to treason.

As anyone who has looked at Henry's accounts will be aware, the vernacular phrase most frequently found among the Latin entries is '*souveyne vous de moi*'. This can be translated as 'remember me' but it also can be read as the name of the forget-me-not flower. It appears in at least a dozen entries in Henry's accounts between 1391 and 1398.[10] For instance, his goldsmith's account for 1391–2 records a payment for a wide belt for Henry 'made in the form of a trail of *soveigne vous de moy* hanging copiously with gilded silver leaves and fronds'.[11] In the embroidery section of the same account we may read of 'a mantle and short loose gown for the lord of velvet motlee with St John's Wort and *soveyne vous de moy*'.[12] There are later references on this same folio to hundreds of gilded silver 'leaves of *soveigne vous de moy*'. These relate to pictorial representations of flowers. Several entries in later accounts make this explicit; for example, 'for mending a collar of the lord in the form of flowers of *souveyne vous de moi* . . . with a swan newly enamelled', and 'for a collar of esses and flowers of *souveyne vous de moys*'.[13] These flowers obviously trailed all over Henry's clothes and livery chains, and his swan badges hung from chains of golden forget-me-nots.

The ubiquity and exclusive use of these flowers of *souveyne vous de moi* suggest that they are a rebus (a picture representing a word or phrase), standing for the motto 'remember me'. A rebus is a common feature of heraldic emblazons, livery collars and banners at this time. Thomas Mowbray's livery collars incorporated *mulberry* leaves; Thomas of Woodstock's banner included a *woodstock*. Evidence that the flowers indeed stood for a motto and were not purely a design feature is to be found in Henry's separate use of *souveignez* (without any reference to flowers) in at least two instances. Descriptions of the windows in his new buildings at Eltham Palace state that they incorporated the motto '*soueignex vous de moy*'.[14] And his wedding present to his second wife was a jewelled collar 'engraved with the motto *soviegnez* [*sic*] and the letter S'.[15] This last example is a particularly striking juxtaposition of the *soveignez* motto and the esses. Similar juxtapositions may be found among references to Henry's own collars, such as 'for a collar of esses and flowers of *souveyne vous de moys*'.[16] Thus there can be little doubt that the esses in the Lancastrian livery collar relate to the motto *souveignez vous de moi*. The Lancastrian collar should be understood as an exhortation for the family to remember someone.

Without further evidence we can only speculate as to who should be remembered. An intimate source is not ruled out by the use of 'vous' (not 'tu'), as it could be an exhortation to several people to 'remember me'. It is possible that the phrase (as a Lancastrian motto) dates from 1368, long before the invention of the livery collar, and is connected with an exhortation by Blanche (Henry's mother) to her children and husband to remember her. Such an explanation would explain why Henry particularly was described as 'the one who wears the S', and it fits with the fact that John chose to be buried by her side, not beside his other wives. Alternatively we might suggest these were final words spoken to John of Gaunt by Edward III or the Black Prince. Further research might clarify the date at which the motto 'Remember me' was adopted by the Lancastrians, and this might strengthen or weaken the above suggestions. However, we are unlikely ever to know its exact source and relevance.

A far more important question arises from an implication of the above analysis. What is the origin and relevance of the motto which does *not* relate to the esses, 'sovereign'? The document on which the seal with this motto (in the form 'so / ve / rey / ne') is first found is dated Leominster 31 July 1399.[17] That document describes Henry as duke of Lancaster, naturally. But the seal itself describes him as 'Sir Henry of Lancaster, duke of Hereford, earl of Derby and Northampton, lord of Brecon' (see plate 12). The seal was thus made sometime between his creation as duke of Hereford (29 September 1397) and the death of his father (3 February 1399). There is no record of Richard granting the use of this motto to Henry so it would appear that Henry assumed it for himself. As noted above, it is unlikely that he did so at the time the seal was created, during Richard's reign. But it is quite possible that it was engraved as an addition on his return to England, probably after his oath-swearing at Doncaster.[18] This would explain the basis on which Henry appointed the earl of Northumberland as warden of the Marches of Scotland on 2 August 1399, while Richard was still king, for the grant was authenticated with this seal.[19] The implication would be that, at Doncaster, Henry agreed to become regent: to allow Richard to remain king in name and lineal right while he (Henry) henceforth exercised sovereign power (as the regent and Richard's heir apparent). Whether Henry formally did divide these two aspects of kingship – the title of king and royal sovereignty – prior to his accession is not proven (and might not be provable) but it would explain many things and must be considered one of the most important historical questions from the summer of 1399 yet to be answered.

NOTES

Short titles or abbreviations in the notes are fully described in the select bibliography. All manuscript references relate to documents in The National Archives (TNA) unless otherwise stated. All places of publication are London unless otherwise stated.

Author's Note

1. Goodman, *John of Gaunt*, p. 67.

Introduction

1. *CH*, iii, p. 7.
2. *LK*, pp. 6–7.
3. Manning (ed.), *Life and Raigne of King Henrie IIII*, p. 19.
4. *CH*, iii, p. 9.
5. *CH*, iii, p. 5.
6. *CH*, iii, p. 74.
7. Ramsay, *Lancaster and York*, i, p. 142.
8. *CH*, iii, p. 74.
9. Edward V – king for just two months – is the only king to have been the subject of just one biographical study, but he was not crowned. Nor did he hold a parliament. At the time of writing, Henry is the subject of Kirby's book, and his life up to 1399 is the subject of Mary Bruce's, *The Usurper King*. Every other post-Conquest king of England has been the subject of at least two serious biographies.
10. Kirby, p. 42.
11. *LK*, p. 7.
12. *LK*, p. 20.
13. *LK*, p. 133.
14. *Henry IV* by Bryan Bevan (1994) has little literary merit and less historical understanding. The other, *The Usurper King* by Mary Bruce (1986) is much better but it deals only with Henry's life up to 1399. Bruce rarely strays from traditional assumptions about Henry and Richard, quick to repeat post-Shakespearian orthodox judgements against him for his 'usurpation' and slow to question the traditional, more sympathetic view of Richard II.
15. Chrimes, Ross & Griffiths (eds), *Fifteenth-Century England*, xii.
16. Since writing this I have heard from Professor Anthony Tuck that he has recently completed a political biography of Henry IV.
17. This statement is based on the assumption that Henry I had no part in the death

of William II, and that John's claim to take precedence over his nephew, Arthur, was lawful.

18. Eric Homberger, *Times Higher Education Supplement*, 9 October 1987, p. 11, quoted in *CB*, v. The McFarlane quotation following this comes from the same source.

19. The quotation comes from Philip K. Wilson, *Surgery, Skin and Syphilis: Daniel Turner's London (1667–1741)*, Clio Medica 54 (Amsterdam, 1999), p. 5, quoting Raphael Samuel, *Theatres of Memory 1: Past and Present in Contemporary Culture* (1994), p. 4.

20. The quotation comes from P. A. Johnson, *Duke Richard of York* (Oxford, 1988), preface page. It is reminiscent of McFarlane's own 'the formal records alone survive; behind them lies a tangle of human motives . . . and these are not revealed.' *CB*, v.

21. 'The Limits of Medieval Biography', conference at the University of Exeter, July 2003. This 'conclusion' is drawn from my notes of the paper delivered by the keynote speaker (Professor Pauline Stafford), which was endorsed by almost all those who took part.

1: The Hatch and Brood of Time

1. *KC*, p. 209.
2. *SAC*, p. 419.
3. *EHD*, p. 132.
4. Saul, p. 70.
5. *SAC*, p. 431; see *ibid.*, p. 419, for the heat of the day and the drinking.
6. *KC*, p. 211, says two hundred. Walsingham, however, says six hundred men-at-arms and six hundred archers. See *SAC*, p. 423.
7. *EHD*, p. 135; Saul, p. 68.
8. *SAC*, p. 425.
9. This specific reference dates from many years later. See Kirby, p. 19. For references to Ferrour as retained in the king's service, see *CPR 1377–81*, pp. 126, 586.
10. *EHD*, p. 135. See Saul, p. 65, n. 39.
11. Dunn, *Great Rising*, p. 102.
12. See Appendix One.
13. For more on Richard II's view of the past, see Ormrod, 'Richard II's Sense of English History'.
14. Smallwood, 'Prophecy of the Six Kings'. For an early version, prior to the revised text written in the *Brut* (written probably on an annual basis up to 1333), see Taylor, *Political Prophecy*, pp. 160–64.
15. These elements of the prophecy are taken from the transcript of British Library, Harley 746 in Taylor, *Political Prophecy*, pp. 160–64, not the later version (*c.* 1333) in *Brut*, i, pp. 72–6
16. *Brut*, i, p. 75.
17. *Froissart*, ii, pp. 678, 709. Because of the timing of this anecdote, it seems probable that Burghersh was blaming the eventual rule of the lamb on the immorality of the woman whom the prince had married, Richard II's mother. Either the lamb was a consequence of the union, or the prince would be judged for marrying an immoral woman.
18. *Revolution*, p. 140.

19. Morgan, 'Apotheosis of a warmonger'; *PK*, p. 394.

20. Keiser, 'Edward III and the Alliterative "Morte Arthure"'.

21. *PK*, pp. 427–9.

22. *PK*, p. 266.

23. Alison McHardy, 'Personal portrait', p. 11.

24. McHardy, 'Personal portrait', p. 12.

25. *Froissart*, ii, p. 166.

26. *The Poetical Works of Geoffrey Chaucer* (Aldine ed., 1845), v, p. 283. The last line has been modernised slightly, from 'Nas sene so blissfull a tresore'.

27. Goodman, *John of Gaunt*, p. 46.

28. Wylie, iv, p. 331.

29. Goodman, *John of Gaunt*, p. 46.

30. Goodman, *Katherine Swynford*, p. 11. He suggests that Blanche, being so named, might have had the duchess as her godmother. If so she must have been born before 1368, and been older than Thomas. However, it is possible that another Blanche stood as her godmother, or that she was named after the late duchess by her mother. Given-Wilson & Curteis, *Royal Bastards*, p. 148, notes that John stood godfather to her, but states that she was younger than her brother.

31. Goodman, *John of Gaunt*, p. 49. He had married Constanza in September 1371. He was authorised to use the Castilian royal title in January 1372.

32. As noted in Goodman, *Katherine Swynford*, p. 11, John's return in November 1371 – the same month as Sir Hugh Swynford died – almost certainly rules out the often-mentioned possibility that they started their affair during her husband's lifetime.

33. For example, *Register 1372–76*, i, pp. 208–9, 211.

34. *ODNB*, under 'Mowbray, Thomas (I)'.

35. For Richard's character see McHardy, 'Personal portrait'; Saul, chapter seventeen.

36. At the age of seventeen Richard built a small lodge on an island in the Thames near Sheen Palace, which one can only see as an attempt to remove himself from court life and find either privacy or isolation. See Mathew, *Court*, p. 33.

37. In 1372 and early 1373 John spent practically all his time either at Hertford Castle or his London palace, and so would have spent many weeks in Henry's company. His register has him at Hertford throughout March, in August and from October through to early March 1373, with occasional visits to the Savoy. He spent Holy Week 1373 at Hertford prior to departing with an army to France.

38. *Register 1372–76*, i, p. 169.

39. The dates of birth of the Beauforts are open to doubt. The dates 1373–7 for all four, put forward by Simon Walker in *ODNB* (under 'Swynford, Katherine'), seems to be far too compact a range, especially given John of Gaunt's absence in France for over a year, not to mention the fact that John's liaison with Katherine was illicit. Armitage-Smith gives a more likely range of 1373–9. See Armitage-Smith, p. 389.

40. For the illegitimate child by Marie de Saint-Hilaire see Given-Wilson & Curteis, *Royal Bastards*, p. 147.

41. *Register 1372–76*, ii, p. 191. The gifts were to (1) his brother the prince, (2) the princess, (3) his wife, the queen of Castile, (4) his brother Edmund, earl of Cambridge, (5–7) Henry, Philippa and Elizabeth, (8) the countess of Cambridge, (9) Lady Poynings, (10) Lady Segrave, (11) his niece, the countess of March, (12)

Lady de la Warre, (13) Lady Courtenay, (14) Lord Latimer, (15) Alan Buxeille, (16) Louis Clifford, (17) 'Monsieur Richard', (18) Nicholas Sharnesfield, (19) Simon Burley, (20) John d'Ypres, (21) William Menowe, (22) John Clanvowe, (23) the queen of Castile's lady, (24) the governess of his children (Katherine Swynford), (25) John Darcy, (26) 'Senche, a buttoner'.

42. *Register 1372–76*, i, p. 251.

43. *Signet Letters*, pp. 4, 51 (Latin and French), 148 (English), 152 (English), 191 (French), 194 (English).

44. See W. L. Warren, *King John* (1961), pp. 48–9 for the legitimacy of this.

45. Galbraith (ed.), *Anonimalle*, p. 83.

46. Bennett, 'Edward III's Entail', p. 585; *Froissart*, i, p. 509.

47. *SAC*, p. 39.

48. *SAC*, p. 41.

49. British Library: Cotton Charter XVI 63.

50. Bennett considers the possibility that it is a fifteenth-century forgery and concludes that it is 'inconceivable'. See Bennett, 'Edward III's Entail', p. 584.

51. There is no indication of the date when Henry was given the courtesy title of Derby; the earliest reference to him as such is the 12 April 1377 writ for the preparation of robes for his knighting at Windsor. See Galway, 'Alice Perrers' son John', p. 243. His father continued to use the title and to receive the profits of the Derby estates for several years.

52. There is no evidence to suggest Henry was in the royal household prior to 1376. However, it would appear that he had already left the custody of Katherine Swynford before 25 July 1376. See *Register 1372–76*, ii, p. 302.

53. Saul, p. 454, for Arundel. *ODNB*, under 'Mowbray, Thomas (I)' and 'Vere, Robert de'.

54. Saul, p. 35.

55. For Henry acting as his father's lieutenant, see *Register 1379–83*, i, xlvii.

56. McHardy, 'Personal portrait', p. 24.

57. DL 28/1/1 fol. 3v. This mentions gilded spangles purchased for the jousts in January 1382. While this payment does not necessarily relate to his taking part in the jousting, just his intention to be there, it has to be noted that spangles were also bought for the 1 May jousts at Hertford, at which Henry definitely did take part. The account includes a payment 'for six lances for the lord on the last day of April for the jousts which were at Hertford on the first day of May 6s' on fol. 6r, and goes on to record payments for armour and points for the armour used by Henry on this occasion.

58. Mortimer, 'Henry IV's Date of Birth'.

59. Montendre's 1376 appointment appears in *ODNB*, under 'Henry IV'; his wages amounted to a shilling per day in 1381–2. See DL 28/1/1 fol. 7r–9v.

60. *LC*, p. 153.

61. *Register 1379–83*, i, p. 152 (no. 463); *CP*, iv, p. 325.

62. On 29 November 1380, at Henry's request, the king pardoned Thomas Bate of Brynsford for the killing of a man. *CPR 1377–81*, p. 561.

63. On 7 November 1379 John wrote to his receiver in the county of Norfolk demanding that Henry's allowance be paid to Hugh Waterton, Henry's treasurer, for the last Michaelmas term. This shows that Henry's own household had been established

by then, but even so it could have operated to support Henry while he was with the king, in the same way that Henry had his own household and budget even when he was in his father's household. Further evidence is required for us to be certain of Henry's independence from Richard's household by this stage.

64. For the minstrels see *LK*, p. 16. For the inclusion of the king in Henry's list of annual 1 January gifts, see for example DL 28/1/2 fol. 17r; DL 28/1/4 fol. 18r.

2: *All Courtesy from Heaven*

1. See *ODNB*, under 'Henry IV', for the date of 5 February. The article in the same work on Thomas of Woodstock states that the marriage 'undoubtedly took place in 1380'.

2. Kirby, p. 17.

3. Holmes, *Estates*, p. 24.

4. See Goodman, *John of Gaunt*, p. 276, for a discussion of Froissart's reliability on the haste of the wedding.

5. Kirby notes that the Inquisitions Post Mortem relating to her father's estate (he dying on 16 January 1373) give her age as two, three or four. On 22 December 1384 she proved herself to be of age (fourteen). See Kirby, p. 18 n. 1. In addition, Mary made an age-related Maundy Thursday payment in 1388 to eighteen poor women (DL 28/1/2 fol. 26r) It would appear almost certain, therefore, that she was born in late 1369 or early 1370, and so eleven years old at the time of her marriage.

6. Alexander & Binski (eds), *Age of Chivalry*, pp. 501–4.

7. Summerson, 'English Bible'.

8. *Register 1379–83*, i, p. 179.

9. Given-Wilson & Curteis, *Royal Bastards*, p. 149.

10. DL 28/1/1.

11. DL 28/1/1 fol. 5r. See also Appendix Three for a note on Wylie's mistranscription of this.

12. DL 28/1/1 fol. 4v. These spangles were made of gilt copper.

13. *LK*, p. 22.

14. *LK*, p. 21.

15. For example, Edward III ordered 21,800 gold threads, costing £8 3s 4d, just for two jousting harnesses for a tournament at Clipstone in the first year of his reign, when he was fourteen. See E 101/383/3.

16. E 101/393/10 m. 1.

17. DL 28/1/1, fol. 5v.

18. For a photograph of Edward III's handwriting, see *PK*, second plate section; also Charles George Crump, 'The arrest of Roger Mortimer and Queen Isabel', *EHR*, xxvi (1911), pp. 331–2. For Richard II, see Saul, illustration no. 7. The letters are relatively neat but awkwardly formed. For Henry, see C 81/1358 4b.

19. It is cautiously said that he could 'at least quote a Latin tag' (Summerson, 'English Bible', p. 111). But given the grammar-based education of the period, it is unlikely that he would have learnt to write so well if he had not learnt Latin. He also owned a number of books in Latin, and wrote pithy Latin statements in his own hand.

20. Summerson, 'English Bible', p. 113. The Greek gloss might have been supplied by a clerk who came with the emperor of Byzantium in 1400. Several Greek clerks were in the party which went to Eltham, where Henry kept his books, and they spent several months in England. Permission was given to thirteen Greeks, 'lately sent to the king by the emperor of Constantinople' to leave England on 29 March 1403 (*Syllabus*, ii, p. 547).

21. *CB*, p. 2.

22. Gower, quoted in Grady, 'Lancastrian Gower', p. 560.

23. Wylie, iv, p. 138.

24. *LK*, p. 23; Kirby, p. 203.

25. *IH*, p. 116.

26. *Creton*, p. 61.

27. Trowell, 'Recorder-Player', pp. 83–4.

28. DL 28/1/2 fol. 9v (cover for his harp [*cither*]); fol. 25v (strings [*cordarum*]). Although his wife paid for the strings, she bought a total of forty-eight, first a set of eight, then three dozen and four.

29. DL 28/1/5 fol. 27r.

30. Although musicologists differ in their opinions on whether Henry or his son wrote this piece, it is nevertheless a striking example of what a king was capable of, despite all the other commitments on his time. Wilkins, 'Music and poetry', p. 188, states that it seems likely that 'Roy Henry' was Henry IV. The authors of Henry's entry in *ODNB* agree. On the other hand, some writers (such as the author of the entry in *Gothic*, p. 157) link the compilation of the manuscript with a musician who may be later associated with Henry's son, Thomas, and thus supposes that the 'Roy Henry' authorship indicates that the two pieces were written after 1413 by Henry V. However, this argument rests on the assumption that the compiler of the manuscript himself knew which King Henry had written it. If the compiler was – as may be reasonably presumed – working from a copy which was simply marked 'by King Henry', unless he had first-hand information as to which king had written it he could have done little more than copy his source. Thomas died in 1421; it is thus more likely that someone working for him had picked up a piece of music written by Thomas's much-loved father and not Henry V, with whom Thomas had a difficult relationship before 1413. In addition, when two kings were likely to be confused, the practice was for 'King Henry' to relate to the father and for the author to be more specific when describing the son, e.g. 'King Henry the son of King Henry'. For these reasons, it is more likely that the composer was Henry IV than his son.

31. DL 28/1/2 fol. 15v.

32. DL 28/1/2 fol. 25v. The entry, which follows a payment for harp strings, reads 'Et pro 1 ferr' empt' pro d'na' pro cantic' regul' xd'. See also Wylie, iv, p. 159.

33. Saul, pp. 16, 249–50; *idem*, 'Kingship', p. 45.

34. Reitemeier, 'Born to be a tyrant?', p. 147.

35. Saul, 'Kingship', p. 48.

36. Saul, p. 76.

37. Tuck, p. 88.

38. This was on 11 July 1382. See Dunn, 'Mortimer inheritance', esp. pp. 160–61.

39. Given-Wilson, 'Richard II and his Grandfather's Will', p. 327; Tuck, pp. 72–3.

40. Goodman, 'Richard II's councils', p. 63. Archbishop Stratford had cited the case of Rehoboam in countering the *libellus famosas* in his argument with Edward III in 1341.

41. Walsingham describes Richard rummaging in the Tower for relics of his ancestors. See Ormrod, 'Richard II's Sense of English History', p. 100.

42. Perroy (ed.), *Diplomatic Correspondence*, no. 95.

43. *PROME*, 1383 February, item 18.

44. *WC*, pp. 44–5. This was attended only by the king and queen, the new chancellor, the treasurer, the keeper of the privy seal, Henry's uncle, Edmund, and John of Gaunt, but as Henry was in the household of the latter, it is likely that they met.

45. *WC*, p. 54.

46. Tuck, p. 88; Given-Wilson, 'Richard II and the Higher Nobility', p. 121.

47. Henry returned with his father in February 1384, as shown by the king granting on 19 February that Edmund Loveney – presumably a relation of Henry's clerk, William Loveney – should be relieved of his duties in respect of his age (over sixty years) in response to a request from Henry. See *CPR 1381–85*, p. 374. John had returned at the start of February. See Goodman, *John of Gaunt*, p. 99.

48. *ODNB*, under 'Henry IV'.

49. If the confirmation of the grant from John to Henry of the manor of Soham can be taken as evidence of Henry being with John, then it would appear that Henry did travel north in March 1384. See *LC*, p. 153. John of Gaunt arrived at Newcastle upon Tyne on 24 March. See *WC*, p. 59.

50. *WC*, p. 67.

51. *WC*, p. 69.

52. *SAC*, p. 727.

53. *WC*, pp. 69–81.

54. *WC*, p. 85.

55. *WC*, p. 93.

56. Henry may have been with him but, if so, he was there in an unofficial capacity as Richard had not named him on the commission to treat with the French.

57. Tuck, p. 79.

58. *WC*, p. 113.

59. *ODNB*, under 'Joan of Kent', presumably using *SAC*, pp. 751.

60. *SAC*, pp. 755–7.

61. Regarding this summons, see Saul, p. 144, and the articles by Palmer and Lewis there cited.

62. Saul, p. 143.

63. *SAC*, pp. 763.

64. *WC*, pp. 127–9; Goodman, *John of Gaunt*, p. 104.

65. *SAC*, pp. 763.

66. Saul, p. 116.

67. *SAC*, p. 759.

68. *Royal Wills*, p. 78.

69. This is the usual interpretation of the thirteen kings (see Cherry & Stratford, *Westminster Kings*, p. 68). Richard was making oblations to the saint-king Edward the Confessor before this, as shown by his offerings at the shrine on his return from Scotland in 1385 (*WC*, pp. 133). But this ignores Harold II. Unless Harold was included and

Richard II not, thirteen is one king too few. On this point, there were in addition two extra large figures (according to *HKW*, i, p. 528) which might have been St Edmund and St Edward, the two English saint-kings. Both of these kings appear as saints on the Wilton Diptych, and had significance for Richard's vision of kingship. This explanation would suggest how Richard II and Harold II might have been incorporated into the design: Edward the Confessor appeared as a large figure elsewhere. However, the *Issues* for this same term (Michaelmas 1385) note that there was an image in the likeness of Richard at the end of Westminster Hall, over which a tabernacle was placed, and also 'two images in the likeness of the king and "Houell", these being placed at the end of the king's great hall within the Palace of Westminster'. See *Issues*, pp. 228–9. It is likely that the two extra large figures were Richard and the mysterious Houell (Hywel?), and these were separate to the thirteen which would have included Edward the Confessor to Edward III. This is more in keeping with Richard's character: to present himself separately to his royal ancestors, rather than placing himself simply and humbly at the end of a long line of kings.

70. Palmer, 'Parliament of 1385', pp. 481–2.
71. This compromise is known as 'the Bill'; the original list of demands is known as 'the Advice'. See *PROME*, 1385 October, appendix; Palmer, 'Parliament of 1385', pp. 483–4.
72. This is different from the commission of nine who had negotiated the compromise, known as the Bill. See Palmer, 'Parliament of 1385', p. 485.
73. *WC*, p. 141. As for the unsuccessful earldoms, Palmer points out that normally all peers were created on the same day. De Vere's elevation three weeks after the others, together with the lack of financial award, suggests that parliament tried to stop his elevation. See Palmer, 'Parliament of 1385', pp. 478–9. He achieved the dukedom of Ireland the following year.
74. Goodman, *John of Gaunt*, p. 106.
75. *CB*, p. 1.
76. *CCR 1385–9*, p. 56.
77. The date of John's departure is given as 9 July in *WC*, p. 165, and 8 July in *KC*, p. 341.

3: The Summons of the Appellant's Trumpet

1. For example, in November 1386, Richard invited the Lords Appellant to drink wine with him in a private chamber at the height of the crisis (*LC*, p. 27). He dined twice with John of Gaunt in the parliament of 1385, despite trying to have him murdered earlier in the year and accusing him of treason on the Scottish campaign. He also dined with the Lords Appellant after they had executed his friends in the Merciless Parliament.
2. According to Allmand, p. 7, Henry and Mary were both at Monmouth in the summer of 1386.
3. The official responsibilities of Waterton and Bache at this time are stated explicitly in DL 28/1/2 fol. 28, dated 24 September 1387.
4. The names of those who were with Henry are based on those who appear in the accounts of 1387–8 and who had been in his service from an earlier date. See Appendix Three for date of birth of Henry V.

5. DL 28/1/2 fol. 28.
6. *PROME*, 1386 October, item 6.
7. *PK*, p. 158.
8. This response, it should be emphasised, is a statement of Gloucester's position. There is no record of what he actually said at this time.
9. The *Eulogium* continuator states that it was at Michael de la Pole's request that Richard dissolved parliament. Since we know that Richard left and went to Eltham, it seems reasonable to assume that the two events – de la Pole's advice and the king's departure – were connected. See *Eulogium*, iii, p. 359.
10. He was not only a son of Edward III, he had formerly been a keeper of the realm, albeit in name alone, at the age of five in 1360, when he was the only one of Edward III's sons left in England.
11. This date is established by taking Knighton's 'three days' between the meeting and Richard's appearance in parliament, and working back from 24 October, the date he replaced the chancellor and treasurer. See *KC*, p. 361.
12. *KC*, p. 359.
13. *KC*, p. 361.
14. 'Succession'. See also Appendix Two.
15. Contrast this view, in the wake of Richard declaring that the Mortimers were his heirs, not Henry, with McFarlane's view that we do not know why Henry sided with the opposition in 1387, in *LK*, pp. 28–9.
16. See Appendix Three. Mary gave birth to their second son, Thomas, in the autumn of 1387.
17. Henry made a grant to his chamberlain, Hugh Waterton, there on 26 June. See *CPR 1396–99*, p. 70.
18. Although evidence for Henry's whereabouts is slight (prior to Michaelmas, when his 1387–8 account book starts), he does not appear on the charter witness lists for 1387, nor does he appear in any other context at court.
19. Richard attended this ceremony on this day, according to Saul, p. 171.
20. *KC*, p. 395. The questions appear in full in the twenty-fifth article against the king's friends, in the Merciless Parliament. See *PROME*, February 1388, part 2, item 25.
21. *WC*, p. 191.
22. *WC*, p. 207. But see also Saul, p. 175, where it is pointed out that the judges claimed that it had been the earl of Kent who revealed the strategy to the opposition lords.
23. *LC*, p. 23.
24. *WC*, p. 209.
25. *SAC*, p. 831.
26. *WC*, pp. 211–13.
27. On 18 November 1387 one John Stapeldon received a pardon for murder at his request. See *CPR 1385–89*, p. 368.
28. See Appendix Three. Mary left London on 25 November. See DL 28/1/2 fol. 25v.
29. See DL 28/1/2 fol. 15v. 'Medicines brought for the lord [Henry] on two occasions from Master John Middleton when the lord was ill with the pox, 11s 4d'. The account also has 'to the same master for medicines bought for the lord's use at the same time, 27s 8d' and adds payments for medicines for two of Henry's servants who were ill as well. There is also a payment to a London woman 'for making a long double-thickness shirt for the lord in the time he was sick of the

pox' (fol. 15r). The two other men in his household 'gravely ill' suggests that the form of pox was a viral infection, like chickenpox. As to the question why Mowbray also did not join the Appellants at this point if illness was the reason Henry delayed, it is possible that he was waiting to see what Henry would do. The twenty-one-year-old Mowbray would have looked a very odd fourth Appellant if Henry had not also joined.

30. The longer sections in Henry's 1387–8 account book (DL 28/1/2), such as those for saddles and repair of saddles, indicate that the entries are mainly chronological. On this basis, although they are mostly undated, we may use the relative positions of entries to develop an approximate itinerary. In almost every case (with one exception) the first item under the section heading was bought in London. It would appear likely therefore that Henry was at London or Westminster for the whole period between the start of the accounts (29 September) and 18 November (*CPR 1385–89*, p. 368). Leaving London in late November or early December (his wife left on the 25 November), he seems to have passed through Hertford (fol. 16r), on his way to Huntingdon, where he met the other Appellant Lords (12 December). According to the order of his wife's letters to him from Kenilworth (fol. 26r), he went next to Northampton and then Daventry. His route then seems to have been through Banbury (from which a horse of his was later returned to him), Woodstock (where he paid for an expensive 'woodknife'), to Radcot Bridge (20 December). Following the encounter with de Vere, he and his fellow Appellants went via Oxford to Notley Abbey, according to Mary's letters (fol. 26r), and his own nearby manor of Henton (fol. 27r), on the way to St Albans (24–25 December). The Appellants then returned to London on 27 December (*SAC*, p. 847).

31. *LC*, p. 29; *WC*, p. 219.

32. DL 28/1/2 fol. 26r.

33. The best account of the campaign is in J. N. L. Myres, 'The Campaign of Radcot Bridge, 1387', *EHR*, xlii (1927), pp. 20–33.

34. The expense of despatching the letter is noted in DL 28/1/2 fol. 26r.

35. *KC*, p. 421.

36. *KC*, pp. 421–5.

37. Mortimer was the earl's steward and had fought in his retinue earlier that same year. He is not mentioned in Henry's accounts. The *WC* indicates that he was sent ahead by Arundel. See J. L. Gillespie, 'Thomas Mortimer and Thomas Molyneux: Radcot Bridge and the Appeal of 1397', *Albion*, 7 (1975), pp. 162–3; *WC*, p. 223.

38. *SAC*, p. 839; *KC*, p. 423.

39. Knighton notes one other man and a boy were killed. *KC*, p. 425.

40. *SAC*, p. 843; *WC*, p. 223.

41. DL/28/1/2 fol. 27v. The total cost of these animals and carts was £81 6s 11d. This is described as replacement of dead animals and wine bought for the lord's work on fol. 29v.

42. DL 28/1/2 fol. 14r.

43. *KC*, p. 427.

44. 'Deposition', p. 157. See also Gloucester's confession in *PROME*, 1397 September, part 2, item 7.

45. *WC*, p. 229.

46. *SAC*, p. 847; *KC*, p. 427. Mowbray was asked to remain at the Tower too.

47. DL 28/1/2 fol. 16v (for the presents). See Note 73 for Richard never forgiving Henry for 1386–8.

48. See for example DL 28/1/2 fol. 4v, 5r, 14v, 15r, amongst other appearances. Bagot also supplied Mary with information about the Cambridge parliament (fol. 29v).

49. Favent's claim is supported by the exchange of cloth of gold brocade mentioned in Henry's accounts in relation to this parliament. See DL 28/1/2 fol. 5v. Interestingly, the divorced wife of Robert de Vere (a granddaughter of Edward III) was also mentioned as having this livery. Thomas of Woodstock had been particularly upset by de Vere setting his royal bride (Thomas's niece) aside.

50. *IH*, p. 103.

51. It was perhaps inspired by the story of St Edward the Confessor's appeal of treason against Earl Godwin as related in the popular *Brut* chronicle. See *Brut*, i, p. 129.

52. Such language seems to have been chosen specifically to play upon Richard's liking for Edward II, using terms which were reminiscent of the man who forced Edward II to abdicate, Roger Mortimer.

53. *PROME*, 1388 February, introduction. All four were sentenced to hang. Berners and Beauchamp were spared the rope on account of their noble birth, Burley on account of his service to the Black Prince.

54. *WC*, p. 329.

55. DL 28/1/2 fol. 4r.

56. A pardon was granted at Henry's request on 15 June at Westminster (*CPR 1386–89*, p. 461). Although this does not prove his presence, his accounts indicate he was still at Westminster on the 9th.

57. DL 28/1/2 fol. 13v. At the end of a section in his accounts dealing with his armour, there is an entry: 'for ten lances bought on account of the lord's crossing over into Scotland, each 20d, [*total*] 16s 8d'. This directly follows a payment 'for twelve lances bought at the time of riding against the duke of Ireland 18s'. See also DL 28/1/2 fol. 15v: 'for carriage of the lord's harness, jugs, tents, lances and other diverse harness from London to Leicester by a cart bought when the lord crossed over towards Scotland 14s 5d'.

58. *Syllabus*, ii, p. 515; DL 28/1/2 fol. 5r.

59. *Froissart*, ii, p. 571.

60. Following on from the earlier tentative reconstruction of Henry's itinerary in 1387–8, it is probable that his journey north to fight the Scots began before he knew about the summons to the Cambridge parliament, which was issued on 28 July. Therefore he had probably left London by the time of Richard's order on 13 August to the chancellor of the duchy of Lancaster to order the people of the duchy to meet the king to ride against the Scots. Henry seems to have travelled from London to Leicester (fol. 15v) and got as far as Lenton in Nottinghamshire, where he bought two horses (fol. 17v), but there is no evidence that he travelled any further. He probably returned via Leicester and Coventry (fol. 8v) to Kenilworth (fol. 6v, 17r) prior to going to the Cambridge parliament which started on 9 September and which he seems to have attended in part at least (*CPR 1385–89*, p. 510; C 53/162 no. 15).

61. See previous note (for Kenilworth) and Wylie, iv, p. 159 (for Melton). See also Appendix Six.

62. Tuck, 'Cambridge Parliament', esp. p. 233.

63. DL 28/1/3 fol. 14v. Henry's accounts have many references to the Lancastrian 'esses' collar, including some very particular descriptions which demonstrate that Henry was using the livery collar during Richard's reign. See Appendix Seven.

64. 12 Richard II, cap. 13.

65. The parliament started on 9 September and lasted until 17 October. If Henry was there for the duration, it raises the question of when his son John was conceived, considering he was born on 20 June 1389 (implying conception around 27 September 1388). Henry was probably at Cambridge on 28 September, as that day a man was pardoned at his request (*CPR 1385–89*, p. 510). He may have turned up late as a result of his illness that summer. Mary was at Kenilworth on 16 September (DL 28/1/2 fol. 29r), about seventy-five miles or three days ride from Cambridge. She seems not to have travelled to Cambridge with Henry, for she gave a servant of William Bagot 6s 8d for bringing her news of the parliament. Thus if Henry did not arrive until the 23rd, he could have been at Kenilworth until the 20th, and his son be only a week overdue. Such tardiness would not have been very unusual: Bishop Fordham was still on his way to parliament on the 27th (Tuck, 'Cambridge Parliament', p. 232). However, this suggestion does not entirely solve the problem of when Henry attended, for he supposedly witnessed a charter at Cambridge on 16 October (C 53/162 no. 15) and yet granted two charters of his own at Kenilworth on 17 and 18 October (*CPR 1396–99*, pp. 122, 547). Taking this problem in conjunction with the conception problem, it is more likely that the baby was premature, and that the charter was actually witnessed by Henry sometime earlier in the Cambridge parliament and not enrolled until 16 October, by which time he had returned to Kenilworth.

66. The earls of Arundel and Warwick both witnessed a charter granted at Westminster on 18 November (C 53/162 no. 25). Six days later a pardon for manslaughter was granted at Henry's request to his clerk, William Loveney (*CPR 1385–89*, p. 531). The latter request could have been communicated by letter, but it also might indicate his presence. Normally such grants were made when Henry was present.

67. Tuck, pp. 136–7.

68. *CCR 1385–89*, p. 571.

69. *LC*, p. 52.

70. Saul, p. 203.

71. *CCR 1385–8*, p. 676; Saul, p. 203; *LC*, p. 52. It met in the Marcolf Chamber.

72. Henry did not witness the charter of 28 May at Westminster (C 53/162 no. 17). He was back at Kenilworth by 12 June (*CPR 1396–99*, p. 518).

73. *PROME*, 1397 September, part 1, item 53 shows Richard never forgave Henry for Radcot Bridge. Henry's response in the Record and Process acknowledged this lack of reconciliation.

4: Iron Wars

1. Henry was still at Kenilworth on 1 July (*CPR 1396–99*, p. 122). He was at Clarendon on 13 September for a council meeting (*PC*, p. 11) and at Westminster on

14 November (C 53/162 nos 3, 10 & 11). There is no direct evidence that Henry rode to join John but it would have been usual and respectful.

2. Goodman, *John of Gaunt*, p. 144.

3. Both Henry and his father attended the meeting of the privy council at Reading on 10 December 1389. See *PC*, p. 17.

4. Richard's request to Jagiello of Poland to grant Henry safe-conduct was dated January 1390. See du Boulay, 'Expeditions to Prussia', p. 155.

5. Jean le Maingre (1366–1421) was the second to bear this nickname. His father – also Jean le Maingre – had borne it at the time of Edward III's 1355 campaign. See *PK*, p. 315.

6. *Foedera*, vii, pp. 665–6.

7. This is the description in Moranville (ed.), *Chronographia*, pp. 97–100. Froissart, who describes each set of strokes, or courses, in minute detail, states that each of the three champions had his own war target, but Froissart is mistaken as to dates and many other events in relation to this tournament.

8. From his poetic description of the jousts taking place in May – not March – it is clear that Froissart was not there himself, but was using a source which had mistakenly copied *Martii* for *Maii*.

9. Froissart gives the same names for the first day's joust, on Monday 21 March, only differing in that his source mistakenly names Peter Shirbourne, not Thomas Swinburn. Swinburn was shortly afterwards given custody of Guines Castle (E 101/69/1/282).

10. Froissart and the Saint-Denis chronicler differ on the number and names of the participants. They have six in common: Thomas Messendon, Thomas Balquet, John Lancaster, Thomas Talbot, Thomas Clifton and Nicholas Cliston/Clinton [*recte*: Clifton] (although Froissart mistakenly has John Talbot instead of Thomas and William Clifton instead of Thomas). In addition, Saint-Denis names Thomas Querry, Nicholas Saton [*recte*: St John?], William Heron [*recte*: Gerard Heron?] and William Stadon. Froissart names instead William Seimort [Seymour], Godfrey de Seca, John Bolton and two squires, 'Navarton' and 'Sequaqueton'.

11. The Saint-Denis chronicler names thirteen; Froissart names eight of these and adds three others.

12. The Saint-Denis chronicler names seven; Froissart names three of these and adds six others.

13. The anonymous poem 'The Jousts of St Inglevert', printed in Lettenhove's edition of Froissart's chronicles, agrees that Henry's joust was towards the end of the tournament but states that it took place on Wednesday 16 April (Tuck, 'Henry IV and chivalry', p. 57). However, in 1390, 16 April fell on a Saturday, so this chronology was probably drawn up in a different year, with poetic effect in mind, and is not reliable. The date here is inferred from the Saint-Denis chronicle.

14. Sarcasm seems to have been a common form of wit in the fourteenth century. Edward II as a young man had written letters to his French relations relating how he would give them a pack of slow hounds 'who can well catch a hare if they find it asleep, for we know that you take delight in lazy hounds'. Similarly, Roger Mortimer had made a sarcastic joke to the earl of Lancaster in 1328: when accused of impoverishing the realm he had replied that if Lancaster knew how to enrich them, he would be welcome at court. See Mortimer, *Greatest Traitor*, p. 214.

15. *Expeditions*, p. 34. As for the Lord de Saimpy taking no further part, this is implied by the two other knights alone taking on challengers after Henry's company met them.

16. Saint-Denis is the source for this compliment. The date adopted here contradicts most writers on the subject. The jousting did not begin on 1 March, as some chronicles state, but on 21 March. Obviously it went on beyond the end of the month. If the tournament actually lasted 'thirty days', however, the first day was the first of three days of ceremonies and feasts, i.e. 18 March (according to Saint-Denis). Wednesday 13 April was the twenty-seventh day. Froissart (although his source left after the first four days) states that the English departed from Calais on a Saturday. The Saturday after the 13th would have indeed been the thirtieth day of the tournament. Henry would have had an obligation to be at Windsor for the Order of the Garter feast on 23 April, and so probably did not leave any later than this. The Saint-Denis chronicler notes Ralph Rochford, Thomas Toty and John Dalyngrigge – all esquires in Henry's service in 1390 – jousted on the last day of the tournament, and so Henry probably remained for the duration.

17. Moranville (ed.), *Chronographia*, pp. 97–100.

18. *Expeditions*, p. 1. His accounts and other documents at this time normally only name him as earl of Derby. The writ ordering their auditing (*ibid.*, p. 2) also has all four titles, so it was probably in regular use by 1390.

19. Du Boulay, 'Expeditions to Prussia', p. 162. Richard had certainly tried to restrict some of those taking part in the St Inglevert jousts from going on crusade. See *Foedera*, vii, pp. 665–6.

20. The situation was a complicated one, and never static. For a background on the shifting alliances see du Boulay, 'Expeditions to Prussia', pp. 156–60, especially p. 158, where the question of whether this was really a crusade is discussed.

21. Details of the participants in the Prussian crusades have been drawn from Keen, 'Chaucer's Knight', pp. 50–56; *LC*, p. 2.

22. C 53/162 no. 2. The date conflicts with *Expeditions*, xxxv and xlii, but the charter witness list in this case is a more reliable guide than Toulmin Smith's estimate.

23. *Expeditions*, p. 19.

24. *Expeditions*, pp. 21–2.

25. *PK*, p. 346.

26. For example, in August 1403 his cousin the duke of York gave him a present of pike, bream and tench; that same year he gave him another present of '6 fresh salmon and 12 bream'. Wylie, iv, p. 206.

27. *Expeditions*, pp. 19–20.

28. There is no indication that his family came 'to see him off'. But he and Mary did give alms together at Lincoln, and the amounts they gave were large for oblations: 10s and 6s 8d. Furthermore these payments appear just after those for getting the ship ready. See *Expeditions*, p. 27.

29. The three hundred men is often quoted and disputed. It is probably not an over-estimate, if one takes into consideration menial servants and also the number of sailors on the boat.

30. According to the Saint-Denis chronicler, Thomas Swynford fought with Henry in his party; Peter Bucton and Richard Dancaster took part on the next day of jousting, and Thomas Toty, John Dalyngrigge and Robert Rochford took part on

the last day. It seems likely that John Clifton and Roger Langford had also taken part in the jousts, as suggested by the chronicler's references to John Claquefort (which appears as 'Cliston' in Froissart) and Roger Long.

31. Henry had his chess board brought to him on the *reyse*. See *Expeditions*, p. 49. For his gambling with dice, see *ibid.*, pp. 28, 31, 35, 107, 109, 110, 115. For his backgammon see pp. 113, 178, 264. For *jeu de paume*, see *ibid.*, p. 263.

32. *Expeditions*, p. 164.

33. Du Boulay describes this as mainly 'an archer victory' but there were few recorded archers in the English force. Having said that, at Vilnius there was an English 'gunner-archer', so it seems that some English archers and gunners were not on Henry's payroll. This might explain why the sources state that Henry had three hundred men with him and yet many fewer appear in his accounts. On this matter see *Expeditions*, xliv.

34. Henry later rewarded an English esquire for first planting the flag above Vilnius. See du Boulay, 'Expeditions to Prussia', pp. 164–5; *Expeditions*, p. 105.

35. *WC*, p. 449.

36. Goodman, *John of Gaunt*, p. 148. One of the men, Thomas Rempston, later served in Henry's retinue, so he was at least half-successful, if not wholly so.

37. Wylie, iv, p. 153.

38. *Expeditions*, p. 107. Clearly Mary was responsible for naming the boy, as she not only gave him her father's name, but Henry's Prussian accounts note he was called Humphrey.

39. The famous declaration by Henry in 1407 that 'I too am a child of Prussia' was made to Prussian envoys and may have been a diplomatic nicety. Even so it supports the view here. See du Boulay, 'Expeditions to Prussia', p. 153.

40. *Expeditions*, p. 108. Postage is one of the few services which is actually cheaper in monetary terms today than it was in the fourteenth century.

41. For instance, Henry paid rewards of twenty shillings to 'diverse French musicians' who played for him on 10 November. *Expeditions*, p. 107.

42. *Expeditions*, p. 114 (one mark) and p. 115 (half a Prussian mark, roughly 3s 2d, according to the calculations directly beneath this entry) were paid to Hans.

43. An earlier (1372) reference to imported 'beer' (as opposed to ale) appears in A. H. Thomas (ed.), *Plea and Memoranda Rolls 1364–1381* (Cambridge, 1929), p. 147. For references to Henry buying continental 'beer' as well as English ale ('*servisia*') see *Expeditions*, p. 85.

44. Kirby, p. 33.

45. *Expeditions*, p. 111.

46. *Expeditions*, p. 113.

47. *Expeditions*, p. 116.

48. DL 28/1/3 fol. 23r. See du Boulay, 'Expeditions to Prussia', p. 170.

49. He landed at Hull by 30 April, when his war account ends.

50. See for example du Boulay, 'Expeditions to Prussia', p. 167, where this question is addressed.

51. *WC*, pp. 445–9.

52. For the lances see DL 28/1/3 fol. 11v; for the date see *ibid.*, fol. 16v. This was to take place at an as yet unidentified place, *Brembeltee*.

53. Henry was at London on 7 July, as shown by his giving a gift there (DL 28/1/3

fol. 20v). The Kennington tournament may have been on 10 July, as on or about that day the king gave him two pieces of armour.

54. DL 28/1/3 fol. 18r.
55. DL 28/1/3 fol. 17v.
56. *WC*, pp. 475, 479, 483–5; *SAC*, p. 913.
57. DL 28/1/3 fol. 20v (*lewt* and *fithele*).
58. DL 28/1/3 fol. 17v. The present included a hundred 'koynes'.
59. *WC*, pp. 477; *SAC*, p. 913.
60. *PROME*, 1391 November, introduction.
61. On 3 December his horses were led to Hertford. See DL 28/1/3 fol. 16v.

5: As Far as to the Sepulchre of Christ

1. *SAC*, p. 917.
2. DL 28/1/3 fol. 20v.
3. DL 28/1/3 fol. 20v. He gave a mark each to two of John's minstrels, and to two of his own minstrels.
4. Although the new calendar year did not start until 25 March, and the new regnal year not until 22 June, it was traditional for lords and ladies to exchange presents on 1 January and call them New Year gifts.
5. DL 28/1/3 fol. 16r.
6. DL 28/1/3 fol. 15v. It should be noted that Thomas, duke of Gloucester, also used the swan as a livery badge, it being used in right of the descendants of the Bohun family.
7. DL 28/1/3 fol. 19r. If the amounts he paid as rewards to the men who delivered these presents is an indication of the esteem in which he held the giver and their present, it is noticeable that Richard's messenger received only one mark (13s 4d) while the queen's received £1, and so did the duchess of Lancaster's and the countess of Hereford's valets. His father's messenger, Master Ludvig the goldsmith, received £2. To the duke and duchess of Gloucester's and Thomas Mowbray's valets he gave a mark each, and to his sister's half a mark.
8. *King's Council*, p. 493.
9. *WC*, p. 485; *King's Council*, pp. 494–5.
10. Armitage-Smith, p. 346; *Froissart*, ii, p. 516; Goodman, *John of Gaunt*, p. 150. It should be remembered that Henry was not an official member of this embassy.
11. See *Froissart*, ii, p. 518, for the full extent of these precise arrangements.
12. Henry sent ahead to his London wardrobe to send him six horses at Rochester on 18 April, so he had returned by then. DL 28/1/3 fol. 16v–17r.
13. After returning from Calais, Henry attended the Order of the Garter festivities at Windsor on 23 April, then returned to London where he was on 10 May (DL 28/1/3 fol. 18v, 20v). I have not found any definitive evidence that he was at Stamford, but it is likely in view of his father's presence, and the fact that so many gentry were summoned. See *WC*, pp. 489–91.
14. *WC*, pp. 493–5.
15. See for example the list of creditors in DL 28/1/3 fol. 21v.
16. *Expeditions*, xlvii.
17. *Expeditions*, p. 161.

18. Du Boulay, 'Expeditions to Prussia', p. 167, states that they met at Danzig but does not cite the source, and I cannot find this in the accounts. The payment of £400 was made at Königsberg.

19. They were the daughters of Blanche de Valois, daughter of Charles de Valois, whose half-brother Philip de Valois was Henry's great-great-grandfather.

20. *Expeditions*, pp. 187–8, 194, 260.

21. It was while he was at Prague that he marked the anniversary of the death of Thomas, Lord Clifford, who had died on 4 October 1391 on an island in the Mediterranean on his way to Jerusalem. This may have inspired Henry's journey, not least because he also gave alms in memory of Thomas when at Rhodes, later on the expedition. See *Expeditions*, pp. 275, 312; *WC*, p. 480.

22. In *Expeditions*, lix, Toulmin Smith mentions that Henry received a pair of leggings embroidered with the king's livery; when he had them repaired the following year, it was noted that they were a gift from the king. See DL 28/1/5 fol. 15v.

23. *Expeditions*, p. 207.

24. *Calendar of State Papers and Manuscripts Relating to English Affairs Existing in the Archives and Collections of Venice . . . 1202–1509* (1864), p. 33.

25. *IH*, p. 105. Capgrave states that the doge went with him to Jerusalem. This is not correct.

26. This estimate is based on the presumption that they stopped to pray at Zara principally because it was Christmas Day. The approximate 250-mile stages on the outgoing journey are marked by stops on Vis, Corfu, the Peloponnese, Rhodes, Cyprus and Jaffa. They were eighty-eight days away from Venice, and ten of these were spent in the Holy Land. Probably a few more were spent on Cyprus and Rhodes. This leaves about seventy sailing days, or about five weeks in each direction. Hence the estimate of stopping every six days. It should be noted that they stopped more frequently on the way back. Also it should be noted that it is not clear that they stopped at Cyprus on the way out; Toulmin Smith thought they did not. The anonymous *Informacion for pylgrymes*, printed by Wynkyn de Worde in 1500 but written in about 1430, states that John Moreson sailed straight from Rhodes to Jaffa.

27. *RHL*, i, p. 422.

28. Tuck suggests that they may have travelled by donkeys but no payment for donkeys appears in his accounts. See Tuck, 'Henry IV and Chivalry', p. 61.

29. This and subsequent material about the medieval pilgrimages in the Holy Land is from the anonymous medieval printed book, *Informacion for pylgrymes* (unpaginated).

30. DL 28/1/4 fol. 18r.

31. *Expeditions*, lxvii.

32. *Expeditions*, p. 234. Sir Nicholas Harris Nicolas, 'Observations of the Origin and History of the Badge and Mottoes of Edward Prince of Wales', *Archaeologia*, 31 (1846), p. 365, mentions some armorial bearings at Venice which include the ostrich feathers, swan badge, esses livery collar and a hart. These are supposed to represent Thomas Mowbray, who died in Venice in 1399. However, although the esses livery collar and ostrich feathers might have belonged to either man, the swan was Henry's personal badge and the hart was that of his wife. It is possible that this relates to arms left by Henry. Henry's arms were placed in St Mark's by

Mowbray Herald. Henry also bought collars while in Venice (*Expeditions*, lxviii, p. 280).

33. Wylie, iv, p. 128.

34. Hinds (ed.), *State Papers . . . Milan*, i, p. 2.

6: Curst Melancholy

1. *SAC*, p. 945. Although Walsingham states that the king did nothing, he did send the earl of Huntingdon and Sir John Stanley to threaten the insurgents with forfeiture if they created trouble. See Goodman, *John of Gaunt*, p. 153. However, this was a very weak response. See Saul, pp. 219–20.

2. There are no indications as to Henry's whereabouts in his own accounts; hence it would appear that he left his own household and joined that of his father soon after arriving in London.

3. *PROME*, 1394 January, item 20. Goodman, *John of Gaunt*, p. 153, states that Talbot was captured prior to this interrogation, which took place some time before the January 1394 parliament, but he was still at large at the time of the parliament, as Richard gave orders for him to be apprehended. See Goodman, *John of Gaunt*, p. 172, n. 46, for John of Gaunt's whereabouts. A detailed note of proceedings against Talbot appears in Tuck, p. 167, n. 3.

4. John was at Beverley in Yorkshire on 28 August; Henry was at Peterborough on 2 September. See Goodman, *John of Gaunt*, p. 172, n. 46; DL 28/1/5 fol. 16v. He was at Peterborough again on 12 December (*CPR 1396–99*, p. 501), and probably had simply stayed with Mary there during the intervening period.

5. DL 28/1/4 fol. 14v–15r. For Thomas Beaufort being equipped at Henry's expense, see *ibid.*, fol. 14v. The date of the Hertford tournament is given on fol. 16v.

6. DL 28/1/4 fol. 20v.

7. DL 28/1/4 fol. 18v.

8. He was still there on 12 January: *CPR 1396–99*, p. 469.

9. Goodman, *John of Gaunt*, p. 153, quoting DL 28/1/4.

10. DL 28/1/4 fol. 19v.

11. For this argument, see *SAC*, p. 957; *PROME*, 1394 January, introduction and item 11. Also see *Froissart*, ii, p. 495, where the disagreement between Gloucester and Arundel against John over France is mentioned, although it needs to be remembered that Gloucester was one of John's negotiators in 1393, and so can hardly have been as firmly against the peace deal as Froissart suggests.

12. Goodman, *John of Gaunt*, p. 153; Tuck, p. 169.

13. This had been the case in Edward III's reign even when that meant appointing an infant, as had happened in 1338 (when the keeper, Edward of Woodstock, was only eight), and in 1345 (when Lionel of Antwerp was only six), and in 1359 (when Thomas of Woodstock was only four).

14. *CCR 1392–96*, p. 325; *LK*, p. 40.

15. *LC*, p. 156. Henry gave the collar after his return in 1393; it is shown on Gower's tomb effigy.

16. It is not certain that Henry returned to Hertford; however as that is where his wife was and where his father returned to (Armitage-Smith, p. 448), it is likely.

17. Goodman, *John of Gaunt*, p. 154; Armitage-Smith, p. 429.

18. Armitage-Smith, p. 449; Goodman, *John of Gaunt*, p. 155.

19. There is considerable doubt about the date of Mary's death, and all we can say for certain is that she died in June or very early July 1394. *ODNB* states (under 'Henry IV') that Mary died 'perhaps on 4 July, the date her anniversary was celebrated in 1406'. This is supported by *WC*, p. 521, which states that 'about the beginning of July the countess of Derby died in childbed and was buried at Leicester'. However, Knighton (*KC*, p. 551) records that she was buried on Monday 6 July, the Monday being supported by Walsingham (*SAC*, p. 961), and this is surely too soon after the 4th for her to have died that day. Although the Westminster chronicler states that Anne died on 7 June and was buried on the 9th – dates followed by Goodman in his *John of Gaunt* (p. 155) – Anne was actually buried on 3 August, as noted by the editors of the *WC*, p. 520, n. 3). *HBC* states that Mary died on '? 4 June', but does not explain why this date has been chosen. It may be that the editors guessed that the 4 July date was an error for 4 June, which would allow enough time for the funeral preparations. If so, this would explain why Walsingham mentions Mary's death after Constanza's and before Anne's.

20. It is tempting to say that his naming his first daughter after the mother he had never known says much for his regard for her, despite the tragedy of her death. However, it is impossible to be certain about this. The English royal family, like several medieval families, continued naming traditions in which a lord's eldest daughter was named after his mother and his second daughter after one of his grandmothers. John had done this in naming his eldest daughter Philippa and his second daughter Elizabeth; Henry followed the same pattern.

21. *ODNB*, under 'Henry IV'.

22. See *Issues*, p. 321, for the likeness commissioned by Henry V. Richard's commission to the coppersmiths was dated on 24 April 1395. He had shortly before contracted (on 1 April) the masons Henry Yevele and Stephen Lote to make the tomb at Westminster for his wife Anne (*Syllabus*, ii, p. 527). Payment to Yevele and Lote was made on 14 July 1397 (*Issues*, p. 264).

23. Goodman, *John of Gaunt*, p. 155.

24. This might have been a coincidence, but in a letter in which John protested his honesty and loyalty to the king in connection with the royal estate, and coming so soon after John requested that Henry be recognised as the heir, it may well be that the succession was the key matter discussed.

25. By this time the earls of March were so far behind in the order of succession – habitually given an inferior status to Henry – that they hardly featured on the magnates' map of the succession. Every potential beneficiary of Edward III's entail was given precedence over the Mortimers. See 'Succession', p. 330.

26. Tuck, p. 166; Goodman, *John of Gaunt*, p. 155.

27. *Royal Household*, p. 392.

28. *PROME*, 1394 January, item 20; Tuck, p. 167, n. 3, which details his arrest and escape.

29. *LC*, p. 155.

30. *LK*, p. 40.

31. *ODNB*, under 'Henry IV'.

32. *PROME*, 1395 January, introduction.

33. Cronin, 'Twelve Conclusions', pp. 292–304; *PC*, p. 59.

34. He was still in London at the beginning of April. C 53/165 nos 4–5 (dated 30 March and 1 April respectively).

35. DL 28/1/5 fol. 8r. Those who had accompanied him on his crusade who were still with him were John Brother, Robert Crakyll, William Bingley and Master John Nakerer (*Expeditions*, pp. 112, 133, 137, 141–2). The new musicians were John Alayn, piper, John Aleyn, trumpeter, and Gilbert Waferer.

36. DL 28/1/5 fol. 3r (robe); 26v (gift).

37. F. J. Furnivall (ed.), *The Babees Boke* (1868), p. 180.

38. DL 28/1/5 fol. 28v; see also Appendix One. He gave alms and clothes to twenty-nine paupers on this occasion.

39. The date Henry sent the messenger was 18 March. See DL 28/1/5 fol. 27r.

40. DL 28/1/5 fol. 9r, 22r–v, 27v, 29r. This suggests she was in her twenty-fourth year at the time of her death, as Henry's donation to twenty-nine paupers on Maundy Thursday suggests this accountant (or Henry) calculated age as of next birthday.

41. DL 28/1/5 fol. 29r. The curtains are mentioned on fol. 12r. They were taken to Leicester, as shown by a reference on fol. 27v.

42. DL 28/1/5 fol. 29r. The earliest entry in the *OED* to a close-stool is 1410.

43. *King's Council*, p. 504; for the barge, see DL 28/1/5 fol. 28r.

44. *King's Council*, pp. 135–7, 504–5; *Froissart*, ii, pp. 572–7.

45. C 53/165 nos 3 and 10.

46. *CCR 1392–96*, p. 448.

47. DL 28/1/5 fol. 27v. The journey took him three weeks. Henry's saddle was repaired while at Plympton. See *ibid.*, fol. 22v.

48. *CPR 1396–99*, p. 542.

49. For his presence in Exeter, see DL 28/1/5 fol. 27v. The messenger was on the road for thirteen days and left London on 24 October. Henry was probably in London from 28 November to 23 December, during which time he was paying his London bargemen (fol. 28r). Cotton and a urinal were bought for him in London on 4 December (fol. 30r).

50. Henry ordered new lances to be bought for the joust at Christmas at Hertford. DL 28/1/5 fol. 22v. There are fewer payments than usual in this account.

51. *HA*, ii, p. 219. Although Walsingham mentions that Richard held Christmas at Langley, and that this was where he met John, it was not necessarily at Christmas that the meeting took place. Richard stayed at King's Langley until 7 January. See Saul, p. 473.

52. Goodman, *John of Gaunt*, p. 156.

53. See the articles on *ODNB* (under 'John of Gaunt', 'Swynford, Katherine'), and Goodman, *Katherine Swynford*.

54. Goodman, *John of Gaunt*, p. 156.

55. Goodman, *John of Gaunt*, p. 157.

56. C 53/166 nos 4 & 5.

57. As stated in *Froissart*, ii, p. 610.

58. This was when he witnessed a royal charter at Westminster. C 53/166 no. 6.

59. Wylie, quoting Michael Ducas, *Historia Byzantina* (1649), states that Henry was present at Nicopolis, in command of 1,000 archers. There is no corroboration of this, however. Froissart does not mention Henry's participation on the Nicopolis Crusade, and nor is there any reference in his accounts. In addition, he could not have fought

on 25 September at Nicopolis (in modern Bulgaria, about seventy-five miles from Bucharest) and been at Calais in early October. His accounts mention the purchase of medicines for him early in 1396, which might more correctly explain his absence from court. See Wylie, i, pp. 6, 157; iv, p. 171.

60. Fier-a-Bras de Vertain was given a grant for life of forty marks a year on 7 July 1396. Presuming that this precedes his visiting Henry, it is reasonable to connect Henry's appearance at court on the 25th with the king's refusal (at the request of John of Gaunt) to allow Henry to depart. See *Froissart*, ii, p. 610; *CPR 1396–99*, p. 12.

7: By Envy's Hand and Murder's Bloody Axe

1. *Froissart*, ii, p. 618. For Henry's expenses in Calais, see DL 28/1/9 fol. 4r–8v.
2. Saul, p. 229. There is a detailed description of the meeting in *Annales*, pp. 188–94.
3. *Froissart*, ii, p. 618; DL 28/1/9 fol. 4r (for Henry at Saint-Omer).
4. He was at Dover Castle on 15 November. *CCR 1396–99*, p. 73.
5. DL 28/1/9 fol. 5r (hay bought for his horses at Dartford, 19 November).
6. DL 28/1/9 fol. 13v.
7. DL 28/1/9 fol. 7v.
8. For example, the gifts of velvet from the count of Virtue in DL 28/1/5 fol. 9r–v (for the year 1395–6).
9. Hinds (ed.), *State Papers . . . Milan*, i, p. 2. This relates to Henry before his exile. Negotiations probably began in late 1397, as the marriage was a rumour circulating in Siena in early March 1398. See Bueno de Mesquita, 'Foreign Policy', pp. 634–5.
10. *Froissart*, ii, pp. 604–7.
11. On 2 January 1397, Thomas Mowbray and Thomas Holland were preparing a force of 150 lances and 500 archers to help the French; the earl of Huntingdon was also preparing to go. Bueno de Mesquita, 'Foreign Policy', pp. 628–9.
12. *PROME*, January 1397, item 10.
13. For Richard's mental state, see Saul, especially chapter 17 (and pp. 459–60 for the identification of his 'narcissism'), and Steel, *Richard II*. Alison McHardy comments on both of these views in her 'Personal Portrait', and adds further very interesting observations. For a view on how the idea of Richard's insanity arose, see Stow, 'Stubbs, Steel and Richard II'.
14. Bueno de Mesquita, 'Foreign Policy', pp. 630–32; *Annales*, p. 199.
15. The Evesham chronicler, in *CR*, p. 54.
16. The earliest reference yet noticed of Edward being described as 'the king's brother' appears in his commission to negotiate with France dated 27 February 1397 (*Syllabus*, p. 530). Thereafter he is usually so described in official documents, including patent letters and royal charters. He is described as 'our very dear brother' in C 53/167 nos 5–10 (23 April, 1 May and 9 May 1399), 16–17 (13 and 24 April 1398). This is also the way he is named in Richard's will. See *Royal Wills*, pp. 196, 199.
17. For adoptive brotherhood in medieval England, see Pierre Chaplais, *Piers Gaveston: Edward II's Adoptive Brother* (Oxford, 1994), pp. 6–22.
18. For instance Alison McHardy states that it is 'notable' that Robert de Vere 'had no successor' as Richard's favourite, ignoring this adoption of Rutland. See

McHardy, 'Personal Portrait', p. 30. The adoption is also ignored by the author of the *ODNB* article on Edward and the second edition of *CP*, and by most other writers on the subject of Richard II's life.

19. DL 28/1/9 fol. 8r, DL 28/1/9 fol. 21v (Leicester, March 1397); DL 28/1/6 fol. 25v, DL 28/1/9 fol. 12r, 16r (Tutbury, April 1397). The foregoing are tentative, based on payments for household expenses which indicate his presence, such as large amounts of expensive fish being delivered to Tutbury between 30 March and 14 April (DL 28/1/9 fol. 21v). He was at Leicester on 1 May 1397 (*CPR 1396–99*, p. 122). He was still in London on 7 March (DL 28/1/6 fol. 30v).

20. The commission to negotiate a marriage between Henry and Navarre was dated 28 February 1397. *Syllabus*, p. 530.

21. DL 28/1/9 fol. 15r.

22. The story given in *Traïson* – that Gloucester and Arundel were arrested following a plot staged with Henry, Warwick and Mowbray, Thomas Arundel, the abbot of St Albans (Thomas of Woodstock's godfather) and the prior of Westminster – is a muddled version of the events of 1387 rehashed in order to explain why Richard took action against these lords in 1397. Richard's accusations in 1397 specifically refer to the events of 1387–8. In addition, by 1397, the abbot of St Albans was dead. In addition to a sound debunking of this story in Tuck, pp. 184–6, it is worth noting that the plot is supposed to have been concocted at Arundel, and Henry is said to have been present. It is difficult to find a space in his itinerary to attend a meeting at Arundel. Following the parliament of January 1397 he travelled north and remained in the Midlands until June, when he was at Hertford, and two weeks later he was with Richard at Westminster. He remained with the king for a month and travelled back again to the Midlands until the time of parliament. He could at some point have made a dash to Arundel but there are no signs of such a journey in his accounts, nor of messengers being sent to Arundel.

23. C 53/167 no. 25 (5 July). John Bernard and Philip Young were paid wages by Henry when they were with him in the king's household from 6 July to 1 August. At 3d per day each, the payment of 13s 6d suggests they were in constant attendance at that time. Similarly Thomas Young and John Aderstone were with Henry in the king's household (at wages of 4d per day between them) for twenty-seven days (as they received 9s). Thomas Ferro was with Henry in the king's household from 14 July to 10 August; John Waurin from 6 July to 1 August. See DL 28/1/9 fol. 16r.

24. Saul, p. 367.

25. Sharpe, *City of London, Letter-Book H*, p. 437.

26. DL 28/1/9 fol. 20v. Richard was at Nottingham on 5 July (Saul, p. 473), having probably just arrived there. He was at Lutterworth on 14 August. For the assembly see Goodman, *John of Gaunt*, p. 159.

27. *CPR 1396–99*, p. 191.

28. *CPR 1396–99*, p. 192.

29. There were 312 royal archers in Richard's personal bodyguard, according to Tuck, p. 187, quoting E 159/175 r. 9 and E 101/42/10. For his raising of two thousand archers in Cheshire, see *ibid.*, p. 186. For chroniclers' accounts of the presence of two thousand archers see *CR*, p. 57. The combined forces of the king, John, Edmund and Henry might account for Usk's statement that there were four thousand archers present.

30. For the date of the announcement, see Tait, 'Did Richard II Murder the Duke of Gloucester?', pp. 208–10; Wright, 'Death of the Duke of Gloucester', p. 277. *Gregory's Chronicle* – a London chronicle – placing the date of death 'around Bartholomewtide' (25 August) is an indication of when the news was circulated in London.

31. The duke's death was certainly announced while he was still alive. This is evident in the confession of a witness to his murder, John Hall, and it is supported by the fact that Richard sent writs to enquire into the estates of the late duke of Gloucester on 7 September, but his confession was made in Calais on 8 September. See *PROME*, 1399 September, item 92 (8 September); *CFR 1391–99*, p. 224 (7 September); Wright, 'Richard II and the death of the duke of Gloucester', pp. 276–7.

32. *PROME*, 1397 September, item 1; *Vita*, p. 138. The biblical quotation is from Ezekiel, chapter 37, verse 22.

33. Tuck, p. 190.

34. *CR*, p. 56.

35. The order of events followed here is that from the monk of Evesham's chronicle. This contradicts the order of the parliament rolls, but makes better sense. See *CR*, p. 57; *PROME*, 1397 September: introduction.

36. That this was choreographed in advance is made very likely by the fact that Bussy had been with the king throughout that summer, and had been one of the knights present at the arrest of Thomas of Woodstock.

37. The parliament rolls note only four, but the impeachment of Mortimer and Cobham followed.

38. *PROME*, 1399 September: appendix, quoting A. H. Thomas & I. D. Thornley (eds), *The Great Chronicle of London* (1938), pp. 76–7.

39. *CR*, pp. 54–60.

40. *PROME*, 1397 September, appendix. This was probably a private vendetta, but Hawkeston was pardoned by Richard in October 1398 and continued to serve and be protected by Richard, regardless of this act of murder.

8: The Breath of Kings

1. DL 28/1/6 fol. 22v.

2. I am very grateful to Dr Margaret Pelling for the information about bezoar stones.

3. *PROME*, 1397 September, item 53.

4. This plot has been seen as doubtful by some historians, partly because of the creation of Henry as duke of Hereford has inclined them to believe that Henry was in favour in 1397 (Tuck, pp. 184–5), and partly because of the unlikelihood that Thomas Holland, duke of Surrey, should seek to encompass the destruction of his uncle John Holland, duke of Exeter, or that William Scrope should try to plot against his erstwhile friend, John of Gaunt (Goodman, *John of Gaunt*, p. 162). As has been shown in the main text, even the award of a dukedom is not good evidence of favour under the dissembling Richard. With regard to the other objections, the disinheritance of the Lancastrians through the reversal of the pardon against Thomas of Lancaster goes some way to bolster Henry's claim. Wiltshire and Salisbury (two of the antagonists) were not of Lancastrian descent

but most of the victims were. John Holland's wife was, being Henry's sister. So too was Thomas Mowbray. John Beaufort was inclined to support the Lancastrians, being Henry's half-brother. William Scrope – newly raised to an earldom – simply, gratefully and sycophantically did what he thought the king wanted him to do, regardless of his earlier friendship with John. So did Surrey. Richard's cousin and adopted brother, Edward, duke of Aumale, is the one whose position is not clear. He was not of Lancastrian descent, and in 1399 Bagot claimed at his trial that Edward had expressed a wish for Henry's destruction. His inclusion amongst the intended victims is as yet unexplained.

5. Given-Wilson, 'Richard II, Edward II', p. 563. It is not clear when Henry told John of the conversation with Mowbray. On 19 November, Henry had spent a day with the king at Woodstock; on 12 December he was at Peterborough (DL 28/1/10 fol. 9r; *CPR 1396–99*, p. 501). It is most likely that he met Mowbray and had this conversation when returning to London in early December. His accounts mention a two-day trip from London to Windsor in December, and such a journey would have taken him through Brentford. He had met his father by Christmas at the latest, for both men were at Leicester on Christmas Eve and Christmas Day (*CPR 1396–99*, pp. 535, 513; Goodman, *John of Gaunt*, p. 161).

6. This was probably at Christmas. Henry and his father were at Leicester, Richard at Coventry, just fourteen miles away. See *CPR 1396–99*, pp. 535, 513; Goodman, *John of Gaunt*, p. 161; Saul, p. 473.

7. *Annales*, p. 219.

8. Given-Wilson, 'Richard II, Edward II', p. 559. This is also mentioned in *Adam Usk*, p. 49.

9. Goodman, *John of Gaunt*, p. 163. Bagot received a livery collar and other gifts from Henry in 1387. See TNA DL 28/1/2 fol. 4v, 5r, 14v, 15r.

10. Goodman, *John of Gaunt*, p. 163; Given-Wilson, 'Richard II, Edward II', p. 559.

11. *CPR 1396–99*, p. 280. This was dated 25 January 1398. It is noticeable that this was granted *before* the session of parliament. It therefore was not covered by the same special protection against revocation which Richard afforded all the Acts of the forthcoming parliament. At the time of granting this pardon Richard may already have been planning to revoke it.

12. *PROME*, 1397 September, item 44.

13. *PROME*, 1397 September, item 54.

14. *Traïson*, p. 142.

15. *CCR 1396–99*, p. 249.

16. Those standing bail are named in *Traïson*, p. 142.

17. *Adam Usk*, pp. 39–41.

18. DL 28/1/6 fol. 40r. Wool was bought for Henry's close-stool at Worcester in March (Richard was there on 3 March). Cotton and urinals, bought for him at Bristol, appear in an entry directly after this one, which probably relates to his being there with the king on 27 March (*CPR 1396–99*, p. 361). Cotton was bought for his close-stool in London on 20 April. For Richard's itinerary, see *Revolution*, p. 128.

19. *Traïson*, p. 147. Henry had prefaced his bill on 30 January with the words 'making protestation to enlarge or reduce it at all times, and as often as I please or as need may be, saving always the substance of my libel' (*PROME*, 1397 September, item 53). Given that he did 'enlarge' his accusation at Windsor, it seems likely that he

already knew in January what he would later say: that Mowbray was responsible for bringing about the death of his uncle, Thomas, duke of Gloucester.

20. *Froissart*, ii, p. 661.

21. *CR*, pp. 103–4. The date originally set was a Monday in August. This was later changed to Monday 16 September.

22. DL 28/1/6 fol. 40r–v. The first instance is spelled *Astirlabr' de laton* and the second *Astirlabl' de laton*. For Richard's astronomical quadrants, see *Revolution*, p. 140.

23. DL 28/1/6 fol. 40v.

24. DL 28/1/6 fol. 41r.

25. DL 28/1/6 fol. 42r.

26. DL 28/1/6 fol. 41r.

27. Brian Robinson, *Silver Pennies and Linen Towels* (1992), p. 28.

28. Given-Wilson, 'Richard II, Edward II', p. 565.

29. *Froissart*, ii, p. 663.

30. DL 28/1/6 fol. 43r.

31. *Froissart*, ii, p. 664.

32. *Revolution*, p. 125; *CPR 1396–99*, p. 499.

33. DL 28/1/10 fol. 20r; DL 28/1/6 fol. 40v (4 & 9 July, London). John was at Rothwell on 17 July (Goodman, *John of Gaunt*, p. 165). Henry's house in Bishopsgate Street appears regularly in his accounts. On this folio there is a payment for a key for the keeper of the close-stools of the lord in this house. He also had a house in Holborn. His wardrobe office was based at Barnard Castle at this time; previously it had been in Coleman Street. For his other houses, see Wylie, iv, p. 140.

34. *CCR 1396–99*, p. 324. Mowbray's gaoler at Windsor was ordered at the same time to release him for the purpose of meeting the king. Mowbray had previously been transferred from Windsor to the office of the king's wardrobe in London, which is probably why Froissart states he was a prisoner in the Tower. He was taken back to Windsor for the Garter ceremonies by Richard, and probably remained there afterwards, until July. See *Revolution*, p. 125.

35. Given-Wilson, 'Richard II, Edward II', p. 566.

36. The description of the duel is taken from *Traïson*, pp. 142–62.

37. *Froissart*, ii, p. 663.

38. Froissart notes the superior arms of Henry over Mowbray. See *Froissart*, ii, p. 663.

39. *Adam Usk*, p. 51; *Traïson*, p. 151.

40. This quotation is a composite of the two versions, one in *Traïson*, pp. 156–8, and the other in *PROME*, 1397 January, part 2, item 11. The latter is written in retrospect and had been slightly modified here for the sake of consistency.

41. There was a precedent for Richard's actions. The first Duke Henry had claimed that Otto, duke of Brunswick, had tried to ambush him while on crusade in 1351–2, and had challenged him to a duel at Cologne. The French king, John II, had tried to reconcile both parties, just as Richard had Henry and Mowbray, but had failed. The duel had then gone ahead, in Paris. But at the last moment, when both Henry and Otto were mounted and about to charge, John decided that the quarrel was of insufficient importance to justify bloodshed, and took the matter into his own hands. Richard had now employed the same strategy to discredit both Henry and Mowbray.

42. Strohm, *Hochon's Arrow*, p. 83, quoting Hardyng.

43. *CPR 1396–99*, p.514; *Traïson*, pp. 158–9. They were at Nuneaton with Richard on the 20th.

44. Kirby, p. 49, Goodman, *John of Gaunt*, p. 165, and *Revolution*, p. 135, all agree with Shakespeare on this point. They might be right, but I have yet to find any evidence of such a commutation. Henry's charges against Richard in 1400 only mention the ten-year period.

45. DL 28/1/6 fol. 36r. Mary had had her Latin primer repaired when in London in 1387 just before Thomas was born.

46. DL 28/1/6 fol. 24r. Henry's present to Richard in this year was a gold tablet with an image of St John the Baptist. St John was one of Richard's favourite saints. See *Revolution*, p. 130.

47. *CPR 1396–99*, p. 425.

48. *Syllabus*, ii, p. 533; *CPR 1396–99*, pp. 469–70, 499, 537.

49. *Froissart*, p. 667.

50. *Revolution*, pp. 123–4.

51. *Revolution*, p. 130; *CR*, p. 31.

52. *LK*, p. 47; *Revolution*, p. 185.

53. Kirby, pp. 49–50.

54. Kirby, p. 49; *Syllabus*, ii, p. 533.

55. *Froissart*, ii, p. 674.

56. *Froissart*, pp. 668–9.

57. Wylie, iv, p. 138.

58. *CR*, p. 106.

59. Froissart notes that she was twice widowed but states that she was not more than twenty-three; she was born in 1367, the same year as Henry.

60. The date of this address is difficult. *Revolution*, p. 137, suggests it might have been an added task of Salisbury's mission at the end of October. Creton gives the date as Christmas. See *Creton*, p. 171.

61. *Froissart*, ii, p. 680.

62. Although Froissart states that the marriage proposal postdates the death of John of Gaunt, the earl of Salisbury's authority to go to Paris dates from late October (*Revolution*, p. 137; *Syllabus*, ii, p. 533). It also makes sense chronologically if Henry made plans to leave France after his marriage plans had collapsed; it would be strange if he was planning to leave France before concluding the arrangements.

63. Froissart states the letter was carried by one 'chevalier Dinorth' (*Froissart*, ii, p. 675). This was probably John [de] Norbury. His name sometimes appears in contemporary records as 'Northbury'.

64. *PROME*, 1399 October, appendix; *Revolution*, p. 139.

65. About twenty years later, the Scottish chronicler Andrew Wyntoun wrote an account of the final meeting between Richard and John. He described the king speaking courteously to the dying duke, and, having comforted him, left on his bed some private letters (Goodman, *John of Gaunt*, p. 166). Given the fact that John was dying, either they must have related to his own past – perhaps some treasonable activity which Richard had discovered – or they must have been connected to his last hopes: his sons' futures, and in particular his lifelong hope that Henry would inherit the crown. We can only speculate now as to what the letters contained, but the most likely candidates from our knowledge are (1) a document relating to

John's birth, which in 1376 was said to be doubtful (see *PK*, p. 184). If Richard believed such a document, he might have felt an obligation to remove Henry from the line of succession as Henry was not sufficiently royal. (2) The original of Edward III's entail, by the terms of which Henry would be Richard's heir. (3) Edward I's settlement of the throne made at Amesbury in 1290 (see Appendix Two), by the terms of which Edmund Mortimer would arguably have been the heir.

66. *Revolution*, p. 141. This is unlikely to be a mistake, due to the positioning of the entry in the account roll.

67. Bennett suggests that John's request was due to a fear of being buried alive. However, it follows a similar request by Henry, duke of Lancaster, in 1361, who asked that his body not be buried or embalmed for three weeks (*Royal Wills*, p. 83). Both men were members of the royal family, but both were mindful of fake death announcements concerning members of the royal family. Duke Henry had learnt from the untrustworthy announcement of Edward II's death in 1327, and John had the additional example of the false announcement of the death of his brother in 1397. Hence John's request is more likely a consequence of his heir, Henry, being so far away. John probably wanted him to have the chance to confirm that he was actually dead, not simply announced as such.

68. E 361/5. This date is two days after that announced by Richard in January, to accommodate his request for a period of forty days between death and burial.

69. Bagot's message to Henry *in France* was sent after a conversation with Richard at Langley in March 1399. Richard was there on 9–10 March (Saul, p. 474) and left soon after for London, where he was on the 15th for the funeral. If Bagot sent his message to Henry in France on or about 10 March, and Henry received it in France, as he later acknowledged, he was not in London on the 15th. *Vita*, pp. 150–51, confirms that, at the time of the death, Henry remained overseas. The French chronicles do not indicate that he returned for the funeral, rather that he departed only when he returned to England in July.

70. *PROME*, 1399 October, appendix.

71. *Froissart*, p. 676.

72. *CR*, p. 105.

73. *Annales*, p. 233 ('*vehementer odire*'). Walsingham himself had hated John of Gaunt, and so this explanation of Richard's treatment of John's son should be given weight accordingly.

74. For Richard's demand to be addressed as your majesty, and the novelty of this, see Saul, 'Vocabulary'; McHardy, 'Personal Portrait', pp. 20, 23. For his references to Aumale as his 'brother' see 'Succession', pp. 333–4.

9: The Virtue of Necessity

1. 'Succession', pp. 333–4.

2. See the remarks at the end of Appendix Two.

3. Manning (ed.), *John Hayward's The Life and Raigne*, pp. 1–5.

4. *Vita*, p. 150; *Revolution*, p. 148; *CR*, p. 31.

5. This order was made the day after Henry's pardons were revoked, 19 March 1399. *CCR 1396–99*, pp. 488–9.

6. Obviously he would not have known the date of the death until some time later. Nevertheless he may well have claimed he had seen this vision when he saw Henry.

7. *CR*, p. 106.

8. *Monstrelet*, i, pp. 18–19. This is inaccurately dated 17 June 1396.

9. *CR*, p. 112.

10. See *Monstrelet*, i, p. 21: 'the principal cause of your seeking our friendship, and requesting this alliance to be made, was your dislike of your uncle of Burgundy, which we can prove . . .'. This was in Henry's second letter to the duke, of April 1403. In 1407 Louis was murdered by the duke of Burgundy's son.

11. See *Froissart*, pp. 686–8; *CR*, pp. 32, 111.

12. *CR*, p. 111.

13. Robert Bruce had been the last man to defeat the king, but, by his own definition, he was a Scot and owed no allegiance to Edward II. Simon de Montfort had been the last Englishman to do so, at the battle of Lewes, in 1264.

14. The date is open to debate, but 4 July is the most likely, especially as York's letters of 28 June presumed that Henry was still in France, and these were probably issued very shortly after the intelligence was received. See *CR*, pp. 33, 118; *Revolution*, p. 154; Saul, p. 408; Kirby, p. 54.

15. *CR*, p. 32. Edmund believed Henry was in Picardy at the time, and about to attack Calais first.

16. Biggs, 'Edmund Langley, duke of York', p. 258.

17. For Walsingham's estimate of no more than fifteen 'fighting men', including the knights of his own household, see *CR*, p. 117. He adds that there were no more than ten or twelve ships. Adam Usk estimates that he had no more than three hundred men with him in all. For the estimate of 'perhaps no more than a hundred or so', see *Revolution*, p. 154. The Evesham chronicler notes that Henry had sixty followers, but he includes men who were already in England; the Kirkstall chronicler states one hundred. Ten ships does suggest more than a hundred men, but of course Walsingham might have been mistaken in the number of ships.

18. Ravenspur is directly across the estuary from Grimsby. If the message that Henry had landed travelled from Grimsby, it would have taken more than two days to cover the 161 miles to London. Urgent messages normally travelled about sixty miles per day. The fastest on record – news of the death of Edward I – travelled at over eighty miles per day, but this was a royal messenger who would have been able to benefit from changes of horses at a number of places. If the weather was good and there was a local official who wished to send the news at high speed to London, the message would have taken between two and three days to reach Edmund. On 7 July Edmund ordered the defence of Nottingham Castle. This might relate to Edmund's receipt of the news of Henry's landing.

19. The letters are mentioned by the Saint-Denis chronicler. See *CR*, p. 110.

20. *CR*, p. 34; Biggs, 'Edmund Langley, duke of York', p. 259; Castor, *King, Crown and Duchy*, p. 26.

21. *CR*, p. 192.

22. Taylor (ed.), *Kirkstall Abbey Chronicles*, p. 122.

23. For numbers in Henry's paid army, see *CR*, pp. 252–3.

24. *CR*, p. 118, quoting Walsingham. The translation has been slightly modernised.
25. *CB*, p. 11; Neville, 'Scotland, the Percies and the law', p. 82; Arvangian, 'Northern Nobility and the Consolidation', p. 123.
26. *CR*, pp. 40, 192, quoting the Dieulacres chronicler. The 'relics of Bridlington' might refer to a portable reliquary, or even a bible taken from Bridlington Priory; it does not mean necessarily that he swore the oath at Bridlington.
27. *Revolution*, p. 155; Sherborne, 'Perjury', p. 220.
28. *CR*, p. 192; *Creton*, p. 180; Sherborne, 'Perjury', p. 218.
29. *CR*, pp. 194–5; Sherborne, 'Perjury', p. 219.
30. See Appendix Seven.
31. *CR*, p. 166, quoting Corpus Christi College, Cambridge, MS 59.
32. *Traïson*, pp. 180–81.
33. Biggs, 'Edmund Langley, duke of York', p. 261, n. 43.
34. *CR*, p. 35; *Revolution*, p. 159; Biggs, 'Edmund Langley, duke of York', p. 260; *Annales*, p. 244.
35. *Traïson*, p. 186.
36. *Traïson*, p. 186.
37. *Adam Usk*, p. 139.
38. Wylie, iv, p. 138.
39. Wylie, iv, p. 145.
40. *CR*, p. 156.
41. There are four reasons underlying this suggestion for Edward of York and two for Thomas Percy. With regard to Edward: his father had already decided long before their meeting at Berkeley Castle to capitulate to Henry, and it is likely that he communicated his decision via a messenger to his son in Ireland. Second, in Ireland Edward had acted against Richard, doing his best to impede Richard's return (according to Creton, who was with Richard and Edward in Ireland; see *Creton*, p. 55). Third, even though Edward was his adoptive brother, Richard left him behind when he fled north. Fourth, he immediately joined Henry after Richard's flight. With regard to Thomas Percy, not only had his brother and nephew already joined Henry, he too rushed to join them after Richard's flight. So, in looking for the protagonists behind the plot in South Wales against Richard, these two men are the prime suspects.
42. Sherborne, 'Perjury', p. 221. Henry's role as steward is also mentioned by the Dieulacres chronicler shortly afterwards. See *Revolution*, p. 163.
43. Nicolas, 'Badge and Mottoes', p. 365.
44. *Creton*, p. 125. Adam Usk thought Archbishop Arundel was at Conway in person, but he might have simply been following the Record and Process, which was probably created to suggest this. It is very unlikely that Arundel was present. See *CR*, p. 38; Sherborne, 'Perjury', pp. 229–30.
45. It is worth noting that, although historians have frequently claimed that Northumberland perjured himself by his promises to Richard, it is likely that he acted in good faith. He had been present at Doncaster when Henry had promised not to seize the throne, so he probably believed that the promises he made now to Richard would be fulfilled. And a parliament *was* summoned to take place at Westminster, so both elements of his promise were honestly made.
46. *CR*, pp. 145–7.

47. *Creton*, pp. 155–63. *Traïson*, pp. 202–6, supports this, and greatly amplifies Richard's lament.

48. *Revolution*, p. 173; *Traïson*, p. 212.

49. *Creton*, p. 179; *Traïson*, p. 215.

50. *Creton*, pp. 180–81; *Traïson*, p. 215.

51. This point was made by David Starkey in his television history series *Monarchy*. However, Henry did not have to be king to 'do what he could'. Similarly his appointment of Northumberland as warden of the Scottish Marches on 2 August is not proof of kingly intentions (as claimed in Boardman, *Hotspur*, p. 99), being a necessary expedient in view of the Scots' threat, and in line with Henry's 'sovereign' power (not necessarily the same as 'royal'; see Appendix Seven).

52. *PROME*, 1399 September, part 1, item 53. In addition, two chronicles note Henry's claim through descent from Henry III, see *CR*, p. 166; *Adam Usk*, p. 71.

53. One of these chronicles, the continuator of the *Eulogium*, mentions this claim in relation to John of Gaunt's request for Henry to be recognised as heir to the throne in 1394. However, this is hardly likely to have been voiced at this time as it would imply that Richard himself was not the legitimate king in 1394. Rather it should be regarded as an interpolation by the continuator's successor, added to the first-state chronicle in or after 1400, by a writer who presumed that the Crouchback legend underlay John's claim that Henry should be given preference to the earl of March, and that this was why Henry had claimed the throne by inheritance from Henry III in 1399. See *Eulogium*, iii, pp. 369–70; 'Succession'.

54. *Adam Usk*, pp. 65–7.

55. *Royal Wills*, p. 16.

56. Philip Vache, who had served Richard II, was possibly a surviving witness. He (or a man of the same name) entered Henry's service in 1403. Given-Wilson, *Royal Household*, p. 290. One of the men with Henry, John d'Aubridgecourt, was the son of one of the witnesses of Edward III's entail.

57. *Foedera*, ii, p. 497.

58. *SAC*, pp. 39–41.

59. See Appendix Two.

60. One account specifically states that Henry claimed the throne as 'the nearest male heir and worthiest blood-descendant of Henry III', *CR*, p. 166. John's claim in 1199 had prevailed not only over Arthur but also Arthur's sister, Eleanor, daughter of Geoffrey, John's older brother. Eleanor died in 1241. Thus, if this can be considered to reflect practice before 1290, Henry III's throne was inheritable only by and through males.

61. Henry himself used parliament to recognise his settlements of the throne in 1406, contrary to earlier examples. It is also interesting that the Record and Process states that Richard had asked that Henry succeed him.

62. *CR*, p. 187.

63. This meeting is described in *Traïson*, pp. 216–18.

64. The council met on or before 28 September. *CR*, pp. 162–3.

65. *Revolution*, p. 175. On this day official documents ceased to bear the regnal year.

66. Rumours of Richard's illegitimacy were in circulation at this time. See *Creton*, p. 179; *Revolution*, p. 176.

67. *PROME*, 1399 October, introduction.
68. *CR*, p. 165. The Record and Process suggests a more reserved and considered response but this was probably written up some while later, and refracted through the lens of justifying the proceedings.
69. *CR*, p. 166.
70. One might add the unspoken right of conquest to make the tripartite claim to which Chaucer and Gower allude and of which Wylie made much. Wylie, i, addendum (facing xvi).
71. *Creton*, p. 201. York and his sons were Richard's designated heirs, so this may have represented an attempt to circumvent Richard's settlement of the throne on the house of York.
72. *Revolution*, p, 183.
73. *CR*, p. 190–91. As Given-Wilson notes, the outburst is doubtful. Although Carlisle was present, and soon after fell into disfavour, his supposed speech implies that Henry had assumed the throne before Richard had been judged. However, all references to opposition speeches have been removed from the 'Record and Process'.

10: High Sparks of Honour

1. *CR*, p. 185; *PROME*, 1399 October, item 53.
2. *Adam Usk*, p. 73.
3. Although the number of knights created is not known for certain, at least one well-informed source gives the number as fifty. It is possible that this was a direct reference to the jubilee of the foundation of the Order of the Garter. See Wylie, i, p. 43; *Adam Usk*, p. 71; *Annales*, p. 291; *PK*, pp. 427–9 (for 1349 as the date of the foundation of the Order of the Garter).
4. *PK*, p. 21.
5. Strohm, *Hochon's Arrow*, pp. 84–5.
6. *Adam Usk*, p. 73. Creton has Westmorland holding the sceptre. See *Creton*, p. 207.
7. *Creton*, pp. 208–9; *Adam Usk*, p, 73.
8. *PROME*, 1399 October, part 1, item 2.
9. *CR*, p. 113.
10. For example, *RHL*, i, p. 23 (a letter to Albert, count of Hainault, dated 1400).
11. For Kingston, see *RHL*, i, p. 158. For his sons, Henry and John regularly wrote to him with the same salutation, for example: Henry in January 1405 and John several times in 1407 (*RHL*, ii, pp. 20, 223, 227, 231, 235). It is likely that Henry V picked up his own devotion to the Trinity at least partly as a result of his father's influence. The younger Henry's regard for the Trinity is already apparent in his letter of 11 March 1405 (*PC*, i, p. 249). For Joan, who wrote praying that the Holy Spirit would keep him in February 1400, see *RHL*, i, p. 20). Other examples are the letter to Henry from the earl of March in 1404 (*ibid.*, p. 434) and the letter from the officers of the staple at Calais (*RHL*, ii, p. 283). A systematic search would no doubt reveal many more such references.
12. For example, *PROME*, 1404 January, item 17; 1406 March, part 1, item 38.
13. Henry certainly used the prince's feathers in his own seals at this time. Nicolas, 'Badge and Mottoes', pp. 365–6.

14. On Edward's reputation at this time as the greatest king who had ever ruled England see Morgan, 'Apotheosis', especially p. 868.

15. *Revolution*, p. 185.

16. *Adam Usk*, p. 73. This may have been a misquotation of the second coronation oath, 'to cause impartial and honest justice and discretion, with mercy and truth, to be done in all your judgements, according to your power'. *PROME*, 1399 October, part 1, item 17.

17. The letter was dated 2 November, at Linlithgow (*RHL*, i, p. 10), but Henry's declaration on 10 November suggests that that was when it was received.

18. When the lords expressed support for his intended expedition, he 'most graciously thanked the said lords in his own words, and said to them that he would never refrain from committing his body and his blood to this expedition, or to any other for the salvation of his realm, if God gave him life'. See *PROME*, 1399 October, part 1, item 80. For a full account of the Scottish expedition of 1400, see Brown, 'English campaign in Scotland', pp. 40–54.

19. *Waurin*, pp. 42–3.

20. *Revolution*, p. 195.

21. For Bucton's role, see Johnstone, 'Richard II's departure from Ireland', p. 799.

22. *CR*, p. 202.

23. *CR*, p. 203.

24. *CR*, p. 212.

25. *CR*, pp. 204–5.

26. Disembowelling alive, with the victim's entrails being burned, had been the sentence meted out by Hugh Despenser on Llewelyn Bren in 1317 and (probably in revenge) by Roger Mortimer on Hugh Despenser in 1326. It was carried out again on Sir Thomas Blount in January 1400, with a particularly graphic description being included in *Waurin*, pp. 39–40.

27. *PROME*, 1399 October, introduction.

28. *PROME*, 1399 October, part 1, item 73.

29. Wylie, i, p. 111. For Knaresborough Castle see Taylor (ed.), *Kirkstall Abbey Chronicles*, p. 82. Morgan, 'Shadow of Richard II', pp. 1–2, gives a selection of the other places mentioned in various chronicles for Richard's location; given the secrecy surrounding his custody, it is difficult to be certain as to his whereabouts.

30. C 53/167 no. 1. For earlier witnessings, see Given-Wilson, 'Royal Charter Witness Lists', esp. tables 7 and 13. For later witnessings, see Biggs, 'Royal Charter Witness Lists', pp. 407–23, esp. pp. 417–19.

31. *Traïson*, pp. 229.

32. *Traïson*, pp. 233–4.

33. *CR*, p. 236.

34. *PC*, i, p. 107.

35. *Brut*, ii, p. 360; *CR*, p. 224, n. 1.

36. McNiven, 'Cheshire rising', pp. 387–8.

37. Brown, 'Reign of Henry IV', pp. 5–6.

38. *Waurin*, p. 41.

11: A Deed Chronicled in Hell

1. *Waurin*, pp. 39–43; Wylie, i, p. 107.
2. *PC*, i, pp. 102–3.
3. *Foedera*, viii, p. 124.
4. *PC*, i, p. 3.
5. Wylie, i, p. 115.
6. The early February council minutes would have mentioned the escape if this was the specific reason for their doubt as to the king's death. Henry made a payment of 100 marks on 17 February for bringing Richard's corpse to London (*Issues*, p. 275). The face was clearly exhibited in St Paul's Cathedral (for two days), and in the main thoroughfare, Cheapside, for two hours, and later at Westminster Abbey, as stated by a number of chroniclers, including the well-informed Walsingham, who states that the cerecloth was removed from his forehead to his neck (*Annales*, p. 331) and a contemporary London chronicler who seems to have been a witness (*EC*, p. 21). A very great number of individuals in London saw the corpse (McNiven, 'Rebellion, sedition', p. 95). Significantly, the earl of Northumberland and the archbishop of York later issued manifestos attesting to the death. The earl was one of Henry's most trusted confidants in February 1400 and both he and the archbishop were present at the council meeting when Richard's death was discussed. They therefore had direct access to information about the physical cause and date of the ex-king's death. Finally, Jean Creton, one of the few chroniclers who believed that Richard had not died, went to see the supposedly living king in Scotland in 1402 and discovered him to be an imposter (*CR*, pp. 240–41; Dillon, 'Remarks', pp. 78–83). To this we might add the circumstantial detail that, had the imposter really been Richard, it would be out of character for him to exist quietly and modestly in Scotland for so many years.
7. Respectively, these are the views of Given-Wilson in *PROME*, 1399 October, introduction; Saul, p. 425; *Revolution*, p. 192.
8. For example, see Palmer, 'French chronicles, 2', pp. 399–400.
9. Amyot, 'Inquiry', pp. 425–8.
10. Jean Creton returned from Scotland to France in 1402 with a story about Richard's violent death. See Dillon, 'Remarks', p. 78; Palmer, 'French chronicles, 1', p, 162.
11. *Traïson*, pp. 233–4.
12. *CR*, p. 241. The date has probably been drawn from Walsingham.
13. *Brut*, ii, p. 360.
14. *CR*, p. 244.
15. *EC*, p. 21; 'Deposition', p. 174.
16. *Adam Usk*, p. 91. Usk names the keeper as 'Sir N. Swynford'.
17. *Annales*, p. 331.
18. *PC*, i, xxxi and p. 111. The minute refers to pardons for crimes committed 'before the feast of the Purification of our lady last past' (2 February 1400). Although Wylie states that the council minute dates from 8 February at the latest, the *CPR* text of the letters to the sheriffs by which he derived this *terminus ante quem* gives their date as 24 February 1400, as Nicolas states, not 8 February as Wylie claims on the basis of *Foedera* (Wylie, i, p. 115; *Foedera*, viii, p. 125). As the minute includes so many provisions for the security of the kingdom, it is

likely to be connected with the 9 February minutes, which mention Faryngton, the French king's letter and the likelihood of war. However, Henry was clearly present at the meeting on 9 February, whereas he was not present at the meeting which discussed the eventuality of the king's death. It is likely therefore that Wylie is right to date this council meeting to 3–8 February, although not for the reasons stated.

19. 'En primes si R. nadgairs Roy soit uncore vivant a ce que len suppose quil est ordenez soit quil soit bien et seurement gardez pur sauvacion de lestat du Roi et de son Roiaume.' This appears printed in *PC*, i, p. 107. The text was checked against the original in the British Library: Cotton, Cleopatra F iii, fol. 14a. It also appears in Strohm, *England's Empty Throne*, p. 104. As Nicolas noted at the time of editing this document, it suggests that Henry and the council were bystanders to the death, not the instigators of it. His thoughts on the subject have largely been ignored subsequently, probably because he did not fully explain them. In recent years this document has been construed as tacit advice from the king's council to terminate Richard's life (e.g. Burden, 'How do you bury a deposed king?', p. 39; Strohm, *Empty Throne*, p. 104).

20. 'Quant a le primer article il semble au Conseil expedient de parler au Roi qen cas que R. nadgairs Roy &c soit uncore vivant quil soit mys en seuretee aggreable a les seigneurs du roiaume & sil soit alez de vie a trespassement qadonques soit il monstrez overtement au people au fin quils ent puissent avoir conissance.' *PC*, i, pp. 111–12. A similar but briefer entry appears in British Library, Cotton Cleopatra F iii, fol. 14b: this is damaged but seems to say 'Sur le primer article soit ple au Roi qen cas que R. vivant &c quil soit mys en seurete . . . [*edge of page*] les seignurs Et que sil soit mort qadonques il soit monstrer overtement au poeples quils en puissent avoir conissance.' The fuller version suggests the matter was deliberated without the king being present.

21. This was usual for council meetings at this period. Harriss, *Shaping the Nation*, p. 77.

22. If a report of the public execution of the lookalike Maudeleyn had triggered the French king's belief in the death, Charles would have accused Henry of killing Richard directly. There is no such accusation; rather there is a quiet and sombre reflection on Richard's death.

23. Bucton took Richard to Knaresborough after the parliament (which ended on 19 November). This seems to be based on first-hand information, as Knaresborough is only eighteen miles away from Kirkstall, and the chronicler adds that he does not know where Richard was taken afterwards, proving he was not reliant on the official version of the death. See Taylor (ed.), *Kirkstall Abbey Chronicles*, p. 82.

24. *Traïson*, p. 248.

25. For the nationality of the author, see Palmer, 'French Chronicles, 1', pp. 163–4. Palmer suggests he was in the service of the duke of Burgundy, as his dialect is West Flanders, Picard or Walloon. He was based in London as he gives descriptions of places in terms of their distance from the city. He or his source seems to have been with Henry and the militia army on the common outside London on 6 January, as he gives details about the times of people coming and going, the earls of Arundel and Warwick among them. See *Traïson*, pp. 235–6, 248, 253–4.

26. *Issues*, p. 276. One man to go to Pontefract from London was reimbursed 6s 8d

in this same account. The payment to Loveney – £3 6s 8d – indicates that he may have had as many as eight or nine men with him, if they were reimbursed for their expenses at the same rate. This visit must have been after 4 January, when Loveney was with the king in London (*CCR* 1399–1402, p. 34).

27. Rogers, 'Royal Household', p. 755.

28. *CR*, pp. 194–5.

29. Although it should be noted that the fifteen days of starvation in the Percy manifesto was probably an exaggeration. If Richard died on 14 February, and Richard started to go without water on 31 January, then Henry would have had to give the order on 28 January, which is before he could have heard from France about the French king's belief in Richard's death.

30. '*Festiationis causa*'. This detail is not in *Issues* but appears in Wylie, i, p. 115.

31. A garbled version of such a precautionary order might be preserved in the account given in *Froissart*, which states that Henry promised he would not kill Richard unless he took part in a plot to oust him. See *Froissart*, ii, p. 708.

32. Wylie, i, p. 117.

33. *Creton*, p. 221.

34. For example, Burden, 'How do you bury a deposed king?'; Strohm, *Empty Throne*, chapter four; Morgan, 'Shadow of Richard II'.

35. Richard had ordered another tomb to be moved to make way for his, so it would have been quite acceptable for Henry to move Richard and Anne's tomb to Langley, or elsewhere in Westminster Abbey. See *HKW*, i, pp. 487–8.

36. Duffy, *Royal Tombs*, p. 157.

37. *Issues*, p. 276.

38. He was at Eltham on 26 February, 8 and 16 March and 8 April but must have returned to London at some point to attend the Mass for Richard at St Paul's between 8 and 16 March. *Signet Letters*, p. 21; *Syllabus*, ii, p. 538.

39. Details of Henry's work at Eltham are to be found in *HKW*, ii, pp. 935–6.

40. *RHL*, i, pp. 25–7. The offer was for negotiators to meet at Kelso on 5 January. Robert III claimed two months later that he had received the letter too late to send representatives. The first offer had been made in September 1399, before Henry's accession.

41. *RHL*, i, pp. 23–5. The letter was dated 18 February, at Dunbar Castle. It would have taken at least ten days to cover the distance to Eltham in winter. Henry's safe-conduct to Dunbar was dated 8 March.

42. *RHL*, i, pp. 28–9. The nature of this information was reported by word of mouth and thus is unfortunately unknown to us. Its importance can be gauged from the fact that it could not safely be written in a letter to the king.

43. *PC*, i, pp. 118–20; Pistono, 'Confirmation of the twenty-eight-year truce', pp. 353–65.

44. Brown, 'English Campaign in Scotland', pp. 44–5. This is comparable with the size of the armies led to Scotland in 1314, 1335 and 1385.

45. Wylie, iv, pp. 230, 232.

46. Brown, 'English Campaign in Scotland', p. 43. *Signet Letters*, p. 23, states they were offering peace on the lines agreed between Edward I and Robert Bruce. However, there was no such treaty. The text of Henry's letter, printed in *PC*, i, p. 123, shows that he did not specify Edward I but 'our well-remembered ancestor, Edward, formerly king of England'.

47. She had been married to John Holland, duke of Exeter, who had died at the hands of the mob in Essex after the Epiphany Rising.

48. *PROME*, 1402 September, item 16.

49. *PC*, i, p. 169.

50. *Annales*, pp. 332–3; Wylie, i, p. 132. The naval successes included the capture of Sir Robert Logan, the Scottish admiral, and David Seton, a secretary of Robert III, who was carrying letters to France.

51. *Eulogium*, iii, p. 387; Brown, 'English Campaign in Scotland', p. 44.

52. *Revolution*, p. 203.

53. Rogers, 'Royal Household', p. 72–4.

54. Dyer, *Standards of Living*, p. 263; Rogers, 'Royal Household', p. 54.

55. Henry continued southwards until he arrived at Northampton. He may have heard about the Welsh rising earlier in the month, before the proclamation of Glendower. See *Vitae*, pp. 167, 212, n. 492.

12: The Great Magician

1. The story of the land dispute which was not settled in parliament comes from Thomas Walsingham's *Annales*, p. 333. The letters between Glendower and Reginald Grey are printed in *RHL*, i, pp. 35–8. See also *Glyn Dŵr*, p. 102.

2. Wylie, i, p. 144.

3. *ODNB*, under 'Glyn Dŵr, Owain'.

4. *CPR 1399–1401*, p. 555. He was at Shrewsbury on the 15th and 16th, Shifnal on the 18th.

5. Boardman suggests that Henry might have averted further rebellion if he had 'made any effort' to enquire into the grievances of Glendower and the Welsh people (Boardman, *Hotspur*, p. 119).

6. *Revolution*, p. 203.

7. Wylie, iv, pp. 141, n. 8, 263.

8. Wylie, iv, p. 263.

9. Wylie, i, p. 158.

10. *Adam Usk*, p. 119.

11. Details of the tournament have been drawn from an article by John Priestley, 'Christmas day and knights', in the November 2006 issue of *Heritage Today*, the English Heritage magazine, pp. 28–31. See also Nicol, 'Byzantine Emperor'.

12. Wylie, iv, pp. 129–30.

13. *Issues*, p. 282.

14. This figure is drawn from Rogers, 'Political crisis', p. 89. Rogers' claim that this amounted to more than Richard II's household had spent in its last three years does not seem to be borne out by Given-Wilson's more recent study. See *Royal Household*, pp. 76–92, 94 (in particular), 107–8, 271.

15. Wylie, iv, pp. 315–18. According to Given-Wilson in *PROME*, 1401 January, introduction, Pope Boniface VIII had recommended in 1298 that burning should be adopted throughout Christendom. Given-Wilson adds that the Lollard William Swinderby 'fully expected to be burned' at his trial in 1382.

16. Usually depictions of burnings are without the barrel. John Badby, who suffered

the same fate as Sawtre nine years later, was described as being burned in a barrel by the contemporary Thomas Walsingham. See *CM*, p. 376.

17. Rogers, 'Political Crisis', pp. 87–8; Castor, *King, Crown and Duchy*, pp. 30–31.

18. Brown, 'Commons and the council', p. 3.

19. *PROME*, 1401 January, introduction; Kirby, pp. 112–13; Rogers, 'Political Crisis'.

20. His attempts to limit the anti-Welsh legislation were restricted to granting a pardon to all those who had taken part in Glendower's rising – except William and Rees ap Tudor, and Glendower himself – and a three-year limit on the period during which Welshmen could not sue Englishmen in Wales.

21. *PROME*, 1401 January, item 48.

22. *Adam Usk*, p. 131.

23. Harriss, *Shaping the Nation*, p. 496, describes this as an 'open letter'. However, it was written at Henry's own request: in Repingdon's words, 'when, with a heavy heart, I last departed from your presence, your excellent majesty requested me, your humble servant, to inform you without delay of anything I might hear . . .' (*Adam Usk*, p. 137) . . . 'I am saying no more than I have already said to you by word of mouth, when I was in your presence' (*ibid*., p. 143). It seems to have been a private letter, written for Henry's information and with his approval, which later came to Usk's attention, perhaps through the offices of the archbishop of Canterbury.

24. It appears in *Adam Usk*, pp. 137–43.

25. Wylie iv, pp. 198–9.

26. Gwilym Dodd, 'Henry IV's Council', p. 100.

27. *Issues*, p. 284.

28. Wylie, 'Dispensation', pp. 96–7. Edmund was in his eleventh year on 15 January 1412.

29. Otway-Ruthven, *Medieval Ireland*, p. 341. Thomas was officially appointed on 27 June and arrived on 13 November.

30. *Adam Usk*, p. 135; Wylie, i, pp. 228–9.

31. *RHL*, pp. 73–6.

32. To add to the six chapters of the 1401 statute concerning the Welsh, on 18 March a further ordinance for Wales was issued. This added a number of precautionary measures but these arose from petitions presented in the parliament to prevent a reoccurrence of Glendower's rising. It cannot therefore be said to have greatly extended what was agreed in parliament.

33. Wylie, i, pp. 212–18; *Adam Usk*, p. 129.

34. *ODNB*, under 'Glyn Dŵr, Owain'. The reference to *PC*, ii, p. 55, quoted indicates that Glendower was in the Carmarthenshire/Cardiganshire area in May, not June.

35. *Signet Letters*, p. 28.

36. *RHL*, i, p. 71.

37. *PC*, i, pp. 156–64; Kirby, pp. 127–8.

38. *Adam Usk*, p. 135.

39. *PC*, i, p. 154; Kirby, p. 128. This was made up of £13,000 for Calais, £5,000 for Ireland, £10,000 for Aquitaine, £8,000 for returning Isabella, £24,000 in annuities granted by the king, £16,000 to repay loans, £16,000 for the wardrobe, and £38,000 for the war in Scotland, the campaigns in Wales and the defence of the sea. See also *Royal Household*, p. 129.

40. Rutland was created lieutenant of Aquitaine on 28 August. *CP*, xii, 2, p. 903.

41. Wylie confused Henry's itinerary in Wales in 1401 with that of 1400. Henry was at Hereford on 10–11 October 1401, and then at Llandovery on the 14th (see Wylie, i, p. 243; *Signet Letters*, p. 31; Kirby, p. 130). He returned to England via Worcester (where he was on the 27th), not Shrewsbury and Shifnal as Wylie states, mistakenly placing the undated *rotulus viagii* of 2 Henry IV at the start of 3 Henry IV.

42. *Adam Usk*, p. 145.

43. *Adam Usk*, pp. 149–53.

13: Uneasy Lies the Head

1. *Annales*, p. 337; *EC*, p. 23; *Eulogium*, iii, p. 389.

2. *HA*, ii, p. 248. *Vitae*, p. 171, adds the details that the attempted assassination took place in early September 1401 at Westminster and that the murderous contraption was placed in the king's bed by a member of Queen Isabella's household, who confessed to the crime and was later pardoned.

3. It may be noted that (1) high-status beds did not normally have straw mattresses at this time, (2) Henry was at Windsor, not Westminster, in early September 1401, and (3) Isabella and her household had left Westminster several months earlier. Nevertheless, the story is unlikely to have been a complete fiction, and certainly not one started by the king himself (despite Paul Strohm's assertion in Strohm, *Empty Throne*, p. 64), for no element of this story can have rebounded to the benefit of the king's public image.

4. *Vitae*, p. 171; Dyer, *Standards of Living*, p. 263.

5. Kirby, p. 127.

6. *Adam Usk*, p. 147.

7. *PC*, p. 178.

8. *PC*, p. 178.

9. *ODNB*, under 'Joan of Navarre'.

10. Froissart states that he went to Brittany and met her at Nantes on his way to Spain. See *Froissart*, ii, p. 687; Strickland, *Lives*, ii, pp. 60–61.

11. *RHL*, i, pp. 19–20.

12. For example, see Kirby, p. 136. 'Whether or not its terms are more effusive than common courtesy required is not easy to determine', Kirby says, even though he must have realised that no other extant letter addressed to Henry is exclusively devoted to expressions of goodwill towards him. 'At least Henry might assume on the receipt of this that the duchess was not ill-disposed towards him,' he adds, with cautiousness so extreme it is comical.

13. *PC*, i, p. 188.

14. *ODNB*, under 'Joan of Navarre'.

15. In addition to Henry's two love matches we might add his father's first and third marriages (to Blanche and Katherine), his uncle's (the Black Prince and Joan of Kent), his aunt's (Isabella and Enguerrand de Coucy) and his sister's (Elizabeth and John Holland). The last three especially were choices made out of affection, not political gain.

16. Morgan, 'Shadow of Richard II', p. 17.

17. *EC*, p. 26; *Annales*, p. 339.
18. The prior of Launde's arrest is placed just before Trinity (21 May) by Walsingham. See *Annales*, p. 339.
19. Wylie, i, p. 277.
20. The dialogue here has been modernised from *EC*, pp. 24–5. The execution is also mentioned by Walsingham (*Annales*, p. 340).
21. Strohm, *Empty Throne*, pp. 107–8.
22. *EC*, p. 24.
23. *Issues*, p. 286.
24. Morgan, 'Shadow of Richard II', p. 13.
25. *Syllabus*, ii, p. 545.
26. Given-Wilson & Curteis, *Royal Bastards*, p. 145.
27. *Annales*, p. 340.
28. The dialogue has been modernised from *EC*, pp. 24–5. The date is from Wylie, i, p. 278. Walsingham says 'a few days after 25 May' in *Annales*, p. 341.
29. First a London jury failed to condemn them, then so did a Holborn jury. Eventually they were found guilty by the men of Islington. They were drawn to Tyburn and there hanged, the master giving a devout sermon before he died, exclaiming his innocence and forgiving his killers. Another friar made a scaffold speech in which he declared that he never intended 'to slay the king and sons but to make them dukes of Lancaster, as they should be'. *EC*, pp. 25–6.
30. Various writers give various dates for this battle, and differ as to whether it was led by Glendower in person. This date and Glendower's presence in person are from *Glyn Dŵr*, p. 107.
31. *Annales*, p. 341.
32. Boardman, *Hotspur*, p. 145.
33. See Wylie, iv, p. 289, for his itinerary at this time. Between 25 June and 15 August 1402 he stayed at Berkhamsted (Hertfordshire), Market Harborough (Leicestershire), Lilleshall (Shropshire), Ravendale (Lincolnshire), Lichfield and Burton-on-Trent (Staffs), Tideswell and Darley (Derbyshire) and Nottingham, as well as many places in between.
34. *Adam Usk*, p. 161.
35. Wylie, i, p. 293 (for the prisoners); *PROME*, 1402 September, item 16.
36. Rogers, 'Royal Household' (Ph.D. thesis), p. 90.
37. Signed and sealed at Coucy, 7 August 1402. *Monstrelet*, i, p. 16; *Waurin*, pp. 64–6.
38. Henry's reply was dated London 5 December 1402. See *Monstrelet*, i, pp. 16–18; *Waurin*, pp. 67–70.
39. Orléans' second letter was dated 22 March 1403. See *Monstrelet*, i, pp. 19–20 (has incorrect date of 26 March 1402); *Waurin*, pp. 73–7. Henry received it on the last day of April.
40. Henry's reply to Orléans' second letter was undated. See *Monstrelet*, i, pp. 21–3; *Waurin*, pp. 77–85.
41. Wylie, i, p. 309.
42. *Signet Letters*, p. 41.
43. Radford, 'An unrecorded royal visit', p. 259.
44. Wylie, i, p. 310 (where it is given as five hundred marks) and ii, p. 288.
45. Radford, 'An unrecorded royal visit', p. 262; *Issues*, p. 305.

46. For his fool see *Issues*, p. 284.
47. For this aspect of her character, see her refusal to allow her husband to send their little son as a hostage to the lord de Clisson, in Strickland, *Lives*, ii, p. 57.
48. Strohm, *Empty Throne*, p. 157.
49. *Issues*, p. 286.

14: A Bloody Field by Shrewsbury

1. See the speech attributed to the Percys in *Eulogium*, iii, pp. 396–7.
2. Particularly Adam Orleton, bishop of Hereford in the reign of Edward II, William Melton, archbishop of York during the time of Mortimer's rule, John Stratford, archbishop of Canterbury during the Crisis of 1341, William Wykeham in relation to John of Gaunt in the 1370s, and Thomas Arundel himself in 1386. I am indebted to W. M. Ormrod, 'Rebellion of Archbishop Scrope and the Tradition of Opposition to Royal Taxation', for further ideas about this.
3. Boardman, *Hotspur*, p. 149.
4. *Brut*, ii, p. 548.
5. *EC*, p. 27.
6. *EHD*, p. 192. *Adam Usk*, p. 161. He fathered four children by her in the seven years after being taken captive, so the marriage must have taken place reasonably soon afterwards. The failure of parliament to appeal on his behalf suggests his loyalty was in doubt in October 1402. Edmund declared his allegiance to Glendower in a letter to Sir John Greyndour dated 13 December 1402.
7. *CPR 1401–5*, p. 213.
8. *PC*, pp. 203–4.
9. *PC, Privy Council*, pp. 204–5.
10. See 1 Maccabees, chapter 2; see also 1 Maccabees, chapter 14, verses 29–32, regarding Mathathias's son, Simon, who had resisted invasions and spent much money in defending the country for the glory of the kingdom. The allusion to Hotspur – if intended – is fitting.
11. This is presuming that the letter was sent on the same day it was written, 26 June, and took five days to reach him from Healaugh, in North Yorkshire, about 220 miles distant.
12. *Signet Letters*, pp. 48–9; *PC*, i, pp. 206–7. For Elmyn or Helmyng Leget and his antecedents see T. F. Tout, 'Firearms in England and the Fourteenth Century', *EHR*, 26 (1911), p. 669.
13. Wylie notes a payment on 17 July 1403 of £8,108 for wages to four barons, twenty knights, 476 esquires and 2,500 archers. This could not relate to the present gathering, summoned to Lichfield the previous day, as the exchequer did not pay wages in advance; it might relate to the army Henry took into Wales the previous autumn. But it is perhaps indicative of the size of force which he was used to gathering, and the number of archers especially should be noted.
14. Philip Morgan, 'Memories of the Battle of Shrewsbury'. One of the major accounts of the battle bears a number of correlations with the classical text of Lucan, and therefore probably reflects the way the chronicler hoped his account would be understood rather than what actually happened.
15. It is normally said that Henry personally reached Shrewsbury first (e.g. 'Deposition',

p. 178). This is unlikely. According to Capgrave, *Chronicle of England*, p. 282, Hotspur began to besiege Shrewsbury. If so, and if Henry was not personally at Shrewsbury but with the main army behind, this would explain how he forced a battle by arriving afterwards, and stayed the night before the battle at Haughmond Abbey, to the north-east of Berwick Field.

16. See Appendix Four.

17. 'Deposition', p. 179.

18. *Waurin*, p. 60.

19. Capgrave, *Chronicle of England*, p. 282 (rebel army); *HA*, ii, p. 257 (royal army). Most modern writers tend to estimate that there were twelve to fourteen thousand men in the king's army and ten thousand with Hotspur, but these figures are little more than educated guesses.

20. It is normally assumed that the battle was fought on a north–south axis. Given that the prince advanced from Shrewsbury and Henry from Haughmond, it is more likely that the initial confrontation was either east–west or northwest–southeast. No single source is reliable enough, and the combined narratives are too contradictory to be certain of this point.

21. *CR*, pp. 194–5. See also *Eulogium*, iii, p. 397.

22. *Eulogium*, iii, p. 397.

23. 'Deposition', p. 179.

24. *Waurin*, p. 61.

25. This interpretation is supported by the most accurate of the chronicles to describe the battle, the Dieulacres chronicle. See 'Deposition', p. 180.

26. 'Deposition', p. 180. Other sources, describing Stafford's death with the other notables, have transposed his demise to a later stage of the battle, fighting alongside Blount and the king.

27. *Annales*, p. 367.

28. *Brut*, ii, p. 549.

29. *Waurin*, p. 62.

30. The charge of the thirty knights is reported in *Eulogium*, iii, p. 397 and *EC*, p. 28.

31. Boardman, *Hotspur*, p. 203, argues on the strength of a reference in Gregory's chronicle to Stafford dying in the king's coat armour, that 'Stafford was the only man to adopt this changed role'. However *Adam Usk*, p. 171, mentions two men in the king's armour, and *Brut*, ii, p. 549, specifically mentions that Blount was wearing the king's coat armour. Although some writers assume Stafford was killed alongside Blount, for the two are mentioned together in some sources, this is only because they were the most notable casualties on the king's side. According to the Dieulacres account, Stafford was killed by a Percy arrow, a scenario very likely in view of his leading the vanguard.

32. 'Deposition', p. 181.

33. See Appendix Four.

34. The statement that the bodies were spread over an area of three miles dates from a much later charter, and possibly relates to how far away the furthest bodies were from the battlefield; these were probably men cut down fleeing the battle. Wylie, i, p. 363.

35. It is usually said that the initiative for the church was local, and only later taken up by the king. This is true in so far as it was a local cleric who presented the

petition to Henry in 1406 to alienate the land for the church. However, petitions do not always demonstrate the petitioner's initiative. Many were as the result of a prior discussion with the king. *Adam Usk*, p. 171, states that Henry swore to build a chapel there for the souls of the dead. It may be that the 1406 petition merely marks the formal beginning of the bureaucratic paper trail, a response by a designated man to Henry's initiative.

36. *Waurin*, pp. 63–4. The text ends 'he maintained and loved justice above all things, and besides was a very handsome prince, learned, and eloquent, courteous, valiant and brave in arms, and in short was filled with every virtue such as was none of his predecessors before his time'.

37. Wylie, iv, p. 366.

38. *Eulogium*, iii, p. 397; *Annales*, pp. 372–3.

39. Given-Wilson, 'Quarrels of Old Women'.

40. *EHD*, p. 195.

15: Treason's True Bed

1. Quoted from Chris Given-Wilson's translation of the Durham newsletter in *PROME*, 1404 January, appendix.

2. *PROME*, 1404 January, introduction.

3. *Eulogium*, iii, p. 400. The gaoler is unnamed. It would either have been Thomas Swynford or Robert Waterton.

4. *PROME*, 1404 January, introduction.

5. It was the sixth plot if one counts Glendower's rising as a plot, and does not count the story about the barbed metal implement in his bed. The other four were the Epiphany Rising (1400), the poisoned saddle (1400), the friars' conspiracy (1402) and the Percy revolt (1403).

6. For the countess of Oxford's plot, see Ross, 'Seditious Activities'; Morgan, 'Shadow of Richard II', pp. 19–22; Wylie, i, pp. 417–28.

7. Wylie, i, p. 437; *Syllabus*, p. 550. It is not clear if Hawley was mayor at this time (Hugh R. Watkin, *Dartmouth* (Devonshire Association, 1935), p. 184, has no names of mayors for 1402–4).

8. Morgan, 'Shadow of King Richard', p. 21.

9. Wylie, i, pp. 431–2.

10. He was captured before 19 June 1404. See *PROME*, 1404 January, appendix; *Adam Usk*, pp. 176–7.

11. *EC*, p. 30.

12. *Eulogium*, iii, p. 402.

13. Kirby, p. 172.

14. However, Kirby, p. 174, prefers the idea that it was called 'unlearned' because of the attack on Church property by ignorant men.

15. *PC*, i, p. 233.

16. *PROME*, 1404 October, items 14–23.

17. Pelham was a Lancastrian retainer. Thomas Neville, Lord Furnival, was the brother of the earl of Westmorland.

18. *Annales*, p. 399.

19. During his 1402 campaign in Wales, he had the boys temporarily transferred to

the custody of his trusted servant Hugh Waterton at Berkhamsted. See *ODNB*, under 'Mortimer, Edmund (V)'.

20. The date is uncertain. Walsingham and Otterburne both say the Friday after St Valentine – 20 February – but as Wylie says, this must be a week late (Wylie, ii, p. 41). Henry knew of the plot in the early morning of Sunday 15 February (*Signet Letters*, p. 191) and Lady Despenser had been arrested by 17 February (Wylie, ii, p. 43). It is therefore likely that the date was the Friday *before* St Valentine (13 February): a copyist's error is probably to blame.

21. *Signet Letters*, p. 191.

22. *CP*, xii/2, p. 903.

23. *Glyn Dŵr*, p. 167. With regard to Glendower's faith in prophecy, it is interesting that he employed a 'master of Brut' at this time. See *ODNB*, under 'Glyn Dŵr, Owain'.

24. *Brut*, i, pp. 75–76. This version postdates the fall of Edward II. The story is the same as in the earliest known version written down about 1312. See Taylor, *Political Prophecy*, pp. 163–4; Smallwood, 'Prophecy of the Six Kings', pp. 571–92.

25. *Glyn Dŵr*, pp. 167–9. These boundaries too were based on Welsh prophetic writing, the Welsh Triads delineating the 'Three Realms of Britain'.

26. As shown by Glendower in renouncing the allegiance of the Welsh Church to Rome the following year (1406) and by Henry in countenancing the confiscation of the temporalities of the Church in October 1404 and executing various high-ranking clergymen in 1402, 1405 and 1408.

27. For Dafydd Gam's attempt to kill Glendower during his first parliament, see *Glyn Dŵr*, p. 226.

28. *PC*, i, p. 249.

29. *Glyn Dŵr*, p. 119; *PC*, pp. 250–51.

30. Wylie, ii, p. 93.

31. The fifteen knights are named by Walsingham. See *Annales*, pp. 400–401.

32. *Syllabus*, ii, p. 553.

33. The date of the battle of Usk is disputed. Adam Usk – a man born in Usk – records that it was fought on 12 March 1405, and he gives several correct details about the battle (*Adam Usk*, p. 213). Shortly after giving this news he refers to being robbed by Welshmen in whom he had placed his trust, so, although he was writing on the Continent, he was probably well informed. However, the end of his entry, in which he relates how Gruffydd died of plague in the Tower six years later, shows that Usk himself, or a later copyist, introduced other details into his manuscript. It is likely therefore that the date of 12 March (the feast of St Gregory) was inserted later, arising out of a confusion with the *eve* of St Gregory, when the prince defeated the Welsh at Grosmont. Walsingham gives the date of the battle of Usk as 5 May (*Annales*, p. 399), and this is altogether more likely, as *Glyn Dŵr*, pp. 226, 223, agrees.

34. Walker, 'Yorkshire Risings', p. 161; *Annales*, p. 400.

35. *PC*, p. 264.

36. See Walker, 'Yorkshire Risings', for the rising as 'a series of loosely connected and largely spontaneous risings . . . best treated as three separate, and perhaps sequential, episodes'.

37. *PROME*, 1406 March, part 2, item 2.

38. Ormrod, 'Rebellion of Archbishop Scrope', Nottingham 2006.

39. Walker, 'Yorkshire Risings', pp. 164–5.

40. Walker, 'Yorkshire Risings', p. 172.

41. Both Walsingham and the continuator of the *Eulogium* refer to Westmorland and the archbishop drinking together. See *Annales*, p. 406, and *Eulogium*, iii, p. 406.

42. *EC*, p. 32, refers to the king sending a host to Westmorland.

43. *Badby*, p. 123.

44. *Eulogium*, iii, p. 407.

45. When news of Lord Bardolph's secret flight north was revealed, Gascoigne was one of the two members whom the council sent to enquire, specifically because Henry had 'a special confidence in him'. See *PC*, i, p.

46. *Badby*, p. 124.

16: Smooth Comforts False

1. The various accounts are summarised in Wylie, ii, pp. 246–52 and analysed in more detail in McNiven, 'Henry IV's health', pp. 747–59.

2. McNiven, 'Henry IV's health', p. 757. See also McNiven's conclusion on p. 759. The investigation included an examination of his nasal passages, which would have disintegrated after eight years of leprosy.

3. *PC*, i, p. 275.

4. *PK*, p. 432.

5. The only statement by the king himself regarding his disease is a letter to the council, which would not have been made public. See *Signet Letters*, pp. 125–6.

6. The 1397 treatment of a plaster was purchased from the London grocer William Chichele. See Wylie, iv, p. 153.

7. *Adam Usk*, p. 243.

8. Wylie, iv, p. 153; Appendix Six.

9. Rawcliffe, *Medicine and Society*, p. 47.

10. *CPR 1399–1401*, p. 255. See Appendix Six.

11. Biggs, 'Politics of health', p. 191; *idem*, 'An Ill and Infirm King'.

12. The documents used for the comparison were C 81/1358 no. 4b and C 81/1362 no. 46.

13. Wylie, ii, p. 267; iii, p. 112. Wylie's reference to 10,000 lb. of copper being purchased for cannon in 1402 later ended up as 'the king's own great gun' of 4.5 tons. There is no direct evidence for Henry having a gun of this weight. Even if he is right, a cannon of 4.5 tons would have been very difficult to transport from Nottingham to Aberystwyth via Hereford (as in Wylie, iv, p. 234). The two-ton cannon called 'The Messenger' is more likely to have been the largest then employed.

14. Wylie, ii, p. 272.

15. For the year 1405 there are no fewer that 302 signet letters extant, calendared in *Signet Letters*, pp. 62–115. This is by far the largest number for any single year (37 are extant for 1402, 82 for 1403, 42 for 1404, 165 for 1406, 24 for 1407, 14 for 1408, 19 for 1409, 12 for 1410 and 3 for 1412). Although the irregularities of creation (for which see Kirby, p. 210) and the vagaries of survival mean that this is a poor method of measuring actual work undertaken, it is worth noting that

in 1405 itself, 176 signet letters date from before 8 June 1405 and 146 are dated afterwards, indicating that Henry sustained a high level of business despite his illness.

16. This took place at Lambeth on 26 December. Philippa was married in October 1406 at Lund. She never saw any of her family again.

17. The essential reading for this is Biggs, 'Politics of health'.

18. According to Biggs, thirty-six of the seventy-four county members in the 1406 parliament were royal retainers, with a further nine being retainers of royalist lords (Biggs, 'Politics of health', pp. 203–4). According to Dodd, 'Conflict or Consensus', p. 123, the figure was twenty-eight retainers but a total of fifty-nine Lancastrian supporters. There were 167 borough members (*PROME*, 1406 March, introduction). Thus even if all the county members were pro-Lancastrian they would still have been outnumbered by the borough representatives. Indeed, one explanation of why the majority of the county members were Lancastrian is that Henry ordered the sheriffs to choose sympathetic men to bolster his position against the rebellious borough representatives.

19. To be specific: the 22 May arrangements, which can be connected with the king's physical condition, cannot be connected with the commons, being the king's own reaction to his illness; the 22 December arrangements (the Thirty-One Articles) cannot be connected to the king's illness, given that his condition had improved and these articles were far harsher on the king than the earlier ones.

20. *Signet Letters*, p. 124.

21. *CPR* 1405–8, p. 170.

22. Wylie, iv, p. 295.

23. *Signet Letters*, p. 125.

24. *Signet Letters*, pp. 125–6.

25. This would imply that he led his army to Berwick after the Yorkshire Rising in this same state, and then campaigned in Wales in poor health.

26. He stayed at the Tower, Lambeth, Eltham and Dowgate. The only places away from the river he stayed at between 11 November 1405 and the opening of parliament (1 March 1406) were Hertford Castle (11–17 December, 30 January–3 February, 21–26 February) and Waltham Abbey (29–30 January). See Wylie, iv, p. 295; *Signet Letters*, pp. 104–23.

27. *PK*, p. 430. See also Appendix Six. I have been unable to identify a large cadre of physicians attending the king at this time. Biggs, 'Politics of health', p. 192, suggests he may have been attended by as many as five.

28. Henry was at Westminster on Saturday 8 May (*PROME*, 1406 March, item 29), Wednesday 12 May (C 53/175, no. 4), Friday 14, Saturday 15, Saturday 22 and Monday 14 May (*PROME*, 1406 March, item 29, supported by C 53/ 175, no. 2), Wednesday 2 June (C 53/175, no. 3), Monday 7 June (*PROME*, 1406 March, item 38), and Saturday 19 June (*PROME*, 1406 March, item 41). The last day of this session was the day of the trial of Lord Bardolph and the earl of Northumberland.

29. *PROME*, March 1406, item 31.

30. *Eulogium*, iii, p. 409.

31. See Appendix Five. It is possible that Henry travelled by carriage; however, evidence is lacking on this point.

32. Biggs, 'Politics of health', p. 198; Kirby, p. 203. The abbot and the monks met the king at the lower gate of the monastery. He dropped to his knees and kissed their crucifix. Having been sprinkled with holy water, he was led into the church and up to the high altar, where he heard a short service, sang a hymn and listened to the abbot's address. There he kissed the sacred relics. He spent the night in the abbot's lodging, and rose early the next morning to attend two Masses in St Mary's Chapel (it being a Sunday, 22 August). He processed with the choir around the cloister and went back to the abbot's lodging for breakfast with his sons Thomas and Humphrey. Having dined with the abbot and the lords and knights in his party, he received two visitors: Philip Repingdon, his old confessor, now bishop of Lincoln, and Lord Willoughby, who had been with him on his crusade in Prussia. After their departure he spent the rest of the day reading in the abbey library.

33. Bede, *A History of the English Church and People*, trans. Leo Sherley-Price (rev. ed., 1968), pp. 158–62.

34. *PROME*, March 1406, introduction.

35. *PC*, i, p. 295.

36. This figure of £2,500 has been taken by some writers to represent the total expenses but the source – Kirby – states that it relates to the county members alone (Kirby, p. 206). The expense was about £34 per member for all three sessions (120 days), an average of 5s 8d per day. This is a little in excess of the 4s per day to which Walsingham states the knights and their deputies attending parliament in 1410 were entitled (*CM*, p. 379). In addition, there were 167 burgesses summoned in 1406, and they were also permitted to reclaim expenses. Had they done so in the same proportion as the county members, that would have added a further £5,462 to the bill, making a total in the region of £8,000, nearly a quarter of the £37,000 implicit in a grant of a tenth and a fifteenth. The forty-nine or so lords usually summoned were not entitled to reclaim expenses, and nor were the forty-seven parliamentary archbishops, bishops, abbots and priors.

37. Kirby, p. 206; *Annales*, p. 418.

38. *Brut*, ii, p. 367.

39. Given-Wilson, *Royal Household*, p. 141.

40. Wright, 'Recovery of royal finance in 1407', pp. 71–80.

41. *Badby*, p. 144.

42. Kirby, p. 210; Allmand, p. 42.

43. *CCR 1405–9*, p. 261.

44. *PROME*, 1407 March, appendix, item 1.

45. *CPR 1405–9*, pp. 361–2.

46. Biggs, 'An Ill and Infirm King'.

47. See Appendix Five.

48. Wylie, iv, pp. 296–7. His route via Worksop (*Signet Letters*, p. 146) shows that on this occasion he did not sail up the River Trent to Nottingham.

49. 1 Peter, chapter ii, verse 17.

50. *PROME*, 1407 October, item 5.

51. Kirby, p. 215, claims Henry was in Gloucester on 20 October; however, the parliament roll states that when parliament assembled on 24 October, having been

adjourned on the 20th, the chancellor spoke 'in the presence of the lords spiritual and temporal', and not 'in the presence of the king and the lords and commons'. The king is not mentioned as being present until the presentation of the Speaker the following day.

52. A radically alternative view is put forward by Douglas Biggs in 'An Ill and Infirm King', specifically that in terms of the political management of the commons 'Arundel's machinations must be counted a complete failure'. Biggs bases this judgement on an assumption that Arundel's ploy to have a committee of powerful lords speak to the commons proved a failure, and that the storm of protest which greeted his use of the lords to set the level of taxation was 'the greatest concession to any house of commons before the Civil War'. I would counter that, with regard to the first of these, the lords' committee was not a ploy of Arundel's but a direct result of a request from the commons (*PROME*, 1407 October, item 18). Nor is there any evidence that it proved a failure; in fact it seems to have been successful, for no detrimental repercussions resulting from this meeting are recorded on the parliament roll. With regard to the second point, the storm of protest was not sufficient to inhibit the granting of the substantial tax and wool subsidy, or even to delay the grant. Indeed, the fact that it took Arundel just eleven working days (from Monday 21 November to Friday 2 December) to persuade the commons to grant a tax significantly larger than that granted in the Long Parliament, which took more than 120 days of parliamentary time, has to be counted extremely efficient political management, especially considering that many members of the Long Parliament were also present at Gloucester. In lifting the restrictions on the king and the council, and securing a large grant so rapidly in the face of the commons' opposition, Arundel has to be counted wholly successful. As for the concession to the commons of their right in future to discuss the affairs of the realm without the king being present, it is arguable that this merely confirmed what was already the practice, and had been since 1399 if not 1376.

53. For his sexual proclivity, see *Eulogium*, iii, p. 410. He claimed to have fathered all the French queen's children.

54. Wylie, iii, p. 93.

55. *PROME*, 1406 March, part 2, item 9.

56. The confirmation 'by the king' was dated at Gloucester, but it would appear that by this date he had already set out for Eltham. He was at Cirencester on the 8th and Windsor on the 14th, and back at Westminster on the 18th. See *Syllabus*, p. 559; *Signet Letters*, p. 147.

17: Golden Care

1. Wylie, iii, pp. 146–52.

2. *Issues*, pp. 307–8. The payment of £13 6s 8d to Simon Flete on 17 January 1408 was followed up by a final payment on completion of the work on 16 March: it is this latter entry which specifies that Henry himself invented this cannon.

3. Wylie, iv, p. 230.

4. Wylie, iv, pp. 230–32.

5. It is worth noting that the document which famously misled generations of historians into believing that English ships were equipped with iron and brass cannon

as early as 1338 dates not from that year but from 12 Henry IV (1410–11). See Tout, 'Firearms in England', p. 669.

6. Wylie, iv, p. 157.

7. *EHD*, p. 201.

8. According to *Signet Letters*, p. 148, he was at Leicester on 16 March. The same day he was at Nottingham, twenty-five miles to the north, where he gave royal assent to the election of the abbot of Selby (according to *Syllabus*, ii, p. 560). Covering this distance in one day would mean that he was either fit enough to ride long-distance, carried in a litter, or travelled by carriage between Leicester and Nottingham.

9. These were York, Bishopthorpe, Cawood, Selby and Wheelhall. Rothwellhaigh, Pontefract and Newstead Priory are not on rivers: these he must have travelled to by road. See Wylie, iv, p. 297.

10. *Signet Letters*, p. 148. Kirby, p. 224, placed this letter in the following year. He corrected this view when editing the letter for *Signet Letters*. For Birdsnest Lodge see *HKW*, ii, p. 901.

11. McNiven, 'Henry IV's health', p. 761. The date is based on the assumption that the collapse postdates the proclamation that Henry would be at Nottingham on 12 August to oversee a tournament (*Syllabus*, p. 561).

12. For Usk's relationship with the archbishop see *Adam Usk*, pp. 247–9.

13. *Adam Usk*, p. 243.

14. The Black Prince is usually said to have died of dysentery (Richard Barber, *The Black Prince* (Stroud, 2003), p. 214, and in *ODNB*, under 'Edward of Woodstock'). There are very few sources for his symptoms. One of the two referenced by Barber (Thompson (ed.), *Chronicon Angliae*, pp. 88–9) does suggest that he had 'bloody flux' or dysentery at the end of his life, but it was not necessarily the underlying illness. Indeed, it was probably not. Lethal cases of dysentery killed the medieval sufferer within weeks (Henry V being an example). The same chronicler who states that the Black Prince had dysentery also states that four thousand people died of the disease in a single year in Gascony in 1411 (*CM*, p. 380). In marked contrast, the Black Prince had a wasting disease which left him increasingly debilitated for about eight years. With regard to the possible connectedness of the prince's disease and Henry's it should be noted that both the prince and Henry retained their mental composure to the end of their lives. The Black Prince's infection was probably picked up on campaign in Castile. Henry was of course in regular contact with representatives from Iberia – his half-sister was the queen of Castile, his eldest sister was the queen of neighbouring Portugal, and his wife maintained contact with her homeland of Navarre – so it is quite possible that he had caught the disease from an ambassador. Neither man had children after the onset of their illnesses, but neither man seems to have foreshortened his wife's life, so neither man is likely to have suffered a highly contagious or sexually transmitted disease.

15. For the pain of his sickness, see *EHD*, p. 207.

16. Wylie, iv, p. 231.

17. Wylie, iv, p. 233.

18. *Royal Wills*, p. 203. The spelling has been modernised.

19. *LK*, pp. 217–19.

20. He witnessed three royal charters in 1408. Biggs, 'Witness Lists', p. 421.

21. Wylie, iv, p. 349.

22. *Royal Wills*, pp. 203–7. There were others, unnamed, also at the making of the will.

23. *Signet Letters*, p. 150. The signet letter from Henry was sent on 22 February; the council sent the letter in his name as if he witnessed it being sealed with his privy seal in person at Westminster on 26 March at Westminster. See *RHL*, ii, p. 240.

24. The privy seal writ predates the patent letter by five days. See *Signet Letters*, p. 150.

25. He appropriated revenues from four nearby churches in order to endow the church, for which he later came in for criticism, especially from Wylie, who compared this religious foundation with Eton and King's College at Cambridge, both founded by Henry VI. See Wylie, iii, p. 243.

26. *Signet Letters*, p. 152.

27. *Signet Letters*, p. 152. The spelling has been modernised and the grammar slightly changed for the sake of readability.

28. Williams (ed.), *Correspondence of Bekyngton*, ii, p. 368.

29. Wylie, iii, p. 252.

30. Williams (ed.), *Bekyngton*, ii, p. 366.

31. *Brut*, ii, p. 369.

32. Allmand, pp. 41–2.

33. For example, *Badby*, pp. 151–2; *ODNB*, under 'Thomas of Lancaster'.

34. It was Henry V who brought Richard II's body back from King's Langley to be buried at Westminster, and the story goes that he had always been fond of Richard, who had knighted him in Ireland in 1399. Likewise they may have had different views about Hotspur, many of whose servants and followers came to be employed by the prince. See Kirby, p. 227.

35. Allmand, p. 397; *PROME*, 1423 October, item 35. Henry Beaufort seems to have taken against her too. See *PROME*, 1426 February, introduction.

36. Allmand, pp. 49–50; *PROME*, 1411 November, introduction, quoting A. H. Thomas & I. D. Thornley (eds), *The Great Chronicle of London* (1938), p. 90.

37. That this was intentional is made likely by the fact that it had been Edward III's entail which had brought John of Gaunt's children closer to the throne than his older siblings'.

38. Such a view is outlined in *EC*, p. 37, where it is dated to 1412–13, and A. H. Thomas & I. D. Thornley (eds), *The Great Chronicle of London* (1938), p. 90, where it is dated to 1411. Such an opinion is likely to have been held for some while before this.

39. It should be noted that Thomas of Lancaster and Henry Beaufort were unfriendly towards one another at this time. In 1411, when Thomas obtained dispensation to marry John Beaufort's widow, Henry Beaufort attempted to stop him. See Kirby, p. 234; Allmand, p. 53; *CB*, pp. 64–5.

40. *CB*, p. 48.

41. Wylie, iv, pp. 298–9. It is perhaps significant that he is not known to have stayed with Henry Beaufort in this year, although he had stayed with him in previous years.

42. *CB*, p. 44.

43. *CB*, p. 49; Wylie, iii, p. 284. Kirby, p. 225, gives 19 December.

44. The king travelled eleven miles per day, slow by normal standards but a rare example of sustained road travel at this time in his life. See Appendix Five.

45. For a view supporting the sustained friendship between Henry and Archbishop Arundel at this time, see *Badby*, pp. 149–50, 188. An alternative reading is suggested in Allmand, p. 42. This is that Arundel was dismissed because he 'may not have been high in the royal favour'. Two reasons are given by Allmand for this tentative suggestion: that he had not always been a firm supporter of the king and that Henry did not appreciate the archbishop's restrictions on his financial practices. The first of these is difficult to see, given Arundel's pro-royal role in parliaments throughout the reign, especially that of 1407. The second is speculation. What is not in doubt is that the close bonds between Henry and Arundel in 1407 grew – if anything – closer in 1408 and 1409, when Arundel was chancellor and leader of the council. Henry wrote notes in his own hand in these two years thanking him for his work, and often stayed at the archbishop's own houses. (Henry is known to have stayed at Lambeth, for example, in January, February, March, April and May 1410: see *Badby*, p. 188; Wylie, iv, p. 299). In March 1409 he granted Arundel the royal castle of Queenborough, and later that year the royal manor of Sheen (*Badby*, p. 156). The archbishop was with him in his sicknesses in 1408 and 1409, and witnessed his will on 21 January 1409. It is also striking that Arundel witnessed almost every charter on C 53/178 (10–12 Henry IV) even after he was no longer chancellor. The only exception is no. 9, sealed on 12 November 1409 (no. 10, dated 17 February 1410 having no witnesses). Other strong evidence for the reading given in the text here – that Arundel resigned against the king's will – is Henry IV's emphatic support for Arundel in his argument with Oxford University in 1411 and the fact that Henry brought back Arundel as chancellor when he reasserted his own authority at the end of 1411. It is far more likely that in December 1409 Arundel was no longer able to tolerate the assertiveness of the young prince, who sacked him as chancellor on the day after Henry IV died.

46. Henry is not known to have visited Southwark Palace in 1409 or 1410 (unlike 1408). In later years, Henry Beaufort was questioned in parliament over his loyalty to Henry, and at the end of the reign he was widely thought to have tried to persuade the king to abdicate. For obvious reasons, it would be quite understandable if Henry had always been a little cautious of his father's other son called Henry.

47. It would appear that the king's half-brother was trying to undermine the king's friend in ecclesiastical as well as political matters. See *Badby*, pp. 153–4.

48. For Thomas Beaufort as the member of the prince's party 'most acceptable to the king', see *Badby*, p. 202.

49. *CM*, pp. 377–9; *PROME*, 1410 January, introduction and appendix.

50. For a full discussion of this scheme see *Badby*, pp. 192–5.

51. *CM*, p. 379.

52. *Badby*, p. 207.

53. *Royal Wills*, pp. 208–11.

54. According to Kirby, p. 230, only these three attended a meeting on 8 February 1410.

55. Kirby, p. 241. The existence of this measure is known only from its annulment. That councillors swore to abide by the Thirty-One Articles again, and that this was struck from the record is not impossible. Some such measure would explain

how the prince and the council was able to overrule the king in his assent to the fifteenth article of the commons petition of 23 April.

56. *Signet Letters*, p. 154.

57. C 53/178. Of the seven which fall in 1410 (nos 2–8), only two were granted by the king in person, and both of these were during the first session of parliament. The remainder were granted on the strength of a privy seal writ.

18: In That Jerusalem

1. Given-Wilson, *Royal Household*, p. 137. The importance to Henry can be gauged from his statement in 1407, when he declared that those currently serving him should be paid their annuities as a priority, over and above recipients of grants in earlier years.

2. *PC*, ii, p. 7. These were in addition to the prince and the three officers (treasurer, chancellor and keeper of the privy seal).

3. *PC*, ii, pp. 8–12.

4. Wylie, iii, p. 431.

5. *Signet Letters*, p. 154.

6. Kirby, p. 236.

7. On 29 November 1410 Henry appointed ambassadors to negotiate with representatives of Castile and France. The same day he separately licensed the prince to grant safe-conducts to the ambassadors of the duke of Burgundy, even though he himself was happy to issue safe-conducts to the French negotiators. In addition, he directed the instructions to the French embassy to be sealed with the great seal and the privy seal (both controlled by members of the council) but not the signet, his personal seal. Although the split with the council was some way off, the difference in policy towards France was perhaps clear to Henry long before the dispute became open. See Nicols, *Privy Council*, ii, pp. 5–6; *Syllabus*, ii, p. 566.

8. Allmand, p. 48.

9. Wylie, iv, p. 36; Allmand, p. 48.

10. Wylie, iv, p. 38.

11. For example, Kirby, p. 238, and Wylie, iv, p. 40. McNiven in 'Health' allows that problems with the prince may have been the real reason. It should be noted that the king was well enough and sane enough at this time to write letters in his own hand (for which see *Signet Letters*, p. 155).

12. *Syllabus*, p. 568 (ships); *PROME*, 1411 November, introduction (summons). If Wylie, iv, p. 41, is correct in stating that plans for the parliament were being made as early as 28 August, this might suggest that the council was planning to hold a parliament in Henry's absence, in which case there can be little doubt that the purpose was to gain parliamentary approval for his deposition.

13. *PROME*, 1411 November, introduction.

14. Kirby, p. 234; Allmand, p. 53; *CB*, pp. 64–5.

15. *Eulogium*, iii, pp. 420–1. In addition there is the prince's open letter of 1412, which accuses others of claiming this about him (for which see *CM*, p. 384) and similar claims in February 1426 against Henry Beaufort regarding his disloyalty to Henry IV. The latter accusation was on the testimony of Henry V himself, who reported

to his brother Humphrey that when Henry IV had been extremely ill, Henry Beaufort had said to him that the king, being so racked with illness that he was not *compos mentis* or able to speak, was not capable of governing his people, and so he urged him to take the government and crown upon himself (*PROME*, 1426 February, appendix).

16. *PROME*, 1411 November, introduction, quoting J. A. Giles (ed.), *Incerti Scriptoris Chronicon Angliae* (1848), p. 63.

17. *PROME*, 1411 November, item 25.

18. *PROME*, 1411 November, item 26.

19. *CCR 1409–13*, p. 311. The sole exceptions were Owen Glendower and Thomas Ward of Trumpington (the man impersonating Richard II in Scotland).

20. Henry's final council is named in *PC*, ii, pp. 31 (twice, once without Lord Roos), 36 and 38. Bowet was appointed on 6 January 1412 (Wylie, iv, p. 52). See also *King's Council*, p. 164, where it is stated that the duke of Clarence was a member of the council. This is unlikely, as he was abroad from shortly after his creation as duke.

21. Allmand, p. 61. On p. 54 Allmand suggests that Henry chose to support the Armagnacs because he wished to demonstrate his independence from his son's policy in supporting Burgundy. However, Henry is unlikely to have made his mind up on which faction to support only in the wake of dismissing his son; it is far more likely that this was a bone of contention leading to the prince's dismissal.

22. For enmity between the duke of Brittany (son of the queen of England) and Burgundy, see *Monstrelet*, i, p. 209. In addition, it should be noted that Arthur of Brittany, son of Queen Joan of England, had been brought up in the household of the duke of Orléans (Wylie, iv, p. 67). For the alliances between the Armagnacs and Navarre, Gascony, Brittany and Aragon see *CM*, p. 382.

23. Representatives of the duke of Burgundy were in England discussing the potential marriage alliance from 1 February to 4 March 1412. Henry had given them safe-conducts on 11 January 1412 and appointed negotiators to deal with them on 10 February. The Armagnacs sent negotiators on 24 January; they received safe-conducts on 6 February. See *Syllabus*, ii, p. 569; Wylie, iv, p. 64.

24. *CM*, p. 385.

25. C 53/179 no. 7.

26. The prince received one thousand marks on 18 February (Wylie, iv, p. 51); payments for their services also went to the prince's treasurer, Henry Scrope, and the earls of Arundel and Warwick. Allmand, p. 53, quoting E 404/27/168–9, 214, 268.

27. C 53/179 nos 5, 6. The earlier of these was the foundation by the duke of York of the great collegiate church at Fotheringay. That Henry visited Windsor in the meantime is suggested by the itinerary in Wylie, iv, p. 301.

28. As Henry declared on 16 May. See *Syllabus*, p. 571.

29. For the naming of the prince as a supporter of the king on this expedition, see *CM*, p. 386.

30. C 53/179 no. 2. This took place on 5 July 1412, four days before Thomas of Lancaster was created duke of Clarence. Extraordinarily, these creations were the only ones in the whole of Henry IV's reign (except passing the royal and Lancastrian titles to his son and heir in 1399). It is surprising that until now he had not raised

his younger sons to dukedoms, even though parliament had urged him to do so regularly since 1406. There are two obvious reasons why he had been reluctant. One was that he could not afford to endow his sons with the lands required to maintain them in the dignity of dukes. The other was the lesson of Richard's reign, in which so many dukes had been created that the dignity had been cheapened.

31. C 53/179 no. 5.

32. *CM*, p. 386.

33. Wylie, iv, pp. 92–3.

34. *CM*, p. 386, has 29 June. Wylie, iv, p. 90, states that the prince was at the bishop of London's house from 30 June to 11 July. There are several accounts of what took place in his meeting with his father, but it seems that two separate meetings have been confused by contemporary writers: one following the prince's letter of 17 June and the other following accusations of the prince's sequestration of the money for Calais in September. Wylie associates the prince drawing a dagger in the king's presence and asking the king to kill him to the late June reconciliation; Allmand and *ODNB* (under 'Henry IV') date it to the September one. The closeness of the suspicions harboured by the king in the *First English Life of Henry V* to those mentioned by Walsingham in relation to June, combined with the presence of the earl of Ormond (who sailed to France with the duke of Clarence in August), favour the late June meeting. See Wylie, iv, pp. 53, 90–91; Allmand, pp. 57–8; C. L. Kingsford (ed.), *The First English Life of Henry V* (Oxford, 1911), pp. 11–12; *EHD*, p. 206; *CM*, p. 387.

35. Wylie, iv, p. 90; John Stow, *Chronicle of England* (1615), p. 339. But note Wylie's word of caution on not finding Ormond's testimony in Stow's supposed source.

36. *EHD*, p. 206.

37. John Stow, *Chronicle of England* (1615), p. 340. Whether this scene relates to the reconciliation in late June or early July, or to a second meeting of the king and his son in late September, is not certain. However, a meaningful reconciliation did take place between Henry and his son at this time, followed by a show of reconciliation between Henry Beaufort and Thomas of Lancaster. On 13 July 1412 Henry Beaufort received a pardon which specifically named him as executor of his brother's will, reflecting on his dispute with Thomas (*CPR* 1408–13, p. 420).

38. Wylie, iv, p. 72.

39. *PC*, ii, p. 33; Wylie, iv, p. 77, has different figures, taken from the St Denis chronicle.

40. *PC*, ii, pp. 34–5. This is undated but it includes a reference to paying wages to the prince for the service of sixty men-at-arms for 203 days from 9 March, i.e. to 25 September.

41. Walsingham also claims this in relation to the June reconciliation. In relation to these earlier claims, Arundel had received a general pardon on 15 June (*Syllabus*, ii, p. 571). Walsingham gives very little information for the last year of the king's life, however, and is less reliable as an authority for this period.

42. *PC*, ii, pp. 37–8.

43. Wylie, iv, p. 102.

44. *EHD*, p. 206.

45. Wylie, iv, p. 38, n. 1.
46. Or the Bethlehem Chamber, according to Elmham, a royal chaplain. See Wright (ed.), *Political Poems*, ii, pp. 122.
47. *Brut*, ii, p. 372; *EHD*, p. 207.
48. *Monstrelet*, i, pp. 239–40; *Waurin*, pp. 166–7. Monstrelet was Waurin's source (Gransden, *Historical Writing II*, pp. 289, 291–2). Monstrelet himself does not fail to compliment Henry on his virtues; he describes him as 'a valiant knight, eager and subtle against his enemies', and states that the prince was 'honourably crowned', so the bias of the story was not his own. But we should be suspicious of the veracity of a French tale which casts the Lancastrians in an unworthy light and conflicts with what was recorded in England.
49. Gransden, *Historical Writing II*, pp. 389–90.
50. *IH*, p. 124.
51. Capgrave, *Chronicle of England*, pp. 302–3.
52. See *ODNB*, under 'Henry IV' and 'Elmham, Thomas'; Wright (ed.), *Political Poems*, ii, pp. 118–23.
53. *Foedera*, ix, pp. 9–10; *Issues*, pp. 334–5. Henry V purchased his father's goods on 15 May for £25,000 so he could 'perform his will'. Henry V had not managed to pay all his father's debts by the time of his own death in 1422. Further evidence that Henry made his second will on his deathbed may be found in *Brut*, ii, p. 372.

19. That I and Greatness were Compelled to Kiss

1. *PK*, p. 401.
2. *Waurin*, pp. 63–4.

Appendix One

1. For Henry V, whose birth is sometimes wrongly assigned to August 1387, see Appendix Three.
2. For a history of the royal Maundy ceremony, see the two books by Brian Robinson, *Royal Maundy* (1977), and *Silver Pennies and Linen Towels* (1992).

Appendix Two

1. *CR*, p. 166.

Appendix Three

1. Kirby, p. 16; *Register 1379–1383*, i, pp. 180, 222, 232; ii, p. 309. This last shows that Mary's mother was paid for her daughter's upkeep for a year on 31 January 1382, presumably in advance. See also *CPR* 1381–85, p. 95: this shows that Mary was still living with her mother on 6 February 1382.
2. *LK*, p. 17.
3. Wylie, iv, p. 166. The use of both English and Latin is common in Wylie's appendices.

4. Wylie, iv, p. 167.
5. Alison Weir, *Britain's Royal Families* (Pimlico edn, 2002), p. 124.
6. DL 28/1/1 fol. 5r.
7. *CIPM*, xvii, pp. 376–80. Odd IPMs also give his age as fourteen or sixteen, but most agree on '15 and more'.
8. John Rylands Library, French MS 54; Allmand, pp. 7–8.
9. Allmand, p. 7.
10. DL 28/1/2 fol. 20v., noted in Wylie, iv, p. 159. A payment to the midwife who assisted at Thomas's birth is also noted in this account, as are cloth, kirtles, tunics and sandals for Thomas as well as his older brother.
11. DL 28/1/2 fol. 28. This is an indenture between Henry of Lancaster's chamberlain and treasurer, dated 24 September 1386.
12. E 101/404/23 fol. 3r.
13. Allmand, p. 8. Also see the ages for Henry cited in Wylie, iii, p. 324.
14. DL 28/1/2 fol. 17r.
15. *ODNB*, under 'John of Lancaster', *CP*, ii, p. 70.
16. *Expeditions*, p. 107.
17. Wylie, iii, p. 248.
18. Goodman, *John of Gaunt*, p. 155.
19. Wylie, 'Dispensation of John XXIII for a son of Henry IV', pp. 96–7. Edmund was in his eleventh year on 15 January 1412. It is not known why he was called 'le Bourd' ('the joke', or 'the deceipt'), nor whom the mother might have been. He was educated in London.

Appendix Four

1. *Waurin*, p. 60.
2. Given-Wilson, *Usk*, p. 171; Wylie, i, p. 363.
3. 'Deposition', pp. 80–81.
4. *Brut*, ii, p. 549.
5. For example, the contemporary Wigmore chronicle in the library of the University of Chicago (MS 224). I am indebted to Dr Philip Morgan for this detail.
6. It may be worth noting that a mass grave of 159 feet in length and 9 feet in depth and width (IX instead of LX) would be sufficient to bury about a thousand corpses if piled four deep.
7. *Eulogium*, iii, p. 397.
8. Capgrave, *Chronicle of England*, p. 283; *Annales*, p. 367.
9. On the side of the rebels, five dead knights can be identified, including those executed after the battle. These are Henry Percy himself, the earl of Worcester, Sir Richard Venables, Sir Richard de Vernon and Sir Gilbert Halsall (the last being named in the Dieulacres chronicle). On the king's side, ten men of substance can be identified as killed in the battle: the earl of Stafford and Sir Walter Blount (according to *Brut*, ii, p. 549), Hugh Schirle, John Clifton, John Cockayne, Nicholas Ganville, John Calverley, John Massy, lord of Podington, Hugh Mortimer and B. Gousile (according to *Annales*, p. 369). *The Brut* also incorrectly includes Sir John Stanley, who was only wounded. See also Wylie, iv, p. 303 for other men from Cheshire and Lancashire at the battle.

Appendix Five

1. Biggs, 'Politics of health', p. 197.
2. Places and dates drawn from Biggs, 'Politics of health', p. 205.
3. Places and dates drawn from Wylie, iv, p. 291.
4. Wylie has Henry at Shrewsbury on 20 July; however, there is no evidence he was in the town. He was probably at Haughmond Abbey, five miles away.
5. Kirby, p. 213; Douglas Biggs, 'An Ill and Infirm King'.
6. Except where stated otherwise, places and dates drawn from Wylie, iv, pp. 296–7.
7. *Signet Letters*, p. 145.
8. *Signet Letters*, p. 146.
9. Douglas Biggs, 'An Ill and Infirm King'.
10. E 101/405/14 fol. 7v. These were made of brass and cost 50s each. This was about four times the normal price of a saddle.
11. DL 28/1/3 fol. 13v. These cost 33s 4d each.
12. Wylie, iv, p. 299.

Appendix Six

1. DL 28/1/2 fol. 15v. Twice medicines were bought for him on Middleton's advice.
2. DL 28/1/2 fol. 26r. The author of Melton's entry in *ODNB* is mistaken in stating that this service was performed on behalf of Henry. The payment occurs in the section of the account devoted to Lady Derby, and the text reads *domine* not *domini*.
3. *Expeditions*, p. 110.
4. *Expeditions*, p. 164.
5. Rawcliffe, *Medicine and Society*, p. 106. Here Rawcliffe states that Malvern was contracted from 1393; in her entry on Malvern in *ODNB* she states that he was employed from 1395.
6. He was with Henry at the execution of Scrope and present at the examination of John Badby on 2 January 1409. See Wylie, ii, p. 238.
7. Rawcliffe, *Medicine and Society*, p. 112; *CPR 1399–1401*, p. 228; *CPR 1401–1405*, pp. 9, 345 (Royal Mint); *CPR 1405–8*, pp. 22, 170.
8. E 101/404/21 fol. 45r.
9. *Syllabus*, ii, p. 544.
10. He may have been the same man as Richard Grisby, abbot of Dore, who received a safe-conduct to travel abroad in 1411. See *CCR 1409–13*, p. 160.
11. *CPR 1408–13*, p. 28. He arrived by the end of September 1408 (Wylie, iv, p. 231).
12. *CPR 1408–13*, p. 363.
13. *Syllabus*, p. 570; *CPR 1408–13*, p. 392 (denization), 397 (death). Henry wrote a close letter on his behalf on 4 April 1412 (*CCR 1409–13*, p. 269). Easter 1412 fell on 3 April, so presumably he died unexpectedly on or about the 4th.
14. Rawcliffe, *Medicine and Society*, p. 123. For Elias de Sabato see Wylie, iv, p. 231; *Syllabus*, p. 566; C. H. Talbot, *Medicine in Medieval England* (1967), p. 205. D'Alcobasso received the prebend of West Thurrock and the deanery of Wimborne Minster in February 1412: see Wylie, iii, p. 232; *CPR 1408–13*, pp. 363, 391, 392, 410.
15. Biggs, 'Politics of health', p. 192.
16. Wylie, iv, p. 204; Rawcliffe, *Medicine and Society*, p. 140.

17. Patricia Basing (ed.), *Parish Fraternity Register: Fraternity of the Holy Trinity . . .*, London Record Society 18 (1982), xvii.
18. E 101/404/21 fol. 45.
19. *CPR 1399–1401*, p. 255.

Appendix Seven

1. DL 28/1/2 fol. 14v. The entry refers to 'swages', very probably esses.
2. Wylie, iv, p. 116. See also the references in the note on the same page to the Lancastrian collar of the 1380s and 1390s being composed of esses.
3. It is possible that the carved collar of esses on the supposed effigy of Sir Thomas Swynford, Katherine Swynford's first husband, who died in 1371, is the earliest extant example of a livery collar. However, it is not certain that the grave is his, nor is it known for certain when the effigy was made. Sometimes a grave went for decades unmarked by an effigy (as in the case of Henry IV's first wife, Mary, who died in 1394 and whose effigy was not made until 1413). As Swynford's widow was still alive, and may have initially thought she would be buried with her husband, it is quite possible that the effigy was not carved until after Katherine had married John of Gaunt in 1396.
4. *Gothic*, p. 206.
5. Wylie, iv, p. 116.
6. Duffy, *Royal Tombs*, p. 204; Nicolas, 'Badge and Mottoes', p. 367.
7. There is a reference to a bishop's *sovereign* archbishop in 1352. The meaning of highest authority is the same as in the secular case. The word also appears with respect to the king's *sovereign* territory, and wool being the sovereign merchandise (i.e. most important).
8. DL 27/310, dated 1394; DL27 /313, dated 1395. I am grateful to Adrian Ailes for these references.
9. Those for 1393–4 include a payment for 'a gold collar made for the lord of seventeen letters of 's' in the form of feathers with roundels and writing in the same with a swan in a ring' (DL 28/1/4 fol. 16v), and those for 1397–8 include a payment for 'a collar in esses and flowers of *soveyne vous de moy*' (DL 28/1/6 fol. 22v).
10. There is at least one reference, and often two or three, to '*souveyne vous de moi*' in the following folios: DL 28/1/3 fol. 14v & 15v, DL 28/1/4 fol. 15v & 16r; DL 28/1/6 fol. 22v, 23r & 23v.
11. DL 28/1/3 fol. 15v.
12. DL 28/1/3 fol. 14v.
13. DL 28/1/3 fol. 14v ('a short loose gown of the lord of black velvet in the form of a curve of swages of *Soveyne vous de moy*'); DL 28/1/4 fol. 16r; DL 28/1/5 fol. 23r; DL 28/1/6 fol. 22v; DL 28/1/4 fol. 15v also has '*ad modum souveyne vous de moys*'.
14. *HKW*, ii, p. 935.
15. Radford, 'An unrecorded royal visit', p. 262; *Issues*, p. 305. The collar is possibly the one shown adorning Joan's effigy in Canterbury Cathedral.
16. DL 28/1/3 fol. 14v.
17. Nicolas, 'Badge and Mottoes', p. 365.
18. In this matter, compare the feathers on Henry's seal with those on that of the

Black Prince, on which it was modelled (reproduced in this volume, as plate twelve, from Nicolas, 'Badge and Mottoes', p. 362). The prince's does not have the motto. Engraved additions to seal matrices were not uncommon. Kings' first great seals were often just altered copies of their predecessors'.

19. *CR*, p. 40.

SELECT BIBLIOGRAPHY AND LIST OF ABBREVIATIONS

Works which are abbreviated in the notes are here given under both the abbreviation and the editor's or author's name. All places of publication are London unless otherwise stated.

Adam Usk: Chris Given-Wilson (ed.), *The Chronicle of Adam Usk* (Oxford, 1997)

J. Alexander & P. Binski (eds), *The Age of Chivalry: Art in Plantagenet England 1200–1400* (1987)

Allmand: Christopher Allmand, *Henry V* (1992)

Thomas Amyot, 'An Inquiry concerning the Death of Richard the Second', *Archaeologia*, 20 (1824), pp. 425–8

Annales: H. T. Riley (ed.), *Johannis de Trokelowe et Henrici de Blaneforde ... chronica et annales*, Rolls Series, 28 (1866)

Armitage-Smith: Sydney Armitage-Smith, *John of Gaunt* (1904)

Sydney Armitage-Smith (ed.), *John of Gaunt's Register 1372–1376*, Camden Society, Third Series 20–21 (2 vols, 1911)

Art of Kingship: Anthony Goodman and James Gillespie (eds), *Richard II: the Art of Kingship* (Oxford, 1999)

Mark Arvangian, 'Henry IV, the Northern Nobility and the Consolidation', in *Establishment*, pp. 117–38

R. L. Atkinson, 'Richard II and the Death of the Duke of Gloucester', *EHR*, 38 (1923), pp. 563–4

Authority & Subversion: Linda Clark (ed.), *Authority and Subversion*, The Fifteenth Century 3 (Woodbridge, 2003)

Badby: Peter McNiven, *Heresy and Politics in the Reign of Henry IV: the Burning of John Badby* (Woodbridge, 1987)

J. F. Baldwin, *The King's Council in England During the Middle Ages* (Oxford 1913, reprinted 1969)

Madeleine Barber, 'John Norbury (*c.*1350–1414): an Esquire of Henry IV', *EHR*, lxviii (1953), pp. 66–76

Caroline M. Barron, 'The Quarrel of Richard II with London, 1392–7', in *RRII*, pp. 173–201

J. M. W. Bean, 'Henry IV and the Percies', *History*, 44 (1959), pp. 212–27

Michael Bennett, *Richard II and the Revolution of 1399* (Stroud, 1999)

Michael Bennett, 'Edward III's Entail and the Succession to the Crown, 1376–1471', *EHR*, 113 (1998), pp. 580–609

Douglas Biggs, ' "A wrong whom conscience and kindred bid me to right": a reassessment of Edmund Langley, duke of York, and the usurpation of Henry IV', *Albion*, 26 (1994), pp. 253–72

Douglas Biggs, 'An Ill and Infirm King: Henry IV, Health and the Gloucester Parliament of 1407' (paper delivered at Nottingham 2006)

Douglas Biggs, 'Royal Charter Witness Lists for the Reign of Henry IV, 1399–1413', *EHR*, 119 (2004), pp. 407–23

Douglas Biggs, 'The politics of health: Henry IV and the Long Parliament of 1406', in *Establishment*, pp. 185–206

BIHR: *Bulletin of the Institute of Historical Research*

BJRL: *Bulletin of the John Rylands [University] Library [of Manchester]*

James Black, 'Henry IV's Pilgrimage', *SQ*, 34: 1 (1983), pp. 18–26

Andrew W. Boardman, *Hotspur: Henry Percy, Medieval Rebel* (Stroud, 2003)

F. W. D. Brie (ed.). *The Brut* (2 vols, Oxford, 1906–8).

A. L. Brown, 'The Commons and the council in the reign of Henry IV', *EHR*, 79 (1964), pp. 1–30

A. L. Brown, 'The English campaign in Scotland, 1400' in H. Hearder & H. Loyn (eds), *British Government and Administration: Studies Presented to S. B. Chrimes* (Cardiff, 1974), pp. 40–54

A. L. Brown, 'The reign of Henry IV', in Chrimes, Ross, and Griffiths (eds), *Fifteenth Century England* (2nd edn, Stroud, 1995)

R. A. Brown, H. M. Colvin & A. J. Taylor, *History of the King's Works: the Middle Ages* (2 vols, 1963)

Bruce, Mary, *The Usurper King* (1986)

Brut: F. W. D. Brie (ed.). *The Brut* (2 vols, Oxford, 1906–8)

D. M. Bueno de Mesquita, 'The Foreign Policy of Richard II: some Italian letters', *EHR*, 56 (1941), pp. 628–37

Joel Burden, 'How do you bury a deposed king?' in *Establishment*, pp. 35–54

Calendar of the Charter Rolls Preserved in the Public Record Office, 1226–1516 (6 vols, 1903–27)

John Capgrave, *The Chronicle of England* (1858)

Helen Castor, *The King, the Crown and the Duchy of Lancaster* (Oxford, 2000)

CB: G. L. Harriss, *Cardinal Beaufort: a Study of Lancastrian Ascendancy and Decline* (Oxford, 1988)

CCR: *Calendar of the Close Rolls*

CFR: *Calendar of the Fine Rolls*

CH: William Stubbs, *Constitutional History of England* (3rd edn, 3 vols, Oxford, 1884)

John Cherry & Neil Stratford, *Westminster Kings and the Medieval Palace of Westminster* (1995)

S. B. Chrimes, C. D. Ross, and R. A. Griffiths (eds), *Fifteenth Century England* (1972)

CIPM: *Calendar of Inquisitions Post Mortem*

M. V. Clarke & V. H. Galbraith, 'The Deposition of Richard II', *BJRL*, 14 (1930), pp. 125–81

CM: David Preest & James G. Clark (eds), *The Chronica Maiora of Thomas Walsingham, 1376–1422* (Woodbridge, 2005)

G. E. Cokayne, revised by V. Gibbs, H. A. Doubleday, D. Warrand, Lord Howard de Walden and Peter Hammond (eds), *The Complete Peerage of England, Scotland, Ireland, Great Britain and the United Kingdom extant, extinct or dormant* (14 vols, 1910–98)

CP: *Complete Peerage* [*see entry under* Cokayne, G. E.]

CPR: *Calendar of the Patent Rolls*

CR: Chris Given-Wilson (ed.), *Chronicles of the Revolution, 1397–1400* (Manchester, 1993)

Creton: J. Webb (ed.), 'Metrical History', *Archaeologia*, 20 (1824), pp. 13–239

H. S. Cronin, 'The Twelve Conclusions of the Lollards', *EHR*, 22 (1907), pp. 292–304

D. Crook, 'Central England and the revolt of the earls, January 1400', *BIHR*, 64 (1991), pp. 403–10

J. D. Griffith Davies, *Henry IV* (1935)

J. D. Griffiths Davies (ed.), *An English Chronicle of the Reigns of Richard II, Henry IV, Henry V and Henry VI*, Camden Society, Old Series 64 (1856)

Richard G. Davies, 'Some Notes from the Register of Henry de Wakefield, Bishop of Worcester, on the Political Crisis of 1386–88', *EHR*, 86 (1971), pp. 547–58

R. R. Davies, *The Revolt of Owain Glyn Dŵr* (Oxford, 1995)

'Deposition': M. V. Clarke & V. H. Galbraith, 'The Deposition of Richard II', *BJRL*, 14 (1930), pp. 125–81

Frederick Devon (ed.), *Issues of the Exchequer* (1837)

P. W. Dillon, 'Remarks on the Manner of the Death of King Richard the Second', *Archaeologia*, 28 (1840), pp. 78–83

Gwilym Dodd & Douglas Biggs, *Henry IV: the Establishment of the Regime* (Woodbridge, 2003)

Gwilym Dodd (ed.), *The Reign of Richard II* (Stroud, 2000)

Gwilym Dodd, 'Henry IV's Council, 1399–1406' in *Establishment*, pp. 95–116

Gwilym Dodd, 'Conflict or Consensus: Henry IV and Parliament, 1399–1406', in Tim Thornton (ed.), *Social Attitudes and Political Structures in the Fifteenth Century* (Stroud, 2000), pp. 118–49

F. R. H. Du Boulay, 'Henry of Derby's expeditions to Prussia, 1390–1 and 1392', in *RRII*, pp. 153–72

Mark Duffy, *Royal Tombs of Medieval England* (Stroud, 2003)

Alastair Dunn, 'Henry IV and the Politics of Resistance in Early Lancastrian England, 1399–1413' in *Authority & Subversion*, pp. 5–24

Alastair Dunn, 'Richard II and the Mortimer inheritance', in Chris Given-Wilson (ed.), *Fourteenth Century England II* (Woodbridge, 2002), pp. 159–70

Alistair Dunn, *The Great Rising of 1381* (Stroud, 2002)

Christopher Dyer, *Standards of Living in the Later Middle Ages* (Cambridge, revised edn, 1998)

EC: J. D. Griffiths Davies (ed.), *An English Chronicle of the Reigns of Richard II, Henry IV, Henry V and Henry VI*, Camden Society, Old Series 64 (1856)

ECC: V. J. Scattergood and J. W. Sherborne, *English Court Culture in the Later Middle Ages* (1983)

EHD: A. R. Myres (ed.), *English Historical Documents iv: 1327–1485* (1969)

EHR: *English Historical Review*

Establishment: Gwilym Dodd & Douglas Biggs, *Henry IV: the Establishment of the Regime, 1399–1406* (Woodbridge, 2003)

Eulogium: F. S. Haydon (ed.), *Eulogium (Historiarum sive Temporis): Chronicon ab Orbe Condito usque ad Annum Domini MCCCLXVI* (3 vols, 1858–63)

Expeditions: Lucy Toulmin Smith (ed.), *Expeditions to Prussia and the Holy Land made by Henry Earl of Derby . . . in the Years 1390–1 and 1392–3*, Camden Society, New Series 52 (1894)

Robert J. Fehrenbach, 'The Characterization of the King in 1 Henry IV', *SQ*, 30: 1 (1979), pp. 42–50

C. D. Fletcher, 'Narrative and Political Strategies at the Deposition of Richard II', *JMH*, 30 (2004), pp. 323–41

Foedera: Thomas Rymer (ed.), *Foedera, conventiones, literae, et cujuscunque generis acta publica* (20 vols, 1704–35).

C. J. Ford, 'Piracy or policy: crisis in the channel, 1400–1403', *Transactions of the Royal Historical Society*, Fifth Series, 29 (1979), pp. 63–78

Froissart: Thomas Johnes (ed.), *Chronicles of England, France, Spain and the adjoining countries . . . by Sir John Froissart* (2 vols, 1848)

V. H. Galbraith (ed.), *Anonimalle Chronicle 1333–1381* (Manchester, 1927)

Margaret Galway, 'Alice Perrers' son John', *EHR*, 65 (1951), pp. 242–6

J. L. Gillespie, 'Thomas Mortimer and Thomas Molyneux: Radcot Bridge and the Appeal of 1397', *Albion*, 7 (1975), pp. 161–73

Chris Given-Wilson, *The Royal Household and the King's Affinity: Service, Politics and Finance in England 1360–1413* (1986)

Chris Given-Wilson (ed.), *Chronicles of the Revolution, 1397–1400* (Manchester, 1993)

Chris Given-Wilson (ed.), *Parliamentary Rolls of Medieval England* (CD ROM edn, Woodbridge, 2005)

Chris Given-Wilson (ed.), *The Chronicle of Adam Usk* (Oxford, 1997)

Chris Given-Wilson, 'The Manner of King Richard's Renunciation: a Lancastrian Narrative?', *EHR*, 108 (1993), pp. 365–70

Chris Given-Wilson, 'Quarrels of Old Women: Lancaster and Valois in the Reign of Henry IV' (paper delivered at Nottingham 2006)

Chris Given-Wilson, 'Richard II and his Grandfather's Will', *EHR*, 93 (1978), pp. 320–37

Chris Given-Wilson, 'Richard II and the Higher Nobility' in *Art of Kingship*, pp. 107–28

Chris Given-Wilson, 'Richard II, Edward II and the Lancastrian Inheritance', *EHR*, 109 (1994), pp. 553–71

Chris Given-Wilson, 'Royal Charter Witness Lists 1327–1399', *Medieval Prosopography*, 12 (1991), pp. 35–94

Chris Given-Wilson & Alice Curteis, *Royal Bastards* (1984)

Glyn Dŵr: R. R. Davies, *The Revolt of Owain Glyn Dŵr* (Oxford, 1995)

Anthony Goodman, 'Richard II's councils', in *Art of Kingship*, pp. 59–82

Anthony Goodman, *John of Gaunt: the Exercise of Princely Power in Fourteenth-Century Europe* (1992)

Anthony Goodman, *Katherine Swynford* (Lincoln, 1994)

Anthony Goodman, *The Loyal Conspiracy: the Lords Appellant under Richard II* (1971)

Anthony Goodman, 'John of Gaunt', in Mark W. Ormrod (ed.), *England in the Fourteenth Century: Proceedings of the 1985 Harlaxton Symposium* (Woodbridge, 1986), pp. 67–87

Anthony Goodman & James Gillespie (eds), *Richard II: the Art of Kingship* (Oxford, 1999)

Gothic: Richard Marks & Paul Williamson (eds), *Gothic Art for England 1400–1547* (2003)

Frank Grady, 'The Lancastrian Gower and the Limits of Exemplarity', *Speculum*, 70, 3 (1995), pp. 552–75

Antonia Gransden, *Historical Writing in England II, c. 1307 to the Early Sixteenth Century* (1982)

HA: H. T. Riley (ed.), *Thomae Walsingham Quondam Monachi S. Albani Historia Anglicana* (2 vols, 1863–4)

Sir William Hardy and Edward L. C. P. Hardy (eds), *A Collection of the Chronicles and Ancient Histories ... by John de Waurin, Lord of Forestel ... 1399–1422* (1887)

T. D. Hardy (ed.), *Syllabus ... of Rymer's Foedera* (3 vols, 1869–85)

Gerald Harriss, *Cardinal Beaufort: a study of Lancastrian Ascendancy and Decline* (Oxford, 1988)

Gerald Harriss, *Shaping the Nation: England 1360–1461* (Oxford, 2005)

F. S. Haydon (ed.), *Eulogium (Historiarum sive Temporis): Chronicon ab Orbe Condito usque ad Annum Domini MCCCLXVI* (3 vols, 1858–63)

John Hayward: *see Manning*

HBC: Sir Maurice Powicke & E. B. Fryde (eds), *Handbook of British Chronology* (2nd ed., 1961)

L. C. Hector & Barbara Harvey, *The Westminster Chronicle 1381–1394* (Oxford, 1982)

Allen B. Hinds (ed.), *Calendar of State Papers Existing in the Archives and Collections of Milan* (1912)

F. C. Hingeston (ed.), *The Book of the Illustrious Henries by John Capgrave* (1858)

F. C. Hingeston (ed.), *The Chronicle of England by John Capgrave* (1858)

F. C. Hingeston (ed.), *Royal and Historical Letters During the Reign of Henry IV, King of England and France and Lord of Ireland* (2 vols, 1860, 1964)

HKW: R. A. Brown, H. M. Colvin & A. J. Taylor, *History of the King's Works: the Middle Ages* (2 vols, 1963)

G. A. Holmes, *Estates of the Higher Nobility* (Cambridge, 1957)

IH: F. C. Hingeston (ed.), *The Book of the Illustrious Henries by John Capgrave* (1858)

Issues: Frederick Devon (ed.), *Issues of the Exchequer* (1837)

JMH: *Journal of Medieval History*

Thomas Johnes (ed.), *Chronicles of England, France, Spain and the adjoining countries ... by Sir John Froissart* (2 vols, 1848)

Thomas Johnes (ed.), *The Chronicles of Enguerrand de Monstrelet* (2 vols, 1853)

J. Gwynfor Jones, 'Government and the Welsh Community: the North-East Borderland in the Fifteenth Century', in H. Hearder & H. Loyn (eds), *British Government and Administration: Studies Presented to S. B. Chrimes* (Cardiff, 1974), pp. 55–68

Dorothy Johnstone, 'Richard II's departure from Ireland, July 1399', *EHR*, 98 (1983), pp. 785–805

KC: G. H. Martin (ed.), *Knighton's Chronicle 1337–1396* (Oxford, 1995)

Maurice Keen, 'Chaucer's Knight: the English Aristocracy and the Crusade', in *ECC*, pp. 45–61

George R. Keiser, 'Edward III and the Alliterative "Morte Arthure"', *Speculum* 48, 1 (1973), pp. 37–51

H. A. Kelly, 'English Kings and the Fear of Sorcery', *Mediaeval Studies*, 39 (1977), pp. 206–38

King's Council: J. F. Baldwin, *The King's Council in England During the Middle Ages* (Oxford 1913, reprinted 1969)

C. L. Kingsford (ed.), *The First English Life of Henry V* (Oxford, 1911), pp. 11–12

Kirby: J. L. Kirby, *Henry IV of England* (1970)

J. L. Kirby (ed.), *Calendar of Signet Letters of Henry IV and Henry V* (1978)

Gaillard Lapsley, 'The Parliamentary Title of Henry IV', *EHR*, 49 (1934), pp. 423–49, 577–606

LC: Anthony Goodman, *The Loyal Conspiracy: the Lords Appellant under Richard II* (1971)

LK: K. B. McFarlane, *Lancastrian Kings and Lollard Knights* (Oxford, 1972)

E. C. Lodge & Robert Somerville, *John of Gaunt's Register 1379–1383*, Camden Society, Third Series 56–57 (2 vols, 1937)

John J. Manning (ed.), *The First and Second Parts of John Hayward's The Life and Raigne of King Henrie IIII*, Camden Fourth Series, 42 (1991)

Richard Marks & Paul Williamson (eds), *Gothic Art for England 1400–1547* (2003)

G. H. Martin (ed.), *Knighton's Chronicle 1337–1396* (Oxford, 1995)

Gervase Mathew, *The Court of Richard II* (1968)

K. B. McFarlane, *Lancastrian Kings and Lollard Knights* (Oxford, 1972)

K. B. McFarlane, 'England: the Lancastrian Kings, 1399–1461', in C. W. Previté-Orton and Z. N. Brooke (eds), *The Cambridge History of Medieval Europe, vol 8: the Close of the Middle Ages* (Cambridge, 1936), pp. 362–93

J. W. McKenna, 'The Coronation Oil of the Yorkist Kings', *EHR*, 82 (1967), pp. 102–4

J. W. McKenna, 'Popular Canonization as Political Propaganda: the Cult of Archbishop Scrope', *Speculum*, 45, 4 (1970), pp. 608–23

Alison McHardy, 'A personal portrait of Richard II' in *Reign*, pp. 11–32

Peter McNiven, *Heresy and Politics in the Reign of Henry IV: the Burning of John Badby* (Woodbridge, 1987)

Peter McNiven, 'The betrayal of Archbishop Scrope', *BJRL*, 54 (1971), pp. 172–213

Peter McNiven, 'The Cheshire rising of 1400', *BJRL*, 52 (1969–70), pp. 375–96

Peter McNiven, 'The problem of Henry IV's health, 1405–1413', *EHR*, 100 (1985), pp. 397, 765–6

Monstrelet: Thomas Johnes (ed.), *The Chronicles of Enguerrand de Monstrelet* (2 vols, 1853)

H. Moranville (ed.), *Chronographia Regum Francorum* (Paris, 1893)

D. A. L. Morgan, 'The political after-life of Edward III: the apotheosis of a warmonger' *EHR*, 112 (1997), pp. 856–81

Philip Morgan, 'Henry IV and the shadow of Richard II', in R. E. Archer (ed.), *Crown, Government and People in the Fifteenth Century* (Stroud, 1995)

Philip Morgan, 'Memories of the Battle of Shrewsbury' (paper delivered at Nottingham 2006)

Ian Mortimer, *The Greatest Traitor: the life of Sir Roger Mortimer, 1st Earl of March, Ruler of England 1327–30* (2003)

Ian Mortimer, *The Perfect King: the Life of Edward III, Father of the English Nation* (2006)

Ian Mortimer, 'Richard II and the Succession to the Crown', *History*, 303 (2006), pp. 320–36

Ian Mortimer, 'Henry IV's Date of Birth and the Royal Maundy', *Historical Research* (forthcoming)

A. R. Myres (ed.), *English Historical Documents vol. 4: 1327–1485* (1969)

J. N. L. Myres, 'The Campaign of Radcot Bridge, 1387', *EHR*, 92 (1927), pp. 20–33

Cynthia J. Neville, 'Scotland, the Percies and the law in 1400', in *Establishment*, pp. 73–94

J. Nichols (ed.), *A Collection of All the Wills Now Known to be Extant of the Kings and Queens of England ...* (1780, reprinted New York, 1969)

Donald M. Nicol, 'A Byzantine Emperor in England: Manuel II's visit to London in 1400–1401', *University of Birmingham Historical Journal*, 12, 2 (1970), pp. 204–25

Sir (Nicholas) Harris Nicolas (ed.), *Proceedings and Ordinances of the Privy Council of England* (7 vols, 1834–7)

Sir Nicholas Harris Nicolas, 'Observations of the Origin and History of the Badge and Mottoes of Edward Prince of Wales', *Archaeologia*, 31 (1846)

Nottingham 2006: papers delivered at the July 2006 symposium on Henry IV at the University of Nottingham. Note: these may be expected to be published by the York Medieval Press, in a successor volume to *Establishment*.

ODNB: *Oxford Dictionary of National Biography from the earliest times to the year 2000* (on-line edition, Oxford, 2004, with corrections and additions)

W. Mark Ormrod, 'Rebellion of Archbishop Scrope and the Tradition of Opposition to Royal Taxation' (paper delivered at Nottingham 2006)

W. Mark Ormrod, 'Richard II's Sense of English History', in *Reign*, pp. 97–110

A. J. Otway-Ruthven, *A History of Medieval Ireland* (1968, rep. 1993)

J. J. N. Palmer, 'The authorship, date and historical value of the French chronicles on the Lancastrian revolution', *BJRL*, 61 (1978–9), pp. 145–81, 398–421

J. J. N. Palmer, 'The parliament of 1385 and the constitutional crisis of 1386', *Speculum*, 46 (1971) pp. 477–90

PC: Sir Harris Nicolas (ed.), *Proceedings and Ordinances of the Privy Council of England* (7 vols, 1834–7)

E. Perroy (ed.), *Diplomatic Correspondence of Richard II*, Camden Society, Third Series 48 (1933)

Stephen P. Pistono, 'Henry IV and Charles VI: the confirmation of the twenty-eight-year truce', *JMH*, 3 (1977), pp. 353–65

Stephen P. Pistono, 'Henry IV and the Privateers', *EHR*, 80 (1975), pp. 322–30

PK: Ian Mortimer, *The Perfect King: the Life of Edward III, Father of the English Nation* (2006)

A.J. Pollard, 'The Lancastrian constitutional experiment revisited: Henry IV, Sir John Tiptoft and the parliament of 1406', *Parliamentary History*, 14 (1995), pp. 103–19

Sir Maurice Powicke & E.B. Fryde (eds), *Handbook of British Chronology* (2nd ed., 1961)

David Preest & James G. Clark (eds), *The Chronica Maiora of Thomas Walsingham, 1376–1422* (Woodbridge, 2005)

PROME: Chris Given-Wilson (ed.), *Parliamentary Rolls of Medieval England* (CD ROM ed., Woodbridge, 2005)

Cecily Radford, 'An unrecorded royal visit to Exeter', *Transactions of the Devonshire Association*, 63 (1931), 255–63

Sir James Ramsay, *Lancaster and York* (2 vols, 1892)

Carole Rawcliffe, *Medicine and Society in Later Medieval England* (1999)

Register 1372–76: Sydney Armitage-Smith (ed.), *John of Gaunt's Register 1372–1376*, Camden Society, Third Series 20–21 (2 vols, 1911)

Register 1379–83: E. C. Lodge & Robert Somerville, *John of Gaunt's Register 1379–1383*, Camden Society, Third Series 56–57 (2 vols, 1937)

Reign: Gwilym Dodd (ed.), *The Reign of Richard II* (Stroud, 2000)

Arnd Reitemeier, 'Born to be a tyrant? The childhood and education of Richard II', in Chris Given-Wilson (ed.), *Fourteenth Century England II* (Woodbridge, 2002), p. 147–58

Revolution: Michael Bennett, *Richard II and the Revolution of 1399* (Stroud, 1999)

RHL: F. C. Hingeston (ed.), *Royal and historical letters during the reign of Henry IV, King of England and France and Lord of Ireland* (2 vols, 1860, 1964)

H. T. Riley (ed.), *Johannis de Trokelowe et Henrici de Blaneforde ... chronica et annales*, Rolls Series, 28 (1866)

H. T. Riley (ed.), *Thomae Walsingham Quondam Monachi S. Albani Historia Anglicana* (2 vols, 1863–4)

Alan Rogers, 'The political crisis of 1401', *Nottingham Mediaeval Studies*, 12 (1968), pp. 85–96

Alan Rogers, 'Henry IV: the commons and taxation', *Medieval Studies*, 31 (1969), pp. 44–70

Alan Rogers, 'Parliamentary Appeals of Treason in the Reign of Richard II', *American Journal of Legal History*, 8, 2 (1964), pp. 95–124

Alan Rogers, 'The Royal Household of Henry IV' (unpublished PhD thesis, University of Nottingham, 1966)

James Ross, 'Seditious Activities: the Conspiracy of Maud de Vere, Countess of Oxford, 1403–4' in *Authority & Subversion*, pp. 25–42

Royal Household: Chris Given-Wilson, *The Royal Household and the King's Affinity: Service, Politics and Finance in England 1360–1413* (1986)

Royal Wills: J. Nichols (ed.), *A Collection of All the Wills Now Known to be Extant of the Kings and Queens of England . . .* (1780, reprinted New York, 1969)

RRII: F. R. H. du Boulay and C. M. Barron (eds), *The reign of Richard II: essays in honour of May McKisack* (1971)

Owen Ruffhead (ed.), *Statutes at Large, from Magna Charta to the End of the Last Parliament in Eight Volumes*, vol. 1 (1763)

Thomas Rymer (ed.), *Foedera, conventiones, literae, et cujuscunque generis acta publica* (20 vols, 1704–35)

SAC: John Taylor, Wendy R. Childs & Leslie Watkiss (eds), *The St Albans Chronicle: the Chronica Maiora of Thomas Walsingham, 1376–1394* (Oxford, 2003)

T. A. Sandquist, 'The holy oil of St Thomas of Canterbury', in T. A. Sandquist and M. R. Powicke (eds), *Essays in medieval history presented to Bertie Wilkinson* (Toronto, 1969), pp. 330–44

Saul: Nigel Saul, *Richard II* (1997)

Nigel Saul, 'The Kingship of Richard II' in *Art of Kingship*, pp. 37–58

G. O. Sayles, 'The Deposition of Richard II: Three Lancastrian Narratives', *BIHR*, 54 (1981), pp. 257–65

V. J. Scattergood & J. W. Sherborne, *English Court Culture in the Later Middle Ages* (1983)

Reginald R. Sharpe, *Calendar of the Letter-Books of the City of London, Letter-Book H* (1907)

James Sherborne, 'Perjury and the Lancastrian Revolution of 1399', *Welsh History Review*, 14 (1988), pp. 217–41

Signet Letters: J. L. Kirby (ed.), *Calendar of Signet Letters of Henry IV and Henry V* (1978)

T. M. Smallwood, 'Prophecy of the Six Kings', *Speculum*, 60 (1985), pp. 571–92

Lucy Toulmin Smith (ed.), *Expeditions to Prussia and the Holy Land made by Henry Earl of Derby . . . in the Years 1390–1 and 1392–3*, Camden Society, New Series 52 (1894)

J. H. Spry, 'A brief account of the examination of the tomb of King Henry

IV in the cathedral of Canterbury, August 21 1832', *Archaeologia*, 26 (1836), pp. 440–5

SQ: Shakespeare Quarterly

A. E. Stamp, 'Richard II and the Death of the Duke of Gloucester', *EHR*, 38 (1923), pp. 249–51

A. E. Stamp, 'Richard II and the Death of the Duke of Gloucester', *EHR*, 47 (1932), p. 453

Anthony Steel, *Richard II* (Cambridge, 1941)

Anthony Steel, 'English Government Finance, 1377–1413', *EHR*, 51 (1936), pp. 29–51, 577–97

Anthony Steel, 'Receipt Roll Totals under Henry IV and Henry V', *EHR*, 47 (1932), pp. 204–15

George B. Stow (ed.), *Historia Vitae et Regni Ricardi Secundi* (Pennsylvania, 1977)

George B. Stow, 'Stubbs, Steel and Richard II as Insane: the Origin and Evolution of an English Historiographical Myth', *Proceedings of the American Philosophical Society*, 143, 4 (1999), pp. 601–38

Jenny Stratford, 'The Royal Library in England Before the Reign of Edward IV', in Nicholas John Rogers (ed.), *England in the Fifteenth Century: Proceedings of the 1992 Harlaxton Symposium* (Stamford, 1994), pp. 187–97

Agnes Strickland, *Lives of the Queens of England* (8 vols, 1882)

Paul Strohm, *England's Empty Throne: Usurpation and the Language of Legitimation 1399–1422* (1998)

Paul Strohm, *Hochon's Arrow: the Social Imagination of Fourteenth Century Texts* (Princeton, 1992)

William Stubbs, *Constitutional History of England* (3rd ed., 3 vols, Oxford, 1884)

'Succession': Ian Mortimer, 'Richard II and the Succession to the Crown', *History*, 91: 303 (2006), pp. 320–36

Henry R. T. Summerson, 'An English Bible and other books belonging to Henry IV', *BJRL*, 79, 1 (1997), pp. 109–15

Syllabus: T. D. Hardy (ed.), *Syllabus . . . of Rymer's Foedera* (3 vols, 1869–85)

James Tait, 'Did Richard II Murder the Duke of Gloucester?' in T. F. Tout and James Tait (eds), *Historical Essays by Members of the Owens College Manchester* (1902)

John Taylor (ed.), *The Kirkstall Abbey Chronicles*, Thoresby Society 42 (1952)

John Taylor, Wendy R. Childs & Leslie Watkiss (eds), *The St Albans Chronicle: the Chronica Maiora of Thomas Walsingham, 1376–1394* (Oxford, 2003)

Rupert Taylor, *The Political Prophecy in England* (New York, 1911; reprinted 1967)

E. M. Thompson (ed.), *Chronicon Angliae* (1874)

T. F. Tout, 'Firearms in England in the Fourteenth Century', *EHR*, 26 (1911), pp. 666–702

Traïson: Benjamin Williams (ed.), *Chronicque de la Traïson et Mort de Richart Deux Roy Dengleterre* (1846)

Brian Trowell, 'Henry IV, Recorder-Player', *The Galpin Society Journal*, 10 (1957), pp. 83–4

Tuck: Anthony Tuck, *Richard II and the English Nobility* (1973)

Anthony Tuck, 'The Cambridge Parliament, 1388', *EHR*, 84 (1969), pp. 225–43

Anthony Tuck, 'Henry IV and chivalry', in *Establishment*, pp. 55–72

Anthony Tuck, 'Henry IV and Europe: a dynasty's search for recognition', in R. H. Britnell and A. J. Pollard (eds), *The McFarlane legacy* (1995), pp. 107–25

Vita: George B. Stow (ed.), *Historia Vitae et Regni Ricardi Secundi* (Pennsylvania, 1977)

Simon Walker, 'The Yorkshire Risings of 1405: texts and contexts', in *Establishment*, pp. 161–84

Thomas Walsingham: *see HA, CM & Thompson (ed.)*

Waurin: Sir William Hardy & Edward L. C. P. Hardy (eds), *A Collection of the Chronicles and Ancient Histories . . . by John de Waurin, Lord of Forestel . . . 1399–1422* (1887)

WC: L. C. Hector & Barbara Harvey, *The Westminster Chronicle 1381–1394* (Oxford, 1982)

J. Webb (ed.), 'Metrical History', *Archaeologia*, 20 (1824), pp. 13–239

Nigel Wilkins, 'Music and poetry at court: England and France in the Late Middle Ages', in *EEC*, pp. 183–204

B. Wilkinson, 'The Deposition of Richard II and the Accession of Henry IV', *EHR*, 54 (1939), pp. 215–39

Benjamin Williams (ed.), *Chronicque de la Traïson et Mort de Richart Deux Roy Dengleterre* (1846)

George Williams (ed.), *Official Correspondence of Thomas Bekyngton* (2 vols, 1872)

Edmund Wright, 'Henry IV, the Commons and the recovery of royal finance in 1407', in Rowena Archer and Simon Walker (eds), *Rulers and Ruled in Late Medieval England* (1995), pp. 71–80

H. G. Wright, 'Richard II and the Death of the Duke of Gloucester', *EHR*, 47 (1932), pp. 276–80

H. G. Wright, 'The Protestation of Richard II in the Tower in September, 1399', *BJRL*, 23 (1939), pp. 151–65

Thomas Wright (ed.), *Political Poems and Songs Relating to English History* (2 vols, 1859–61)

Wylie: James Hamilton Wylie, *A History of England under Henry the Fourth* (4 vols, 1884–98)

James Hamilton Wylie, 'Dispensation of John XXIII for a son of Henry IV "propter defectum natalium"', *EHR*, 19 (1904), pp. 96–7

Alfred Benjamin Wyon and Allan Wyon, *The Great Seals of England* (1887)

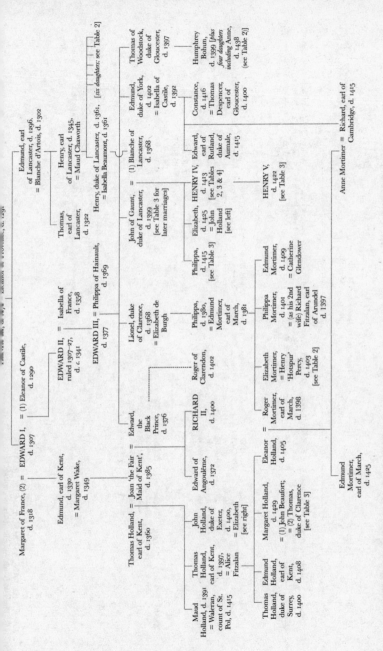

Table 1: THE ENGLISH ROYAL FAMILY BEFORE 1399

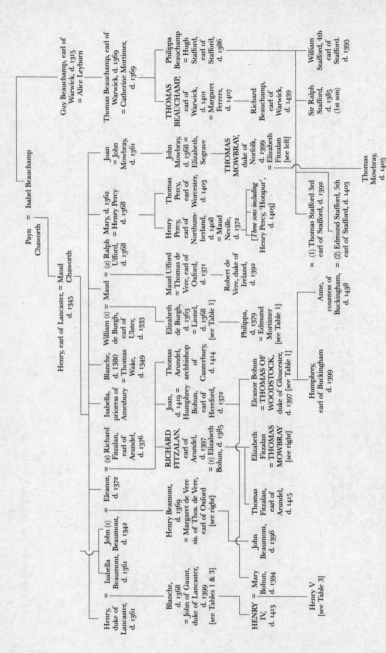

Table 2: THE LANCASTRIAN FAMILY NETWORK
N.B. The five Lords Appellant are in capitals.

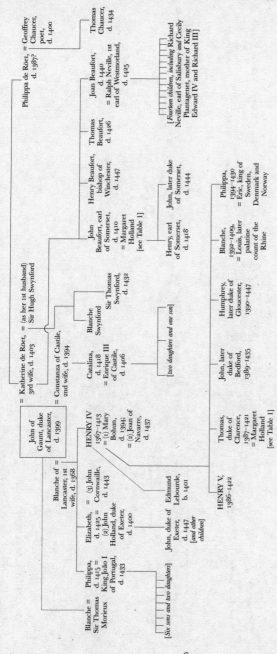

Philippa de Röet, = Geoffrey
d. 1387?   Chaucer,
                poet,
                d. 1400

Thomas
Chaucer,
d. 1434

Joan Beaufort,
d. 1440
= Ralph Neville, 1st
earl of Westmorland,
d. 1425

[Fourteen children, including Richard
Neville, earl of Salisbury and Cecily
Plantagenet, mother of King
Edward IV and Richard III]

Thomas
Beaufort,
d. 1426

Henry Beaufort,
bishop of
Winchester,
d. 1447

John Beaufort, earl
of Somerset,
d. 1410
= Margaret
Holland
[see Table 1]

John, later duke
of Somerset,
d. 1444

Henry, earl
of Somerset,
d. 1418

Philippa,
1394–1430
= Eric, king of
Sweden,
Denmark and
Norway

Blanche,
1392–1409,
= Louis, later
count palatine
of the
Rhine

= Katherine de Röet, = (as her 1st husband)
3rd wife, d. 1403   Sir Hugh Swynford

= Constanza of Castile,
2nd wife, d. 1394

Blanche
Swynford

Sir Thomas
Swynford,
d. 1432

Catalina,
d. 1418
= Enrique III
of Castile,
d. 1406

[two daughters and one son]

Humphrey,
later duke of
Gloucester,
1390–1447

John, later
duke of
Bedford,
1389–1435

John of
Gaunt, duke
of Lancaster,
d. 1399

HENRY IV
1367–1413
= (1) Mary
Bohun,
d. 1394;
= (2) Joan of
Navarre,
d. 1437

Thomas,
duke of
Clarence,
1387–1421
= Margaret
Holland
[see Table 1]

HENRY V,
1386–1422

Blanche of =
Lancaster; 1st
wife, d. 1368

Elizabeth, = (3) John
d. 1425   Cornwaille,
= (2) John d. 1443
Holland, duke
of Exeter,
d. 1400

John, duke of
Exeter,
d. 1447
[and other
children]

Edmund
Lebourde,
b. 1401

Philippa,
d. 1415 =
King João I
of Portugal,
d. 1433

Blanche =
Sir Thomas
Morieux

[Six sons and two daughters]

Table 3: THE ENGLISH ROYAL FAMILY AFTER 1399

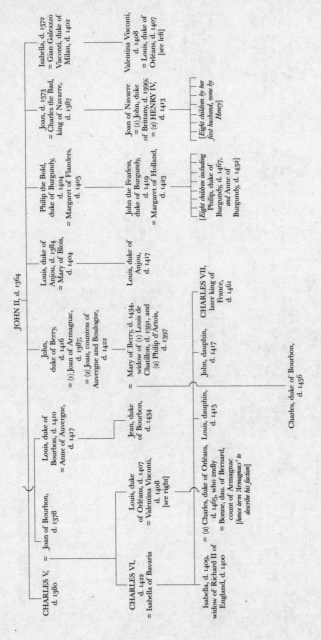

JOHN II, d. 1364

CHARLES V, = Joan of Bourbon,
d. 1380   d. 1378

Louis, duke of
Bourbon, d. 1410
= Anne of Auvergne,
d. 1417

Jean, duke
of Bourbon,
d. 1434

Charles, duke of Bourbon,
d. 1456

John,
duke of Berry,
d. 1416
= (1) Joan of Armagnac,
d. 1387;
= (2) Joan, countess of
Auvergne and Boulogne,
d. 1422

= Mary of Berry, d. 1434,
widow of (1) Louis de
Chatillon, d. 1391, and
(2) Philip d'Artois,
d. 1397

Louis, duke of
Anjou, d. 1384
= Mary of Blois,
d. 1404

Louis, duke of
Anjou,
d. 1417

Philip the Bold,
duke of Burgundy,
d. 1404
= Margaret of Flanders,
d. 1405

John the Fearless,
duke of Burgundy,
d. 1419
= Margaret of Holland,
d. 1423

[Eight children including
Philip, duke of Burgundy, d. 1467,
and Anne of
Burgundy, d. 1432]

Joan, d. 1373
= Charles the Bad,
king of Navarre,
d. 1387

Joan of Navarre
= (1) John, duke
of Brittany, d. 1399;
= (2) HENRY IV,
d. 1413

[Eight children by her
first husband, none by
Henry]

Isabella, d. 1372
= Gian Galeazzo
Visconti, duke of
Milan, d. 1402

Valentina Visconti,
d. 1408
= Louis, duke of
Orléans, d. 1407
[see left]

CHARLES VI,
d. 1422
= Isabella of Bavaria

Louis, duke
of Orléans, d. 1407
= Valentina Visconti,
d. 1408
[see right]

Isabella, d. 1409,
widow of Richard II of
England, d. 1400

= (2) Charles, duke of Orléans,
d. 1465, who 2ndly
= Bonne, dau. of Bernard,
count of Armagnac
[hence term 'Armagnac' to
describe this faction]

Louis, dauphin,
d. 1415

John, dauphin,
d. 1417

CHARLES VII,
later king of
France,
d. 1461

Table 4: THE FRENCH ROYAL FAMILY

462

INDEX

Dates in brackets after the name relate to lifespan; dates after titles and offices relate to date of entitlement or appointment; date spans are only given for those whose title or office proved to be temporary.

INDEX